NON-DISCRIMINATION AND EQUALITY IN THE VIEW OF THE UN HUMAN RIGHTS TREATY BODIES

NON-DISCRIMINATION AND EQUALITY IN THE VIEW OF THE UN HUMAN RIGHTS TREATY BODIES

WOUTER VANDENHOLE

intersentia
Antwerpen – Oxford

Distribution for the UK:
Hart Publishing
Salter's Boat Yard
Folly Bridge
Abingdon Road
Oxford OX1 4LB
UK
Tel: + 44 1865 24 55 33
Fax: + 44 1865 79 48 82

Distribution for North America:
Gaunt Inc.
Gaunt Building
3011 Gulf Drive
Holmes Beach
Florida 34217-2199
USA
Tel: + 1 941 778 5211
Fax: + 1 941 778 5252

Distribution for Switzerland and Germany:
Schulthess Verlag
Zwingliplatz 2
CH-8022 Zürich
Switzerland
Tel: + 41 1 251 93 36
Fax: + 41 1 261 63 94

Distribution for other countries:
Intersentia Publishers
Groenstraat 31
BE-2640 Mortsel
Belgium
Tel: + 32 3 680 15 50
Fax: + 32 3 658 71 21

Non-Discrimination and Equality in the View of the UN Human Rights Treaty Bodies
Wouter Vandenhole

Omslagontwerp: Danny Juchtmans
Illustratie: Joachim Vandenhole

ISBN 90-5095-500-2
D/2005/7849/85
NUR 828

FOREWORD

In February 2002, I embarked upon a research project on the convergence of the procedures of the UN human rights treaty bodies. This research was boosted by the UN Secretary General's *Agenda for Reform.* As pressure for harmonization of the reporting procedures grew, the research's practical relevance increased. The results of this scientific journey were reflected in the book entitled *The Procedures Before the UN Human Rights Treaty Bodies: Convergence or Divergence?*[1]

This research continues along similar lines. After having explored the convergence in procedural law, we then expanded our research question to substantive law, with a particular focus on the principles of equality and non-discrimination. As most of the UN core human rights treaties contain provisions on non-discrimination and equality, the principles of non-discrimination and equality might be expected to be the most conducive to convergence and harmonisation.

I am heavily indebted to Paul Lemmens, my mentor and the head of the Institute for Human Rights at the K.U.Leuven (Belgium). He has relentlessly and without any reservations allowed and encouraged me to devote all my time to this exciting but time-consuming research topic. I am equally grateful to Willem van Genugten, the head of the Center for Transboundary Legal Development at Tilburg University (The Netherlands), whose outstanding research centre I currently belong to.

This research was generously funded by the Research Council of the K.U.Leuven.

Leuven, June 2005

Wouter Vandenhole

1 Wouter Vandenhole, *The Procedures Before the UN Human Rights Treaty Bodies: Convergence or Divergence?*, 2004, Antwerp, Intersentia, 331 and xx p.

TABLE OF CONTENTS

INTRODUCTION

Equality is without doubt one of the central principles of human rights law and of the UN core human rights treaties in particular. This has been reaffirmed time and again. Equality has been claimed to be "the most important principle imbuing and inspiring the concept of human rights", along with liberty,[2] the "dominant and recurring theme of international human rights law",[3] "one of the most frequently declared norms of international human rights law",[4] and "one of the major themes of most UN core human rights treaties".[5]

Two of the UN core human rights treaties are exclusively devoted to the issue of equality and non-discrimination, *i.e.* the International Convention on the Elimination of All Forms of Racial Discrimination (ICERD) and the Convention on the Elimination of All Forms of Discrimination Against Women (CEDAW). All others, but the Convention Against Torture and Other Cruel, Inhuman or Degrading Treatment or Punishment (CAT), explicitly prohibit discrimination on a number of grounds.

The lead question in this book is whether and to what extent the UN human rights treaty bodies, each of which supervises the implementation of one of the core human rights treaties, tend to interpret and apply the principle of equality and non-discrimination in a similar vein. The analysis draws on the treaty texts and all 'decisions' taken by the Committees, *i.e.* general comments/recommendations, concluding observations/comments adopted at the end of the examination of state reports, views/decisions adopted in individual complaints procedures and other relevant documents.

The initial research hypothesis was that convergence in the interpretation and application of the principle of equality and non-discrimination among the UN human rights treaty bodies was very likely to take place. All treaties (but CAT) share a provision on equality and non-discrimination, which in some cases is to a considerable extent similarly worded. Being "congruent substantive provisions", equality and non-

---

2 Manfred Nowak, *U.N. Covenant on Civil and Political Rights. CCPR Commentary*, Kehl, Engel, 1993, 458.

3 Anne Bayefski, "The Principle of Equality or Non-Discrimination in International Law, 11 *Human Rights Law Journal* 1990/1-2, 2.

4 *Ibid.*, 1.

5 Bertrand G. Ramcharan, "Equality and Nondiscrimination" in Louis Henkin (ed.), *The International Bill of Rights. The Covenant on Civil and Political Rights*, New York, Columbia University Press, 1981, 246.

discrimination have been identified as a topic that might lend itself to being reported upon in the so-called common core document.[6]

The conclusions that are drawn from the research here undertaken do not fully confirm this research hypothesis. Spontaneous harmonization in the interpretation and application of equality and non-discrimination seems to have occurred less than initially assumed. The human rights treaty bodies do show a number of commonalities in their approach to equality and non-discrimination: gender equality features prominently in the work of most of them for example, and the Committee on the Elimination of Discrimination against Women may have influenced some of the other Committees in their understanding of gender discrimination. However, in terms of analytical sophistication and degree of detail in recommendations, for instance, they tend to exhibit quite divergent practices. The Human Rights Committee has had to decide on a considerable number of complaints of discrimination. It tends to take a rather judge-like approach in its concluding observations too, with quite a detailed analysis and recommendations. The Committee on the Elimination of Racial Discrimination, which has remained most faithful to its original mandate of racial discrimination, seems to have benefited in the analysis of state reports much less of its individual complaints procedure than the HRC has. The Committee on Economic, Social and Cultural Rights seems to have devoted surprisingly little detailed attention to equality and non-discrimination in its concluding observations, though these principles might be a forceful instrument to further the realisation of economic, social and cultural rights. It is too early to say whether the recent adoption of a general comment on gender equality will represent a turning point. Commensurate with the very wide-running and detailed approach of the Convention itself, the Committee on the Elimination of Discrimination against Women has covered a wide range of issues. It may, therefore, sometimes prove difficult to apply an equality and non-discrimination analysis. Finally, the Committee on the Rights of the Child has paid sustained and explicit attention to the principles of non-discrimination and equality, which have been identified as one of the four general principles of the Convention on the Rights of the Child. It seems to have focused on some of the black holes of UN equality law, for example by taking up discrimination based on disability.

The reasons for the relatively low degree of spontaneous harmonization of the Committees' interpretation of non-discrimination and equality may be manifold, and

---

6 See UN Doc. HRI/MC/2004/3, *Guidelines on an Expanded Core Document and Treaty-Specific Targeted Reports and Harmonized Guidelines on Reporting Under the International Human Rights Treaties. Report of the Secretariat.* The common core document would contain detailed background information on human rights implementation, as well as substantive information on the congruent provisions. The common core document would constitute a common first part of each report presented to any treaty body.

rather difficult to identify. Some are recalled here. First, the UN human rights Committees have a very diverse mandate. Whereas for two of them non-discrimination and equality is the overarching perspective and the core issue to be treated, for others equality and non-discrimination are only one among many other issues. Moreover, for most Committees, the non-discrimination and equality provisions are parasitic, *i.e.* limited to the rights covered in the treaty. Only the Covenant on Civil and Political Rights contains a general free-standing prohibition of discrimination. Secondly, not all Committees have as yet made an attempt to systematise their thoughts on equality and non-discrimination, for instance, in a general comment/recommendation. Such systematisation might help to address issues of discrimination and equality under the reporting procedure in a more sustained and coherent fashion. Thirdly, Committees may feel less need in practice to harmonize their work in relation to non-discrimination and equality, than they have felt with regard to their procedures. This may be exemplified by the fact that the Meetings of Chairpersons and Inter-Committee Meetings have mainly focused on procedural harmonisation, and seem to have discussed to a lesser extent substantive issues.

This book starts off by briefly outlining the different treaty regimes on equality and non-discrimination. In a second chapter, conceptual issues of equality and non-discrimination are examined for each of the UN human rights treaty bodies. In particular, it explores how discrimination is understood, and to what extent all Committees use concepts as *de facto* and *de jure* discrimination, direct and indirect discrimination, intentional and non-intentional discrimination, multiple discrimination, systemic inequality and private discrimination. In a third chapter, the grounds of discrimination commonly referred to are scrutinized in greater detail. In addition, an overview is given of the issues that are usually addressed under a given ground. It is here that differences in approach become overtly clear. Divergence is confirmed in the fourth chapter that tackles the question which obligations ensue from the principles of equality and non-discrimination. Here again, the Committees sometimes take quite different approaches. An attempt is made to insert a degree of comparability by structuring the obligations along the well-known threefold typology commonly used under the International Covenant on Economic, Social and Cultural Rights *i.e.* obligations to respect, to protect and to fulfil. The latter disaggregates into sub-obligations to facilitate, to promote and to provide. In the final chapter, some of the implications of the Committees' divergent approach towards equality and non-discrimination are explored in light of the current wave of reform of the reporting procedure.

CHAPTER I.
TREATY REGIMES

All but one of the seven UN core human rights treaties contain explicit provisions on equality and non- discrimination.[7] The International Convention on the Elimination of All Forms of Racial Discrimination (ICERD) and the Convention on the Elimination of All Forms of Discrimination Against Women (CEDAW) are explicitly devoted to a particular form of discrimination, *i.e.* racial discrimination and sex/gender-based discrimination.

The International Covenant on Civil and Political Rights (CCPR) contains the most comprehensive non-discrimination guarantees,[8] including an independent or free-standing non-discrimination clause. On the contrary, the International Covenant on Economic, Social and Cultural Rights (CESCR), the Convention on the Rights of the Child (CRC) and the Convention on the Protection of All Migrant Workers and Members of Their Families (CMW) only contain a so-called accessory, subordinate or parasitic provision. This means that the equality and non-discrimination provision in the latter treaties is not autonomous, but only applies with regard to the rights set forth in the treaty concerned.[9]

The CRC and the CMW contain an equality and non-discrimination provision with respect to the rights of the particular vulnerable group they are concerned with, *i.e.* children, and migrant workers and members of their families. The Convention Against Torture and Inhuman or Degrading Treatment or Punishment (CAT) is the only UN core human rights treaty that lacks equality and non-discrimination provisions.[10]

---

7 The exception being the Convention Against Torture and Inhuman or Degrading Treatment or Punishment.

8 Lord Lester of Herne QC and Sarah Joseph, "Obligations of Non-Discrimination" in David Harris and Sarah Joseph (ed.), *The International Covenant on Civil and Political Rights and United Kingdom Law*, Oxford, Clarendon Press, 1995, 563.

9 Similarly, article 14 of the European Convention on Human Rights (E.C.H.R.) is of an accessory nature. Protocol No. 12, which entered into force on 1 April 2005, complements this treaty provision now with an independent prohibition of discrimination. For more details on equality and non-discrimination in the E.C.H.R., see *e.g.* Oddný Mjöll Arnadóttir, *Equality and Non-Discrimination under the European Convention on Human Rights*, The Hague, Martinus Nijhoff Publishers, 2003, 265 p., and in particular 33-41.

10 Discrimination is however mentioned in the definition of torture in article 1, para. 1 CAT, as the reason why severe pain or suffering might be inflicted on a person (see further in this chapter).

A. THE INTERNATIONAL CONVENTION ON THE ELIMINATION OF ALL FORMS OF RACIAL DISCRIMINATION (ICERD)

The ICERD is exclusively dedicated to racial discrimination. Therefore, all of its substantive rights provisions in part I refer to aspects of racial discrimination.

Article 1, para. 1 ICERD defines racial discrimination in the following way:[11]

> In this Convention, the term "racial discrimination" shall mean any distinction, exclusion, restriction or preference based on race, colour, descent, or national or ethnic origin which has the purpose or effect of nullifying or impairing the recognition, enjoyment or exercise, on an equal footing, of human rights and fundamental freedoms in the political, economic, social, cultural or any other field of public life.

According to the CERD, "the words 'based on' do not bear any meaning different from 'on the grounds of' in preambular paragraph 7."[12] As will be discussed in chapter II, the definition of racial discrimination offered in article 1 extends beyond measures which are explicitly discriminatory, "to encompass measures which are not discriminatory at face value but are discriminatory in fact and effect, that is, if they amount to indirect discrimination."[13]

Article 1, para. 2 ICERD allows for differentiation between citizens and non-citizens, albeit that discrimination against any particular nationality is prohibited in matters of nationality, citizenship or naturalization (art. 1, para. 3 ICERD):

> 2. This Convention shall not apply to distinctions, exclusions, restrictions or preferences made by a State Party to this Convention between citizens and non-citizens.
>
> 3. Nothing in this Convention may be interpreted as affecting in any way the legal provisions of States Parties concerning nationality, citizenship or naturalization, provided that such provisions do not discriminate against any particular nationality.

---

11 See UN Doc. HRI/GEN/1/Rev.7/Add.1, General Recommendation No. 30 (2004): *Discrimination Against Non Citizens*, para. 1: "Article 1, paragraph 1, of the Convention defines racial discrimination".

12 See UN Doc. HRI/GEN/1/Rev.7, General Recommendation XIV (1993), *Definition of Discrimination (Art. 1, par. 1)*, para. 1.

13 UN Doc. CERD/C/66/D/31/2003, Communication No. 31/3003, *L.R. v. Slovakia*, para. 10.4.

CERD had already pointed out that article 1, para. 2 was to "be construed so as to avoid undermining the basic prohibition of discrimination."[14] In a 2004 general recommendation on discrimination against non-citizens, it has clarified that the exception in art. 1, para. 2 ICERD is nowadays to be understood very restrictively (see further chapter III).[15]

Article 1, para. 4 ICERD provides for the possibility of taking affirmative action, *i.e.* special measures for the purpose of securing adequate advancement of certain racial or ethnic groups or individuals requiring such protection, as may be necessary in order to ensure such groups or individuals equal enjoyment or exercise of human rights and fundamental freedoms. Such measures should not, however, lead to the maintenance of separate rights for different racial groups and should not be continued after the objectives for which they were taken, have been achieved.

Article 2 ICERD reads:

> 1. States Parties condemn racial discrimination and undertake to pursue by all appropriate means and without delay a policy of eliminating racial discrimination in all its forms and promoting understanding among all races, and, to this end:
> (a) Each State Party undertakes to engage in no act or practice of racial discrimination against persons, groups of persons or institutions and to ensure that all public authorities and public institutions, national and local, shall act in conformity with this obligation;
> (b) Each State Party undertakes not to sponsor, defend or support racial discrimination by any persons or organizations;
> (c) Each State Party shall take effective measures to review governmental, national and local policies, and to amend, rescind or nullify any laws and regulations which have the effect of creating or perpetuating racial discrimination wherever it exists;
> (d) Each State Party shall prohibit and bring to an end, by all appropriate means, including legislation as required by circumstances, racial discrimination by any persons, group or organization;
> (e) Each State Party undertakes to encourage, where appropriate, integrationist multiracial organizations and movements and other means of eliminating barriers between races, and to discourage anything which tends to strengthen racial division.
>
> 2. States Parties shall, when the circumstances so warrant, take, in the social, economic, cultural and other fields, special and concrete measures to ensure the adequate development and protection of certain racial groups or individuals belonging to them, for the purpose of guaranteeing them the full and equal enjoyment of human rights and fundamental freedoms. These measures shall in no case entail as a consequence the maintenance of unequal or separate rights for different racial groups after the objectives for which they were taken have been achieved.

---

14 UN Doc. HRI/GEN/1/Rev.7, General Recommendation XIV (1993), *Definition of Discrimination (Art. 1, par. 1)*, para. 2.

15 UN Doc. HRI/GEN/1/Rev.7/Add.1, General Recommendation No. 30 (2004), *Discrimination Against Non Citizens.*

The Committee has pointed out the compulsory nature of the provisions of article 2 of the Convention,[16] and stressed that article 2, paragraph 1, (d) "makes it an obligation for States parties to prohibit racial discrimination committed not only by individuals but 'by any persons, group or organization'".[17]

Article 3 ICERD deals with racial segregation and apartheid and the undertaking of states to prevent, prohibit and eradicate all practices of this nature in territories under their jurisdiction.

Article 4, which proscribes the dissemination of ideas of racial superiority, and of organized activity likely to incite persons to racial violence, is considered to be one of the core articles of ICERD.[18] It reads:

> States Parties condemn all propaganda and all organizations which are based on ideas or theories of superiority of one race or group of persons of one colour or ethnic origin, or which attempt to justify or promote racial hatred and discrimination in any form, and undertake to adopt immediate and positive measures designed to eradicate all incitement to, or acts of, such discrimination and, to this end, with due regard to the principles embodied in the Universal Declaration of Human Rights and the rights expressly set forth in article 5 of this Convention, inter alia:
> (a) Shall declare an offence punishable by law all dissemination of ideas based on racial superiority or hatred, incitement to racial discrimination, as well as all acts of violence or incitement to such acts against any race or group of persons of another colour or ethnic origin, and also the provision of any assistance to racist activities, including the financing thereof;
> (b) Shall declare illegal and prohibit organizations, and also organized and all other propaganda activities, which promote and incite racial discrimination, and shall recognize participation in such organizations or activities as an offence punishable by law;
> (c) Shall not permit public authorities or public institutions, national or local, to promote or incite racial discrimination.

The Committee has repeatedly stressed the mandatory nature of these provisions.[19] It is an obligation of each state party to adopt immediate and positive measures

---

16 UN Doc. CERD/C/304/Add.12, para. 18 (Korea).

17 UN Doc. CERD/C/304/Add.71, para. 8 (Costa Rica). See also further chapter II.

18 UN Doc. CERD/C/62/CO/9, para. 12 (Slovenia).

19 UN Doc. HRI/GEN/1/Rev.7, General Recommendation XV (1993), *Organized Violence Based on Ethnic Origin (Art. 4)*, para. 2; General Recommendation VII (1985), *Legislation to Eradicate Racial Discrimination (Art. 4)*, para. 1; UN Doc. CERD/C/LUX/CO/13, para. 16 (Luxembourg); UN Doc. A/57/18, para. 461 (Yemen); UN Doc. A/57/18, para. 376 (Hungary); UN Doc. CERD/C/304/Add.105, para. 9 (Slovenia); UN Doc. CERD/C/304/Add.54, para. 17 (Cambodia); UN Doc. CERD/C/304/Add.42, para. 25 (Burundi); UN Doc. CERD/C/304/Add.35, para. 18 (Denmark); UN Doc. CERD/C/304/Add.34, para. 24 (Philippines); UN Doc. CERD/C/304/Add.33, para. 19 (Algeria); UN Doc. CERD/C/304/Add.20, para. 23 (United Kingdom); UN Doc. CERD/C/304/Add.19, para. 20 (Mauritius); UN Doc. CERD/C/304/Add.12, para. 19 (Korea); UN Doc. CERD/C/304/Add.1, paras. 9 and 14 (Colombia); UN Doc. A/50/18, para. 391 (Mexico); UN Doc. A/49/18, para. 408 (Iceland); UN Doc. A/49/18, para. 261 (Norway); UN Doc. A/49/18, para. 202 (Sweden); UN Doc. A/48/18, para. 231 (Korea).

designed to eradicate all incitement to or acts of racial discrimination.[20] States are also to enact specific penal legislation,[21] not merely as a means to ensure protection against existing violations, but as a preventive measure.[22] Criminalization of racial insults should be unconditional: a restrictive of "broad publicity" or "wider dissemination" required for the criminalization of racial insults, was considered not to be fully in conformity with the requirements of article 4 and 6 ICERD.[23] In accordance with article 4(b), legislation is to be adopted that declares illegal and prohibits any organization which promotes or incites to racism and racial discrimination.[24] The focus should be on the prohibition of racist organizations rather than on the prohibition of activities conducted by racist organizations.[25] Finally, in an individual communication the Committee has stressed the need to balance freedom of expression with the requirements of the Convention to prevent and eliminate all forms of racial discrimination, particularly in the context of statements made by members of political parties.[26]

Whereas article 1, paragraph 1, of the Convention only refers to the political, economic, social and cultural *fields*, article 5 ICERD lists more specifically the civil, political, economic, social and cultural rights in respect of which states undertake to prohibit and to eliminate racial discrimination in all its forms and to guarantee the right to everyone, without distinction as to race, colour, or national or ethnic origin, to equality before the law:[27]

> (a) The right to equal treatment before the tribunals and all other organs administering justice;
> (b) The right to security of person and protection by the State against violence or bodily harm, whether inflicted by government officials or by any individual group or institution;
> (c) Political rights, in particular the right to participate in elections – to vote and to stand for election – on the basis of universal and equal suffrage, to take part in the Government as well as in the conduct of public affairs at any level and to have equal access to public service;
> (d) Other civil rights, in particular:
>   (i) The right to freedom of movement and residence within the border of the State;
>   (ii) The right to leave any country, including one's own, and to return to one's country;
>   (iii) The right to nationality;
>   (iv) The right to marriage and choice of spouse;

20 UN Doc. CERD/C/304/Add.49, para. 13 (Lebanon).
21 UN Doc. CERD/C/304/Add.76, para. 9 (Colombia).
22 UN Doc. CERD/C/304/Add.96, para. 5 (Tonga).
23 UN Doc. CERD/C/62/D/25/2002, Communication No. 25/2002, *Ahmad Najaati Sadic v. Denmark*, para. 6.8.
24 UN Doc. CERD/C/60/CO/2, para. 14 (Belgium).
25 UN Doc. A/57/18, para. 335 (Canada). Compare with UN Doc. CERD/C/LUX/CO/13, para. 16 (Luxembourg).
26 UN Doc. CERD/C/63/D/27/2002, Communication No. 27/2002, *Kamal Quereshi v. Denmark*, para. 9.
27 See UN Doc. HRI/GEN/1/Rev.7, General Recommendation XIV (1993), *Definition of Discrimination (Art. 1, par. 1)*, para. 3.

(v) The right to own property alone as well as in association with others;
(vi) The right to inherit;
(vii) The right to freedom of thought, conscience and religion;
(viii) The right to freedom of opinion and expression;
(ix) The right to freedom of peaceful assembly and association;
(e) Economic, social and cultural rights, in particular:
(i) The rights to work, to free choice of employment, to just and favourable conditions of work, to protection against unemployment, to equal pay for equal work, to just and favourable remuneration;
(ii) The right to form and join trade unions;
(iii) The right to housing;
(iv) The right to public health, medical care, social security and social services;
(v) The right to education and training;
(vi) The right to equal participation in cultural activities;
(f) The right of access to any place or service intended for use by the general public, such as transport, hotels, restaurants, cafes, theatres and parks.

In the words of CERD:

> Article 5 of the Convention contains the obligation of States Parties to guarantee the enjoyment of civil, political, economic, social and cultural rights and freedoms without racial discrimination. Note should be taken that the rights and freedoms mentioned in article 5 do not constitute an exhaustive list.
>
> [...] Article 5 of the Convention, apart from requiring a guarantee that the exercise of human rights shall be free from racial discrimination, does not of itself create civil, political, economic, social or cultural rights, but assumes the existence and recognition of these rights.[28]

The Committee gave a far more extensive interpretation to article 5 ICERD in its concluding observations on Malawi. It first reminded Malawi of the fact that article 5 of the Convention implied the existence and recognition of civil, political, economic, social and cultural rights and submitted then "that full respect for human rights is the necessary framework for the efficiency of measures adopted to combat racial discrimination."[29]

In its jurisprudence, CERD has stressed that the right under article 5 (a) ICERD to equal treatment before the tribunals – without distinction as to race, colour or national or ethnic origin – applies to all types of judicial proceedings, including trial by jury. Inimical remarks made by a juror which can be seen as an indication of racial prejudice

---

28 UN Doc. HRI/GEN/1/Rev.7, General Recommendation XX (1996), *Non-Discriminatory Implementation of Rights and Freedoms (Art. 5)*, para. 1. See also UN Doc. CERD/C/39/D/2/1989, Communication No. 2/1989, *Demba Talibe Diop v. France*, para. 6.4.

29 UN Doc. CERD/C/63/CO/12, para. 7 (Malawi).

may thus be sufficient to disqualify a juror.[30] Due attention is to be given to the impartiality of jurors, and every effort is to be made more generally to prevent any form of racial bias from entering into judicial proceedings, which might result in adversely affecting the administration of justice on the basis of equality and non-discrimination.[31] The Committee has also found that municipal resolutions prohibiting Roma from settling, represent a violation of article 5 (d)(i) ICERD.[32] With regard to article 5 (e), the Committee has clarified that it has no mandate to see to it that economic, social and cultural rights are established; its task is rather to monitor implementation of these rights once they have been granted on equal terms.[33]

Article 6 guarantees effective protection and remedies against acts of racial discrimination, as well as the right to seek reparation or satisfaction for damage resulting from racial discrimination. It reads:

> States Parties shall assure to everyone within their jurisdiction effective protection and remedies, through the competent national tribunals and other State institutions, against any acts of racial discrimination which violate his human rights and fundamental freedoms contrary to this Convention, as well as the right to seek from such tribunals just and adequate reparation or satisfaction for any damage suffered as a result of such discrimination.

In the established jurisprudence of the Committee, "the terms of article 6 do not impose upon States parties the duty to institute a mechanism of sequential remedies in cases of alleged racial discrimination."[34] In other words, it is not necessary to provide remedies up to and including the Supreme Court level.

Finally, article 7 ICERD imposes the obligation to take educational and promotional measures to combat prejudices which lead to racial discrimination and to promote understanding, tolerance and friendship among nations and racial or ethnical groups. It reads:

> States Parties undertake to adopt immediate and effective measures, particularly in the fields of teaching, education, culture and information, with a view to combating prejudices which lead to racial discrimination and to promoting understanding, tolerance and friendship among nations and racial or ethnical groups, as well as to propagating the purposes and principles of the Charter

---

30 UN Doc. CERD/C/44/D/3/1991, Communication No. 3/1991, *Michel L.N. Narrainen v. Norway*, paras. 9.2 and 9.4.

31 *Ibid.*, para. 10.

32 UN Doc. CERD/C/57/D/13/1998, Communication No. 13/1998, *Anna Koptova v. Slovakia*, para. 10.1.

33 UN Doc. CERD/C/39/D/2/1989, Communication No. 2/1989, *Demba Talibe Diop v. France*, para. 6.4.

34 UN Doc. CERD/C/63/D/27/2002, Communication No. 27/2002, *Kamal Quereshi v. Denmark*, para. 7.5; UN Doc. CERD/C/36/D/1/1984, Communication No. 1/1984, *Dogan v. The Netherlands*, para. 9.4.

of the United Nations, the Universal Declaration of Human Rights, the United Nations Declaration on the Elimination of All Forms of Racial Discrimination, and this Convention.

B. THE INTERNATIONAL COVENANT ON CIVIL AND POLITICAL RIGHTS (CCPR)

Equality and non-discrimination is a cross-cutting theme in the CCPR.[35] The Covenant contains a number of provisions dealing with non-discrimination and equality. The core provisions are article 2, para. 1 and articles 3 and 26. Ramcharan identified five related principles in these three provisions:

- the principle of equal enjoyment of rights;
- the general principle of equality and the corollary principle of equality between men and women;
- the principle of equality before the law;
- the principle of equal protection of the law;
- and the principle of non-discrimination.[36]

Article 2, para. 1 CCPR prohibits discrimination[37] in the exercise of the Covenant's rights on a number of grounds. It reads:

> Each State Party to the present Covenant undertakes to respect and to ensure to all individuals within its territory and subject to its jurisdiction the rights recognized in the present Covenant, without distinction of any kind, such as race, colour, sex, language, religion, political or other opinion, national or social origin, property, birth or other status.

Article 3 CCPR addresses gender equality in particular:

> The States Parties to the present Covenant undertake to ensure the equal right of men and women to the enjoyment of all civil and political rights set forth in the present Covenant.

The express provision on gender equality in article 3 CCPR, which was added in the General Assembly, was included for emphasis,[38] in order to reinforce this fundamental principle.[39]

---

35 Raija Hanski and Martin Scheinin (ed.), *Leading Cases of the Human Rights Committee*, Turku, Åbo Akademi University, 2003, 329.

36 Ramcharan, supra note 5, 250.

37 For more details on the use of the words "discrimination" and "distinction" in the CCPR and the CESCR, in light of the drafting history, see Ramcharan, supra note 5, 251 and 258-259.

38 *Ibid.*, 251.

39 Nowak, supra note 2, 67.

It has been pointed out that this specific provision on the equal right of men and women is the only provision which is not just providing protection against discrimination, but the guarantee of equality.[40] The underlying assumption is that there is a qualitative difference between the prohibition of discrimination and the guarantee of equality. As Nowak puts it, article 3 is "formulated with a positive goal in mind".[41] The question arises whether this difference in formulation gives rise to different legal effects, *i.e.* whether additional duties flow from this positive formulation.[42] According to Nowak, "[a]rticle 3 does not afford increased protection in the event of gender-specific discrimination."[43] In chapter II, the question whether equality and non-discrimination have a different meaning will be addressed in more detail.

Both articles 2 and 3 CCPR limit the scope of the rights to be protected against discrimination to those set forth in the CCPR.[44] They have therefore been said to be of a parasitic[45] or accessory[46] character: a violation of these provisions can be found "only in conjunction with the concrete exercise (but not necessarily violation) of one of the substantive rights ensured by the Covenant."[47]

By contrast, article 26 CCPR holds an independent[48] or free-standing prohibition of discrimination, guaranteeing equality before the law and equal protection of the law:

> All persons are equal before the law and are entitled without any discrimination to the equal protection of the law. In this respect, the law shall prohibit any discrimination and guarantee to all persons equal and effective protection against discrimination on any ground such as race, colour, sex, language, religion, political or other opinion, national or social origin, property, birth or other status.

---

40 Lester and Sarah, supra note 8, 565.

41 Nowak, supra note 2, 67.

42 *Ibid.*, 67 and 69.

43 *Ibid.*, 69 and 71. In UN Doc. CCPR/C/34/D/202/1986, Communication No. 202/1986, *Ato del Avellanal v. Peru*, para. 10.2, the HRC does not seem to distinguish between the guarantees offered by article 3 and 26.

44 UN Doc. HRI/GEN/1/Rev.7, General Comment No. 18 (1989), *Non-Discrimination*, para. 12; for a comparison with the largely similar situation under article 14 E.C.H.R., see UN Doc. CCPR/C/78/D/998/2001, Communication No. 998/2001, *Althammer et al. v. Austria*, para. 8.4.

45 David Harris, "The International Covenant on Civil and Political Rights and the United Kingdom: An Introduction" in David Harris and Sarah Joseph (ed.), *The International Covenant on Civil and Political Rights and United Kingdom Law*, Oxford, Clarendon Press, 1995, 18, footnote 92.

46 Nowak, supra note 2, 28 and 34-36.

47 *Ibid.*, 28; UN Doc. CCPR/C/12/D/35/1978, Communication No. 35/1978, *Aumeeruddy-Cziffra et al. v. Mauritius*, para. 9.2 (b) 2 (i).

48 See most recently in UN Doc. CCPR/C/80/D/1115/2002, Communication No. 1115/2001, *Petersen v. Germany*, para. 6.7.

The HRC has held consistently that "Equal protection of the law is guaranteed without the need to identify a specific ground."[49] As article 26 derives from the principle of equal protection of the law without discrimination, it follows that legislation and the application thereof should not be discriminatory. Article 26 is a guarantee for persons regarding equal and effective protection against discrimination.[50]

Article 26 has been interpreted as requiring equality in any area of law, not just in those within the ambit of CCPR rights.[51] It is not limited to rights which are provided for in the Covenant, but is truly an autonomous right.[52] It is a "free-standing guarantee of non-discrimination in relation to all rights",[53] whether or not independently guaranteed in the CCPR. This liberal interpretation of article 26 has allowed the HRC to examine all kinds of complaints about violations outside the scope of the civil and political rights guaranteed under the CCPR, predominantly in relation to issues of social security. It is therefore not a duplication of the guarantee in article 2; its scope goes clearly beyond it.[54]

Article 26 prohibits discrimination in law and in fact in any field regulated and protected by public authorities.[55] The HRC has thus examined issues of discrimination under article 26 CCPR with regard to the right of conscientious objection, severance pay, the right to social security (unemployment benefit,[56] disability pensions, survivors'

49 See *e.g.* UN Doc. CCPR/C/77/D/983/2001, Communication No. 983/2001, *Love v. Australia*, para. 8.2; UN Doc. CCPR/C/71/D/819/1998, Communication No. 819/1998, *Kavanagh v. Ireland*, para. 10.3.

50 UN Doc. CCPR/C/29/D/172/1984, Communication No. 172/1984, *Broeks v. The Netherlands*, paras. 12 and 12.4.

51 Harris, supra note 45, 17.

52 See *e.g.* UN Doc. CCPR/C/75/D/854/1999, Communication No. 854/1999, *Wackenheim v. France*, para. 6.6.

53 Bayefski, supra note 3, 3; Sarah Joseph, Jenny Schultz and Melissa Castan, *The International Covenant on Civil and Political Rights. Cases, Materials, and Commentary*, Oxford, Oxford University Press, 2004 (2nd edition), 686. Compare with Hanski and Scheinin, supra note 35, 325.

54 UN Doc. HRI/GEN/1/Rev.7, General Comment No. 18 (1989), *Non-Discrimination*, para. 12; UN Doc. CCPR/C/75/D/854/1999, Communication No. 854/1999, *Wackenheim v. France*, para. 6.6; UN Doc. CCPR/C/29/D/182/1984, Communication No. 182/1984, *Zwaan-de Vries v. The Netherlands*; para. 12.3; UN Doc. CCPR/C/29/D/180/1984, Communication No. 180/1984, *Danning v. The Netherlands*; paras. 12.2 and 12.3; UN Doc. CCPR/C/29/D/172/1984, Communication No. 172/1984, *Broeks v. The Netherlands*; para. 12.3.

55 UN Doc. HRI/GEN/1/Rev.7, General Comment No. 18 (1989), *Non-Discrimination*, para. 12; UN Doc. CCPR/C/74/D/677/1996, Communication No. 677/1996, *Teesdale v. Trinidad and Tobago*, para. 9.8; UN Doc. CCPR/C/29/D/182/1984, Communication No. 182/1984, *Zwaan-de Vries v. The Netherlands*, para. 12.3; UN Doc. CCPR/C/29/D/180/1984, Communication No. 180/1984, *Danning v. The Netherlands*, para. 12.3; UN Doc. CCPR/C/29/D/172/1984, Communication No. 172/1984, *Broeks v. The Netherlands*, paras. 12.2 and 12.3.

56 UN Doc. CCPR/C/55/D/454/1991, Communication No. 454/1991, *Pons v. Spain*, para. 9.3; UN Doc. CCPR/C/29/D/180/1984, Communication No. 180/1984, *Danning v. The Netherlands*.

pensions,[57] children benefits, veteran's pensions), education subsidies, employment, public-health insurance, access to relevant information with regard to restitution claims (equal access to remedies),[58] and the right to property[59] (see further).[60] Article 26 covers not only entitlements which individuals entertain vis-à-vis the state, but also obligations assumed by them pursuant to law.[61]

The HRC has confirmed the free-standing nature of article 26 also in its examination of state reports. In its concluding observations on Switzerland, it held:

> The Committee regrets the maintenance of Switzerland's reservation to article 26 of the Covenant, which limits the applicability of the principle of the equality of all persons before the law and of the prohibition of discrimination to only those rights which are contained in the Covenant, whereas article 26 of the Covenant, as interpreted by the Committee, extends it to every area regulated and protected by the public authorities.[62]

It is generally accepted that the list of discriminatory grounds in article 26 CCPR is not limitative. In other words, differential treatment based on other grounds might equally be found to be discriminatory (see further chapter III on the grounds of discrimination). However, differential treatment based on one of the enumerated grounds creates a higher justificatory threshold:

> The Committee reiterates its constant jurisprudence that the right to equality before the law and to the equal protection of the law without any discrimination does not make all differences of treatment discriminatory. [...]. A different treatment based on one of the specific grounds enumerated in article 26, clause 2 of the Covenant, however, places a heavy burden on the State party to explain the reason for the differentiation.[63]

In its early jurisprudence, the HRC stressed that claimants had to establish that "their different treatment was attributable to their belonging to any identifiably distinct category which could have exposed them to discrimination on account of any of the grounds enumerated or "other status" referred to in article 26 of the Covenant."[64]

---

57 UN Doc. CCPR/C/44/D/415/1990, Communication No. 415/1990, *Pauger v. Austria.*

58 UN Doc. CCPR/C/76/D/757/1997, Communication No. 757/1997, *Pezoldova v. The Czech Republic*, para. 11.6.

59 UN Doc. CCPR/C/54/D/516/1992, Communication No. 516/1992, *Simunek et al. v. The Czech Republic*, para. 11.3.

60 For an overview of issues and cases, see *e.g.* Joseph, Schultz and Castan, supra note 53, 686-687 and Lester and Joseph, supra note 8, 571.

61 UN Doc. CCPR/C//D/273/1989, para. 6.5, Communication No. 273/1989, *B.d.B. v. The Netherlands.*

62 UN Doc. CCPR/C/79/Add.70, para. 11 (Switzerland).

63 UN Doc. CCPR/C/74/D/919/2000, Communication No. 919/2000, *Müller and Engelhard v. Namibia*, para. 6.7.

64 UN Doc. CCPR/C/35/D/273/1988, Communication No. 273/1988, *B.d.B. et al. v. The Netherlands*, para. 6.7.

Equality before the law and equal protection of the law is an obligation of immediate application. In *Zwaan – de Vries v. The Netherlands* on alleged discrimination between women and men in granting unemployment benefits, the government of The Netherlands had submitted that the elimination of discrimination in the economic, social and cultural field was subject to progressive realization and the state's available resources. The HRC rebutted:

> [...] the International Covenant on Civil and Political Rights would still apply even if a particular subject-matter is referred to or covered in other international instruments, [...] as in the present case, the International Covenant on Economic, Social and Cultural Rights. Notwithstanding the interrelated drafting history of the two covenants, it remains necessary for the Committee to apply fully the terms of the International Covenant on Civil and Political Rights. The Committee observes in this connection that the provisions of article 2 of the International Covenant on Economic, Social and Cultural Rights do not detract from the full application of article 26 of the International Covenant on Civil and Political Rights.[65]

More generally speaking, the HRC has paid little attention to budgetary constraints,[66] with some exceptions. In the *Cavalcanti* case, it accepted that the requirement that applicants for unemployment benefits are unemployed at the time of application, was reasonable and objective.[67] Similarly, in the case of *Snijder v. the Netherlands*, it accepted as a justification of differential treatment of those who had to make personal contributions (*i.e.* those in residential care) and those who were not required to do so (*i.e.* those not in residential care) the affordability of the insurance scheme.[68]

The HRC has made clear that although article 26 CCPR is applicable to social security legislation, it does not per se contain any obligation with regard to matters that may be provided for by legislation. In other words, article 26 CCPR *for instance* does not require enacting pension legislation. However, if a state does adopt social security legislation, this legislation must comply with article 26 CCPR.[69]

---

65 UN Doc. CCPR/C/35/D/218/1986, Communication No. 218/1986, *Vos v. The Netherlands*, para. 11.2; UN Doc. CCPR/C/29/D/182/1984, Communication No. 182/1984, *Zwaan-de Vries v. The Netherlands*, para. 12.1; UN Doc. CCPR/C/29/D/180/1984, Communication No. 180/1984, *Danning v. The Netherlands*, para. 12.1.

66 See *e.g.* some cases on social security benefits (UN Doc. CCPR/C/29/D/172/1984, Communication No. 172/1984, *Broeks v. The Netherlands*; UN Doc. CCPR/C/66/D/786/1997, Communication No. 786/1997, *Vos v. The Netherlands*) and a case on funding of private religious schools (UN Doc. CCPR/C/67/D/694/1996, Communication No. 694/1996, *Waldman v. Canada*).

67 UN Doc. CCPR/C/49/D/418/1990, Communication No. 418/1990, *Cavalcanti Araujo-Jongen v. The Netherlands*, para. 7.4.

68 UN Doc. CCPR/C/63/D/651/1995, Communication No. 651/1995, *Snijders et al. v. The Netherlands*, para. 8.3.

69 See *e.g.* UN Doc. CCPR/C/44/D/415/1990, Communication No. 415/1990, *Pauger v. Austria*, para. 7.2; UN Doc. CCPR/C/49/D/418/1990, Communication No. 418/1990, *Cavalcanti Araujo-Jongen v. The Netherlands*, para. 7.3.

Complaints with respect to violations of economic, social and cultural rights have very often been declared admissible. It is however only with regard to a few distinctions that a violation was found on the merits,[70] *i.e.* the requirement for a married woman but not for a married man to prove that she was a breadwinner in order to receive unemployment benefits;[71] a different pension regime for Senegalese and French veterans;[72] the differentiation between widowers and widows for granting a survivor's pension;[73] a lower pension for male civil servants than for female civil servants;[74] or a distinction with regard to social security benefits between children born either in wedlock or after a given date also out of wedlock on the one hand, and out of wedlock prior to that date on the other hand[75] (see also further). Most of these violations relate to gender discrimination. Schmidt observed in 1995 that the HRC had sought "quietly to 'back-peddle' on this jurisprudence, by limiting the instances in which no objective and justifiable objectives for differences of treatment in social security matters were found to be present."[76] Former Committee member Higgins stated that article 26 had been interpreted "very cautiously, particularly where there [were] public funds at issue, such as in the field of welfare benefits."[77] Harris considered the possible retreat from the position that legal equality in respect of economic and social rights was to be provided immediately, a "regrettable, retrograde step."[78] Although some individual members of the HRC seem willing to take this "regrettable step" (see further for references), the Committee has confirmed its earlier position in the recent case of *Derksen v. The Netherlands.*

Article 26 CCPR has a triple content: it guarantees equality before the law and equal protection of the law, and it imposes the duty to protect from discrimination.[79] The

70 Joseph, Schultz and Castan, supra note 53, 688

71 UN Doc. CCPR/C/29/D/182/1984, Communication No. 182/1984, *Zwaan-de Vries v. The Netherlands.*

72 UN Doc. CCPR/C/35/D/196/1985, Communication No. 196/1985, *Gueye et al. v. France*, para. 9.5.

73 UN Doc. CCPR/C/65/D/716/1996, Communication No. 716/1996, *Pauger v. Austria*, para. 10.2; UN Doc. CCPR/C/44/D/415/1990, Communication No. 415/1990, *Pauger v. Austria*, para. 7.4.

74 UN Doc. CCPR/C/66/D/786/1997, Communication No. 786/1997, *Vos v. The Netherlands*, paras. 7.6 and 8.

75 UN Doc. CCPR/C/80/D/976/2001, Communication No. 976/2001, *Derksen v. The Netherlands*, para. 9.3.

76 See Markus Schmidt, "The Complementarity of the Covenant and the European Convention on Human Rights –Recent Developments" in David Harris and Sarah Joseph (ed.), *The International Covenant on Civil and Political Rights and United Kingdom Law*, Oxford, Clarendon Press, 1995, 637-638, and the references found there.

77 Rosalie Higgins, "Foreword" in David Harris and Sarah Joseph (ed.), *The International Covenant on Civil and Political Rights and United Kingdom Law*, Oxford, Clarendon Press, 1995, xvii.

78 Harris, supra note 45, 18.

79 According to Opsahl, "The text of article 26 thus enshrines – or less respectfully, lumps together – three related concepts: Equality before the law, equal protection of the law, and protection against discrimination" which are said to have their origins respectively in the 18th, 19th and 20th century (Torkel Opsahl, "Equality in Human Rights Law with Particular Reference to Art. 26 of the

formal claim of *equality before the law* requires equality in the application and enforcement of the law:[80] legal administrators – judges, administrative officials – are not to apply legislation in a discriminatory manner.[81] It is an issue of discussion whether the discretionary power to commute sentences might be in the field of application of article 26.[82]

The requirement of *equal protection of the law* is directed at the national legislator, who is to grant legal rights and duties to all without discrimination, and who should not adopt or maintain discriminatory legislative standards.[83] Bossuyt qualifies this equality in law as substantive equality.[84] More often, substantive equality denotes not so much equality in law but equality in fact (see further chapter II). Nowak integrates both approaches when he argues that equal protection of the law requires from the state to ensure substantive equality by way of legislation.[85]

Nowak has submitted that the requirement of equal protection of the law contains both positive and negative aspects, in that the legislator would be required to both refrain from discrimination when enacting laws, and to afford effective *protection against discrimination*.[86] The latter element can also be understood as a third and separate obligation, *i.e.* the duty to prohibit discrimination by private persons.[87] In the view of Bossuyt, the first sentence of article 26 has (indirect) horizontal effect, in that it contains an obligation to take measures in order to prevent private persons or organisations from violating the principle of equality. The second sentence imposes the obligation to prohibit private discrimination, if necessary by extending the legal protection offered.[88]

Some other articles in the CCPR equally prohibit discrimination in specific circumstances. Article 4, para. 1 CCPR prohibits discrimination with relation to derogations:

International Covenant of Civil and Political Rights" in Manfred Nowak, Dorothea Steurer and Felix Ermacora (ed.), *Fortschritt im Bewusstsein der Grund- und Menschenrechte: Festschrift für Felix Ermacora*, Kehl am Rhein, Engel, 1988, 52).

80 Lester and Joseph, supra note 8, 566.

81 Nowak, supra note 2, 466-467.

82 UN Doc. CCPR/C/74/D/677/1996, Communication No. 677/1996, *Teesdale v. Trinidad and Tobago*. According to three dissenters, it does (see partly dissenting opinions of Kretzmer and Shearer, and of Yrigoyen).

83 Lester and Joseph, supra note 8, 566. This interpretation seems to be supported by *inter alia* Ramcharan (Ramcharan, supra note 5, 255), Nowak (supra note 2, 468) and Bossuyt (Marc Bossuyt, "Het gelijkheidsbeginsel in de internationale pacten inzake mensenrechten" in André Alen and Paul Lemmens (ed.), *Gelijkheid en non-discriminatie*, Antwerp, Kluwer, 1991, 38).

84 Bossuyt, supra note 83, 37.

85 Nowak, supra note 2, 469.

86 *Ibid.*, 468.

87 See *e.g.* Lester and Joseph, supra note 8, 566.

88 Bosssuyt, supra note 83, 44.

> In time of public emergency which threatens the life of the nation and the existence of which is officially proclaimed, the States Parties to the present Covenant may take measures derogating from their obligations under the present Covenant to the extent strictly required by the exigencies of the situation, provided that such measures are not inconsistent with their other obligations under international law and do not involve discrimination solely on the ground of race, colour, sex, language, religion or social origin.

Article 14, para. 1, first sentence CCPR guarantees equality before courts and tribunals. It reads: "All persons shall be equal before the courts and tribunals." Equality before the court includes equal access to the court.[89] In the view of the HRC, it is unnecessary to examine a possible violation of article 14 if there is already a finding of a violation under article 26.[90] Therefore, the guarantee of article 14, para. 1, first sentence seems to be covered also by article 26 CCPR. The HRC has held that article 14 applies too with regard to the right to social security.[91] It thus seems to accord the same autonomous position to article 14 as it does to article 26. Both guarantees are therefore not inherently limited to the rights protected in the CCPR.

Article 20, para. 2 CCPR requires the prohibition by law of advocacy of hatred that constitutes incitement to discrimination:

> Any advocacy of national, racial or religious hatred that constitutes incitement to discrimination, hostility or violence shall be prohibited by law.

Some provisions impose positive obligations,[92] *i.e.* with regard to equality in marriage and child protection. Article 23, para. 4 CCPR reads:

> States Parties to the present Covenant shall take appropriate steps to ensure equality of rights and responsibilities of spouses as to marriage, during marriage and at its dissolution. In the case of dissolution, provision shall be made for the necessary protection of any children.

Article 24, para. 1 CCPR reads:

> Every child shall have, without any discrimination as to race, colour, sex, language, religion, national or social origin, property or birth, the right to such measures of protection as are required by his status as a minor, on the part of his family, society and the State.

---

89 UN Doc. HRI/GEN/1/Rev.7, General Comment No. 13 (1984), *Article 14 (Administration of Justice)*, para. 3.

90 UN Doc. CCPR/C/71/D/819/1998, Communication No. 819/1998, *Kavanagh v. Ireland*, para. 10.3.

91 UN Doc. CCPR/C/60/D/552/1993, Communication No. 552/1993, *Kall v. Poland*, paras. 13.2.

92 UN Doc. HRI/GEN/1/Rev.7, General Comment No. 18 (1989), *Non-Discrimination*, para. 5. See also further, chapter IV.

Finally, Article 25 CCPR guarantees for every *citizen* the right to take part in public affairs, and the right to vote and to be elected without discrimination on any of the prohibited grounds. It equally provides for equal access to public service:

> Every citizen shall have the right and the opportunity, without any of the distinctions mentioned in article 2 and without unreasonable restrictions:
> (a) To take part in the conduct of public affairs, directly or through freely chosen representatives;
> (b) To vote and to be elected at genuine periodic elections which shall be by universal and equal suffrage and shall be held by secret ballot, guaranteeing the free expression of the will of the electors;
> (c) To have access, on general terms of equality, to public service in his country.

Equality and non-discrimination are prominently present in the general comment the HRC has devoted to article 25. In this general comment, the Committee explains that no distinctions are permitted between citizens in the enjoyment of their political rights on the grounds of race, colour, sex, language, religion, political or other opinion, national or social origin, property, birth or other status. Distinctions between those who are entitled to citizenship by birth and those who acquire it by naturalization may raise questions of compatibility with article 25.[93] Where a mode of direct participation by citizens is established, no distinction should be made between citizens as regards their participation on the grounds mentioned in article 2, paragraph 1.[94] Persons who are otherwise eligible to stand for election should not be excluded by unreasonable or discriminatory requirements such as education, residence or descent, or by reason of political affiliation. No person should suffer discrimination or disadvantage of any kind because of that person's candidacy.[95] Conditions relating to nomination dates, fees or deposits should be reasonable and not discriminatory.[96] The drawing of electoral boundaries and the method of allocating votes should not distort the distribution of voters or discriminate against any group and should not exclude or restrict unreasonably the right of citizens to choose their representatives freely.[97]

With regard to access to public service, in order to ensure it on general terms of equality, the criteria and processes for appointment, promotion, suspension and dismissal must be objective and reasonable. Affirmative measures may be taken in appropriate cases to ensure that there is equal access to public service for all citizens. Basing access to public service on equal opportunity and general principles of merit, and providing secured tenure, ensures that persons holding public service positions are free from political interference or pressures. It is of particular importance to ensure that persons

93 *Ibid.*, para. 3. Compare with Ramcharan, supra note 5, 263.
94 *Ibid.*, para. 6.
95 *Ibid.*, para. 15.
96 *Ibid.*, para. 16.
97 *Ibid.*, para. 21.

do not suffer discrimination in the exercise of their rights under article 25, subparagraph (c), on any of the grounds set out in article 2, paragraph 1.[98]

The HRC has developed some jurisprudence under article 25 (c), in particular on the dismissal of civil servants and judges. It has held that

> the principle of access to public service on general terms of equality implies that the State has a duty to ensure that it does not discriminate against anyone. This principle is all the more applicable to persons employed in the public service and to those who have been dismissed.[99]

Also,

> access to public service on general terms of equality encompasses a duty, for the State, to ensure that there is no discrimination on the ground of political opinion or expression. This applies *a fortiori* to those who hold positions in the public service.[100]

On the other hand, it has pointed out rightfully that article 25 (c) does not entitle every citizen to obtain guaranteed employment in the public service: it only guarantees access on general terms of equality.[101] A complaint was lodged to the HRC by a Polish former officer of the Civic Militia. Posts of members of the Civic Militia had retroactively been reclassified as security police posts. The HRC reached the conclusion that no violation had taken place, for the complainant had not been singled out for reclassification of his post, the posts of all members of the security police had been abolished without distinction or differentiation; and he had not been precluded from access to civil service during the verification procedure.[102] On the contrary, the dismissal of judges by Presidential Decree after a war in an effort to cleanse the judiciary, but without following disciplinary procedures was found to be in violation of article 25 (c) read in conjunction with article 14, para. 1 and of art. 2, para. 1 CCPR.[103] Equally, the dismissal of a judge before the expiry of his term, without effective judicial protections, and targeting the judge in person was found to be an attack on the independence of

---

98 *Ibid.*, para. 23.

99 UN Doc. CCPR/C/78/D/933/2000, Communication No. 933/2000, *Adrien Mundyo Busyo et al. v. Congo*, para. 5.2.

100 UN Doc. CCPR/C/57/D/422/1990, Communication No. 422/1990, *Adimayo M. Aduayom T. Diasso and Yawo S. Dobou v. Togo*, para. 7.5.

101 UN Doc. CCPR/C/60/D/552/1993, Communication No. 552/1993, *Kall v. Poland*, paras. 13.2 and 13.6.

102 *Ibid.*, paras. 13.3-13.5.

103 UN Doc. CCPR/C/78/D/933/2000, Communication No. 933/2000, *Adrien Mundyo Busyo et al. v. Congo*, para. 5.2.

the judiciary and in violation of the right of access, on general terms of equality, to public service.[104]

Finally, the lack of remedies to challenge the illegal dismissal of a school director was also found to be in violation of art. 25 (c) in conjunction with article 2 CCPR.[105]

C. THE INTERNATIONAL COVENANT ON ECONOMIC, SOCIAL AND CULTURAL RIGHTS (CESCR)

The CESCR contains two provisions on non-discrimination. Its articles 2 and 3 are broadly similar to those in the CCPR.[106] Art. 2, para. 2 CESCR reads:

> The States Parties to the present Covenant undertake to guarantee that the rights enunciated in the present Covenant will be exercised without discrimination of any kind as to race, colour, sex, language, religion, political or other opinion, national or social origin, property, birth or other status.

Similar to article 2, para. 2 CCPR, the provision of article 2 CESCR does not contain an autonomous or free-standing right to be free from discrimination; it only prohibits discrimination in the exercise of the substantive rights it contains, and is therefore to be linked to the enjoyment of a substantive right.[107] For that purpose, it might be sufficient, however, that the subject falls within the general scope of a substantive right. It is thus possible that discrimination in the enjoyment of a substantive right amounts to a violation of art. 2, para. 2 without there being a simultaneous violation of the substantive right.[108]

The CESCR contains a similarly phrased specific provision on equal rights of men and women. Article 3 CESCR reads:

---

104 UN Doc. CCPR/C/78/D/814/1998, Communication No. 814/1998, *Pastukhov v. Belarus*, para. 7.3.

105 UN Doc. CCPR/C/75/D/641/1995, Communication No. 641/1995, *Gedumbe v. Congo*, paras 5.2 and 5.3.

106 Ramcharan points out that art. 2 CESCR refers to "discrimination", whereas art. 2 CCPR refers to "distinction". This appears to be one of the inconsistencies due to changing membership and shifting coalitions in the Third Committee of the General Assembly at the time of drafting (see Ramcharan, supra note 5, 251).

107 UN Doc. E/C.12/2005/3, General Comment No. 16 (2005), Article 3: The Equal Right of Men and Women to the Enjoyment of All Economic, Social and Cultural Rights, para. 2.

108 Magdalena Sepúlveda, *The Nature of the Obligations under the International Covenant on Economic, Social and Cultural Rights*, Antwerp, Intersentia, 2003, 380-381. This position is fully in line with the one taken by the HRC and the E.Ct.H.R. on the accessory non-discrimination clauses their respective treaties contain.

> The States Parties to the present Covenant undertake to ensure the equal right of men and women to the enjoyment of all economic, social and cultural rights set forth in the present Covenant.

Article 3 imposes the double obligation of gender equality in and before the law. Equality in the law is to be respected by the legislature. Equality before the law is to be respected by administrative agencies, court and tribunals when applying the law.[109] In Sepúlveda's view, article 3 holds an additional and more specific requirement.[110] This was confirmed by the Committee in its 2005 general comment on this article. The Committee states that it goes beyond the prohibition of discrimination in art. 2, para. 2, albeit that both articles are integrally related and mutually reinforcing: the elimination of discrimination is fundamental to the enjoyment of economic, social and cultural rights on the basis of equality.[111]

It is generally assumed that the rights enumerated in the CESCR are subject to progressive realization, in light of available resources, as provided for in general terms in article 2, para. 1. However, the CESCR Committee has stressed that the prohibition of discrimination is not susceptible to progressive realization; it is an obligation of immediate effect.[112]

Non-discrimination features prominently in every of the Committee's general comments on a substantive right. It has been said that the right to housing cannot be seen in isolation from *inter alia* the principle of non-discrimination,[113] and the enjoyment of the right to adequate housing should *e.g.* not be subjected to any form of discrimination (entitlement to adequate housing regardless of age, economic status, group or other affiliation or status and other such factors).[114] Any discrimination in access to food, as well as to means and entitlements for its procurement with the purpose or effect of nullifying or impairing the equal enjoyment or exercise of economic, social and cultural rights constitutes a violation of the Covenant.[115] Non-discrimination and equality have been said to be one of the essential features of the rights to edu-

---

109 UN Doc. E/C.12/2005/3, General Comment No. 16 (2005), *Article 3: The Equal Right of Men and Women to the Enjoyment of All Economic, Social and Cultural Rights*, para. 9.

110 Sepúlveda, supra note 108, 404.

111 UN Doc. E/C.12/2005/3, General Comment No. 16 (2005), *Article 3: The Equal Right of Men and Women to the Enjoyment of All Economic, Social and Cultural Rights*, paras. 2 and 3.

112 *Ibid.*, para. 16; UN Doc. HRI/GEN/1/Rev.7, General Comment No. 3 (1990), *The Nature of States Parties' Obligations*, paras. 1 and 32. Compare with UN Doc. E/C.12/1/Add.103, para. 38 (Italy), specifically as far as equal pay for work of equal value is concerned. See also further chapter II.

113 UN Doc. HRI/GEN/1/Rev.7, General Comment No. 4 (1991), *The Right to Adequate Housing (Art. 11(1) of the Covenant)*, para. 9.

114 *Ibid.*, para. 6.

115 UN Doc. HRI/GEN/1/Rev.7, General Comment No. 12 (1999), *The Right to Adequate Food (Art. 11)*, para. 18.

cation,[116] health[117] and water,[118] and part of the core obligation pertaining to these rights.[119] Particular attention has also been paid to non-discrimination in the more recent general comments under the heading of "Special topics of broad application".[120]

D. THE CONVENTION ON THE ELIMINATION OF ALL FORMS OF DISCRIMINATION AGAINST WOMEN (CEDAW)

In the view of the CEDAW Committee, the articles 1 to 5 and 24 CEDAW form the general interpretative framework for all of the Convention's substantive articles. Three obligations are central to this general interpretative framework:

1° to ensure that there is no direct or indirect discrimination in law, and that women are protected against discrimination;

2° to improve the *de facto* position of women through concrete and effective policies and programmes; and

3° to address prevailing gender relations and the persistence of gender-based stereotypes.[121]

Article 1 CEDAW mirrors article 1 ICERD. It prohibits sex discrimination with regard to all civil, political, economic, social and cultural rights. Article 1 CEDAW reads:

---

116 UN Doc. HRI/GEN/1/Rev.7, General Comment No. 13 (1999), *The Right to Education (Art. 13)*, para. 6.

117 UN Doc. HRI/GEN/1/Rev.7, General Comment No. 14 (2000), *The Right to the Highest Attainable Standard of Health (Art. 12)*, para. 12.

118 UN Doc. HRI/GEN/1/Rev.7, General Comment No. 15 (2002), *The Right to Water (Arts. 11 and 12 of the International Covenant on Economic, Social and Cultural Rights)*, para. 12.

119 *Ibid.*, para. 37 (b): to ensure the right of access to water and water facilities and services on a non-discriminatory basis, especially for disadvantaged or marginalized groups; General Comment No. 14 (2000), *The Right to the Highest Attainable Standard of Health (Art. 12)*, para. 43: to ensure the right of access to health facilities, goods and services on a non-discriminatory basis, especially for vulnerable or marginalized groups; General Comment No. 13 (1999), *The Right to Education (Art. 13)*, para. 57: to ensure the right of access to public educational institutions and programmes on a non-discriminatory basis.

120 See UN Doc. HRI/GEN/1/Rev.7, General Comment No. 15 (2000), *The Right to Water (Arts. 11 and 12 of the International Covenant on Economic, Social and Cultural Rights)*, paras. 13-16; General Comment No. 14 (2000), *The Right to the Highest Attainable Standard of Health (Art. 12)*, paras. 18-19; General Comment No. 13 (1999), *The Right to Education (Art. 13)*, paras. 31-37.

121 UN Doc. HRI/GEN/1/Rev.7, General Recommendation No. 25 (2004), *On Article 4, paragraph 1, of the Convention on the Elimination of All Forms of Discrimination against Women – Temporary Special Measures*, para. 7.

> For the purposes of the present Convention, the term "discrimination against women" shall mean any distinction, exclusion or restriction made on the basis of sex which has the effect or purpose of impairing or nullifying the recognition, enjoyment or exercise by women, irrespective of their marital status, on a basis of equality of men and women, of human rights and fundamental freedoms in the political, economic, social, cultural, civil or any other field.

Articles 2 and 3 impose a comprehensive obligation to eliminate discrimination, whereas articles 5 to 16 contain more specific obligations.[122]

Article 2 CEDAW reads:

> States Parties condemn discrimination against women in all its forms, agree to pursue by all appropriate means and without delay a policy of eliminating discrimination against women and, to this end, undertake:
> (a) To embody the principle of the equality of men and women in their national constitutions or other appropriate legislation if not yet incorporated therein and to ensure, through law and other appropriate means, the practical realization of this principle;
> (b) To adopt appropriate legislative and other measures, including sanctions where appropriate, prohibiting all discrimination against women;
> (c) To establish legal protection of the rights of women on an equal basis with men and to ensure through competent national tribunals and other public institutions the effective protection of women against any act of discrimination;
> (d) To refrain from engaging in any act or practice of discrimination against women and to ensure that public authorities and institutions shall act in conformity with this obligation;
> (e) To take all appropriate measures to eliminate discrimination against women by any person, organization or enterprise;
> (f) To take all appropriate measures, including legislation, to modify or abolish existing laws, regulations, customs and practices which constitute discrimination against women;
> (g) To repeal all national penal provisions which constitute discrimination against women.

Article 2 is one of the Convention's core articles. The CEDAW Committee regards article 2 as a fundamental and core provision of the Convention,[123] and considers any reservation to that article to be contrary to the object and purpose of the Convention and incompatible with international law.[124]

Article 3 stipulates:

> States Parties shall take in all fields, in particular in the political, social, economic and cultural fields, all appropriate measures, including legislation, to ensure the full development and advan-

122 UN Doc. HRI/GEN/1/Rev.7, General Recommendation No. 19 (1992), *Violence against Women*, para. 10.

123 UN Doc. A/52/38/Rev.1 (part II), para. 433 (Bangladesh). Compare with UN Doc. A/56/38 (part II), para. 74 (Singapore), in which the Committee declared "articles 2 and 16 [to be] the very essence of obligations under the Convention".

124 UN Doc. A/52/38/Rev.1, para. 59 (Morocco). Compare also with UN Doc. A/56/38 (part I), para. 327 (Egypt); UN Doc. A/55/38 (part II), para. 186 (Iraq).

cement of women, for the purpose of guaranteeing them the exercise and enjoyment of human rights and fundamental freedoms on a basis of equality with men.

Articles 4 CEDAW allows states parties to take affirmative action ("temporary special measures" in the language of CEDAW) and special measures:[125]

1. Adoption by States Parties of temporary special measures aimed at accelerating de facto equality between men and women shall not be considered discrimination as defined in the present Convention, but shall in no way entail as a consequence the maintenance of unequal or separate standards; these measures shall be discontinued when the objectives of equality of opportunity and treatment have been achieved.
2. Adoption by States Parties of special measures, including those measures contained in the present Convention, aimed at protecting maternity shall not be considered discriminatory.

Article 5 concerns the elimination of social prejudices and traditional practices, and article 6 focuses on trafficking and sexual exploitation of women.

Articles 7 to 9 of part II of CEDAW deal with equality of women and men in political and public life,[126] in international representation and participation, and with regard to nationality of women and their children. Articles 10 to 13 of part III cover the equal rights of women and men in the fields of education (article 10), employment (article 11), access to health care services throughout the life cycle[127] (article 12) and other areas of economic and social life (article 13). Article 14 specifically addresses the situation of rural women. Article 15 contains provisions on equality before the law and equal legal capacity. Article 16 aims at eliminating discrimination against women in marriage and family relations.[128] The Committee considers article 16 critical to the full enjoyment by women of their rights.[129]

---

125 See also UN Doc. HRI/GEN/1/Rev.7, General Recommendation No. 25 (2004), *On Article 4, paragraph 1, of the Convention on the Elimination of All Forms of Discrimination against Women – Temporary Special Measures.*

126 In UN Doc. HRI/GEN/1/Rev.7, General Recommendation No. 23 (1997), *Political and Public Life*, para. 5, the CEDAW Committee has clarified that all areas of public and political life are envisaged: "Article 7 obliges States parties to take all appropriate measures to eliminate discrimination against women in political and public life and to ensure that they enjoy equality with men in political and public life. The obligation specified in article 7 extends to all areas of public and political life and is not limited to those areas specified in subparagraphs (a), (b) and (c). [...]."

127 See also UN Doc. HRI/GEN/1/Rev.7, General Recommendation No. 24 (1999), *Article 12 of the Convention on the Elimination of All Forms of Discrimination against Women – Women and Health*, para. 2.

128 See also UN Doc. HRI/GEN/1/Rev.7, General Recommendation No. 21 (1994), *Equality in Marriage and Family Relations.*

129 UN Doc. A/52/38/Rev.1 (part II), para. 433 (Bangladesh). See also higher under article 2 CEDAW.

E. THE CONVENTION AGAINST TORTURE AND OTHER CRUEL, INHUMAN OR DEGRADING TREATMENT OR PUNISHMENT (CAT)

CAT is the only UN core human rights treaty that does not contain any explicit prohibition of discrimination (see higher). Reference is however made to discrimination in the definition of torture in article 1, para. 1 CAT, as the reason why severe pain or suffering might be inflicted on a person:

> For the purposes of this Convention, the term "torture" means any act by which severe pain or suffering, whether physical or mental, is intentionally inflicted on a person for such purposes as obtaining from him or a third person information or a confession, punishing him for an act he or a third person has committed or is suspected of having committed, or intimidating or coercing him or a third person, or for any reason based on discrimination of any kind, when such pain or suffering is inflicted by or at the instigation of or with the consent or acquiescence of a public official or other person acting in an official capacity.

The absence of an explicit prohibition of discrimination does not mean that the Committee Against Torture (CAT Committee) ignores issues of discrimination. It appointed for instance, among its members a thematic rapporteur on discriminatory practices in May 1998.[130] When dealing with individual complaints, issues of discrimination have sometimes been raised and/or addressed.[131]

F. THE CONVENTION ON THE RIGHTS OF THE CHILD (CRC)

Four general principles inspire the Convention on the Rights of the Child, one of which is non-discrimination.[132] Being a general principle of the CRC, the principle of non-

130 UN Doc. A/55/44, para. 25.

131 Issues of gender equality have been mentioned in passing in a case of forced return to Iran, a country where there was a danger that the women concerned would be subjected to torture upon return (*i.e.* stoning for adultery) (see UN Doc. CAT/C/25/D/149/1999, Communication No. 149/1999, *A.S. v. Sweden*, para. 8.7).

132 See *e.g.* UN Doc. HRI/GEN/1/Rev.7, General Comment No. 5 (2003), *General Measures of Implementation of the Convention on the Rights of the Child (arts. 4, 42 and 44, para. 6)*, paras. 4 and 12; General Comment No. 1 (2001), *The Aims of Education*, para. 6. Compare with UN Doc. CRC/C/15/Add.223, para. 28 (Indonesia); UN Doc. CRC/C/15/Add.207, para. 23 (Sri Lanka); UN Doc. CRC/C/15/Add.202, para. 23 (Haiti); UN Doc. CRC/C/15/Add.199, para. 23 (Romania); UN Doc. CRC/C/15/Add.197, para. 29 (Korea); UN Doc. CRC/C/15/Add.196, para. 21 (Estonia).

discrimination applies irrespective of budgetary resources.[133] The Committee has also stressed that the guarantee of non-discrimination applies to "each child within [the state party's] jurisdiction".[134]

Art. 2 CRC, which contains the prohibition of discrimination, reads:

> 1. States Parties shall respect and ensure the rights set forth in the present Convention to each child within their jurisdiction without discrimination of any kind, irrespective of the child's or his or her parents' or legal guardian's race, colour, sex, language, religion, political or other opinion, national, ethnic or social origin, property, disability, birth or other status.
> 2. States Parties shall take all appropriate measures to ensure that the child is protected against all forms of discrimination or punishment on the basis of the status, activities, expressed opinions, or beliefs of the child's parents, legal guardians, or family members.

Here too, as is the case with most general non-discrimination provisions in other UN core human rights treaties, the prohibition of discrimination is an accessory right. It cannot be invoked independently, but only with regard to the "rights set forth in the Convention".

G. THE CONVENTION ON THE PROTECTION OF THE RIGHTS OF ALL MIGRANT WORKERS AND MEMBERS OF THEIR FAMILIES (CMW)

The CMW contains several references to the principle of non-discrimination. Article 1, para. 1 CMW reads:

> The present Convention is applicable, except as otherwise provided hereafter, to all migrant workers and members of their families without distinction of any kind such as sex, race, colour, language, religion or conviction, political or other opinion, national, ethnic or social origin, nationality, age, economic position, property, marital status, birth or other status.

Article 7 CMW provides:

> States Parties undertake, in accordance with the international instruments concerning human rights, to respect and to ensure to all migrant workers and members of their families within their territory or subject to their jurisdiction the rights provided for in the present Convention without

---

133 UN Doc. CRC/C/15/Add. 20, para. 19 (France); UN Doc. CRC/C/15/Add. 1, para. 14 (Bolivia). Compare with the position taken by the CERD, the HRC, the CESCR Committee and the CEDAW Committee, which have equally submitted that the realization of the principle of non-discrimination is not subject to progressive realization.

134 UN Doc. CRC/C/15/Add.178, para. 6 (Belgium).

> distinction of any kind such as to sex, race, colour, language, religion or conviction, political or other opinion, national, ethnic or social origin, nationality, age, economic position, property, marital status, birth or other status.

Again, non-discrimination is not an independent but an accessory right. It therefore only applies in relation to the rights provided for in the CMW.

Article 18, para. 1 CMW provides for equality before the law with nationals of the state concerned for migrant workers and members of their families. Articles 25 CMW guarantees equal treatment in respect of remuneration and other conditions of work and terms of employment. No derogation from the principle of equality of treatment is permissible in private contracts of employment. Article 27 CMW extends the principle of equality of treatment to social security, provided migrant workers and members of their families fulfil the requirements provided for by the applicable legislation of the state concerned and the applicable treaties.

The CMW entered into force on 1 July 2003 only, and the CMW Committee has not yet started the examination of state reports. It is therefore too early to comment on the CMW Committee's interpretation of the provisions on non-discrimination.

H. CONCLUSIONS

The treaty regimes on non-discrimination and equality do not point unequivocally to convergence or congruence. On the one hand, little overall convergence in the provisions on non-discrimination and equality of six UN core human rights treaties[135] can be pinpointed. Some contain a definition of discrimination (ICERD and CEDAW), others do not; some focus exclusively on (an aspect of) non-discrimination (ICERD and CEDAW), others deal with a range of rights, among which non-discrimination and equality. One contains a general self-standing prohibition of discrimination (CCPR), the others contain only an accessory right to non-discrimination (CESCR, CRC, CMW); some are devoted exclusively to gender equality (CEDAW), others contain an explicit guarantee for equality between men and women (CCPR and CESCR) and still others refer to sex as one of the prohibited grounds, etc. Furthermore, the list of prohibited grounds differs from treaty to treaty (CCPR and CESCR contain an identical list; CRC and CMW list more prohibited grounds).

On the other hand, it is also obvious that some "clusters of commonality" can be detected, *i.e.* common definitions, concepts, grounds or provisions among some of the seven

[135] All apart from CAT, which does not really contain a non-discrimination provision.

core UN human rights treaties. First of all, ICERD and CEDAW – the two treaties exclusively dedicated to non-discrimination – share a similar definition of discrimination, *i.e.* any distinction, exclusion or restriction made on the basis of certain grounds which has the purpose or effect of nullifying or impairing the recognition, enjoyment or exercise, on an equal footing, of human rights and fundamental freedoms in the political, economic, social, cultural or any other field. The other core human rights treaties do not contain a definition of discrimination.[136]

Secondly, all but one of the general non-discrimination provisions is of an accessory or parasitic nature. They only apply in relation to the rights listed in the treaty concerned. The only exception to this rule is article 26 CCPR, which is an independent or free-standing provision on non-discrimination.

Thirdly, the field of application of the non-discrimination provisions extends in principle in all treaties at least to all people within a state's territory and subject to its jurisdiction. The CCPR and the CMW explicitly refer to territory and jurisdiction. The CRC refers only to jurisdiction. ICERD, CESCR and CEDAW are silent on this matter. ICERD explicitly allows for differentiation between citizens and non-citizens,[137] as does the CCPR with regard to political rights (art. 25) and CESCR with regard to economic rights in developing countries (art. 2, para. 3).

Fourthly, sex/gender discrimination is a very prominent issue, not only in the treaty dedicated to this particular type of discrimination (CEDAW), but also in the CCPR and the CESCR. Their common article 3 reads that the states parties undertake to ensure the equal right of men and women to the enjoyment of all rights set forth in the respective Covenants.

Fifthly, equality before the law is guaranteed by the following congruent provisions: article 5, (a) ICERD, articles 14, para. 1 and 26 CCPR, article 15 CEDAW and article 18, para. 1 CMW.

Finally, the four core human rights treaties that do not focus specifically on one form of discrimination (CCPR, CESCR, CRC and CMW) enumerate to a large extent the same prohibited grounds of discrimination, such as race, colour, sex, language, religion, political or other opinion, national or social origin, property, birth or other status. In addition to this list, which covers all the prohibited grounds of the two 1966 Covenants (CCPR and CESCR), the CRC and in particular the CMW contain a

---

136 In chapter II, the definitions used by each of the Committees will be examined.

137 Albeit that the CERD has severely restricted this kind of differentiation in its 2004 general recommendation on this issue.

number of other prohibited grounds of discrimination, such as ethnic origin (CRC and CMW), disability (CRC), conviction, nationality, age, economic position and marital status (CMW). The grounds of discrimination will be discussed at great length in chapter III, but first we will turn to the concept of discrimination and equality, and the qualifiers employed by the UN human rights treaty bodies.

CHAPTER II. THE CONCEPT OF EQUALITY AND NON-DISCRIMINATION

A. DEFINITIONS AND QUALIFIERS

1. DEFINITIONS

There is no universally accepted definition of discrimination, or equality. Nor do the seven core UN human rights treaties offer a common definition of discrimination or equality. ICERD and CEDAW hold a specific definition of discrimination (the former on racial discrimination, the latter on gender discrimination), while the other treaties do not define discrimination at all.

Broadly speaking, two types of definition of discrimination can be distinguished. On the one hand, there is the definition that features in article 1, para. 1 ICERD and article 1 CEDAW. This definition qualifies as discrimination any distinction, exclusion, restriction or preference based on a number of grounds which has the purpose or effect of nullifying or impairing the recognition, enjoyment or exercise, on an equal footing, of human rights and fundamental freedoms in the political, economic, social, cultural or any other field of public life. On the other hand, there is a now widely used and generally accepted definition of discrimination,[138] also by the European Court of Human Rights,[139] which contains four elements or criteria to determine whether differential treatment is justifiable and does not amount to discrimination.[140] These four elements are the following:

---

138 This definition has been qualified by *inter alia* Sepúlveda as "the international law principle of non-discrimination," see Sepúlveda, supra note 108, 418.

139 The European Court of Human Rights introduced this working definition in the famous *Belgian Linguistics Case* (E.Ct.H.R, *Belgian Linguistics Case*, 23 July 1968, Series A, No. 6, para. 10: a differentiation has an objective and reasonable justification if it pursues a legitimate aim, and if there is proportionality between the means used and the aim sought to be realised.

140 See *e.g.* P. Van Dijk and G.J.H. Van Hoof, *Theory and Practice of the European Convention on Human Rights*, The Hague, Kluwer Law International, 1998, 719; Katarina Frostell, "Gender Difference and the Non-Discrimination Principle in the CCPR and the CEDAW" in Lauri Hannikainen and Eeva Nykänen (ed.), *New Trends in Discrimination Law – International Perspectives*, Turku, Turku Law School 1999, 34; Bayefski, supra note 3, 11-18.

- whether there is differential treatment;
- of equal cases (comparability test);
- whether there is an objective and reasonable justification (justification test);
- whether there is proportionality between aim and means (proportionality test).

A second inconclusive issue is whether non-discrimination and equality are simply synonyms,[141] or whether both terms are qualitatively different, whereby equality not only linguistically may incorporate more positive obligations[142] but also entails other and/or more legal effects.[143]

The two above-mentioned questions will be used as entry points to scrutinize the UN human rights treaty bodies' conceptions of equality and non-discrimination in the latter part of this chapter.

2. QUALIFIERS

Equality and non-discrimination are often further qualified with twin adjectives like *de jure* and *de facto* equality and discrimination, intentional and non-intentional discrimination, direct and indirect discrimination, and the concepts of multiple discrimination, systemic or structural inequality and private discrimination. These qualifiers are shortly introduced. Their appearance and meaning in the Committees' decisions will be checked hereafter.

a. *De Jure and De Facto Discrimination and Equality*

De jure or legal discrimination refers to discrimination in laws and policies. *De facto* discrimination denotes discrimination in practice.

Similar qualifiers are used with regard to the concept of equality. *De jure* or formal equality refers to equal treatment of similarly situated individuals.[144] *De facto* or substantive equality hints at equality of results. It therefore "accepts departures from strict equality in order to ameliorate the position of disadvantaged groups in society, or to

---

141 See *e.g.* Bayefski, supra note 3, 1; Opsahl, supra note 79, 52-53.

142 See *e.g.* Lester and Joseph, supra note 8, 565; Joseph, Schultz and Castan, supra note 53, 681. Compare with Paul Lemmens, "Gelijkheid en non-discriminatie in het internationale recht: synthese" in André Alen and Paul Lemmens (ed.), *Gelijkheid en non-discriminatie*, Antwerp, Kluwer, 1991, 89-90, and Ramcharan, supra note 5, 252.

143 For Nowak's negative answer on the latter question as far as the CCPR is concerned, see higher chapter I.

144 Frostell, supra note 140, 29, as taken from Vierdag and McKean.

guarantee the rights of those not equally situated".[145] Bossuyt does not seem to equate *de jure* equality with formal equality, and *de facto* equality with substantive equality. In his understanding of article 26 CCPR, *de jure equality* encompasses both formal equality (equality before the law, *i.e.* in the application of laws) and substantive equality (equality in the law).[146] *De facto equality* does not so much refer to substantive equality (equality in the law), but to equality in practice.[147] The crucial shift in meaning takes place here with regard to the concept of substantive equality, which is not understood as equality of results or equality in practice, but as equality in the law.

b. *Intentional and Non-Intentional Discrimination*

Discriminatory intent is not a necessary element of discrimination. Discrimination can occur on purpose, or distinctions can be discriminatory as an unintended outcome or effect. The definition in both ICERD and CEDAW refers to both kinds of discrimination ("with purpose or effect").[148]

c. *Direct and Indirect Discrimination*

The twin concepts of direct and indirect discrimination originate from the European Community legal order.[149] Direct discrimination occurs when differential treatment takes place that is directly connected with a person's association with one of the protected categories.[150] It involves the less favourable treatment on prohibited grounds of an *individual* compared to someone else in comparable circumstances.[151] Indirect discrimination occurs when a neutral measure is having a disparate and discriminatory effect on different *groups* of people,[152] and cannot be justified by reasonable and objective criteria. In the case of indirect discrimination, treating unequals equally leads to unequal results which can have the effect of fostering inequality. Indirect discrimination deals with institutional and structural biases.[153] Lester and Joseph suggest that the proof of direct discrimination is determined by comparison between individuals,

145 *Ibid.*, 30, as taken from the PCIJ's 1935 Advisory Opinion on *Minority Schools in Albania.*
146 Compare with Opsahl, supra note 79, 53.
147 Bossuyt, supra note 83, 37 and 45. See also higher in chapter I.
148 Article 1, para. 1 CERD; article 1 CEDAW.
149 Frostell, supra note 140, 37 and 43.
150 UN Doc. E/CN.4/2004/40, *Analytical study of the High Commissioner for Human Rights on the Fundamental Principle of Non-Discrimination in the Context of Globalization*, para. 12.
151 Lester and Joseph, supra note 8, 575.
152 Compare with Lester and Joseph, supra note 8, 575; Joseph, Schultz and Castan, supra note 53, 694: a practice, rule, requirement or condition is neutral on its face but impacts disproportionately upon particular groups, without any objective justification.
153 UN Doc. E/CN.4/2004/40, *Analytical study of the High Commissioner for Human Rights on the Fundamental Principle of Non-Discrimination in the Context of Globalization*, para. 12.

whereas the proof of indirect discrimination is determined by comparison between groups.

Discriminatory purpose is sometimes equated with direct discrimination, and discriminatory effect with indirect discrimination. According to Frostell, these equations are wrong. Indirect discrimination may well be unintentional.[154] While conceptually these qualifiers may be different, in practice it seems extremely difficult to distinguish between them (see further).

No reference is made to indirect discrimination in the treaty texts.[155] The concept has however been used by all Committees discussed.

d. Multiple Discrimination

Multiple discrimination concerns discrimination on several prohibited grounds simultaneously. Quite often, multiple discrimination takes place on the grounds of sex/gender in combination with another ground. All Committees but the HRC have explicitly used the concept of multiple discrimination in their analyses.

e. Systemic Inequality

Sometimes the concept of systemic inequality is invoked. Systemic inequality has been said to occur due to the influence of "dominant societal values" which are "always male, heterosexual and able-bodied", and "reflect a state's prevalent race, religion, and language."[156]

f. Private Discrimination

Private discrimination occurs when third parties, rather than the state party itself, discriminate. The lead question here is whether and to what extent the state party in which private discrimination occurs, can be held responsible therefore. Due attention will be paid to this issue in chapter IV, under the obligation to protect.

B. THE COMMITTEES

In what follows, the conceptualization of equality and non-discrimination by the fully operational UN human rights treaty bodies will be examined, with the exception of

154 Frostell, supra note 140, 51.
155 *Ibid.*, 44.
156 Joseph, Schultz and Castan, supra note 53, 735.

the CAT Committee, for the reasons explained above. Attention will be paid to the definition of discrimination and the qualifiers used.

1. CERD

a. *Definition*

As pointed out earlier, ICERD is one of the two UN core human rights treaties that contain a definition of discrimination. Article 1, para. 1 ICERD reads:

> In this Convention, the term "racial discrimination" shall mean any distinction, exclusion, restriction or preference based on race, colour, descent, or national or ethnic origin which has the purpose or effect of nullifying or impairing the recognition, enjoyment or exercise, on an equal footing, of human rights and fundamental freedoms in the political, economic, social, cultural or any other field of public life.

The Committee has stressed the rather broad scope of this definition of racial discrimination.[157]

A distinction is said to be contrary to ICERD if it has either the purpose or the effect of impairing particular rights and freedoms.[158] According to CERD, this is confirmed by the obligation placed upon states parties by article 2, paragraph 1 (c), to nullify any law or practice which has the effect of creating or perpetuating racial discrimination.[159] It has further clarified that "the definition of racial discrimination in article 1 expressly extends beyond measures which are explicitly discriminatory, to encompass measures which are not discriminatory at face value but are discriminatory in fact and effect, that is, if they amount to indirect discrimination."[160]

In two situations, differentiation of treatment does not constitute discrimination, *i.e.* if the criteria for such differential treatment, judged against the objectives and purposes of the Convention, are legitimate, or if it amounts to special measures as provided for in article 1, para. 4 ICERD.[161] The legitimacy of criteria depends on their effects, and more in particular whether or not particular actions have an unjustifiable disparate

157 UN Doc. CERD/C/304/Add.42, para. 10 (Burundi); UN Doc. CERD/C/304/Add.34, para. 11 (Philippines).
158 See also further under the qualifiers of intentional and non-intentional discrimination.
159 UN Doc. HRI/GEN/1/Rev.7, General Recommendation XIV (1993), *Article 1, paragraph 1 of the Convention*, para. 1.
160 UN Doc. CERD/C/66/D/31/2003, Communication No. 31/3003, *LR. v. Slovakia*, para. 10.4.
161 UN Doc. HRI/GEN/1/Rev.7, General Recommendation XIV (1993), *Article 1, paragraph 1 of the Convention*, para. 2.

impact on a group distinguished by one of the grounds enumerated in article 1, para. 1 ICERD, *i.e.* race, colour, descent, or national or ethnic origin:

> In considering the criteria that may have been employed, the Committee will acknowledge that particular actions may have varied purposes. In seeking to determine whether an action has an effect contrary to the Convention, it will look to see whether that action has an unjustifiable disparate impact upon a group distinguished by race, colour, descent, or national or ethnic origin.[162]

Quite recently, the Committee seems to have embraced the more commonly used definition of discrimination too. In its 2005 concluding observations on Australia, it referred to the need for "an objective and reasonable justification for differential treatment", and submitted that

> differential treatment [...] would constitute discrimination if the criteria for such differentiation, judged in the light of the objectives and purposes of the Convention, are not applied pursuant to a legitimate aim, and are not proportional to the achievement of that aim.[163]

Similarly, in *Sefic v. Denmark*, it concluded that the requirement to speak Danish in order to be able to obtain a car insurance was based on reasonable and objective grounds, and did not therefore constitute racial discrimination.[164]

Several characteristics of the principle of non-discrimination have been highlighted. First of all, CERD has pointed out that the principle of non-discrimination is not subject to the availability of resources.[165] The other Committees have taken a similar stance (see further). Secondly, no derogations to the principle of non-discrimination are allowed.[166]

b. *Qualifiers*

i. *De Jure* and *De Facto*

De facto discrimination has been a major issue of concern for the CERD in the examination of state reports. It has expressed concern about *de facto* racial discrimina-

162 *Ibid.*
163 UN Doc. CERD/C/AUS/CO/14, para. 24 (Australia).
164 UN Doc. CERD/C/66/D/32/2003, Communication No. 32/2003, *Sefic v. Denmark*, para. 7.2.
165 UN Doc. CERD/C/65/CO/4, para. 16 (Madagascar).
166 UN Doc. A/57/18, para. 300 (Botswana).

tion and (school[167] or residential[168]) segregation,[169] in particular towards (ethnic) minorities,[170] indigenous people,[171] Amerasian children and against Korean women married to asylum seekers.[172] One source of *de facto* discrimination towards certain groups of immigrants might be the "two-speed" integration that sometimes occurs, *i.e.* the easier acceptance of some groups over others in a society.[173]

In recent years, the *de facto* segregation of and discrimination against Roma has been at the centre of the CERD's attention.[174] Issues of concern have been the *de facto* segregation of Roma children in education[175] (segregation in special schools,[176] including special remedial classes for mentally disabled children),[177] housing[178] and employment.[179] It has been noted that the *de facto* discrimination the Roma face in the enjoyment of their economic, social and cultural rights increases their vulnerability in a context of economic crisis.[180]

The Committee has equally expressed concern over the persistence of *de facto* caste-based discrimination:

> It notes in particular concern over information on the existence of segregated residential areas for Dalits, social exclusion of inter-caste couples, restriction to certain types of employment, and denial of access to public spaces, places of worship and public sources of food and water, as well as allegation, that public funds were used for the construction of separate water taps for Dalits.[181]

Finally, it has encouraged states to ensure *de facto* equal access to the courts to all persons, including members of minority and ethnic groups.[182]

---

167 UN Doc. CERD/C/64/CO/7, para. 12 (The Netherlands); UN Doc. CERD/C/304/Add.104, para. 14 (The Netherlands).
168 UN Doc. CERD/C/64/CO/2, para. 13 (Brazil); UN Doc. CERD/C/304/Add.76, para. 22 (Colombia); UN Doc. CERD/C/304/Add.103, para. 14 (Sweden).
169 UN Doc. CERD/C/304/Add.24, para. 19 (Germany).
170 UN Doc. CERD/C/65/CO/6, para. 9 (Portugal); UN Doc. CERD/C/304/Add.29, para. 17 (Bulgaria).
171 UN Doc. CERD/C/62/CO/2, paras. 11 and 13 (Ecuador); UN Doc. A/50/18, para. 304 (Guatemala).
172 UN Doc. CERD/C/304/Add.65, para. 13 (Republic of Korea).
173 UN Doc. CERD/C/65/CO/6, para. 11 (Portugal).
174 UN Doc. CERD/C/65/CO/7, para. 9 (Slovakia); UN Doc. CERD/C/63/CO/4, para. 9 (Czech Republic); UN Doc. CERD/C/304/Add.67, para. 11 (Portugal).
175 UN Doc. CERD/C/304/Add.109, para. 10 (Czech Republic).
176 UN Doc. CERD/C/304/Add.47, para. 13 (Czech Republic).
177 UN Doc. CERD/C/65/CO/7, para. 8 (Slovakia).
178 UN Doc. CERD/C/304/Add.109, para. 10 (Czech Republic).
179 UN Doc. A/49/18, para. 503 (Spain).
180 UN Doc. CERD/C/304/Add.29, para. 8 (Bulgaria); UN Doc. CERD/C/304/Add.4, para. 12 (Hungary).
181 UN Doc. CERD/C/64/CO/5, para. 12 (Nepal).
182 UN Doc. CERD/C/60/CO/3, para. 17 (Costa Rica).

ii. Intentional and Non-Intentional

The distinction between intentional and non-intentional discrimination is overtly present in the definition of discrimination given in article 1 ICERD, which refers to differential treatment which has the *purpose or effect* of impairing the recognition, on an equal footing, of human rights and fundamental freedoms. The Committee, in its general recommendation No. XIV of 1993, emphasized that the decisive factor for concluding whether or not a particular action is discriminatory is its "unjustifiable disparate impact upon a group distinguished by race, colour, descent, or national or ethnic origin."[183]

In its concluding observations too, it has stressed that the definition of racial discrimination under article 1, paragraph 1, of the Convention includes the effect as well as the purpose of an act,[184] and it has cautioned states for rules and practices which might be discriminatory in effect, such as the so-called "two-weeks rule" that was applied to restrict foreign domestic workers legal stay in the Hong Kong Special Administrative Region,[185] the establishment of special reception classes for non-Danish speaking school children, attempts of municipalities to prevent undue concentrations of ethnic minority families in "socially-burdened" urban neighbourhoods,[186] rules restricting certain occupations to French nationals,[187] or restrictive provisions with regard to asylum-seekers.[188]

The CERD also has had the opportunity to examine a complaint about discrimination in the examination and quota system in Australia for overseas-trained doctors. All overseas-trained doctors were subjected to the quota system, and were required to sit written and clinical examinations, irrespective of their race or national origin. The Committee concluded that even if the system had a favourable effect for doctors trained in Australian and New Zealand medical schools, it did not necessarily constitute discrimination on the basis of race or national origin since all overseas-trained doctors were subjected to the same quota system, and were required to sit the same examinations, and since medical students in Australia did not share a single national origin.[189]

---

183 UN Doc. HRI/GEN/1/Rev.7, General Recommendation XIV (1993), *Article 1, paragraph 1 of the Convention*, para. 2. See also *e.g.* UN Doc. CERD/C/AUS/CO/14, paras. 13 and 20.

184 UN Doc. CERD/C/304/Add.20, para. 18 (United Kingdom); UN Doc. A/56/18, para. 393 (United States).

185 UN Doc. A/56/18, para. 248 (China).

186 UN Doc. CERD/C/304/Add.3, paras. 10-11 (Denmark).

187 UN Doc. A/49/18, para. 152 (France).

188 UN Doc. CERD/C/AZE/CO/4, para. 13: priority concern; UN Doc. A/48/18, para. 448 (Germany).

189 UN Doc. CERD/C/54/D/8/1996, Communication No. 8/1996, *B.M.S. v. Australia*, para. 9.2.

iii. Direct and Indirect

Sometimes, the Committee seems to recognize the existence of indirect discrimination, but without labelling it as such. In Brazil, illiterate citizens did not have the right to be elected to public office. This rule was in fact discriminatory for the indigenous, black and mestizo groups, among whom illiteracy was found in particular. The Committee expressed its concern

> over the fact that illiterate citizens, who are found especially among the indigenous, black or mestizo groups, do not have the right to be elected to public office. In light of article 5(c) of the Convention, the Committee recommends that the State party adopt adequate measures to combat illiteracy and allow all citizens the enjoyment of all political rights, in particular the right to be elected to public office.[190]

More often, it has mentioned indirect discrimination directly and explicitly, for instance, when welcoming new legislation in which direct and indirect discrimination were prohibited,[191] when asking to include in a next periodic report statistical information on prosecutions launched and punishment awarded in cases of offences which had a bearing on racial discrimination, including indirect discrimination,[192] when asking to implement effective measures to address direct and indirect discrimination,[193] or when expressing concern over direct and indirect forms of discrimination in recruitment procedures,[194] or over an inadequate definition of indirect discrimination in domestic law.[195] It was equally concerned

> that policies and practices such as the housing dispersal policy, the quota system for the admission of minority children to certain crèches and nurseries, and the reported prohibition of the use of the mother tongue in some of these establishments may, though aimed at facilitating integration, lead to indirect discrimination against minorities and refugees.[196]

Recently, it has unequivocally confirmed that indirect discrimination is forbidden under ICERD:

> As indirect discrimination is forbidden under the Convention, the Committee draws the attention of the State party on the ethnic dimension that these inequalities (i.e. regional distribution of resources) could have.[197]

---

190 UN Doc. CERD/C/64/CO/2, para. 20 (Brazil).
191 UN Doc. CERD/C/64/CO/8, para. 9 (Sweden); UN Doc. A/57/18, para. 372 (Hungary).
192 UN Doc. A/56/18, para. 350 (Trinidad and Tobago).
193 UN Doc. CERD/C/60/CO/6, para. 5 (Jamaica).
194 UN Doc. CERD/C/304/Add.46, para. 12 (The Netherlands).
195 UN Doc. CERD/C/63/CO/7, para. 8 (Latvia).
196 UN Doc. CERD/C/60/CO/5, para. 12 (Denmark).
197 UN Doc. CERD/C/65/CO/4, para. 16 (Madagascar). Compare with UN Doc. CERD/C/AUS/CO/14, para. 20.

CERD has defined indirect discrimination as "discriminatory in fact and effect." It thus seems to equate indirect discrimination with non-intentional discrimination. Indirect discrimination can only be assessed by fully taking into account the particular context and circumstances, "as by definition indirect discrimination can only be demonstrated circumstantially."[198]

iv. Multiple Discrimination

Double or multiple discrimination has been recognized relatively recently by CERD in some of its general recommendations, and the concept is now also used as an analytical concept in CERD's concluding observations. Typically, double or multiple discrimination is based simultaneously on gender, in combination with discrimination of minorities (in particular Roma), descent-based discrimination, or discrimination based on social, national or ethnic origin.

No explicit mention was made of multiple discrimination in the 2000 general recommendation on the gender-related dimensions of racial discrimination, although the concept was implicitly recognized by the very subject of the general recommendation itself.[199] In 2001, the Committee for the first time used the concept of double discrimination.[200] It has made clear that multiple discrimination falls within the scope of the Convention,[201] and expressed concern about double or multiple discrimination against women belonging to ethnic minorities (*i.e.* discrimination based on gender as well as ethnic or national origin, race or descent).[202] It has asked states to address the issue in their action plan on the rights of women,[203] and to establish special programmes aimed at facilitating their social enhancement.[204] CERD has equally paid attention to double or multiple discrimination against Roma women,[205] and women belonging to vulnerable groups.[206] Only once, the Committee has invoked the problem of

---

198 UN Doc. CERD/C/66/D/31/2003, Communication No. 31/3003, *LR. v. Slovakia*, para. 10.4.

199 UN Doc. HRI/GEN/1/Rev.7, General Recommendation No. XXV (2000), *Gender Related Dimensions of Racial Discrimination.*

200 UN Doc. CERD/C/304/Add.78, para. 10 (Uruguay).

201 UN Doc. CERD/C/60/CO/1, para. 9 (Austria).

202 UN Doc. HRI/GEN/1/Rev.7, General Recommendation XXIX (2002), *Article 1, paragraph 1, (Descent)*, paras. 11-12; UN Doc. CERD/C/IRL/CO/2, para. 23; UN Doc. A/57/18, para. 443 (Senegal); UN Doc. A/57/18, para. 357 (Estonia); UN Doc. CERD/C/304/Add.78, para. 10 (Uruguay).

203 UN Doc. CERD/C/62/CO/2, para. 15 (Ecuador).

204 UN Doc. CERD/C/304/Add.78, para. 16 (Uruguay).

205 UN Doc. HRI/GEN/1/Rev.7, General Recommendation No. XXVII (2002), *Discrimination against Roma*, para. 6; UN Doc. CERD/C/65/CO/7, para. 6 (Slovakia); UN Doc. CERD/C/65/CO/6, para. 13 (Portugal).

206 UN Doc. CERD/C/64/CO/5, para. 16 (Nepal).

double discrimination with regard to another group in addition to women, *i.e.* children.[207]

v. Systemic Inequality

Rather exceptionally, CERD has referred to structural discrimination and inequality, in particular with regard to black and mestizo communities, and to indigenous peoples in Latin America.[208]

vi. Private Discrimination

Without explicitly using the notion of "private discrimination", CERD has referred repeatedly to discrimination in the private sector, or by private persons.[209] It has pointed out that racial segregation may arise without any initiative or direct involvement by the public authorities.[210] ICERD contains specific provisions that make it mandatory for a state to criminalise racial discrimination (see further chapter IV, under the obligation to protect).

2. HRC

a. Definition

As pointed out by the HRC in its general comment No. 18 on non-discrimination, the CCPR does not offer any definition of discrimination.[211] Fully in line with the definition of discrimination found in ICERD and CEDAW, the HRC has adopted the following definition of discrimination:

---

207 UN Doc. A/57/18, para. 404 (Mali). The Committee has refrained from making clear however what constitutes "double discrimination" against children, *i.e.* on which double ground this discrimination would be based.

208 UN Doc. CERD/C/64/CO/2, para. 12 (Brazil); UN Doc. CERD/C/304/Add.11, para. 8 (Brazil); UN Doc. CERD/C/304/Add.1, para. 10 (Colombia).

209 UN Doc. HRI/GEN/1/Rev.7, General Recommendation XX (1996), *Non-Discriminatory Implementation of Rights and Freedoms (Art. 5)*, para. 5; UN Doc. CERD/C/60/CO/14, para. 16 (Switzerland); UN Doc. A/56/18, para. 434 (Liberia); UN Doc. A/56/18, para. 269 (Cyprus); UN Doc. A/56/18, para. 247 (China); UN Doc. CERD/C/304/Add.102, para. 21 (United Kingdom); UN Doc. CERD/C/304/Add.84, para. 14 (Haiti); UN Doc. CERD/C/304/Add.71, para. 8 (Costa Rica); UN Doc. CERD/C/304/Add.64, para. 9 (Austria); UN Doc. CERD/C/304/Add.24, para. 17 (Germany); UN Doc. CERD/C/304/Add.22, paras. 12 and 19 (Belarus); UN Doc. CERD/C/304/Add.20, para. 20 (United Kingdom); UN Doc. CERD/C/304/Add.9 (United Kingdom).

210 UN Doc. HRI/GEN/1/Rev.7, General Recommendation XIX (1995), *Racial Segregation and Apartheid (Art. 3)*, paras. 3-4. See also UN Doc. CERD/C/64/CO/7, para. 12 (The Netherlands); UN Doc. CERD/C/64/CO/2, para. 13 (Brazil).

211 UN Doc. HRI/GEN/1/Rev.7, General Comment No. 18 (1989), *Non-Discrimination*, para. 6.

> While these conventions deal only with cases of discrimination on specific grounds, the Committee believes that the term "discrimination" as used in the Covenant should be understood to imply any distinction, exclusion, restriction or preference which is based on any ground such as race, colour, sex, language, religion, political or other opinion, national or social origin, property, birth or other status, and which has the purpose or effect of nullifying or impairing the recognition, enjoyment or exercise by all persons, on an equal footing, of all rights and freedoms.[212]

As will be explained in more detail below, discriminatory intent is not required in order to qualify a differentiation as discriminatory.

In the same 1989 general comment No. 18, the Committee added another, much more commonly used definition of discrimination, which has also been the working definition of the Committee in its jurisprudence:

> not every differentiation of treatment will constitute discrimination, if the criteria for such differentiation are reasonable and objective and if the aim is to achieve a purpose which is legitimate under the Covenant.[213]

This final paragraph of the general comment draws on the definition of the HRC in its established jurisprudence that "differentiation based on reasonable and objective criteria does not amount to prohibited discrimination",[214] or that a differentiation

---

212 *Ibid.*, para. 7.

213 UN Doc. HRI/GEN/1/Rev.7, General Comment No. 18 (1989), *Non-Discrimination*, para. 13.

214 UN Doc. CCPR/C/80/D/1115/2002, Communication No. 1115/2001, *Petersen v. Germany*, para. 6.8; UN Doc. CCPR/C/74/D/965/2000, Communication No. 965/2000, *Karakurt v. Austria*, para. 8.3; UN Doc. CCPR/C/74/D/919/2000, Communication No. 919/2000, *Müller and Engelhard v. Namibia*, para. 6.7; UN Doc. CCPR/C/71/D/819/1998, Communication No. 819/1998, *Kavanagh v. Ireland*, para. 10.2; UN Doc. CCPR/C/72/D/855/1999, Communication No. 855/1999, *Schmitz-de-Jong v. The Netherlands*, para. 7.2; UN Doc. CCPR/C/67/D/666/1995, Communication No. 651/1995, Communication No. 666/1995, *Foin v. France*, para. 10.3; UN Doc. CCPR/C/64/D/602/1994, Communication No. 602/1994, *Hoofdman v. The Netherlands*, para. 11.4; UN Doc. CCPR/C/63/D/651/1995, Communication No. 651/1995, *Snijders et al. v. The Netherlands*, para. 8.4; UN Doc. CCPR/C/51/D/425/1990, para. 7.2; Communication No. 425/1990, *Doesburg Lannooij Neefs v. The Netherlands*, UN Doc. CCPR/C/49/D/418/1990, Communication No. 418/1990, *Cavalcanti Araujo-Jongen v. The Netherlands*, para. 7.4; UN Doc. CCPR/C/46/D/406/1990, Communication No. 406/1990, *Oulajin and Kaiss v. The Netherlands*, para. 7.3; UN Doc. CCPR/C/44/D/395/1990, Communication No. 395/1990, *Sprenger v. The Netherlands*, paras. 7.2 and 7.4; UN Doc. CCPR/C/44/D/415/1990, Communication No. 415/1990, *Pauger v. Austria*, para. 7.3; UN Doc. CCPR/C/35/D/218/1986, Communication No. 218/1986, *Vos v. The Netherlands*, para. 11.3; UN Doc. CCPR/C/29/D/180/1984, Communication No. 180/1984, *Danning v. The Netherlands*, para. 13; UN Doc. CCPR/C/29/D/182/1984, Communication No. 180/1984, *Zwaan-de Vries v. The Netherlands*, para. 13; UN Doc. CCPR/C/29/D/172/1984, Communication No. 172/1984, *Broeks v. The Netherlands*, para. 13. Compare with UN Doc. CCPR/CO/72/MCO, para. 17 (Monaco): differences in treatment based on objective and reasonable criteria, do not take the form of discrimination. See also UN Doc. HRI/GEN/1/Rev.7, General Comment No. 23 (1994), *Article 27*, para. 6.2.

which is compatible with the provisions of the CCPR and based on reasonable grounds does not amount to prohibited discrimination,[215] or still put differently, that "distinctions must be justified on reasonable and objective grounds, in pursuit of an aim that is legitimate under the Covenant".[216]

As explained above, the definition of discrimination most commonly in use applies four tests or criteria in order to decide whether differential treatment is acceptable or not. The first test is that of the comparability of the situations invoked. The HRC seems to have relied on this comparability test in order to find that a complaint on the differentiation between soldiers and civilians in relation to their ability to appeal against a summons was inadmissible. It pointed out that "the author ha[d] not claimed that the Netherlands military penal procedures [were] not being applied equally to all Netherlands citizens serving in the Netherlands armed forces."[217] This seems to suggest that as different legislative regimes were in place (one for civilians and one for citizens while doing their compulsory military service), whereby the exigencies of military services may require restrictions on some rights of individuals, no comparability of situations can be alleged. Similarly, the HRC declared inadmissible a complaint about different social security regimes for civilians and conscientious objectors performing alternative service. States are allowed to have compulsory national service, which entails only modest pecuniary payments. Neither did the Committee accept the comparability of the situation civilians are in on the one hand, and conscripts are in on the other hand.[218] No comparability was accepted either in a case on pension entitlements of former Dutch citizens living in different countries abroad. The Committee

---

215 UN Doc. CCPR/C/57/D/586/1994, Communication No. 586/1994, *Adam v. The Czech Republic*, para. 12.4; UN Doc. CCPR/C/54/D/516/1992, Communication No. 516/1992, *Simunek et al. v. The Czech Republic*, para. 11.5; UN Doc. CCPR/C/55/D/454/1991, Communication No. 454/1991, *Pons v. Spain*, para. 9.4. Compare with the Committee's statement of concern "about the vagueness of the concept of "reasonable discrimination", which, in the absence of objective criteria, is incompatible with article 26 of the Covenant." (UN Doc. CCPR/C/79/Add.102, para. 11 (Japan)).

216 UN Doc. CCPR/C/77/D/983/2001, Communication No. 983/2001, *Love v. Australia*, para. 8.2. Compare with UN Doc. CCPR/C/75/D/932/2000, Communication No. 932/2000, *Gillot et al. v. France*, para. 13.5: not all differentiation constitutes discrimination if it is based on objective and reasonable criteria and the purpose sought is legitimate under the CCPR; UN Doc. CCPR/C/37/D/208/1986, Communication No. 208/1986, *Singh Bhinder v. Canada*, para. 6.1: the requirement is to be regarded as reasonable and directed towards objective purposes that are compatible with the Covenant; UN Doc. CCPR/C/40D299/1988, Communications Nos. 298 and 299/1988, *Lindgren v. Sweden*, para. 10.4: reasonable and objective criteria and made for a purpose that is legitimate under the Covenant.

217 UN Doc. CCPR/C/32/D/267/1987, Communication No. 267/1987, *M.J.G. v. The Netherlands*, para. 3.2. See Bayefski, supra note 3, 14.

218 UN Doc. CCPR/C/37/D/297/1988, Communication No. 297/1988, *H.A.E.d.J. v. The Netherlands*, para. 8.2.

pointed out that "the categories of persons being compared [were] distinguishable".[219] Finally, it has observed that "the different treatment for different remedies according to the seriousness of the offence does not necessarily constitute discrimination."[220] Underlying this observation seems to be the assumption that it concerns different situations.

Comparability of situations was accepted in a case in which a differentiation was made among conscientious objectors on the basis of the nature of their particular beliefs, *i.e.* Jehovah's Witnesses and other conscientious objectors. The HRC held that equal treatment is to be given to all conscientious objectors "holding equally strong convictions to military and substitute service."[221] The Committee seems similarly to have accepted the comparability of situations both when the advantaged group is a comparable minority as when the advantaged group is a majority.[222] It has not yet had the occasion to express itself on the issue whether substantially different situations necessitate different treatment.[223]

A second criterion in order to determine whether or not differential treatment amounts to discrimination, pertains to the question whether the differentiation made is permissible or not. The Committee's jurisprudence on the permissibility or legitimacy of distinctions has been developed on a case-by-case basis, and is therefore difficult to systematize. As some observers have pointed out, "findings of 'reasonableness' and 'objectivity' [have been accompanied] with sparse reasoning,"[224] and the "reasonable and objective" test is potentially very subjective.[225] Whether the test has actually been applied subjectively is a matter of debate.[226] Whereas some have concluded that it has led to "uneven and confused application",[227] others have submitted that the HRC has taken a very cautious interpretation, particularly where public funds

---

219 UN Doc. CCPR/C/60/D/658/1995, Communication No. 658/1995, *Van Oord v. The Netherlands*, para. 8.5.

220 UN Doc. CCPR/C/80/D/1101/2002, Communication No. 1101/2002, *Alba Cabriada v. Spain*, para. 6.7.

221 UN Doc. CCPR/C/48/D/402/1990, Communication No. 402/1990, *Brinkhof v. The Netherlands*, paras. 9.3 and 9.4.

222 UN Doc. CCPR/C/67/D/694/1996, Communication No. 694/96, *Waldham v. Canada*; see also Joseph, Schultz and Castan, supra note 53, 681.

223 The issue arose in UN Doc. CCPR/C/82/D/944/2000, Communication No. 944/2000, *Mahabir v. Austria*, para. 8.6, in which a foreign prisoner who was to be deported directly following his release, complained that compulsory contributions to the unemployment scheme amounted to discrimination. The HRC did not examine the merits of the complaint for lack of exhaustion of domestic remedies.

224 Lester and Joseph, supra note 8, 586.

225 Joseph, Schultz and Castan, supra note 53, 700.

226 The legitimacy of the prolongation of civilian service (see further) may be an outstanding example of a rather versatile application of the "reasonable and objective" criterion.

227 Bayefski, supra note 3, 14.

were at issue.[228] It is undoubtedly true that the Committee moved extremely carefully in the area of welfare benefits, in which the requirement of a reasonable and objective basis does not seem a difficult test to meet. Even then, some Committee members expressed their concerns about the lack of restraint:

> With regard to the application of article 26 of the Covenant in the field of economic and social rights, it is evident that social security legislation, which is intended to achieve aims of social justice, necessarily must make distinctions. It is for the legislature of each country, which best knows the socio-economic needs of the society concerned, to try to achieve social justice in the concrete context. Unless the distinctions made are manifestly discriminatory or arbitrary, it is not for the Committee to re-evaluate the complex socio-economic data and substitute its judgement for that of the legislatures of States parties.
>
> Furthermore it would seem to us that it is essential to keep one's sense of proportion. With respect to the present cases, we note that the authors are asking for child benefits not only for their own children – to which they are entitled under the legislation of the Netherlands – but also for siblings, nephews and nieces, for whom they claim to have accepted responsibility and hence consider as dependants. On the basis of the information before the Committee, such demands appear to run counter to a general sense of proportion, and their denial by the government concerned cannot be considered unreasonable in view of the budget limitations which exist in every social security system. While States parties to the Covenant may wish to extend benefits to such wide-ranging categories of dependants, article 26 of the Covenant does not require them to do so.[229]

Moreover, in almost all social security cases in which the HRC did find a violation, discomfort had already been expressed by the state,[230] most often exemplified by legislative changes either before the submission of the complaint,[231] or in between the date of submission of the complaint and the date the Committee adopted it views.[232]

---

228 Higgins, supra note 77, xvii-xviii.

229 Individual opinion of Committee members Herndl, Müllerson, N'Diaye and Sadi in UN Doc. CCPR/C/46/D/406/1990, Communication Nos. 406 and 426/90, *Oulajin and Kaiss v. The Netherlands*. Compare with the individual opinion of Committee member Ando in UN Doc. CCPR/C/80/D/976/2001, Communication No. 976/2001, *Derksen v. The Netherlands*: "Consequently, the Human Rights Committee needs to be especially prudent in applying its article 26 to cases involving economic and social rights, which States parties to the International Covenant on Economic, Social and Cultural Rights are to realize without discrimination but step-by-step through available means."

230 See Higgins, supra note 77, xviii.

231 See *e.g.* UN Doc. CCPR/C/80/D/976/2001, Communication No. 976/2001, *Derksen v. The Netherlands*, para. 9.3.

232 See UN Doc. CCPR/C/44/D/415/1990, Communication No. 415/1990, *Pauger v. Austria*; para. 7.4: "Such a differentiation is not reasonable, as is implicitly acknowledged by the State party when it points out that the ultimate goal is to achieve full equality between men and women in 1995."; UN Doc. CCPR/C/29/D/172/1984, Communication No. 172/1984, *Broeks v. The Netherlands*, para. 14; UN Doc. CCPR/C/29/D/182/1984, Communication No. 182/1984, *Zwaan-de Vries v. The Netherlands*, para. 14: "Such a differentiation is not reasonable, and this seems to have been effectively

Therefore, "[t]he nature of the right to which the discrimination claim is attached may impact on the HRC's decision on whether a distinction is reasonable and therefore permissible under the Covenant."[233]

The reasonableness of a distinction seems also to be determined by the prohibited ground of discrimination implied. As Bayefski put it: "The technique of tailoring the stringency of evaluations of the legitimacy of distinctions to particular grounds" is a feature of the HRC's jurisprudence, which it has in common with other international legal sources.[234] Differential treatment on grounds of gender and race generally seem to entail a higher threshold of justification (see also chapter III where the prohibited grounds of discrimination are discussed).

Violations of the non-discrimination principle for lack of objective and reasonable grounds for differential treatment were found in the following cases. Most violations were based on unjustifiable distinctions on the basis of sex/gender, and nationality or citizenship.

Very early in its existence, in 1981, the HRC found that different residence rights for alien wives and husbands were arbitrary and hence discriminatory. Whereas foreign husbands of Mauritian citizens could only obtain a limited, temporary residence permit, foreign wives had the right to free access to Mauritius and enjoyed immunity from deportation.[235]

In two landmark cases against the Netherlands, the Committee concluded that the so-called "breadwinner assumption"[236] as a basis for differentiation between men and women was not reasonable in relation to unemployment benefits.[237] Equally, a different pension regime for men and women, whereby full pension benefits were granted to widowers only if they had no other source of income, whereas such a "no income" requirement was not applicable to widows (as it was assumed that only the husband had been gainfully employed), was judged not reasonable.[238] The HRC decided also

acknowledged even by the State party by the enactment of a change in law on 29 April 1985, with retroactive effect to 23 December 1984."

233 Joseph, Schultz and Castan, supra note 53, 688.

234 Bayefski, supra note 3, 18.

235 UN Doc. CCPR/C/12/D/35/1978, Communication No. 35/1978, *Aumeeruddy-Cziffra et al. v. Mauritius*, para. 9.2 (b), 2, (i) and (ii).

236 Under the bread winner assumption, a man was assumed to be the breadwinner and did not have to prove this in order to obtain unemployment benefits; a woman however was only entitled to unemployment benefits if she could prove that she was the breadwinner.

237 UN Doc. CCPR/C/29/D/182/1984, Communication No. 182/1984, *Zwaan-de Vries v. The Netherlands*, para. 14; UN Doc. CCPR/C/29/D/172/1984, Communication No. 172/1984, *Broeks v. The Netherlands*, para. 14.

238 UN Doc. CCPR/C/44/D/415/1990, Communication No. 415/1990, *Pauger v. Austria*, para. 7.4.

that the fact that a married male former civil servant whose pension accrued before 1985 was lower than the pension paid to a married female former civil servant whose pension accrued at the same date, was not justifiable.[239] Differential treatment of unmarried heterosexual partners and same-sex partners was equally found to be discriminatory for lack of reasonable and objective grounds.[240]

In a relatively recent case, the HRC found that the differentiation between men and women in the possibility of choosing one partner's surname on marriage was not based on reasonable grounds. It thereby rejected the state's argument that there was a long-standing tradition in this regard.[241]

Cases of differential treatment between married and unmarried people have been accepted as reasonable (see further), except in cases of indirect discrimination. In *Derksen v. The Netherlands*, the Committee held that the distinction with regard to social security benefits between children born either in wedlock or after a given date also out of wedlock on the one hand, and out of wedlock prior to that date on the other hand, was not based on reasonable grounds and constituted (indirect) discrimination. In the view of the Committee, the termination of ongoing discrimination in respect of children who had no say in whether their parents choose to marry or not, should have taken place by extending the application of the new law, which was aimed at remedying the situation, to them, albeit not necessarily with retroactive effect.[242]

The HRC also held that the different pension regime for Senegalese and French veterans was discriminatory. It argued that the basis for pension was not nationality, but the service provided.[243] Administrative inconvenience or the risk of abuse could not justify unequal treatment.[244] Similarly, though the HRC has accepted that bilateral treaties based on reciprocity between states may justify certain differences in pension entitlements, bilateral treaties can only have limited force as justification for a differentiation based on nationality.[245] The Committee further restricted its jurisprudence

---

239 UN Doc. CCPR/C/66/D/786/1997, Communication No. 786/1997, *Vos v. The Netherlands*, paras. 7.5 and 7.6.

240 UN Doc. CCPR/C/78/D/94/2000, Communication No. 941/2000, *Young v. Australia*, para. 10.4. This decision was foreshadowed in a concurring opinion of Lallah and Scheinin in UN Doc. CCPR/C/75/D/902/1999, Communication No.902/1999, *Joslin et al. v. New Zealand*.

241 UN Doc. CCPR/C/74/D/919/2000, Communication No. 919/2000, *Müller and Engelhard v. Namibia*, para. 6.8. In this case, the proportionality test was also applied (see further).

242 UN Doc. CCPR/C/80/D/976/2001, Communication No. 976/2001, *Derksen v. The Netherlands*, para. 9.3.

243 UN Doc. CCPR/C/35/D/196/1985, Communication No. 196/1985, *Gueye et al. v. France*, para. 9.5.

244 *Idem*.

245 See UN Doc. CCPR/C/60/D/658/1995, Communication No. 658/1995, *van Oord v. The Netherlands*, para. 8.5 for the justificatory potential. In this case, the HRC seemed to suggest that privileges that respond to separately negotiated bilateral treaties which necessarily reflect agreements based on reciprocity, are differentiations based on reasonable and objective criteria.

on this matter in *Karakurt v. Austria*. In this case, it held that a distinction between aliens with regard to "a close and natural incident of employment", namely the right to stand for election to the relevant work-council, on the basis of citizenship alone, was not reasonable.[246] It argued that an international agreement that confers preferential treatment to some aliens does not constitute in itself sufficient ground for differentiation.[247]

In a number of cases in the aftermath of the collapse of the Berlin Wall, it was found that the requirement in law for citizenship (and permanent residence) as a necessary condition for restitution or compensation for confiscations by the authorities, made an arbitrary and consequently discriminatory distinction between individuals who were equally victims of prior state confiscation.[248] The HRC clarified that the basis for property rights was not based on citizenship (or residence), and that it was incompatible with the CCPR to require victims of political persecution for which a state was responsible, to permanently return.[249]

The HRC was equally unable to find a reasonable and objective justification for differential (and preferential) treatment between Roman Catholic religious schools, which were publicly funded as a distinct part of the public education system, and schools of Jewish faith, which were private by necessity. It underlined that if public funding was given to religious schools, this was to be done without discrimination.[250]

A decision to try a person before special courts without reasons to be given (*i.e.* enjoying unfettered discretion), and with a very restricted possibility of judicial review (restricted to the most exceptional and virtually non-demonstrable circumstances) was found not to be based on reasonable and objective grounds.[251]

Finally, the Committee rejected the legitimacy of justifications for differentiation between conscientious objectors and military, and among conscientious objectors. The exemption of only one group of conscientious objectors (*i.e.* Jehovah's Witnesses)

---

246 UN Doc. CCPR/C/74/D/965/2000, Communication No. 965/2000, *Karakurt v. Austria*, para. 8.4.

247 *Idem*. The HRC admitted itself that this ruling was possibly at odds with its position taken in *van Oord v. The Netherlands*. See also Hanski and Scheinin, supra note 35, 326.

248 UN Doc. CCPR/C/73/D/774/1997, Communication No. 774/1997, *Brok v. The Czech Republic*, para. 7.3; UN Doc. CCPR/C/74/D/747/1997, Communication No. 747/1997, *Des Fours Walderode v. Czech Republic*, para. 8.4; UN Doc. CCPR/C/54/D/516/1992, Communication No. 516/1992, *Simunek et al. v. The Czech Republic*, para. 11.6.

249 UN Doc. CCPR/C/54/D/516/1992, Communication No. 516/1992, *Simunek et al. v. The Czech Republic*, para. 11.6; UN Doc. CCPR/C/57/D/586/1994, Communication No. 586/1994, *Adam v. The Czech Republic*, paras. 12.5 and 12.6.

250 UN Doc. CCPR/C/67/D/694/1996, Communication No. 694/1996, *Waldman v. Canada*, paras. 10.5-10.6.

251 UN Doc. CCPR/C/71/D/819/1998, Communication No. 819/1998, *Kavanagh v. Ireland*, para. 10.2.

and the inapplicability of the exemption for all others was found not reasonable.[252] Equally, doubling the period of alternative service for administrative convenience, *i.e.* in order to be able to test the sincerity of the individual's convictions, was not sufficient a justification. Elements that might justify differential treatment could be the nature of the specific service concerned or the need for a special training in order to accomplish that service.[253]

In a number of other cases, the HRC did accept the justifications invoked as objective and reasonable. In a case in which the prolongation of the term for alternative service, resulting in different terms of service for conscientious objectors and military, was challenged, the Committee concluded that the new arrangement was based on reasonable and objective criteria. The reason for the prolongation of the term for alternative service was to facilitate the administration of alternative service. There was also some benefit in it though for conscientious objectors, for they were no longer to convince the examination board of the genuineness of their beliefs, and for the new regime allowed a broader range of individuals potentially to opt for the possibility of alternative service.[254]

In some Swedish cases of differential treatment in according educational subsidies (*i.e.* financial assistance to parents for their children's textbooks and meals) to public schools, but not to private ones, the Committee submitted that the state could not be deemed to be under an obligation to provide the same benefits to private schools, for the preferential treatment given to public sector schooling was reasonable and based on objective criteria. At the core of the Committee's viewpoint was the fact that the private system was not subject to state supervision,[255] and that the parents were free

---

252 UN Doc. CCPR/C/48/D/402/1990, Communication No. 402/1990, *Brinkhof v. The Netherlands*, para. 9.4. The Committee nevertheless did not find a violation, as it concluded that the complainant was not a victim of the violation.

253 UN Doc. CCPR/C/67/D/666/1995, Communication No. 666/1995, *Foin v. France*, para. 10.3; UN Doc. CCPR/C/67/D/689/1996, Communication No. 689/1996, *Maille v. France*, para. 10.4; UN Doc. CCPR/C/69/D/690/1996, Communication No. 690/1996, *Venier and Nicolas v. France*, para. 10.4. The majority position was refuted by three members in a dissenting opinion. They believed that there were other relevant facts that justified differentiation, such as the wide choice of posts, the choice of one's own employer, the higher remuneration, and the absence of the burdens of military service for people taking alternative service.

254 UN Doc. CCPR/C/39/D/295/1988, Communication No. 295/88, *Järvinen v. Finland*, paras. 6.4 and 6.5; see also Joseph, Schultz and Castan, supra note 53, 709. As pointed out higher, the legitimacy of the prolongation of civilian service may not be the best illustration of the objectivity and predictability of the "reasonable and objective" criterion.

255 UN Doc. CCPR/C/32/D/ 191/1985, Communication No. 191/1985, *Blom v. Sweden*, paras. 10.2 and 10.3.

to choose not to avail themselves of benefits which were generally open to all (*i.e.* in public schools).[256]

In some cases concerning social security benefits, most often against The Netherlands, the Committee held that the differential treatment of men of women was based on objective and reasonable grounds. It has been observed quite rightly that the HRC seems to be rather reluctant to find a violation with regard to the limited or no retroactive remedying of discrimination in social security matters.[257] In *Vos v. The Netherlands*, the Committee concluded that the rule whereby a disabled woman was shifted from disability benefits to widow benefits upon the death of her husband (the application of which was disadvantageous in her particular case) was based on objective and reasonable criteria, "especially bearing in mind that both statutes under which Mrs. Vos qualified for benefits aim at ensuring to all persons falling thereunder, subsistence-level income."[258] In another case, the Committee held that the requirement of being unemployed at the time of application for unemployment benefits is reasonable and objective, "in view of the purposes of the legislation in question, namely to provide assistance to persons who are unemployed".[259] Whereas this rule may be sound in general, it was less so in the particular case. In fact, the claim related to past discriminatory provisions in application of the famous breadwinner criterion.[260] This discriminatory provisions were abolished at a given moment in time. Retroactive claims for unemployment benefits were possible, but only if the applicant was still unemployed on the date of application.

The HRC also found that differential treatment of married and cohabitant persons was reasonable, as the decision to enter into a legal status by marriage, which provides

256 UN Doc. CCPR/C/40D299/1988, Communication Nos. 298 & 299/1988, *Lindgren v. Sweden*, paras. 10.2 and 10.3. This free choice argument has also been used in the contexts of differential treatment between married and unmarried couples concerning their eligibility for social security benefits. The Committee has not condoned however every differential treatment among private schools (see higher, UN Doc. CCPR/C/67/D/694/1996, Communication No. 694/1996, *Waldman v. Canada*, para. 10.5).

257 See *e.g.* UN Doc. CCPR/C/51/D/484/1991, Communication No. 484/1991, *Pepels v. The Netherlands*, paras. 7.3-7.5 and the cases cited in footnote 259.

258 UN Doc. CCPR/C/35/D/218/1986, Communication No. 218/1986, *Vos v. The Netherlands*, para. 12. For a critique, see Bayefski, supra note 3, 15: "[T]he decision fails entirely to recognize that this legislative distinction bore the hallmarks of classic stereotyping of women with its accompanying consequences of degradation and second-class status. It was based on outmoded assumptions about women and their role in society; [...] it categorized women in terms of their relationship with men, refusing to address them as persons in their own right – even where those relationships had ended a quarter of a century earlier."

259 UN Doc. CCPR/C/49/D/418/1990, Communication No. 418/1990, *Cavalcanti Araujo-Jongen v. The Netherlands*, para. 7.4. Compare with UN Doc. CCPR/C/48/D/478/1991, Communication No. 478/1991, *A.P.L.-v.d.M. v. The Netherlands*, para. 6.4 (inadmissibility decision: no claim under art. 2).

260 *I.e.* the assumption that men generally were breadwinners, whereas women were not.

for certain benefits and for certain duties and responsibilities, was said to be entirely free. By choosing not to enter into marriage, one did not assume the full extent of the duties and responsibilities incumbent on married persons. Therefore, a different treatment between married and cohabitant persons was considered reasonable.[261] Similarly, according lower benefits to parents and children sharing a household, than to other persons sharing a household, was held to be neither unreasonable nor arbitrary, for the costs of living were reduced by sharing a household with parents, and a mutual obligation to provide support in the costs of living was imposed on parents and children in civil law.[262]

Differential treatment in according child benefits for natural and foster children was accepted to draw on an objective distinction between natural children and foster children. As to the reasonableness criterion, it was held that the requirement for foster parents to be involved in the upbringing of the foster children as a precondition to granting of benefits was not unreasonable.[263] In practice, the granting of benefits for foster children who were not living with the foster parent was therefore excluded. This situation was more commonly to be found with migrant workers than with Dutch nationals. In the view of the Committee however, "the scope of article 26 of the Covenant does not extend to differences resulting from the equal application of common rules in the allocation of benefits."[264]

The Committee has also had to decide whether it is acceptable that some people are required to make personal contributions to an insurance scheme, whereas others are not. It held that:

> the requirement that individuals, when benefiting from the [...] insurance scheme, pay a personal contribution towards the costs of residential care, is as such not in violation of the principle of equality before the law.[265]

---

261 UN Doc. CCPR/C/80/D/976/2001, Communication No. 976/2001, *Derksen v. The Netherlands*, para. 9.2; UN Doc. CCPR/C/64/D/602/1994, Communication No. 602/1994, *Hoofdman v. The Netherlands*, para. 11.4; UN Doc. CCPR/C/44/D/395/1990, Communication No. 395/1990, *Sprenger v. The Netherlands*; para. 7.2; UN Doc. CCPR/C/29/D/180/1984, Communication No. 180/1984, *Danning v. The Netherlands*, para. 14. In her concurring individual opinion, Evatt pointed out quite rightly that cohabitees were considered as a family unit for other purposes (UN Doc. CCPR/C/64/D/602/1994, Communication No. 602/1994, *Hoofdman v. The Netherlands*).

262 UN Doc. CCPR/C/51/D/425/1990, Communication No. 425/1990, *Doesburg Lannooij Neefs v. The Netherlands*, para. 7.4. The second element of the argument is not given explicitly by the Committee. It simply refers to the explanations given by The Netherlands.

263 UN Doc. CCPR/C/46/D/406/1990, Communication Nos. 406 and 426/90, *Oulajin and Kaiss v. The Netherlands*, para. 7.4.

264 *Id.*, para. 7.5. See also further under the heading of indirect discrimination.

265 UN Doc. CCPR/C/63/D/651/1995, Communication No. 651/1995, *Snijders et al. v. The Netherlands*, para. 8.3.

With regard to the question whether these personal contributions were calculated objectively and without arbitrariness, the Committee held that the distinction between single persons (who were required to pay income-related contributions) and married or cohabitating persons (who paid a fixed contribution) was objective and reasonable, for it had its basis "in the factual circumstances of life of persons benefiting from the scheme".[266] The Committee did not pronounce itself on the issue whether it was justifiable that the same ceiling for personal contributions applied for single persons and couples alike, as the applicants were not found to be victims themselves (*i.e.* they were not paying the maximum amount).[267]

Equally, the imposition of an age limitation (*i.e.* 60 years) for obtaining an entitlement to rate reductions as a partner to a pensioner above the age of 65 was found to be an objective criterion of differentiation that had been applied reasonably.[268]

The distinction between an unemployed substitute judge who is not a civil servant on leave and one who is (and can therefore return to civil service) for being eligible for unemployment benefits was judged not to be arbitrary or unreasonable.[269] Gender quotas for the nomination of candidates to the Belgian High Council of Justice were equally found to have a reasonable and objective justification.[270]

A third criterion employed in the more common definition of non-discrimination is the principle of proportionality. In the 1990s, it was submitted by some authors that the HRC predominantly stressed the establishment of differential treatment and a justification, and much less the comparability and proportionality, contrary to what had been done usually by other judicial bodies using this definition of discrimination.[271] As clarified above, for a long time,the reasonable and objective criterion was not interpreted in terms of proportionality and the existence of a legitimate aim, as has been the case for example in the approach of the European Court of Human Rights.[272]

Proportionality was however explicitly taken into account by the HRC in more recent cases. *Gillot v. France* dealt with a local referendum about the future of New Caledonia.

---

266 *Id.*, para. 8.4. Married or cohabiting persons left behind a partner who continued to live in the common household, and therefore did not save the same amount of money as a single person did in residential care.

267 *Ibid.*, para. 8.5.

268 UN Doc. CCPR/C/72/D/855/1999, Communication No. 855/1999, *Schmitz-de-Jong v. The Netherlands*, para. 7.2.

269 UN Doc. CCPR/C/55/D/454/1991, Communication No. 454/1991, *Pons v. Spain*, para. 9.5.

270 UN Doc. CCPR/C/81/D/943/2000, Communication No. 943, *Jacobs v. Belgium*, para. 9.3.

271 Frostell, supra note 140, 473-474; Lemmens, supra note 142, 89.

272 As exemplified *e.g.* in the *Belgian Linguistics Case*, see supra, note 139.

The question arose whether it was reasonable to limit participation in local referenda to persons concerned by the future of New Caledonia who had proven sufficiently strong ties to the territory. The HRC accepted that the restrictions in terms of length of residence and ties to the territory did respect the criterion of proportionality, as they were strictly limited *ratione loci* to local ballots on self-determination.[273] It submitted: "evaluation of any restrictions must be effected on a case-by-case basis, having regard in particular to the purpose of such restrictions and the principle of proportionality".[274] An objective criterion for differentiation was said to be one that "did not have the purpose or effect of establishing different rights for different ethnic groups or groups distinguished by their national extraction."[275] In *Jacobs v. Belgium*, the HRC found that the imposition of gender quota for appointment to the High Council of Justice, whereby at least 4 out of 11 appointees had to belong to each sex, was not disproportionate in that particular case.[276]

Some months earlier, the HRC had already hinted at the proportionality test in other case. It had thus held in a case on the differentiation between men and women to choose their partner's surname upon marriage that "at any rate the reason for the distinction [had] no sufficient importance in order to outweigh the generally excluded gender-based approach".[277] In other words, the differential treatment of men and women was not thought to be proportional to the stated purpose of legal security. The proportionality test has also been used by the HRC for interpreting the reasonableness of restrictions to the right to privacy.[278]

As to the difference in meaning between non-discrimination and equality, the HRC has not really taken a firm stance on the issue. In an individual concurring opinion to *Young v. Australia*, Committee members Wedgwood and DePasquale pointed out that that case, which was on equal treatment of same-sex partners and unmarried heterosexual partners with regard to entitlement to pension benefits, raised the question of positive rights to equal treatment, *i.e.* whether there is an obligation for states to accommodate same-sex relationships on par with more traditional forms of civil union. Both Committee members went a long way in explaining the limits of the

---

273 UN Doc. CCPR/C/75/D/932/2000, Communication No. 932/2000, *Gillot et al. v. France*, paras. 13.16-13.17.

274 *Ibid.*, para. 13.2.

275 *Ibid.*, para. 13.11.

276 UN Doc. CCPR/C/81/D/943/2000, Communication No. 943/2000, *Jacobs v. Belgium*, para. 9.5.

277 UN Doc. CCPR/C/74/D/919/2000, Communication No. 919/2000, *Müller and Engelhard v. Namibia*, para. 6.8

278 UN Doc. CCPR/C/50/D/488/1992, Communication No. 488/1992, *Nicholas Toonen v. Australia*, para. 8.3: "The Committee interprets the requirement of reasonableness to imply that any interference with privacy must be proportional to the end sought and be necessary in the circumstances of any given case."

Committee's decision in the case at hand, and seemed to suggest that the Committee had mainly reached it decision due to the lack of arguments of the state.[279] The recognition of positive rights to equal treatment as such did not, however, appear to be questioned. The limits rather pertained to the question as to whether there are positive rights to equal treatment for the specific groups of same-sex partners. In fact, the recognition of positive rights to equality should not come as a surprise in the context of article 26, which explicitly refers to equality.

b. *Qualifiers*

i. *De Jure* and *De Facto*

Like all other Committees, the HRC distinguishes between discrimination in law and in fact. In its general comment on non-discrimination, it pointed out that:

> Reports of many States parties contain information regarding legislative as well as administrative measures and court decisions which relate to protection against discrimination in law, but they very often lack information which would reveal discrimination in fact. When reporting on articles 2 (1), 3 and 26 of the Covenant, States parties usually cite provisions of their constitution or equal opportunity laws with respect to equality of persons. While such information is of course useful, the Committee wishes to know if there remain any problems of discrimination in fact, which may be practised either by public authorities, by the community, or by private persons or bodies.[280]

In its concluding observations, the Committee has rather frequently referred to discrimination in fact with regard to women[281] and minorities.[282] Occasionally, the HRC has hinted at discrimination in fact in its views on individual complaints. It has repeated that "article 26 of the Covenant prohibits discrimination in law and in fact".[283] It has also held that the requirement for workers in federal employment to wear hard hats for safety reasons did not constitute *de facto* discrimination for members of the Sikh religion.[284]

---

[279] UN Doc. CCPR/C/78/D/941/2000, Communication No. 941/2000, *Young v. Australia.*

[280] UN Doc. HRI/GEN/1/Rev.7, General Comment No. 18 (1989), *Non-Discrimination*, para. 9.

[281] UN Doc. CCPR/CO/83/KEN, para. 10 (Kenya); UN Doc. CCPR/CO/69/KWT, para. 8 (Kuwait); UN Doc. CCPR/C/79/Add.84, para. 13 (Iraq); UN Doc. CCPR/C/79/Add.76, para. 24 (Colombia); UN Doc. CCPR/C/79/Add.66, para. 13 (Brazil); UN Doc. CCPR/C/79/Add.62, para. 9 (Zambia); UN Doc. CCPR/C/79/Add.45, para. 19 (Libya); UN Doc. CCPR/C/79/Add.44, para. 9 (Morocco); UN Doc. CCPR/C/79/Add.42, para. 8 (Nepal); UN Doc. CCPR/C/79/Add.27, para. 7 (Norway).

[282] UN Doc. CCPR/CO/72/CZE, para. 8 (Czech Republic).

[283] UN Doc. CCPR/C/74/D/677/1996, Communication No. 677/1996, *Teesdale v. Trinidad and Tobago*, para. 9.8.

[284] UN Doc. CCPR/C/37/D/208/1986, Communication No. 208/1986, *Singh Bhinder v. Canada*, para.6.2. This case seems to be rather one of indirect discrimination, as reference is made to "legislation which, on the face of it, is neutral in that it applies to all persons without distinction, [but which] is said to operate in fact in a way which discriminates against persons of the Sikh religion." (para. 6.1.)

ii. Intentional and Non-Intentional

The HRC does not consider discriminatory intent to be an essential characteristic of discrimination.[285] A distinction is thus made between discrimination that is discriminatory in purpose, and that which is discriminatory only in effect.[286] The definition of discrimination formally adopted in its general comment on non-discrimination reads:

> [T]he Committee believes that the term "discrimination" as used in the Covenant should be understood to imply any distinction, exclusion, restriction or preference which is based on any ground such as race, colour, sex, language, religion, political or other opinion, national or social origin, property, birth or other status, and *which has the purpose or effect* of nullifying or impairing the recognition, enjoyment or exercise by all persons, on an equal footing, of all rights and freedoms. (my emphasis)[287]

In line with this formal adoption of a definition of discrimination in which a discriminatory intention is not required to qualify a distinction as discrimination ("with the purpose or effect"), the HRC's jurisprudence too shows that discriminatory intent is not required to qualify a distinction as discrimination. The Committee thus found a discrimination while recognizing at the same time that the state concerned "had not intended to discriminate".[288] It took a very clear stance on the issue in *Adams v. the Czech Republic*:

> the intent of the legislature is not alone dispositive in determining a breach of article 26 of the Covenant. A politically motivated differentiation is unlikely to be compatible with article 26. But an act which is not politically motivated may still contravene article 26 if its effects are discriminatory.[289]

---

285 See e.g. UN Doc. CCPR/C/29/D/182/1984, Communication No. 182/1984, *Zwaan-de Vries v. The Netherlands*, paras. 15-16. For a possibly less unequivocal opinion of the HRC on the issue, see *Järvinen v. Finland*, in which the HRC concluded that the introduction of a longer term for alternative service than for military service was based on objective and reasonable criteria, *inter alia* because the relevant legislation "had no discriminatory purpose" (see UN Doc. CCPR/C/39/D/295/1988, Communication No. 295/1988, *Järvinen v. Finland*, para. 6.4). It is unclear whether the Committee in this case simply added this additional argument to support its view that no discrimination had taken place, or whether it wanted to enhance its analysis by not requiring discriminatory purpose for discrimination to take place, while at the same time accepting that discriminatory intent might be one among several of the elements to be taken into account when considering whether a particular distinction was based on objective and reasonable criteria.

286 UN Doc. CCPR/C/75/D/932/2000, Communication No. 932/2000, *Gillot et al. v. France*, para. 13.11.

287 UN Doc. HRI/GEN/1/Rev.7, General Comment No. 18 (1989), *Non-Discrimination*, para. 7.

288 UN Doc. CCPR/C/29/D/182/1984, Communication No. 182/1984, *Zwaan-de Vries v. The Netherlands*, para. 16 and UN Doc. CCPR/C/29/D/172/1984, Communication No. 172/84, *Broeks v. The Netherlands*, para. 16.

289 UN Doc. CCPR/C/54/D/516/1992, Communication No. 516/1992, *Simunek et al. v. The Czech Republic*, para. 11.7.

Similarly, it stated that:

> a violation of article 26 can also result from the discriminatory effect of a rule or measure that is neutral at face value or without intent to discriminate. However, such indirect discrimination can only be said to be based on the grounds enumerated in Article 26 of the Covenant if the detrimental effects of a rule or decision exclusively or disproportionaly affect persons having a particular race, colour, sex, language, religion, political or other opinion, national or social origin, property, birth or other status.[290]

On the other hand, the HRC does not seem to accept that the intention to discriminate is always a sufficient condition, and automatically implies a violation. In *Simunek v. the Czech Republic*, the Committee left some space by submitting that a politically motivated differentiation was *unlikely*, but not impossible, to be compatible with art. 26.[291] However, discriminatory intent seems to be an aggravating factor. In *Diergaardt v. Namibia*, the HRC decided that prohibiting civil servants to communicate in a minority language – *i.e.* Afrikaans, formerly the official language – was in violation of art. 26, apparently because the authors had alleged that the measures had been *intentionally targeted* against Afrikaans.[292] It should be noted however that this conclusion was reached in the absence of any state response, and with five dissenters. Similarly, after it had found that a ban on the throwing of dwarfs was a differentiation which was based on objective and reasonable criteria and necessary in order to protect public order, the HRC did not find a violation of article 26 CCPR allegedly for the author had not established that the differentiation had been discriminatory *in purpose*.[293]

iii. Direct and Indirect

Indirect discrimination was for the first time explicitly recognized by the HRC in 2003, in a case concerning the abolition of household benefits said to be affecting to a greater extent retired persons than active employees:

> a violation of article 26 can also result from the discriminatory effect of a rule or measure that is neutral at face value or without intent to discriminate. However, such indirect discrimination can only be said to be based on the grounds enumerated in Article 26 of the Covenant if the detrimental effects of a rule or decision exclusively or disproportionaly affect persons having a

290 UN Doc. CCPR/C/78/D/998/2001, Communication No. 998/2001, *Althammer et al. v. Austria*, para. 10.2.

291 UN Doc. CCPR/C/54/D/516/1992, Communication No. 516/1992, *Simunek et al. v. The Czech Republic*, para. 11.7.

292 UN Doc. CPR/C/69/D/760/1997, Communication No. 760/1997, *Diergaardt et al. v. Namibia*, para. 10.10.

293 UN Doc. CCPR/C/75/D/854/1999, Communication No. 854/1999, *Wackenheim v. France*, paras. 7.4 and 7.5.

> particular race, colour, sex, language, religion, political or other opinion, national or social origin, property, birth or other status.[294]

Likewise, in *Derksen v. The Netherlands*, in which the question arose whether the refusal of benefits to the surviving parent of a half-orphan born outside marriage constituted discrimination, the HRC held:

> [A]rticle 26 prohibits both direct and indirect discrimination, the latter notion being related to a rule or measure that may be neutral on its face without intent to discriminate but which nevertheless results in discrimination because of its exclusive or disproportionate adverse effect on a certain category of persons.[295]

Committee member Rodley seemed to question the whole doctrine of indirect discrimination in his individual opinion.[296]

Before 2003, observers agreed that the Committee's position was not clear and that it took a rather uncertain approach.[297] Some observers speculated whether indirect discrimination was not recognised with regard to social security benefits only.[298]

Initially, the Committee had left some room for indirect discrimination. In *Singh Bhinder v. Canada*, the Committee had for the first time recognized the possibility of indirect discrimination (qualified as "*de facto* discrimination"). It had noted that legislation which on the face of it was neutral in that it applied to all persons without distinction, operated in fact in a way which discriminated against members of the Sikh religion.[299] In a case of differential treatment in 1989 with regard to social security benefits, it had held that "differences in result of the uniform application of laws do not *per se* constitute prohibited discrimination" (my emphasis). In the case at hand, the HRC was of the view that "the unfavourable result complained of [...] follow[ed] from the application of a uniform rule to avoid overlapping in the allocation of social

---

294 UN Doc. CCPR/C/78/D/998/2001, Communication No. 998/2001, *Althammer et al. v. Austria*, para. 10.2. It did not find a violation, for the measure was found to be based on objective and reasonable grounds.

295 UN Doc. CCPR/C/80/D/976/2001, Communication No. 976/2001, *Derksen v. The Netherlands*, para. 9.3.

296 He argued: "The already vulnerable doctrine of indirect discrimination that the Committee is here applying is being subjected to intolerable pressure in being asked to sustain the Committee's argument."

297 Bayefski, supra note 3, 10; Lester and Joseph, supra note 8, 576.

298 Sarah Joseph, Jenny Schultz and Melissa Castan, *The International Covenant on Civil and Political Rights. Cases, Materials, and Commentary*, Oxford, Oxford University Press, 2000 (1st edition), 535.

299 UN Doc. CCPR/C/37/D/208/1986, Communication No. 208/1986, *Singh Bhinder v. Canada*, para. 6.1. It did not find a violation as it found the legislation to be reasonable and directed towards objective purposes that were compatible with the Covenant.

security benefits." As this rule was believed to be based on objective and reasonable criteria, the Committee held that no violation had taken place.[300]

In four cases concerning social security benefits dealt with between 1988 and 1992, it dismissed complaints about the differences in result of the equal application of laws in the allocation of social security benefits, arguing that "the scope of article 26 of the Covenant [did] not extend to differences resulting from the equal application of common rules in the allocation of benefits."[301]

In the years immediately preceding the explicit recognition of indirect discrimination, although it had not invoked the concept explicitly, it had referred to it,[302] and it had subsumed indirect discrimination under discrimination *de facto*.[303] With the decision in *Althammer*, it now seems clear that the HRC recognizes indirect discrimination if the detrimental effects of the impugned rule or decision exclusively or disproportionaly affect persons belonging to a particular group against which discrimination is prohibited in article 26, and if they are not based on objective and reasonable grounds.[304]

In its concluding observations, the HRC has only once hinted at indirect discrimination, and even then it seemed to refer to the wording of a domestic body's recommendations in that regard.[305]

---

300 UN Doc. CCPR/C/35/D/218/1986, Communication No. 218/1986, *Vos v. The Netherlands*, paras. 11.3 and 12.

301 UN Doc. CCPR/C/46/D/406/1990, Communication Nos. 406 and 426/90, *Oulajin and Kaiss v. The Netherlands*, para. 7.5; compare with UN Doc. CCPR/C/37/D/297/1988, Communication No. 297/1988, *H.A.E.d.J. v. The Netherlands*, para. 8.2, which mentions explicitly *social security* benefits. Two communications were declared inadmissible on the same grounds: see UN Doc. CCPR/C/48/D/478/1991, Communication No. 478/1991, *A.P.L.-v.d.M. v. The Netherlands*, para. 6.4; UN Doc. CCPR/C/32/D/212/1986, Communication No. 212/1986, *P.P.C. v. The Netherlands*, para. 6.2.

302 See Frostell, supra note 140, 46-48. In *e.g.* UN Doc. CCPR/C/49/D/418/1990, Communication No. 418/1990, *Cavalcanti Araujo-Jongen v. The Netherlands*, para. 7.4, the Committee noted that the author argued that the amended law still *indirectly* discriminated against her; in UN Doc. CCPR/C/39/D/295/1988, Communication No. 295/88, *Järvinen v. Finland*, para. 6.5, the Committee expressed its *awareness* of the fact that the impact of the legislative differentiation worked to the detriment of genuine conscientious objectors, after having found in para. 6.4 that the *ratio legis* of the act had no discriminatory purpose.

303 Frostell, supra note 140, 48. Compare with Joseph, Schultz and Castan, supra note 53, 694.

304 UN Doc. CCPR/C/78/D/998/2001, Communication No. 998/2001, *Althammer et al. v. Austria*, para. 10.2.

305 UN Doc. CCPR/C/79/Add.21, para. 6 (Ireland): "With respect to the issue of gender equality, the Committee welcomes the recommendations of the Second Commission on the Status of Women aimed at eliminating direct and indirect discrimination based on sex, including, in particular, the proposed deletion of article 41.2.2 of the Constitution".

iv. Multiple Discrimination

Double discrimination was referred to, albeit implicitly, in the HRC's general comment on gender equality:

> Discrimination against women is often intertwined with discrimination on other grounds such as race, colour, language, religion, political or other opinion, national or social origin, property, birth or other status.[306]

Multiple discrimination was also implicitly recognized a couple of times by the HRC in its concluding observations with regard to discrimination on the grounds of belonging to a minority group in combination with either gender (*i.e.* Arab women in Israel),[307] or living in rural areas.[308]

However, it has never been used explicitly as a concept of analysis.

v. Systemic Discrimination

Until recently, systemic discrimination had never been recognized literally by the HRC, though it had referred to situations in its concluding observations that might be qualified as systemic discrimination. The Committee had probably come closest to recognizing systemic discrimination in its references to affirmative action[309] and in its general comment No. 28 on the equality of rights between men and women.[310] In the Committee's most recent concluding observations on Kenya however, systemic discrimination against women was mentioned explicitly for the first time.[311]

As has been pointed out correctly by Joseph, Schultz and Castan, it might be rather unlikely to find references to systemic discrimination in individual complaints.[312]

---

306 UN Doc. HRI/GEN/1/Rev.7, General Comment No. 28 (2000), *The Equality of Rights Between Men and Women*, para. 30.

307 UN Doc. CCPR/CO/78/ISR, para. 23 (Israel); UN Doc. CCPR/C/79/Add.93, para. 15 (Israel).

308 UN Doc. CCPR/CO/75/MDA, para. 19 (Moldova).

309 UN Doc. HRI/GEN/1/Rev.7, General Comment No. 18 (1989), *Non-Discrimination*, para. 10.

310 UN Doc. HRI/GEN/1/Rev.7, General Comment No. 28 (2000), *Article 3: The Equality of Rights Between Men and Women*, *e.g.* paras. 5 and 24.

311 UN Doc. CCPR/CO/83/KEN, para. 10 (Kenya) (priority concern). For earlier references to discrimination that might have been labelled as systemic, see *e.g.* UN doc. CCPR/C/79/Add.81, paras. 15-17 (India): women and people of lower casts; UN Doc. CCPR/C/79/Add.110, para. 12 (Poland): inequality between the sexes in remuneration.

312 Joseph, Schultz and Castan, supra note 53, 735.

vi. Private Discrimination

The HRC has not referred to private discrimination as a concept. It has however paid due attention to discrimination in the private sector or in private life, particularly against women (see further chapter IV under the obligation to protect).

3. CESCR COMMITTEE

a. Definition

The CESCR Committee subscribes to the definition contained in CERD and CEDAW. In its 1994 general comment on the rights of the disabled, it defined "disability-based discrimination" as

> any distinction, exclusion, restriction or preference, or denial of reasonable accommodation based on disability which has the effect of nullifying or impairing the recognition, enjoyment or exercise of economic, social or cultural rights.[313]

Similarly, in the reporting guidelines for states on article 6, discrimination is defined as

> any distinctions, exclusions, restrictions or preferences, be it in law or in administrative practices or in practical relationships, between persons or groups of persons, made on the basis of race, colour, sex, religion, political opinion, nationality or social origin, which have the effect of nullifying or impairing the recognition, enjoyment or exercise of equality of opportunity or treatment in employment or occupation.[314]

Similarly, the CESCR Committee defined discrimination against women, literally as defined in article 1 CEDAW, as:

> any distinction, exclusion or restriction made on the basis of sex which has the effect or purpose of impairing or nullifying the recognition, enjoyment or exercise by women, irrespective of their marital status, on the basis of equality of men and women, of human rights and fundamental freedoms in the political, economic, social, cultural, civil or any other field.[315]

---

313 UN Doc. HRI/GEN/1/Rev.7, General Comment No. 5 (1994), *Persons with Disabilities*, para. 15.

314 UN Doc. E/C.12/1991/1, *Revised General Guidelines Regarding the Form and Contents of Reports to Be Submitted by States Parties under Articles 16 and 17 of the International Covenant on Economic, Social and Cultural Rights*, article 6, para. 3 (a).

315 UN Doc. E/C.12/2005/3, General Comment No. 16 (2005), *Article 3: The Equal Right of Men and Women to the Enjoyment of All Economic, Social and Cultural Rights*, para. 11.

Elements of this definition also appear in other general comments (as well as in some concluding observations):[316]

> any discrimination in access to food, as well as to means and entitlements for its procurement, on the grounds of race, colour, sex, language, age, religion, political or other opinion, national or social origin, property, birth or other status with the purpose or effect of nullifying or impairing the equal enjoyment or exercise of economic, social and cultural rights constitutes a violation of the Covenant.[317]

> By virtue of article 2.2 and article 3, the Covenant proscribes any discrimination in access to health care and underlying determinants of health, as well as to means and entitlements for their procurement, on the grounds of race, colour, sex, language, religion, political or other opinion, national or social origin, property, birth, physical or mental disability, health status (including HIV/AIDS), sexual orientation and civil, political, social or other status, which has the intention or effect of nullifying or impairing the equal enjoyment or exercise of the right to health.[318]

> The Covenant proscribes any discrimination on the grounds of race, colour, sex, age, language, religion, political or other opinion, national or social origin, property, birth, physical or mental disability, health status (including HIV/AIDS), sexual orientation and civil, political, social or other status, which has the intention or effect of nullifying or impairing the equal enjoyment or exercise of the right to water.[319]

Until 2005, the Committee had never explicitly stated that distinctions made on the basis of objective and reasonable criteria did not amount to discrimination. As a consequence, for a long time it has been unclear whether the CESCR Committee accepted this more commonly-used definition of discrimination. In the view of Sepúlveda, concluding observations showed the Committee's use of the latter definition.[320] She also submitted that it was not necessary to expressly provide a reasoning along these lines when the arbitrariness of the distinction was evident.[321] In our view, until recently, the Committee sent out a rather ambiguous message. In its 2001 concluding observations on the Japanese second periodic report *e.g.*, it expressed concern that the state interpreted "the principle of non-discrimination as being subject to [...] 'reasonable' or 'rationally justifiable' exceptions."[322] Whereas this rather looks as a rejection of the

---

316 UN Doc. E/C.12/1/Add.107, para. 45 (China).

317 UN Doc. HRI/GEN/1/Rev.7, General Comment No. 12 (1999), *The Right to Adequate Food (Art. 11)*, para. 18.

318 UN Doc. HRI/GEN/1/Rev.7, General Comment No. 14 (2000), *The Right to the Highest Attainable Standard of Health (Art. 12)*, para. 18.

319 UN Doc. HRI/GEN/1/Rev.7, General Comment No. 15 (2002), *The Right to Water (Arts. 11 and 12 of the International Covenant on Economic, Social and Cultural Rights)*, para. 13.

320 Sepúlveda, supra note 108, 385.

321 *Ibid.*, 386, footnote 31.

322 UN Doc. E/C.12/1/Add.67, para. 12 (Japan).

definition of discrimination in which differential treatment can be allowed on reasonable and objective grounds, it then told Japan that

> the principle of non-discrimination, as laid down in article 2 (2) of the Covenant, is an absolute principle and can be subject to no exception, unless the distinction is based on objective criteria.[323]

However, in its definition of direct gender discrimination in its recent general comment No. 16, the Committee clearly referred to the criterion of objective justification.[324] It therefore seems rather likely that in the future the CESCR Committee too will make use of the working definition of discrimination that is common to the other Committees.

The Committee does not seem to have attached different legal obligations to the concepts of non-discrimination and equality so far.

The CESCR Committee has stressed both the immediate character as well as the wide scope of the obligation not to discriminate. As to the immediate character of the obligation, the Committee has submitted repeatedly that the prohibition against discrimination is subject to neither progressive realization[325] nor the availability of resources, and that it applies fully and immediately[326] to all aspects of the rights in the Covenant and encompasses all internationally prohibited grounds of discrimination.[327] This does not exclude however that the state has a margin of discretion in adopting appropriate measures in order to comply with this immediate obligation.[328]

---

323 *Ibid.*, para. 39. Similarly, the Committee hinted at the reasonable and objective grounds definition in its concluding observations on the initial report of Croatia, in which it expressed concern that the granting of citizenship had not been governed by "fair and objective non-discriminatory criteria." (UN Doc. E/C.12/1/Add. 73, para. 11 (Croatia)).

324 UN Doc. E/C.12/2005/3, General Comment No. 16 (2005), *Article 3: The Equal Right of Men and Women to the Enjoyment of All Economic, Social and Cultural Rights*, para. 12.

325 UN Doc. E/C.12/1/Add.67, para. 12 (Japan).

326 UN Doc. HRI/GEN/1/Rev.7, General Comment No. 15 (2002), *The Right to Water (Arts. 11 and 12 of the International Covenant on Economic, Social and Cultural Rights)*, para. 17; General Comment No. 14 (2000), *The Right to the Highest Attainable Standard of Health (Art. 12)*, para. 30; General Comment No. 13 (1999), *The Right to Education (art. 13)*, paras. 31 and 43; General Comment No. 11 (1999), *Plans of Action for Primary Education (Article 14 Covenant)*, para. 10; General Comment No. 3 (1990), *The nature of States parties' obligations (Art. 2, para. 1, of the Covenant)*, para. 1. See also UN Doc. E/2001/22, para. 496 (Yugoslavia).

327 UN Doc. HRI/GEN/1/Rev.7, General Comment No. 13 (1999), *The Right to Education (Art. 13)*, para. 31. Compare with UN Doc. E/C.12/2005/3, General Comment No. 16 (2005), *Article 3: The Equal Right of Men and Women to the Enjoyment of All Economic, Social and Cultural Rights*, paras. 1 and 32.

328 UN Doc. E/C.12/2005/3, General Comment No. 16 (2005), *Article 3: The Equal Right of Men and Women to the Enjoyment of All Economic, Social and Cultural Rights*, para. 32.

Sometimes, the Committee has made a distinction between *de jure* and *de facto* discrimination, and has submitted that (only) *de jure* discrimination is to be eliminated fully and immediately.[329] The reason why the Committee can put this so unequivocally is obvious: "many measures, such as most strategies and programmes designed to eliminate [...] discrimination, can be pursued with minimum resource implications through the adoption, modification or abrogation of legislation or the dissemination of information."[330] A state is to take immediate steps to eliminate *de facto* discrimination as soon as possible.[331] In line with this position, it considers as a violation of the right to education the failure *to take measures* which address *de facto* educational discrimination.[332] A distinction between the obligation to immediately eliminate *de jure* discrimination, and to take immediate steps to eliminate *de facto* discrimination as soon as possible was made in the Limburg Principles.[333]

As to its scope, the Committee has taken the position that the principle of non-discrimination "extends to all persons of school age residing in the territory, including non nationals, and irrespective of their legal status."[334] The Committee found explicit support for this position in article 2 CRC and article 3 (e) of the UNESCO Convention against Discrimination in Education.[335] Probably lacking such explicit support in other

329 UN Doc. E/C.12/1/Add.12, para. 16 (Zimbabwe).

330 UN Doc. HRI/GEN/1/Rev.7, General Comment No. 14 (2000), *The Right to the Highest Attainable Standard of Health (Art. 12)*, para. 18.

331 Sepúlveda, supra note 108, 396-397; See *e.g.* UN Doc. HRI/GEN/1/Rev.7, General Comment No. 15, *The Right to Water (Arts. 11 and 12 of the International Covenant on Economic, Social and Cultural Rights)*, para. 14.

332 UN Doc. HRI/GEN/1/Rev.7, General Comment No. 13 (1999), *The Right to Education (Art. 13)*, para. 59.

333 *Limburg Principles on the Implementation of the International Covenant on Economic, Social and Cultural Rights*, UN Doc. E/C.12/2000/13 and *Human Rights Quarterly*, Vol. 9, no. 2, 1987, pp. 122-135, Nos. 37-38. The *Limburg Principles on the Implementation of the International Covenant on Economic, Social and Cultural Rights* are principles that a group of distinguished experts in international law agreed upon during a meeting in Maastricht from 2 to 6 June 1986. They were believed by the participants to reflect the then present state of international law, except when otherwise indicated.
See also Sepúlveda, supra note 108, 396-397.

334 UN Doc. HRI/GEN/1/Rev.7, General Comment No. 13 (1999), *The Right to Education (Art. 13)*, para. 34.

335 Article 2 CRC reads: "1. States Parties shall respect and ensure the rights set forth in the present Convention to each child within their jurisdiction without discrimination of any kind, irrespective of the child's or his or her parent's or legal guardian's race, colour, sex, language, religion, political or other opinion, national, ethnic or social origin, property, disability, birth or other status. 2. States Parties shall take all appropriate measures to ensure that the child is protected against all forms of discrimination or punishment on the basis of the status, activities, expressed opinions, or beliefs of the child's parents, legal guardians, or family members."
Article 3 (e) UNESCO Convention against Discrimination in Education reads: "In order to eliminate and prevent discrimination within the meaning of this Convention, the States Parties thereto undertake to give foreign nationals resident within their territory the same access to education as that given to their own nationals."

legal documents, it has not taken such a bold stance with regard to other economic, social and cultural rights.

b. Qualifiers

i. *De Jure* and *De Facto*

Similar to the other Committees, the CESCR Committee frequently distinguishes between *de jure* and *de facto* equality and/or discrimination, both in its general comments and its concluding observations. The main focus is however on practice and *de facto discrimination*.[336]

In its general comment on article 3 CESCR, the Committee has explained the difference between *de facto* and *de jure* equality:

> De jure (or formal) equality and de facto (or substantive) equality are different but interconnected concepts. Formal equality assumes that equality is achieved if a law or policy treats men and women in a neutral manner. Substantive equality is concerned, in addition, with the effects of laws, policies and practices and with ensuring that they do not maintain, but rather alleviate, the inherent disadvantage that particular groups experience.[337]

In many other general comments, the existence of both *de jure* and *de facto* discrimination is recalled,[338] and the prohibition of discrimination in law and in fact with regard to accessibility of water, health, education and food has been stressed.[339] *De facto* equality has been recognized as a legitimate cause for affirmative action in the field of education.[340] States are to monitor closely education so as to identify and take measures to redress any *de facto* discrimination.[341]

---

336 See also UN Doc. HRI/GEN/2/Rev.2, *Reporting Guidelines*, paras. 9 (a), 15 (c), 17 (a), 37 (a) and 60 (a).

337 UN Doc. E/C.12/2005/3, General Comment No. 16 (2005), *Article 3: The Equal Right of Men and Women to the Enjoyment of All Economic, Social and Cultural Rights*, para. 7.

338 UN Doc. HRI/GEN/1/Rev.7, General Comment No. 5 (1994), *Persons with Disabilities*, para. 15.

339 UN Doc. HRI/GEN/1/Rev.7, General Comment No. 15 (2002), *The Right to Water (Arts. 11 and 12 of the International Covenant on Economic, Social and Cultural Rights)*, paras. 12 (c) (iii) and 14; General Comment No. 14 (2000), *The Right to the Highest Attainable Standard of Health (Art. 12)*, paras. 12 (b) (i) and 50; General Comment No. 13 (1999), *The Right to 3ducation (art. 13)*, para. 6 (b); General Comment No. 12 (1999), *The Right to Adequate Food (Art. 11)*, para. 19.

340 UN Doc. HRI/GEN/1/Rev.7, General Comment No. 13 (1999), *The Right to Education (Art. 13)*, para. 32.

341 *Ibid.*, para. 37.

The Committee has expressed concern about certain forms of *de jure* or legal discrimination[342], in particular against women,[343] children born out of wedlock,[344] salaried domestic workers,[345] internal migrants[346] and minority groups.[347] The CESCR Committee has equally highlighted the (persistence of)[348] *de facto* discrimination, in particular against marginalized and vulnerable groups in society,[349] children born out of wedlock,[350] ethnic (minority)[351] groups, indigenous people,[352] minority groups, and internal migrants,[353] especially in the fields of employment, housing and education.[354] In response to the French report, the Committee underlined that it:

> [was] of the opinion that the fact that all individuals are guaranteed equal rights in the State party and that they are all equal before the law does not mean that minorities do not have the right to exist and to be protected as such in the State party. The Committee emphasizes that equality before the law is not always adequate to ensure the equal enjoyment of human rights, and in particular economic, social and cultural rights, by certain minority groups in a country.[355]

Particular concern has also been expressed repeatedly about the (persistence of)[356] *de facto* inequality or discrimination between women and men,[357] owing to the perpetuation of traditional stereotypes and lack of implementation of legislative guarantees of equality,[358] or to traditional practices such as arranged marriages of children and forced marriages of widows with a late husband's brother.[359]

---

342 UN Doc. E/C.12/1/Add.16, para. 14 (Dominican Republic).
343 UN Doc. E/C.12/1/Add.98, para. 14 (Kuwait).
344 UN Doc. E/C.12/1995/17, para. 19 (Algeria).
345 UN Doc. E/C.12/1/Add.60, para. 16 (Bolivia).
346 UN Doc. E/C.12/1/Add.107, para. 79 (China).
347 UN Doc. E/C.12/1/Add.67, para. 13 (Japan).
348 UN Doc. E/C.12/1/Add.79, para. 14 (United Kingdom).
349 UN Doc. E/C.12/1/Add.92, paras. 8 and 27 (Yemen).
350 UN Doc. E/C.12/1995/17, para. 19 (Algeria).
351 UN Doc. E/C.12/1/Add.65, para. 12 (Ukraine); UN Doc. E/C.12/1/Add.19, para. 12 (United Kingdom).
352 UN Doc. E/C.12/1/Add.100, para. 13 (Ecuador); UN Doc. E/C.12/1/Add.30, para. 16 (Switzerland).
353 UN Doc. E/C.12/1/Add.107, paras. 15 and 79 (China).
354 UN Doc. E/C.12/1/Add.104, para. 15 (Azerbaijan); UN Doc. E/C.12/1/Add.67, para. 13 (Japan).
355 UN Doc. E/C.12/1/Add.73, para. 15 (France).
356 UN Doc. E/C.12/1/Add.98, para. 14 (Kuwait); UN Doc. E/C.12/1/Add.95, para. 13 (Democratic People's Republic of Korea); UN Doc. E/C.12/1/Add.19, para. 12 (United Kingdom); UN Doc. E/C.12/1/Add.18, para. 14 (Uruguay).
357 UN Doc. E/C.12/1/Add.100, para. 15 (Ecuador); UN Doc. E/C.12/1/Add.93, para. 12 (Guatemala); UN Doc. E/C.12/1/Add.66, para. 17 (Nepal); UN Doc. E/C.12/1/Add.62, para. 15 (Senegal); UN Doc. E/C.12/1/Add.60, para. 15 (Bolivia); UN Doc. E/C.12/1/Add.57, para. 13 (Honduras); UN Doc. E/C.12/1/Add.38, para. 17 (Argentina); UN Doc. E/C.12/1/Add.30, paras. 16-17 (Switzerland); UN Doc. E/C.12/1/Add.8, para. 11 (Finland); UN Doc. E/C.12/1995/13, para. 21 (Norway); UN Doc. E/C.12/1995/4, para. 9 (Portugal); UN Doc. E/C.12/1993/15, para. 8 (Iceland).
358 UN Doc. E/C.12/1/Add.100, para. 13 (Ecuador).
359 UN Doc. E/C.12/1/Add.12, para. 10 (Zimbabwe).

ii. Intentional and Non-Intentional

The CESCR Committee does not seem to use the twin concepts of intentional and non-intentional discrimination. It has referred however to discrimination in purpose or in effect in its general comments (see above).

iii. Direct and Indirect

The CESCR Committee has on two occasions only referred to indirect discrimination in its concluding observations.[360] It recommended Belgium to revise the "cohabitation rule" in the unemployment insurance regime in order to eliminate its indirect discriminatory impact on women,[361] and expressed concern about ongoing direct and indirect discrimination of the Gypsy minority in Romania.[362]

In its general comment on disability, the Committee referred to 'subtle' forms of discrimination such as segregation and isolation achieved through the imposition of physical and social barriers."[363] In two of its more recent general comments, the Committee has spelled out the risk of hidden (not 'overt') discrimination, both with regard to investments in health and water:

> Inappropriate resource allocation can lead to discrimination that may not be overt. For example, investments should not disproportionately favour expensive water supply services which are often accessible only to a small, privileged fraction of the population, rather than investing in services and facilities that benefit a far larger part of the population.[364]

It equally referred to 'covert' discrimination in its general comment No. 16 on article 3 CESCR.[365] In the latter general comment, it defined for the first time the concepts of direct and indirect discrimination. Direct discrimination is said to occur "when a difference in treatment relies directly and explicitly on distinctions based exclusively on sex and characteristics of men or of women, which cannot be justified objectively."[366] Indirect discrimination on the other hand "occurs when a law, policy or programme does not appear to be discriminatory on its face, but has a discriminatory

---

360 See also Sepúlveda, supra note 108, 388-389.

361 UN Doc. E/C.12/1/Add.54, para. 22 (Belgium).

362 UN Doc. E/C.12/1994/4, para. 12 (Romania).

363 UN Doc. HRI/GEN/1/Rev.7, General Comment No. 5 (1994), *Persons with Disabilities*, para. 15.

364 UN Doc. HRI/GEN/1/Rev.7, General Comment No. 15 (2002), *The Right to Water (Arts. 11 and 12 of the International Covenant on Economic, Social and Cultural Rights)*, para. 14. An almost similar wording was used with regard to health care, see UN Doc. HRI/GEN/1/Rev.7, General Comment No. 14 (2000), *The Right to the Highest Attainable Standard of Health (Art. 12)*, para. 19.

365 UN Doc. E/C.12/2005/3, General Comment No. 16 (2005), *Article 3: The Equal Right of Men and Women to the Enjoyment of All Economic, Social and Cultural Rights*, para. 5.

366 *Ibid.*, para. 12.

effect when implemented."[367] Indirect discrimination seems therefore to be understood as non-intentional discrimination.

iv. Multiple Discrimination

Double or multiple discrimination has been referred to explicitly in the two general comments concerning the economic, social and cultural rights of particular groups only, *i.e.* people with disabilities and the elder people. In both cases, it was submitted that gender in combination with another ground, *i.e.* age or disability, may lead to double discrimination.[368] In its general comment on equality of men and women, the Committee hinted at the concept of multiple discrimination by submitting that

> Many women experience distinct forms of discrimination, due to the intersection of sex with such factors as race, colour, language, religion, political and other opinion, national or social origin, property, birth, or other status, such as age, ethnicity, disability, marital, refugee or migrant status, resulting in compounded disadvantage.[369]

In its concluding comments, the Committee seems to have hinted at double discrimination, without explicitly invoking the concept however, with regard to disability and ethnic origin.[370]

v. Systemic Discrimination

The CESCR Committee does not use the term systemic discrimination as such. It has, however, repeatedly referred to persistent patterns of (societal) discrimination and to institutionalized discrimination. Pervasive culturally-ingrained discrimination[371] and persistent patterns of (societal) discrimination were identified against women and

---

367 *Ibid.*, para. 13.

368 UN Doc. HRI/GEN/1/Rev.7, General Comment No. 6 (1995), *The Economic, Social and Cultural Rights of Older Persons*, para. 20; UN Doc. HRI/GEN/1/Rev.7, General Comment No. 5 (1994), *Persons with Disabilities*, para. 19.

369 UN Doc. E/C.12/2005/3, General Comment No. 16 (2005), *Article 3: The Equal Right of Men and Women to the Enjoyment of All Economic, Social and Cultural Rights*, para. 5.

370 UN Doc. E/C.12/1/Add.90, para. 32 (Israel): undertake effective measures to combat discrimination against persons with disabilities (access to public facilities; access to basic services and employment), with particular attention to persons with disabilities from the Arab sector.

371 UN Doc. E/C.12/1/Add.3, para. 33 (Guatemala).

girls,[372] children born out of wedlock,[373] and against ethnic minorities[374] indigenous peoples[375] and Roma.[376] Institutionalized discrimination has been used in the context of racial discrimination[377] and the Palestinian conflict.[378] Systematic discrimination was detected in Viet Nam, where persons from certain groups, such as children of war victims and decorated families, received preferential treatment.[379]

vi. Private Discrimination

Private acts of discrimination have in particular been highlighted in relation to race[380] and the Gypsy minority.[381]

4. CEDAW COMMITTEE

Initially, little clarification on the concept of discrimination was given. The Committee started to use the word "discrimination" more in its concluding comments from 1998 onwards, and has greatly clarified the concept since 1998-1999. It tends to focus on *de facto* equality (hence the emphasis on implementation, assessment of measures and educational measures), and on indirect (hence the emphasis on the definition in CEDAW, which includes discrimination in effect) and structural discrimination.

---

372 UN Doc. E/C.12/1/Add.92, para. 9 (Yemen); UN Doc. E/C.12/1/Add.71, para. 14 (Algeria); UN Doc. E/C.12/1/Add.61, para. 20 (Togo); UN Doc. E/C.12/1/Add.55, para. 16 (Morocco): in national legislation, particularly in family and personal status law, as well as inheritance law; UN Doc. E/C.12/1/Add.53, para. 12 (Portugal): in the fields of employment and equality of wages and opportunity with men; UN Doc. E/C.12/1/Add.28, para. 12 (Cyprus); UN Doc. E/C.12/1/Add.1, para. 7 (Paraguay).

373 UN Doc. E/C.12/1/Add.55, para. 23 (Morocco).

374 UN Doc. E/C.12/1/Add.61, para. 20 (Togo).

375 UN Doc. E/C.12/1/Add.93, para. 11 (Guatemala): with regard to access to, *inter alia*, land ownership, work, education, health services and adequate nutrition and housing; UN Doc. E/C.12/1/Add.57, para. 14 (Honduras): especially in the field of employment, and the protection of traditional ancestral and agricultural lands.

376 UN Doc. E/C.12/1/Add.97, para. 11 (Greece).

377 UN Doc. E/C.12/1/Add.16, para. 14 (Dominican Republic).

378 UN Doc. E/C.12/1/Add.27, para. 11 (Israel): large-scale and systematic confiscation of Palestinian land and property by the State and the transfer of that property to private Jewish agencies constitute an institutionalized form of discrimination because these agencies by definition would deny the use of these properties to non-Jews.

379 UN Doc. E/C.12/1993/8, para. 11 (Viet Nam).

380 UN Doc. E/C.12/1/Add.74, para. 9 (Croatia); UN Doc. E/C.12/1/Add.58, para. 30 (China: Hong Kong); UN Doc. E/C.12/1/Add.16, para. 31 (Dominican Republic).

381 UN Doc. E/C.12/1994/4, para. 12 (Romania).

a. Definition

Article 1 CEDAW defines discrimination. It reads:

> Any distinction, exclusion or restriction made on the basis of sex which has the effect or purpose of impairing or nullifying the recognition, enjoyment or exercise by women, irrespective of their marital status, on a basis of equality of men and women, of human rights and fundamental freedoms in the political, economic, social, cultural, civil or any other field.

As pointed out earlier, this definition resembles closely the one given in ICERD. In its concluding comments, the CEDAW Committee has stressed that any domestic definition of discrimination should include differentiation with both the purpose or effect of discrimination, as specified in article 1 CEDAW.[382] The definition is said to prohibit both direct and indirect discrimination,[383] by public as well as private actors.[384]

It is not clear whether the CEDAW Committee accepts the widely-used pragmatic definition of discrimination (*i.e.* differential treatment in a comparable situation without a reasonable and objective justification). In its 1998 concluding comments on the Peruvian report, it expressed concern at a clause which defined discrimination as "the act of according different treatment to people, without there being any objective and reasonable justification", and recommended that "any objective and reasonable justification" be used only as a basis for the implementation of temporary special measures which accelerated the *de facto* equality between women and men.[385]

For the CEDAW Committee, the elimination of discrimination and the promotion of equality are "two different but equally important goals in the quest for women's empowerment."[386] CEDAW is said to include the obligation for states to eliminate discrimination against women and to ensure *de jure* and *de facto* equality of women and men.[387]

---

382 UN Doc. A/53/38/Rev.1 (part II), para. 372 (Korea).

383 UN Doc. A/55/38 (part II), para. 91 (Moldova); UN Doc. A/56/38 (part I), para. 87 (Kazakhstan); UN Doc. A/56/38 (part I), para. 166 (Uzbekistan); UN Doc. A/56/38 (part I), para. 253 (Mongolia); UN Doc. A/56/38 (part II), para. 118 (Guinea); UN Doc. A/57/38 (part I), para. 87 (Estonia).

384 UN Doc. A/54/38/Rev.1 (part II), para. 50 (Belize); UN Doc. A/54/38/Rev.1 (part II), para. 94 (Georgia).

385 UN Doc. A/53/38/Rev.1 (part II), paras. 319-320 (Peru).

386 UN Doc. A/57/38 (part II), para. 146 (Belgium).

387 See *e.g.* UN Doc. A/58/38 (part II), para. 332 (Ecuador); UN Doc. A/58/38 (part II), para. 71 (Costa Rica).

b. Qualifiers

The CEDAW Committee tends to use rather frequently a variety of qualifiers simultaneously. With regard to a number of states it has held that there was a

> lack of understanding of discrimination against women as a multifaceted phenomenon that entails indirect and unintentional as well as direct and intentional discrimination. This understanding is a sine qua non of comprehensive analyses and for policy analysis for the effective elimination of discrimination against women in both de jure and de facto terms.[388]

i. *De Jure* and *De Facto*

The twin concepts of *de jure* and *de facto* equality (or legal and substantive equality) feature often together in the decisions of the CEDAW Committee, and are commonly used as a standard expression.[389] In a standard final paragraph of its concluding comments, the Committee has requested since early 1997 the wide dissemination of its concluding comments in the country concerned in order to make the people aware of the steps that have been taken to ensure *the jure* and *de facto* equality.[390]

Adherence to formal or *de jure* equality is welcomed,[391] and *de jure* equality is recognized as an essential prerequisite for achieving *de facto* equality of women.[392] At the same time, it is submitted that the insistence on formal or *de jure* equality "tends to impede a proper understanding of the complex issue of discrimination, such as structural and indirect discrimination, which further compounds the situation of de facto inequality of women."[393]

---

388 UN Doc. A/57/38 (part II), para. 279 (Ukraine); UN Doc. A/54/38/Rev.1 (part I), para. 113 (Kyrgyzstan).

389 See *e.g.* UN Doc. A/58/38 (part I), para. 362 (Canada); UN Doc. A/55/38 (part I), para. 225 (Congo); UN Doc. A/54/38/Rev.1 (part II), paras. 297 and 299 (United Kingdom and Northern Ireland); UN Doc. A/53/38/Rev.1 (part II), para. 118 (South Africa); UN Doc. A/53/38/Rev.1 (part I), para. 238 (Bulgaria).

390 See *e.g.* UN Doc. A/52/38/Rev.1 (part I), para. 122 (Slovenia). Since 1998, government administrators and politicians have been targeted in particular, see *e.g.* UN Doc. A/53/38/Rev.1 (part I), para. 79 (Azerbaijan) and most recently so in UN Doc. CEDAW/C/PAR/CC/3-5, para. 42 (Paraguay); UN Doc. CEDAW/C/DZA/CC/2, para. 49 (Algeria); UN Doc. CEDAW/C/LAO/CC/1-5, para. 47 (Laos).

391 UN Doc. A/54/38/Rev.1 (part I), para. 63 (Algeria); UN Doc. A/52/38/Rev.1, para. 91 (Slovenia); UN Doc. A/52/38/Rev.1, para. 89 (Slovenia); UN Doc. A/49/38, para. 354 (Zambia).

392 UN Doc. A/58/38 (part I), para. 250 (El Salvador).

393 UN Doc. A/53/38/Rev.1 (part I), para. 232 (Bulgaria).

Concern is expressed that *de facto* inequalities between women and men (*de facto* discrimination)[394] are not addressed,[395] and that a gap between *de facto* and *de jure* equality persists.[396]

De facto equality is interpreted by the Committee as substantive equality.[397] *De facto* or substantive equality have their logical corollary in the equality of results.[398] *De facto* equality for women in all spheres of life is welcomed and encouraged,[399] and the absence of full *de facto* equality between women and men is regretted.[400]

The close link with indirect discrimination becomes clear in the analysis of the shared root causes of *de facto* inequality and indirect discrimination, *i.e.* the overarching tendency to conceive of women as mothers and within the context of the family, rather than as individuals and independent actors in the public sphere.[401] The lack of a proper understanding of the complex issue of discrimination, such as indirect discrimination, is also believed to further compound the situation of *de facto* inequality of women.[402] The non-incorporation of gender in all discussions of equality may contribute to concealment and perpetuation of, in particular, *de facto* inequality.[403] Moreover, the persistence of deep-seated social and cultural attitudes inhibits the attainment of *de facto* equality.[404]

---

394 UN Doc. A/53/38/Rev.1 (part I), para. 391 (Mexico); UN Doc. A/52/38/Rev.1 (Part I), para. 86 (Slovenia).

395 UN Doc. A/56/38 (part II), para. 49 (Andorra); UN Doc. A/54/38/Rev.1 (part I), para. 159 (Liechtenstein); UN Doc. Doc. A/53/38/Rev.1 (part I), para. 186 (Czech Republic).

396 UN Doc. CEDAW/C/DZA/CC/2, para. 33 (Algeria); UN Doc. A/56/38 (part II), para. 256 (Viet Nam); UN Doc. A/56/38 (part II), para. 120 (Guinea); UN Doc. A/56/38 (part I), para. 55 (Burundi); UN Doc. A/53/38/Rev.1 (part I), para. 286 (Indonesia); UN Doc. A/53/38/Rev.1 (part I), para. 60 (Azerbaijan); UN Doc. A/52/38/Rev.1, para. 145 (Saint Vincent and the Grenadines); UN Doc. A/52/38/Rev.1, para. 72 (Morocco); UN Doc. A/50/38, para. 149 (Chile).

397 UN Doc. HRI/GEN/1/Rev.7, General Recommendation No. 25 (2004), *On Article 4, paragraph 1, of the Convention on the Elimination of All Forms of Discrimination against Women – Temporary Special Measures*, paras. 8, 11, 14, 15, 18, 35.

398 *Ibid.*, para. 9.

399 UN Doc. A/52/38/Rev.1 (part II), para. 265 (Antigua and Barbuda); UN Doc. A/52/38/Rev.1 (part II), para. 116 (Namibia); UN Doc. A/52/38/Rev.1 (part I), para. 343 (Canada); UN Doc. A/52/38/Rev.1 (part II), para. 344 (Italy); UN Doc. A/49/38, para. 658 (h) (New Zealand); UN Doc. A/49/38, para. 367 (Zambia).

400 UN Doc. A/54/38/Rev.1 (part II), para. 2232 (Chile).

401 UN Doc. A/53/38/Rev.1 (part II), para. 74 (Slovakia); UN Doc. A/53/38/Rev.1 (part I), para. 184 (Czech Republic). Compare with UN Doc. A/53/38/Rev.1 (part I), para. 103 (Croatia), in which it was submitted that a careful and gender-sensitive analysis of the emphasis on motherhood vis-à-vis women's roles in the public sphere was needed to assure *de facto* gender equality.

402 UN Doc. A/53/38/Rev.1 (part I), para. 232 (Bulgaria).

403 UN Doc. A/53/38/Rev.1 (part I), para. 106 (Croatia).

404 UN Doc. A/54/38/Rev.1 (part I), para. 157 (Liechtenstein).

The proclaimed aim of affirmative action ('temporary special measures' in the language of CEDAW) is to accelerate *de facto* equality between men and women.[405] A purely formal legal or programmatic approach is deemed insufficient to achieve women's *de facto* equality with men. Non-identical treatment is therefore required,[406] in particular in those areas where women's *de facto* equality does not improve at the desired pace.[407] The application of temporary special measures is one of the means to realize *de facto* equality for women, rather than an exception to the norms of non-discrimination and equality.[408]

ii. Intentional and Non-Intentional

The CEDAW Committee has referred a number of times to unintentional discrimination. It has recommended legislation and policies that are directed at countering both intentional and unintentional discrimination.[409] Unintentional discrimination has been said to be "the result of outmoded practices and procedures which inadvertently promote men."[410]

iii. Direct and Indirect

In the current view of the CEDAW Committee,[411] the definition of discrimination in article 1 CEDAW prohibits both direct and indirect discrimination,[412] by public as well

405 Article 4, para. 1 CEDAW; UN Doc. HRI/GEN/1/Rev.7, General Recommendation No. 5 (1988), *Temporary Special Measures*; UN Doc. A/54/38/Rev.1 (part I), para. 165 (Liechtenstein); UN Doc. A/53/38/Rev.1 (part II), para. 75 (Slovakia). In these concluding comments, the Committee links temporary special measures with structural discrimination and accelerated *de facto* equality.

406 UN Doc. HRI/GEN/1/Rev.7, General Recommendation No. 25 (2004), *On Article 4, paragraph 1, of the Convention on the Elimination of All Forms of Discrimination against Women – Temporary Special Measures*, para. 8.

407 UN Doc. A/52/38/Rev.1 (part II), para. 355 (Italy). Compare also with UN Doc. A/52/38/Rev.1 (part II), para. 265 (Antigua and Barbuda), where the Committee suggested to utilize article 4 CEDAW in accelerating *de facto* equality for women.

408 UN Doc. HRI/GEN/1/Rev.7, General Recommendation No. 25 (2004), *On Article 4, paragraph 1, of the Convention on the Elimination of All Forms of Discrimination against Women – Temporary Special Measures*, para. 14. In 1998, the Committee seemed to have a somehow different understanding of temporary special measures. It argued that temporary special measures, being the establishment of programmes that advantage women more than men, require undermining formal equality for a certain period of time in order to achieve *de facto* equality in the long term (UN Doc. A/53/38/Rev.1 (part I), para. 234 (Bulgaria)).

409 UN Doc. A/54/38/Rev.1 (part I), para. 284 (China); UN Doc. A/54/38/Rev.1 (part I), para. 114 (Kyrgyzstan).

410 UN Doc. HRI/GEN/1/Rev.7, General Recommendation No. 23 (1997), *Political and Public Life*, para. 15.

411 Initially, it was not clear whether indirect discrimination was a distinct category, see Frostell, supra note 140, 51-52.

412 UN Doc. A/58/38 (part II), para. 358 (Japan); UN Doc. A/55/38 (part II), para. 91 (Moldova); UN Doc. A/53/38/Rev.1 (part II), para. 319 (Peru).

as private actors.[413] Differential treatment which is discriminatory in effect is labelled indirect discrimination[414] or discrimination of effect.[415] Discrimination in effect seems therefore to be equated with indirect discrimination.[416]

In general recommendation No. 25 (2004) on temporary special measures, it was submitted to be a central obligation for states to ensure that there is no direct or indirect discrimination in laws, in order to eliminate discrimination against women.[417] The concept of indirect discrimination is explained in an endnote:

> Indirect discrimination against women may occur when laws, policies and programmes are based on seemingly gender-neutral criteria which in their actual effect have a detrimental impact on women. Gender-neutral laws, policies and programmes unintentionally may perpetuate the consequences of past discrimination. They may be inadvertently modelled on male lifestyles and thus fail to take into account aspects of women's life experiences which may differ from those of men. These differences may exist because of stereotypical expectations, attitudes and behaviour directed towards women which are based on the biological differences between women and men. They may also exist because of the generally existing subordination of women by men.

In the view of the Committee, the overemphasis on legal protection and the insistence on formal or de *jure* equality, and the cultural promotion of motherhood and family roles for women, rather than an emphasis on women as individuals in their own right and as independent actors in the public sphere, reflects a misunderstanding of such critical concepts as gender roles, indirect discrimination and *de facto* inequality,[418] and is a major obstacle to the implementation of the Convention.[419] The understanding of discrimination against women as a multifaceted phenomenon that entails indirect and unintentional as well as direct and intentional discrimination is considered "a sine qua non of comprehensive analyses and for policy analysis for the effective elimination of discrimination against women in both *de jure* and de facto terms."[420] The close link between structural and indirect discrimination has been stressed in the context of participation of women in public life:[421]

---

413 UN Doc. A/54/38/Rev.1 (part II), para. 50 (Belize).

414 UN Doc. A/54/38/Rev.1 (part II), paras. 300-301 (United Kingdom and Northern Ireland).

415 UN Doc. A/58/38 (part II), para. 264 (France); UN Doc. A/57/38 (part III), para. 186 (Guatemala).

416 The CEDAW Committee used both terms to indicate distinguishable modes of discrimination however in UN Doc. A/54/38/Rev.1 (part I), para. 284 (China); UN Doc. A/54/38/Rev.1 (part I), para. 113 (Kyrgyzstan).

417 UN Doc. HRI/GEN/1/Rev.7, General Recommendation No. 25 (2004), *On Article 4, paragraph 1, of the Convention on the Elimination of All Forms of Discrimination against Women – Temporary Special Measures*, para. 7.

418 UN Doc. A/56/38 (part II), para. 39 (Andorra); UN Doc. A/53/38/Rev.1 (part II), para. 74 (Slovakia); UN Doc. A/53/38/Rev.1 (part I), para. 232 (Bulgaria).

419 UN Doc. A/53/38/Rev.1 (part I), para. 184 (Czech Republic).

420 UN Doc. A/54/38/Rev.1 (part I), para. 113 (Kyrgyzstan).

421 UN Doc. A/54/38/Rev.1 (part I), para. 319 (China-Hong Kong).

> [T]he view that women themselves bear full responsibility for their low level of participation in public life suggests a lack of understanding of indirect and structural discrimination and its impact on women.[422]

The Committee has paid a lot of attention to the variety of measures to be taken in order to address indirect discrimination. In general terms, states are expected to include in domestic legislation a prohibition of discrimination against women, encompassing both direct and indirect discrimination in line with article 1 of the Convention.[423] Policies and efforts are to be directed at preventing and countering both direct and indirect discrimination against women and achieving *de facto* gender equality.[424] Anti-discrimination laws, as well as laws on violence against women, should be accompanied by sensitisation measures in order to be able to combat effectively indirect discrimination and eradicate traditional stereotypes.[425] Among the target groups are judges, lawyers and law enforcement personnel.[426] Temporary special measures may be needed to overcome systemic and indirect discrimination against women.[427]

In particular with regard to employment, states are encouraged to prevent direct and indirect discrimination.[428] They are recommended to assess the potential for indirect discrimination against women in the recruitment, training and professional development opportunities offered to women, and in the promotion and dismissal of women.[429] Marginalization of women in the labour market through the institutionalisation of temporary work for women,[430] the sex segregation of the labour market,[431] a disproportionate number of women occupied in part-time employment[432] and lower wages for women[433] are all factors that contribute to indirect discrimination in the labour market.[434]

---

422 UN Doc. A/53/38/Rev.1 (part I), para. 102 (Croatia).

423 UN Doc. A/58/38 (part II), para. 358 (Japan); UN Doc. A/54/38/Rev.1 (part I), para. 316 (China-Hong Kong); UN Doc. A/52/38/Rev.1 (part II), para. 357 (Italy); UN Doc. A/52/38/Rev.1 (part II), para. 172 (Israel); UN Doc. A/52/38/Rev.1 (part I), para. 108 (Slovenia).

424 UN Doc. A/57/38 (part II), para. 280 (Ukraine); UN Doc. A/56/38 (part II), para. 84 (Singapore); UN Doc. A/53/38/Rev.1 (part I), para. 113 (Croatia).

425 UN Doc. A/58/38 (part I), para. 165 (Congo); UN Doc. A/54/38/Rev.1 (part II), para. 258 (Spain); UN Doc. A/52/38/Rev.1 (part II), para. 349 (Italy).

426 UN Doc. A/52/38/Rev.1 (part II), para. 357 (Italy).

427 UN Doc. A/54/38/Rev.1 (part II), para. 190 (Ireland).

428 UN Doc. A/58/38 (part II), para. 175 (Morocco); UN Doc. A/57/38 (part II), para. 201 (Tunisia); UN Doc. A/56/38 (part I), para. 272 (Mongolia).

429 UN Doc. A/56/38 (part I), para. 182 (Uzbekistan); UN Doc. A/54/38/Rev.1 (part II), para. 262 (Spain).

430 UN Doc. A/52/38/Rev.1, para. 106 (Slovenia).

431 UN Doc. A/54/38/Rev.1 (part II), para. 94 (Georgia).

432 UN Doc. A/52/38/Rev.1 (part II), para. 350 (Italy); UN Doc. A/51/38, para. 96 (Iceland).

433 UN Doc. A/51/38, para. 217 (Cuba).

434 UN Doc. CEDAW/C/TUR/CC/4-5, para. 35 (Turkey).

States have been recommended to provide women with effective remedies against indirect discrimination,[435] especially in the area of employment.[436]

The CEDAW Committee has sometimes expressed concern about *hidden* discrimination, *e.g.* in social security and taxation between different groups of women,[437] or in training programmes.[438] The fact that part-time work has sometimes been raised as an issue of indirect discrimination,[439] and sometimes as an issue of hidden discrimination[440] might suggest that indirect or hidden discrimination are basically the same. The Committee has however also listed them as different forms of discrimination.[441]

iv. Multiple Discrimination

The concept of double or multiple discrimination is well-known to the CEDAW Committee, and frequently invoked. Generally speaking, the Committee has identified double or multiple discrimination based on sex/gender and one or more other grounds, such as disability,[442] ethnicity or the belonging to a minority group (such as Roma women, Kurdish women),[443] ethnicity and race,[444] or race, ethnicity and religious affiliation.[445]

In many other cases, the Committee has however refrained from invoking explicitly double or multiple discrimination.[446] Sometimes, it has referred to the "particular

---

435 UN Doc. A/54/38/Rev.1 (part II), paras. 300-301 (United Kingdom and Northern Ireland).

436 UN Doc. A/55/38 (part I), para. 360 (Belarus).

437 UN Doc. A/51/38, para. 190 (Belgium).

438 UN Doc. A/55/38 (part II), para. 144 (Lithuania).

439 Supra note 432.

440 UN Doc. A/51/38, para. 187 (Belgium).

441 UN Doc. A/52/38/Rev.1, para. 108 (Slovenia): ongoing revision of laws should take account of hidden, indirect and structural discrimination.

442 See UN Doc. HRI/GEN/1/Rev.7, General Recommendation No. 18 (1991), *Disabled Women*: "disabled women, who suffer from a double discrimination linked to their special living conditions".

443 UN Doc. A/58/38 (part II), para. 365 (Japan); UN Doc. A/58/38 (part I), para. 413 (Norway); UN Doc. A/57/38 (part III), para. 293 (Greece); UN Doc. A/56/38 (part II), para. 205 (Netherlands); UN Doc. A/56/38 (part I), para. 305 (Finland); UN Doc. A/52/38/Rev.1, para. 180 (Turkey).

444 UN Doc. A/55/38 (part I), para. 317 (Germany).

445 UN Doc. A/58/38 (part II), para. 275 (France); UN Doc. A/58/38 (part I), para. 122 (Switzerland).

446 UN Doc. A/58/38 (part II), para. 425 (New Zealand): immigrant, refugee and minority women; UN Doc. A/57/38 (part I), para. 49 (Fiji): indigenous Fijian women; UN Doc. A/56/38 (part II), para. 356 (Sweden): immigrant, refugee and minority women in Sweden; UN Doc. A/55/38 (part I), para. 68 (India): women who belong to particular castes or ethnic or religious groups; UN Doc. A/54/38/Rev.1 (part II), para. 305 (United Kingdom and Northern Ireland): women belonging to ethnic minorities; UN Doc. A/53/38/Rev.1 (part II), para. 136 (South Africa): rural women in rural areas in South Africa; UN Doc. A/53/38/Rev.1 (part I), para. 389 (Mexico): indigenous women; UN Doc. A/52/38/Rev.1 (part II), para. 390 (Australia): Aboriginal and Torres Strait Islander women in Australia.

vulnerability of certain groups of women to discrimination" or "particularly disadvantaged women", but without explicitly using the concept of multiple discrimination.[447]

In its 2004 general recommendation on temporary special measures, the Committee noted that certain groups of women suffer from multiple discrimination, based on race, ethnic or religious identity, disability, age, class, caste or other factors (including rural women).[448] It submitted that states may need to take specific temporary special measures to eliminate such multiple discrimination.[449]

v. Systemic Inequality

In the view of the Committee, systemic inequality or structural discrimination originates from "traditional attitudes by which women are regarded as subordinate to men or as having stereotyped roles",[450] and of social and cultural structures and institutions.[451] The underlying causes of discrimination against women, and of their inequality are to be addressed. A conceptual approach is needed, so that historically-determined male paradigms of power and life patterns do no longer dominate the lives of women and men.[452]

The concept of structural discrimination is often, but not always,[453] mentioned in connection with indirect discrimination.[454]

In case of (indirect and) structural discrimination, the government, rather than women themselves have primary responsibility for implementing strategies to eliminate such

---

447 UN Doc. A/55/38 (part II), para. 207 (Iraq): women belonging to ethnic minorities, including Kurds, Turkmens and Asssyrians; UN Doc. A/50/38, para. 389 (Finland): minority women.

448 UN Doc. HRI/GEN/1/Rev.7, General Recommendation No. 25 (2004), *On Article 4, paragraph 1, of the Convention on the Elimination of All Forms of Discrimination against Women – Temporary Special Measures*, para. 38.

449 *Ibid.*, para. 12. For an illustration, see UN Doc. A/52/38/Rev.1, para. 180 (Turkey), in which the Committee was deeply concerned that no special temporary measures had been put in place to redress the situation of Kurdish women.

450 UN Doc. HRI/GEN/1/Rev.7, General Recommendation No. 19 (1992), *Violence Against Women*, para. 10.

451 UN Doc. HRI/GEN/1/Rev.7, General Recommendation No. 25 (2004), *On Article 4, paragraph 1, of the Convention on the Elimination of All Forms of Discrimination against Women – Temporary Special Measures*, para. 11.

452 *Ibid.*, para. 10.

453 UN Doc. A/53/38/Rev.1 (part I), para. 251 (Bulgaria).

454 UN Doc. A/54/38/Rev.1 (part II), para. 190 (Ireland); UN Doc. A/53/38/Rev.1 (part I), para. 232 (Bulgaria); UN Doc. A/52/38/Rev.1, para. 108 (Slovenia).

forms of discrimination.[455] One strategy for effectively addressing structural discrimination against women is the adoption of temporary special measures.[456]

vi. Private Discrimination

Article 1 of the Convention, which provides a definition of discrimination, covers direct and indirect discrimination by public as well as private actors.[457] The Committee has recommended to prevent and eliminate discrimination against women in the private sphere,[458] *e.g.* with regard to gender-based violence (see also further under the obligation to protect).[459] Affirmative action is also to be considered for the private sector,[460] and should cover governmental actors as well as private organizations or enterprises.[461] The office of the ombudsman should be allowed to address complaints about gender discrimination in the private sphere and the private sector.[462]

5. CRC COMMITTEE

a. Definition

The CRC does not contain a definition of discrimination. The CRC Committee seems to lean towards the definition of discrimination in terms of differential treatment in similar cases without an objective and reasonable justification. It invoked this definition most explicitly in its concluding comments on the Belgian report, in which it said that "the general principle of non-discrimination in the Convention prohibits differences in treatment on grounds that are arbitrary and objectively unjustifiable."[463]

The CRC Committee has not taken an explicit stance on the relationship between the concepts of non-discrimination and equality.

---

455 UN Doc. A/53/38/Rev.1 (part I), paras. 102 and 113 (Croatia).

456 UN Doc. A/54/38/Rev.1 (part II), para. 190 (Ireland); UN Doc. A/54/38/Rev.1 (part I), para. 165 (Liechtenstein); UN Doc. A/53/38/Rev.1 (part II), paras. 75-76 (Slovakia).

457 UN Doc. A/54/38/Rev.1 (part II), para. 50 (Belize).

458 UN Doc. A/57/38 (part I), para. 275 (Sri Lanka); UN Doc. A/57/38 (part I), para. 47 (Fiji); UN Doc. A/55/38 (part I), para. 316 (Germany); UN Doc. A/53/38/Rev.1 (part II), para. 229 (Tanzania); UN Doc. A/53/38/Rev.1 (part I), para. 416 (Mexico).

459 UN Doc. HRI/GEN/1/Rev.7, General Comment No. 19 (1992), *Violence Against Women*, para. 9. Compare with Communication No. 2/2003, *A.T. v. Hungary*, para. 9.2.

460 UN Doc. A/53/38/Rev.1 (part I), para. 404 (Mexico).

461 UN Doc. HRI/GEN/1/Rev.7, General Comment No. 25 (2004), *On Article 4, paragraph 1, of the Convention on the Elimination of All Forms of Discrimination against Women – Temporary special measures*, para. 31.

462 UN Doc. A/53/38/Rev.1 (part I), para. 156 (Zimbabwe).

463 UN Doc. CRC/C/15/Add.178, para. 6 (Belgium).

Being a general principle of the CRC, the principle of non-discrimination applies irrespective of budgetary resources.[464] The Committee has also stressed that the guarantee of non-discrimination applies to "each child within [the state party's] jurisdiction".[465]

b. *Qualifiers*

i. *De Jure* and *De Facto*

Apart from occasional *de jure* discrimination,[466] (the persistence of) *de facto* discrimination has been the CRC Committee's major concern.[467] It has expressed concern at *de facto* discrimination against certain groups of children,[468] in particular children belonging to ethnic and national groups or minorities,[469] especially Roma,[470] foreign children,[471] refugee and internally displaced children,[472] indigenous children,[473] *Dalit* children,[474] children and families living in poverty,[475] children in conflict with the law, street children, children living in rural areas and also children who have migrated from the rural areas and are living in the capital without official registration,[476] disabled

464 UN Doc. CRC/C/15/Add. 20, para. 19 (France); UN Doc. CRC/C/15/Add.1, para. 14 (Bolivia). Compare with the position taken by the HRC, the CESCR Committee and the CEDAW Committee, which have equally submitted that the realization of the principle of non-discrimination is not subject to progressive realization.

465 UN Doc. CRC/C/15/Add.178, para. 6 (Belgium).

466 UN Doc. CRC/C/15/Add.147, para. 39 (Lesotho); UN Doc. CRC/C/15/Add.44, para. 12 (Senegal).

467 UN Doc. CRC/C/15/Add.236, para. 23 (Liberia); UN Doc. CRC/C/15/Add.218, para. 25 (Madagascar); UN Doc. CRC/C/15/Add.202, para. 25 (Haiti); UN Doc. CRC/C/15/Add.193, para. 23 (Burkina Faso); UN Doc. CRC/C/15/Add.179, para. 27 (Niger); UN Doc. CRC/C/15/Add.171, para. 24 (Gabon).

468 UN Doc. CRC/C/15/Add.215, para. 21 (Canada); UN Doc. CRC/C/15/Add.213, para. 27 (Kazakhstan).

469 UN Doc. CRC/C/15/Add.260, para. 35 (Nepal); UN Doc. CRC/C/15/Add.226, para. 24 (Germany); UN Doc. CRC/C/15/Add.219, para. 26 (Brunei Darussalam); UN Doc. CRC/C/15/Add.182, para. 22 (Switzerland); UN Doc. CRC/C/15/Add.157, para. 30 (Bhutan).

470 UN Doc. CRC/C/15/Add.243, paras. 21 and 23 (Croatia); UN Doc. CRC/C/15/Add.240, para. 60 (France); UN Doc. CRC/C/15/Add.201, para. 28 (Czech Republic); UN Doc. CRC/C/15/Add.162, para. 19 (Portugal); UN Doc. CRC/C/15/Add.140, para. 19 (Slovakia).

471 UN Doc. CRC/C/15/Add.243, paras. 21 and 23 (Croatia); UN Doc. CRC/C/15/Add.226, paras. 23-24 (Germany); UN Doc. CRC/C/15/Add.182, paras. 21-22 (Switzerland).

472 UN Doc. CRC/C/15/Add.260, para. 35 (Nepal); UN Doc. CRC/C/15/Add.199, para. 54 (Romania).

473 UN Doc. CRC/C/15/Add.260, para. 35 (Nepal); UN Doc. CRC/C/15/Add.232, para. 26 (El Salvador).

474 UN Doc. CRC/C/15/Add.260, para. 36 (Nepal).

475 UN Doc. CRC/C/15/Add.263, para. 22 (Mongolia); UN Doc. CRC/C/15/Add.235, para. 21 (Sao Tome and Principe); UN Doc. CRC/C/15/Add.162, para. 19 (Portugal).

476 UN Doc. CRC/C/15/Add.263, para. 22 (Mongolia); UN Doc. CRC/C/15/Add.260, para. 35 (Nepal).

children,[477] children born out of wedlock,[478] and girls.[479] *De facto* gender discrimination was equally detected in the sharing of parental responsibilities and child custody.[480]

Only once, it linked *de facto* discrimination with xenophobia directed at certain minority groups of children, such as children belonging to ethnic minorities, refugee and asylum-seeking children, children belonging to migrant families, children with disabilities and those belonging to socially and economically disadvantaged families.[481]

Efforts are to be undertaken to prevent and eliminate all forms of *de facto* discrimination against children,[482] including through the adoption of a proactive and comprehensive strategy.[483]

ii. Intentional and Non-Intentional

The CRC Committee does not use the twin concept of intentional and unintentional discrimination.

iii. Direct and Indirect

The concept of indirect discrimination has been referred to, but rather occasionally. In its general comment on the aims of education, the Committee mentioned "overt or hidden" discrimination.[484] In its concluding observations however, it has consis-

---

477 UN Doc. CRC/C/15/Add.263, para. 22 (Mongolia); UN Doc. CRC/C/15/Add.260, para. 35 (Nepal); UN Doc. CRC/C/15/Add.258, para. 55 (Philippines); UN Doc. CRC/C/15/Add.252, para. 50 (Belize); UN Doc. CRC/C/15/Add.235, para. 21 (Sao Tome and Principe); UN Doc. CRC/C/15/Add.232, para. 26 (El Salvador); UN Doc. CRC/C/15/Add.184, para. 19 (St. Vincent and the Grenadines); UN Doc. CRC/C/15/Add.88, para. 16 (DPR Korea). It equally expressed concern about *de facto* discrimination between children born with disability and children who become disabled as a result of disease or an accident in the Swiss home care support system (UN Doc. CRC/C/15/Add.182, para. 43 (Switzerland)).

478 UN Doc. CRC/C/15/Add.44, para. 12 (Senegal).

479 UN Doc. CRC/C/15/Add.260, para. 35 (Nepal); UN Doc. CRC/C/15/Add.258, para. 20 (Philippines); UN Doc. CRC/C/15/Add.232, para. 26 (El Salvador); UN Doc. CRC/C/15/Add.167, para. 30 (Uzbekistan); UN Doc. CRC/C/15/Add.143, paras. 20-21 (Liechtenstein); UN Doc. CRC/C/15/Add.136, para. 22 (Tajikistan); UN Doc. CRC/C/15/Add.119, para. 24 (Armenia).

480 UN Doc. CRC/C/15/Add.236, paras. 36 and 37 (Liberia); UN Doc. CRC/C/15/Add.127, para. 25 (Kyrgyzstan).

481 UN Doc. CRC/C/15/Add.151, paras. 26-27 (Denmark).

482 UN Doc. CRC/C/15/Add.262, para. 19 (Norway); UN Doc. CRC/C/15/Add.259, para. 26 (Bosnia and Herzegovina).

483 UN Doc. CRC/C/15/Add.263, para. 23 (Mongolia).

484 UN Doc. HRI/GEN/1/Rev.7, General Comment No. 1 (2001), *The Aims of Education*, para. 10.

tently used the terms direct and indirect discrimination.[485] Indirect discrimination was mainly found to affect girls[486] and children born out of wedlock.[487]

iv. Multiple Discrimination

Multiple discrimination has been noted only rarely, *i.e.* with regard to girls in general,[488] and with regard to girls with disabilities in particular.[489]

v. Structural Discrimination

The CRC Committee seems to prefer the term social[490] or societal discrimination[491] to indicate long-standing and in-built discrimination. It has referred once to institutional discrimination.[492]

vi. Private Discrimination

The issue of private discrimination has mainly arisen in the context of discriminatory traditional customs and social attitudes.[493] The Committee has insisted on appropriate

---

485 UN Doc. CRC/C/15/Add.222, para. 70 (Georgia); UN Doc. CRC/C/15/Add.212, para. 25 (Syrian Arab Republic); UN Doc. CRC/C/15/Add.209, para. 23 (Libyan Arabic Jamahiriya); UN Doc. CRC/C/15/Add.145, para. 29 (Egypt); UN Doc. CRC/C/15/Add.125, para. 29 (Jordan); UN Doc. CRC/C/15/Add.123, para. 21 (Iran).

486 UN Doc. CRC/C/15/Add.211, para. 25 (Morocco); UN Doc. CRC/C/15/Add.148, para. 23 (Saudi Arabia); UN Doc. CRC/C/15/Add.116, paras. 32-33 (Sierra Leone).

487 UN Doc. CRC/C/15/Add.211, para. 25 (Morocco); UN Doc. CRC/C/15/Add.148, para. 23 (Saudi Arabia).

488 UN Doc. CRC/C/15/Add.258, para. 20 (Philippines).

489 UN Doc. CRC/C/15/Add.172, paras. 25 and 48 (Mozambique).

490 UN Doc. CRC/C/15/Add.266, para. 32 (Yemen); UN Doc. CRC/C/15/Add.246, para. 41 (Angola); UN Doc. CRC/C/15/Add.232, para. 46 (El Salvador); UN Doc. CRC/C/15/Add.228, para. 27 (India); UN Doc. CRC/C/15/Add.179, para. 27 (Niger); UN Doc. CRC/C/15/Add.98, para. 30 (Austria).

491 UN Doc. CRC/C/15/Add.261, para. 50 (Ecuador); UN Doc. CRC/C/15/Add.255, para. 25 (Togo); UN Doc. CRC/C/15/Add.253, paras. 28 and 45 (The Bahamas);UN Doc. CRC/C/15/Add.244, para. 26 (Kyrgyzstan); UN Doc. CRC/C/15/Add.242, para. 27 (Botswana); UN Doc. CRC/C/15/Add.238, paras. 21 and 36 (Dominica); UN Doc. CRC/C/15/Add.233, para. 24 (Panama); UN Doc. CRC/C/15/Add.231, para. 24 (Japan); UN Doc. CRC/C/15/Add.224, paras. 22 and 39 (Guyana); UN Doc. CRC/C/15/Add.223, para. 30 (Indonesia); UN Doc. CRC/C/15/Add.221, para. 40 (Bangladesh); UN Doc. CRC/C/15/Add.220, para. 23 (Singapore); UN Doc. CRC/C/15/Add.204, paras. 20 and 47 (Eritrea); UN Doc. CRC/C/15/Add.197, para. 50 (Korea); UN Doc. CRC/C/15/Add.191, para. 53 (Ukraine); UN Doc. CRC/C/15/Add.177, para. 36 (Guinea-Bissau); UN Doc. CRC/C/15/Add.172, para. 48 (Mozambique); UN Doc. CRC/C/15/Add.170, para. 33 (Greece); UN Doc. CRC/C/15/Add.144, para. 30 (Ethiopia); UN Doc. CRC/C/15/Add.110, para. 65 (Russian Federation).

492 UN Doc. CRC/C/15/Add.200, para. 22 (Viet Nam).

493 UN Doc. CRC/C/15/Add.115, para. 9 (India); UN Doc. CRC/C/15/Add.80, para. 7 (Uganda); UN Doc. CRC/C/15/Add.24, para. 11 (Honduras); UN Doc. CRC/C/15/Add.18, paras. 8 and 16 (Pakistan); UN Doc. CRC/C/15/Add.14, para. 15 (Namibia); UN Doc. CRC/C/15/Add.3, para. 6 (Viet Nam).

legislation that protects against and outlaws discrimination by private persons.[494] With regard to the practice of "untouchability", caste- and tribe-motivated abuse it has recommended to prosecute also private actors who are responsible for such practices or abuses.[495]

6. CONCLUSIONS

a. *Definition*

Broadly speaking, two definitions of discrimination are in use with the UN human rights treaty bodies. One definition can be found in both ICERD and CEDAW, and defines discrimination as any distinction, exclusion or preference on prohibited grounds, with the purpose or effect of impairing the equal enjoyment of rights. A second definition, which has been used by the European Court of Human Rights since its earliest case-law on equality and non-discrimination, defines discrimination as the differential treatment in comparable situations without an objective and reasonable justification.

Four Committees for which discrimination has been at the core of their work, *i.e.* the CERD, HRC, CESCR Committee and CEDAW Committee, have paid at least lip service to the definition found in ICERD and CEDAW. Only the CRC Committee does not seem to have embraced the above-mentioned definition. Most Committees have however also used the other definition. CERD has invoked since early 2005 the more commonly used definition of discrimination too. The HRC has done this very explicitly in its views on individual complaints. The CEDAW has not as yet used the more pragmatic definition. The CESCR Committee has never explicitly invoked the definition, but has come close to it in its 2005 general comment on gender equality.

To the extent that the Committees have paid attention to a possible difference in meaning between non-discrimination and equality, whereby equality would imply more positive obligations, they have not gone a long way in clarifying the differences. Regardless of the terminology, all have identified negative and positive obligations for the state (see further chapter IV on obligations). The HRC has recognized positive rights to equality, which comes as no surprise as articles 3 and 26 explicitly refer to equality. The CEDAW Committee has recognized that the elimination of discrimination and the promotion of equality are two different goals, but it has not further

494 UN Doc. CRC/C/15/Add.227, para. 31 (Netherlands and Aruba); UN Doc. CRC/C/15/Add.205, para. 27 (Cyprus).

495 UN Doc. CRC/C/15/Add.228, para. 28 (India).

clarified the differences. The CESCR and CRC Committee do not seem to have taken an explicit position on the issue.

All five Committees have submitted that the principle of non-discrimination is not subject to the availability of resources; it is of immediate application. The CESCR Committee may be willing to soften somewhat the positive obligation to realize *de facto* equality by making it subject to available resources and progressive realization.

b. Qualifiers

Qualifiers have been most in vogue with the CEDAW Committee, and least by the CESCR and CRC Committee. The added value of the use of different sets of qualifiers is not always clear, as the Committees tend to blur *e.g.* unintentional and indirect discrimination.

i. *De Jure* and *De Facto* Discrimination

De jure, legal or formal equality has been opposed to *de facto*, substantive equality or equality in practice. All Committees distinguish between *de jure* and *de facto* equality and discrimination, mainly to emphasise issues of *de facto* discrimination. CERD has expressed concern about *de facto* discrimination within its mandate of racial discrimination. The HRC has mainly done so with regard to women and minorities, and predominantly in its concluding observations. The CEDAW Committee has put a strong emphasis on *de facto* equality, whereas the CESCR and CRC Committee may have stressed instances of *de facto* discrimination.

ii. Intentional and Non-Intentional Discrimination

Discriminatory intent is not a necessary element of discrimination. Discrimination can occur on purpose, or differentiation can be discriminatory as an unintended outcome or effect. Both CERD and CEDAW include discrimination on purpose or in effect in their definition of discrimination. The CERD, HRC and CEDAW Committee have explicitly referred to intentional and unintentional discrimination. The CESCR and the CRC Committee have not as such, although the CESCR Committee recognizes both discrimination on purpose or in effect.

iii. Direct and Indirect Discrimination

As explained higher, direct discrimination occurs when differential treatment takes place that is directly connected with a person's association with one of the protected categories (race, sex, ...). Indirect discrimination occurs when a neutral measure is having a disparate and discriminatory effect on different *groups* of people, and cannot be justified by reasonable and objective criteria.

All Committees have invoked indirect discrimination to a larger or lesser extent, either in their jurisprudence, their general comments/recommendations, or their concluding comments/observations. All Committees have equated the concept of indirect discrimination with unintentional discrimination. The CEDAW Committee has further intertwined indirect or non-intentional discrimination with *de facto* equality and systemic inequality, without clear conceptual distinctions. One may therefore wonder how helpful these qualifiers have been for clarifying the different aspects under which discrimination may occur.

iv. Multiple Discrimination

The concept of double or multiple discrimination refers to discrimination based on more than one ground. The only Committee that has so far not used the concept is the HRC, although it has hinted at the phenomenon. All other Committees discussed here have referred to double or multiple discrimination. The common ground of discrimination invoked has been gender/sex, combined with a limited (CERD) or an extended list of other grounds (CESCR, CEDAW and CRC Committee). Double or multiple discrimination has thus always gender-based discrimination at its core, in combination with one of the other grounds.

v. Structural or Systemic Inequality

Most Committees, except for the HRC,[496] have to a certain extent integrated the notion of structural or systemic inequality in their analysis of inequality and discrimination. The CRC Committee tends to refer to social or societal discrimination. As was pointed out by some observers, "CEDAW has exhibited the greatest awareness of systemic inequality",[497] which may explain its outspoken position on the need for affirmative action in many fields (see further chapter IV under the obligation to fulfil-provide).

vi. Private Discrimination

Private discrimination has explicitly been taken into account by all Committees (see also further in chapter IV, where the obligation for states to protect against discrimination by third parties is discussed).

---

496 The HRC only recently invoked the concept in one set of concluding observations.
497 Joseph, Schultz and Castan, supra note 53, 736.

c. *Convergence or Divergence?*

Whereas some elements point to convergence and harmonisation, others illustrate divergence in the Committees' understanding of non-discrimination and equality. Without rejecting the definition of discrimination contained in ICERD and CEDAW, all Committees seem to turn to the more pragmatic definition of discrimination (*i.e.* no differential treatment of equal cases without an objective and reasonable justification) for application in concrete circumstances. The way this definition of discrimination is operationalised differs tremendously, however. While the HRC has developed a rich jurisprudence on each of the criteria or tests, the other Committees have only started to explore this pragmatic definition of non-discrimination. None of the Committees has paid much attention to a conceptual distinction between the principles of equality and non-discrimination. All have emphasized that the principles of equality and non-discrimination are to be realized immediately, independently of available resources.

As to the use of qualifiers in order to analyse discrimination, the CESCR and CRC Committee have generally been most restrictive in using them, while the CEDAW Committee has invoked most frequently a number of qualifiers. All Committees clearly distinguish between *de jure* and *de facto* discrimination and equality. They all pay attention to private discrimination. All Committees seem also to acknowledge that no discriminatory intent is required in order to qualify differential treatment as discriminatory. The HRC has refrained from referring to double or multiple discrimination. Major differences exist as to the degree which systemic inequality has been invoked in. Terminology has not been identical either, with some Committees referring to systemic inequality and others to social, societal or structural discrimination.

The twin concepts of unintentional and non-intentional discrimination have only been used by the CERD, HRC and CEDAW Committee. All Committees have mentioned indirect discrimination. The analytical clarification to be derived from the use of the twin concepts of intentional and non-intentional discrimination on the one hand, and of direct and indirect discrimination on the other hand, by these Committees may be extremely limited however, as no sharp conceptual lines have been drawn between the concepts. Moreover, the CESCR Committee and CRC Committee seem to use indirect discrimination to denote unintentional discrimination.

In sum, as in chapter I, no unequivocal conclusions can be drawn on convergence and harmonisation in the Committees' use of definitions and qualifiers for non-discrimination and equality.

CHAPTER III. PROHIBITED GROUNDS OF DISCRIMINATION

A. GROUNDS

Two of the UN core human rights treaties, ICERD and CEDAW, prohibit discrimination on a specific ground. ICERD is concerned with racial discrimination, *i.e.* discrimination on grounds of race, colour, descent, and national or ethnic origin. CEDAW focuses on sex/gender discrimination.

Four other and more general UN core human rights treaties share a large common core of prohibited grounds of discrimination.[498] Grounds of discrimination in common to the two 1966 Covenants – the CCPR and CESCR – are race, colour, sex, language, religion, political or other opinion, national or social origin, property, birth or other status. The reason for selection of these criteria as prohibited grounds of differentiation is to be sought in the fact that these grounds have no relevance to merit or social value. Some are innate (colour, race, sex) while the others are social generic categories.[499] In addition to the list of the CCPR and the CESCR, the CRC and even more so the CMW contain a number of additional grounds, such as ethnic origin (CRC and CMW),[500] disability (CRC) and conviction, nationality, age, economic position and marital status (CMW). These two most recent core human rights treaties codify to a certain degree additional grounds of discrimination that had been identified by some of the UN Committees over the years.

As to the importance of the enumerated prohibited grounds of discrimination, it has been pointed out that the enumeration is open-ended and not exhaustive, in particular through the phrase "or other status".[501] This has been confirmed in practice, for the

---

498 CAT does not contain any explicit provision on discrimination.

499 Ramcharan, supra note 5, 253.

500 Compare with ICERD.

501 Sepúlveda, supra note 108, 391. Bayefsky on the contrary submits that the core human rights treaties operate under a list of fixed grounds, in *contradistinction* to the Universal Declaration of Human Rights and the European Convention on Human Rights. The latter are said to prohibit discrimination on the basis of an indeterminate number of grounds, as they clearly refer to the prohibition of discrimination of any kind or of any ground (see Bayefski, supra note 3, 5).

Committees have accepted additional grounds indeed. Differential treatment based on one of the enumerated grounds may create a higher justificatory threshold though (see above, chapter I).

A consequence of the open-ended number of grounds is that "[d]etermining whether a given distinction violates the non-discrimination provision will *never* concern whether the given distinction is covered by the non-discrimination provision or not."[502] On the one hand, the fact that differential treatment is based on one of the prohibited grounds will not be sufficient to qualify it as discrimination. On the other hand, if differential treatment is not covered by one of the explicitly-listed prohibited grounds, it may still be discriminatory treatment. In other words, the ground of discrimination will never be decisive in itself to establish whether a distinction or differentiation is of a discriminatory character.[503]

B. THE COMMITTEES

1. CERD

The focus of ICERD is on racial discrimination, *i.e.* discrimination based on race, colour, descent, or national or ethnic origin (article 1, para. 1 ICERD). CERD does not accept any hierarchy among the categories mentioned, they are all on an equal footing:

> The Committee is therefore concerned that the emerging situation may lead to inconsistencies in discrimination laws and differential levels of protection according to the categorization of discrimination (i.e. race, ethnic origin, colour, nationality, etc.), and create difficulties for the general public as well as law enforcement agencies.
>
> The Committee recommends that the State party extend the amending regulations to cover discrimination on the grounds of colour and nationality. In this context, the Committee also recommends that the State party consider introducing a single comprehensive law, consolidating primary and secondary legislations, to provide for the same protection from all forms of racial discrimination, enshrined in article 1 of the Convention.[504]

CERD has pointed out that references to "visible minorities" in Canadian anti-discrimination policy, *i.e.* basically to non-white persons, did not appear to cover fully

---

502 Bayefski, supra note 3, 5.
503 Bossuyt, supra note 83, 35.
504 UN Doc. CERD/C/63/CO/11, para. 15 (United Kingdom).

the scope of article 1 of the Convention.[505] The scope of article 1 ICERD is broader than "visible minorities", which notion could be argued to relate primarily to the ground of colour. As to the term "descent", the Committee has repeatedly stated "that the term 'descent' in article 1, paragraph 1, of the Convention does not solely refer to 'race' and has a meaning and application which complement the other prohibited grounds of discrimination."[506] Indigenous peoples have been explicitly mentioned as being covered by article 1, para. 1 ICERD.[507]

The other prohibited grounds of discrimination that are common to the core human rights treaties, but which do not feature in the ICERD, are quite logically not referred to.[508] The only exception is sex/gender. For the Committee, the reason is obvious:

> Racial discrimination does not always affect women and men equally or in the same way. There are circumstances in which racial discrimination only or primarily affects women, or affects women in a different way, or to a different degree than men. Such racial discrimination will often escape detection if there is no explicit recognition or acknowledgement of the different life experiences of women and men, in areas of both public and private life.[509]

Women can be affected particularly by racial discrimination on purpose or in effect:

> Certain forms of racial discrimination may be directed towards women specifically because of their gender, such as sexual violence committed against women members of particular racial or ethnic groups in detention or during armed conflict; the coerced sterilization of indigenous women; abuse of women workers in the informal sector or domestic workers employed abroad by their employers. Racial discrimination may have consequences that affect primarily or only women, such as pregnancy resulting from racial bias-motivated rape; in some societies women victims of such rape may also be ostracized. Women may also be further hindered by a lack of access to remedies and complaint mechanisms for racial discrimination because of gender-related impediments, such as gender bias in the legal system and discrimination against women in private spheres of life.[510]

In recognizing the particular gender dimension in the context of racial discrimination, the Committee has integrated – initially implicitly, but by now also explicitly – the

---

505 UN Doc. A/57/18, para. 328 (Canada).

506 UN Doc. HRI/GEN/1/Rev.7, General Recommendation XXIX (2002), *Article 1, paragraph 1, (Descent)*, preamble.

507 UN Doc. HRI/GEN/1/Rev.7, General Recommendation XXIV (1999), *Reporting of Persons Belonging to Different Races, National/Ethnic Groups, or Indigenous Peoples (Art. 1)*, para. 1.

508 On one occasion, the Committee seems to have expressed concern about the rural-urban divide, when referring to "the social and cultural inequalities that continue to affect rural populations" (UN Doc. A/57/18, para. 398 (Mali)).

509 UN Doc. HRI/GEN/1/Rev.7, General Recommendation XXV (2000), *Gender Related Dimensions of Racial Discrimination*, para. 1.

510 *Ibid.*, para. 2.

concept of double or multiple discrimination in its analysis of discrimination (see also higher, chapter II).

a. Race

Racial discrimination is used as a generic term. The Committee thus expressed the opinion that a solution for Kosovo was to include a high degree of autonomy as a means to eliminate all forms of racial discrimination.[511] Similarly, it expressed concern about racial discrimination against inhabitants who were not ethnic Kyrgyz – in particular against the Russian-speaking minority – in the fields of employment and housing.[512] Issues of racial discrimination that related more strongly to the ground of race included the granting of some form of British nationality only to Asian residents of Hong Kong whereas full citizenship status was usually conferred upon a predominantly white population living in another dependent territory,[513] and the operation of parallel systems of private schools for pupils whose parents who could afford them and public schools for others resulting in a racially segregated school system.[514]

In the Committee's concluding observations on state reports, race as such has extremely seldom been explicitly mentioned as a prohibited ground of discrimination. Attention has nevertheless been paid to the fact that race is to be included as a ground for discrimination in domestic law.[515]

b. Nationality

Nationality or citizenship is not mentioned as such as a prohibited ground of discrimination under ICERD. Article 1, para. 2, explicitly excepts from the definition of racial discrimination differentiation between citizens and non citizens. Article 1, para. 3 qualifies article 1, para. 2 however in that, among non citizens, states are not to discriminate against any particular nationality.[516]

In its recent 2004 general recommendation on discrimination against non citizens, CERD has rather drastically reduced the permissibility of differential treatment of non

---

511 UN Doc. CERD/C/304/Add.50, para. 20 (Yugoslavia).
512 UN Doc. CERD/C/304/Add.77, para. 7 (Kyrgyzstan).
513 UN Doc. CERD/C/304/Add.9 (United Kingdom).
514 UN Doc. CERD/C/304/Add.4, paras. 11 and 17 (Zimbabwe).
515 UN Doc. CERD/C/304/Add.12, para. 18 (Korea).
516 See UN Doc. HRI/GEN/1/Rev.7, General Recommendation XI (1993), *Non-Citizens (Art. 1)*, para. 1, now replaced by UN Doc. HRI/GEN/1/Rev.7/Add.1, General Recommendation XXX (2004), *Discrimination Against Non Citizens* (see para. 39).

citizens. Article 1, para. 2 is to be construed so as to avoid undermining the basic prohibition of discrimination:

> hence, it should not be interpreted to detract in any way from the rights and freedoms recognized and enunciated in particular in the Universal Declaration of Human Rights, the International Covenant on Economic, Social and Cultural Rights and the International Covenant on Civil and Political Rights.[517]

In 1996, CERD had held already that the exception allowing for differential treatment between citizens and non citizens did not extend to all human rights mentioned in article 5 ICERD. The right to equal treatment before tribunals had been mentioned by way of illustration:

> Many of the rights and freedoms mentioned in article 5, such as the right to equal treatment before tribunals, are to be enjoyed by all persons living in a given State; others such as the right to participate in elections, to vote and to stand for election are the rights of citizens.[518]

In its 2004 general recommendation, CERD has seriously limited the scope of the exception contained in article 1, para. 2 ICERD by submitting in a much more general way that human rights are, in principle, to be enjoyed by all persons, and that equality between citizens and non citizens in the enjoyment of human rights is to be guaranteed to the extent recognized under international law.[519] This position seems to imply that apart from the right to participate in elections, to vote and to stand for elections – rights which are mentioned as such by the Committee as allowing for confinement to citizens – differentiation between citizens and non citizens with regard to human rights is no longer permissible. However, "a general reference to foreigners does not [...] single out a group of persons, contrary to article 1 of the Convention, on the basis of a specific race, ethnicity, colour, descent or national or ethnic origin", and does therefore not amount to an act of racial discrimination.[520]

Elements of this restrictive approach were already foreshadowed in the Committee's concluding observations. It thus asked Latvia to review the differential treatment of citizens and non citizens, mostly persons belonging to ethnic groups, in the field of economic, social and cultural rights, so as to eliminate any unjustifiable differences.[521]

---

517 UN Doc. HRI/GEN/1/Rev.7/Add.1, General Recommendation XXX (2004), *Discrimination Against Non Citizens*, para. 2.

518 UN Doc. HRI/GEN/1/Rev.7, General Recommendation XX (1996), *Non-Discriminatory Implementation of Rights and Freedoms (Art. 5)*, para. 3.

519 UN Doc. HRI/GEN/1/Rev.7/Add.1, General Recommendation XXX (2004), *Discrimination Against Non Citizens*, para. 3. Compare with UN Doc. CERD/C/63/CO/11, para. 15 (United Kingdom), where the United Kingdom was asked to include nationality as a prohibited ground of discrimination.

520 UN Doc. CERD/C/66/D/33/2003, Communication No. 33/2003, *Quereshi v. Denmark*, para. 7.3.

521 UN Doc. CERD/C/304/Add.79, para. 23 (Latvia).

It similarly expressed concern about a significant number of persons who had been living in Slovenia since independence without Slovenian citizenship, that might have been deprived under certain circumstances of their pensions, of apartments they were occupying, and of health care and other rights.[522] Even with regard to political rights, CERD had raised critical questions:

> The Committee recognizes that political rights can be legitimately limited to citizens. Nevertheless, noting that most non-citizens have been residing in Latvia for many years, if not for their whole lives, the Committee strongly recommends that the State party consider facilitating the integration process by making it possible for all non-citizens who are long-time permanent residents to participate in local elections.[523]

The question arises on the basis of which specific ground discrimination against non citizens might be prohibited. Nationality or citizenship is not explicitly mentioned as a prohibited ground in ICERD. Given the exception of article 1, para. 2 ICERD, the ground of "national origin" does not seem to be applicable either. Nor is it possible to refer to an open-ended ground of "other status" for lack of any such clause in ICERD.[524] In its concluding observations, CERD tends to refer to the whole set of prohibited grounds under ICERD, *i.e.* race, colour, descent, national or ethnic origin,[525] or simply raises the issue of discriminatory treatment of non nationals without invoking any ground.[526]

Even in the – meanwhile severely restricted – cases in which differential treatment between citizens and non citizens is allowed, states are not to discriminate against any particular nationality (article 1, para. 3 ICERD). As to the ground that can be invoked for prohibiting discrimination on the basis of nationality *among* non citizens, the Committee itself seems to refer to national origin:

> notes with concern that the State party does not appear to guarantee freedom of marriage between nationals and non nationals unless the latter are nationals of States members of the Gulf Cooperation Council. Such a distinction, based upon national origin, does not, in the Committee's view, appear to be consistent with article 5 (d) (iv) of the Convention.[527]

---

522 UN Doc. CERD/C/62/CO/9, para. 14 (Slovenia).

523 UN Doc. CERD/C/63/CO/7, para. 12 (Latvia).

524 In a partly dissenting opinion, HRC members Rodley and Scheinin have argued that distinctions based on citizenship are to be addressed under the notion of "other status", and not under "any of the grounds of discrimination covered by article 1, paragraph 1, of the CERD" while referring to article 1, para. 2 ICERD (UN Doc. CCPR/C/74/D/965/2000, Communication No. 965/2000, *Karakurt v. Austria*).

525 UN Doc. CERD/C/AUS/CO/14, para. 14 (Australia); UN Doc. CERD/C/AZE/CO/4, para. 13 (Azerbaijan).

526 See *e.g.* UN Doc. CERD/C/BHR/CO/7, para. 14 (Bahrain).

527 UN Doc. CERD/C/60/CO/11, para. 14 (Qatar).

Differentiation among non citizens on the basis of their nationality is here deemed to be unacceptable differential treatment on the ground of national origin. Citizenship or nationality therefore seems to be covered by the term "national origin" in these circumstances. This leads to the rather ambiguous result that differentiation between citizens and non citizens is not covered by the notion of "national origin" (see article 1, para. 2 ICERD), whereas differentiation among non citizens on the basis of their nationality may well be.[528]

The Committee has rejected differential treatment *among* non citizens with regard to *inter alia* access to citizenship, visa, asylum procedures and removal, marriage, employment and education.

With regard to access to citizenship and naturalization, the Committee has established some principles. First, states are to ensure that particular groups of non citizens are not discriminated against.[529] Members of Roma communities have been mentioned explicitly.[530] States are to pay due attention to possible barriers that may exist for long-term or permanent residents.[531] The Committee recommended *e.g.* to Croatia that measures be taken to ensure that former long-term residents of Croatia, particularly persons of Serb origin and other minorities, were able to reclaim their status as citizens and/or residents on a non-discriminatory basis.[532] Also, denial of citizenship for long-term or permanent residents, resulting in creating disadvantage in access to employment and social benefits was considered to be discrimination. With regard to the excessive delays in the processing of applications for citizenship, in particular those of ethnic Serbs, the Committee pointed to the loss of social and educational benefits for the applicants.[533]

---

528 This situation is to be distinguished from the one in which differentiation among non citizens is made on other grounds than citizenship. The United Kingdom *e.g.* usually conferred full citizenship status upon a predominantly white population living in a dependent territory. To the Asian residents of Hong Kong it granted however only some form of British nationality. The Committee noted that full citizenship status was not granted to Asians and that judgements on applications for citizenship appeared to vary according to the country of origin. For CERD, this led to the assumption that elements of racial discrimination were revealed (see UN Doc. CERD/C/304/Add.9 (United Kingdom)).

529 UN Doc. HRI/GEN/1/Rev.7/Add.1, General Recommendation XXX (2004), *Discrimination Against Non Citizens*, para. 13. Compare with UN Doc. CERD/C/65/CO/8, para. 14 (Tajikistan); UN Doc. CERD/C/62/CO/7, para. 15 (Russian Federation); UN Doc. CERD/C/60/CO/4, para. 14 (Croatia); UN Doc. A/56/18, para. 334 (Sri Lanka); UN Doc. CERD/C/304/Add.70, para. 14 (Syrian Arab Republic).

530 UN Doc. HRI/GEN/1/Rev.7, General Recommendation XXVII (2000), *Discrimination against Roma*, para. 4.

531 UN Doc. HRI/GEN/1/Rev.7/Add.1, General Recommendation XXX (2004), *Discrimination Against Non Citizens*, para. 13.

532 UN Doc. CERD/C/60/CO/4, para. 14 (Croatia).

533 UN Doc. CERD/C/304/Add.55, para. 11 (Croatia).

Secondly, deprivation of citizenship on the basis of any of the enumerated grounds in ICERD is a violation of the right to non-discriminatory enjoyment of the right to nationality.[534] In a number of cases, the Committee has requested states to ensure the right to acquire a nationality for children of mixed couples without any discrimination.[535] Quite often, children with a father of foreign nationality are denied citizenship.[536] Also, in case immigration quotas are used, the quota system is to be applied without discrimination based on race or ethnic or national origin.[537] No differential treatment based on citizenship or immigration status is permissible in the granting of visas.[538] Asylum procedures are not to discriminate between asylum seekers.[539]

Thirdly, statelessness is to be reduced, in particular among children.[540]

Fourthly, the status of former citizens of predecessor states who reside within the jurisdiction of a state party is to be regularized.[541] The Committee recommended for instance, that Estonia conduct a thorough investigation into possible barriers which existed, both in terms of the naturalization procedure and in relation to lack of motivation to apply for citizenship. They also called for a speedy resolution of the issue concerning the difficulties in obtaining citizenship for children born in Estonia of long-term residents whose legal status had not yet been determined,[542] and recommended that applications for citizenship by former Soviet Union military personnel residing in Estonia be considered on a case-by-case basis.[543] It recommended that Latvia streamline the process of naturalization for all those who applied for citizenship, encouraged it to keep the criteria for eligibility under review,[544] and recommended to regularize as soon as possible the status of persons who did not qualify for citizenship and were not registered as residents, in order to avoid discrimination against them.[545]

---

534 UN Doc. HRI/GEN/1/Rev.7/Add.1, General Recommendation XXX (2004), *Discrimination Against Non Citizens*, para. 14.

535 UN Doc. A/57/18, para. 464 (Yemen).

536 UN Doc. CERD/C/BHR/CO/7, para. 17 (Bahrain); UN Doc. CERD/C/65/CO/5, para. 18 (Mauritania); UN Doc. CERD/C/65/CO/4, para. 15 (Madagascar); UN Doc. CERD/C/64/CO/1, para. 16 (Bahamas); UN Doc. CERD/C/62/CO/8, para. 14 (Saudi Arabia); UN Doc. A/56/18, para. 288 (Egypt); UN Doc. CERD/C/304/Add.92, para. 12 (Zimbabwe).

537 UN Doc. CERD/C/304/Add.98, para. 11 (Estonia).

538 UN Doc. CERD/C/AUS/CO/14, paras. 22 and 24 (Australia).

539 UN Doc. CERD/C/AZE/CO/4, para. 13 (Azerbaijan): priority concern.

540 UN Doc. HRI/GEN/1/Rev.7/Add.1, General Recommendation XXX (2004), *Discrimination Against Non Citizens*, para. 16. Compare with UN Doc. CERD/C/64/CO/3, para. 13 (Lebanon).

541 UN Doc. HRI/GEN/1/Rev.7/Add.1, General Recommendation XXX (2004), *Discrimination Against Non Citizens*, para. 17.

542 UN Doc. A/57/18, para. 353 (Estonia).

543 *Ibid.*, para. 354 (Estonia).

544 UN Doc. CERD/C/304/Add.79, para. 21 (Latvia).

545 *Ibid.*, para. 22 (Latvia).

The removal of *non citizens* should not discriminate amongst them on the basis of ethnic or national origin.[546] With regard to the right to marriage,[547] and in the fields of employment[548] and education,[549] the Committee has pointed out instances of differential treatment based on citizenship which were considered to be contrary to the Convention. Sometimes, CERD has identified particular groups of non citizens, such as Palestinian refugees, as being treated discriminatorily in comparison with other non citizens.[550]

Finally, supplementary conditions attached to the exercise of rights by naturalized citizens as compared to citizens by birth have been judged inconsistent with the Convention.[551]

c. *Ethnic Origin*

In its general recommendation on the right to self-determination, CERD has emphasized that "[g]overnments are to represent the whole population without distinction as to race, colour, descent or national or ethnic origin."[552] It added:

> Governments should be sensitive towards the rights of persons belonging to ethnic groups, particularly their right to lead lives of dignity, to preserve their culture, to share equitably in the fruits of national growth and to play their part in the Government of the country of which they are citizens. Also, Governments should consider, within their respective constitutional frameworks, vesting persons belonging to ethnic or linguistic groups comprised of their citizens, where appropriate, with the right to engage in activities which are particularly relevant to the preservation of the identity of such persons or groups.[553]

For analytical purposes, discrimination on the basis of ethnic origin against *minorities* is here dealt with under a separate heading. Discrimination against people on the basis of their belonging to a minority is not mentioned as such in ICERD. CERD tends to treat discrimination against minorities as a distinct theme, regardless of which prohibited grounds are involved.

---

546 UN Doc. CERD/C/64/CO/4, para. 11 (Libya).
547 UN Doc. CERD/C/60/CO/11, para. 14 (Qatar); UN Doc. CERD/C/304/Add.96, para. 8 (Tonga).
548 UN Doc. CERD/C/64/CO/4, para. 14 (Libya); UN Doc. CERD/C/63/CO/7, para. 14 (Latvia).
549 UN Doc. CERD/C/304/Add.114, para. 15 (Japan).
550 UN Doc. CERD/C/64/CO/3, para. 12 (Lebanon).
551 UN Doc. CERD/C/60/CO/11, para. 12 (Qatar).
552 UN Doc. HRI/GEN/1, Rev.7, General Recommendation XXI (1996), *Right to Self-Determination*, para. 4.
553 *Ibid.*, para. 5.

i. Minorities

CERD has pronounced itself on a number of issues, such as the recognition and definition of minorities, discrimination among minorities, discrimination against members of minorities in particular fields, and discrimination against Roma as a minority that requires particular attention.

States are encouraged to adopt legislation on minorities.[554] The definition of national minorities should not be too restrictive, for a narrow definition may limit the scope of an integration programme and have the effect of transforming a policy of integration into a policy of assimilation.[555] For example, to require an ethnic group to have lived on the state's soil for at least a century, in order to be recognized as a minority was thought to be very restrictive.[556] Likewise, concern was expressed about references to "visible minorities" in regard to Canadian anti-discrimination policy, since this term was considered not to cover fully the scope of article 1 of the Convention.[557]

An issue of particular concern is discrimination *among* minorities. With regard to political representation, all minority groups are to be included, and fair and adequate representation of all groups of minorities is to be ensured.[558] Consideration might be given to the inclusion of more members of minority nationalities in positions of leadership at all levels.[559] Also, no discrimination should take place against persons or groups of persons belonging to minority groups that enjoy a lower level of protection from a state party.[560] The criteria on the basis of which the distinction between minorities (national minorities, linguistic minorities, ethnic minorities, tribal minorities) is based, may be in need of reconsideration, and the state is to ensure that members of the different minority communities enjoy the same rights, especially in the cultural field.[561]

CERD has expressed concern about the treatment of members of minorities in different domains. Attitudes and acts of racial violence against persons belonging to minority groups are to be prevented and countered effectively,[562] as well as any *de facto*

554 UN Doc. CERD/C/304/Add.120, para. 9 (Georgia).
555 UN Doc. A/57/18, para. 355 (Estonia).
556 UN Doc. CERD/C/304/Add.4, para. 13 (Hungary).
557 UN Doc. A/49/18, para. 324 (Canada).
558 UN Doc. CERD/C/60/CO/4, para. 10 (Croatia).
559 UN Doc. CERD/C/304/Add.15, para. 24 (China).
560 UN Doc. CERD/C/304/Add.105, para. 8 (Slovenia).
561 UN Doc. CERD/C/63/CO/1, para. 14 (Albania).
562 UN Doc. CERD/C/AZE/CO/4, para. 10 (Azerbaijan): priority concern; UN Doc. CERD/C/IRL/CO/2, para. 11 (Ireland); UN Doc. CERD/C/LUX/CO/13, para. 14 (Luxemburg); UN Doc. CERD/C/304/Add.47, paras. 8 and 16 (Czech Republic).

segregation of minorities.[563] In the area of the administration of justice, a particularly high incarceration rate of members of ethnic or national minorities might be a reflection of their unequal treatment before the courts and all other organs administering justice.[564] The Committee has recalled that a distinctive religion is integral to the identity of several minorities.[565]

CERD also pays particular attention to the economically, socially and educationally disadvantaged position many members of minorities find themselves in,[566] and the unequal enjoyment of economic, social and cultural rights they benefit from.[567] The economic, social and cultural development of disadvantaged ethnic and tribal minorities and groups is to be pursued, and the participation of these minorities in such development is to be encouraged.[568] In addition to health care[569] and housing,[570] equal opportunity in public service and private employment is a central preoccupation of the Committee.[571] Concern has been expressed about equal working conditions[572] and equal remuneration[573] of members of minorities, the scope of language requirements in relation to employment, particularly in the private sector,[574] the rate of participation of minorities in the labour market[575] and in business,[576] the unemployment rates for members of minorities, and direct and indirect forms of discrimination in recruitment procedures.[577] Participation of ethnic minorities in the elaboration of cultural and educational policies is to be facilitated.[578] With regard to education,[579] states are encouraged to ensure education and teaching in the mother tongue of minorities, wherever possible,[580] and in any case elementary education in their own languages,[581] and to include the history and culture of the relevant minority nationalities

563 UN Doc. CERD/C/304/Add.29, para. 17 (Bulgaria).
564 UN Doc. A/56/18, para. 395 (United States).
565 UN Doc. A/56/18, para. 244 (China).
566 UN Doc. A/56/18, para. 395 (United States).
567 UN Doc. A/57/18, para. 357 (Estonia).
568 UN Doc. CERD/C/304/Add.83, para. 14 (Iran).
569 UN Doc. A/57/18, para. 357 (Estonia).
570 UN Doc. CERD/C/304/Add.36, para. 17 (Poland).
571 UN Doc. A/57/18, para. 357 (Estonia); UN Doc. CERD/C/304/Add.36, para. 17 (Poland).
572 UN Doc. CERD/C/304/Add.15, paras. 16 and 29 (China).
573 UN Doc. A/57/18, para. 356 (Estonia); UN Doc. CERD/C/304/Add.15, para. 29 (China).
574 UN Doc. A/57/18, para. 356 (Estonia).
575 UN Doc. CERD/C/304/Add.46, para. 12 (Netherlands).
576 UN Doc. CERD/C/304/Add.15, para. 16 (China).
577 UN Doc. CERD/C/304/Add.46, para. 12 (Netherlands).
578 UN Doc. CERD/C/AZE/CO/4, para. 14 (Azerbaijan).
579 UN Doc. A/57/18, para. 357 (Estonia); UN Doc. CERD/C/304/Add.46, para. 12 (The Netherlands).
580 UN Doc. A/56/18, para. 376 (Ukraine); UN Doc. CERD/C/304/Add.48, para. 18 (Ukraine).
581 UN Doc. CERD/C/AZE/CO/4, para. 14 (Azerbaijan); UN Doc. CERD/C/304/Add.43, para. 24 (Russian Federation).

in the school curricula.[582] Equal opportunities for access to education at all levels are to be guaranteed.[583] Special attention is to be paid to any adverse effect that economic development and national modernization may have on the enjoyment of the right to culture, particularly of minority nationalities.[584]

Roma have received particular attention from CERD, predominantly as a minority, but also as an ethnic group (see further). States are to pay particular attention to the situation of Roma women and children.[585]

Recommendations have ranged from adopting a comprehensive programme of action to promote and protect the rights of the Roma population,[586] to granting citizenship[587] or the status of minority. The latter recommendation concerned Roma populations who had resided on the territory for an extended period of time and who had become sedentary. Effective consultation on this issue with representatives of the Roma population was deemed necessary. At the same time, concern was expressed with regard to the possible inappropriate consequences of a policy of encouraging Roma to apply for stateless status.[588]

Discrimination against Roma has been highlighted in the fields of housing, education, transport and employment.[589] Concern was expressed that the Roma suffered from persistent marginalization and that an economic crisis affected them disproportionately, due to *de facto* discrimination in the enjoyment of their economic, social and cultural rights.[590] In addition to expressly outlawing discrimination,[591] states are to take additional measures at the national and municipal levels to improve the situation of the Roma minority, with a view to preventing social exclusion and discrimination against them.[592] Efforts should be made to strengthen the implementation of measures of affirmative action.[593]

---

582 UN Doc. A/56/18, para. 245 (China); UN Doc. CERD/C/304/Add.15, paras. 17 and 30 (China).

583 UN Doc. A/56/18, para. 245 (China); UN Doc. CERD/C/304/Add.43, para. 24 (Russian Federation); UN Doc. CERD/C/304/Add.15, paras. 17 and 30 (China).

584 UN Doc. CERD/C/304/Add.15, para. 31 (China).

585 UN Doc. CERD/C/304/Add.103, para. 11 (Sweden).

586 UN Doc. CERD/C/304/Add.36, para. 17 (Poland).

587 UN Doc. CERD/C/304/Add.47, paras. 14 and 20 (Czech Republic).

588 UN Doc. A/56/18, para. 309 (Italy). In its earlier recommendations, the Committee had asked that more attention to the situation of Roma in Italy be given, with a view to averting discrimination against them (UN Doc. CERD/C/304/Add.68, para. 15 (Italy)).

589 UN Doc. CERD/C/304/Add.109, para. 9 (Czech Republic); UN Doc. CERD/C/304/Add.107, para. 10 (Finland); UN Doc. CERD/C/304/Add.47, para. 12 (Czech Republic).

590 UN Doc. CERD/C/304/Add.29, para. 8 (Bulgaria).

591 UN Doc. CERD/C/304/Add.47, para. 12 (Czech Republic).

592 UN Doc. CERD/C/304/Add.107, para. 10 (Finland).

593 UN Doc. CERD/C/304/Add.29, para. 14 (Bulgaria).

As to discrimination against Roma in the workplace, most of whom have relatively little training and education, states are encouraged to adopt or make more effective legislation prohibiting discrimination in employment and all discriminatory practices in the labour market.[594] Adequate job-training initiatives and the implementation of affirmative action programmes is deemed necessary.[595] Concerns have also been expressed that Roma encounter difficulties in applying for social benefits.[596]

A major problem within the educational system is the practice of segregation of Roma children, through their placement in special schools (*e.g.* for mentally disabled children).[597] States are called upon to facilitate the integration of pupils into mainstream education.[598] On the other hand, to states choosing to integrate Roma children into the regular schooling system, recommendations have been made to take appropriate measures to meet the specific educational needs of Roma children,[599] and to respect and accommodate the specific cultural background of these children.[600] Other problems relate to low enrolment rates, high drop-out rates, poor performance rates[601] and a considerably lower level of participation in secondary and higher education.[602] The recruitment and training of Roma teachers has been encouraged.[603]

In light of the fact that a disproportionately large number of Roma suffered higher mortality rates, had poorer nutrition levels, and low levels of awareness of maternal and child health, as well as poor access to clean drinking water and adequate sanitation, and high exposure to environmental pollution, the Committee recommended Slovakia to ensure that the Roma enjoyed the full right to health and health care and to prioritize and target social services for them.[604] The same state was also asked to review legislation regulating local residence permits and investigate promptly and thoroughly incidents of discrimination in access to housing after two municipalities had issued decrees banning Roma from their territory.[605]

---

594 UN Doc. CERD/C/65/CO/2, para. 10 (Belarus).
595 UN Doc. CERD/C/304/Add.110, para. 13 (Slovakia).
596 UN Doc. CERD/C/304/Add.29, para. 8 (Bulgaria).
597 UN Doc. CERD/C/60/CO/4, para. 11 (Croatia); UN Doc. CERD/C/304/Add.110, para. 11 (Slovakia); UN Doc. CERD/C/304/Add.109, para. 10 (Czech Republic); UN Doc. CERD/C/304/Add.47, para. 13 (Czech Republic).
598 UN Doc. CERD/C/304/Add.110, para. 11 (Slovakia).
599 UN Doc. CERD/C/304/Add.36, para. 18 (Poland).
600 UN Doc. A/56/18, para. 311 (Italy).
601 UN Doc. CERD/C/60/CO/4, para. 11 (Croatia); UN Doc. CERD/C/304/Add.110, para. 11 (Slovakia).
602 UN Doc. CERD/C/304/Add.47, para. 13 (Czech Republic); UN Doc. CERD/C/304/Add.38, para. 10 (Former Yugoslav Republic of Macedonia).
603 UN Doc. CERD/C/60/CO/4, para. 11 (Croatia).
604 UN Doc. CERD/C/304/Add.110, para. 14 (Slovakia).
605 *Ibid.*, para. 9 (Slovakia).

Other common problems are the denial of access to and service in public places such as restaurants, pubs, discotheques and similar establishments,[606] ill-treatment by the police and racially motivated violence. In response to the former problem, CERD has recommended states to strictly apply relevant legislation and regulations providing for sanctions, to adequately train law enforcement bodies (also regarding the provisions of ICERD)[607] and to sensitivize the judiciary.[608] Recruitment of members of minority groups into the police has equally been suggested.[609] In response to racially motivated violence against members of the Roma community,[610] the Committee has insisted on prevention and prosecution.[611]

Other minority groups that have enjoyed the Committee's particular attention are *inter alia* the Korean minority in Japan[612] and the Crimean Tatars in Ukraine.[613]

ii. Ethnic or Racial Origin

Ethnic or racial origin is an important prohibited ground of discrimination in CERD's practice. Issues include the identification as members of a particular ethnic group, categorization of ethnic groups, and many forms of discrimination against people belonging to ethnic groups.

Identification with a particular ethnic or racial group is, if no justification exists to the contrary, to be based upon self-identification by the individual concerned.[614] As to the recognition and categorization of ethnic or racial groups, the Committee has spelt out the principle that the same criteria should be applied to all groups, for the application of different criteria in order to determine ethnic groups, leading to the recognition of some and refusal to recognize others, may give rise to differential treatment for various groups within a country's population:[615]

---

606 UN Doc. CERD/C/304/Add.107, para. 10 (Finland); UN Doc. CERD/C/304/Add.47, para. 12 (Czech Republic).

607 UN Doc. CERD/C/304/Add.47, para. 10 (Czech Republic); UN Doc. CERD/C/304/Add.29, para. 10 (Bulgaria).

608 UN Doc. A/57/18, para. 379 (Hungary).

609 UN Doc. CERD/C/60/CO/14, para. 12 (Switzerland); UN Doc. A/57/18, para. 379 (Hungary).

610 UN Doc. CERD/C/304/Add.110, para. 10 (Slovakia); UN Doc. CERD/C/304/Add.29, para. 9 (Bulgaria).

611 UN Doc. CERD/C/304/Add.109, para. 12 (Czech Republic); UN Doc. CERD/C/304/Add.68, para. 14 (Italy).

612 UN Doc. CERD/C/304/Add.114, paras. 16 and 18 (Japan).

613 UN Doc. A/56/18, para. 374 (Ukraine); UN Doc. CERD/C/304/Add.48, para. 15 (Ukraine).

614 UN Doc. HRI/GEN/1/Rev.7, General Recommendation VIII (1990), *Identification With a Particular Racial or Ethnic Group (Art.1, par.1 & 4)*. Compare with UN Doc. CERD/C/304/Add.42, para. 10 (Burundi).

615 UN Doc. HRI/GEN/1/Rev.7, General Recommendation XXIV (1999), *Reporting of Persons Belonging to Different Races, National/Ethnic Groups, or Indigenous Peoples (Art. 1)*, para. 3.

> [...] a number of States parties recognize the presence on their territory of some national or ethnic groups or indigenous peoples, while disregarding others. Certain criteria should be uniformly applied to all groups, in particular the number of persons concerned, and their being of a race, colour, descent or national or ethnic origin different from the majority or from other groups within the population.[616]

In line with this principle, CERD has recommended to a number of states to review their categorization of ethnic groups so as to grant them all equal status and protection.[617]

Most concerns however deal not so much with differentiation and discrimination among ethnic groups, but with discrimination of persons belonging to ethnic groups,[618] particularly in the field of economic, social and cultural rights.[619] While ethnic groups should not be discriminated against with respect to economic development and national modernization, members of such ethnic groups should not be deprived of their right to their own culture, in particular their traditional ways of life.[620] As to education, concern has been expressed about the fact that ethnic groups are under-represented in most areas of education,[621] and states have been urged to maintain the possibility for the various ethnic groups of receiving instruction in their languages,[622] or to study those languages at different educational levels without prejudice to the learning of the official language, as well as of using their mother tongue in private and in public.[623] Training of teachers for minority languages in public establishments should be provided for.[624] With regard to the right of health, and in light of allegations of forced sterilization of mountain ethnic minority women, the Committee has asked

616 *Ibid.*, para. 2.

617 UN Doc. A/56/18, para. 337 (Sri Lanka); UN Doc. CERD/C/304/Add.73, para. 16 (Mongolia); UN Doc. CERD/C/304/Add.49, para. 12 (Lebanon); UN Doc. CERD/C/304/Add.25, para. 25 (Pakistan); UN Doc. CERD/C/304/Add.24, para. 14 (Germany).

618 UN Doc. A/56/18, para. 418 (Viet Nam); UN Doc. CERD/C/304/Add.73, para. 17 (Mongolia); UN Doc. CERD/C/304/Add.65, para. 17 (Republic of Korea); UN Doc. CERD/C/304/Add.12, para. 20 (Republic of Korea).

619 UN Doc. CERD/C/IRL/CO/2, para. 21 (Ireland); UN Doc. CERD/C/62/CO/2, para. 13 (Ecuador); UN Doc. CERD/C/60/CO/9, para. 12 (Moldova); UN Doc. CERD/C/60/CO/2, para. 18 (Belgium); UN Doc. CERD/C/304/add.116, para. 13 (Sudan); UN Doc. CERD/C/304/Add.102, para. 19 (United Kingdom); UN Doc. CERD/C/304/Add.103, para. 16 (Sweden); UN Doc. CERD/C/304/Add.75, para. 10 (Azerbaijan); UN Doc. CERD/C/304/Add.35, para. 20 (Denmark); UN Doc. CERD/C/304/Add.9 (United Kingdom).

620 UN Doc. CERD/C/304/Add.15, para. 18 (China).

621 UN Doc. CERD/C/304/Add.46, para. 13 (The Netherlands); UN Doc. CERD/C/304/Add.38, para. 15 (Former Yugoslav Republic of Macedonia).

622 UN Doc. CERD/C/304/Add.51, para. 13 (Armenia); UN Doc. CERD/C/304/Add.46, para. 13 (The Netherlands).

623 UN Doc. CERD/C/304/Add.98, para. 12 (Estonia); UN Doc. CERD/C/304/Add.79, para. 26 (Latvia).

624 UN Doc. CERD/C/304/Add.38, para. 15 (Former Yugoslav Republic of Macedonia).

for clarification on the impact of population-planning policies on the enjoyment of reproductive rights by persons belonging to ethnic minorities.[625]

CERD has highlighted instances of political disenfranchisement of a large segment of the ethnic minority population[626] and of under-representation of ethnic minorities in political institutions[627] and the public administration.[628] Representation should be proportionate to their respective percentages in the population.[629]

States are to ensure that access to places or services intended for use by the general public is not denied to any person on grounds of national or ethnic origin.[630]

The Committee has noted with serious concern that among the victims of death in custody were a disproportionate number of members of minority groups, that police brutality appeared to affect members of minority groups disproportionately, that allegations of police brutality and harassment were not vigorously investigated and perpetrators, once guilt was established, not appropriately punished.[631] It has recommended to prevent and prosecute any act or manifestation of racial discrimination or xenophobia, including acts of violence against ethnic groups.[632] The Committee has urged states to address not only private racial violence, but also private discrimination against ethnic groups, *e.g.* by private insurance carriers.[633]

States have also been asked to reconsider the requirement to record ethnic origin in passports.[634]

The provision of basic and equal assistance is to be ensured to all asylum-seekers, without distinction as to race or ethnic and national origin,[635] and a quota system for refugees is to be applied without discrimination based on race or ethnic origin.[636]

---

625 UN Doc. A/56/18, para. 417 (Viet Nam).
626 UN Doc. A/56/18, para. 397 (United States).
627 UN Doc. CERD/C/IRL/CO/2, para. 22 (Ireland); UN Doc. CERD/C/304/Add.120, para. 13 (Georgia); UN Doc. CERD/C/304/Add.55, para. 7 (Croatia).
628 UN Doc. CERD/C/304/Add.93, para. 12 (Denmark); UN Doc. CERD/C/304/Add.9 (United Kingdom).
629 UN Doc. CERD/C/304/Add.55, para. 14 (Croatia); UN Doc. CERD/C/304/Add.38, para. 7 (Former Yugoslav Republic of Macedonia).
630 UN Doc. CERD/C/304/Add.66, para. 16 (Finland); UN Doc. CERD/C/304/Add.7, para. 28 (Finland).
631 UN Doc. CERD/C/304/Add.9 (United Kingdom).
632 UN Doc. CERD/C/304/Add.67, para. 13 (Portugal).
633 UN Doc. CERD/C/304/Add.24, para. 16 (Germany).
634 UN Doc. CERD/C/304/Add.79, para. 24 (Latvia).
635 UN Doc. CERD/C/60/CO/1, para. 14 (Austria).
636 UN Doc. CERD/C/304/Add.66, para. 17 (Finland).

Numerous ethic groups have been taken care of, ranging from the ethnic Serbs in Croatia,[637] to persons of Arab ethnic origin in Israel[638] and to ethnic Vietnamese in Cambodia.[639]

iii. Indigenous Origin

CERD has made clear that discrimination against indigenous people is to be considered as racial discrimination:

> Particular concern is expressed that the State party does not seem to perceive that pervasive discrimination being suffered by the 56 indigenous groups living in Mexico falls under the definition given to racial discrimination in article 1 of the Convention. The description of their plight merely as an unequal participation in social and economic development is inadequate.[640]

In its general recommendation on indigenous people, the Committee has affirmed that discrimination against indigenous peoples falls under the scope of the Convention (paras. 1 and 2), and it has referred to the specific ground of *indigenous origin or identity* (para. 4 (b)).[641] Indigenous origin is not mentioned explicitly in ICERD. Elsewhere, discrimination against indigenous people seems to have subsumed under discrimination on the grounds of ethnic origin.

The latter appears to be the case with regard to the identification of individuals with indigenous groups. In referring to its general recommendation on identification with a particular ethnic or racial group, CERD emphasized that the criterion of self-identification was to be accorded adequate weight:

> The Committee considers that by relying mainly, if not exclusively, on the criteria of the language spoken and the taxes levied on a person's ancestors, the State party is not taking into account to a sufficient degree the criterion of self-identification. Accordingly, the Committee suggests that the State party give more adequate weight to self-identification by the individual, as indicated in general recommendation VIII.[642]

Elsewhere, it expressed concern at the absence of a specific categorization of the indigenous population as a separate ethnic group in official statistics on the population, and it encouraged the government to include the indigenous population in any

---

637 UN Doc. CERD/C/304/Add.55, paras. 10 and 16 (Croatia).

638 UN Doc. CERD/C/304/Add.45, paras. 16, 17 and 19 (Israel).

639 UN Doc. CERD/C/304/Add.54, paras. 11, 12 and 18 (Cambodia).

640 UN Doc. A/50/18, para. 382 (Mexico).

641 UN Doc. HRI/GEN/1/Rev.7, General Recommendation XXIII (1997), *The Rights of Indigenous Peoples*.

642 UN Doc. CERD/C/63/CO/5, para. 11 (Finland).

statistical data as a separate ethnic group.[643] It also worried about Denmark's denial of the identity and continued existence of the Inughuit as a separate ethnic or tribal entity.[644]

With regard to indigenous origin too, as with ethnic origin, the Committee has stressed that no discrimination should take place among different groups of indigenous origin.[645]

In paragraph 4 of its general recommendation on the rights of indigenous peoples, CERD focused on five aspects of recognition and protection.[646] It has also recommended to ratify[647] and implement[648] ILO Convention No. 169 concerning Indigenous and Tribal Peoples in Independent Countries.

In this general recommendation, it called first of all upon states to recognize and respect indigenous distinct culture, history, language and way of life as an enrichment of the state's cultural identity and to promote its preservation.[649] In light of past practices such as the forced separation of indigenous children from their families,[650] a reconciliation process may have to be conducted, so as to lead to meaningful reconciliation, genuinely embraced by both the indigenous population and the population at large.[651]

Secondly, it asked to ensure that members of indigenous peoples were free and equal in dignity and rights and free from any discrimination, in particular that based on indigenous origin or identity.[652] Instances of discrimination based on indigenous origin

---

643 UN Doc. A/56/18, para. 351 (Trinidad and Tobago).

644 UN Doc. CERD/C/60/CO/5, para. 18 (Denmark).

645 UN Doc. A/57/18, para. 301 (Botswana): recognition and representation of all tribes in Botswana on an equal basis.

646 This general recommendation takes a very progressive approach, and seems to have been inspired by the UN Draft Declaration on Indigenous People. For more background information, see *e.g.* Koen De Feyter, *World Development Law. Sharing Responsibility for Development,* Antwerp, Intersentia, 2001, 158-159.

647 UN Doc. CERD/C/304/Add.103, para. 13 (Sweden); UN Doc. CERD/C/304/Add.11, paras. 20-21 (Brazil); UN Doc. CERD/C/304/Add.7, para. 23 (Finland).

648 UN Doc. CERD/C/65/CO/1, para. 16 (Argentina); UN Doc. A/56/18, para. 400 (United States).

649 UN Doc. HRI/GEN/1/Rev.7, General Recommendation XXIII (1997), *The Rights of Indigenous Peoples,* para. 4 (a). Compare with UN Doc. A/57/18, para. 305 (Botswana); UN Doc. CERD/C/304/Add.54, para. 19 (Cambodia).

650 Qualified by the Committee as "racially discriminatory practice," see UN Doc. CERD/C/304/Add.101, para. 13 (Australia).

651 UN Doc. CERD/C/AUS/CO/14, para. 25 (Australia); UN Doc. CERD/C/304/Add.101, para. 12 (Australia).

652 UN Doc. HRI/GEN/1/Rev.7, General Recommendation XXIII (1997), *The Rights of Indigenous Peoples,* para. 4 (b).

have arisen in particular with regard to legal proceedings and law enforcement. The Committee thus highlighted a discriminatory approach to law enforcement towards indigenous people in Australia, as exemplified by the disproportionately high rate of incarceration of indigenous people, due to mandatory sentencing schemes that appeared to target offences (*i.e.* minor property offences) that were committed disproportionately by indigenous Australians.[653] It also seeks clarification of the reasons for maintaining a system of separate prison facilities for members of the indigenous population.[654] With respect to the right to equal treatment before the courts, the Committee has been concerned that legislation had not been translated into indigenous languages, that interpreters were not in practice available to monolingual indigenous people[655] and that members of indigenous peoples were not guaranteed the right to express themselves in their own languages during legal proceedings.[656]

Thirdly, indigenous peoples are to be provided with conditions allowing for a sustainable economic and social development compatible with their cultural characteristics.[657] The Committee has repeatedly expressed concern at the serious discrimination indigenous peoples face in respect of the enjoyment of their civil, political, economic, social and cultural rights.[658] It has highlighted the lack of a social security system which took into account the specific needs of indigenous peoples,[659] major shortcomings in the health services,[660] racial discrimination on the job market (access to jobs and promotions),[661] and the high rate of illiteracy among indigenous communities.[662] States were called upon to improve the economic and social situation of their indigenous population,[663] *inter alia* by expanding the economic and social infrastructure to the rural areas where many indigenous communities were situated,[664] but were also to prevent harm against them, *e.g.* due to deforestation.[665] With regard to the right of access to all public places, legislation prohibiting the owners of establish-

653 UN Doc. CERD/C/AUS/CO/14, paras. 20-21 (Australia); UN Doc. CERD/C/304/Add.101, paras. 15 and 16 (Australia).

654 UN Doc. CERD/C/304/Add.17, paras. 13 and 18 (Venezuela).

655 UN Doc. CERD/C/304/Add.69, para. 17 (Peru).

656 UN Doc. CERD/C/304/Add.30, paras. 11 and 25 (Mexico).

657 UN Doc. HRI/GEN/1/Rev.7, General Recommendation XXIII (1997), *The Rights of Indigenous Peoples*, para. 4 (c).

658 UN Doc. CERD/C/AUS/CO/14, para. 19 (Australia); UN Doc. A/56/18, para. 421 (Viet Nam); UN Doc. CERD/C/304/Add.101, para. 18 (Australia); UN Doc. CERD/C/304/Add.69, para. 12 (Peru); UN Doc. CERD/C/304/Add.11, para. 14 (Brazil); UN Doc. A/50/18, para. 386 (Mexico); UN Doc. A/50/18, paras. 305 and 310 (Guatemala).

659 UN Doc. CERD/C/304/Add.112, para. 12 (Argentina).

660 UN Doc. CERD/C/304/Add.69, para. 19 (Peru); UN Doc. CERD/C/304/Add.17, para. 17 (Venezuela).

661 UN Doc. CERD/C/304/Add.69, para. 20 (Peru).

662 UN Doc. A/50/18, para. 311 (Guatemala).

663 UN Doc. A/50/18, para. 380 (Mexico).

664 UN Doc. CERD/C/304/Add. 10, para. 20 (Bolivia).

665 UN Doc. CERD/C/304/Add.53, para. 17 (Cameroon).

ments open to the public from screening their clients on racial grounds was not deemed sufficient; such a prohibition was to be accompanied by a form of penalty.[666]

Fourthly, states are to ensure that members of indigenous peoples have equal rights in respect of effective participation in public life, and that no decisions directly relating to their rights and interests are taken without their informed consent.[667] The political rights of members of indigenous groups are not always protected,[668] and they are under-represented in Parliament, in the public service and in public life, particularly among judges and in the administration of justice.[669] Lack of identity papers or lack of recognition of their citizenship may deprive indigenous people of the possibility of exercising their civic and political rights.[670] In its concluding observations, CERD has encouraged states to take appropriate measures to enable indigenous persons to participate in elections and to provide them with equal access to employment in the public service.[671] It has stressed repeatedly the need to ensure effective consultation of and participation by indigenous communities in decisions affecting them, including those on their land rights and those pertaining to the management of natural resources.[672]

Fifthly and finally, states are to ensure that indigenous communities can exercise their rights to practise and revitalize their cultural traditions and customs and to preserve and to practise their languages.[673] Measures may have to be taken, especially in the field of education, in order to encourage knowledge of the history, language and culture of indigenous peoples.[674] Indigenous people should be offered the possibility of a bilingual and bicultural education.[675] With regard to the Sami, the Committee has insisted on measures in order to ensure the use by Sami of their own language,[676] and

666 UN Doc. CERD/C/304/Add.69, para. 21 (Peru).
667 UN Doc. HRI/GEN/1/Rev.7, General Recommendation XXIII (1997), *The Rights of Indigenous Peoples*, para. 4 (d). UN Doc. CERD/C/AUS/CO/14, para. 11 (Australia): priority concern.
668 UN Doc. CERD/C/304/Add.30, para. 13 (Mexico).
669 UN Doc. CERD/C/304/Add.21, para. 21 (Guatemala); UN Doc. A/50/18, para. 305 (Guatemala).
670 UN Doc. CERD/C/304/Add.69, para. 18 (Peru); UN Doc. CERD/C/304/Add.54, para. 19 (Cambodia).
671 UN Doc. CERD/C/304/Add.32, para. 25 (Panama); UN Doc. CERD/C/304/Add.30, para. 24 (Mexico).
672 UN Doc. CERD/C/AUS/CO/14, paras. 16-17 (Australia): priority concern; UN Doc. CERD/C/60/CO/3, para. 13 (Costa Rica); UN Doc. A/57/18, para. 304 (Botswana); UN Doc. A/56/18, para. 400 (United States); UN Doc. CERD/C/304/Add.112, para. 10 (Argentina); UN Doc. CERD/C/304/Add.54, paras. 13 and 19 (Cambodia).
673 UN Doc. HRI/GEN/1/Rev.7, General Recommendation XXIII (1997), *The Rights of Indigenous Peoples*, para. 4 (e). Compare with UN Doc. CERD/C/64/CO/9, para. 22 (Suriname).
674 UN Doc. CERD/C/64/CO/4, para. 15 (Libya).
675 UN Doc. CERD/C/304/Add.30, para. 17 (Mexico); UN Doc. CERD/C/304/Add.17, para. 16 (Venezuela); UN Doc. A/50/18, para. 386 (Mexico).
676 UN Doc. CERD/C/304/Add.103, para. 12 (Sweden); UN Doc. CERD/C/304/Add.37, para. 19 (Sweden); UN Doc. CERD/C/304/Add.7, para. 12 (Finland): in the Sami parliament.

to enable Sami children to pursue their studies at the primary and secondary levels in their mother tongue.[677] However, women's rights are to be respected, irrespective of the community they belong to, especially where marriage is concerned.[678]

CERD has also drawn attention to the special importance for the culture and spiritual values of indigenous peoples of their relationship with the land.[679] In line with the expressed cultural importance of land, it has called upon states

> to recognize and protect the rights of indigenous peoples to own, develop, control and use their communal lands, territories and resources and, where they have been deprived of their lands and territories traditionally owned or otherwise inhabited or used without their free and informed consent, to take steps to return those lands and territories. Only when this is for factual reasons not possible, the right to restitution should be substituted by the right to just, fair and prompt compensation. Such compensation should as far as possible take the form of lands and territories.[680]

This concern has been echoed in numerous concluding observations. States are to adopt, in consultation with indigenous peoples, a general land tenure policy and effective legal procedures to recognize indigenous peoples' titles to land and demarcate territorial boundaries.[681] Measures are also to be adopted to safeguard indigenous rights over ancestral lands, especially sacred sites,[682] and to recognize and protect, in practice, the right of indigenous peoples to own, develop, control and use their lands, territories and resources.[683] In decisions affecting their land rights, the "informed consent" of indigenous peoples is to be sought.[684] Where indigenous peoples have been deprived of their lands and territories traditionally owned or otherwise inhabited or used without their free and informed consent, steps are to be taken to return those lands and territories.[685] Restitution of those lands that have been occupied by non-

---

677 UN Doc. CERD/C/304/Add.7, para. 24 (Finland).

678 UN Doc. CERD/C/64/CO/9, para. 25 (Suriname).

679 UN Doc. CERD/C/65/CO/1, para. 16 (Argentina); UN Doc. CERD/C/304/Add.71, para. 18 (Costa Rica).

680 UN Doc. HRI/GEN/1/Rev.7, General Recommendation XXIII (1997), *The Rights of Indigenous Peoples*, para. 5.

681 UN Doc. CERD/C/65/CO/1, para. 16 (Argentina); UN Doc. CERD/C/64/CO/2, para. 15 (Brazil); UN Doc. CERD/C/64/CO/9, para. 12 (Suriname).

682 UN Doc. CERD/C/65/CO/1, para. 16 (Argentina).

683 UN Doc. CERD/C/64/CO/9, para. 11 (Suriname); UN Doc. CERD/C/64/CO/2, para. 15 (Brazil); UN Doc. CERD/C/63/CO/8, para. 18 (Norway); UN Doc. CERD/C/63/CO/2, para. 13 (Bolivia); UN Doc. A/56/18, para. 335 (Sri Lanka); UN Doc. CERD/C/304/Add.54, para. 13 (Cambodia).

684 UN Doc. CERD/C/304/Add.101, para. 9 (Australia); UN Doc. CERD/C/304/Add.54, para. 19 (Cambodia).

685 UN Doc. CERD/C/63/CO/2, para. 13 (Bolivia); UN Doc. CERD/C/304/Add.39, para. 24 (Argentina).

indigenous persons should be made possible.[686] In case this is impossible, compensation should be offered.[687]

Before awarding any forestry or mining concessions, consultation is to take place and efforts are to be made to reach agreements with the peoples concerned, as far as possible.[688] Merely consulting indigenous communities prior to exploiting the resources falls short of meeting CERD's requirements; prior informed consent of these communities is to be sought, and the equitable sharing of benefits to be derived from such exploitation is to be ensured.[689] A legislative framework which clearly sets forth the broad principles governing the exploitation of land, including the obligation to abide by strict environmental standards, is to be adopted, and an independent body is to be set up in order to conduct environmental impact surveys before any operating licenses are issued, and to conduct health and safety checks on small-scale and industrial gold-mining.[690]

States are to examine ways and means to facilitate the establishment of proof of indigenous people's title over land in procedures before the courts.[691] Indigenous and tribal peoples should be granted the right of appeal to the courts, or any independent body specially created for that purpose, in order to uphold their traditional rights and their right to be consulted before concessions are granted, and to be fairly compensated for any damage.[692]

Before the adoption of the general recommendation in 1997, the Committee's concluding observations with regard to the land rights of indigenous peoples had been less far-reaching and sometimes slightly vague. It had stressed the importance that land held for indigenous peoples and their spiritual and cultural identity, and had suggested that the provisions of ILO Convention No. 169 be used as a guideline for resolving land distribution issues.[693] With regard to land delimitation, distribution and restitution problems, it had insisted on finding just and equitable solutions and on the protection of indigenous inhabitants from all forms of discrimination.[694] It had equally

686 UN Doc. CERD/C/60/CO/3, para. 11 (Costa Rica).

687 UN Doc. CERD/C/65/CO/1, para. 16 (Argentina).

688 UN Doc. CERD/C/64/CO/9, para. 13 (Suriname).

689 UN Doc. CERD/C/62/CO/2, para. 16 (Ecuador).

690 UN Doc. CERD/C/64/CO/9, para. 15 (Suriname).

691 UN Doc. CERD/C/AUS/CO/14, para. 17 (Australia): priority concern; UN Doc. A/57/18, para. 330 (Canada).

692 UN Doc. CERD/C/64/CO/9, para. 14 (Suriname).

693 UN Doc. CERD/C/304/Add.21, para. 31 (Guatemala).

694 UN Doc. CERD/C/304/Add.30, para. 27 (Mexico); UN Doc. CERD/C/304/Add.21, para. 30 (Guatemala); UN Doc. CERD/C/304/Add.11, paras. 20-21 (Brazil); UN Doc. A/50/18, para. 386 (Mexico).

recommended to investigate and monitor the impact of the work of mining companies, including foreign ones, as well as the impact of the development of tourism, on the enjoyment of basic rights by indigenous peoples.[695]

The Committee has quite consistently paid attention to the land rights of the Sami people. It has urged states to find an adequate settlement of the land dispute together with the Sami people,[696] in a manner that did justice to the claims of the Sami.[697] It has also recommended a clear policy and legislation recognizing traditional Sami land rights and reflecting the centrality of reindeer husbandry to their way of life.[698] It therefore has expressed concern about activities authorized by state bodies in Sami reindeer-breeding areas which might threaten Sami culture and their traditional way of life,[699] such as mining and other economic interests of national and international companies.[700]

In quite a number of cases, the Committee has expressed concern about basic physical security of indigenous people and the impact of an armed conflict on their livelihood.[701] It has condemned instances of violence, summary executions, threats and forcible recruitment into the armed forces, intimidation and other serious human rights violations against indigenous people.[702] It has insisted on systematic prosecution of those responsible for such crimes, regardless of whether they were members of private militias or state officials, on effective preventive measures, including the training of members of the police force and the army, and on compensation for the victims of such acts.[703]

d. *Descent*

Descent is explicitly mentioned as one of the prohibited grounds of discrimination in article 1, para. 1 ICERD. In the view of the Committee, the term "descent" has a meaning and application which complement the other prohibited grounds of discrimination, and does not refer solely to race or ethnic or national origin.[704]

---

695 UN Doc. CERD/C/304/Add.32, para. 23 (Panama).
696 UN Doc. CERD/C/63/CO/5, para. 12 (Finland); UN Doc. CERD/C/304/Add.107, para. 11 (Finland).
697 UN Doc. CERD/C/304/Add.66, para. 14 (Finland).
698 UN Doc. CERD/C/304/Add.103, para. 13 (Sweden); UN Doc. CERD/C/304/Add.7, para. 23 (Finland).
699 UN Doc. CERD/C/304/Add.107, para. 11 (Finland).
700 UN Doc. CERD/C/304/Add.7, paras. 11-12 (Finland).
701 UN Doc. CERD/C/304/Add.30, para. 19 (Mexico).
702 *Ibid.*, para. 26 (Mexico); UN Doc. CERD/C/304/Add.21, para. 13 (Guatemala); UN Doc. A/50/18, para. 307 (Guatemala).
703 UN Doc. CERD/C/304/Add.30, para. 26 (Mexico).
704 UN Doc. HRI/GEN/1/Rev.7, General Recommendation XXIX (2002), *Article 1, paragraph 1 of the Convention (Descent)*, preamble; UN Doc. CERD/C/304/Add.118, para. 11 (Bangladesh); UN Doc. CERD/C/304/Add.114, para. 8 (Japan).

"[D]iscrimination based on "descent" includes discrimination against members of communities based on forms of social stratification such as caste and analogous systems of inherited status which nullify or impair their equal enjoyment of human rights."[705] In other words, castes falls within the scope of ICERD.[706]

The Committee has extremely rarely referred to discrimination based on descent outside the context of castes.[707] With regard to caste-based discrimination, it has repeatedly expressed concern over the persistence thereof.[708] Recommendations include the implementation of practical and substantive measures to eradicate the practice of the caste system, including measures for the prevention of caste-motivated abuse and the prosecution of state and private actors responsible for such abuse, and affirmative measures to advance and protect persons subjected to caste-based discrimination.[709] Special measures are to be taken to prevent acts of discrimination towards persons belonging to castes, and, in cases where such acts have been committed, to conduct thorough investigations, to punish those found responsible and to provide just and adequate reparation to the victims.[710]

e. *Religion*

Discrimination on religious grounds has only exceptionally and succinctly been touched upon. This may not come as a surprise, for religious discrimination is not explicitly within the mandate of CERD. The Committee mainly seems to have raised issues of religious discrimination when these intersect with racial discrimination,[711] *i.e.* when religious freedom is not ensured without discrimination and only some religions enjoy legal status.[712]

f. *Gender*

Occasionally, and increasingly so in recent years, CERD has paid attention to discrimination against women belonging to minority and other vulnerable groups, such

---

705 UN Doc. HRI/GEN/1/Rev.7, General Recommendation XXIX (2002), *Article 1, paragraph 1 of the Convention (Descent)*, preamble.

706 UN Doc. CERD/C/304/Add.118, para. 11 (Bangladesh); UN Doc. CERD/C/304/Add.13, para. 14 (India).

707 UN Doc. CERD/C/65/CO/4, para. 17 (Madagascar).

708 UN Doc. CERD/C/64/CO/5, para. 12 (Nepal); UN Doc. CERD/C/304/Add.108, para. 11 (Nepal); UN Doc. CERD/C/304/Add.13, para. 23 (India).

709 UN Doc. CERD/C/304/Add.108, para. 11 (Nepal); UN Doc. CERD/C/304/Add.13, para. 26 (India).

710 UN Doc. CERD/C/304/Add.13, para. 27 (India).

711 UN Doc. CERD/C/IRL/CO/2, para. 18 (Ireland): priority concern; UN Doc. CERD/C/63/CO/11, para. 20 (United Kingdom); UN Doc. CERD/C/304/Add.9 (United Kingdom).

712 UN Doc. CERD/C/60/CO/15, para. 5 (Turkmenistan); UN Doc. A/57/18, para. 282 (Armenia).

as migrant workers,[713] who often happen to be the victim of multiple discrimination.[714] Gender discrimination against male foreign spouses with regard to the acquisition of nationality has equally been noted with concern.[715] Foreign men should be able to acquire nationality in the same way as foreign women.[716]

g. *Conclusions*

CERD has limited itself by and large to the enumerated grounds in ICERD, *i.e.* race, colour, descent, and national or ethnic origin. Race, colour and descent have been referred to rather exceptionally. The ground of descent has been limited to caste. The Committee has submitted that all grounds are equally important.

Most attention has gone to discrimination based on ethnic origin. Issues covered include the identification as members of a particular ethnic group, the categorization of ethnic groups, and many forms of discrimination against people belonging to ethnic groups. Discrimination against indigenous peoples, which has enjoyed the particular attention of the Committee, seems to have been addressed most frequently under this ground, although CERD has never specified whether indigenous origin constitutes a specific ground or rather forms part of ethnic origin. Discrimination of minorities has been dealt with as a cross-cutting issue, which may be based on different grounds. CERD's focus has been inter alia on the identification as members of a particular minority, discrimination among minorities, and on issues of housing, education, transport and employment. Discrimination against Roma has been singled out as a matter requiring particular attention.

Discrimination based on the grounds of nationality has been a challenging issue. ICERD explicitly allows for differential treatment of non citizens. However, CERD has recently seriously restricted the permissibility of discrimination on the basis of nationality in its 2004 general recommendation on the issue.

Occasionally, it has paid attention to religious grounds for discrimination in intersection with racial discrimination. Gender discrimination in combination with racial discrimination has gained more attention in recent years, both against women and men.

---

713 UN Doc. CERD/C/BHR/CO/7, para. 15 (Bahrain): priority concern.

714 See higher in chapter II for references to multiple discrimination; UN Doc. CERD/C/IRL/CO/2, para. 23 (Ireland).

715 UN Doc. CERD/C/BHR/CO/7, para. 17 (Bahrain); UN Doc. CERD/C/64/CO/1, para. 16 (Bahamas); UN Doc. CERD/C/62/CO/8, para. 14 (Saudi Arabia); UN Doc. CERD/C/304/Add.92, para. 12 (Zimbabwe).

716 UN Doc. CERD/C/BHR/CO/7, para. 17 (Bahrain).

2. HRC

As pointed out higher, the CCPR contains a whole list of prohibited grounds of discrimination, *i.e.* race, colour, sex, language, religion, political or other opinion, national or social origin, property, birth or other status.

As far as individual complaints are concerned, initially the HRC may have been rather restrictive in applying other grounds than those explicitly enumerated.[717] Over the years however, it has accepted many new grounds under the open category of "other status", such as nationality, descent, health status, civilian status, military status, etc.[718] The non-exhaustive nature of permissible grounds does not imply that every distinction between individuals raises an issue of discrimination. In order for complaints about discrimination to be admissible, authors of a communication are to claim that their differential treatment "was attributable to their belonging to any identifiably distinct category which could have exposed them to discrimination on account of any of the grounds enumerated or "other status" referred to in article 26 of the Covenant."[719] Comparably, in the context of indirect discrimination, the Committee submitted:

> [I]ndirect discrimination can only be said to be based on the grounds enumerated in Article 26 of the Covenant if the detrimental effects of a rule or decision exclusively or disproportionaly affect persons having a particular race, colour, sex, language, religion, political or other opinion, national or social origin, property, birth or other status.[720]

The test thus seemed to be whether there was an identifiable distinct category, a group united by a common "other" status.[721] In *van Oord v. The Netherlands*,[722] the HRC may have introduced a new test for "other status", *i.e.* whether a relevant distinction exists between the categories of persons being compared.[723]

---

717 Frostell, supra note 140, 39.

718 Joseph, Schultz and Castan mention age, nationality, marital status, dwarfism, place of residence within a state, a distinction between foster and natural children, a difference between students at public and private schools, a difference between employed and unemployed persons, a difference between people performing their compulsory national service in a military or in a non-military capacity, and a distinction between households shared by close relatives and households shared by others (supra note 53, 690-693).

719 UN Doc. CCPR/C/35/D/273/1988, Communication No. 273/1989, *B.d.B. v. The Netherlands*, para. 6.7; UN Doc. CCPR/C/35/D/218/1986, *Vos v. The Netherlands*, Communication No. 218/1986, individual opinion of Committee members Aguilar and Wennergren, para. 1.

720 UN Doc. CCPR/C/78/D/998/2001, Communication No. 998/2001, *Althammer v. Austria*, para. 10.2.

721 UN Doc. CCPR/C//D/273/1989, Communication No. 273/1989, *B.d.B. v. The Netherlands*, para. 6.7.

722 UN Doc. CCPR/C/60/D/658/1995, Communication No. 658/1995, *van Oord v. The Netherlands*, para. 8.5.

723 For a critique, see Joseph, Schultz and Castan, supra note 53, 690.

Over the years, it has become clear that the grounds issue is not an issue of major concern for the Committee in deciding on individual complaints. Joseph, Schultz and Castan find it "arguable that the issue of 'grounds' should be considered as an aspect relating to the permissibility or the reasonableness of the impugned distinction."[724] Although that might imply that the grounds issue is completely subsumed by the issue of reasonableness, the grounds remain important in that they help to establish or disprove reasonableness.[725] Hanski and Scheinin have read in *Kavanagh v. Ireland* a possible turning point that may redirect attention away from the grounds issue. In that case, independent meaning was given to the first sentence of article 26 CCPR, which ensures equal protection of the law. In the words of Hanski and Scheinin:

> In this case, the Committee gave independent meaning for the first sentence of Article 26, ensuring to all persons 'the equal protection of the law'. Without having to identify any specific basis for a differentiation or any category of persons the Committee took the view that the executive's decision to put the author on trial before a special court was as such in violation of Article 26 in the absence of proper justification.[726]

Different treatment based on one of the specific grounds enumerated in article 26, para. 2 CCPR has been said to place a heavy burden on the state to explain the reason for differentiation.[727] Differences in importance of the grounds seems to have been accepted too. Suspect distinctions calling for stricter scrutiny are racial distinctions and differential treatment based on sex/gender.[728] In the view of Joseph, Schultz and Castan, a common characteristic of the more important grounds is that the ground describes a group which has historically suffered from unjustifiable discrimination, and is therefore vulnerable to such treatment.[729]

---

724 *Ibid.*, 693.

725 *Idem.* and the references there.

726 Hanski and Scheinin, supra note 35, 328.

727 UN Doc. CCPR/C/74/D/919/2000, Communication No. 919/2000, *Müller and Engelhard v. Namibia*, para. 6.7. In para. 6.8, the Committee referred to the importance of the principle of equality between men and women.

728 As was pointed out by Lester and Joseph, the HRC has held consistently by consensus that distinctions based on sex are in violation of the CCPR, with the exception of indirect discrimination based on sex with regard to social security laws (Lester and Joseph, supra note 8, 590). As to the latter, after initial recognition it seems to have taken a different position (see supra).
See *e.g.* UN Doc. CCPR/C/74/D/919/2000, Communication No. 919/2000, *Müller and Engelhard v. Namibia*; UN Doc. CCPR/C/65/D/716/1996, Communication No. 716/1996, *Pauger v. Austria*; UN Doc. CCPR/C/66/D/786/1997, Communication No. 786/1997, *Vos v. The Netherlands*; UN Doc. CCPR/C/44/D/415/1990, Communication No. 415/1990, *Pauger v. Austria*; UN Doc. CCPR/C/29/D/172/1984, Communication No. 172/1984, *Broeks v. the Netherlands*; UN Doc. CCPR/C/29/D/182/1984, Communication No. 182/1984, *Zwaan-de Vries v. The Netherlands*; UN Doc. CCPR/C/12/D/35/1978, Communication No. 35/1978, *Aumeeruddy-Cziffra et.al. v. Mauritius*.

729 Joseph, Schultz and Castan, supra note 53, 693.

De facto, most cases of alleged discrimination have been based on either sex/gender or nationality.[730] Some of the other grounds have either never been invoked (such as colour or property), or only rarely.

In its concluding observations, the HRC has accepted at least as broad a range of prohibited grounds of discrimination as it has in its views. In its recent concluding observations on Trinidad and Tobago *e.g.*, it requested the state to extend the provisions of its Equal Opportunities Act to those suffering discrimination on grounds of age, sexual orientation, pregnancy or infection with HIV/AIDS.[731]

In what follows, the grounds of discrimination will be discussed in their order of appearance in the articles 2 and 26 CCPR.

a. Race

Racial discrimination has been invoked only twice in individual communications. Both complaints were found inadmissible.[732]

The Committee does not seem to have paid particular attention to the ground of race in its concluding observations, except for generic references to racial discrimination. It has condemned incitement to racial hatred or intolerance (in combination with article 20), racial violence and rioting[733] and racially inspired police violence.[734]

b. Colour

Discrimination on the basis of colour has not acquired any distinct meaning, neither in the individual complaints procedure nor in the reporting procedure.

---

730 Hanski and Scheinin, supra note 35, 327.

731 UN Doc. CCPR/CO/70/TTO, para. 11 (Trinidad and Tobago).

732 In *E.H. v. Finland*, the complainant submitted that on the ground of belonging to the Roma minority she had received a heavier sentence than another Finnish woman for a similar offence. The complaint was not sufficiently substantiated (she failed *e.g.* to furnish the Committee with copies of any judicial decisions) and so the Committee decided that she had no claim under art. 2 (UN Doc. CCPR/C/26/D/170/1984, Communication No. 170/1984, *E.H. v. Finland*). As Lester and Joseph have pointed out, national or social origin rather than race might have been a more appropriate ground to be invoked in this case (Lester and Joseph, supra note 8, 567). In *C.J. v. Canada*, the HRC held a complaint about racial discrimination in the field of employment inadmissible for failure to exhaust domestic remedies, but it made also clear that "there [did] not appear to be evidence in substantiation of the author's claim to be a victim of racial discrimination." (UN Doc. CCPR/C/OP/1, Communication No. 19/1977, *C.J. v. Canada*).

733 UN Doc. CCPR/CO/73/CH, para. 8 (Switzerland); UN Doc. CCPR/CO/73/UK;CCPR/CO/73/UKOT, para. 11 (UK and Overseas Territories): priority concern; UN Doc. CCPR/CO/72/CZE, para. 11 (Czech Republic).

734 UN Doc. CCPR/CO/78/PRT, para. 8 (Portugal): priority concern.

c. *Sex/Gender*

i. Sex/Gender

Sex or gender equality is a central issue in the CCPR, which contains a specific provision on it (*i.e.* art. 3 CCPR, see higher chapter I). Sex/gender is probably the most important ground of alleged discrimination in individual cases, both qualitatively (*i.e.* the weight given to the ground of sex, see higher) and quantitively (the number of complaints about sex discrimination)[735]. In the HRC's concluding observations, it is by far the most important ground in terms of the attention paid to it in almost each and every set of concluding observations concerning a particular country, and as a whole. Since the HRC started to identify priority concerns in March 2001, the compliance with which states are to submit information on within one year,[736] it has rather frequently done so for issues of sex-based discrimination. Very often, the issue of sex/gender discrimination is addressed in a cluster devoted to women's rights. Sometimes, no sharp distinction seems to be made between women's rights in general and the issue of gender equality and non-discrimination in particular.

As to the concept of sex/gender, the Committee's views offer no conclusive answer to the question whether the HRC equates sex with gender, or whether it attaches specific meaning to the notion of gender. In *Müller and Engelhard v. Namibia*, it referred almost exclusively to the concept of gender rather than sex.[737] In its concluding observations, the notion of gender seems to have acquired full recognition by now. The HRC seems to use the two concepts interchangeably.

The following differential treatment based on sex/gender has been held to be discriminatory in the Committee's views: legislation that does not offer the same level of protection of the family to men and women (*i.e.* expelling for security reasons from Mauritius, foreign spouses of Mauritian women, but not foreign spouses of Mauritian men);[738] legislation that women automatically can assume surnames of their husbands on marriage whereas men have to go through specified procedures of application;[739] legislation that women are to prove that they are the breadwinner in order to receive

[735] Hanski and Scheinin, supra note 35, 329.

[736] For more details on the identification of priority concerns, see Vandenhole, supra note 1, 97-98.

[737] UN Doc. CCPR/C/74/D/919/2000, Communication No. 919/2000, *Müller and Engelhard v. Namibia*, paras. 6.7 (differentiation on the basis of gender) and 6.8 (sex-based approach).

[738] UN Doc. CCPR/C/12/D/35/1978, Communication No. 35/78, *Aumeeruddy-Cziffra et.al. v. Mauritius*, para. 9.2.

[739] UN Doc. CCPR/C/74/D/919/2000, Communication No. 919/2000, *Müller and Engelhard v. Namibia*, para. 6.8.

unemployment benefits whereas men are not;[740] and legislation that prevents married women from representing marital property before the courts.[741] Instances of sex discrimination against men have equally been recognized, *e.g.* legislation that provides for a lower pension for male civil servants than for female civil servants[742] or for widowers than for widows.[743]

The HRC has identified as sources of gender-based discrimination law, traditions and customs,[744] and persistent attitudes and prejudices,[745] such as attitudes based on traditional roles,[746] and the assignment of domestic roles to women,[747] such as household tasks and rearing of children.[748]

A broad range of fields of discrimination has been covered in the Committee's concluding observations, dealing with all aspects of social, economic and political life,[749] and in the public and private sector alike.[750] A central concern of the HRC is to ensure equality of opportunity.[751] A good summary overview can be found in the Committee's

---

740 UN Doc. CCPR/C/29/D/182/1984, Communication No. 182/1984, *Zwaan-de Vries v. The Netherlands*, para. 14; UN Doc. CCPR/C/29/D/172/1984, Communication No. 172/1984, *Broeks v. The Netherlands*, para. 14.

741 UN Doc. CCPR/C/34/D/202/1986, Communication No. 202/1986, *Graciela Ato del Avellanal v. Peru*, para. 10.

742 UN Doc. CCPR/C/66/D/786/1997, Communication No. 786/1997, *Vos v. The Netherlands*, paras. 7.6 and 8.

743 UN Doc. CCPR/C/65/D/716/1996, Communication No. 716/1996, *Pauger v. Austria*, para. 10.2; UN Doc. CCPR/C/44/D/415/1990, Communication No. 415/1990, *Pauger v. Austria*, para. 7.4.

744 UN Doc. CCPR/CO/83/KEN, para. 10 (Kenya) (priority concern); UN Doc. CCPR/C/79/Add.82, para. 4 (Senegal); UN Doc. CCPR/C/79/Add.74, para.21 (Bolivia); UN Doc. CCPR/C/79/Add.71, para. 3 (Gabon); UN Doc. CCPR/C/79/Add.62, para. 3 (Zambia); UN Doc. CCPR/C/79/Add.51, para. 5 (Yemen); UN Doc. CCPR/C/79/Add.44, para. 4 (Morocco); UN Doc. CCPR/C/79/Add.36, para. 3 (Togo); UN Doc. CCPR/C/79/Add.33, para. 3 (Cameroon).

745 UN Doc. CCPR/CO/71/UZB, paras. 19-20 (Uzbekistan); UN Doc. CCPR/C/79/Add.120, para. 8 (Mongolia); UN Doc. CCPR/C/79/Add.50, para. 5 (United States of America).

746 UN Doc. CCPR/C/79/Add.52, para. 11 (Ukraine).

747 UN Doc. CCPR/C/79/Add.54, para. 14 (Russian Federation).

748 UN Doc. A/55/40, para. 29 (Ireland); UN Doc. CCPR/C/79/Add.70, para. 12 (Switzerland).

749 UN Doc. CCPR/CO/70/GAB, paras. 8-9 (Gabon); UN Doc. CCPR/C/79/Add.118, para. 9 (Congo); UN Doc. CCPR/C/79/Add.84, para. 13 (Iraq); UN Doc. CCPR/C/79/Add.76, para. 37 (Colombia); UN Doc. CCPR/C/79/Add.71, para. 19 (Gabon); UN Doc. CCPR/C/79/Add.65, para. 29 (Nigeria); UN Doc. CCPR/C/79/Add.62, para. 21 (Zambia); UN Doc. CCPR/C/79/Add.52, para. 22 (Ukraine); UN Doc. CCPR/C/79/Add.45, para. 19 (Lybia) ; UN Doc. CCPR/C/79/Add.40, para. 16 (Slovenia); UN Doc. CCPR/C/79/Add.1, para. 6 (Algeria).

750 UN Doc. CCPR/CO/80/DEU, paras. 13-14 (Germany); UN Doc. CCPR/CO/79/LVA, para. 14 (Latvia); UN Doc. CCPR/CO/76/EGY, para. 7 (Egypt); UN Doc. CCPR/CO/75/YEM, para. 13 (Yemen): priority concern; UN Doc. CCPR/CO/72/MCO, para. 8 (Monaco); UN Doc. CCPR/CO/72/CZE, para. 12 (Czech Republic); UN Doc. CCPR/CO/71/HRV, para. 21 (Croatia); UN Doc. CCPR/CO/71/DOM, para. 21 (Dominican Republic).

751 UN Doc. CCPR/C/79/Add.109, para. 18 (Mexico).

general comment on the equality of rights between men and women,[752] which represents a gender-sensitive reading of the CCPR.

In the area of labour law and employment,[753] the Committee has focused on equality of opportunity and conditions of employment.[754] As to equality of opportunity, issues arise such as whether women have a professional activity outdoors,[755] women's access to the labour market and the participation of women in professions,[756] and gender concentration in certain professions.[757] Particular attention has been paid to the public administration and the judiciary,[758] the armed forces,[759] the private economic sector[760] and senior posts in the public and private sector.[761] With regard to working conditions,

752 In UN Doc. HRI/GEN/1/Rev.7, General Comment No. 28 (2000), *The Equality of Rights Between Men and Women.*

753 UN Doc. CCPR/C/79/Add.48, para. 27 (Paraguay); UN Doc. CCPR/C/79/Add.3, para. 3 (Belgium).

754 UN Doc. CCPR/CO/77/MLI, para. 13 (Mali); UN Doc. CCPR/CO/76/TGO, para. 22 (Togo); UN Doc. CCPR/CO/74/HUN, para. 9 (Hungary); UN Doc. CCPR/CO/71/DOM, para. 21 (Dominican Republic); UN Doc. CCPR/CO/70/DNK, para. 14 (Denmark); UN Doc. CCPR/CO/69/KGZ, para. 13 (Kyrgyzstan); UN Doc. CCPR/C/79/Add.116, para. 11 (Cameroon); UN Doc. CCPR/C/79/Add.114, para. 12 (Korea); UN Doc. CCPR/C/79/Add.113, para. 12 (Morocco); UN Doc. CCPR/C/79/Add.108, para. 17 (Cambodia); UN Doc. CCPR/C/79/Add.100, para. 15 (Armenia); UN Doc. CCPR/C/79/Add.98, para. 10 (Iceland); UN Doc. CCPR/C/79/Add.96, para. 13 (Macedonia); UN Doc. CCPR/C/79/Add.88, para. 10 (Cyprus); UN Doc. CCPR/C/79/Add.86, para. 10 (Lithuania); UN Doc. CCPR/C/79/Add.47, para. 26 (New Zealand); UN Doc. CCPR/C/79/Add.45, para. 6 (Lybia); UN Doc. CCPR/C/79/Add.30, para. 11 (Romania).

755 UN Doc. A/55/40, para. 505 (Australia); UN Doc. CCPR/C/79/Add.101, para. 5 (Libya); UN Doc. CCPR/C/79/Add.99, para. 4 (Belgium); UN Doc. CCPR/C/79/Add.70, para. 8 (Switzerland) UN Doc. CCPR/C/79/Add.35, para. 7 (Jordan).

756 UN Doc. CCPR/CO/82/POL, para. 10 (Poland); UN Doc. CCPR/C/79/Add.121, para. 13 (Guyana); UN Doc. CCPR/C/79/Add.120, para. 8 (Mongolia); UN Doc. CCPR/C/79/Add.109, para. 12 (Poland); UN Doc. CCPR/C/79/Add.66, paras. 13 and 30(Brazil); UN Doc. CCPR/C/79/Add.62, para. 9 (Zambia); UN Doc. CCPR/C/79/Add.54, para. 14 (Russian Federation); UN Doc. CCPR/C/79/Add.44, para. 9 (Morocco); UN Doc. CCPR/C/79/Add.61, para. 7 (Spain); UN Doc. CCPR/C/79/Add.37, para. 5 (Italy).

757 UN Doc. CCPR/C/79/Add.112, para. 7 (Norway).

758 UN Doc. CCPR/CO/80/DEU, para. 13 (Germany); UN Doc. CCPR/CO/72/GTM, para. 25 (Guatemala); UN Doc. CCPR/CO/71/HRV, para. 21 (Croatia); UN Doc. CCPR/CO/70/VEN, para. 21 (Venezuela); UN Doc. CCPR/CO/69/KGZ, para. 13 (Kyrgyzstan); UN Doc. CCPR/C/79/Add.117, para. 16 (China – Hong Kong); UN Doc. CCPR/C/79/Add.25, para. 13 (Iran); UN Doc. A/55/40, para. 505 (Australia); UN Doc. CCPR/C/79/Add.103, para. 5 (Austria); UN Doc. CCPR/C/79/Add.102, para. 5 (Japan); UN Doc. CCPR/C/79/Add.80, para. 5 (France); UN Doc. CCPR/C/79/Add.75, para. 8 (Georgia); UN Doc. CCPR/C/79/Add.73, para. 7 (Germany); UN Doc. CCPR/C/79/Add.21, para. 22 (Ireland).

759 UN Doc. CCPR/C/79/Add.93, para. 15 (Israel); UN Doc. CCPR/C/79/Add.103, para. 5 (Austria).

760 UN Doc. CCPR/C/79/Add.44, para. 9 (Morocco); UN Doc. CCPR/C/79/Add.40, para. 16 (Slovenia); UN Doc. CCPR/C/79/Add.37, para. 5 (Italy).

761 UN Doc. CCPR/CO/83/MUS, para. 8 (Mauritius); UN Doc. CPR/CO/82/ALB, para. 11 (Albania): priority concern; UN Doc. CCPR/CO/82/POL, para. 10 (Poland); UN Doc. CCPR/CO/75/MDA, para. 17 (Moldova); UN Doc. CCPR/CO/74/HUN, para. 9 (Hungary); UN Doc. CCPR/CO/72/PRK, para. 27 (Democratic People's Republic of Korea); UN Doc. CCPR/C/79/Add.111, para. 7 (Romania); UN Doc. CCPR/C/79/Add.91, para. 10 (Finland); UN Doc. CCPR/C/79/Add.81, para. 17 (India); UN Doc. CCPR/C/79/Add.80, para. 14 (France); UN Doc. CCPR/C/79/Add.17, para. 3 (Niger).

the focus has primarily been on equal remuneration for work of equal value.[762] The HRC has qualified harassment in the workplace as discrimination.[763] The Committee has also expressed concern at compulsory retirement for women,[764] and at the different retirement ages for men and women, resulting in lower pensions for women.[765]

The issue of women's participation has equally arisen with regard to public affairs,[766] political life[767] and civil society,[768] and rather exceptionally in particular with the basic issue of women's right to vote.[769]

---

762 UN Doc. CCPR/CO/83/MUS, para. 8 (Mauritius); UN Doc. CCPR/CO/82/FIN, para. 9 (Finland); UN Doc. CCPR/CO/82/POL, para. 10 (Poland); UN Doc. CCPR/CO/79/RUS, para. 9 (Russian Federation); UN Doc. CCPR/CO/80/DEU, para. 13 (Germany); UN Doc. CCPR/CO/79/LVA, para. 14 (Latvia); UN Doc. A/55/40, para. 29 (Ireland); UN Doc. CCPR/C/79/Add.117, para. 16 (China – Hong Kong); UN Doc. CCPR/C/79/Add.116, para. 11 (Cameroon); UN Doc. CCPR/C/79/Add.115, para. 10 (Portugal-Macau); UN Doc. CCPR/C/79/Add.114, para. 12 (Korea); UN Doc. CCPR/C/79/Add.109, para. 12 (Poland); UN Doc. CCPR/C/79/Add.101, para. 17 (Libya); UN Doc. CCPR/C/79/Add.98, para. 10 (Iceland); UN Doc. CCPR/C/79/Add.94, para. 12 (Italy); UN Doc. CCPR/C/79/Add.91, para. 10 (Finland); UN Doc. CCPR/CO/77/EST, para. 6 (Estonia); UN Doc. CCPR/C/79/Add.93, para. 8 (Israel); UN Doc. CCPR/C/79/Add.77, para. 12 (Portugal-Macau); UN Doc. CCPR/C/79/Add.70, paras. 12 and 23 (Switzerland); UN Doc. CCPR/C/79/Add.58, paras. 13 and 22 (Sweden); UN Doc. CCPR/C/79/Add.54, para. 14 (Russian Federation); UN Doc. CCPR/C/79/Add.52, para. 11 (Ukraine); UN Doc. CCPR/C/79/Add.47, para. 26 (New Zealand); UN Doc. CCPR/C/79/Add.42, para. 8 (Nepal); UN Doc. CCPR/C/79/Add.28, para. 10 (Japan); UN Doc. CCPR/C/79/Add.26, para. 5 (Iceland); UN Doc. CCPR/C/79/Add.2, para. 4 (Colombia).

763 UN Doc. CCPR/CO/70/ARG, para. 15 (Argentina); UN Doc. CCPR/C/79/Add.63, para. 33 (Guatemala).

764 UN Doc. CCPR/C/79/Add.102, para. 5 (Japan).

765 UN Doc. CCPR/C/79/Add.109, para. 13 (Poland).

766 UN Doc. CCPR/CO/83/KEN, para. 10 (Kenya) (priority concern); UN Doc. CCPR/CO/81/LIE, para. 7 (Liechtenstein); UN Doc. CCPR/CO/71/HRV, para. 21 (Croatia); UN Doc. CCPR/CO/71/DOM, para. 21 (Dominican Republic); UN Doc. CCPR/CO/69/KGZ, para. 13 (Kyrgyzstan); UN Doc. CCPR/C/79/Add.113, para. 12 (Morocco); UN Doc. CCPR/C/79/Add.109, para. 18 (Mexico); UN Doc. CCPR/C/79/Add.101, para. 5 (Libya); UN Doc. CCPR/C/79/Add.100, para. 15 (Armenia); UN Doc. CCPR/C/79/Add.99, para. 4 (Belgium); UN Doc. CCPR/C/79/Add.94, para. 12 (Italy); UN Doc. CCPR/C/79/Add.93, para. 15 (Israel); UN Doc. CCPR/C/79/Add.81, para. 17 (India); UN Doc. CCPR/C/79/Add.62, para. 9 (Zambia); UN Doc. CCPR/C/79/Add.61, para. 7 (Spain); UN Doc. CCPR/C/79/Add.52, para. 11 (Ukraine); UN Doc. CCPR/C/79/Add.45, para. 6 (Lybia); UN Doc. CCPR/C/79/Add.48, para. 27 (Paraguay); UN Doc. CCPR/C/79/Add.44, para. 9 (Morocco); UN Doc. CCPR/C/79/Add.40, para. 9 (Slovenia); UN Doc. CCPR/C/79/Add.37, paras. 5 and 19 (Italy); UN Doc. CCPR/C/79/Add.35, para. 7 (Jordan); UN Doc. CCPR/C/79/Add.30, para. 11 (Romania)UN Doc. CCPR/C/79/Add.22, para. 9 (Hungary).

767 UN Doc. CCPR/CO/83/MUS, para. 8 (Mauritius); UN Doc. CPR/CO/82/ALB, para. 11 (Albania): priority concern; UN Doc. CCPR/CO/77/MLI, para. 13 (Mali); UN Doc. CCPR/CO/76/TGO, para. 22 (Togo); UN Doc. CCPR/CO/74/HUN, para. 9 (Hungary); UN Doc. CCPR/CO/72/GTM, para. 25 (Guatemala); UN Doc. CCPR/CO/70/VEN, paras. 21 (Venezuela); UN Doc. A/55/40, para. 29 (Ireland); UN Doc. CCPR/C/79/Add.120, para. 8 (Mongolia); UN Doc. CCPR/C/79/Add.111, para. 7 (Romania); UN Doc. CCPR/C/79/Add.108, para. 17 (Cambodia).

768 UN Doc. CCPR/CO/71/UZB, paras. 19-20 (Uzbekistan).

769 UN Doc. CCPR/CO/69/KWT, paras. 9-10 (Kuwait).

In the broad area of marriage and family relations,[770] recurrent themes have been women's rights to and in marriage:[771] *i.e.* difference in minimum age for girls and boys;[772] levirat;[773] polygamy;[774] transmission of nationality to children;[775] different age for registration of children by unmarried minors;[776] child custody[777] and parental authority;[778] parental consent for marriage of minor children;[779] issues of divorce, custody and

770 UN Doc. CCPR/CO/83/MUS, para. 6 (Mauritius); UN Doc. CCPR/C/79/Add.82, para. 12 (Senegal); UN Doc. CCPR/C/79/Add.84, para. 13 (Iraq); UN Doc. CCPR/C/79/Add.80, para. 11 (France); UN Doc. CCPR/C/79/Add.72, para. 14 (Peru); UN Doc. CCPR/C/79/Add.62, paras. 9 and 21 (Zambia); UN Doc. CCPR/C/79/Add.51, paras. 14 and 20 (Yemen); UN Doc. CCPR/C/79/Add.25, para. 13 (Iran).

771 UN Doc. CCPR/CO/77/MLI, para. 10 (Mali): priority concern; UN Doc. CCPR/CO/79/LKA, para. 19 (Sri Lanka); UN Doc. CCPR/CO/76/TGO, paras. 21 (Togo); UN Doc. CCPR/CO/75/YEM, para. 7 (Yemen): priority concern; UN Doc. CCPR/CO/72/MCO, para. 9 (Monaco); UN Doc. CCPR/CO/70/SYR, para. 18 (Syria); UN Doc. CCPR/CO/70/GAB, paras. 8-9 (Gabon); UN Doc. CCPR/CO/KWT, para. 7 (Kuwait); UN Doc. CCPR/C/79/Add.121, para. 13 (Guyana); UN Doc. CCPR/C/79/Add.116, para. 9 (Cameroon); UN Doc. CCPR/C/79/Add.113, para. 12 (Morocco); UN Doc. CCPR/C/79/Add.109, para. 18 (Mexico); UN Doc. CCPR/C/79/Add.104, para. 17 (Chile); UN Doc. CCPR/C/79/Add.97, para. 12 (Tanzania); UN Doc. CCPR/C/79/Add.95, para. 13 (Algeria); UN Doc. CCPR/C/79/Add.88, para. 10 (Cyprus); UN Doc. CCPR/C/79/Add.85, para. 11 (Sudan); UN Doc. CCPR/C/79/Add.81, para. 17 (India); UN Doc. CCPR/C/79/Add.78, paras. 18-19 (Lebanon); UN Doc. CCPR/C/79/Add.62, paras. 9 and 21 (Zambia); UN Doc. CCPR/C/79/Add.51, para. 20 (Yemen); UN Doc. CCPR/C/79/Add.44, para. 9 (Morocco); UN Doc. CCPR/C/79/Add.43, para. 10 (Tunisia); UN Doc. CCPR/C/79/Add.42, para. 8 (Nepal); UN Doc. CCPR/C/79/Add.45, para. 6 (Lybia).

772 UN Doc. CCPR/CO/77/MLI, para. 10 (Mali); UN Doc. CCPR/CO/80/SUR, para. 18 (Suriname); UN Doc. CCPR/CO/76/TGO, para. 21 (Togo); UN Doc. CCPR/CO/75/YEM, para. 10 (Yemen): priority concern; UN Doc. CCPR/CO/72/MCO, para. 12 (Monaco): the minimum age for marriage is to be 18 years; UN Doc. CCPR/CO/KWT, para. 7 (Kuwait); UN Doc. CCPR/C/79/Add.116, para. 10 (Cameroon); UN Doc. CCPR/C/79/Add.113, para. 12 (Morocco); UN Doc. CCPR/C/79/Add.102, para. 16 (Japan); UN Doc. CCPR/C/79/Add.97, para. 13 (Tanzania); UN Doc. CCPR/C/79/Add.89, para. 12 (Zimbabwe).

773 UN Doc. CCPR/CO/77/MLI, para. 10 (Mali): priority concern.

774 UN Doc. CCPR/CO/83/KEN, para. 10 (Kenya) (priority concern); UN Doc. CCPR/CO/82/MAR, para. 33 (Morocco); UN Doc. CCPR/CO/77/MLI, para. 10 (Mali): priority concern; UN Doc. CCPR/CO/76/TGO, paras. 21 (Togo); UN Doc. CCPR/CO/75/YEM, para. 9 (Yemen): priority concern; UN Doc. CCPR/CO/70/GAB, paras. 8-9 (Gabon); UN Doc. CCPR/CO/KWT, paras. 7-8 (Kuwait); UN Doc. CCPR/C/79/Add.116, para. 10 (Cameroon); UN Doc. CCPR/C/79/Add.113, para. 12 (Morocco); UN Doc. CCPR/C/79/Add.101, para. 17 (Libya); UN Doc. CCPR/C/79/Add.95, para. 13 (Algeria); UN Doc. CCPR/C/79/Add.82, para. 12 (Senegal); UN Doc. CCPR/C/79/Add.65, para. 25 (Nigeria).
In UN Doc. HRI/GEN/1/Rev.7, General Comment No. 28 (2000), *The Equality of Rights Between Men and Women*, para. 24, the HRC has unequivocally stated that polygamy is an inadmissible discrimination against women.

775 UN Doc. CCPR/CO/76/EGY, para. 10 (Egypt); UN Doc. CCPR/CO/75/YEM, para. 11 (Yemen): priority concern; UN Doc. CCPR/CO/72/MCO, para. 10 (Monaco); UN Doc. CCPR/C/79/Add.101, para. 17 (Libya); UN Doc. CCPR/C/79/Add.44, para. 9 (Morocco); UN Doc. CCPR/C/79/Add.43, paras. 10 and 18 (Tunisia); UN Doc. CCPR/C/79/Add.42, para. 8 (Nepal).

776 UN Doc. CCPR/C/79/Add.90, para. 11 (Uruguay).

777 UN Doc. CCPR/C/79/Add.43, paras. 10 and 18 (Tunisia).

778 UN Doc. CCPR/C/79/Add.11, para. 12 (Tanzania).

779 UN Doc. CCPR/C/79/Add.43, paras. 10 and 18 (Tunisia).

maintenance;[780] adultery;[781] and the right to remarry.[782] Wife inheritance,[783] forced marriage[784] and female genital mutilation[785] have been qualified as being "against equality rights of women."[786] Inheritance rights,[787] property and land rights,[788] and income tax[789] have equally preoccupied the Committee. The HRC has also expressed concern about the fact that women were kept in detention because of rejection by their family.[790]

Another cluster of concerns pertains to women's freedom of movement,[791] *e.g.* their right to leave the house[792] or the country,[793] issues of immigration,[794] applications for

---

780 UN Doc. CCPR/CO/82/MAR, para. 33 (Morocco); UN Doc. CCPR/CO/77/MLI, para. 10 (Mali): priority concern; UN Doc. CCPR/CO/76/EGY, para. 8 (Egypt); UN Doc. CCPR/CO/72/MCO, para. 9 (Monaco); UN Doc. CCPR/C/79/Add.121, para. 13 (Guyana); UN Doc. CCPR/C/79/Add.113, para. 12 (Morocco); UN Doc. CCPR/C/79/Add.109, para. 18 (Mexico); UN Doc. CCPR/C/79/Add.101, para. 17 (Libya); UN Doc. CCPR/C/79/Add.97, para. 12 (Tanzania); UN Doc. CCPR/C/79/Add.81, para. 17 (India); UN Doc. CCPR/C/79/Add.72, para. 16 (Peru); UN Doc. CCPR/C/79/Add.62, para. 9 (Zambia); UN Doc. CCPR/C/79/Add.44, para. 9 (Morocco); UN Doc. CCPR/C/79/Add.101, para. 5 (Libya); UN Doc. CCPR/C/79/Add.93, para. 29 (Israel); UN Doc. CCPR/C/79/Add.43, para. 6 (Tunisia).

781 UN Doc. CCPR/CO/70/VEN, para. 22 (Venezuela).

782 *Idem*; UN Doc. CCPR/C/79/Add.109, para. 18 (Mexico); UN Doc. CCPR/C/79/Add.102, para. 16 (Japan).

783 UN Doc. CCPR/CO/83/KEN, para. 10 (Kenya) (priority concern).

784 UN Doc. CCPR/CO/83/UZB, para. 24 (Uzbekistan); UN Doc. CCPR/C/79/Add.65, paras. 25 and 29 (Nigeria).

785 UN Doc. CCPR/CO/83/KEN, para. 12 (Kenya); UN Doc. CCPR/CO/82/BEN, para. 11 (Benin): priority concern; UN Doc. CCPR/CO/77/MLI, para. 11 (Mali): priority concern; UN Doc. CCPR/CO/75/YEM, para. 6 (Yemen): priority concern; UN Doc. CCPR/C/79/Add.89, para. 12 (Zimbabwe); UN Doc. CCPR/C/79/Add.65, para. 29 (Nigeria).

786 Compare with article 16 CEDAW and the CEDAW Committee's approach (see further in this chapter).

787 UN Doc. CCPR/CO/83/KEN, para. 10 (Kenya) (priority concern); UN Doc. CCPR/CO/82/MAR, para. 33 (Morocco); UN Doc. CCPR/CO/77/MLI, para. 10 (Mali); UN Doc. CCPR/CO/76/TGO, para. 22 (Togo); UN Doc. CCPR/CO/76/EGY, para. 10 (Egypt); UN Doc. CCPR/CO/70/GAB, paras. 8-9 (Gabon); UN Doc. CCPR/C/79/Add.121, para. 13 (Guyana); UN Doc. CCPR/C/79/Add.116, para. 9 (Cameroon); UN Doc. CCPR/C/79/Add.106, para. 10 (Lesotho); UN Doc. CCPR/C/79/Add.101, para. 17 (Libya); UN Doc. CCPR/C/79/Add.89, para. 12 (Zimbabwe); UN Doc. CCPR/C/79/Add.82, para. 12 (Senegal); UN Doc. CCPR/C/79/Add.84, para. 13 (Iraq); UN Doc. CCPR/C/79/Add.81, para. 17 (India); UN Doc. CCPR/C/79/Add.62, para. 9 (Zambia); UN Doc. CCPR/C/79/Add.45, para. 12 (Lybia); UN Doc. CCPR/C/79/Add.44, para. 9 (Morocco); UN Doc. CCPR/C/79/Add.42, para. 8 (Nepal); UN Doc. CCPR/C/79/Add.25, para. 13 (Iran); UN Doc. CCPR/C/79/Add.119, para. 7 (United Kingdom – Crown Dependencies).

788 UN Doc. CCPR/CO/83/KEN, para. 10 (Kenya) (priority concern); UN Doc. CCPR/C/79/Add.106, para. 10 (Lesotho); UN Doc. CCPR/C/79/Add.104, para. 17 (Chile); UN Doc. CCPR/C/79/Add.97, para. 12 (Tanzania); UN Doc. CCPR/C/79/Add.56, para. 25 (Sri Lanka); UN Doc. CCPR/C/79/Add.11, para. 12 (Tanzania).

789 UN Doc. CCPR/CO/72/NET, para. 15 (Netherlands).

790 UN Doc. CCPR/CO/75/YEM, para. 12 (Yemen): priority concern.

791 UN Doc. CCPR/C/79/Add.101, para. 17 (Libya).

792 UN Doc. CCPR/CO/75/YEM, para. 8 (Yemen): priority concern; UN Doc. CCPR/C/79/Add.51, para. 14 (Yemen).

793 UN Doc. CCPR/C/79/Add.78, paras. 18-19 (Lebanon); UN Doc. CCPR/C/79/Add.44, para. 9 (Morocco); UN Doc. CCPR/C/79/Add.35, para. 7 (Jordan).

794 UN Doc. CCPR/C/79/Add.88, para. 10 (Cyprus).

asylum,[795] admittance and deportation,[796] the registration of alien husbands of women citizens,[797] and the acquisition of nationality.[798]

In the area of justice, equal access to legal services is to be guaranteed to women.[799] The Committee has identified many problematic issues in the field of criminal justice, including the absence of a penalty if a rapist marries the raped woman,[800] the lack of prosecution of rape,[801] and sexual exploitation of foreign women.[802] Violence against women, including domestic violence,[803] gained growing attention in the latter half of the 1990s.[804] The Committee has qualified trafficking of women as a violation of *inter alia* art. 3 CCPR.[805]

In the broad field of economic and social rights, it has expressed concern about the lower life expectancy of women,[806] restrictions on abortion[807] and the lack of equal

795 UN Doc. CCPR/CO/70/DNK, para. 14 (Denmark).

796 UN Doc. CCPR/CO/72/NET, para. 23 (Netherlands).

797 UN Doc. A/55/40, para. 29 (Ireland).

798 UN Doc. CCPR/CO/75/YEM, para. 11 (Yemen): priority concern; UN Doc. CCPR/C/79/Add.88, para. 10 (Cyprus); UN Doc. CCPR/C/79/Add.45, para. 12 (Lybia); UN Doc. CCPR/C/79/Add.35, para. 7 (Jordan).

799 UN Doc. A/55/40, para. 505 (Australia); UN Doc. CCPR/C/79/Add.40, para. 16 (Slovenia); UN Doc. CCPR/C/79/Add.39, para. 20 (Cyprus); UN Doc. CCPR/C/79/Add.11, para. 12 (Tanzania).

800 UN Doc. CCPR/CO/76/EGY, para. 9 (Egypt); UN Doc. CCPR/CO/72/GTM, paras. 24 (Guatemala); UN Doc. CCPR/CO/70/VEN, para. 20 (Venezuela); UN Doc. CCPR/C/79/Add.120, para. 8 (Mongolia); UN Doc. CCPR/C/79/Add.113, paras. 12 and 14 (Morocco); UN Doc. CCPR/C/79/Add.97, paras. 11 and 15 (Tanzania); UN Doc. CCPR/C/79/Add.78, paras. 18-19 (Lebanon); UN Doc. CCPR/C/79/Add.72, para. 15 (Peru); UN Doc. CCPR/C/79/Add.48, paras. 16 and 27 (Paraguay); UN Doc. CCPR/C/79/Add.42, para. 8 (Nepal).

801 UN Doc. CCPR/CO/83/ISL, para. 11 (Iceland): priority concern.

802 UN Doc. CCPR/CO/72/NET, para. 10 (The Netherlands).

803 UN Doc. CCPR/CO/83/MUS, para. 10 (Mauritius); UN Doc. CCPR/CO/83/UZB, para. 23 (Uzbekistan); UN Doc. CCPR/CO/83/ISL, para. 12 (Iceland); UN Doc. CPR/CO/82/ALB, para. 10 (Albania); UN Doc. CCPR/CO/82/POL, para. 11 (Poland); UN Doc. CCPR/CO/82/MAR, para. 28 (Morocco); UN Doc. CCPR/CO/82/BEN, para. 9 (Benin).

804 UN Doc. CCPR/CO/79/RUS, para. 9 (Russian Federation); UN Doc. CCPR/CO/78/SVK, para. 9 (Slovakia); UN Doc. CCPR/CO/77/MLI, para. 12 (Mali): priority concern; UN Doc. CCPR/CO/80/LTU, para. 9 (Lithuania): priority concern; UN Doc. CCPR/CO/80/SUR, para. 12 (Suriname); UN Doc. CCPR/CO/80/DEU, para. 14 (Germany); UN Doc. CCPR/CO/79/LVA, para. 13 (Latvia); UN Doc. CCPR/CO/75/YEM, para. 6 (Yemen): priority concern; UN Doc. CCPR/CO/75/VNM, para. 17 (Viet Nam); UN Doc. CCPR/CO/72/CZE, para. 14 (Czech Republic); UN Doc. CCPR/CO/71/UZB, paras. 19-20 (Uzbekistan): priority concern; UN Doc. CCPR/CO/70/ARG, para. 15 (Argentina); UN Doc. CCPR/C/79/Add.118, para. 10 (Congo); UN Doc. CCPR/C/79/Add.101, para. 17 (Libya); UN Doc. CCPR/C/79/Add.94, para. 19 (Italy); UN Doc. CCPR/C/79/Add.81, para. 16 (India). See also Joseph, Schultz and Castan, supra note 53, 738-739.

805 UN Doc. CCPR/CO/83/GRC, para. 10 (Greece); UN Doc. CPR/CO/82/ALB, para. 15 (Albania); UN Doc. CCPR/CO/81/SEMO, para. 16 (Serbia and Montenegro); UN Doc. CCPR/CO/80/LTU, para. 14 (Lithuania); UN Doc. CCPR/CO/80/SUR, para. 13 (Suriname); UN Doc. CCPR/CO/72/CZE, para. 13 (Czech Republic).

806 UN Doc. CCPR/C/79/Add.42, para. 8 (Nepal).

807 UN Doc. CCPR/C/79/Add.97, para. 15 (Tanzania).

access to all methods of family planning[808] with regard to the right to health. It has also paid attention to education,[809] including academic enrolment,[810] and to poverty among women.[811]

ii. Marriage, Pregnancy, Childbirth

The HRC seems to consider discrimination on the basis of marriage, pregnancy and childbirth as sex/gender discrimination. It has expressed concern about dismissals on ground of marriage, pregnancy or childbirth,[812] and on the requirement of pregnancy and sterilisation certificates.[813] Under the articles 3 and 26 CCPR, it has equally pronounced itself on the lack of registration of customary marriages, and customary married women's deprivation of rights with regard to inheritance and land ownership.[814]

iii. Sexual Orientation

Sexual orientation has been considered to be included in the concept of sex, rather than to be falling under "other status".[815] The mere refusal to provide for marriage between homosexual couples was not considered to constitute a violation.[816] However, differential treatment of same-sex partners on the one hand, who were excluded from pension benefits, and of married or unmarried heterosexual partners on the other hand, who were granted such benefits as they were considered to be surviving dependants of military service personnel, was held to be in violation of article 26 CCPR.[817]

---

808 UN Doc. CCPR/C/79/Add.109, para. 11 (Poland).

809 UN Doc. CCPR/CO/82/MAR, para. 26 (Morocco); UN Doc. CCPR/CO/77/MLI, para. 13 (Mali); UN Doc. CCPR/CO/69/KGZ, para. 13 (Kyrgyzstan); UN Doc. CCPR/C/79/Add.117, para. 16 (China – Hong Kong); UN Doc. CCPR/C/79/Add.116, para. 11 (Cameroon); UN Doc. CCPR/C/79/Add.108, para. 17 (Cambodia); UN Doc. CCPR/C/79/Add.97, para. 12 (Tanzania); UN Doc. CCPR/C/79/Add.96, para. 13 (Macedonia); UN Doc. CCPR/C/79/Add.88, para. 10 (Cyprus); UN Doc. CCPR/C/79/Add.70, para. 12 (Switzerland); UN Doc. CCPR/C/79/Add.62, para. 9 (Zambia); UN Doc. CCPR/C/79/Add.44, para. 9 (Morocco); UN Doc. CCPR/C/79/Add.42, para. 8 (Nepal); UN Doc. CCPR/C/79/Add.101, para. 5 (Libya); UN Doc. CCPR/C/79/Add.75, para. 8 (Georgia).

810 UN Doc. A/55/40, para. 505 (Australia).

811 UN Doc. CCPR/CO/79/RUS, para. 9 (Russian Federation).

812 UN Doc. CCPR/C/79/Add.102, para. 5 (Japan).

813 UN Doc. CCPR/C/79/Add.66, para. 30 (Brazil).

814 UN Doc. CCPR/CO/81/NAM, para. 9 (Namibia): priority concern.

815 UN Doc. CCPR/C/78/D/94/2000, Communication No. 941/2000, *Young v. Australia*, para. 10.4; UN Doc. CCPR/C/50/D/488/1992, Communication No. 488/1992, *Nicholas Toonen v. Australia*, para. 8.7. For a critique, see Joseph, Schultz and Castan, supra note 53, 691.

816 UN Doc. CCPR/C/75/D/902/1999, Communication No.902/1999, *Joslin et al. v. New Zealand*, para. 8.3.

817 UN Doc. CCPR/C/78/D/941/2000, Communication No. 941/2000, *Young v. Australia*, para. 10.4.

In its concluding observations, the HRC has raised the issue of discrimination on grounds of sexual orientation,[818] and identified issues of discrimination against same-sex partners with regard to the minimum age of consent for sexual relations,[819] the penalization of sexual relations between adult, consenting same-sex partners[820] carried out in private,[821] and the prohibition of immigration for persons deemed to be homosexuals.[822] The possibility of registration of partnerships was welcomed.[823]

d. *Language*

Discrimination on the basis of language was accepted in the case of *Diergaardt v. Namibia*. Prohibiting civil servants to communicate in a minority language – *i.e.* Afrikaans, formerly the official language – was held to be in violation of art. 26.[824] In other cases of alleged discrimination on the ground of language, no violation was found.[825]

In its concluding observations, the HRC has predominantly paid attention to language as a ground of discrimination from the perspective of minorities (see further).

e. *Religion*

No discrimination on religious grounds has been found so far in individual complaints. In *Singh Bhinder v. Canada*, the Committee held that the requirement for all

---

818 UN Doc. CCPR/CO/83/GRC, para. 19 (Greece); UN Doc. CCPR/CO/82/POL, para. 18 (Poland); UN Doc. CCPR/CO/81/NAM, para. 22 (Namibia).

819 UN Doc. CCPR/C/79/Add.103, para. 13 (Austria).

820 UN Doc. CCPR/CO/83/KEN, para. 27 (Kenya).

821 UN Doc. CCPR/CO/76/EGY, para. 19 (Egypt); UN Doc. CCPR/C/79/Add.104, para. 20 (Chile); UN Doc. CCPR/C/79/Add.88, para. 11 (Cyprus); UN Doc. CCPR/C/79/Add.50, para. 22 (United States of America).

822 UN Doc. CCPR/C/79/Add.89, para. 24 (Zimbabwe).

823 UN Doc. CCPR/C/79/Add.27, para. 7 (Norway).

824 UN Doc. CPR/C/69/D/760/1997, Communication No. 760/1997, *Diergaardt et al. v. Namibia*, para. 10.10. Compare with UN Doc. CCPR/CO/81/NAM, para. 21 (Namibia), in which the HRC expressed concern that those persons who did not speak the official language might be discriminated against in the administration of public affairs and in the administration of justice.

825 The Committee held that the prohibition to use commercial advertising outdoors in other than the French language in Quebec was not discriminatory, as this prohibition applied to French speakers as well as English speakers, so that a French speaking person wishing to advertise in English, in order to reach those of his or her clientele who are English speaking, was neither able to do so (UN Doc. CCPR/C/47/D/359/1989, Communication Nos. 359/1989, 385/1989, *Ballantyne, Davidson & Mcintyre v. Canada*, para. 11.5).
The services of an interpreter were available under French law to those unable to speak or understand French. The Breton complainant was found to be sufficiently proficient in the court's language (*i.e.* French), and therefore no discrimination on the basis of language was found to have taken place in refusing him an interpreter (UN Doc. CCPR/C/41/D/221/1987, Communication Nos. 221/1987, 323/1988, *Cadoret & Le Bihan v. France*, para. 5.8).

workers in federal service, including for people of the Sikh religion, to wear a hard hat was compatible with the Covenant.[826]

In its concluding observations, the HRC has expressed concern about the special status accorded to some religions in public law.[827] No differentiation between religions should be made on account of their recognition as official religion or belief,[828] or their registration/recognition.[829] Registration requirements[830] or practices[831] are not to be discriminatory. Preferential treatment, such as financial subsidies or benefits accorded, or the entitlement to own property and receive foreign funding, that is granted to a particular religious denomination constitutes religious discrimination.[832]

Religious discrimination may take place in education,[833] employment (by allowing religious bodies directing hospitals and schools to discriminate in certain circumstances on the ground of religion in employing persons whose functions are not religious),[834] or the restitution of Church property.[835] Members of religious communities might be discriminated against positively (through economic privileges)[836] or negatively. In the latter case, issues of discrimination relate to access (eligibility for public office;[837] participation in (presidential) elections)[838] as well as to the freedom to practice and manifest one's religion[839] or to exercise one's right to religious education.[840] The Committee has also expressed concern about the effect of mechanisms for monitoring new religious movements on the actual enjoyment of religious freedom on equal terms by members of all denominations in Poland.[841]

---

826 *E.g.* UN Doc. CCPR/C/37/D/208/1986, Communication No. 208/1986, *Singh Bhinder v. Canada*, para. 6.2.

827 UN Doc. CCPR/C/79/Add.104, para. 24 (Chile).

828 UN Doc. CCPR/C/79/Add.100, para. 19 (Armenia); UN Doc. CCPR/C/79/Add.25, para. 22 (Iran).

829 UN Doc. CCPR/CO/81/BEL, para. 26 (Belgium); UN Doc. CCPR/CO/72/CZE, para. 22 (Czech Republic).

830 UN Doc. CCPR/CO/80/LTU, para. 16 (Lithuania); UN Doc. CCPR/C/79/Add.87, para. 18 (Lithuania).

831 UN Doc. CCPR/CO/74/HUN, para. 14 (Hungary).

832 UN Doc. CCPR/CO/81/LIE, para. 13 (Liechtenstein); UN Doc. CCPR/CO/77/LUX, para. 7 (Luxemburg); UN Doc. CCPR/CO/70/ARG, para. 15 (Argentina); UN Doc. CCPR/C/79/Add.103, para. 15 (Austria); UN Doc. CCPR/C/79/Add.100, para. 19 (Armenia); UN Doc. CCPR/C/79/Add.93, para. 28 (Israel); UN Doc. CCPR/C/79/Add.11, para. 8 (Luxemburg).

833 UN Doc. CCPR/C/79/Add.107, para. 16 (Costa Rica); UN Doc. CCPR/C/79/Add.85, para. 23 (Sudan).

834 UN Doc. A/55/40, para. 22 (Ireland).

835 UN Doc. CCPR/CO/74/HUN, para. 14 (Hungary).

836 UN Doc. CCPR/C/79/Add.25, para. 22 (Iran).

837 UN Doc. CCPR/C/79/Add.43, para. 10 (Tunisia); UN Doc. CCPR/C/79/Add.25, para. 22 (Iran).

838 UN Doc. CCPR/C/79/Add.43, para. 18 (Tunisia).

839 *Ibid.*, para. 13 (Tunisia); UN Doc. CCPR/C/79/Add.25, para. 22 (Iran).

840 UN Doc. CCPR/C/79/Add.31, para. 13 (Costa Rica).

841 UN Doc. CCPR/C/79/Add.109, para. 24 (Poland).

A different issue concerns discrimination against Muslim women in the fields of marriage and inheritance due to the non-application of general civil law.[842]

f. *Political or Other Opinion*

Discrimination on the basis of political opinion has been found in a number of individual complaints. In *Kang v. Korea*, the Committee held that the "oath of law-abidance system", which was applied in a discriminatory fashion with a view to alter the political opinion of an inmate, by offering inducements of preferential treatment within prison and improved possibilities of parole, restricted freedom of expression and of manifestation of belief on the discriminatory basis of political opinion.[843] Discrimination on the ground of political opinions and open criticism of, and opposition to, the Government and the ruling political party was found to have taken place in *Oló Bahamonde v. Equatorial Guinea.*[844] In *Nuri Jazairi v. Canada*, the Committee held that the absence of protection against discrimination on the basis of political belief raises an issue under the Covenant, and that the absence of a remedy for a victim of discrimination on political grounds in the field of employment might constitute a violation. It considered the complaint in the particular case however hypothetical. A minority considered the absence of political opinion as a prohibited ground of discrimination in the domestic legal order to be in violation of the CCPR.[845] Differential treatment of conscientious objectors on the basis of their conviction of conscience, compared to those fulfilling their military service,[846] might be considered under the ground of "other opinion". The exemption from military service of only one group of conscientious objectors, *i.e.* Jehovah's Witnesses, can also be said to be based on opinion.[847]

---

842 UN Doc. CCPR/CO/83/GRC, para. 8 (Greece).

843 UN Doc. CCPR/C/78/D/878/1999, Communication No. 878/1999, *Kang v. Korea*, para. 7.2.

844 UN Doc. CCPR/C/49/D/468/1991, Communication No. 468/91, *Oló Bahamonde v. Equatorial Guinea*, para. 9.5. For differentiation based on political opinion in a more distant sense, *i.e.* according priority in recruitment to former civil servants dismissed on political, ideological or trade union grounds under the previous regime, see UN Doc. CCPR/C/30/D/198/1985, Communication No. 198/1985, *Stalla Costa v. Uruguay*, para. 10.

845 UN Doc. CCPR/C/82/D/958/2000, Communication no. 958/2000, *Nuri Jazairi v. Canada*, para. 7 and dissenting opinion, para. 6.

846 UN Doc. CCPR/C/67/D/689/1996, Communication No. 689/1996, *Maille v. France*, para. 10.4; UN Doc. CCPR/C/69/D/690/1996, Communication No. 690/1996, *Venier and Nicolas v. France*, para. 10.4; UN Doc. CCPR/C/67/D/666/1995, Communication No. 666/1995, *Foin v. France*, para. 10.3; UN Doc. CCPR/C/39/D/295/1988, Communication No. 295/1988, *Järvinen v. Finland*, para. 6.5.

847 The Committee has not really examined the ground of the alleged discrimination in this case (UN Doc. CCPR/C/48/D/402/1990, Communication No. 402/1990, *Brinkhof v. the Netherlands*).

In the Committee's concluding observations, issues of discrimination on the basis of political opinion have arisen with regard to access to media[848] and the right of access to public service.[849] As to conscientious objection, very much the same issues as in the individual complaints procedure have been dealt with, *i.e.* the grounds and eligibility for alternative service,[850] and the treatment of conscientious objectors compared to those fulfilling military service.[851] The HRC has expressed concern about the terms of alternative service,[852] and stressed that it should not be punitive[853] nor discriminatory,[854] and be of the same length as military service.[855]

g. *National or Social Origin*

In its concluding observations, the HRC has expressed concern about discrimination on the basis of ethnic origin on the labour market;[856] with regard to access to public service, and in the administration, the army, the police, the gendarmerie, the security forces and the judiciary;[857] with regard to the conduct of public affairs,[858] stop and search practices,[859] deportation,[860] refusal of access to public places,[861] education[862] and housing.[863] The HRC has expressed particular concern about the disproportionate number of Roma children who are assigned to special schools designed for mentally

848 UN Doc. CCPR/CO/76/TGO, para. 17 (Togo); UN Doc. CCPR/CO/75/MDA, para. 14 (Moldova).

849 UN Doc. CCPR/C/79/Add.59, paras. 14 and 26 (Estonia).

850 UN Doc. CCPR/CO/82/FIN, para. 14 (Finland); UN Doc. CCPR/CO/80/LTU, para. 16 (Lithuania); UN Doc. CCPR/CO/73/UKR, para. 20 (Ukraine); UN Doc. CCPR/CO/71/VEN, para. 26 (Venezuela); UN Doc. CCPR/CO/69, para. 18 (Kyrgyzstan); UN Doc. CCPR/C/79/Add.111, para. 17 (Romania); UN Doc. CCPR/C/79/Add.91, para. 21 (Finland): preferential treatment of Jehova's witnesses; UN Doc. CCPR/C/79/Add.87, para. 19 (Lithuania).

851 UN Doc. CCPR/CO/75/VNM, para. 17 (Viet Nam); UN Doc. CCPR/CO/73/AZE, para. 21 (Azerbaijan); UN Doc. CCPR/CO/71/DOM, para. 21 (Dominican Republic); UN Doc. CCPR/C/79/Add.88, para. 17 (Cyprus).

852 UN Doc. CCPR/CO/79/LVA, para. 15 (Latvia); UN Doc. CCPR/CO/74/GEO, para. 18 (Georgia); UN Doc. CCPR/CO/69, para. 18 (Kyrgyzstan); UN Doc. CCPR/C/79/Add.39, paras. 10 and 19 (Cyprus).

853 UN Doc. CCPR/CO/82/POL, para. 15 (Poland); UN Doc. CCPR/CO/80/LTU, para. 16 (Lithuania).

854 UN Doc. CCPR/CO/82/FIN, para. 14 (Finland); UN Doc. CCPR/CO/82/MAR, para. 22 (Morocco).

855 UN Doc. CCPR/CO/79/RUS, para. 9 (Russian Federation).

856 UN Doc. CCPR/CO/80/DEU, para. 21 (Germany); UN Doc. CCPR/CO/74/SWE, para. 13 (Sweden); UN Doc. CCPR/CO/72/GTM, para. 29 (Guatemala); UN Doc. CCPR/C/79/Add.58, para. 5 (Sweden).

857 UN Doc. CCPR/CO/78/PRT, para. 8 (Portugal): priority concern; UN Doc. CCPR/CO/73/UK;CCPR/CO/73/UKOT, para. 13 (United Kingdom and Overseas Territories); UN Doc. CCPR/C/79/Add.56, para. 40 (Sri Lanka); UN Doc. CCPR/C/79/Add.41, para. 14 (Burundi).

858 UN Doc. CCPR/C/79/Add.56, para. 40 (Sri Lanka); UN Doc. CCPR/C/79/Add.41, para. 14 (Burundi).

859 UN Doc. CCPR/C/79/Add.55, para. 14 (United Kingdom).

860 UN Doc. CCPR/CO/80/DEU, para. 21 (Germany).

861 UN Doc. CCPR/CO/74/SWE, para. 13 (Sweden); UN Doc. CCPR/CO/70/DNK, para. 14 (Denmark).

862 UN Doc. CCPR/CO/80/DEU, para. 21 (Germany); UN Doc. CCPR/CO/72/GTM, para. 29 (Guatemala).

863 UN Doc. CCPR/CO/80/DEU, para. 21 (Germany).

disabled children. The use of stereotypes based on the child's ethnic group in placement decisions is in contravention of article 26 of the Covenant.[864]

The HRC has condemned the circulation of a list of persons grouped on the basis of their ethnic origin.[865]

h. Birth

Differential treatment with regard to foster and natural children as to entitlements to family allowances, *i.e.* the requirement that a foster parent be involved in the upbringing of its foster child as a precondition to the granting of benefits, has been found not to be contrary to article 26 CCPR.[866] Indirect discrimination was found against children born out of wedlock with regard to social security benefits. The surviving parent of a half-orphan was not entitled to orphan benefits under previous legislation. Under new 1996 legislation, the surviving parent was, but only in case the child was born after the date of entry into force of that legislation. The Committee held that the exclusion of previously-born children out of wedlock out of the application of the new law amounted to indirect discrimination.[867]

In its concluding observations, the HRC has consistently held that all discrimination against children out of wedlock was to be abolished,[868] in particular also with regard to inheritance rights.[869] It has repeatedly welcomed equal rights for children born in and out of wedlock.[870] Children born out of registered customary marriages are to be granted the same rights as those born out of a marriage under civil law.[871]

---

864 UN Doc. CCPR/CO/78/SVK, para. 18 (Slovakia): priority concern; UN Doc. CCPR/CO/74/HUN, para. 7 (Hungary): priority concern; UN Doc. CCPR/CO/72/CZE, para. 9 (Czech Republic): priority concern.

865 UN Doc. CCPR/C/79/Add.15, paras. 7 and 9 (Croatia).

866 UN Doc. CCPR/C/46/D/406/1990, Communication Nos. 406/90 and 426/90, *Oulajin and Kaiss v. The Netherlands.*

867 UN Doc. CCPR/C/80/D/976/2001, Communication No. 976/2001, *Derksen v. The Netherlands*, para. 9.3.

868 UN Doc. CCPR/CO/77/LUX, para. 9 (Luxemburg); UN Doc. CCPR/CO/73/UK; CCPR/CO/73/UKOT, para. 30 (UK and Overseas Territories); UN Doc. CCPR/CO/72/MCO, para. 11 (Monaco); UN Doc. CCPR/CO/72/NET, para. 21 (Netherlands); UN Doc. CCPR/C/79/Add.102, para. 12 (Japan); UN Doc. CCPR/C/79/Add.101, para. 18 (Libya); UN Doc. CCPR/C/79/Add.98, para. 11 (Iceland); UN Doc. CCPR/C/79/Add.28, para. 17 (Japan).

869 UN Doc. CCPR/C/79/Add.80, para. 25 (France).

870 UN Doc. CCPR/C/79/Add.119, para. 7 (United Kingdom – Crown Dependencies); UN Doc. CCPR/C/79/Add.102, para. 4 (Japan); UN Doc. CCPR/C/79/Add.60, para. 6 (Mauritius); UN Doc. CCPR/C/79/Add.29, para. 5 (Malta); UN Doc. CCPR/C/79/Add.3, para. 3 (Belgium).

871 UN Doc. CCPR/CO/81/NAM, para. 9 (Namibia): priority concern.

i. Other Status

Finally, article 26 CCPR also mentions the open-ended ground of "other status". What is to be considered as "other status" has been decided in the Committee's decisions on a case-by-case basis.[872] The test criterion is not fully clear (see above). Initially, it seemed to be whether there was an identifiable distinct category, a group united by a common "other" status.[873] The HRC may however have introduced a new test for "other status" in *van Oord v. The Netherlands*,[874] *i.e.* whether a relevant distinction exists between the categories of persons being compared.[875]

i. Nationality

In the Committee's views on individual communications, nationality or citizenship has been identified as a prohibited ground of discrimination, with regard to the restitution of confiscated property,[876] pension rights[877] and the capacity to stand for the election of work councils.[878] There has been some debate as to whether differential treatment based on nationality falls under the ground of "national or social origin", or rather under "other status".[879] Lester and Joseph question the equation of nationality with national origin. They submit that nationality refers to one's administrative status as a certain state's citizen, whereas national origin refers to one's ethnic background.[880] In *Karakurt v. Austria*, the dissenting Committee members Rodley and Scheinin submitted in the same vein that distinctions based on citizenship fell under the notion of "other status".[881] The majority of the Committee, by accepting Austria's reservation, according to which article 26 CCPR did not exclude different treatment of Austrian citizens and aliens, as was also permissible under article 1, para. 2 ICERD, considered the complaint of discrimination in light of the grounds of discrimination enumerated in ICERD, *i.e.* race, colour, descent or national or ethnic origin. The discussion in

---

872 Lester and Joseph, supra note 8, 568; Joseph, Schultz and Castan, supra note 53, 689.

873 UN Doc. CCPR/C//D/273/1989, Communication No. 273/1989, *B.d.B. v. The Netherlands*, para. 6.7.

874 UN Doc. CCPR/C/60/D/658/1995, Communication No. 658/1995, *van Oord v. The Netherlands*, para. 8.5.

875 For a critique, see Joseph, Schultz and Castan, supra note 53, 690.

876 UN Doc. CCPR/C/74/D/747/1997, Communication No. 747/1997, *Des Fours Walderode v. The Czech Republic*, para. 8.4; UN Doc. CCPR/C/57/D/586/1994, Communication No. 586/94, *Adam v. The Czech Republic.*

877 UN Doc. CCPR/C/35/D/196/1985, Communication No. 196/1985, *Gueye v. France*, para. 9.4.

878 UN Doc. CCPR/C/74/D/965/2000, Communication No. 965/2000, *Karakurt v. Austria.*

879 This question has also arisen under the CESCR, see Sepúlveda, supra note 108, 393.As pointed out higher, the complaint about differential treatment of a woman of Roma origin, which was phrased as being based on the ground of race, should rather have referred to national origin (supra note 732).

880 Lester and Joseph, supra note 8, 568, footnote 33.

881 UN Doc. CCPR/C/74/D/965/2000, Communication No. 965/2000, *Karakurt v. Austria.* They found support for this view in the Committee's decision in UN Doc. CCPR/C/35/D/196/1985, Communication No. 196/1985, *Gueye v. France*, para. 9.4.

Karakurt v. Austria was not purely of theoretical or conceptual importance. If citizenship was a self-standing issue under the CCPR, falling under the notion of "other status" and unrelated to the grounds of discrimination enumerated by article 1, para. 1 ICERD, the Committee would not be barred by the reservation (as it accepted it was) from assessing whether a distinction based on citizenship was *per se* incompatible with article 26. The majority held in the present case that only a distinction *among* aliens concerning the capacity to stand for the election for a work council solely on the basis of a different nationality was not reasonable.[882]

In its concluding observations too, the Committee has frequently addressed discrimination based on nationality or citizenship. It has identified as not permissible distinctions between citizens and non-citizens,[883] between citizens by birth and citizens by naturalization,[884] and among aliens.[885] In a number of cases, the HRC has also pinpointed discrimination in the acquisition of nationality for certain groups.[886] The Baltic states in particular have tended to keep a large proportion of people as non-citizens, who by law are treated neither as foreigners nor as stateless persons but as a distinct category of persons with long-lasting and effective ties with the country, but without the rights that come with full citizenship.[887]

ii. Descent

On two occasions, the HRC has paid attention to discrimination based on caste.[888] Although Joseph, Schultz and Castan suggest that discrimination based on descent

---

882 UN Doc. CCPR/C/74/D/965/2000, Communication No. 965/2000, *Karakurt v. Austria*, para. 8.4.

883 UN Doc. CCPR/CO/82/MAR, para. 32 (Morocco): transmission of nationality is treated differently between children of a Moroccan versus a non-Moroccan father; UN Doc. CCPR/CO/81/LIE, para. 9 (Liechtenstein); UN Doc. CCPR/C/79/Add.59, para. 26 (Estonia); UN Doc. CCPR/C/79/Add.28, para. 9 (Japan); UN Doc. CCPR/C/79/Add.102, para. 17 (Japan): it is a penal offence for non citizen permanent residents not to carry documentation at all times; UN Doc. CCPR/C/79/Add.28, para. 9 (Japan); UN Doc. CCPR/CO/72/NET, para. 23 (The Netherlands): non citizen domestic workers are not given the same protection by labour laws as citizen workers; UN Doc. CCPR/CO/73/AZE, para. 20 (Azerbaijan): applying the principle of reciprocity for guaranteeing the CCPR rights to non citizens is contrary to the principle of non-discrimination. Also, to guarantee immediate access to legal representation only to citizens is a reason for concern.

884 UN Doc. CCPR/CO/69/KWT, paras. 27, 29 and 32-33 (Kuwait). Limitation in the retention of one's name of origin (UN Doc. CCPR/C/79/Add.26, para. 10 (Iceland)) or in access to certain positions in public life (UN Doc. CCPR/C/79/Add.66, para. 28 (Brazil)) are not permissible.

885 UN Doc. CCPR/CO/78/PRT, para. 17 (Portugal): resident and non-resident aliens; UN Doc. CCPR/CO/73/CH, para. 15 (Switzerland): aliens with and without papers (priority concern).

886 UN Doc. CCPR/CO/72/MCO, para. 17 (Monaco); UN Doc. CCPR/CO/71/SYR, para. 27 (Syria): priority concern; UN Doc. CCPR/CO/69/KWT, paras. 27, 29 and 32-33 (Kuwait); UN Doc. CCPR/C/79/Add.53, para. 27 (Latvia).

887 UN Doc. CCPR/CO/79/LVA, para. 18 (Latvia): priority concern; UN Doc. CCPR/CO/77/EST, para. 14 (Estonia): priority concern.

888 UN Doc. CCPR/C/79/Add.81, para. 15 (India); UN Doc. CCPR/C/79/Add.42, paras. 7-8 (Nepal).

may well be covered by the reference to birth in the CCPR,[889] it is preferred here to consider caste-based discrimination under the notion of "other status".[890]

iii. Disability

In its views on individual communications, the Committee has not yet had the opportunity to express itself on the question whether disability is being covered by the concept of "other status".[891] Disability has been referred to a number of times in concluding observations, though.[892]

iv. Civilian or Military Status

For a long time, the HRC has held – always in cases of social security benefits – that civilians and military were not comparable categories, and declared all complaints inadmissible.[893] To the contrary, in a case of solitary confinement of a serviceman for disciplinary reasons, the question arose whether the lawfulness of this detention had had to be decided upon by a court – as was the case for civilians (article 9, para. 4 CCPR). The HRC held:

> [A]s a general proposition, the Covenant does not contain any provision exempting from its application certain categories of persons. According to article 2, paragraph 1, "each State party to the present Covenant undertakes to respect and to ensure to all individuals within its territory and subject to its jurisdiction the rights recognized in the present Covenant, without distinction of any kind, such as race, colour, sex, language, religion, political or other opinion, national or social origin, property, birth or other status." The all-encompassing character of the terms of this article leaves no room for distinguishing between different categories of persons, such as civilians and members of the military, to the extent of holding the Covenant to be applicable in one case but not in the other. Furthermore, the travaux préparatoires as well as the Committee's general comments indicate that the purpose of the Covenant was to proclaim and define certain human rights for all and to guarantee their enjoyment. It is, therefore, clear that the Covenant is not, and should not be conceived of in terms of whose rights shall be protected but in terms of what rights shall be guaranteed and to what extent.[894]

---

[889] Joseph, Schultz and Castan, supra note 53, 691.

[890] In ICERD, descent is explicitly mentioned as one of the prohibited grounds of discrimination.

[891] Lester and Joseph have submitted that disability should also be a protected status (Lester and Joseph, supra note 8, 568).

[892] UN Doc. CCPR/CO/78/ISR, para. 8 (Israel); UN Doc. CCPR/CO/73/UK; CCPR/CO/73/UKOT, para. 5 (UK and Overseas Territories); UN Doc. A/55/40, para. 503 (Australia); UN Doc. CCPR/C/79/Add.57, para. 8 (United Kingdom – Hong Kong).

[893] See UN Doc. CCPR/C/37/D/297/1988, Communication No. 297/88, *H.A.E.d.J. v. The Netherlands*, para. 8.2; UN Doc. CCPR/C/32/D/267/1987, Communication No. 267/1987, *M.J.G. v. The Netherlands*, para 3.2; UN Doc. CCPR/C/31/D/245/1987, Communication No. 245/1987, *R.T.Z. v. The Netherlands*; UN Doc. CCPR/C/59/D/601/1994, Communication No. 601/1994, *Drake and Drake v. New Zealand*.

[894] See UN Doc. CCPR/C/35/D/265/1987, Communication No. 265/1987, *Vuolanne v. Finland*, para. 9.3.

The Committee dealt with the scope of the Convention as such, not with the scope of the non-discrimination provision. However, by invoking the "all-encompassing character of the terms" of the non-discrimination provision to reject a distinction between civilians and members of the military as to the applicability of article 9, para. 4 CCPR, it is hard to see how the Committee could accept that distinction in the application of the non-discrimination provision itself.

v. Other

Other grounds that have been accepted as being covered by the notion of "other status" include marital status,[895] the place of residence within a state,[896] the public or private nature of schools,[897] being employed or unemployed,[898] the composition of households (shared by close relatives or shared by others),[899] age,[900] health status[901] and dwarfism.[902] Most of them have also been recognized by other Committees.

It is striking to see how few complaints pertaining to discrimination on the basis of other status have been found to be well-founded. The widening of the phrase "other

---

895 UN Doc. CCPR/C/64/D/602/1994, Communication No. 602/1994, *Hoofdman v. The Netherlands*; UN Doc. CCPR/C/44/D/395/1990, Communication No. 395/1990, *Sprenger v. The Netherlands*, para. 7.4; UN Doc. CCPR/C/29/D/172/1984, Communication No. 172/1984, *Danning v. The Netherlands*, paras. 14 and 15. See also Frostell, supra note 140, 40; Joseph, Schultz and Castan, supra note 53, 690.

896 UN Doc. CCPR/C/40D299/1988, Communications Nos. 298-299/88, *Lindgren et al. v. Sweden*, paras. 2.5, 4.9, 4.10 and 10.4. According to Lester and Joseph, this is unlikely as a ground on itself (supra note 8, 568, footnote 37). Compare with the distinction between rural and urban areas as to access to public services like education, medical treatment, legal services (UN Doc. CCPR/CO/80/SUR, para. 19 (Suriname); UN Doc. CCPR/CO/75/MDA, para. 19 (Moldova); UN Doc. A/55/40, para. 505 ((Australia); UN Doc. CCPR/C/79/Add.120, para. 15 (Mongolia)).

897 UN Doc. CCPR/C/40D299/1988, Communications Nos. 298-299/1988, *Lindgren et al. v. Sweden*; UN Doc. CCPR/C/32/D/191/1985, Communication No. 191/1985, *Blom v. Sweden*.

898 UN Doc. CCPR/C/48/D/478/1991, Communication No. 478/1991, *A.P.L.-v.d.M. v. The Netherlands*; UN Doc. CCPR/C/49/D/418/1990, Communication No. 418/1990, *Cavalcanti Araujo-Jongens v. The Netherlands*. The former was declared inadmissible, whereas the latter was examined on the merits. Lester and Joseph wonder whether the complaint of *Cavalcanti Araujo-Jongens v. The Netherlands* was declared admissible simply for failure of The Netherlands to raise objections to the admissibility (Lester and Joseph, supra note 8, 568, footnote 38).

899 UN Doc. CCPR/C/51/D/425/1990, Communication No. 425/1990, *Doesburg Lanooij Neefs v. The Netherlands*.

900 In 2003, the Committee for the first time explicitly accepted that age falls under "other status" (UN Doc. CCPR/C/77/D/983/2001, Communication No. 983/2001, *Love v. Australia*, para. 8.2). Committee member Ando disagreed. He was of the opinion that age was not to be included in "other status", as it is applicable to all human species. Earlier, discrimination on the basis of age had been alleged but not established (UN Doc. CCPR/C/39/D/306/1988, Communication No. 306/1988, *J.G. v. The Netherlands*; UN Doc. CCPR/C/72/D/855/1999, Communication No. 855/1999, *Schmitz-de-Jong v. The Netherlands*, para. 7.2).

901 UN Doc. CCPR/C/79/Add.28, para. 10 (Japan).

902 UN Doc. CCPR/C/75/D/854/1999, Communication No. 854/1999, *Wackenheim v. France*, para. 7.4.

status"[903] clearly has not been matched by an equally-expanding number of instances of prohibited discrimination.

j. Minorities

Discrimination against minorities has only arisen in the Committee's concluding observations. It is a cross-cutting issue, in the sense that discrimination against minorities may be based on grounds such as language, religion or ethnic origin. The Committee has stressed that the concept of minorities is a broad one, that extends to ethnic, religious and linguistic minorities.[904] The Roma community is therefore to be accorded recognized minority status.[905] States are to ensure that all members of ethnic, religious and linguistic minorities, whether or not their communities are recognized as national minorities, enjoy effective protection against discrimination. Comprehensive non-discrimination legislation is to be enacted, in order to combat ethnic and other discrimination in all fields of social life and to provide effective remedies to victims of discrimination.[906]

Discriminatory practices against minorities have been identified in the social, cultural and economic fields of public and private life,[907] as is the case with sex/gender discrimination. Members of minorities have generally lower living standards, low levels of participation in national political and social life and high levels of maternal and infant mortality.[908] They are discriminated against in employment, education, health care, housing, penitentiaries, and social programmes and in the private sphere.[909]

The HRC has observed *de facto* discrimination against members of minorities in the area of employment,[910] with significantly lower levels of employment[911] and lower representation in civil service.[912]

---

903 See Bayefski, supra note 3, 6. Lester and Joseph have pointed out that distinctions based on *e.g.* the place of residence within a state, public and private schools or between employed and unemployed, do not relate to personal characteristics of the complainant, as the explicitly enumerated grounds do (Lester and Joseph, supra note 8, 568).

904 UN Doc. CCPR/CO/71/HRV, para. 22 (Croatia); UN Doc. CCPR/C/79/Add.54, para. 40 (Russian Federation); UN Doc. CCPR/C/79/Add.37, para. 11 (Italy).

905 UN Doc. CCPR/CO/71/HRV, para. 22 (Croatia): priority concern.

906 UN Doc. CCPR/CO/81/SEMO, para. 18 (Serbia and Montenegro). Compare with UN Doc. CPR/CO/82/ALB, para. 22 (Albania).

907 UN Doc. CCPR/CO/71/HRV, para. 22 (Croatia); UN Doc. CCPR/C/79/Add.111, para. 6 (Romania).

908 UN Doc. A/55/40, paras. 27-28 (Ireland).

909 UN Doc. CCPR/CO/72/CZE, para. 8 (Czech Republic); compare with UN Doc. CCPR/CO/74/HUN, para. 7 (Hungary); UN Doc. CPR/CO/82/ALB, para. 15 (Albania).

910 UN Doc. CCPR/CO/78/SVK, para. 16 (Slovakia); UN Doc. CCPR/CO/72/CZE, para. 10 (Czech Republic); UN Doc. CCPR/C/79/Add.91, para. 14 (Finland).

911 UN Doc. CCPR/CO/78/PRT, para. 20 (Portugal); UN Doc. CCPR/CO/72/CZE, para. 10 (Czech Republic); UN Doc. CCPR/C/79/Add.93, para. 12 (Israel).

912 UN Doc. CCPR/CO/78/ISR, para. 23 (Israel).

A prominent problem is the lack of access to education.[913] Most Arab Israelis *e.g.*, because they do not join the army, do not enjoy the financial benefits available to Israelis who have served in the army, including scholarships.[914] The gradual transition to Latvian as the language of instruction was a cause of concern for the Committee, because of its expected impact on Russian speakers and other minorities. The Committee also expressed concern about the distinction made in providing state support to private schools based on the language of instruction. Similarly to its position with regard to religion, it has insisted that if state subsidies are provided to private schools, they are to be provided in a non-discriminatory manner.[915]

Considerable inequality and (*de facto*) discrimination have equally been observed in regard to land and housing,[916] health care[917] and social services.[918]

Another issue of concern is the discrimination against members of minorities in regard to language,[919] political participation and representation,[920] residency status,[921] the entry of ethnic origin in passports and identity documents,[922] and special laws.[923] The Committee has also expressed concern about racist attacks,[924] police harassment[925] and xenophobic statements by prominent politicians reflecting discriminatory attitudes vis-à-vis minorities,[926] such as the Roma.[927]

913 UN Doc. CCPR/CO/78/PRT, para. 20 (Portugal); UN Doc. CCPR/CO/78/SVK, para. 16 (Slovakia); UN Doc. CCPR/C/79/Add.111, para. 6 (Romania); UN Doc. CCPR/C/79/Add.102, paras. 13-15 (Japan); UN Doc. CCPR/C/79/Add.50, para. 26 (United States of America).

914 UN Doc. CCPR/C/79/Add.93, para. 12 (Israel).

915 UN Doc. CCPR/CO/79/LVA, para. 20 (Latvia): priority concern.

916 UN Doc. CCPR/CO/78/PRT, para. 20 (Portugal); UN Doc. CCPR/CO/78/SVK, para. 16 (Slovakia); UN Doc. CCPR/C/79/Add.93, paras. 12, 14, 24 and 26 (Israel); UN Doc. CCPR/C/79/Add.91, para. 14 (Finland).

917 UN Doc. CCPR/CO/78/SVK, para. 16 (Slovakia); UN Doc. CCPR/C/79/Add.93, para. 12 (Israel). See also UN Doc. CCPR/CO/78/SVK, para. 12 (Slovakia) with regard to forced sterilization (priority concern).

918 UN Doc. CCPR/CO/78/PRT, para. 20 (Portugal); UN Doc. CCPR/C/79/Add.91, para. 14 (Finland).

919 UN Doc. CCPR/CO/82/POL, para. 20 (Poland); UN Doc. CCPR/CO/79/LVA, paras. 19-21 (Latvia): priority concern; UN Doc. CCPR/CO/77/EST, para. 16 (Estonia): priority concern; UN Doc. CCPR/C/79/Add.102, para. 13-15 (Japan); UN Doc. CCPR/C/79/Add.95, para. 15 (Algeria); UN Doc. CCPR/C/79/Add.93, para. 12 (Israel).

920 UN Doc. CCPR/CO/72/CZE, para. 8 (Czech Republic); UN Doc. CCPR/CO/71/HRV, para. 22 (Croatia): priority concern; UN Doc. A/55/40, paras. 27-28 (Ireland).

921 UN Doc. CCPR/C/79/Add.93, para. 23 (Israel).

922 UN Doc. CCPR/CO/79/LVA, para. 21 (Latvia): priority concern.

923 UN Doc. CCPR/C/79/Add.32, para. 12 (Mexico).

924 UN Doc. CCPR/CO/79/RUS, para. 24 (Russian Federation).

925 UN Doc. CCPR/CO/78/SVK, para. 11 (Slovakia): priority concern; UN Doc. CCPR/CO/72/CZE, para. 15 (Czech Republic).

926 UN Doc. CCPR/CO/79/RUS, para. 24 (Russian Federation).

927 UN Doc. CCPR/CO/78/SVK, para. 17 (Slovakia).

The HRC has paid some attention to the fate of the Roma, albeit in a much less sustained way than the CERD has done. Only recently, it seems to have started paying more systematic attention to this group.[928]

k. *Conclusions*

Unlike CERD, the HRC has acknowledged the unequal importance of the prohibited grounds of discrimination. In principle, the explicitly enumerated grounds are more important than those covered by the notion of "other status". The HRC has made clear also that among the enumerated grounds, some like sex/gender are more important than others.

By and large, the Committee has not taken a fundamentally different approach in its views on individual complaints than it has done in its concluding observations on state reports. In both procedures, it has accepted new grounds as being covered by "other status", such as age, place of residence, descent, health status, disability, civilian status, military status, etc. It remains a contentious issue whether nationality is covered by "national origin" or "other status".

By far the most important ground of discrimination has been sex/gender, which concern is very prominently present in both the HRC's views and concluding observations. Discrimination against both women and men has been addressed in the Committee's decisions. Equality of opportunity in all fields of life has been a major concern, not only in relation to civil and political rights, but also in relation to economic, social and cultural rights. For that reason, the HRC and the CESCR Committee have expressed concern about by and large the same issues of labour (*e.g.* equal opportunity, equal pay for work of equal value), marriage and family relations etc. Women's representation and participation in public life has received more sustained attention from the HRC. In the concluding observations, a broad range of issues has been qualified as discrimination, ranging from sexual harassment on the work floor to polygamy, female genital mutilation, trafficking of women and gender-based violence more generally.

The HRC has established standards as to discrimination based on political or other opinion, in particular with regard to conscientious objection.

Discrimination based on nationality and against minorities enjoys particular attention in the HRC's concluding observations. The importance of these issues is reflected by

---

928 UN Doc. CPR/CO/82/ALB, para. 21 (Albania); UN Doc. CCPR/CO/82/FIN, para. 15 (Finland); UN Doc. CCPR/CO/82/POL, para. 17 (Poland); UN Doc. CCPR/CO/81/SEMO, paras. 18 and 24-25 (Serbia and Montenegro): priority concern.

both the quantity of recommendations and the number of priority concerns pertaining to nationality and minority issues. Discrimination against Roma has become more important recently; education in particular has been identified as a priority concern in recent years.

3. CESCR COMMITTEE

The list of prohibited grounds of discrimination in the CESCR is identical to the one in the CCPR, *i.e.* race, colour, sex, language, religion, political or other opinion, national or social origin, property, birth or other status. In its 2005 general comment on gender equality, the Committee has clarified – albeit non-exhaustively – the meaning of "other status", by referring to age, ethnicity, disability, marital, refugee or migrant status.[929] While ethnicity and refugee or migrant status were here for the first time mentioned under the ground of "other status", other grounds that had already been mentioned in earlier general comments as falling under "other status", such as sexual orientation, health status, nationality or social status, were omitted this time. It may therefore be clear that the Committee tends to accord a broad meaning to the notion of "other status", although there seems to be a limited list of core grounds, such as age, disability and marital status.

Unlike its attention for issues of discrimination in its general comments, the CESCR Committee has paid so far strikingly little attention to issues of discrimination in its concluding observations, with the exception of gender discrimination. As a consequence, the grounds of discrimination have not been a major concern for the Committee either.

a. Race and Colour

Very exceptionally, reference has been made to racial discrimination[930] or discrimination on the basis of colour.[931]

b. Sex

As with the HRC, sex/gender discrimination has strongly preoccupied the CESCR Committee in its concluding observations. It has submitted that the "Covenant is

929 UN Doc. E/C.12/2005/3, General Comment No. 16 (2005), *Article 3: The Equal Right of Men and Women to the Enjoyment of All Economic, Social and Cultural Rights*, paras. 5 and 10.

930 UN Doc. E/C.12/1/Add.107, paras. 45 and 78-79 (China); UN Doc. E/C.12/1/Add.82, para. 35 (Poland); UN Doc. E/C.12/1/Add.58, para. 15 (China: Hong Kong); UN Doc. E/C.12/1/Add.16, para. 14 (Dominican Republic).

931 UN Doc. E/C.12/1/Add.107, para. 45 (China).

predicated on the principles of absolute non-discrimination against women and the full enjoyment of all rights enjoyed by their male counterparts."[932] It has also underlined that measures to address the existing inequality between men and women in public service is a major priority, so that in case of limited resources, a state is to concentrate their use thereon.[933]

The concept of gender seems to be preferred over that of sex.

The CESCR Committee takes as a starting point that the prevalence of certain traditions, customs and cultural practices and the persistence of cultural stereotypes of the role of women leads to discrimination against women and girls,[934] and that the persistence of a traditional male-dominated society is detrimental to gender equality.[935] It has in particular deplored the lack of progress made in combating and eradicating the enduring discriminatory practices against women and girls.[936]

The CESCR Committee, very much in line with the HRC's approach, has identified issues of gender discrimination in a number of fields. In the area of employment,[937] gender discrimination can be found with regard to access to employment,[938] unequal pay for work of equal value,[939] lesser paid jobs and part-time work for women,[940]

---

932 UN Doc. E/C.12/1/Add.15, para. 14 (Libya).

933 UN Doc. E/C.12/1/Add.42, para. 26 (Georgia).

934 UN Doc. E/C.12/1/Add.106, para. 14 (Zambia); UN Doc. E/C.12/1/Add.105, para. 15 (Chile); UN Doc. E/C.12/1/Add.101, para. 11 (Malta); UN Doc. E/C.12/1/Add.78, para. 8 (Benin).

935 UN Doc. E/C.12/1/Add.16, para. 15 (Dominican Republic).

936 UN Doc. E/C.12/1/Add.62, para. 15 (Senegal); UN Doc. E/C.12/1/Add.40, para. 14 (Cameroon).

937 UN Doc. E/C.12/1/Add.107, paras. 17 and 108 (China); UN Doc. E/C.12/1/Add.104, para. 16 (Azerbaijan); UN Doc. E/C.12/1/Add.95, para. 13 (Democratic People's Republic of Korea); UN Doc. E/C.12/1/Add.14, para. 17 (Peru); UN Doc. E/C.12/1/Add.13, para. 15 (Russian Federation); UN Doc. E/C.12/1/Add.10, para. 15 (UK: Hong Kong); UN Doc. E/C.12/1/Add.4, para. 15 (El Salvador); UN Doc. E/C.12/1/Add.2, para. 6 (Spain); UN Doc. E/C.12/1995/17, para. 17 (Algeria); UN Doc. E/C.12/1995/6, para. 8 (Suriname).

938 UN Doc. E/C.12/1/Add.105, para. 16 (Chile); UN Doc. E/C.12/1/Add.101, para. 14 (Malta); UN Doc. E/C.12/1/Add.62, para. 16 (Senegal); UN Doc. E/C.12/1/Add.17, para. 14 (Iraq); UN Doc. E/C.12/1/Add.7/Rev.1, para. 16 (Belarus); UN Doc. E/C.12/1994/5, para. 12 (Morocco); UN Doc. E/C.12/1993/18, para. 6 (Senegal).

939 UN Doc. E/C.12/1/Add.109, para. 12 (Norway); UN Doc. E/C.12/1/Add.107, paras. 81 and 108 (China); UN Doc. E/C.12/1/Add.103, para. 18 (Italy); UN Doc. E/C.12/1/Add.102, para. 14 (Denmark); UN Doc. E/C.12/1/Add.101, para. 11 (Malta); UN Doc. E/C.12/1/Add.18, para. 14 (Uruguay); UN Doc. E/C.12/1/Add.17, para. 14 (Iraq); UN Doc. E/C.12/1/Add.16, para. 15 (Dominican Republic); UN Doc. E/C.12/1/Add.10, para. 17 (UK: Hong Kong); UN Doc. E/C.12/1/Add.8, para. 11 (Finland); UN Doc. E/C.12/1/Add.2, para. 6 (Spain); UN Doc. E/C.12/1/Add.1, para. 10 (Paraguay); UN Doc. E/C.12/1995/14, para. 10 (Mauritius); UN Doc. E/C.12/1995/13, para. 21 (Norway); UN Doc. E/C.12/1995/12, para. 14 (Colombia); UN Doc. E/C.12/1995/4, para. 9 (Portugal); UN Doc. E/C.12/1995/3, para. 11 (Republic of Korea); UN Doc. E/C.12/1994/8, para. 9 (Mauritius); UN Doc. E/C.12/1993/15, para. 8 (Iceland).

940 UN Doc. E/C.12/1/Add.19, para. 12 (United Kingdom).

discriminatory dismissal or hiring,[941] treatment at work,[942] promotion,[943] and representation in senior management positions.[944] The Committee has also expressed concern at the lack of meaningful remedies[945] and of protection afforded to women workers who are victims of discrimination in employment or arbitrary dismissal owing to pregnancy,[946] and the possibly discriminatory effects of imposing different retirement ages for men and women.[947]

In recent concluding observations, the Committee has drawn attention to discrimination in the lack of participation and representation of women in political and administrative bodies and in public service (including the judiciary),[948] and in (certain levels of) decision-making.[949]

With regard to the domestic sphere,[950] discriminatory provisions in civil and family law,[951] on the difference in marriageable ages for men and women,[952] the right freely to choose a spouse,[953] the requirement of a guardian's consent for marriage,[954] the obligation of the wife to obey her husband,[955] the regime of shared assets in marriage,[956] polygamy,[957] the conferring of nationality to children on equal terms,[958] unilateral repudiation by the husband,[959] more severe punishment of women for adultery and

941 UN Doc. E/C.12/1/Add.13, para. 15 (Russian Federation); UN Doc. E/C.12/1995/3, para. 11 (Republic of Korea).

942 UN Doc. E/C.12/1995/4, para. 9 (Portugal).

943 UN Doc. E/C.12/1/Add.67, para. 15 (Japan); UN Doc. E/C.12/1/Add.21, para. 15 (Saint Vincent and the Grenadines); UN Doc. E/C.12/1/Add.19, para. 12 (United Kingdom); UN Doc. E/C.12/1/Add.8, para. 11 (Finland); UN Doc. E/C.12/1995/13, para. 21 (Norway); UN Doc. E/C.12/1994/16, para. 12 (Austria).

944 UN Doc. E/C.12/1/Add.101, para. 14 (Malta).

945 UN Doc. E/C.12/1/Add.13, para. 15 (Russian Federation); UN Doc. E/C.12/1/Add.10, para. 19 (United Kingdom: Hong Kong).

946 UN Doc. E/C.12/1/Add.16, para. 15 (Dominican Republic); UN Doc. E/C.12/1/Add.6, para. 22 (Dominican Republic); UN Doc. E/C.12/1994/5, para. 12 (Morocco).

947 UN Doc. E/C.12/1/Add.105, para. 20 (Chile); UN Doc. E/C.12/1995/15, para. 16 (Ukraine).

948 UN Doc. E/C.12/1/Add.108, para. 15 (Serbia and Montenegro); UN Doc. E/C.12/1/Add.101, para. 11 (Malta); UN Doc. E/C.12/1/Add.95, para. 13 (Democratic People's Republic of Korea).

949 UN Doc. E/C.12/1/Add.107, paras. 17 and 108 (China); UN Doc. E/C.12/1/Add.106, para. 16 (Zambia); UN Doc. E/C.12/1/Add.102, para. 14 (Denmark).

950 UN Doc. E/C.12/1/Add.4, para. 15 (El Salvador).

951 UN Doc. E/C.12/1/Add.106, para. 15 (Zambia); UN Doc. E/C.12/1/Add.17, para. 14 (Iraq); UN Doc. E/C.12/1994/17, para. 7 (Mali); UN Doc. E/C.12/1994/5, para. 12 (Morocco).

952 UN Doc. E/C.12/1/Add.63, para. 31 (Syrian Arab Republic); UN Doc. E/C.12/1995/6, para. 11 (Suriname).

953 UN Doc. E/C.12/1995/17, para. 17 (Algeria).

954 UN Doc. E/C.12/1/Add.71, para. 14 (Algeria).

955 *Idem.*

956 UN Doc. E/C.12/1/Add.66, para. 17 (Nepal).

957 UN Doc. E/C.12/1/Add.71, para. 14 (Algeria).

958 UN Doc. E/C.12/1/Add.66, para. 17 (Nepal); UN Doc. E/C.12/1995/3, para. 10 (Republic of Korea).

959 UN Doc. E/C.12/1/Add.71, para. 14 (Algeria).

"honour crimes",[960] and divorce[961] (*e.g.* the husband's absolute right to keep the conjugal home in the case of divorce;[962] child custody in case of divorce and remarriage)[963] have been highlighted.[964] The absence of legal recognition of *de facto* marriages[965] and the existence of certain family and civil rights on the basis of Sharia law[966] have equally been raised as issues of concern.

Gender-based violence, such as domestic violence that very often targets women, has been qualified as a form of discrimination.[967]

Unequal treatment of women has been identified in personal, property,[968] commercial,[969] succession and social security laws[970] and with regard to inheritance[971] and access to credit and land ownership.[972] The lack of freedom of movement,[973] *e.g.* the need for permission of the husband to work or travel abroad,[974] reflects just another aspect of gender discrimination.

With regard to health, concern has been expressed about the lack of family planning services and the high maternal mortality rate.[975] The Committee has emphasized that in order to eliminate discrimination against women, there is a need to develop and implement a comprehensive national strategy for promoting women's right to health throughout their life span.[976] Implementation of the principle of non-discrimination requires that girls and boys alike have equal access to adequate nutrition, safe environments, and physical as well as mental health services.[977]

---

960 UN Doc. E/C.12/1/Add.63, para. 31 (Syrian Arab Republic).
961 UN Doc. E/C.12/1/Add.90, para. 39 (Israel); UN Doc. E/C.12/1/Add.66, para. 17 (Nepal); UN Doc. E/C.12/1995/7, para. 11 (Philippines).
962 UN Doc. E/C.12/1/Add.71, para. 14 (Algeria).
963 UN Doc. E/C.12/1/Add.66, para. 17 (Nepal).
964 UN Doc. E/C.12/1/Add.17, para. 14 (Iraq).
965 UN Doc. E/C.12/1/Add.16, para. 15 (Dominican Republic).
966 UN Doc. E/C.12/1/Add.15, para. 14 (Libya).
967 UN Doc. E/C.12/2005/3, General Comment No. 16 (2005), *Article 3: The Equal Right of Men and Women to the Enjoyment of All Economic, Social and Cultural Rights*, para. 27; compare with Sepúlveda, supra note 108, 410 and following.
968 UN Doc. E/C.12/1994/17, para. 7 (Mali).
969 UN Doc. E/C.12/1/Add.105, para. 22 (Chile).
970 UN Doc. E/C.12/1/Add.63, para. 31 (Syrian Arab Republic); UN Doc. E/C.12/1994/16, para. 12 (Austria).
971 UN Doc. E/C.12/1/Add.71, para. 14 (Algeria); UN Doc. E/C.12/1/Add.66, para. 17 (Nepal).
972 UN Doc. E/C.12/1/Add.21, para. 15 (Saint Vincent and the Grenadines).
973 UN Doc. E/C.12/1/Add.17, para. 14 (Iraq); UN Doc. E/C.12/1995/17, para. 17 (Algeria).
974 UN Doc. E/C.12/1993/7, para. 6 (Iran).
975 UN Doc. E/C.12/1/Add.16, para. 15 (Dominican Republic).
976 UN Doc. HRI/GEN/1/Rev.7, General Comment No. 14 (2000), *The Right to the Highest Attainable Standard of Health (Art. 12)*, para. 21.
977 *Ibid.*, para. 22.

The prohibition of gender discrimination in access to education[978] and the need for equal educational opportunities[979] has been stressed in reaction to both gender discrimination in (higher) education[980] and gender disparities in illiteracy rates.[981]

c. *National or Social Origin*

The CESCR Committee has paid little attention to discrimination on the basis of national or social origin so far.[982] Minority issues seem to have been subsumed under this ground (with the exception of discrimination against ethnic minorities, see further), rather than to have been addressed as a cross-cutting and multi-based issue of discrimination, as with the CERD and HRC.

The CESCR Committee has occasionally expressed concern about discrimination against members of certain minorities in general,[983] in workplaces, and in schools[984] or education more generally.[985]

Most of its concluding observations on discrimination on the basis of national origin pertain to certain groups, such as Arabs in Israel, the Roma and indigenous people.[986] With regard to the Arabs in Israel, the Committee has insisted on ensuring equality of treatment for all Israeli citizens in relation to all Covenant rights, in particular with respect to employment and wages.[987]

Discriminatory practices against the Roma minority have been identified in the field of housing, health, employment and education,[988] as well as with regard to social

---

978 UN Doc. HRI/GEN/1/Rev.7, General Comment No. 11 (1999), *Plans of Action for Primary Education (Article 14 Covenant)*, para. 6.

979 UN Doc. E/C.12/1/Add.17, para. 24 (Iraq); UN Doc. E/C.12/1/Add.2, para. 6 (Spain); UN Doc. E/C.12/1995/3, para. 10 (Republic of Korea); UN Doc. E/C.12/1993/7, para. 6 (Iran).

980 UN Doc. E/C.12/1/Add.106, para. 32 (Zambia); UN Doc. E/C.12/1/Add.21, para. 15 (Saint Vincent and the Grenadines); UN Doc. E/C.12/1/Add.14, para. 17 (Peru); UN Doc. E/C.12/1995/17, para. 17 (Algeria); UN Doc. E/C.12/1994/6, para. 7 (Iraq).

981 UN Doc. E/C.12/1994/9, para. 17 (Gambia).

982 For an exception, see UN Doc. E/C.12/1/Add.107, para. 45 (China), in which the Committee referred to ethnic or national origin.

983 UN Doc. E/C.12/1/Add.107, para. 38 (China); UN Doc. E/C.12/1/Add.63, para. 13 (Syrian Arab Republic); UN Doc. E/C.12/1/Add.17, para. 13 (Iraq).

984 UN Doc. E/C.12/1994/4, para. 12 (Romania).

985 UN Doc. E/C.12/1994/6, para. 7 (Iraq).

986 For the Crimean Tatars, see UN Doc. E/C.12/1995/15, para. 15 (Ukraine).

987 UN Doc. E/C.12/1/Add.90, para. 32, 36 and 37 (Israel).

988 UN Doc. E/C.12/1/Add.108, paras. 15 and 37 (Serbia and Montenegro); UN Doc. E/C.12/1/Add.103, para. 25 (Italy); UN Doc. E/C.12/1/Add.96, para. 9 (Lithuania); UN Doc. E/C.12/1/Add.81, para. 9 (Slovakia); UN Doc. E/C.12/1/Add.76, para. 12 (Czech Republic); UN Doc. E/C.12/1/Add.35, para. 20 (Ireland); UN Doc. E/C.12/1/Add.8, para. 15 (Finland).

benefits and access to land.[989] Like the CERD and the HRC, albeit rather incidentally, the CESCR Committee has expressed concern at the over-representation of Roma children in "special schools".[990]

Thirdly, discrimination against indigenous peoples,[991] particularly with regard to access to land ownership, housing, health services and sanitation, education, work and adequate nutrition has been highlighted on occasion.[992]

d. *Political Opinion*

Discrimination on the basis of political opinion has only once arisen as an issue before the CESCR Committee, *i.e.* with regard to discrimination in the employment of teachers of the new Länder in Germany after the re-unification.[993]

e. *Religion*

Discrimination on the ground of religion has been addressed in the field of education in Iran,[994] and more generally with regard to the Catholics in Northern Ireland.[995]

f. *Birth*

Discrimination against children born out of wedlock has been a sustained concern of the CESCR Committee.[996]

g. *Other Status*

The CESCR-Committee has given a liberal interpretation to the concept of "other status",[997] partly in line with the HRC. It has counted under "other status" grounds such as disability, age, sexual orientation, health status, nationality, place of residence, social status, ethnicity, marital status, and refugee or migrant status.

---

989 UN Doc. E/C.12/1/Add.37, para. 11 (Albania).
990 UN Doc. E/C.12/1/Add.76, para. 23 (Czech Republic).
991 UN Doc. E/C.12/1/Add.3, para. 10 (Guatemala).
992 UN Doc. E/C.12/1/Add.56, para. 12 (Venezuela).
993 UN Doc. E/C.12/1993/17, para. 8 (Germany).
994 UN Doc. E/C.12/1993/7, para. 5 (Iran).
995 UN Doc. E/C.12/1/Add.19, para. 24 (United Kingdom).
996 UN Doc. E/C.12/1/Add.101, para. 20 (Malta); UN Doc. E/C.12/1/Add.98, para. 42 (Kuwait); UN Doc. E/C.12/1/Add.67, para. 14 (Japan); UN Doc. E/C.12/1/Add.23, para. 40 (Nigeria); UN Doc. E/C.12/1/Add.22, para. 12 (Luxemburg); UN Doc. E/C.12/1/Add.18, para. 13 (Uruguay); UN Doc. E/C.12/1995/17, para. 19 (Algeria); UN Doc. E/C.12/1994/5, para. 16 (Morocco).
997 Sepúlveda, supra note 108, 391.

i. Disability

In its general comment on the rights of the disabled, the Committee submitted that the concept of "other status" clearly applied to discrimination on the grounds of disability – both mental and physical.[998] It also indicated the many fields which the effects of disability-based discrimination can be felt in, thereby stressing in particular, the issue of employment:

> The effects of disability-based discrimination have been particularly severe in the fields of education, employment, housing, transport, cultural life, and access to public places and services.[999]
>
> The field of employment is one in which disability-based discrimination has been prominent and persistent. In most countries the unemployment rate among persons with disabilities is two to three times higher than the unemployment rate for persons without disabilities. Where persons with disabilities are employed, they are mostly engaged in low-paid jobs with little social and legal security and are often segregated from the mainstream of the labour market. The integration of persons with disabilities into the regular labour market should be actively supported by States.[1000]
>
> Disabled workers may not be discriminated against with respect to wages or other conditions if their work is equal to that of non-disabled workers.[1001]

The Committee's concern with disability-based discrimination has also become apparent in some of its concluding observations,[1002] in particular in the fields of work, social security, education and health.[1003]

ii. Age

The CESCR Committee has explicitly added age as a prohibited ground of discrimination. Whereas it refrained in its general comment on the economic, social and cultural rights of older persons from submitting that discrimination on the basis of age is

---

998 UN Doc. HRI/GEN/1/Rev.7, General Comment No. 5 (1994), *Persons With Disabilities*, para. 5; compare with General Comment No. 14 (2000), *The Right to the Highest Attainable Standard of Health (Art. 12)*, para. 18: physical or mental disability; idem in General Comment No. 15 (2002), *The Right to Water (Arts. 11 and 12 of the International Covenant on Economic, Social and Cultural Rights)*, para. 13.

999 UN Doc. HRI/GEN/1/Rev.7, General Comment No. 5 (1994), *Persons With Disabilities*, para. 15.

1000 *Ibid.*, para. 20.

1001 *Ibid.*, para. 25.

1002 UN Doc. E/C.12/1/Add.93, para. 7 (Guatemala); UN Doc. E/C.12/1/Add.90, para. 32 (Israel); UN Doc. E/C.12/1/Add.79, para. 14 (United Kingdom); UN Doc. E/C.12/1/Add.77, para. 15 (Ireland); UN Doc. E/C.12/1/Add.67, para. 25 (Japan); UN Doc. E/C.12/1/Add.58, para. 20 (China: Hong Kong); UN Doc. E/C.12/1/Add.35, para. 20 (Ireland); UN Doc. E/C.12/1/Add.21, para. 14 (Saint Vincent and the Grenadines): UN Doc. E/C.12/1/Add.10, para. 30 (United Kingdom: Hong Kong).

1003 UN Doc. E/C.12/1/Add.107, para. 16 (China).

always and comprehensively prohibited by the CESCR,[1004] it included age in the list of prohibited grounds of discrimination in its general comments on the right to adequate food, the right to water and gender equality.[1005]

Age has been referred to, albeit not very systematically, in the Committee's concluding observations too.[1006]

iii. Sexual Orientation

Sexual orientation has been recognized as a prohibited ground of discrimination in two of the CESCR Committee's more recent general comments and concluding observations.[1007] Unlike the HRC, the CESCR Committee does not seem to bring sexual orientation under the concept of sex.

iv. Health Status

Health status (including HIV/AIDS) equally features in the list of prohibited grounds of discrimination in some of the Committee's more recent general comments, as well as in some of its concluding observations.[1008]

1004 UN Doc. HRI/GEN/1/Rev.7, General Comment No. 6 (1995), *Economic, Social and Cultural Rights of Older Persons*, para. 12: "The Committee notes that while it may not yet be possible to conclude that discrimination on the grounds of age is comprehensively prohibited by the Covenant, the range of matters in relation to which such discrimination can be accepted is very limited. Moreover, it must be emphasized that the unacceptableness of discrimination against older persons is underlined in many international policy documents and is confirmed in the legislation of the vast majority of States. In the few areas in which discrimination continues to be tolerated, such as in relation to mandatory retirement ages or access to tertiary education, there is a clear trend towards the elimination of such barriers. The Committee is of the view that States parties should seek to expedite this trend to the greatest extent possible."

1005 UN Doc. E/C.12/2005/3, General Comment No. 16 (2005), *Article 3: The Equal Right of Men and Women to the Enjoyment of All Economic, Social and Cultural Rights*, paras. 5 and 10; General Comment No. 15 (2002), *The Right to Water (Arts. 11 and 12 of the International Covenant on Economic, Social and Cultural Rights)*, para. 13; General Comment No. 12 (1999), *The Right to Adequate Food (Art. 11)*, para. 18.

1006 UN Doc. E/C.12/1/Add.107, para. 78 (China); UN Doc. E/C.12/1/Add.80, para. 14 (Trinidad and Tobago); UN Doc. E/C.12/1/Add.79, para. 15 (United Kingdom); UN Doc. E/C.12/1/Add.73, para. 12 (Croatia); UN Doc. E/C.12/1/Add.58, paras. 15 and 31 (China: Hong Kong).

1007 UN Doc. HRI/GEN/1/Rev.7, General Comment No. 15 (2002), *The Right to Water (Arts. 11 and 12 of the International Covenant on Economic, Social and Cultural Rights)*, para. 13; General Comment No. 14 (2000), *The Right to the Highest Attainable Standard of Health (Art. 12)*, para. 18. Not however in UN Doc. E/C.12/2005/3, General Comment No. 16 (2005), *Article 3: The Equal Right of Men and Women to the Enjoyment of All Economic, Social and Cultural Rights*, paras. 5 and 10.
See also UN Doc. E/C.12/1/Add.107, para. 78 (China); UN Doc. E/C.12/1/Add.80, para. 14 (Trinidad and Tobago); UN Doc. E/C.12/1/Add.58, paras. 15 and 31 (China: Hong Kong).

1008 UN Doc. HRI/GEN/1/Rev.7, General Comment No. 15 (2002), *The Right to Water (Arts. 11 and 12 of the International Covenant on Economic, Social and Cultural Rights)*, para. 13; General Comment No. 14 (2000), *The Right to the Highest Attainable Standard of Health (Art. 12)*, para. 18. Not however

v. Nationality

The CESCR allows for discrimination against non nationals, albeit it only in developing countries, and only with regard to economic rights recognized in the Covenant, and with due regard to human rights and their national economy (article 2, para. 3 CESCR). The relevance of this provision seems rather minimal, as it has not been invoked, and the Committee has not taken any position on it.[1009] The CRC Committee has recently submitted that this exception does not apply with regard to unaccompanied and separated children (see also further).[1010]

Nationality as a prohibited ground of discrimination has been emphasized in the Committee's general comments on the right to education and the right to water. In the general comment on the right to education, the Committee emphasized the obligation not to discriminate against non nationals with regard to both the right to receive an education and the right to educational freedom. All persons of school age residing in the territory of a state party, including non nationals, and irrespective of their legal status, are to enjoy the right to receive education without discrimination. Moreover, everyone, including non nationals, has the liberty to establish and direct educational institutions.[1011] In its general comment on the right to water, the Committee clarified that refugees and asylum-seekers should be granted the right to water on the same conditions as it is granted to nationals.[1012] In its concluding observations, the Committee has paid attention to discrimination on the basis of nationality[1013] in the fields *inter alia* of wages, social security laws[1014] education,[1015] vocational guidance and training courses,[1016] health[1017] and residence permits.[1018]

---

in General Comment UN Doc. E/C.12/2005/3, No. 16 (2005), *Article 3: The Equal Right of Men and Women to the Enjoyment of All Economic, Social and Cultural Rights*, paras. 5 and 10.
See also UN Doc. E/C.12/1/Add.94, para. 62 (Russian Federation); UN Doc. E/C.12/1/Add.80, para. 14 (Trinidad and Tobago); UN doc. E/C.12/1/Add.71, para. 39 (Algeria); UN Doc. E/C.12/1/Add.15, para. 18 (Libya).

1009 Sepúlveda, supra note 108, 414-415.

1010 General Comment No. 6 (2005), *Treatment of Unaccompanied and Separated Children Outside Their Country of Origin*.

1011 UN Doc. HRI/GEN/1/Rev.7, General Comment No. 13 (1999), *The Right to Education (Art. 13)*, paras. 30 and 34.

1012 UN Doc. HRI/GEN/1/Rev.7, General Comment No. 15 (2002), *The Right to Water (Arts. 11 and 12 of the International Covenant on Economic, Social and Cultural Rights)*, para. 16 (f).

1013 UN Doc. E/C.12/1/Add.27, para. 10 (Israel).

1014 UN Doc. E/C.12/1/Add.98, paras. 12, 13, 31, 32, 34 and 40 (Kuwait); UN Doc. E/C.12/1/Add.17, paras. 17 and 33 (Iraq); UN Doc. E/C.12/1/Add.15, para. 16 (Libya).

1015 UN Doc. E/C.12/1/Add.97, para. 12 (Greece); UN Doc. E/C.12/1/Add.66, para. 29 (Nepal); UN Doc. E/C.12/1/Add.31, para. 49 (Canada).

1016 UN Doc. E/C.12/1/Add.53, para. 19 (Portugal).

1017 UN Doc. E/C.12/1/Add.66, para. 29 (Nepal).

1018 UN Doc. E/C.12/1/Add.107, para. 78 (China); UN Doc. E/C.12/1994/16, para. 11 (Austria).

There seems to have been no conceptual discussion within the Committee as to whether nationality is covered by national origin. Generally, it is assumed that "national origin" refers to ethnic or racial origin, irrespective of nationality.[1019] Nationality is therefore considered here under "other status".

vi. Place of Residence

In its general comment on the right to education, the Committee highlighted that "sharp disparities in spending policies that result in differing qualities of education for persons residing in different geographic locations may constitute discrimination under the Covenant."[1020] It equally expressed concern about regional inequalities more generally,[1021] and about disparities between rural and urban areas,[1022] in particular with regard to access to productive resources[1023] and to clean drinking water, sanitary facilities and electricity.[1024]

vii. Social Status

Occasionally, the CESCR Committee has referred to "discrimination because of social or economic status".[1025] It has expressed concern about widespread discrimination in housing against people with children, and disadvantaged and marginalized groups,[1026] and about the different treatment between domestic helpers and professional migrant workers in allowing them to bring their families to Hong Kong.[1027] To a certain extent, the differences mentioned could have been addressed under the heading of "property", but the Committee seems to have preferred not to do so.

viii. Ethnicity

Ethnicity was explicitly subsumed under "other status" in the Committee's 2005 general comment on gender equality.[1028] In fact, ethnicity could well have been

---

1019 For an early analysis, see Matthew Craven, *The International Covenant on Economic, Social and Cultural Rights. A Perspective on its Development*, Oxford, Clarendon, 1995, 172; Sepúlveda considers the issue devoid of any importance as the Committee has now explicitly recognized nationality as a prohibited ground (Sepúlveda, supra note 108, 393-394).

1020 UN Doc. HRI/GEN/1/Rev.7, General Comment No. 13 (1999), *The Right to Education (Art. 13)*, para. 35.

1021 UN Doc. E/C.12/1/Add.103, para. 20 (Italy).

1022 UN Doc. E/C.12/1994/5, para. 11 (Morocco).

1023 UN Doc. E/C.12/1/Add.64, para. 8 (Panama); UN Doc. E/C.12/1/Add.17, para. 13 (Iraq).

1024 UN Doc. E/C.12/1/Add.55, para. 26 (Morocco).

1025 UN Doc. E/C.12/1/Add.31, para. 51 (Canada).

1026 UN Doc. E/C.12/1/Add.103, para. 25 (Italy); UN Doc. E/C.12/1/Add.102, para. 21 (Denmark); UN Doc. E/C.12/1993/5, para. 18 (Canada).

1027 UN Doc. E/C.12/1994/19, para. 29 (United Kingdom: Hong Kong).

1028 UN Doc. E/C.12/2005/3, General Comment No. 16 (2005), *Article 3: The Equal Right of Men and Women to the Enjoyment of All Economic, Social and Cultural Rights*, paras. 5 and 10.

considered under the ground of national origin, which is commonly interpreted as referring to ethnic or racial origin (see higher under nationality).

In some concluding observations, reference has been made to ethnic discrimination.[1029] The Committee has observed the persistence of a substantially higher rate of unemployment among ethnic minorities, and their disproportionate numbers in lesser paid jobs.[1030]

ix. Marital Status

Marital status was explicitly subsumed under "other status" in the Committee's general comment on gender equality.[1031]

x. Refugee or Migrant Status

Refugee and migrant status were explicitly subsumed under "other status" in the Committee's general comment on gender equality.[1032] This status might be considered to be a further specification of the ground of nationality.

In its concluding observations, the Committee has *inter alia* expressed concern about cases of discrimination faced by persons with an immigrant background in the areas of housing and work.[1033]

h. Conclusions

The CESCR Committee has a less-developed approach to discrimination than for example the HRC. It has so far paid relatively little attention to the issue of discrimination and possible grounds of discrimination, with the exception of gender discrimination. Most "doctrinal" development has taken place in the Committee's general comments, but these doctrinal developments have not always strongly influenced the Committee's approach to discrimination issues in the reporting procedure.

Most systematic attention has been paid to gender discrimination and equality. Like the HRC, the CESCR Committee has attributed gender discrimination to traditions, customs and cultural practices. The CESCR Committee has also addressed very similar issues as the HRC, *e.g.* in the field of labour and employment (equal opportunities,

---

1029 UN Doc. E/C.12/1/Add.108, para. 40 (Serbia and Montenegro).
1030 UN Doc. E/C.12/1/Add.19, para. 12 (United Kingdom).
1031 UN Doc. E/C.12/2005/3, General Comment No. 16 (2005), *Article 3: The Equal Right of Men and Women to the Enjoyment of All Economic, Social and Cultural Rights*, paras. 5 and 10.
1032 *Idem.*
1033 UN Doc. E/C.12/1/Add.109, para. 10 (Norway).

equal pay for work of equal value, representation in senior positions, representation in segment of lower paid and part-time jobs; pregnancy), and marriage and family relations (including *e.g.* same marriageable age; transfer of nationality to children, same rights in marriage, ...). Polygamy and gender-based violence have similarly been qualified as discrimination. Due to its mandate of economic, social and cultural rights, the CESCR Committee has also expressed concern about equal educational opportunities and equal rights to health care (mainly with regard to reproductive health).

Like the HRC, the CESCR Committee has rejected discrimination against children born out of wedlock.

The CESCR Committee has paid considerably less attention to Roma (with the occasional exception of special classes) and other minorities or ethnic groups than the CERD and the HRC have done.

A number of new grounds have been added under "other status", such as disability, age, sexual orientation, health status (including those affected by HIV/AIDS), nationality, place of residence, ethnicity, social status, marital status, and refugee or migrant status. Whereas some were repeatedly claimed to be read under "other status" (disability, age, place of residence, marital status), others have only very recently been explicitly recognized (ethnicity, and refugee or migrant status). On the other hand, previously recognized grounds like sexual orientation, health status, nationality and social status were omitted in the Committee's 2005 general comment. In comparison with the HRC, sexual orientation has been recognized as an independent ground by the CESCR Committee (the HRC subsumes sexual orientation under sex). Social status and refugee or migrant status seem to have been recognized more explicitly as a prohibited ground of discrimination. As to nationality, it is a moot point with both Committees where to best insert this ground from a theoretical perspective. Both Committees have however, recognized unequivocally that nationality is a prohibited ground of discrimination. CERD too has recently adopted a restrictive approach, in which nationality is more often than not a prohibited ground of discrimination. The (very restrictive) exception clause in CESCR with regard to non nationals has not been invoked in practice, and does not seem to play any role.

All in all, the CESCR Committee does not seem to have explored as yet the full potential of equality and non-discrimination in the field of economic, social and cultural rights.

4. CEDAW COMMITTEE

CEDAW prohibits discrimination on the basis of sex only. The CEDAW Committee has given an extensive interpretation to the ground of sex/gender, and has included also sexual orientation, marital status, pregnancy and maternity.[1034]

In comparison with other Committees, the CEDAW Committee has probably been most innovative, being the first to give an extensive interpretation to the concept of gender *discrimination*[1035] by including gender-based violence[1036] into the concept of discrimination. Gender-based violence is defined as violence that is directed against a woman because she is a woman or that affects women disproportionately.[1037]

a. Sex/Gender

i. Sex

The CEDAW Committee uses a broad concept of discrimination. The definition of discrimination in article 1 "includes gender-based violence, that is, violence that is directed against a women because she is a woman or that affects women disproportionately."[1038] "Gender-based violence is a form of discrimination that seriously inhibits women's ability to enjoy rights and freedoms on a basis of equality with men."[1039] Domestic violence against women in particular has been qualified as "a form of discrimination against women and a violation of their human rights".[1040]

In its concluding comments, the CEDAW Committee very often takes the general perspective of women's rights rather than the specific one of gender discrimination.[1041] The CEDAW Committee's concerns regarding issues of gender discrimination in the strict sense often relate to the lack of affirmative action measures. Its suggestions and recommendations address a much wider range of issues. The primary focus in what

---

1034 See Frostell, supra note 139, 42. Compare with the HRC (supra notes 812-813) and the CESCR Committee (supra note 946), which have occasionally done the same predominantly in the context of labour law and employment.

1035 For a discussion, see Frostell, supra note 140, 42, who points out the radicalism of this standpoint, as gender-based violence is a gender practice that lacks an immediate male comparator. Meanwhile, the HRC and the CESCR Committee have done the same (see higher).

1036 UN Doc. HRI/GEN/1/Rev.7, General Recommendation No. 19 (1992), *Violence Against Women*, para. 1.

1037 *Ibid.*, para. 6.

1038 *Ibid.*, paras. 6 and 7.

1039 *Ibid.*, para. 1.

1040 UN Doc. CEDAW/C/TUR/CC/4-5, para. 28 (Turkey); UN Doc. CEDAW/C/DZA/CC/2, para. 32 (Algeria); UN Doc. CEDAW/C/WSM/CC/1-3, para. 25 (Samoa).

1041 See *e.g.* UN Doc. A/55/38 (part I), para. 58 (India): "there is an urgent need to introduce comprehensive legislative reform to promote equality and the human rights of women."

follows will therefore be on issues in relation to which the absence of affirmative action measures was raised, without excluding other themes that have been addressed frequently by the CEDAW Committee.

The CEDAW Committee shows a clear preference for "gender" over "sex", and seems to resort to an exclusive use of the concept of "gender", except when the use of "sex" is more appropriate (*e.g.* in the case of sex-disaggregated data, sex education, or when referring to the notion of sex in domestic legislation).

The Committee has regretted impediments to the full implementation of CEDAW due to reservations,[1042] and asked states to incorporate sex as a ground of discrimination in domestic legislation.[1043] Furthermore, it has insisted on the integration of a holistic approach to women's equality with men in all fields,[1044] including a timetable to monitor and evaluate progress in this regard.[1045] The CEDAW Committee has welcomed affirmative action as a means of closing the gap in gender equality.[1046] It has also commended the adoption of legislation that provides residence permits to individuals who have a well-founded fear of persecution on the basis of gender, particularly in cases that involve discrimination against women.[1047] Frequently, it has expressed concern about the lack of understanding and use of affirmative action measures ("temporary special measures" as they are called in CEDAW) (see further).[1048]

A primary concern of the Committee is the persistence and pervasiveness of patriarchal attitudes and deep-rooted stereotypes regarding the roles and responsibilities of women and men in the family and in society, which leads to disparities in leadership and decision-making in all spheres, including in the family, the community and in public life.[1049] They negatively affect women's enjoyment of their rights in many areas and impede the full implementation of CEDAW, with respect to *inter alia* education, employment, health and participation in decision-making.[1050] The Committee has also

1042 UN Doc. A/56/38 (part II), para. 72 (Singapore).
1043 UN Doc. A/54/38/Rev.1 (part I), para. 114 (Kyrgyzstan); UN Doc. A/50/38, para. 208 (Mauritius).
1044 UN Doc. A/56/38 (part I), para. 92 (Kazakhstan); UN Doc. A/55/38 (part II), para. 96 (Moldova).
1045 UN Doc. A/55/38 (part II), para. 300 (Romania).
1046 UN Doc. A/56/38 (part II), para. 332 (Sweden); UN Doc. A/55/38 (part II), para. 131 (Lithuania); UN Doc. A/53/38/Rev.1 (part I), para. 381 (Mexico); UN Doc. A/52/38/Rev.1 (part II), para. 291 (Argentina); UN Doc. A/52/38/Rev.1 (part II), para. 93 (Namibia).
1047 UN Doc. A/56/38 (part II), para. 334 (Sweden).
1048 UN Doc. A/57/38 (part I), paras. 93 and 95 (Estonia); UN Doc. A/54/38/Rev.1 (part I), para. 193 (Greece); UN Doc. A/54/38/Rev.1 (part I), para. 164 (Liechtenstein); UN Doc. A/54/38/Rev.1 (part I), para. 118 (Kyrgyzstan); UN Doc. A/53/38/Rev.1 (part II), para. 282 (New Zealand); UN Doc. A/52/38/Rev.1 (part II), para. 99 (Namibia).
1049 UN Doc. CEDAW/C/TUR/CC/4-5, para. 29 (Turkey); UN Doc. CEDAW/C/ITA/CC/4-5, para. 25 (Italy); UN Doc. CEDAW/C/DZA/CC/2, para. 35 (Algeria); UN Doc. CEDAW/C/LAO/CC/1-5, para. 27 (Laos).
1050 UN Doc. CEDAW/C/TUR/CC/4-5, para. 29 (Turkey).

expressed deep concern about the portrayal of women in the media and in advertising as sex objects and in stereotypical roles.[1051]

With regard to labour law and employment, the Committee has expressed concern *inter alia* about serious disadvantages women face in the labour market, as reflected in their lower level of participation in the labour force,[1052] women's high unemployment rate, the persistence of strong vertical and horizontal segregation, the significant wage gap between men and women and the lack of implementation of the principle of equal pay for work of equal value, the under representation of women in senior positions, the concentration of women in certain low-wage sectors and in part-time,[1053] the poor working conditions for women in the informal sector, the low participation of women in the formal labour market, persistent wage disparities between women and men and discriminatory practices vis-à-vis domestic workers, such as workdays of 12 hours and remuneration below the minimum wage, the high number of girls performing domestic work without remuneration,[1054] and their concentration in agriculture as unpaid family workers and in unregistered work with low or no income or wages and lack of social security benefits.[1055] Other concerns include the discriminatory treatment of pregnant women in the labour market, the limited provision of paid maternity leave, insufficient attention to policies supporting the sharing of work and family responsibilities between women and men and the lack of adequate childcare services.[1056] It has noted with appreciation, affirmative action measures in the field of employment,[1057] *e.g.* to promote women's employment in senior positions in the public sector.[1058] It has regretted that states did not make use of affirmative action measures to accelerate the equal status of women in the areas of employment and public service,[1059] to redress high rates of unemployment among women,[1060] or to ensure women's employment in non-traditional areas.[1061] To the extent that temporary special measures were only used for non-academic training such as embroidery, industrial sewing etc., the Committee has warned that these would only contribute to keeping women to the feminized sector of the economy.[1062] In its recommendations, the pay

1051 UN Doc. CEDAW/C/ITA/CC/4-5, para. 25 (Italy).
1052 UN Doc. CEDAW/C/WSM/CC/1-3, para. 28 (Samoa).
1053 UN Doc. CEDAW/C/ITA/CC/4-5, para. 29 (Italy); UN Doc. CEDAW/C/CRO/CC/2-3, para. 27 (Croatia).
1054 UN Doc. CEDAW/C/PAR/CC/3-5, para. 30 (Paraguay).
1055 UN Doc. CEDAW/C/TUR/CC/4-5, para. 35 (Turkey).
1056 UN Doc. CEDAW/C/TUR/CC/4-5, para. 35 (Turkey); UN Doc. CEDAW/C/WSM/CC/1-3, para. 28 (Samoa); UN Doc. CEDAW/C/CRO/CC/2-3, para. 27 (Croatia).
1057 UN Doc. A/54/38/Rev.1 (part II), para. 253 (Spain).
1058 UN Doc. A/51/38, para. 179 (Belgium).
1059 UN Doc. A/55/38 (part II), para. 138 (Lithuania); UN Doc. A/52/38/Rev.1, para. 134 (Saint Vincent and the Grenadines).
1060 UN Doc. A/52/38/Rev.1, para. 139 (Saint Vincent and the Grenadines).
1061 UN Doc. A/54/38/Rev.1 (part I), para. 118 (Kyrgyzstan).
1062 UN Doc. A/50/38, para. 213 (Mauritius).

discrimination against women,[1063] access to the labour market,[1064] and the creation of safe and protected jobs for women have been highlighted.[1065]

As to women's equal participation in political and public life,[1066] the CEDAW Committee has deplored the low representation of women in public life and decision-making positions.[1067] It has observed that affirmative action may contribute to increasing the representation of women in public life.[1068] It has regretted the lack of use of affirmative action measures to ensure equitable participation of women in the conduct of public affairs,[1069] and occasionally its lack of significant results.[1070] It has made clear that women should on equal terms with men and without any discrimination, be ensured the opportunities to represent their governments at the international level and to participate in the work of international organizations.[1071]

In 1994, the Committee adopted a general recommendation on equality in marriage and family relations. In this general recommendation, its stressed *inter alia* women's right to choose a domicile on the same basis as a man, migrant women's same rights as men to have their spouses, partners and children join them, and a series of rights with regard to marriage on a basis of equality with men, which are guaranteed in article 16 CEDAW.[1072] In its concluding comments, the Committee has expressed concern at discrimination against women in the field of inheritance,[1073] choice of residence and

---

1063 UN Doc. A/58/38 (part I), para. 430 (Norway); UN Doc. A/54/38/Rev.1 (part II), para. 308 (United Kingdom and Northern Ireland); UN Doc. A/53/38/Rev.1 (part II), para. 334 (Peru); UN Doc. A/51/38, para. 191 (Belgium).

1064 UN Doc. A/53/38/Rev.1 (part II), para. 334 (Peru).

1065 UN Doc. A/52/38/Rev.1, para. 296 (Philippines).

1066 A general recommendation was devoted to this theme, see UN Doc. HRI/GEN/1/Rev.7, General Recommendation No. 23 (1997), *Political and Public Life.*

1067 See most recently in UN Doc. CEDAW/C/TUR/CC/4-5, para. 31 (Turkey); UN Doc. CEDAW/C/ITA/CC/4-5, para. 27 (Italy); UN Doc. CEDAW/C/GAB/CC/2-5, para. 34 (Gabon); UN Doc. CEDAW/C/CRO/CC/2-3, para. 35 (Croatia); UN Doc. CEDAW/C/DZA/CC/2, para. 37 (Algeria); UN Doc. CEDAW/C/DZA/CC/2, para. 37 (Algeria); UN Doc. CEDAW/C/WSM/CC/1-3, para. 26 (Samoa); UN Doc. CEDAW/C/LAO/CC/1-5, para. 33 (Laos).

1068 UN Doc. A/50/38, para. 327 (Uganda).

1069 UN Doc. A/56/38 (part I), para. 134 (Maldives); UN Doc. A/55/38 (part II), para. 138 (Lithuania); UN Doc. A/54/38/Rev.1 (part I), para. 118 (Kyrgyzstan); UN Doc. A/53/38/Rev.1 (part I), para. 188 (Czech Republic); UN Doc. A/53/38/Rev.1 (part I), para. 62 (Azerbaijan); UN Doc. A/52/38/Rev.1, para. 261 (Venezuela); UN Doc. A/52/38/Rev.1 (part II), para. 206 (Luxembourg).

1070 UN Doc. A/52/38/Rev.1 (part II), para. 448 (Bangladesh).

1071 UN Doc. HRI/GEN/1/Rev.7, General Recommendation No. 8 (1988), *Implementation of Article 8 of the Convention.*

1072 UN Doc. HRI/GEN/1/Rev.7, General Recommendation No. 19 (1994), *Equality in Marriage and Family Relations*, paras. 9-10.

1073 UN Doc. CEDAW/C/GAB/CC/2-5, para. 22 (Gabon); UN Doc. A/50/38, para. 332 (Uganda). Compare with UN Doc. HRI/GEN/1/Rev.7, General Recommendation No. 19 (1994), *Equality in Marriage and Family Relations*, para. 35.

profession,[1074] and genital examinations of women without their consent.[1075] With regard to marriage, it has paid attention to different ages of marriage for boys and girls,[1076] low legal age of marriage,[1077] practices as dowry,[1078] early and forced marriage, widowhood practices, and levirate,[1079] and discriminatory practices or provisions with regard to property regimes,[1080] separation and divorce,[1081] child custody,[1082] women's legal guardianship,[1083] the differences in the rights enjoyed by men and women marrying foreign citizens,[1084] as well as in conferring their nationality on their partner upon marriage.[1085] It has insisted on measures so that women and men share domestic work and the care of children equally.[1086]

In the field of economic, social and cultural rights, the Committee has expressed concern about the lack of affirmative action to support women's efforts to break the cycle of poverty.[1087] It has highlighted issues of discrimination of women in *for example,* social security and taxation.[1088] Repeatedly, it has focused on high(er) illiteracy rates of women,[1089] low(er) attendance rates,[1090] women's predominance in traditionally female areas of education and the persistence of stereotypical attitudes.[1091] The Committee has stressed the need for affirmative action for women in education (see also further under the obligation to fulfil-provide).[1092] It has insisted on special measures

1074 UN Doc. CEDAW/C/GAB/CC/2-5, para. 22 (Gabon).
1075 UN Doc. CEDAW/C/TUR/CC/4-5, para. 25 (Turkey).
1076 UN Doc. CEDAW/C/GAB/CC/2-5, para. 22 (Gabon); UN Doc. CEDAW/C/WSM/CC/1-3, para. 34 (Samoa); UN Doc. CEDAW/C/LAO/CC/1-5, para. 39 (Laos); UN Doc. A/51/38, para. 159 (Ethiopia).
1077 UN Doc. CEDAW/C/PAR/CC/3-5, para. 26 (Paraguay).
1078 UN Doc. A/55/38 (part I), para. 69 (India).
1079 UN Doc. CEDAW/C/GAB/CC/2-5, para. 30 (Gabon); UN Doc. CEDAW/C/TUR/CC/4-5, para. 29 (Turkey).
1080 UN Doc. CEDAW/C/TUR/CC/4-5, para. 25 (Turkey); UN Doc. CEDAW/C/WSM/CC/1-3, para. 34 (Samoa).
1081 UN Doc. CEDAW/C/GAB/CC/2-5, para. 22 (Gabon); UN Doc. CEDAW/C/DZA/CC/2, para. 25 (Algeria); UN Doc. CEDAW/C/WSM/CC/1-3, para. 34 (Samoa).
1082 UN Doc. CEDAW/C/GAB/CC/2-5, para. 22 (Gabon); UN Doc. CEDAW/C/DZA/CC/2, para. 25 (Algeria).
1083 UN Doc. CEDAW/C/DZA/CC/2, para. 25 (Algeria).
1084 UN Doc. A/50/38, para. 210 (Mauritius).
1085 UN Doc. CEDAW/C/DZA/CC/2, para. 25 (Algeria); UN Doc. A/52/38/Rev.1, para. 2394 (Venezuela).
1086 UN Doc. A/51/38, para. 300 (Ukraine).
1087 UN Doc. A/53/38/Rev.1 (part I), para. 333 (Dominican Republic).
1088 UN Doc. A/51/38, paras. 187 and 190 (Belgium).
1089 See recently in UN Doc. CEDAW/C/TUR/CC/4-5, para. 33 (Turkey); UN Doc. CEDAW/C/PAR/CC/3-5, para. 36 (Paraguay); UN Doc. CEDAW/C/LAO/CC/1-5, para. 23 (Laos).
1090 See recently in UN Doc. CEDAW/C/TUR/CC/4-5, para. 33 (Turkey); UN Doc. CEDAW/C/GAB/CC/2-5, para. 32 (Gabon).
1091 See recently in UN Doc. CEDAW/C/TUR/CC/4-5, para. 33 (Turkey); UN Doc. CEDAW/C/CRO/CC/2-3, para. 33 (Croatia).
1092 UN Doc. A/56/38 (part I), para. 134 (Maldives); UN Doc. A/55/38 (part II), para. 138 (Lithuania); UN Doc. A/51/38, para. 143 (Ethiopia).

and incentives for girls for the achievement of universal literacy and primary education,[1093] and on the reduction of the very high drop-out rates among girls.[1094] As to health, concern has been expressed about high maternal mortality rates,[1095] women's access to primary health services, particularly reproductive health, family life education and family planning services,[1096] and the enjoyment of reproductive rights by guaranteeing them access to safe abortion services in public hospitals.[1097] With regard to HIV/AIDS, states are to address the gender dimensions of HIV/AIDS, including the power differential between women and men, which is said to often prevent women from insisting on safe and responsible sex practices.[1098] A multifaceted and holistic approach to combating the HIV/AIDS pandemic is to be taken,[1099] and infected women and men must be guaranteed equal enjoyment of their human rights.[1100]

Occasionally, the Committee has insisted on the elimination of all forms of discrimination with respect to ownership, co-sharing and inheritance of land,[1101] and on equality in land distribution and ownership in all aspects of its productive use.[1102]

ii. Gender-Based Violence

As early as 1992, the Committee has subsumed gender-based violence under the concept of gender discrimination.[1103] This was once more reconfirmed in its views on the second complaint it dealt with under the recently-established individual complaints procedure.[1104] It has called upon states to adopt a zero tolerance policy[1105] and to address the issue of gender-based violence in a holistic manner,[1106] through legislation[1107]

1093 UN Doc. A/54/38/Rev.1 (part I), para. 295 (China).

1094 UN Doc. A/53/38/Rev.1 (part II), para. 329-332 (Peru).

1095 UN Doc. CEDAW/C/TUR/CC/4-5, para. 37 (Turkey); UN Doc. CEDAW/C/PAR/CC/3-5, para. 32 (Paraguay); UN Doc. CEDAW/C/WSM/CC/1-3, para. 30 (Samoa).

1096 UN Doc. HRI/GEN/1/Rev.7, General Recommendation No. 24 (1999), *Article 12 of the Convention on the Elimination of All Forms of Discrimination against Women – Women and Health*, para. 2; UN Doc. CEDAW/C/PAR/CC/3-5, para. 32 (Paraguay); UN Doc. CEDAW/C/LAO/CC/1-5, para. 25 (Laos); UN Doc. A/52/38/Rev.1 (part II), para. 450 (Bangladesh); UN Doc. A/51/38, para. 160 (Ethiopia); UN Doc. A/51/38, para. 131 (Paraguay).

1097 UN Doc. A/52/38/Rev.1 (part II), para. 360 (Italy).

1098 UN Doc. A/57/38 (part III), para. 248 (Barbados).

1099 UN Doc. A/56/38 (part I), para. 60 (Burundi).

1100 UN Doc. A/51/38, para. 161 (Ethiopia).

1101 UN Doc. A/57/38 (part III), para. 152 (Uganda).

1102 UN Doc. A/51/38, para. 132 (Paraguay).

1103 UN Doc. HRI/GEN/1/Rev.7, General Recommendation No. 19 (1992), *Violence Against Women*, paras. 1 and 6.

1104 Communication No. 2/2003, *A.T. v. Hungary*, para. 9.2.

1105 UN Doc. A/57/38 (part II), para. 239 (Zambia).

1106 UN Doc. A/55/38 (part I), para. 70 (India); UN Doc. A/52/38/Rev.1 (part II), para. 402 (Australia); UN Doc. A/51/38, para. 104 (Iceland).

1107 UN Doc. A/55/38 (part I), para. 218 (Congo).

(including criminalisation),[1108] awareness-raising and education,[1109] and national plans of action,[1110] and by strengthening enforcement and monitoring of existing laws, policies and mechanisms on violence.[1111] Funding is to be allocated commensurate with the high priority that efforts to combating violence against women should have.[1112] Assistance is to be given to the victims: states are to ensure that victims of violence receive support from the police, understanding of the dynamics of violence against women from judges, counselling and placement in shelters and, in particular, that they be assisted in rebuilding their lives.[1113] The Committee has emphasized the need for a network of crisis centres (including hotlines),[1114] the establishment of victim support centres equipped with legal, medical, psychological and emotional support[1115] and adequately resourced women's shelters.[1116] In addition, women victims of violence are to be provided socio-economic integration measures.[1117] Measures are to be taken to encourage the reporting of violence (*e.g.* through primary health-care providers)[1118] and the submission of complaints, and to provide mechanisms for effective and timely response to such claims.[1119] Procedures should permit prosecution of violence against women independent of victim testimony and omitting the requirement that the complainant's evidence be corroborated.[1120] Women are also to be protected from reprisal where they report their victimization.[1121]

Training is to be offered to legal, health and police personnel.[1122] The incorporation of models of non-violent forms of conflict resolution in education and the media is

---

1108 UN Doc. A/53/38/Rev.1 (part II), para. 234 (Tanzania).
1109 UN Doc. A/53/38/Rev.1 (part II), para. 165 (Nigeria); UN Doc. A/52/38/Rev.1, para. 194 (Turkey).
1110 UN Doc. A/55/38 (part I), para. 70 (India).
1111 UN Doc. A/52/38/Rev.1 (part II), para. 451 (Bangladesh).
1112 UN Doc. A/57/38 (part I), para. 195 (Uruguay).
1113 UN Doc. A/52/38/Rev.1, para. 101 (Slovenia).
1114 UN Doc. A/58/38 (part I), para. 370 (Canada); UN Doc. A/55/38 (part II), para. 264 (Cuba); UN Doc. A/55/38 (part II), para. 190 (Iraq).
1115 UN Doc. A/55/38 (part II), para. 50 (Cameroon); UN Doc. A/55/38 (part I), para. 218 (Congo); UN Doc. A/54/38/Rev.1 (part II), para. 102 (Georgia); UN Doc. A/54/38/Rev.1 (part I), para. 324 (China-Hong Kong); UN Doc. A/54/38/Rev.1 (part I), para. 124 (Kyrgyzstan); UN Doc. A/53/38/Rev.1 (part II), para. 201 (Panama); UN Doc. A/53/38/Rev.1 (part II), para. 80 (Slovakia).
1116 UN Doc. A/58/38 (part I), para. 370 (Canada); UN Doc. A/55/38 (part II), para. 264 (Cuba); UN Doc. A/55/38 (part II), para. 190 (Iraq); UN Doc. A/53/38/Rev.1 (part II), para. 375 (Korea); UN Doc. A/53/38/Rev.1 (part II), para. 165 (Nigeria); UN Doc. A/52/38/Rev.1 (part II), para. 359 (Italy); UN Doc. A/54/38/Rev.1 (part I), para. 286 (China); UN Doc. A/53/38/Rev.1 (part II), para. 234 (Tanzania); UN Doc. A/52/38/Rev.1, para. 194 (Turkey).
1117 UN Doc. A/55/38 (part I), para. 218 (Congo).
1118 UN Doc. A/51/38, para. 104 (Iceland).
1119 UN Doc. A/52/38/Rev.1 (part II), para. 359 (Italy).
1120 UN Doc. A/53/38/Rev.1 (part II), para. 80 (Slovakia).
1121 UN Doc. A/57/38 (part I), para. 285 (Sri Lanka); UN Doc. A/53/38/Rev.1 (part II), para. 165 (Nigeria).
1122 UN Doc. A/55/38 (part II), para. 50 (Cameroon); UN Doc. A/52/38/Rev.1 (part II), para. 359 (Italy).

encouraged.[1123] Public-awareness campaigns are to be launched in order to achieve zero tolerance with regard to all forms of violence against women and girls.[1124]

Female genital mutilation is one among many examples of gender-based violence.[1125] States are urgently to take all appropriate measures, including legislation[1126] and awareness programmes to abolish the practice of female genital mutilation and all other such practices that discriminate against women.[1127] Domestic violence against women too has been qualified as "a form of discrimination against women and a violation of their human rights".[1128] Consistent attention has also been paid to trafficking of women.[1129]

iii. Polygamy

In its general recommendation on equality in marriage and family relations of 1994, the CEDAW Committee unequivocally qualified polygamous marriages as a form of gender discrimination. It submitted that "polygamous marriage contravenes a woman's right to equality with men".[1130] While the Committee in its concluding comments has not always explicitly qualified polygamy as discrimination,[1131] it has done so in a number of instances[1132], and it has consistently urged states to eliminate it.[1133]

1123 UN Doc. A/53/38/Rev.1 (part II), para. 375 (Korea).

1124 UN Doc. A/57/38 (part III), para. 432 (Mexico); UN Doc. A/55/38 (part II), para. 190 (Iraq); UN Doc. A/55/38 (part II), para. 50 (Cameroon).

1125 UN Doc. HRI/GEN/1/Rev.7, General Recommendation No. 19 (1992), *Violence Against Women*, para. 11.

1126 UN Doc. A/58/38 (part I), para. 1190 (Switzerland).

1127 UN Doc. A/51/38, para. 155 (Ethiopia).

1128 UN Doc. CEDAW/C/TUR/CC/4-5, para. 28 (Turkey); UN Doc. CEDAW/C/GAB/CC/2-5, para. 27 (Gabon); UN Doc. CEDAW/C/DZA/CC/2, para. 32 (Algeria); UN Doc. CEDAW/C/WSM/CC/1-3, para. 25 (Samoa); UN Doc. CEDAW/C/LAO/CC/1-5, para. 37 (Laos).

1129 UN Doc. CEDAW/C/ITA/CC/4-5, para. 31 (Italy); UN Doc. CEDAW/C/PAR/CC/3-5, para. 28 (Paraguay); UN Doc. CEDAW/C/CRO/CC/2-3, para. 37 (Croatia).

1130 UN Doc. HRI/GEN/1/Rev.7, General Recommendation No. 19 (1994), *Equality in Marriage and Family Relations*, para. 14.

1131 See *e.g.* UN Doc. A/56/38 (part II), para. 123 (Guinea); UN Doc. A/56/38 (part I), para. 188 (Uzbekistan); UN Doc. A/55/38 (part I), para. 282 (Burkina Faso); UN Doc. A/55/38 (part I), para. 175 (Jordan); UN Doc. A/53/38/Rev.1 (part II), para. 118 (South Africa); UN Doc. A/52/38/Rev.1 (part II), para. 124 (Namibia): "address the issue", "discourage polygamy".

1132 See e.g. UN Doc. CEDAW/C/TUR/CC/4-5, para. 29 (Turkey); UN Doc. A/58/38 (part I), para. 181 (Congo); UN Doc. A/55/38 (part II), para. 192 (Iraq); UN Doc. A/54/38/Rev.1 (part I), para. 91 (Algeria); UN Doc. A/53/38/Rev.1 (part I), paras. 141 and 151 (Zimbabwe).

1133 Most recently e.g. in UN Doc. CEDAW/C/GAB/CC/2-5, paras. 22 and 30 (Gabon); UN Doc. CEDAW/C/DZA/CC/2, para. 25 (Algeria).

iv. Marital Status

Women are to be able to freely choose their own domicile, regardless of their marital status.[1134] Discrimination with regard to full social security coverage between married and unmarried women is to be abolished.[1135]

v. Sexual Orientation

Occasionally, the CEDAW Committee has paid attention to discrimination based on sexual orientation.[1136]

b. Other Grounds

The Committee has referred to *inter alia* religious beliefs, political preferences, age or disability, ethnicity, and differences between rural and urban areas, albeit only rarely.[1137] Reference has been made to these grounds in the exclusive context of discrimination among women.

i. Disability

On at least one occasion, the Committee has invited a state to ensure that disabled women did not suffer from discrimination, in particular in the areas of employment and access to health care and loans.[1138]

ii. Age

The Committee has explicitly referred to age discrimination women were faced with in the labour market.[1139]

iii. Place of Residence

The CEDAW Committee has pointed out that rural women do not have access to the same opportunities for the same services as those in the cities,[1140] *e.g.* with regard to

---

1134 UN Doc. HRI/GEN/1/Rev.7, General Recommendation No. 19 (1994), *Equality in Marriage and Family Relations*, para. 9.

1135 UN Doc. A/51/38, para. 65 (Paraguay).

1136 UN Doc. A/56/38 (part II), para. 334 (Sweden); UN Doc. A/54/38/Rev.1 (part I), paras. 127-128 (Kyrgyzstan); UN Doc. A/49/38, para. 316 (Netherlands).

1137 UN Doc. A/53/38/Rev.1 (part II), para. 372 (Korea); UN Doc. A/52/38/Rev.1 (part II), para. 400 (Australia).

1138 UN Doc. A/58/38 (part II), para. 422 (New Zealand).

1139 UN Doc. CEDAW/C/CRO/CC/2-3, para. 28 (Croatia); UN Doc. A/54/38/Rev.1 (part I), para. 2964 (China).

1140 UN Doc. A/54/38/Rev.1 (part I), para. 278 (China); UN Doc. A/54/38/Rev.1 (part II), para. 137 (Nepal); UN Doc. A/50/38, para. 152 (Chile).

employment outside the home[1141] and working hours,[1142] living conditions,[1143] education,[1144] and health,[1145] which leads to multiple forms of discrimination against rural women.[1146] Programmes and services directed towards rural women are therefore to be strengthened,[1147] so as to reduce discrimination suffered by rural women[1148] and to ensure their economic empowerment, their access to capital and productive resources as well as to health-care services and educational and social opportunities.[1149]

iv. Ethnic Origin

China has been asked to eliminate discrimination against indigenous women.[1150] The marginalized and disadvantaged situation of indigenous women,[1151] Roma women[1152] and women belonging to ethnic minorities[1153] seems to have received increased attention in recent years.

c. Conclusions

CEDAW deals with one particular form of discrimination, *i.e.* sex/gender discrimination. The CEDAW Committee has taken the broad approach of women's rights, rather than the more limited one of discrimination against women, which may explain why discrimination language has very often not been used explicitly. The Committee has subsumed under the concept of gender pregnancy, marital status and sexual orientation. The HRC and the CESCR Committee have taken a similar approach. The CEDAW Committee was also the first to take a broad concept of gender discrimination, including gender-based violence. Here too, the HRC and the CESCR Committee have followed suit.

As to the issues that have been addressed under the heading of gender discrimination, concern has been expressed about pay discrimination, access to the labour market and to senior posts in the field of labour, about women's participation in public and political life, about their rights in and to marriage (including the same marriageable

1141 UN Doc. A/51/38, para. 99 (Iceland).
1142 UN Doc. A/53/38/Rev.1 (part I), para. 149 (Zimbabwe).
1143 UN Doc. A/52/38/Rev.1 (part II), para. 305 (Argentina).
1144 UN Doc. CEDAW/C/LAO/CC/1-5, para. 23 (Laos).
1145 UN Doc. CEDAW/C/LAO/CC/1-5, para. 25 (Laos); UN Doc. A/51/38, para. 123 (Iceland).
1146 UN Doc. CEDAW/C/GAB/CC/2-5, para. 38 (Gabon).
1147 UN Doc. A/52/38/Rev.1 (part II), para. 320 (Argentina).
1148 UN Doc. A/53/38/Rev.1 (part II), para. 173 (Nigeria).
1149 UN Doc. A/57/38 (part II), para. 66 (Suriname); UN Doc. A/56/38 (part II), para. 175 (Guyana); UN Doc. A/56/38 (part I), para. 190 (Uzbekistan); UN Doc. A/56/38 (part I), para. 110 (Kazakhstan).
1150 UN Doc. A/54/38/Rev.1 (part I), para. 333 (China-Hong Kong).
1151 UN Doc. CEDAW/C/PAR/CC/3-5, para. 36 (Paraguay).
1152 UN Doc. CEDAW/C/CRO/CC/2-3, para. 29 (Croatia).
1153 UN Doc. CEDAW/C/LAO/CC/1-5, paras. 21, 23 and 25 (Laos).

age for boys and girls, the transfer of nationality to a foreign partner, and with regard to divorce and property regimes), and in the fields of education and health. Own accents compared to the HRC and the CESCR Committee may be the concern about safe jobs for women, and about HIV/AIDS.

Occasionally, reference has been made to age, disability, place of residence and ethnic origin as prohibited grounds of gender discrimination.

Unique in the CEDAW Committee's approach is its unparalleled emphasis on affirmative action ("temporary special measures"). This point will be explored in greater detail in chapter IV, under the obligation to fulfil-provide.

5. CRC COMMITTEE

As pointed out above, the CRC contains largely the same list of prohibited grounds of discrimination as the CCPR and the CESCR do, with two additional grounds, *i.e.* ethnic origin and disability.

Since 2000, the CRC Committee has included a separate heading in its concluding observations on the general principle of non-discrimination, which is one of the four general principles of the Convention. It has paid particular attention to discrimination based on any of the prohibited grounds with regard to social services like education and health. In its more recent concluding observations, discrimination against children with disabilities has been a major concern which the Committee has raised systematically.

The CRC Committee very often expresses in a general clause its concern at the occurrence of discrimination[1154] (or disparities[1155] or discrepancies)[1156] in the enjoyment of rights (health, education and other social services) against vulnerable groups of

---

1154 See for 2004-2005 *e.g.* UN Doc. CRC/C/15/Add.263, para. 22 (Mongolia); UN Doc. CRC/C/15/Add.261, para. 28 (Ecuador); UN Doc. CRC/C/15/Add.260, para. 35 (Nepal); UN Doc. CRC/C/15/Add.258, para. 20 (Philippines); UN Doc. CRC/C/15/Add.257, para. 29 (Nigeria); UN Doc. CRC/C/15/Add.253, para. 28 (The Bahamas); UN Doc. CRC/C/15/Add.250, para. 18 (Luxembourg); UN Doc. CRC/C/15/Add.244, para. 26 (Kyrgyzstan); UN Doc. CRC/C/15/Add.242, para. 27 (Botswana); UN Doc. CRC/C/15/Add.240, para. 18 (France); UN Doc. CRC/C/15/Add.238, para. 21 (Dominica); UN Doc. CRC/C/15/Add.233, para. 24 (Panama); UN Doc. CRC/C/15/Add.232, para. 25 (El Salvador); UN Doc. CRC/C/15/Add.231, para. 24 (Japan); UN Doc. CRC/C/15/Add.224, para. 22 (Guyana).

1155 See for 2004-2005 *e.g.* UN Doc. CRC/C/15/Add.266, para. 32 (Yemen); UN Doc. CRC/C/15/Add.250, para. 18 (Luxembourg); UN Doc. CRC/C/15/Add.239, para. 27 (People's Republic of Korea); UN Doc. CRC/C/15/Add. 236, para. 23 (Liberia); UN Doc. CRC/C/15/Add.228, para. 25 (India).

1156 UN Doc. CRC/C/15/Add.159, para. 25 (Mauritania); UN Doc. CRC/C/15/Add.155, para. 22 (Ivory Coast); UN Doc. CRC/C/15/Add. 119, para. 24 (Armenia).

children. In the enumerated vulnerable groups of children, some of the prohibited grounds are reflected. Gender discrimination – which is sometimes also mentioned additionally as such[1157] – is addressed in the Committee's concerns about girls[1158] and about particularly vulnerable girl children like child brides[1159] and pregnant girls.[1160] Other grounds frequently invoked include race,[1161] colour,[1162] religion,[1163] national or ethnic origin[1164] (minority children,[1165] tribal children,[1166] children of ethnic minorities,[1167] children belonging to ethnic groups,[1168] Roma and Traveller

---

1157 UN Doc. CRC/C/15/Add.141, para. 23 (Comoros); UN Doc. CRC/C/15/Add.137, para. 32 (Colombia); UN Doc. CRC/C/15/Add.128, para. 27 (Cambodia); UN Doc. CRC/C/15/Add.108, para. 24 (Nicaragua); UN Doc. CRC/C/15/Add.95, para. 17 (Bolivia); UN Doc. CRC/C/15/Add.93, para. 18 (Ecuador); UN Doc. CRC/C/15/Add.14, para. 7 (Namibia).

1158 See for 2004-2005 *e.g.* UN Doc. CRC/C/15/Add.261, para. 28 (Ecuador); UN Doc. CRC/C/15/Add.260, para. 35 (Nepal); UN Doc. CRC/C/15/Add.259, para. 25 (Bosnia and Herzegovina); UN Doc. CRC/C/15/Add.257, para. 29 (Nigeria); UN Doc. CRC/C/15/Add.252, para. 25 (Belize); UN Doc. CRC/C/15/Add.250, para. 18 (Luxembourg); UN Doc. CRC/C/15/Add. 236, para. 23 (Liberia); UN Doc. CRC/C/15/Add.232, para. 25 (El Salvador); UN Doc. CRC/C/15/Add.231, para. 24 (Japan); UN Doc. CRC/C/15/Add.228, para. 25 (India).

1159 UN Doc. CRC/C/15/Add.113, para. 16 (Mali).

1160 UN Doc. CRC/C/15/Add.252, para. 25 (Belize); UN Doc. CRC/C/15/Add.147, para. 25 (Lesotho).

1161 UN Doc. CRC/C/15/Add.137, para. 32 (Colombia).

1162 UN Doc. CRC/C/15/Add.240, para. 18 (France); UN Doc. CRC/C/15/Add.122, para. 18 (South Africa).

1163 UN Doc. CRC/C/15/Add.240, para. 18 (France); UN Doc. CRC/C/15/Add.195, para. 26 (Israel); UN Doc. CRC/C/15/Add.190, para. 26 (Sudan); UN Doc. CRC/C/15/Add.155, para. 22 (Ivory Coast);UN Doc. CRC/C/15/Add.141, para. 23 (Comoros).

1164 UN Doc. CRC/C/15/Add.240, para. 18 (France); UN Doc. CRC/C/15/Add.205, para. 27 (Cyprus); UN Doc. CRC/C/15/Add.169, para. 23 (Lebanon); UN Doc. CRC/C/15/Add.149, para. 32 (Palau).

1165 UN Doc. CRC/C/15/Add.252, para. 25 (Belize); UN Doc. CRC/C/15/Add.231, para. 24 (Japan); UN Doc. CRC/C/15/Add.217, para. 30 (Pakistan); UN Doc. CRC/C/15/Add.216, para. 22 (New Zealand); UN Doc. CRC/C/15/Add.199, para. 25 (Romania); UN Doc. CRC/C/15/Add.195, para. 26 (Israel); UN Doc. CRC/C/15/Add.167, para. 26 (Uzbekistan); UN Doc. CRC/C/15/Add.159, para. 25 (Mauritania); UN Doc. CRC/C/15/Add.152, para. 29 (Turkey); UN Doc. CRC/C/15/Add.130, para. 25 (Suriname); UN Doc. CRC/C/15/Add.90, para. 13 (Japan); UN Doc. CRC/C/15/Add.81, para. 13 (Czech Republic); UN Doc. CRC/C/15/Add. 78, para. 15 (Laos).

1166 UN Doc. CRC/C/15/Add.221, para. 28 (Bangladesh); UN Doc. CRC/C/15/Add.97, para. 18 (Thailand).

1167 UN Doc. CRC/C/15/Add.260, para. 35 (Nepal); UN Doc. CRC/C/15/Add.258, para. 20 (Philippines); UN Doc. CRC/C/15/Add.257, para. 29 (Nigeria); UN Doc. CRC/C/15/Add.250, para. 18 (Luxembourg); UN Doc. CRC/C/15/Add.227, para. 30 (Netherlands and Aruba); UN Doc. CRC/C/15/Add.208, para. 21 (Solomon Islands); UN Doc. CRC/C/15/Add.199, para. 25 (Romania); UN Doc. CRC/C/15/Add.156, para. 26 (Tanzania); UN Doc. CRC/C/15/Add.155, para. 22 (Ivory Coast); UN Doc. CRC/C/15/Add.151, para. 26 (Denmark); UN Doc. CRC/C/15/Add.147, para. 25 (Lesotho); UN Doc. CRC/C/15/Add.69, para. 13 (Myanmar); UN Doc. CRC/C/15/Add.61, para. 12 (Nigeria).

1168 UN Doc. CRC/C/15/Add.236, para. 23 (Liberia); UN Doc. CRC/C/15/Add.190, para. 26 (Sudan); UN Doc. CRC/C/15/Add.171, para. 24 (Gabon); UN Doc. CRC/C/15/Add.164, para. 25 (Cameroon); UN Doc. CRC/C/15/Add.157, para. 28 (Bhutan); UN Doc. CRC/C/15/Add.141, para. 23 (Comoros); UN Doc. CRC/C/15/Add.131, para. 27 (Djibouti); UN Doc. CRC/C/15/Add.128, para. 27 (Cambodia); UN Doc. CRC/C/15/Add.108, para. 24 (Nicaragua); UN Doc. CRC/C/15/Add.102, para. 18 (Yemen); UN Doc. CRC/C/15/Add.95, para. 17 (Bolivia); UN Doc. CRC/C/15/Add.93, para. 18 (Ecuador).

children,[1169] indigenous children),[1170] caste,[1171] property (poverty,[1172] street children[1173]), disability,[1174] birth (born out of wedlock),[1175] health status

[1169] UN Doc. CRC/C/15/Add.250, para. 18 (Luxembourg); UN Doc. CRC/C/15/Add.198, para. 20 (Italy); UN Doc. CRC/C/15/Add.191, para. 29 (Ukraine); UN Doc. CRC/C/15/Add.188, para. 22 (United Kingdom); UN Doc. CRC/C/15/Add.185, para. 27 (Spain); UN Doc. CRC/C/15/Add.180, para. 28 (Belarus); UN Doc. CRC/C/15/Add.146, para. 21 (Lithuania); UN Doc. CRC/C/15/Add.142, para. 23 (Latvia); UN Doc. CRC/C/15/Add.85, para. 14 (Ireland); UN Doc. CRC/C/15/Add.66, para. 12 (Bulgaria); UN Doc. CRC/C/15/Add.41, para. 11 (Italy).

[1170] UN Doc. CRC/C/15/Add.252, para. 25 (Belize); UN Doc. CRC/C/15/Add.232, para. 25 (El Salvador); UN Doc. CRC/C/15/Add.216, para. 22 (New Zealand); UN Doc. CRC/C/15/Add.187, para. 29 (Argentina); UN Doc. CRC/C/15/Add.173, para. 26 (Chile); UN Doc. CRC/C/15/Add.166, para. 27 (Paraguay); UN Doc. CRC/C/15/Add.154, para. 26 (Guatemala); UN Doc. CRC/C/15/Add.137, para. 32 (Colombia); UN Doc. CRC/C/15/Add.130, para. 25 (Suriname); UN Doc. CRC/C/15/Add.113, para. 16 (Mali); UN Doc. CRC/C/15/Add.99, para. 16 (Belize); UN Doc. CRC/C/15/Add.68, para. 15 (Panama).

[1171] UN Doc. CRC/C/15/Add.260, para. 35 (Nepal); UN Doc. CRC/C/15/Add.228, para. 25 (India); UN Doc. CRC/C/15/Add.115, para. 28 (India).

[1172] UN Doc. CRC/C/15/Add.263, para. 22 (Mongolia); UN Doc. CRC/C/15/Add.261, para. 28 (Ecuador); UN Doc. CRC/C/15/Add.258, para. 20 (Philippines); UN Doc. CRC/C/15/Add.257, para. 29 (Nigeria); UN Doc. CRC/C/15/Add.253, para. 28 (The Bahamas); UN Doc. CRC/C/15/Add.235, para. 21 (Sao Tome and Principe); UN Doc. CRC/C/15/Add.208, para. 21 (Solomon Islands); UN Doc. CRC/C/15/Add.206, para. 21 (Zambia); UN Doc. CRC/C/15/Add.202, para. 25 (Haiti); UN Doc. CRC/C/15/Add.199, para. 25 (Romania); UN Doc. CRC/C/15/Add.198, para. 20 (Italy); UN Doc. CRC/C/15/Add.194, para. 27 (Poland); UN Doc. CRC/C/15/Add.191, para. 29 (Ukraine); UN Doc. CRC/C/15/Add.188, para. 22 (United Kingdom); UN Doc. CRC/C/15/Add.187, para. 29 (Argentina)UN Doc. CRC/C/15/Add.180, para. 28 (Belarus); UN Doc. CRC/C/15/Add.178, para. 18 (Belgium); UN Doc. CRC/C/15/Add.174, para. 22 (Malawi); UN Doc. CRC/C/15/Add.173, para. 26 (Chile); UN Doc. CRC/C/15/Add.166, para. 27 (Paraguay); UN Doc. CRC/C/15/Add.160, para. 24 (Kenya); UN Doc. CRC/C/15/Add.159, para. 25 (Mauritania); UN Doc. CRC/C/15/Add.157, para. 28 (Bhutan); UN Doc. CRC/C/15/Add.156, para. 26 (Tanzania); UN Doc. CRC/C/15/Add.155, para. 22 (Ivory Coast); UN Doc. CRC/C/15/Add.154, para. 26 (Guatemala); UN Doc. CRC/C/15/Add.151, para. 26 (Denmark); UN Doc. CRC/C/15/Add.142, para. 23 (Latvia); UN Doc. CRC/C/15/Add.139, para. 28 (Marshall Islands; UN Doc. CRC/C/15/Add.130, para. 25 (Suriname); UN Doc. CRC/C/15/Add.127, para. 21 (Kyrgyzstan); UN Doc. CRC/C/15/Add.124, para. 24 (Georgia); UN Doc. CRC/C/15/Add.119, para. 24 (Armenia); UN Doc. CRC/C/15/Add.106, para. 15 (Benin); UN Doc. CRC/C/15/Add.100, para. 17 (Guinea); UN Doc. CRC/C/15/Add.99, para. 16 (Belize); UN Doc. CRC/C/15/Add.97, para. 18 (Thailand); UN Doc. CRC/C/15/Add.85, para. 14 (Ireland); UN Doc. CRC/C/15/Add.68, para. 15 (Panama); UN Doc. CRC/C/15/Add.41, para. 11 (Italy).

[1173] UN Doc. CRC/C/15/Add.266, para. 32 (Yemen); UN Doc. CRC/C/15/Add.263, para. 22 (Mongolia); UN Doc. CRC/C/15/Add.260, para. 35 (Nepal); UN Doc. CRC/C/15/Add.258, para. 20 (Philippines); UN Doc. CRC/C/15/Add.221, para. 28 (Bangladesh); UN Doc. CRC/C/15/Add.202, para. 25 (Haiti); UN Doc. CRC/C/15/Add.192, para. 26 (Moldova); UN Doc. CRC/C/15/Add.187, para. 29 (Argentina); UN Doc. CRC/C/15/Add.166, para. 27 (Paraguay); UN Doc. CRC/C/15/Add.160, para. 24 (Kenya); UN Doc. CRC/C/15/Add.159, para. 25 (Mauritania); UN Doc. CRC/C/15/Add.156, para. 26 (Tanzania); UN Doc. CRC/C/15/Add.155, para. 22 (Ivory Coast); UN Doc. CRC/C/15/Add.149, para. 32 (Palau); UN Doc. CRC/C/15/Add.147, para. 25 (Lesotho); UN Doc. CRC/C/15/Add.131, para. 27 (Djibouti); UN Doc. CRC/C/15/Add.130, para. 25 (Suriname); UN Doc. CRC/C/15/Add.124, para. 24 (Georgia); UN Doc. CRC/C/15/Add.122, para. 18 (South Africa); UN Doc. CRC/C/15/Add.119, para. 24 (Armenia); UN Doc. CRC/C/15/Add.113, para. 16 (Mali); UN Doc. CRC/C/15/Add.106, para. 15 (Benin); UN Doc. CRC/C/15/Add.99, para. 16 (Belize); UN Doc. CRC/C/15/Add.97, para. 18 (Thailand); UN Doc. CRC/C/15/Add.81, para. 13 (Czech Republic).

[1174] For 2004-2005 see UN Doc. CRC/C/15/Add.266, para. 32 (Yemen); UN Doc. CRC/C/15/Add.263, para. 22 (Mongolia); UN Doc. CRC/C/15/Add.260, para. 35 (Nepal); UN Doc. CRC/C/15/Add.259, para. 25 (Bosnia and Herzegovina); UN Doc. CRC/C/15/Add.258, para. 20 (Philippines); UN Doc.

(HIV/AIDS),[1176] nationality ("sans papiers",[1177] refugee and asylum-seeking children,[1178] foreign children[1179] including unaccompanied minors,[1180] illegal immigrant children,[1181] children of migrant workers[1182]), place of residence (children living in rural and remote areas,[1183] remote islands,[1184] slums[1185] and refugee camps[1186], children residing in the Overseas Departments and Territories,[1187] children living in areas of conflict[1188]),

---

CRC/C/15/Add.257, para. 29 (Nigeria); UN Doc. CRC/C/15/Add.253, para. 28 (The Bahamas); UN Doc. CRC/C/15/Add.252, para. 25 (Belize); UN Doc. CRC/C/15/Add.250, para. 18 (Luxembourg); UN Doc. CRC/C/15/Add.239, para. 27 (People's Republic of Korea); UN Doc. CRC/C/15/Add.236, para. 23 (Liberia); UN Doc. CRC/C/15/Add.235, para. 21 (Sao Tome and Principe); UN Doc. CRC/C/15/Add.232, para. 25 (El Salvador); UN Doc. CRC/C/15/Add.231, para. 24 (Japan).

1175 See *e.g.* in 2004-2005 in UN Doc. CRC/C/15/Add.266, para. 32 (Yemen); UN Doc. CRC/C/15/Add.257, para. 29 (Nigeria); UN Doc. CRC/C/15/Add.240, para. 18 (France).

1176 UN Doc. CRC/C/15/Add.252, para. 25 (Belize); UN Doc. CRC/C/15/Add.199, para. 25 (Romania); UN Doc. CRC/C/15/Add.194, para. 27 (Poland); UN Doc. CRC/C/15/Add.192, para. 26 (Moldova); UN Doc. CRC/C/15/Add.191, para. 29 (Ukraine);. UN Doc. CRC/C/15/Add.147, para. 25 (Lesotho); UN Doc. CRC/C/15/Add.128, para. 27 (Cambodia).

1177 UN Doc. CRC/C/15/Add.240, para. 18 (France).

1178 For 2004-2005 see UN Doc. CRC/C/15/Add.261, para. 28 (Ecuador); UN Doc. CRC/C/15/Add.260, para. 35 (Nepal); UN Doc. CRC/C/15/Add.250, para. 18 (Luxembourg); UN Doc. CRC/C/15/Add.227, para. 30 (Netherlands and Aruba).

1179 UN Doc. CRC/C/15/Add.240, para. 18 (France); UN Doc. CRC/C/15/Add. 216, para. 22 (New Zealand); UN Doc. CRC/C/15/Add.199, para. 25 (Romania); UN Doc. CRC/C/15/Add.163, para. 32 (Qatar); UN Doc. CRC/C/15/Add.155, para. 22 (Ivory Coast); UN Doc. CRC/C/15/Add.142, para. 23 (Latvia).

1180 UN Doc. CRC/C/15/Add.198, para. 20 (Italy); UN Doc. CRC/C/15/Add.178, para. 18 (Belgium); UN Doc. CRC/C/15/Add.45, para. 13 (Portugal).

1181 UN Doc. CRC/C/15/Add.258, para. 20 (Philippines); UN Doc. CRC/C/15/Add.99, para. 16 (Belize); UN Doc. CRC/C/15/Add.97, para. 18 (Thailand); UN Doc. CRC/C/15/Add.45, para. 13 (Portugal).

1182 UN Doc. CRC/C/15/Add.253, para. 28 (The Bahamas); UN Doc. CRC/C/15/Add.252, para. 25 (Belize); UN Doc. CRC/C/15/Add.231, para. 24 (Japan); UN Doc. CRC/C/15/Add.195, para. 26 (Israel); UN Doc. CRC/C/15/Add.187, para. 29 (Argentina); UN Doc. CRC/C/15/Add.185, para. 27 (Spain); UN Doc. CRC/C/15/Add.151, para. 26 (Denmark); UN Doc. CRC/C/15/Add.127, para. 24 (Kyrgyzstan); UN Doc. CRC/C/15/Add.40, para. 12 (Sri Lanka).

1183 See *e.g.* for 2004-2005 UN Doc. CRC/C/15/Add.266, para. 32 (Yemen); UN Doc. CRC/C/15/Add.263, para. 22 (Mongolia); UN Doc. CRC/C/15/Add.260, para. 35 (Nepal); UN Doc. CRC/C/15/Add.259, para. 25 (Bosnia and Herzegovina); UN Doc. CRC/C/15/Add.258, para. 20 (Philippines); UN Doc. CRC/C/15/Add.252, para. 25 (Belize); UN Doc. CRC/C/15/Add.250, para. 18 (Luxembourg); UN Doc. CRC/C/15/Add.239, para. 27 (People's Republic of Korea); UN Doc. CRC/C/15/Add. 236, para. 23 (Liberia).

1184 UN Doc. CRC/C/15/Add.208, para. 21 (Solomon Islands); UN Doc. CRC/C/15/Add.149, para. 32 (Palau); UN Doc. CRC/C/15/Add.139, para. 28 (Marshall Islands).

1185 UN Doc. CRC/C/15/Add.228, para. 25 (India); UN Doc. CRC/C/15/Add.115, para. 28 (India).

1186 UN Doc. CRC/C/15/Add.125, para. 31 (Jordan).

1187 UN Doc. CRC/C/15/Add.240, para. 18 (France).

1188 UN Doc. CRC/C/15/Add.258, para. 20 (Philippines).

age,[1189] and social status[1190] (child labourers,[1191] marginalized adolescents who are neither studying nor working,[1192] children living in institutions,[1193] children in the juvenile justice system,[1194] children in conflict with the law[1195]).

In addition to these general expressions of concern, the CRC Committee has raised issues of discrimination on specific grounds.

a. Race

The Committee has repeatedly expressed concern at racial discrimination,[1196] racism and xenophobia,[1197] and at the use of expressions with racial connotations by state officials, in particular in relation to children belonging to immigrant families (in an irregular situation).[1198] It has regretted that a state regarded as unnecessary any initiatives to prevent and combat racial discrimination given its position that social and ethnic tension, racism and xenophobia were minimal.[1199]

1189 UN Doc. CRC/C/15/Add.199, para. 25 (Romania); UN Doc. CRC/C/15/Add.188, para. 22 (United Kingdom); UN Doc. CRC/C/15/Add.156, para. 26 (Tanzania).

1190 UN Doc. CRC/C/15/Add.239, para. 27 (People's Republic of Korea); UN Doc. CRC/C/15/Add.108, para. 24 (Nicaragua); UN Doc. CRC/C/15/Add.95, para. 17 (Bolivia); UN Doc. CRC/C/15/Add.93, para. 18 (Ecuador).

1191 UN Doc. CRC/C/15/Add.122, para. 18 (South Africa); UN Doc. CRC/C/15/Add.113, para. 16 (Mali); UN Doc. CRC/C/15/Add.40, para. 12 (Sri Lanka).

1192 UN Doc. CRC/C/15/Add.187, para. 29 (Argentina).

1193 UN Doc. CRC/C/15/Add.206, para. 21 (Zambia); UN Doc. CRC/C/15/Add.199, para. 25 (Romania); UN Doc. CRC/C/15/Add.194, para. 27 (Poland); UN Doc. CRC/C/15/Add.192, para. 26 (Moldova); UN Doc. CRC/C/15/Add.191, para. 29 (Ukraine); UN Doc. CRC/C/15/Add.188, para. 22 (United Kingdom); UN Doc. CRC/C/15/Add.180, para. 28 (Belarus); UN Doc. CRC/C/15/Add.174, para. 22 (Malawi); UN Doc. CRC/C/15/Add.167, para. 26 (Uzbekistan); UN Doc. CRC/C/15/Add.160, para. 24 (Kenya); UN Doc. CRC/C/15/Add.156, para. 26 (Tanzania); UN Doc. CRC/C/15/Add.147, para. 25 (Lesotho); UN Doc. CRC/C/15/Add.146, para. 21 (Lithuania); UN Doc. CRC/C/15/Add.136, para. 20 (Tajikistan); UN Doc. CRC/C/15/Add.130, para. 25 (Suriname); UN Doc. CRC/C/15/Add.127, para. 21 (Kyrgyzstan); UN Doc. CRC/C/15/Add.124, para. 24 (Georgia); UN Doc. CRC/C/15/Add.119, para. 24 (Armenia); UN Doc. CRC/C/15/Add.113, para. 16 (Mali); UN Doc. CRC/C/15/Add.106, para. 15 (Benin); UN Doc. CRC/C/15/Add.99, para. 16 (Belize); UN Doc. CRC/C/15/Add.97, para. 18 (Thailand);UN Doc. CRC/C/15/Add.88, para. 11 (DPR Korea).

1194 UN Doc. CRC/C/15/Add.199, para. 25 (Romania); UN Doc. CRC/C/15/Add.188, para. 22 (United Kingdom); UN Doc. CRC/C/15/Add.160, para. 24 (Kenya); UN Doc. CRC/C/15/Add.156, para. 26 (Tanzania); UN Doc. CRC/C/15/Add.130, para. 25 (Suriname); UN Doc. CRC/C/15/Add.124, para. 24 (Georgia); UN Doc. CRC/C/15/Add.122, para. 18 (South Africa); UN Doc. CRC/C/15/Add.113, para. 16 (Mali); UN Doc. CRC/C/15/Add.106, para. 15 (Benin); UN Doc. CRC/C/15/Add.99, para. 16 (Belize); UN Doc. CRC/C/15/Add.90, para. 13 (Japan); UN Doc. CRC/C/15/Add.81, para. 13 (Czech Republic); UN Doc. CRC/C/15/Add.40, para. 12 (Sri Lanka).

1195 UN Doc. CRC/C/15/Add.263, para. 22 (Mongolia).

1196 UN Doc. CRC/C/15/Add.210, para. 23 (Jamaica); UN Doc. CRC/C/15/Add.150, para. 22 (Dominican Republic); UN Doc. CRC/C/15/Add.120, para. 16 (Peru).

1197 UN Doc. CRC/C/15/Add.251, para. 20 (Austria); UN Doc. CRC/C/15/Add.203, para. 22 (Iceland); UN Doc. CRC/C/15/Add.117, para. 15 (Costa Rica); UN Doc. CRC/C/15/Add.110, para. 24 (Russian Federation).

1198 UN Doc. CRC/C/15/Add.198, para. 20 (Italy); UN Doc. CRC/C/15/Add.129, paras. 23-24 (Malta).

1199 UN Doc. CRC/C/15/Add.257, para. 29 (Nigeria).

The CRC Committee seems to use the expression "racial discrimination" in the same way as the CERD does, *i.e.* to denote any form of differential treatment based on race, colour, ethnic or national origin. While referring to the findings of the CERD, the CRC pointed out for example that there were occurrences of racial discrimination affecting children, including the children of some minorities.[1200] Race more strictly construed was referred to when expressing concern about the fact that race was indicated on identity cards,[1201] and that the granting of citizenship to children born in the state was restricted on the basis of racial origin.[1202]

States are to expressly outlaw discrimination on the basis of racial origin,[1203] racially motivated acts,[1204] racial discrimination by private persons in education and employment,[1205] and incitement to racial discrimination and violence.[1206] Prejudices and hostilities towards foreigners among children and adolescents should be prevented by campaigns against racism, xenophobia and related intolerance.[1207]

b. Colour

The Committee has only rarely paid attention to the issue of colour. It has expressed concern about the continued practice of discrimination in some schools, particularly against black children in racially mixed schools,[1208] and about the restriction on granting of citizenship to children born in the state on the basis of colour.[1209] States are to expressly outlaw discrimination on the basis of colour.[1210]

c. Sex/Gender

The CRC Committee seems to use rather consistently the concept of gender rather than of sex,[1211] like most other Committees have done.

1200 UN Doc. CRC/C/15/Add.184, para. 19 (St. Vincent and the Grenadines). Compare with UN Doc. CRC/C/15/Add.198, para. 20 (Italy) and UN Doc. CRC/C/15/Add.178, para. 18 (Belgium).

1201 UN Doc. CRC/C/15/Add.219, para. 26 (Brunei Darussalam).

1202 UN Doc. CRC/C/15/Add.236, para. 32 (Liberia).

1203 *Ibid.*, para. 33 (Liberia).

1204 UN Doc. CRC/C/15/Add.196, para. 24 (Estonia).

1205 UN Doc. CRC/C/15/Add.205, para. 27 (Cyprus).

1206 UN Doc. CRC/C/15/Add.243, para. 21 (Croatia).

1207 UN Doc. CRC/C/15/Add.143, paras. 20-21 (Liechtenstein).

1208 UN Doc. CRC/C/15/Add.122, para. 34 (South Africa).

1209 UN Doc. CRC/C/15/Add.236, para. 32 (Liberia).

1210 *Ibid.*, para. 33 (Liberia).

1211 For exceptions, see *e.g.* UN Doc. CRC/C/15/Add.249, para. 24 (Albania); UN Doc. CRC/C/15/Add.219, paras. 35-36 (Brunei Darussalam); UN Doc. CRC/C/15/Add.212, paras. 32-33 (Syrian Arab Republic).

It has expressed concern at many occasions about traditional stereotypes (*inter alia* relating to the roles and responsibilities of women and men),[1212] and harmful cultural practices (*e.g.* female infanticide, selective abortions, female circumcision, low school enrolment and high drop-out rates, early and forced marriages)[1213] which perpetuate *de facto* discrimination on the grounds of gender.[1214] Discriminatory legislation or the lack of legislative provisions prohibiting gender discrimination has also been a source of concern.[1215] On many other occasions, the CRC Committee has pointed out existing patterns or remaining instances of gender discrimination without reference to their origins.[1216]

Article 2 CRC prohibits discrimination on the grounds of a child's *or its parents' or legal guardians'* sex. The Committee seems to have extended this to "discrimination against women, which may have an impact on their children",[1217] which sometimes seems to have been qualified indirect discrimination.[1218] Multiple forms of discrimina-

---

1212 UN Doc. CRC/C/15/Add.136, para. 22 (Tajikistan); UN Doc. CRC/C/15/Add.127, para. 25 (Kyrgyzstan); UN Doc. CRC/C/15/Add.125, para. 29 (Jordan); UN Doc. CRC/C/15/Add.123, para. 21 (Iran); UN Doc. CRC/C/15/Add.25, para. 22 (Indonesia); UN Doc. CRC/C/15/Add.13, para. 18 (Mexico).

1213 UN Doc. CRC/C/15/Add.115, para. 32 (India); UN Doc. CRC/C/15/Add.107, para. 17 (Chad); UN Doc. CRC/C/15/Add.19, para. 8 (Burkina Faso); UN Doc. CRC/C/15/Add.18, para. 16 (Pakistan).

1214 UN Doc. CRC/C/15/Add.247, para. 26 (Antigua and Barbuda); UN Doc. CRC/C/15/Add.246, para. 21 (Angola); UN Doc. CRC/C/15/Add.239, para. 27 (People's Republic of Korea); UN Doc. CRC/C/15/Add.221, para. 28 (Bangladesh); UN Doc. CRC/C/15/Add.190, paras. 26 and 27 (Sudan); UN Doc. CRC/C/15/Add.183, para. 21 (United Arab Emirates); UN Doc. CRC/C/15/Add.167, para. 30 (Uzbekistan); UN Doc. CRC/C/15/Add.161, para. 24 (Oman); UN Doc. CRC/C/15/Add.153, para. 22 (DRC); UN Doc. CRC/C/15/Add.150, para. 22 (Dominican Republic); UN Doc. CRC/C/15/Add.148, para. 23 (Saudi Arabia); UN Doc. CRC/C/15/Add.131, para. 27 (Djibouti); UN Doc. CRC/C/15/Add.105, para. 19 (Honduras); UN Doc. CRC/C/15/Add.3, para. 6 (Viet Nam).

1215 UN Doc. CRC/C/15/Add.220, para. 23 and 24 (Singapore); UN Doc. CRC/C/15/Add.205, para. 27 (Cyprus); UN Doc. CRC/C/15/Add.172, para. 26 (Mozambique); UN Doc. CRC/C/15/Add.144, para. 31 (Ethiopia); UN Doc. CRC/C/15/Add.141, para. 24 (Comoros); UN Doc. CRC/C/15/Add.131, para. 28 (Djibouti); UN Doc. CRC/C/15/Add.116, paras. 32-33 (Sierra Leone).

1216 UN Doc. CRC/C/15/Add.266, para. 32 (Yemen); UN Doc. CRC/C/15/Add.143, paras. 20-21 (Liechtenstein); UN Doc. CRC/C/15/Add.120, para. 16 (Peru); UN Doc. CRC/C/15/Add.109, para. 18 (Venezuela); UN Doc. CRC/C/15/Add.107, para. 17 (Chad); UN Doc. CRC/C/15/Add.98, para. 16 (Austria); UN Doc. CRC/C/15/Add.91, para. 15 (Maldives); UN Doc. CRC/C/15/Add.86, para. 15 (Micronesia); UN Doc. CRC/C/15/Add.61, para. 12 (Nigeria); UN Doc. CRC/C/15/Add.57, para. 12 (Nepal) UN Doc. CRC/C/15/Add.47, para. 8 (Yemen); UN Doc. CRC/C/15/Add.11, para. 9 (Costa Rica); UN Doc. CRC/C/15/Add.9, para. 12 (El Salvador); UN Doc. CRC/C/15/Add.5, para. 12 (Egypt); UN Doc. CRC/C/15/Add.1, para. 11 (Bolivia).

1217 UN Doc. CRC/C/15/Add.168, para. 28 (Cape Verde); UN Doc. CRC/C/15/Add.147, para. 25 (Lesotho); UN Doc. CRC/C/15/Add.144, para. 30 (Ethiopia).

1218 UN Doc. CRC/C/15/Add.125, para. 29 (Jordan); UN Doc. CRC/C/15/Add.123, para. 21 (Iran); UN Doc. CRC/C/15/Add. 116, paras. 32-33 (Sierra Leone).

tion have been identified with regard to girls in general,[1219] girls with disabilities[1220] and, less explicitly, with regard to girls living in rural areas.[1221]

While stressing that girls are particularly vulnerable to gender discrimination,[1222] the CRC Committee has also paid attention to the "gender bias faced by boys".[1223] It seems to have done so much more systematically than any of the other Committees.[1224] Areas in which the CRC Committee has identified discrimination against boys include the degree of protection against sexual abuse and exploitation,[1225] coverage by the definition of juvenile[1226] and the legal minimum age for sexual consent,[1227] education,[1228] corporal punishment[1229] and placement for adoption.[1230] In the eyes of the Committee, the lower self-esteem of boys and discrimination against them arises from the inappropriate socialization of boys and girls into rigid gender roles, and the resulting determination of family and social attitudes concerning children based on gender.[1231]

The CRC Committee has highlighted domains of particular concern with regard to gender discrimination. These include personal status and marriage, education, health care, and sexual exploitation.

In the context of the family, the CRC Committee has been more attentive than the other Committees to the issue of sex selection, *inter alia* through selective abortion and female infanticide.[1232]

Discriminatory personal status laws have been considered to be "the entry-point of discrimination against women in society."[1233] The Committee has paid sustained attention to direct and indirect discrimination against girls and women with regard to personal status (*i.e.* fostering, marriage, divorce, custody and guardianship of

---

1219 UN Doc. CRC/C/15/Add.258, para. 20 (Philippines).
1220 UN Doc. CRC/C/15/Add.172, para. 25 (Mozambique).
1221 UN Doc. CRC/C/15/Add.110, para. 23 (Russian Federation).
1222 UN Doc. CRC/C/15/Add.172, para. 25 (Mozambique); UN Doc. CRC/C/15/Add.121, para. 13 (Grenada).
1223 UN Doc. CRC/C/15/Add.135, para. 25 (United Kingdom – Overseas Territories).
1224 Some other Committees have pointed out discrimination against men too, see *e.g.* CERD, HRC and CESCR Committee.
1225 UN Doc. CRC/C/15/Add.135, para. 25 (United Kingdom – Overseas Territories); UN Doc. CRC/C/15/Add. 121, para. 14 (Grenada).
1226 UN Doc. CRC/C/15/Add.115, para. 81 (India).
1227 UN Doc. CRC/C/15/Add.135, para. 25 (United Kingdom – Overseas Territories).
1228 *Id.*; UN Doc. CRC/C/15/Add.103, para. 16 (Barbados).
1229 UN Doc. CRC/C/15/Add.116, para. 31 (Sierra Leone).
1230 UN Doc. CRC/C/15/Add.103, para. 16 (Barbados).
1231 UN Doc. CRC/C/15/Add.121, para. 13 (Grenada); UN Doc. CRC/C/15/Add.103, para. 16 (Barbados).
1232 UN Doc. CRC/C/15/Add.228, paras. 33 and 34 (India); UN Doc. CRC/C/15/Add.56, para. 15 (China).
1233 UN Doc. CRC/C/15/Add.145, para. 29 (Egypt).

infants, and inheritance)[1234] and civil status (*e.g.* lack of identity cards for females).[1235] The focus is thereby on the possibly negative effects on the rights of children. For example, the fact that married women have the legal status of minors can, in certain circumstances, negatively affect respect for the rights of their children.[1236] Other issues of concern relate to bridal kidnappings,[1237] early and forced marriages,[1238] honour killings[1239] and the right of women to leave the country.[1240]

The CRC Committee has also paid attention to equal parenting rights[1241] and rights to financial assistance for fathers and mothers.[1242] It has deplored *de facto* gender discrimination in the sharing of parental responsibilities.[1243]

A central concern shared with most other Committees is the fact that women are discriminated against in the passing on of parents' nationality,[1244] *e.g.* when citizenship is not automatically acquired by birth by children of women of a certain state which are married to a non national, as it is where the father is the national of that state. The Committee has pointed out that the right of a child to a nationality without discrimination on the basis of the parents' sex/gender, race, religion or ethnic origin is to be ensured.[1245] A similar issue arises if nationality law does not grant equal

1234 UN Doc. CRC/C/15/Add.255, para. 25 (Togo); UN Doc. CRC/C/15/Add.228, para. 29 (India); UN Doc. CRC/C/15/Add.217, paras. 44-45 (Pakistan); UN Doc. CRC/C/15/Add.211, para. 25 (Morocco); UN Doc. CRC/C/15/Add.172, para. 25 (Mozambique); UN Doc. CRC/C/15/Add.165, para. 25 (Gambia); UN Doc. CRC/C/15/Add.163, para. 30 (Qatar); UN Doc. CRC/C/15/Add.160, para. 24 (Kenya); UN Doc. CRC/C/15/Add.145, para. 29 (Egypt); UN Doc. CRC/C/15/Add.138, paras. 28-29 (Central African Republic); UN Doc. CRC/C/15/Add.115, para. 32 (India); UN Doc. CRC/C/15/Add.96, para. 17 (Kuwait); UN Doc. CRC/C/15/Add.85, para. 11 (Libya); UN Doc. CRC/C/15/Add.61, para. 15 (Nigeria); UN Doc. CRC/C/15/Add.21, para. 11 (Jordan).

1235 UN Doc. CRC/C/15/Add.148, para. 23 (Saudi Arabia).

1236 UN Doc. CRC/C/15/Add.147, paras. 25-26 (Lesotho).

1237 UN Doc. CRC/C/15/Add.244, paras. 26-27 (Kyrgyzstan).

1238 UN Doc. CRC/C/15/Add.217, para. 29 (Pakistan); UN Doc. CRC/C/15/Add.169, para. 24 (Lebanon); UN Doc. CRC/C/15/Add.145, para. 29 (Egypt); UN Doc. CRC/C/15/Add.125, para. 29 (Jordan); UN Doc. CRC/C/15/Add.123, para. 21 (Iran).

1239 UN Doc. CRC/C/15/Add.217, para. 29 (Pakistan); UN Doc. CRC/C/15/Add.152, para. 32 (Turkey).

1240 UN Doc. CRC/C/15/Add.21, para. 11 (Jordan).

1241 UN Doc. CRC/C/15/Add.158, paras. 32-33 (Monaco).

1242 *Id.*, paras. 30-31 (Monaco).

1243 UN Doc. CRC/C/15/Add.236, paras. 36-37 (Liberia).

1244 UN Doc. CRC/C/15/Add.221, paras. 39-40 (Bangladesh); UN Doc. CRC/C/15/Add.158, paras. 20-21 (Monaco); UN Doc. CRC/C/15/Add.145, para. 30 (Egypt); UN Doc. CRC/C/15/Add.85, para. 11 (Libya); UN Doc. CRC/C/15/Add.54, para. 15 (Lebanon); UN Doc. CRC/C/15/Add.21, para. 11 (Jordan).

1245 UN Doc. CRC/C/15/Add.220, para. 30-31 (Singapore); UN Doc. CRC/C/15/Add.219, paras. 35-36 (Brunei Darussalam); UN Doc. CRC/C/15/Add.212, paras. 32-33 (Syrian Arab Republic); UN Doc. CRC/C/15/Add.169, paras. 32-33 (Lebanon); UN Doc. CRC/C/15/Add.163, paras. 41-42 (Qatar); UN Doc. CRC/C/15/Add.161, paras. 33-34 (Oman); UN Doc. CRC/C/15/Add.157, paras. 36-37 (Bhutan); UN Doc. CRC/C/15/Add.145, para. 29 (Egypt); UN Doc. CRC/C/15/Add.125, para. 29 (Jordan).

citizenship status to children of women of a certain state who are married to non nationals.[1246]

In the field of economic, social and cultural rights, the CRC Committee has paid particular attention to the right to education and the right to health. It has emphasized that gender-based discrimination[1247] persists within the educational system[1248] and in the school environment,[1249] which is reflected in girls' notably lower participation rate (preference being given to the education of male children)[1250] and their higher drop-out rate.[1251] In the view of the Committee

> gender discrimination can be reinforced by practices such as a curriculum which is inconsistent with the principles of gender equality, by arrangements which limit the benefits girls can obtain from the educational opportunities offered, and by unsafe or unfriendly environments which discourage girls' participation.[1252]

All children are to be ensured equal access to educational opportunities,[1253] and all necessary measures are to be taken to reduce the drop-out rate of girls.[1254] The aims of education outlined in article 29 of the Convention (*i.e.* human rights) are to be included in school curricula, particularly with respect to equality of the sexes.[1255]

With respect to the right to health, of particular concern to the Committee is gender-based discrimination combined with taboos or negative or judgmental attitudes to sexual activity of girls, often limiting their access to preventive measures and other services. "In the design of HIV/AIDS related strategies, and in keeping with their

---

1246 UN Doc. CRC/C/15/Add.148, para. 23 (Saudi Arabia).

1247 UN Doc. CRC/C/15/Add.255, para. 25 (Togo); UN Doc. CRC/C/15/Add.181, para. 39 (Tunisia); UN Doc. CRC/C/15/Add.46, para. 8 (Holy See).

1248 UN Doc. CRC/C/15/Add.221, para. 65 (Bangladesh); UN Doc. CRC/C/15/Add.49, para. 29 (Yugoslavia). *E.g.* certain vocational courses at the secondary level are restricted by sex (UN Doc. CRC/C/15/Add.175, para. 26 (Bahrain)).

1249 UN Doc. CRC/C/15/Add.221, paras. 63 and 65 (Bangladesh).

1250 UN Doc. CRC/C/15/Add.136, para. 22 (Tajikistan).

1251 UN Doc. CRC/C/15/Add.217, para. 29 (Pakistan); UN Doc. CRC/C/15/Add.208, para. 21 (Solomon Islands); UN Doc. CRC/C/15/Add.197, para. 52 (Korea); UN Doc. CRC/C/15/Add.155, para. 22 (Ivory Coast); UN Doc. CRC/C/15/Add.145, para. 29 (Egypt); UN Doc. CRC/C/15/Add.125, para. 29 (Jordan); UN Doc. CRC/C/15/Add.123, para. 21 (Iran); UN Doc. CRC/C/15/Add.44, para. 12 (Senegal).

1252 UN Doc. HRI/GEN/1/Rev.7, General Comment No. 1 (2001), *The Aims of Education*, para. 10.

1253 UN Doc. CRC/C/15/Add.217, para. 63 (Pakistan); UN Doc. CRC/C/15/Add.144, para. 30 (Ethiopia); UN Doc. CRC/C/15/Add.138, paras. 28-29 (Central African Republic); UN Doc. CRC/C/15/Add.128, para. 28 (Cambodia).

1254 UN Doc. CRC/C/15/Add.94, para. 17 (Iraq); UN Doc. CRC/C/15/Add.57, para. 32 (Nepal).

1255 UN Doc. CRC/C/15/Add.212, para. 47 (Syrian Arab Republic); UN Doc. CRC/C/15/Add.209, para. 40 (Libyan Arabic Jamahiriya); UN Doc. CRC/C/15/Add.203, para. 36 (Iceland); UN Doc. CRC/C/15/Add.178, para. 25 (Belgium); UN Doc. CRC/C/15/Add.148, paras. 39-40 (Saudi Arabia).

obligations under the Convention, State parties must give careful consideration to prescribed gender norms within their societies with a view to eliminating gender-based discrimination as these impact on the vulnerability of both girls and boys to HIV/AIDS. States parties should in particular recognize that discrimination in the context of HIV/AIDS often impacts girls more severely than boys."[1256] In its concluding observations, the CRC Committee has stressed that adolescent girls are more vulnerable to HIV/AIDS.[1257]

Sexual exploitation was until 2001[1258] a major issue: states were to ensure that domestic laws concerning the sexual exploitation of children were gender neutral; they were to provide civil remedies in the event of violations and had to ensure that procedures were simplified so that responses were appropriate, timely, child-friendly and sensitive to victims. Those who exposed violations were to be offered protection.[1259] The criminalization of domestic violence was welcomed as a positive measure to combat gender discrimination and child abuse and ill-treatment.[1260]

Overall, the Committee has mainly stressed the need for public education campaigns to prevent and combat gender discrimination, particularly within the family.[1261] Specific training on the CRC is to be ensured for professional groups working with and for children, including teachers, social workers, health personnel, judges and law enforcement officials.[1262] Local and other leaders might be invited to take a more active role in supporting the efforts to prevent and eliminate discrimination against the girl child and to provide guidance to communities in this regard.[1263]

1256 UN Doc. HRI/GEN/1/Rev.7, General Comment No. 3 (2003), *HIV/AIDS and the Rights of the Child*, para. 6.

1257 UN Doc. CRC/C/15/Add.242, para. 27 (Botswana).

1258 On 25 May 2000, an Optional Protocol on the Sale of Children, Child Prostitution and Child Pornography was adopted. It entered into force on 18 January 2002. States are to submit a separate initial comprehensive report under this optional protocol. Thereafter, states parties to the CRC have to report on it in the reporting procedure under the CRC (see article 12 of the Optional Protocol).

1259 UN Doc. CRC/C/15/Add.145, para. 52 (Egypt); UN Doc. CRC/C/15/Add.140, para. 50 (Slovakia); UN Doc. CRC/C/15/Add.136, para. 23 (Tajikistan).

1260 UN Doc. CRC/C/15/Add.112, para. 5 (Mexico); UN Doc. CRC/C/15/Add.108, para. 10 (Nicaragua).

1261 UN Doc. CRC/C/15/Add.172, para. 26 (Mozambique); UN Doc. CRC/C/15/Add.168, para. 29 (Cape Verde); UN Doc. CRC/C/15/Add.167, para. 31 (Uzbekistan); UN Doc. CRC/C/15/Add.153, para. 23 (Democratic Republic of Congo); UN Doc. CRC/C/15/Add.136, para. 23 (Tajikistan); UN Doc. CRC/C/15/Add.127, para. 26 (Kyrgyzstan); UN Doc. CRC/C/15/Add.73, para. 32 (Ghana); UN Doc. CRC/C/15/Add.11, para. 16 (Costa Rica); UN Doc. CRC/C/15/Add.9, para. 18 (El Salvador).

1262 UN Doc. CRC/C/15/Add.57, para. 26 (Nepal).

1263 UN Doc. CRC/C/15/Add.56, para. 34 (China).

The CRC Committee, more than any of the other Committees, refers explicitly to other Committees' recommendations. It has also referred to general comment No. 28 of the Human Rights Committee on equality between men and women.[1264]

d. *Religion*

Religious discrimination is not a major issue under the CRC. The Committee has occasionally expressed concern about religious discrimination in the context of education.[1265]

e. *Political Opinion*

Discrimination on the grounds of political belief or opinion has been referred to rather rarely.[1266]

f. *Ethnic Origin*

Ethnic origin is explicitly mentioned as a prohibited ground of discrimination in the CRC, like in ICERD, but unlike the CCPR and the CESCR.[1267]

The CRC Committee has expressed concern about the existence and growth of discrimination based on ethnic origin against children belonging to some ethnic groups or ethnic minorities, including against indigenous children.[1268] Issues will only be dealt with here to the extent that the Committee has raised them as strictly ones of discrimination based on ethnic origin. Issues in which minority considerations play as well, will be covered under the cross-cutting heading of minorities (see further). The Committee seems to have invoked rather exceptionally discrimination based on ethnic origin only.

Issues of concern include the requirement to record ethnic origin in passports,[1269] the ineffectiveness of the existing legislation on "unlawful discrimination" and "agitation

---

1264 UN Doc. CRC/C/15/Add.212, para. 26 (Syrian Arab Republic).
1265 UN Doc. CRC/C/15/Add.265, para. 25 (Costa Rica); UN Doc. CRC/C/15/Add.262, para. 18 (Norway).
1266 UN Doc. CRC/C/15/Add.196, para. 29 (Estonia); UN Doc. CRC/C/15/Add.177, para. 21 (Guinea-Bissau); UN Doc. CRC/C/15/Add.157, para. 30 (Bhutan).
1267 In the latter two, reference is made to national origin.
1268 UN Doc. CRC/C/15/Add.262, para. 18 (Norway); UN Doc. CRC/C/15/Add.153, para. 22 (Democratic Republic of Congo); UN Doc. CRC/C/15/Add.109, para. 18 (Venezuela).
1269 UN Doc. CRC/C/15/Add.142, para. 23 (Latvia).

against an ethnic group",[1270] and the fact that killings and other acts committed in armed conflict had frequently been perpetrated on the basis of ethnic origin.[1271]

Effective measures are to be taken to protect children belonging to indigenous and ethnic groups against discrimination,[1272] and to ensure that they enjoy all their rights without discrimination, including equal access to (culturally appropriate) services including health, education, social services, housing, potable water and sanitation.[1273] Regardless of ethnic origin, all children are to be accorded a nationality.[1274] Public awareness campaigns are necessary to combat negative attitudes and misconceptions about indigenous children.[1275]

g. Property

The CRC Committee has paid some attention to discrimination against the poor and low-income families,[1276] but without identifying any particular ground as mentioned in the CRC. It is submitted that poverty-based discriminatory treatment can be qualified as discrimination based on property.

Discriminatory attitudes and disparities can be identified in access to basic services.[1277] The Committee has pointed out that a decrease of public early childhood education centres or the introduction of fees for state health and education services may result in discrimination on the basis of income level.[1278] Also, the practice of considering the "personality" of the child as a criteria for passing sentences may, in its actual application, be discriminatory against children living in poverty.[1279]

On one occasion, the Committee has not hesitated to urge a state to take all appropriate measures to the maximum extent of its available resources, to support families in a difficult economic and/or social situation in order to ensure to the maximum extent

---

1270 UN Doc. CRC/C/15/Add.101, para. 12 (Sweden).
1271 UN Doc. CRC/C/15/Add.133, para. 26 (Burundi).
1272 UN Doc. CRC/C/15/Add.224, para. 58 (Guyana); UN Doc. CRC/C/15/Add.112, para. 29 (Mexico); UN Doc. CRC/C/15/Add.109, para. 30 (Venezuela).
1273 UN Doc. CRC/C/15/Add.265, para. 18 (Costa Rica); UN Doc. CRC/C/15/Add.233, para. 64 (Panama).
1274 UN Doc. CRC/C/15/Add.153, para. 29 (Democratic Republic of Congo).
1275 UN Doc. CRC/C/15/Add.233, para. 64 (Panama); UN Doc. CRC/C/15/Add.70, para. 27 (Syrian Arab Republic).
1276 UN Doc. CRC/C/15/Add.182, para. 47 (Switzerland); UN Doc. CRC/C/15/Add.128, para. 28 (Cambodia).
1277 UN Doc. CRC/C/15/Add.247, para. 26 (Antigua and Barbuda).
1278 UN Doc. CRC/C/15/Add.181, para. 39 (Tunisia); UN Doc. CRC/C/15/Add.136, para. 20 (Tajikistan).
1279 UN Doc. CRC/C/15/Add.1, para. 11 (Bolivia).

possible the survival and development of all children living on its territory, without discrimination.[1280]

h. Disability

The CRC was the first of the core human rights treaties to explicitly include disability as a prohibited ground of discrimination. The CRC Committee has paid sustained and particular attention to disability-based discrimination.

Issues raised have ranged from the persistence of societal[1281] and *de facto*[1282] discrimination[1283] to the explicit prohibition of discrimination on the grounds of disability,[1284] the review of existing policies and practice in relation to children with disabilities, including draft legislation,[1285] the integration within a child-rights policy of the perspectives of the rights of children with disabilities with regard to non-discrimina-

1280 UN Doc. CRC/C/15/Add.146, para. 42 (Lithuania).

1281 UN Doc. CRC/C/15/Add.253, para. 28 (The Bahamas); UN Doc. CRC/C/15/Add.246, para. 41 (Angola); UN Doc. CRC/C/15/Add.238, para. 36 (Dominica); UN Doc. CRC/C/15/Add.232, para. 46 (El Salvador); UN Doc. CRC/C/15/Add.224, para. 39 (Guyana); UN Doc. CRC/C/15/Add.221, para. 55 (Bangladesh); UN Doc. CRC/C/15/Add.204, para. 47 (Eritrea); UN Doc. CRC/C/15/Add.197, para. 50 (Korea); UN Doc. CRC/C/15/Add.190, para. 45 (Sudan); UN Doc. CRC/C/15/Add.177, para. 21 (Guinea-Bissau); UN Doc. CRC/C/15/Add.172, para. 48 (Mozambique); UN Doc. CRC/C/15/Add.19, para. 8 (Burkina Faso).

1282 UN Doc. CRC/C/15/Add.252, para. 50 (Belize); UN Doc. CRC/C/15/Add.210, para. 23 (Jamaica); UN Doc. CRC/C/15/Add.184, para. 19 (St. Vincent and the Grenadines); UN Doc. CRC/C/15/Add.88, para. 16 (DPR Korea).

1283 UN Doc. CRC/C/15/Add.264, para. 45 (Nicaragua); UN Doc. CRC/C/15/Add.263, para. 41 (Mongolia); UN Doc. CRC/C/15/Add.261, para. 49 (Ecuador); UN Doc. CRC/C/15/Add.257, para. 46 (Nigeria); UN Doc. CRC/C/15/Add.246, para. 21 (Angola); UN Doc. CRC/C/15/Add.232, para. 45 (El Salvador); UN Doc. CRC/C/15/Add.228, para. 56 (India); UN Doc. CRC/C/15/Add.206, para. 52 (Zambia); UN Doc. CRC/C/15/Add.186, para. 25 (Netherlands Antilles); UN Doc. CRC/C/15/Add.174, para. 51 (Malawi); UN Doc. CRC/C/15/Add.172, para. 25 (Mozambique); UN Doc. CRC/C/15/Add.169, para. 40 (Lebanon); UN Doc. CRC/C/15/Add.154, para. 38 (Guatemala); UN Doc. CRC/C/15/Add.150, para. 41 (Dominican Republic); UN Doc. CRC/C/15/Add.144, paras. 14 and 30 (Ethiopia); UN Doc. CRC/C/15/Add.138, para. 28 (Central African Republic); UN Doc. CRC/C/15/Add.91, paras. 15 and 35 (Maldives); UN Doc. CRC/C/15/Add.65, para. 13 (Slovenia); UN Doc. CRC/C/15/Add.18, para. 17 (Pakistan); UN Doc. CRC/C/15/Add.9, para. 12 (El Salvador).

1284 UN Doc. CRC/C/15/Add.253, para. 28 (The Bahamas); UN Doc. CRC/C/15/Add.246, para. 22 (Angola); UN Doc. CRC/C/15/Add.227, paras. 30-31 (Netherlands and Aruba); UN Doc. CRC/C/15/Add.224, para. 22 (Guyana); UN Doc. CRC/C/15/Add.220, paras. 23-24 (Singapore); UN Doc. CRC/C/15/Add.200, paras. 22-23 (Viet Nam); UN Doc. CRC/C/15/Add.177, paras. 36-37 (Guinea-Bissau); UN Doc. CRC/C/15/Add.172, para. 26 (Mozambique); UN Doc. CRC/C/15/Add.170, paras. 33-34 (Greece); UN Doc. CRC/C/15/Add.168, paras. 28-29 (Cape Verde); UN Doc. CRC/C/15/Add.144, paras. 14-15, 31 (Ethiopia); UN Doc. CRC/C/15/Add.107, para. 26 (Chad).

1285 UN Doc. CRC/C/15/Add.178, para. 19 (Belgium).

tion,[1286] the adoption of a more proactive approach to eliminate discrimination against children with disabilities,[1287] specific legislation to cater for their special needs and to provide them with appropriate facilities,[1288] and research on the measures required to prevent and combat discrimination on the ground of disability.[1289] The Committee has pointed out that societal discrimination against adults with disabilities limits the opportunities for children with disabilities to achieve full respect for their rights.[1290]

Discrimination can be discerned in the persistence of practices leading to cases of selective infanticide,[1291] and hampers integration and full inclusion in society,[1292] access to basic services (health, education and social care),[1293] and accessibility of buildings and transportation for them.[1294] With regard to education,[1295] discrimination can be encountered in formal educational systems and in many informal educational settings, including in the home.[1296] The Committee has insisted on access to education[1297] and integration into regular schools.[1298] This requires that teachers are trained to educate children with disabilities within regular schools,[1299] that the physical access of children with disabilities to schools and recreational facilities is ensured, and that the number of integrated education programmes at pre-primary, primary, secondary and tertiary levels is increased.[1300] These measures are to be preceded by an assessment of existing

1286 UN Doc. CRC/C/15/Add.224, para. 40 (Guyana); UN Doc. CRC/C/15/Add.190, para. 46 (Sudan); UN Doc. CRC/C/15/Add.184, para. 37 (St. Vincent and the Grenadines); UN Doc. CRC/C/15/Add.61, para. 35 (Nigeria).

1287 UN Doc. CRC/C/15/Add.91, paras. 15 and 35 (Maldives).

1288 UN Doc. CRC/C/15/Add.184, paras. 19-20 (St. Vincent and the Grenadines).

1289 UN Doc. CRC/C/15/Add.56, para. 35 (China).

1290 UN Doc. CRC/C/15/Add.144, para. 30 (Ethiopia).

1291 UN Doc. CRC/C/15/Add.177, para. 37 (Guinea-Bissau); UN Doc. CRC/C/15/Add.56, para. 15 (China).

1292 UN Doc. CRC/C/15/Add.253, para. 45 (The Bahamas); UN Doc. CRC/C/15/Add.245, para. 28 (Equatorial Guinea); UN Doc. CRC/C/15/Add.88, para. 16 (DPR Korea).

1293 UN Doc. CRC/C/15/Add.258, para. 55 (Philippines); UN Doc. CRC/C/15/Add.253, para. 45 (The Bahamas); UN Doc. CRC/C/15/Add.247, para. 26 (Antigua and Barbuda); UN Doc. CRC/C/15/Add.88, para. 16 (DPR Korea); UN Doc. CRC/C/15/Add.57, para. 32 (Nepal).

1294 UN Doc. CRC/C/15/Add.253, para. 45 (The Bahamas).

1295 UN Doc. CRC/C/15/Add.238, para. 36 (Dominica); UN Doc. CRC/C/15/Add.186, para. 52 (Netherlands Antilles); UN Doc. CRC/C/15/Add.169, para. 40 (Lebanon); UN Doc. CRC/C/15/Add.150, para. 41 (Dominican Republic).

1296 UN Doc. HRI/GEN/1/Rev.7, General Comment No. 1 (2001), *The Aims of Education* (2001), para. 10.

1297 UN Doc. CRC/C/15/Add.245, para. 28 (Equatorial Guinea); UN Doc. CRC/C/15/Add.221, para. 55 (Bangladesh); UN Doc. CRC/C/15/Add.144, para. 30 (Ethiopia); UN Doc. CRC/C/15/Add.88, para. 16 (DPR Korea).

1298 UN Doc. CRC/C/15/Add.210, para. 23 (Jamaica); UN Doc. CRC/C/15/Add.209, para. 35 (Libyan Arabic Jamahiriya); UN Doc. CRC/C/15/Add.184, para. 19 (St. Vincent and the Grenadines); UN Doc. CRC/C/15/Add.122, para. 8 (South Africa).

1299 UN Doc. CRC/C/15/Add.232, para. 46 (El Salvador).

1300 UN Doc. CRC/C/15/Add.197, para. 51 (Korea).

disparities in the integration of disabled children in mainstream education, their educational needs and their access to education and other social services.[1301]

With regard to health,[1302] a central issue is effective access to health care and specialized services.[1303] Participation in social and cultural life is equally important.[1304]

In the view of the Committee, an important instrument to combat the culture of discrimination against children with disabilities is awareness-raising and education campaigns aimed at parents, children, teachers, social workers and the general public.[1305]

The Committee has also addressed distinctions between children born with disability and children who have become disabled as far as home care is concerned. It has urged the state to review its home care support system in order to eliminate the *de facto* discrimination between children born with disability and children who had become disabled as a result of disease or an accident.[1306]

i. Birth Status

Discrimination on the basis of birth status, *i.e.* whether a child is born in or out of wedlock, is a prominent issue in the CRC Committee's concluding observations.[1307]

1301 UN Doc. CRC/C/15/Add.197, para. 51 (Korea); UN Doc. CRC/C/15/Add.182, para. 43 (Switzerland).

1302 UN Doc. CRC/C/15/Add.245, para. 28 (Equatorial Guinea).

1303 UN Doc. CRC/C/15/Add.169, para. 40 (Lebanon); UN Doc. CRC/C/15/Add.88, para. 16 (DPR Korea).

1304 UN Doc. CRC/C/15/Add.245, para. 28 (Equatorial Guinea); UN Doc. CRC/C/15/Add.238, paras. 36-37 (Dominica).

1305 UN Doc. CRC/C/15/Add.204, para. 48 (Eritrea); UN Doc. CRC/C/15/Add.197, para. 51 (Korea); UN Doc. CRC/C/15/Add.172, para. 49 (Mozambique); UN Doc. CRC/C/15/Add.170, para. 59 (Greece); UN Doc. CRC/C/15/Add.153, para. 51 (Democratic Republic of Congo); UN Doc. CRC/C/15/Add.150, para. 40 (Dominican Republic); UN Doc. CRC/C/15/Add.140, para. 34 (Slovakia); UN Doc. CRC/C/15/Add.137, para. 51 (Colombia); UN Doc. CRC/C/15/Add.73, para. 32 (Ghana); UN Doc. CRC/C/15/Add.9, para. 18 (El Salvador).

1306 UN Doc. CRC/C/15/Add.182, paras. 42-43 (Switzerland).

1307 UN Doc. CRC/C/15/Add.258, para. 6 (Philippines); UN Doc. CRC/C/15/Add.247, para. 26 (Antigua and Barbuda); UN Doc. CRC/C/15/Add.231, para. 24 (Japan); UN Doc. CRC/C/15/Add.211, para. 25 (Morocco); UN Doc. CRC/C/15/Add.209, para. 23 (Syrian Arabic Jamahiriya); UN Doc. CRC/C/15/Add.202, para. 25 (Haiti); UN Doc. CRC/C/15/Add.161, para. 24 (Oman); UN Doc. CRC/C/15/Add.141, para. 23 (Comoros); UN Doc. CRC/C/15/Add.135, para. 25 (United Kingdom – Overseas Territories); UN Doc. CRC/C/15/Add.125, para. 29 (Jordan); UN Doc. CRC/C/15/Add.123, para. 21 (Iran); UN Doc. CRC/C/15/Add.92, paras. 9 and 27 (Luxembourg); UN Doc. CRC/C/15/Add.211, para. 25 (Morocco); UN Doc. CRC/C/15/Add.209, para. 23 (Syrian Arabic Jamahiriya); UN Doc. CRC/C/15/Add.161, para. 24 (Oman); UN Doc. CRC/C/15/Add.85, para. 11 (Libya); UN Doc. CRC/C/15/Add.21, para. 22 (Jordan); UN Doc. CRC/C/15/Add.19, para. 8 (Burkina Faso).

Concern has been expressed at the use of the terms "illegitimate child" or "natural child" in legislation, administrative instructions and regulations,[1308] the mention of birth out of wedlock in official documents,[1309] the difficulties and humiliation faced by mothers of children born out of wedlock in obtaining travel documents for their children,[1310] procedures for the determination of their name that prevented them of having access to their origins,[1311] their right to a name and to citizenship,[1312] the impossibility to be recognized by a minor parent,[1313] and discriminatory treatment in areas relating to personal status (*e.g.* inheritance, custody and guardianship),[1314] and in accessing basic services.[1315]

Emphasis has been on legislative measures to prevent and eliminate discrimination on grounds of birth.[1316] Public education campaigns, which include religious leaders, may prevent and combat negative societal attitudes towards birth outside marriage.[1317]

j. Other Status

i. Age

Age discrimination[1318] has been raised with regard to the non-applicability of the national minimum wage to young workers above the minimum age of employment.[1319]

1308 UN Doc. CRC/C/15/Add.258, para. 20 (Philippines); UN Doc. CRC/C/15/Add.250, para. 22 (Luxembourg); UN Doc. CRC/C/15/Add.129, paras. 23-24 (Malta); UN Doc. CRC/C/15/Add.92, paras. 9 and 27 (Luxembourg); UN Doc. CRC/C/15/Add.89, para. 14 (Fiji); UN Doc. CRC/C/15/Add.85, para. 12 (Libya).

1309 UN Doc. CRC/C/15/Add.90, para. 14 (Japan).

1310 UN Doc. CRC/C/15/Add.147, para. 25 (Lesotho).

1311 UN Doc. CRC/C/15/Add.62, para. 11 (Uruguay).

1312 UN Doc. CRC/C/15/Add.59, para. 12 (Cyprus).

1313 UN Doc. CRC/C/15/Add.62, para. 11 (Uruguay).

1314 UN Doc. CRC/C/15/Add.258, para. 20 (Philippines); UN Doc. CRC/C/15/Add.219, para. 24 (Brunei Darussalam); UN Doc. CRC/C/15/Add.211, para. 25 (Morocco); UN Doc. CRC/C/15/Add.183, para. 21 (United Arab Emirates); UN Doc. CRC/C/15/Add.175, para. 26 (Bahrain); UN Doc. CRC/C/15/Add.163, para. 30 (Qatar); UN Doc. CRC/C/15/Add.158, para. 20 (Monaco); CRC/C/15/Add.148, para. 23 (Saudi Arabia); UN Doc. CRC/C/15/Add.90, para. 14 (Japan); UN Doc UN Doc. CRC/C/15/Add.85, para. 11 (Libya).

1315 UN Doc. CRC/C/15/Add.247, para. 26 (Antigua and Barbuda).

1316 UN Doc. CRC/C/15/Add.249, para. 24 (Albania); UN Doc. CRC/C/15/Add.231, para. 25 (Japan); UN Doc. CRC/C/15/Add.219, paras. 24-25 (Brunei Darussalam); UN Doc. CRC/C/15/Add.202, para. 26 (Haiti); UN Doc. CRC/C/15/Add.147, para. 26 (Lesotho); UN Doc. CRC/C/15/Add.129, paras. 23-24 (Malta); UN Doc. CRC/C/15/Add.92, paras. 9 and 27 (Luxembourg); UN Doc. CRC/C/15/Add.90, para. 35 (Japan); UN Doc. CRC/C/15/Add.44, para. 25 (Senegal); UN Doc. CRC/C/15/Add.41, para. 16 (Italy); UN Doc. CRC/C/15/Add.39, paras. 7 and 14 (Tunisia).

1317 UN Doc. CRC/C/15/Add.209, paras. 23-24 (Syrian Arabic Jamahiriya).

1318 UN Doc. CRC/C/15/Add.71, para. 66 (New Zealand).

1319 UN Doc. CRC/C/15/Add.188, paras. 55-56 (United Kingdom).

ii. Marital Status

Restrictions applied to unmarried fathers in transmitting citizenship to their children may lead to adverse effects on children of unmarried fathers.[1320]

iii. Pregnancy and Motherhood

Concerns have been raised about pregnant adolescents as far as access to education is concerned,[1321] and about teenage mothers.[1322]

iv. Sexual Orientation

In both its 2003 general comments, one on HIV/AIDS and one on adolescent health, the CRC Committee held explicitly that the grounds of discrimination mentioned in article 2 covered also sexual orientation.[1323] It has however refrained from indicating which of these grounds in particular includes sexual orientation. Drawing from the qualifications by other Committees, sexual orientation might be subsumed under the notions of either "sex" or "other status". The latter option is here preferred.

In its concluding observations, attention for discrimination based on sexual orientation has been less outspoken. It has noted only twice so far a disparity between the ages for sexual consent to heterosexual and homosexual relations and the discrimination it entails.[1324]

v. Health Status

The Committee has interpreted "other status" to cover also the health status, including the HIV/AIDS status of the child or its parents, and the mental health status.[1325]

1320 *Ibid.*, para. 23 (United Kingdom); UN Doc. CRC/C/15/Add.34, para. 12 (United Kingdom).

1321 UN Doc. CRC/C/15/Add.232, para. 57 (El Salvador); UN Doc. CRC/C/15/Add.186, para. 52 (Netherlands Antilles); UN Doc. CRC/C/15/Add.166, para. 27 (Paraguay); UN Doc. CRC/C/15/Add.150, para. 41 (Dominican Republic).

1322 UN Doc. CRC/C/15/Add.135, para. 25 (United Kingdom – Overseas Territories).

1323 UN Doc. HRI/GEN/1/Rev.7, General Comment No. 4 (2003), *Adolescent Health and Development in the Context of the Convention on the Rights of the Child*, para. 2; General Comment No. 3 (2003), *HIV/AIDS and the Rights of the Child*, para. 6.

1324 UN Doc. CRC/C/15/Add.135, para. 25 (United Kingdom – Overseas Territories); UN Doc. CRC/C/15/Add.134, paras. 22-23 (United Kingdom – Isle of Man).

1325 UN Doc. HRI/GEN/1/Rev.7, General Comment No. 4 (2003), *Adolescent Health and Development in the Context of the Convention on the Rights of the Child*, para. 2; General Comment No. 3 (2003), *HIV/AIDS and the Rights of the Child*, para. 7. As to mental health, see also para. 25 of the latter general comment.

Most attention has gone so far to discrimination based on HIV/AIDS.[1326] The effects of discrimination based on HIV/AIDS were spelled out in the Committee's general comment No. 3:

> Discrimination is responsible for heightening the vulnerability of children to HIV and AIDS, as well as seriously impacting the lives of children who are affected by HIV/AIDS, or are themselves HIV infected. Girls and boys of parents living with HIV/AIDS are often the victims of stigma and discrimination as they too are often assumed to be infected. As a result of discrimination children are denied access to information, education (reference to general comment No. 1 on the aims of education), health or social care services or from community life. At its extreme, discrimination against HIV-infected children has resulted in their abandonment by their family, community and/or society. Discrimination also fuels the epidemic by making children in particular those belonging to certain groups like children living in remote or rural areas where services are less accessible, more vulnerable to infection. These children are thereby doubly victimized.[1327]

The Committee has also pointed out that "discrimination in the context of HIV/AIDS often impacts girls more severely than boys."[1328]

Discrimination against children with HIV/AIDS has been highlighted in the areas of education[1329] and health[1330] in particular. States have been encouraged to integrate respect for the rights of the child into their HIV/AIDS policies and strategies,[1331] with a particular emphasis on the Convention's four general principles of non-discrimination, best interests of the child, right to life and respect for the views of the child. They should prevent discrimination against children infected with or affected by

[1326] UN Doc. CRC/C/15/Add.260, para. 69 (Nepal); UN Doc. CRC/C/15/Add.259, para. 53 (Bosnia and Herzegovina); UN Doc. CRC/C/15/Add.257, para. 52 (Nigeria); UN Doc. CRC/C/15/Add.210, para. 44 (Jamaica); UN Doc. CRC/C/15/Add.191, para. 58 (Ukraine); UN Doc. CRC/C/15/Add.186, para. 50 (Netherlands Antilles); UN Doc. CRC/C/15/Add.177, para. 40 (Guinea-Bissau); UN Doc. CRC/C/15/Add.172, para. 52 (Mozambique); UN Doc. CRC/C/15/Add.122, para. 31 (South Africa); UN Doc. CRC/C/15/Add.120, para. 24 (Peru); UN Doc. CRC/C/15/Add.31, para. 27 (Poland).

[1327] UN Doc. HRI/GEN/1/Rev.7, General Comment No. 3 (2003), *HIV/AIDS and the Rights of the Child*, para. 5.

[1328] *Ibid.*

[1329] UN Doc. HRI/GEN/1/Rev.7, General Comment No. 1 (2001), *The Aims of Education*, para. 10; UN Doc. CRC/C/15/Add.210, para. 23 (Jamaica); UN Doc. CRC/C/15/Add.184, para. 19 (St. Vincent and the Grenadines)UN Doc. CRC/C/15/Add.122, para. 8 (South Africa).

[1330] UN Doc. CRC/C/15/Add.209, para. 38 (Libyan Arabic Jamahiriya).

[1331] UN Doc. CRC/C/15/Add.191, para. 59 (Ukraine); UN Doc. CRC/C/15/Add.186, para. 51 (Netherlands Antilles); UN Doc. CRC/C/15/Add.177, para. 41 (Guinea-Bissau); UN Doc. CRC/C/15/Add.172, para. 53 (Mozambique).

HIV/AIDS,[1332] and launch public education campaigns,[1333] particularly for health professionals.[1334]

vi. Nationality

The Committee has explicitly recognized nationality as one of the prohibited grounds of discrimination under the Convention,[1335] without specifying however under which of the enumerated grounds it was to be subsumed. Other Committees have considered "nationality" to be covered by either "national origin" or "other status". For the reasons stated earlier, preference is given to subsume nationality under "other status".

Concern has been expressed at discrimination against non citizen children,[1336] in particular illegal or undocumented ones,[1337] children of migrant families,[1338] and unaccompanied or separated, or refugee, asylum-seeker or migrant children.[1339] Double discrimination might arise against non national children with disabilities.[1340] Issues relate mainly to accessing services like education, health care and social

1332 UN Doc. CRC/C/15/Add.252, para. 57 (Belize).

1333 UN Doc. CRC/C/15/Add.200, para. 46 (Viet Nam).

1334 UN Doc. CRC/C/15/Add.115, para. 51 (India).

1335 UN Doc. CRC/C/15/Add.178, para. 6 (Belgium).

1336 UN Doc. CRC/C/15/Add.243, para. 21 (Croatia); UN Doc. CRC/C/15/Add.226, para. 24 (Germany); UN Doc. CRC/C/15/Add.220, paras. 23-24 (Singapore); UN Doc. CRC/C/15/Add.212, paras. 32-33 (Syrian Arab Republic); UN Doc. CRC/C/15/Add.201, para. 29 (Czech Republic); UN Doc. CRC/C/15/Add.199, para. 54 (Romania); UN Doc. CRC/C/15/Add.183, para. 24 (United Arab Emirates); UN Doc. CRC/C/15/Add.182, para. 21 (Switzerland); UN Doc. CRC/C/15/Add.178, para. 6 (Belgium); UN Doc. CRC/C/15/Add.167, paras. 26 and 28 (Uzbekistan); UN Doc. CRC/C/15/Add.161, paras. 26-27 (Oman); UN Doc. CRC/C/15/Add.158, para. 20-21 (Monaco); UN Doc. CRC/C/15/Add.149, para. 33 (Palau); UN Doc. CRC/C/15/Add.127, para. 21 (Kyrgyzstan); UN Doc. CRC/C/15/Add.85, para. 11 (Libya).

1337 UN Doc. CRC/C/15/Add.265, para. 18 (Costa Rica); UN Doc. CRC/C/15/Add.230, para. 55 (Slovenia); UN Doc. CRC/C/15/Add.212, para. 49 (Syrian Arab Republic); UN Doc. CRC/C/15/Add.209, para. 42 (Libyan Arabic Jamahiriya); UN Doc. CRC/C/15/Add.201, para. 54 (Czech Republic); UN Doc. CRC/C/15/Add.199, para. 54 (Romania); UN Doc. CRC/C/15/Add.196, para. 23 (Estonia); UN Doc. CRC/C/15/Add.186, para. 52 (Netherlands Antilles); UN Doc. CRC/C/15/Add.176, para. 29 (Andorra); UN Doc. CRC/C/15/Add.170, para. 69 (Greece).

1338 UN Doc. CRC/C/15/Add.265, para. 18 (Costa Rica); UN Doc. CRC/C/15/Add.227, para. 30 (Netherlands and Aruba); UN Doc. CRC/C/15/Add.186, paras. 25-26 (Netherlands Antilles); UN Doc. CRC/C/15/Add.150, paras. 22 and 41 (Dominican Republic); UN Doc. CRC/C/15/Add.96, para. 18 (Kuwait); UN Doc. CRC/C/15/Add.85, para. 11 (Libya); UN Doc. CRC/C/15/Add.37, para. 13 (Canada).

1339 For an explicit recognition of this group see the CRC Committee's most recent general comment (General Comment No. 6 (2005), *Treatment of Unaccompanied and Separated Children Outside Their Country of Origin*).

1340 UN Doc. CRC/C/15/Add.175, para. 28 (Bahrain). The Committee has not qualified it that way though.

benefits,[1341] for example through social security laws which effectively deprive non citizens of rights to social security benefits and impose fees which may inhibit access to health and education services.[1342] Furthermore, the services available to illegal-immigrant children are to be expanded beyond the provision of emergency health services.[1343] Concern has also been voiced over discrimination in the definition of the child between citizen and non citizen children (*i.e.* persons under 18 or 16),[1344] and against children adopted abroad, who must wait two years before being formally adopted.[1345]

The Committee has emphasized that the guarantee of non-discrimination in the CRC applies to each child within the state 's jurisdiction, and seems thus to have questioned the acceptability of any declaration under article 2 CRC which might have a discriminatory effect against non citizen children.[1346] Measures required to address discrimination against non citizen children include an effective legal framework for the protection of the rights of refugee and asylum-seeking children,[1347] the strengthening of administrative and judicial measures to prevent and eliminate *de facto* discrimination,[1348] prosecution of those responsible for discrimination and information campaigns.[1349] The latter may have to be targeted at local government and law-enforcement officials.[1350]

With regard to unaccompanied and separated children in particular, the CRC Committee has submitted that the exception of art. 2, para. 3 CESCR (*i.e.* the freedom for developing countries to decide to what extent they guarantee economic rights to

---

1341 UN Doc. CRC/C/15/Add.265, para. 18 (Costa Rica); UN Doc. CRC/C/15/Add.230, para. 55 (Slovenia); UN Doc. CRC/C/15/Add.227, para. 30 (Netherlands and Aruba); UN Doc. CRC/C/15/Add.201, para. 54 (Czech Republic); UN Doc. CRC/C/15/Add.199, para. 54 (Romania); UN Doc. CRC/C/15/Add.188, para. 50 (United Kingdom); UN Doc. CRC/C/15/Add.186, paras. 25-26 and 52 (Netherlands Antilles); UN Doc. CRC/C/15/Add.183, para. 24 (United Arab Emirates); UN Doc. CRC/C/15/Add.176, para. 29 (Andorra); UN Doc. CRC/C/15/Add.167, para. 29 (Uzbekistan); UN Doc. CRC/C/15/Add.161, paras. 26-27 (Oman); UN Doc. CRC/C/15/Add.150, paras. 22-23 and 41 (Dominican Republic); UN Doc. CRC/C/15/Add.149, para. 33 (Palau); UN Doc. CRC/C/15/Add.126, para. 20 (Norway); UN Doc. CRC/C/15/Add.103, para. 15 (Barbados); UN Doc. CRC/C/15/Add.43, para. 19 (Germany). See also General Comment No. 6 (2005), *Treatment of Unaccompanied and Separated Children Outside Their Country of Origin*.

1342 UN Doc. CRC/C/15/Add.167, para. 26 (Uzbekistan); UN Doc. CRC/C/15/Add.127, para. 21 (Kyrgyzstan).

1343 UN Doc. CRC/C/15/Add.101, para. 11 (Sweden).

1344 UN Doc. CRC/C/15/Add.195, paras. 24-25 (Israel).

1345 UN Doc. CRC/C/15/Add.182, paras. 36-37 (Switzerland).

1346 UN Doc. CRC/C/15/Add.178, para. 6 (Belgium).

1347 UN Doc. CRC/C/15/Add.212, para. 49 (Syrian Arab Republic); UN Doc. CRC/C/15/Add.209, para. 42 (Libyan Arabic Jamahiriya); UN Doc. CRC/C/15/Add.126, para. 21 (Norway).

1348 UN Doc. CRC/C/15/Add.226, para. 24 (Germany).

1349 UN Doc. CRC/C/15/Add.170, para. 69 (Greece).

1350 UN Doc. CRC/C/15/Add.110, para. 51 (Russian Federation).

non nationals) does not apply.[1351] Developing states too are therefore to guarantee economic rights to foreign unaccompanied and separated children on an equal footing with nationals.

vii. Place of Residence

The CRC Committee has expressed concern about both interregional[1352] (extending to remote islands[1353] or areas[1354]) and rural-urban discrimination.[1355] Quite often, they are mentioned simultaneously.[1356]

Discrimination between regions may arise in the context of a federal state[1357] or of decentralization or devolution,[1358] or out of persistent unequal social development between regions.[1359] Both for interregional and rural-urban discrimination, the Committee has focused on availability[1360] of and access to basic services,[1361] such as health,[1362]

1351 General Comment No. 6 (2005), *Treatment of Unaccompanied and Separated Children Outside Their Country of Origin.*

1352 UN Doc. CRC/C/15/Add.117, para. 15 (Costa Rica).

1353 UN Doc. CRC/C/15/Add.91, para. 35 (Maldives).

1354 UN Doc. CRC/C/15/Add.255, para. 27 (Togo).

1355 UN Doc. CRC/C/15/Add.265, para. 18 (Costa Rica); UN Doc. CRC/C/15/Add.264, para. 27 (Nicaragua); UN Doc. CRC/C/15/Add.263, para. 16 (Mongolia); UN Doc. CRC/C/15/Add.233, para. 23 (Panama); UN Doc. CRC/C/15/Add.95, para. 17 (Bolivia); UN Doc. CRC/C/15/Add.93, para. 18 (Ecuador); UN Doc. CRC/C/15/Add.5, para. 12 (Egypt).

1356 UN Doc. CRC/C/15/Add.211, para. 25 (Morocco); UN Doc. CRC/C/15/Add.181, paras. 23 and 39 (Tunisia); UN Doc. CRC/C/15/Add.108, para. 24 (Nicaragua); UN Doc. CRC/C/15/Add.102, para. 18 (Yemen); UN Doc. CRC/C/15/Add.67, para. 8 (Ethiopia).

1357 UN Doc. CRC/C/15/Add.251, para. 23 (Austria); UN Doc. CRC/C/15/Add.228, para. 14 (India); UN Doc. CRC/C/15/Add.226, paras. 23-24 (Germany).

1358 UN Doc. HRI/GEN/1/Rev.7, General Comment No. 5 (2003), *General Measures of Implementation of the Convention on the Rights of the Child (Arts. 4, 42 and 44, para. 6)*, para. 41. UN Doc. CRC/C/15/Add.249, para. 10 (Albania); UN Doc. CRC/C/15/Add.182, para. 21 (Switzerland); UN Doc. CRC/C/15/Add.178, para. 10 (Belgium); UN Doc. CRC/C/15/Add.50, para. 16 (Iceland).

1359 UN Doc. CRC/C/15/Add.241, para. 29 (Brazil).

1360 See *e.g.* UN Doc. CRC/C/15/Add.67, para. 8 (Ethiopia).

1361 UN Doc. CRC/C/15/Add.265, para. 18 (Costa Rica); UN Doc. CRC/C/15/Add.190, para. 27 (Sudan); UN Doc. CRC/C/15/Add.110, para. 22 (Russian Federation).

1362 UN Doc. CRC/C/15/Add.241, para. 52 (Brazil); UN Doc. CRC/C/15/Add.212, para. 25 (Syrian Arab Republic); UN Doc. CRC/C/15/Add.161, paras. 26-27 (Oman); UN Doc. CRC/C/15/Add.145, para. 31 (Egypt); UN Doc. CRC/C/15/Add.57, para. 32 (Nepal).

education services[1363] (including quality of education)[1364] and opportunities,[1365]or both[1366], and social care.[1367]

viii. Caste

The CRC Committee has expressed deep concern at persistent and significant social discrimination against children based on caste,[1368] but has not clarified whether it subsumes it under the ground of "ethnic, national or social origin", or rather under "other status". Affirmative action is required to address this kind of discrimination.[1369]

ix. Number of Children

On one occasion, the Committee has raised the issue that under the arrangements with regard to a "three child policy", children from families with more than three children were at a disadvantage with regard to access to social service, financial and other assistance.[1370]

x. Children in Care

The CRC Committee has expressed concern about children's homes receiving children without parental care, which might become places of potential discrimination, because of, *inter alia*, limited access to health care, lack of adequate life skills training, lack of adequately educated professionals, poorness of facilities and lack of adequate resources.[1371]

1363 UN Doc. CRC/C/15/Add.218, para. 58 (Madagascar); UN Doc. CRC/C/15/Add.161, paras. 26-27 (Oman); UN Doc. CRC/C/15/Add.145, para. 31 (Egypt); UN Doc. CRC/C/15/Add.135, para. 44 (United Kingdom – Overseas Territories).

1364 UN Doc. CRC/C/15/Add.232, para. 57 (El Salvador); UN Doc. CRC/C/15/Add.200, paras. 47- 48 (Viet Nam).

1365 UN Doc. CRC/C/15/Add.217, para. 63 (Pakistan); UN Doc. CRC/C/15/Add.212, para. 25 (Syrian Arab Republic); UN Doc. CRC/C/15/Add.200, para. 47 (Viet Nam); UN Doc. CRC/C/15/Add.57, para. 32 (Nepal).

1366 UN Doc. CRC/C/15/Add.190, para. 26 (Sudan); UN Doc. CRC/C/15/Add.120, para. 16 (Peru).

1367 UN Doc. CRC/C/15/Add.57, para. 32 (Nepal).

1368 UN Doc. CRC/C/15/Add.260, para. 36 (Nepal); UN Doc. CRC/C/15/Add.228, paras. 27-28 (India); UN Doc. CRC/C/15/Add.115, paras. 30-31 (India); UN Doc. CRC/C/15/Add.86, para. 15 (Micronesia); UN Doc. CRC/C/15/Add.57, para. 12 (Nepal).

1369 UN Doc. CRC/C/15/Add.228, para. 28 (India); UN Doc. CRC/C/15/Add.115, para. 31 (India).

1370 UN Doc. CRC/C/15/Add.118, paras. 16-17 (Macedonia).

1371 UN Doc. CRC/C/15/Add.259, para. 40 (Bosnia and Herzegovina).

k. *Minorities*

A cross-cutting issue is discrimination against children belonging to minorities, which may be based on national or ethnic origin, language or religion. The Committee has frequently expressed concern at instances of (*de facto*)[1372] and societal[1373] discrimination,[1374] against a broad range of ethnic, national, indigenous, religious, linguistic and cultural minorities,[1375] *e.g.* Roma.[1376] Concerns relate again mainly to access to social services such as health and education,[1377] but are not limited to these issues. The Committee has equally raised minorities' rights to survival and development, to enjoy their own culture and language,[1378] their overrepresentation among low-income and unemployed households, and their under representation in public service,[1379] the higher likelihood to be placed in care,[1380] the lack of birth registration[1381] and the absence of the aims of education as outlined in article 29 of the Convention (*i.e.* ...

1372 UN Doc. CRC/C/15/Add.261, para. 28 (Ecuador); UN Doc. CRC/C/15/Add.243, para. 21 (Croatia); UN Doc. CRC/C/15/Add.240, para. 60 (France).

1373 UN Doc. CRC/C/15/Add.200, para. 22 (Viet Nam); UN Doc. CRC/C/15/Add.170, para. 33 (Greece); UN Doc. CRC/C/15/Add.110, para. 65 (Russian Federation).

1374 UN Doc. CRC/C/15/Add.243, para. 70 (Croatia); UN Doc. CRC/C/15/Add.230, para. 22 (Slovenia); UN Doc. CRC/C/15/Add.228, para. 81 (India); UN Doc. CRC/C/15/Add.144, para. 30 (Ethiopia); UN Doc. CRC/C/15/Add.123, para. 23 (Iran); UN Doc. CRC/C/15/Add.75, para. 16 (Paraguay); UN Doc. CRC/C/15/Add.27, para. 8 (Paraguay).

1375 UN Doc. CRC/C/15/Add.263, para. 70 (Mongolia); UN Doc. CRC/C/15/Add.221, para. 79 (Bangladesh); UN Doc. CRC/C/15/Add.212, para. 47 (Syrian Arab Republic); UN Doc. CRC/C/15/Add.209, para. 40 (Libyan Arabic Jamahiriya); UN Doc. CRC/C/15/Add.203, para. 36 (Iceland); UN Doc. CRC/C/15/Add.196, para. 23 (Estonia); UN Doc. CRC/C/15/Add.178, para. 25 (Belgium); UN Doc. CRC/C/15/Add.170, para. 33 (Greece); UN Doc. CRC/C/15/Add.128, para. 28 (Cambodia); UN Doc. CRC/C/15/Add.117, paras. 15 and 25 (Costa Rica); UN Doc. CRC/C/15/Add.110, para. 65 (Russian Federation); UN Doc. CRC/C/15/Add.105, para. 31 (Honduras); UN Doc. CRC/C/15/Add.90, para. 35 (Japan); UN Doc. CRC/C/15/Add.56, para. 40 (China); UN Doc. CRC/C/15/Add.49, para. 7 (Yugoslavia).

1376 UN Doc. CRC/C/15/Add.249, para. 24 (Albania); UN Doc. CRC/C/15/Add.243, paras. 21 and 70 (Croatia); UN Doc. CRC/C/15/Add.240, para. 60 (France); UN Doc. CRC/C/15/Add.230, para. 22 (Slovenia); UN Doc. CRC/C/15/Add.182, para. 60 (Switzerland); UN Doc. CRC/C/15/Add.162, para. 19 (Portugal); UN Doc. CRC/C/15/Add.49, para. 10 (Yugoslavia); UN Doc. CRC/C/15/Add.31, para. 27 (Poland).

1377 UN Doc. CRC/C/15/Add.200, paras. 22-23 (Viet Nam); UN Doc. CRC/C/15/Add.182, para. 60 (Switzerland); UN Doc. CRC/C/15/Add.175, para. 28 (Bahrain); UN Doc. CRC/C/15/Add.157, para. 30 (Bhutan); UN Doc. CRC/C/15/Add.110, para. 66 (Russian Federation); UN Doc. CRC/C/15/Add.90, para. 13 (Japan); UN Doc. CRC/C/15/Add.87, para. 18 (Hungary); UN Doc. CRC/C/15/Add.56, para. 40 (China).

1378 UN Doc. CRC/C/15/Add.222, para. 70 (Georgia); UN Doc. CRC/C/15/Add.171, para. 69 (Gabon); UN Doc. CRC/C/15/Add.56, para. 40 (China).

1379 UN Doc. CRC/C/15/Add.196, para. 23 (Estonia).

1380 UN Doc. CRC/C/15/Add.34, para. 12 (United Kingdom).

1381 UN Doc. CRC/C/15/Add.128, para. 30 (Cambodia).

equality of religious and ethnic minorities) in the curricula.[1382] Media sometimes contribute to stigmatization and social exclusion by conveying stereotypical messages and distrust of people belonging to minority and/or ethnic groups.[1383] Equality before the law may not be sufficient to ensure equal enjoyment of rights by certain minority groups who may face *de facto* discrimination.[1384] As with gender equality, the CRC Committee has sometimes asked to take due regard of the Human Rights Committee's general comment on the issue.[1385]

Particular attention has been paid to negative stereotypes and (*de facto*)[1386] discrimination against Roma children.[1387] Like the other Committees, the CRC Committee too has expressed concern at the high number of Roma children attending classes for children with special needs (qualifying it as "segregation in education")[1388], instead of their integration into mainstream education, so that special assistance and support can be provided at regular classes,[1389] or for example through pre-school programmes for Romani children to learn the primary language of schooling in their communities.[1390] Other issues include access to health services and to the education system,[1391] their higher mortality rate, their conditions of accommodation[1392] and their lower standard of living.[1393] The Committee has equally noted with concern that some programmes aiming at uplifting Roma communities make a distinction between "autochthonous" and "non-autochthonous" Roma and exclude the latter group.[1394] Affirmative action is required to address discrimination against Roma.[1395]

1382 UN Doc. CRC/C/15/Add.212, para. 47 (Syrian Arab Republic); UN Doc. CRC/C/15/Add.209, para. 40 (Libyan Arabic Jamahiriya); UN Doc. CRC/C/15/Add.203, para. 36 (Iceland); UN Doc. CRC/C/15/Add.178, para. 25 (Belgium).

1383 UN Doc. CRC/C/15/Add.259, para. 25 (Bosnia and Herzegovina).

1384 UN Doc. CRC/C/15/Add.240, para. 60 (France).

1385 UN Doc. CRC/C/15/Add.222, para. 70 (Georgia).

1386 UN Doc. CRC/C/15/Add.162, para. 19 (Portugal).

1387 UN Doc. CRC/C/15/Add.259, para. 75 (Bosnia and Herzegovina); UN Doc. CRC/C/15/Add.230, para. 23 (Slovenia); UN Doc. CRC/C/15/Add.198, para. 54 (Italy); UN Doc. CRC/C/15/Add.162, paras. 19-20 (Portugal); UN Doc. CRC/C/15/Add.98, para. 30 (Austria); UN Doc. CRC/C/15/Add.87, paras. 14-31 (Hungary); UN Doc. CRC/C/15/Add.16, para. 21 (Romania).

1388 UN Doc. CRC/C/15/Add.188, para. 51 (United Kingdom).

1389 UN Doc. CRC/C/15/Add.230, paras. 22-23 (Slovenia).

1390 UN Doc. CRC/C/15/Add.194, para. 53 (Poland); UN Doc. CRC/C/15/Add.191, para. 75 (Ukraine).

1391 UN Doc. CRC/C/15/Add.259, para. 57 (Bosnia and Herzegovina); UN Doc. CRC/C/15/Add.199, para. 64 (Romania); UN Doc. CRC/C/15/Add.198, para. 55 (Italy); UN Doc. CRC/C/15/Add.140, para. 19 (Slovakia); UN Doc. CRC/C/15/Add.87, para. 34 (Hungary).

1392 UN Doc. CRC/C/15/Add.194, para. 52 (Poland); UN Doc. CRC/C/15/Add.192, para. 49 (Moldova); UN Doc. CRC/C/15/Add.191, para. 74 (Ukraine).

1393 UN Doc. CRC/C/15/Add.230, para. 23 (Slovenia); UN Doc. CRC/C/15/Add.188, para. 51 (United Kingdom).

1394 UN Doc. CRC/C/15/Add.230, paras. 22-23 (Slovenia).

1395 UN Doc. CRC/C/15/Add.140, paras. 21-24 (Slovakia).

Recently, the Committee has started to pay attention to discriminatory attitudes and the emergence of racism, xenophobia and related intolerance towards the Muslim community.[1396]

l. Conclusions

Of the UN core human rights treaties, the CRC contains the one but longest list of prohibited grounds of discrimination, in which *inter alia* disability is explicitly mentioned. The CMW holds an even longer list of prohibited grounds, but it is too early to say how that will affect the CMW Committee's practice.[1397]

Gender- and disability-based discrimination are very prominent in the CRC Committee's concluding observations. The issues raised as constituting gender discrimination correspond to a large degree with those raised by the other Committees under this ground (*i.e.* personal and civil status, representation of women in public life, discrimination in labour, health and education...). The attention paid to disability may have real added value, as none of the other Committees have shown any sustained concern for this type of discrimination. Poverty too has attracted more attention from the CRC Committee than from any other committee. Discrimination based on birth, *i.e.* against children born out of wedlock, is squarely within the Committee's mandate and has received the corresponding attention it deserves.[1398]

The CRC Committee has added a significant number of grounds under "other status", such as age, sexual orientation, pregnancy and motherhood, marital status, health status, nationality, place of residence, caste, number of children, and children in care. In comparison with other Committees, discrimination based on health status (in particular against those infected or affected by HIV/AIDS) has received more attention from the CRC Committee. Discrimination based on the place of residence has equally been better developed.

Discrimination against minorities may be based on a number of prohibited grounds, and has been treated accordingly (much in line with the CERD's and HRC's approach). Roma children have received specific attention.

1396 UN Doc. CRC/C/15/Add.258, paras. 91-92 (Philippines); UN Doc. CRC/C/15/Add.250, para. 19 (Luxembourg).

1397 The CMW Committee, which met for the first time in March 2004, had not yet started its substantive work at the time of writing.

1398 Most of the other Committees, with the exception of CERD, have equally paid sustained attention to discrimination against children born out of wedlock.

C. CONCLUSIONS

With regard to the grounds of discrimination, the core UN human rights treaties can be divided into two categories, *i.e.* single issue treaties and comprehensive treaties. ICERD and CEDAW are single issue treaties, the former limiting itself to racial discrimination and the latter to discrimination against women. The CCPR, CESCR, CRC and CMW are comprehensive treaties.[1399] They share a large common core of prohibited grounds of discrimination, *i.e.* race, colour, sex, language, religion, political or other opinion, national or social origin, property, birth or other status. To these grounds is added disability (CRC), ethnic origin (CRC and CMW),[1400] and conviction,[1401] nationality, age, economic position and marital status (CMW). As has become clear by now, the two most recent core human rights treaties codify to a large extent some of the newer important grounds that have been identified by the UN Committees under the notion of "other status".

While CERD has been rather careful and restrictive in added new grounds to its mandate, the CESCR Committee and CRC Committee probably have been most liberal and innovative in adding new grounds of discrimination under the umbrella heading of "other status". Commonly accepted additional grounds include sexual orientation, nationality, marital status, age, disability, health status and place of residence.[1402] The HRC has added *inter alia* civilian and military status.

CERD has explicitly submitted that all grounds are of equal importance. To the contrary, the HRC has clearly differentiated the importance of the grounds in its views, whereby it has attached greater importance to the explicitly enumerated grounds in general, and to gender in particular. The other Committees have not yet taken a position on the issue.

As indicated above, race and colour have received little attention. CERD has paid more attention than other Committees to the grounds of race and colour. This comes as no surprise, as they are squarely within that Committee's mandate.

By far the most prominent and conceptually best-developed ground of discrimination has been sex/gender, which all Committees with the exception of CERD have paid most attention to. Issues addressed range from family and personal status to a broad variety

---

1399 CAT does not contain any explicit provision on discrimination.

1400 Compare with ICERD.

1401 "religion or conviction" (article 7 CMW).

1402 It is to be noted that some of these have been subsumed by some Committees under one of the other grounds of discrimination.

of economic and social rights, including employment, education, health etc. The HRC, CEDAW Committee and recently also the CESCR Committee have paid particular attention to women's participation in public life. Gender has been understood by some Committees (HRC, CEDAW Committee) as to include also sexual orientation. Not surprisingly, the CEDAW Committee has been the first one to give the most extensive interpretation to gender discrimination, including also gender-based violence. It has been followed in this interpretation by the HRC and CESCR Committee.

Discrimination based on political or other opinion belongs to the core business of the HRC; it has elaborated the main principles predominantly with regard to (individual complaints of) conscientious objectors. Grounds like race, religion and language have mainly been referred to when considering discrimination against minorities (see further).

The grounds of national or social origin have been rather well-developed by most Committees (with the exception of the CESCR Committee and CEDAW Committee). Issues of discrimination against ethnic groups, including indigenous peoples, have been addressed under this heading. Quite often, no clear distinction is made between discrimination based on national or ethnic origin, and discrimination that minorities are facing more generally on a variety of grounds not limited to national or ethnic origin. As indicated higher, ethnic origin is explicitly (and in addition to "national or social") mentioned in the CRC and CMW. The CERD, more than any other Committee, has been very focused on this ground.

Property has not explicitly been referred to, but many concerns voiced about discrimination in relation to poverty might be subsumed under this ground. The CESCR Committee seems to have preferred the creation of a new ground under the notion of "other status", *i.e.* social status. The CMW mentions explicitly "economic position" as a prohibited ground.

A common theme to all Committees but the CERD, dealt with under the ground of birth, is instances of discrimination against children born out of wedlock. It has been argued that descent could have been subsumed under this ground too, but that has not happened in practice.

As to the grounds covered by "other status", sexual orientation has by some Committees been subsumed under sex (HRC, CEDAW Committee), while others have recognized it as an independent ground under other status (CESCR Committee, CRC Committee).

Discrimination based on the grounds of nationality has been a challenging issue. Both CERD and CESCR allow for differential treatment of non-citizens, albeit to a different degree. This has never been an issue under CESCR. CERD has recently, at the end of 2004, seriously restricted the permissibility of differentiation on the basis of nationality in its general recommendation on the issue. Discrimination among non nationals is in any event prohibited under the ICERD too. With some Committees (HRC, CESCR Committee), there is some uncertainty as to whether nationality is covered by "national origin" or by "other status". Nationality is a well-developed ground with the CERD, HRC and CRC Committee. Growing attention is being paid to asylum seeking, refugee and migrant status as a specific group of non nationals, in particular by the CESCR Committee and CRC Committee. It is to be expected that the CMW Committee will consider this status to be at the heart of its work.

Marital status has been invoked as a ground of discrimination by most Committees (with the exception of CERD). Is has not been a major ground of discrimination though.

Disability has been accepted as a ground of discrimination by the HRC, CESCR Committee and CEDAW Committee under the notion of "other status". While these Committees have only occasionally referred to it, the CRC has paid particular and sustained attention to discrimination based on disability. This is quite understandably so, as the ground is explicitly enumerated in the CRC.

Age has been recognized as a prohibited ground of discrimination by all Committees dealt with except for CERD. Little elaboration as to issues covered has been done however.

Health status has mainly been used to address discrimination against individuals with HIV/AIDS, but occasionally also with regard to mental health. The CRC has shown most sustained attention for this ground.

Place of residence is a recurring prohibited ground for discrimination in the CRC Committee's concluding observations. Both differential treatment between regions, and between rural and urban areas, have been addressed. Other Committees like the HRC, CESCR Committee and the CEDAW Committee have equally referred to it from time to time.

Discrimination against minorities has been a prominent issue of concern with the CERD, the HRC and the CRC Committee. The CERD has best developed its concerns on this topic. As pointed out before, this is a cross-cutting issue, as it refers often to grounds as ethnic or national origin, religion or language. The CESCR Committee seem to have somewhat neglected this group. Roma have received a lot of attention from the CERD and the CRC Committee in particular. Segregational education has been a common theme to most Committees, including those which have only occasionally paid attention to discrimination against Roma. The HRC paid less sustained attention to discrimination against Roma in the past, but it seems to have become a growing priority concern in recent years.

Two more general conclusions can be drawn. First of all, the majority of the Committees here discussed have a high number of prohibited grounds of discrimination in common, either because they are mentioned in each of the core human rights treaties, or because they have been added by the Committees itself. This high degree of commonality of grounds should, however, not detract attention from the fact that two out of five have a single issue mandate, *i.e.* CERD (racial discrimination) and the CEDAW Committee (discrimination against women). Secondly, after having read all documents pertaining to equality and non-discrimination of all Committees, one cannot escape the conclusion that the Committees' practices of identifying and addressing issues of discrimination under the different grounds, vary considerably. Some Committees like the HRC and CERD raise issues of discrimination systematically and in great detail. The CESCR Committee seems to have resorted to a less systematized approach, and to identify issues of discrimination in more general wording. The CEDAW Committee uses relatively little equality and non-discrimination language, and more women's rights language. The CRC Committee pays sustained attention to discrimination as one of the four general principles of the CRC.

CHAPTER IV. OBLIGATIONS DERIVING FROM THE PRINCIPLES OF NON-DISCRIMINATION AND EQUALITY

A. OBLIGATIONS

In previous chapters, the concepts of discrimination and equality and their qualifiers, and the prohibited grounds of discrimination have been explored. In the present chapter, states' obligations under the principles of non-discrimination and equality are scrutinized.

A now commonly-used typology of state obligations with regard to economic, social and cultural rights distinguishes between the obligation to respect, to protect and to fulfil. The latter is composed of sub-obligations to facilitate, to promote and to provide.[1403] It is submitted that this threefold typology of state obligations – which is usually mainly used to identify obligations relating to economic, social and cultural rights only – can be applied usefully with regard to all human rights, including non-discrimination and equality. This typology can be considered to be a further refinement of the common distinction between negative and positive obligations, and between vertical and (indirect) horizontal effects. The threefold typology will be deployed as an analytical and structuring tool for this chapter. As many suggestions and recommendations are case and country specific, their structuring along the threefold typology of obligations greatly facilitates comparison. The obligation to respect requires the state to refrain from interference, *i.e.* not to take any discriminatory action. In order to respect the right to non-discrimination, states are under an obligation not to adopt any discriminatory legislation or practices, and to amend or repeal discriminatory legislation as well as to bring to an end discriminatory practices or measures. The obligation to protect imposes a duty on the state to prevent third parties from discriminating. The obligation to fulfil requires the state to adopt appropriate legislative, administrative, budgetary, judicial, promotional and other measures towards the full realization of the right to equality. The sub-obligation to

1403 See e.g. UN Doc. E/C.12/2005/3, General Comment No. 16 (2005), *Article 3: The Equal Right of Men and Women to the Enjoyment of All Economic, Social and Cultural Rights*, para. 17.

facilitate necessitates the state to take positive measures to assist individuals to enjoy their right to equality. Such measures may consist of legislation, plans of action, strategies and programmes. A second important way of facilitating equality is through making available effective recourse in case of violations. The obligation to promote obliges a state to take steps to ensure that there is appropriate education and awareness raising concerning non-discrimination and equality. Finally, the obligation to provide comes into play when individuals or groups are unable, for reasons beyond their control, to realize the right to equality themselves by the means at their disposal.[1404] The closest a state can come to actually providing equality may be through affirmative action.[1405]

As will be clarified in greater detail for each of the Committees where and if relevant, affirmative action[1406] is intended to accelerate *de facto* equality, by redressing disadvantage suffered by some groups due to entrenchment of discrimination in society.[1407] Affirmative action typically implies differential treatment for a period of time in favour of certain persons or groups. Affirmative action should not lead to the maintenance of separate rights for different groups, and should not be continued after the intended objectives have been achieved, as the non-discrimination principle remains applicable.[1408]

In light of article 2, para. 1 CESCR, it is assumed that economic, social and cultural rights may only be realized progressively. However, all Committees have emphasized the immediate character of the obligation to abstain from discrimination. This obli-

---

1404 See the CESCR Committee's general comments, *e.g.* UN Doc. HRI/GEN/1/Rev.7, General Comment No. 15 (2002), *The Right to Water (Arts. 11 and 12 of the International Covenant on Economic, Social and Cultural Rights)*, paras. 20-29; General Comment No. 14 (2000), *The Right to the Highest Attainable Standard of Health (Art. 12)*, para. 33; General Comment No. 13 (1999), *The Right to Education (Art. 13)*, para. 47; General Comment No. 12, *The Right to Adequate Food (Art. 11)*, para. 15.

1405 Affirmative action is here used to indicate preferential treatment of certain groups during a limited period of time because of *de facto* discrimination. It is therefore not a synonym of positive measures, as Joseph, Schultz and Castan suggest, who distinguish between affirmative action and reverse discrimination (Joseph, Schultz and Castan, supra note 53, 728), or as Hanski and Scheinin use it (Hanski and Scheinin, supra note 35, 328).

1406 Synonyms are temporary special measures, positive discrimination, reverse discrimination, or preferential treatment. Positive action is used here, for it may create least confusion as to what it actually means. See *e.g.* on affirmative action, UN Doc. E/CN.4/Sub.2/2002/21, *The Concept and Practice of Affirmative Action. Final Report by Mr. Marc Bossuyt, Special Rapporteur, In Accordance with Sub-Commission Resolution 1998/5.*

1407 Joseph, Schultz and Castan, supra note 53, 728.

1408 See further; see also *e.g.* Bossuyt, supra note 83, 44-45. See also Bossuyt's report on affirmative action, UN Doc. E/CN.4/Sub.2/2002/21, *The Concept and Practice of Affirmative Action. Final Report by Mr. Marc Bossuyt, Special Rapporteur, In Accordance with Sub-Commission Resolution 1998/5*, paras. 81-100.

gation is subject to neither progressive realisation nor the availability of resources. As to the elimination of *de facto* discrimination, the CESCR Committee seems to allow for progressive realisation (see higher, chapter II).

No attention will be paid in this chapter to the reporting obligations for states. Suffice it to say that in particular the CESCR Committee[1409] and the CEDAW Committee have insisted on data disaggregated by the prohibited grounds (mainly sex/gender for the CEDAW Committee,[1410] with some extension in recent years to age,[1411] and race and ethnicity[1412]). The CRC Committee has stressed that disaggregated data on children to enable identification of discrimination and/or disparities in the realization of rights, is an essential part of implementation.[1413]

The obligation to withdraw reservations with regard to the non-discrimination principle will equally not be addressed. All Committees have requested the withdrawal of reservations.[1414]

1409 UN Doc. HRI/GEN/1/Rev.7, General Comment No. 13 (1999), *The Right to Education (Art. 13)*, para. 37.

1410 UN Doc. A/58/38 (part II), para. 258 (France); UN Doc. A/58/38 (part I), para. 276 (El Salvador); UN Doc. A/57/38 (part III), para. 448 (Mexico); UN Doc. A/57/38 (part II), para. 114 (Saint Kitts and Nevis); UN Doc. A/56/38 (part II), para. 42 (Andorra); UN Doc. A/54/38/Rev.1 (part II), para. 197 (Ireland); UN Doc. A/54/38/Rev.1 (part II), para. 146 (Nepal); UN Doc. A/54/38/Rev.1 (part I), para. 161 (Liechtenstein); UN Doc. A/53/38/Rev.1 (part II), para. 371 (Korea); UN Doc. A/53/38/Rev.1 (part II), para. 288 (New Zealand); UN Doc. A/53/38/Rev.1 (part II), para. 161 (Nigeria); See UN Doc. A/52/38/Rev.1 (part II), para. 316 (Argentina); UN Doc. A/52/38/Rev.1 (part II), para. 66 (Armenia); UN Doc. A/52/38/Rev.1 (Part I), para. 247 (Venezuela); UN Doc. A/52/38/Rev.1 (Part I), para. 80 (Morocco); UN Doc. A/51/38, para. 88 (Iceland); UN Doc. A/49/38, para. 368 (Zambia); UN Doc. A/49/38, para. 237 (Madagascar).

1411 UN Doc. A/58/38 (part II), para. 376 (Japan); UN Doc. A/57/38 (part II), para. 71 (Suriname).

1412 UN Doc. A/58/38 (part II), para. 134 (Brazil).

1413 UN Doc. HRI/GEN/1/Rev.7, General Comment No. 5 (2003), *General Measures of Implementation of The Convention on the Rights of the Child (Arts. 4, 42 and 44, para. 6)*, para. 48. Until early 2001, it asked states in its concluding observations to collect disaggregated data and other information in order to identify discrimination against children, in particular those belonging to the mentioned vulnerable groups (see *e.g.* UN Doc. CRC/C/15/Add.146, para. 22 (Lithuania); UN Doc. CRC/C/15/Add.142, para. 24 (Latvia); UN Doc. CRC/C/15/Add.139, para. 29 (Marshall Islands).

1414 For CERD, see recently *e.g.* UN Doc. CERD/C/65/CO/2, para. 18 (Belarus); UN Doc. CERD/C/64/CO/1, para. 10 (Bahamas); UN Doc. CERD/C/62/CO/12, para. 5 (Papua New Guinea); UN Doc. CERD/C/62/CO/8, para. 9 (Saudi Arabia); UN Doc. CERD/C/62/CO/3, para. 12 (Fiji); UN Doc. CERD/C/60/CO/14, para. 14 (Switzerland); UN Doc. CERD/C/60/CO/6, para. 7 (Jamaica); UN Doc. CERD/C/60/CO/2, para. 14 (Belgium). For the HRC, see *e.g.* UN Doc. CCPR/CO/80/DEU, para. 10 (Germany); UN Doc. CCPR/C/79/Add.70, para. 23 (Switzerland). For the CESCR Committee, see *e.g.* UN Doc. E/C.12/1/Add.98, para. 28 (Kuwait). For the CEDAW Committee, see *e.g.* UN Doc. CEDAW/C/DZA/CC/2, para. 24 (Algeria); UN Doc. A/58/38 (part II), para. 428 (New Zealand); UN Doc. A/58/38 (part II), para. 252 (France); UN Doc. A/58/38 (part II), para. 159 (Morocco); UN Doc. A/58/38 (part I), para. 301 (Luxembourg); UN Doc. A/58/38 (part I), para. 100 (Switzerland). For the CRC Committee, see *e.g.* UN Doc. CRC/C/15/Add.178, paras. 6-7 (Belgium); UN Doc. CRC/C/15/Add.39, paras. 6 and 10 (Tunisia).

B. THE COMMITTEES

1. CERD

The incorporation of a prohibition of racial discrimination in domestic legislation is a measure that may be required under the obligations to respect, to protect and to fulfil (facilitate). It therefore precedes here a detailed analysis of the different types of obligations.

The inclusion of a general principle of non-discrimination in domestic legislation is not a sufficient response to the requirements of ICERD.[1415] States are to incorporate in their domestic legislation an explicit prohibition of *racial* discrimination, in accordance with the ICERD,[1416] as well as provisions for enforcing the prohibition.[1417] The definition of racial discrimination in their legislation is to be in line with article 1, para. 1 ICERD.[1418] All forms of racial discrimination are to be covered,[1419] including race,[1420] descent,[1421] colour and nationality.[1422] Discrimination in effect is to be included too.[1423] The same protection from all forms of racial discrimination, enshrined in article 1 ICERD, is to be provided for.[1424]

Moreover, ICERD is to be incorporated comprehensively into domestic law,[1425] so that the provisions of the Convention are fully reflected in domestic law.[1426] This requires

---

1415 UN Doc. CERD/C/63/CO/12, para. 7 (Malawi).

1416 UN Doc. CERD/C/65/CO/8, para. 11 (Tajikistan); UN Doc. CERD/C/65/CO/5, para. 10 (Mauritania); UN Doc. CERD/C/65/CO/4, para. 12 (Madagascar); UN Doc. CERD/C/62/CO/7, para. 10 (Russian Federation); UN Doc. CERD/C/304/Add.114, para. 10 (Japan); UN Doc. CERD/C/304/Add.107, para. 8 (Finland); UN Doc. CERD/C/304/Add.33, para. 18 (Algeria); UN Doc. CERD/C/304/Add.19, para. 19 (Mauritius).

1417 UN Doc. CERD/C/304/Add.113, para. 11 (Algeria).

1418 UN Doc. CERD/C/BHR/CO/7, para. 11 (Bahrain); UN Doc. CERD/C/65/CO/3, para. 8 (Kazakhstan); UN Doc. CERD/C/64/CO/1, para. 12 (Bahamas); UN Doc. CERD/C/63/CO/7, para. 8 (Latvia); UN Doc. CERD/C/63/CO/6, para. 11 (Iran); UN Doc. CERD/C/63/CO/4, para. 8 (Czech Republic); UN Doc. CERD/C/60/CO/1, para. 9 (Austria); UN Doc. CERD/C/304/Add.79, para. 19 (Latvia).

1419 UN Doc. CERD/C/60/CO/1, para. 10 (Austria); UN Doc. CERD/C/304/Add.14, para. 15 (Malta).

1420 UN Doc. A/48/18, para. 232 (Korea).

1421 UN Doc. HRI/GEN/1/Rev.7, General Recommendation XXIX (2002), *Article 1, paragraph 1, (Descent)*, para. 3; UN Doc. CERD/C/63/CO/11, para. 25 (United Kingdom).

1422 UN Doc. CERD/C/63/CO/11, para. 15 (United Kingdom).

1423 UN Doc. CERD/C/304/Add.91, para. 13 (France); UN Doc. CERD/C/304/Add.81, para. 14 (Chile).

1424 UN Doc. CERD/C/63/CO/11, para. 15 (United Kingdom).

1425 UN Doc. CERD/C/AUS/CO/14, para. 9 (Australia); UN Doc. CERD/C/IRL/CO/2, para. 9 (Ireland); UN Doc. CERD/C/63/CO/12, para. 7 (Malawi); UN Doc. CERD/C/62/CO/8, para. 10 (Saudi Arabia); UN Doc. CERD/C/60/CO/11, para. 9 (Qatar); UN Doc. A/57/18, para. 298 (Botswana).

1426 UN Doc. CERD/C/304/Add.111, para. 12 (Iceland); UN Doc. CERD/C/304/Add.102, para. 10 (United Kingdom); UN Doc. A/56/18, para. 369 (Ukraine); UN Doc. A/56/18, para. 434 (Liberia).

inter alia the penalization of racial discrimination,[1427] as well as the access to effective protection and remedies through the competent national tribunals and other state institutions against any acts of racial discrimination.[1428] Specific legislation may be required, *inter alia* on the status of languages,[1429] land rights[1430] and in order to protect refugees and asylum-seekers.[1431]

a. *The Obligation to Respect*

The obligation to respect often requires review of legislation that is discriminatory.[1432] In the field of civil rights, states are for instance, to ensure that the right to equal treatment before the law, as defined in article 5 (a) of the Convention, is respected in national and customary judicial proceedings.[1433] Practices restricting freedom of movement and residence of Roma are to be fully and promptly eliminated,[1434] and a state is to abstain from having an offending term on a sign.[1435] States are to abstain from discrimination in purpose or effect in their asylum procedures.[1436] Security procedures and practices at entry points are to be reviewed in order to avoid discriminatory treatment.[1437] The mandatory, automatic and indeterminate character of detention of illegal migrants is to be reviewed.[1438]

Discriminatory provisions are to be modified,[1439] the withdrawal of existing guarantees for indigenous people is to be reconsidered,[1440] and high standards of proof for indigenous people in order to obtain recognition of land titles is to be reviewed.[1441] Enforcement of counter-terrorism legislation should not disproportionately impact on

1427 UN Doc. A/48/18, para. 232 (Korea).
1428 UN Doc. CERD/C/304/Add.114, para. 12 (Japan).
1429 UN Doc. CERD/C/65/CO/3, para. 12 (Kazakhstan).
1430 UN Doc. CERD/C/64/CO/8, para. 12 (Sweden).
1431 UN Doc. CERD/C/64/CO/5, para. 19 (Nepal).
1432 UN Doc. CERD/C/63/CO/11, paras. 11 and 16 (United Kingdom); UN Doc. CERD/C/63/CO/10, para. 7 (Saint Vincent and Grenadines); UN Doc. A/57/18, para. 460 (Yemen); UN Doc. CERD/C/304/Add.113, para. 10 (Algeria); UN Doc. CERD/C/304/Add.83, para. 13 (Iran). See also General Recommendation XXVII (2000), *Discrimination against Roma*, para. 1.
1433 UN Doc. CERD/C/304/Add.97, para. 12 (Rwanda).
1434 UN Doc. CERD/C57/D/13/1998, Communication No. 13/1998, *Anna Koptova v. Slovakia*, para. 10.3.
1435 UN Doc. CERD/C/62/D/26/2002, Communication No. 26/2002, *Stephen Hagan v. Australia*, para. 8.
1436 UN Doc. CERD/C/AZE/CO/4, para. 13 (Azerbaijan): priority concern.
1437 UN Doc. CERD/C/IRL/CO/2, para. 16 (Ireland).
1438 UN Doc. CERD/C/AUS/CO/14, para. 23 (Australia).
1439 UN Doc. CERD/C/BHR/CO/7, para. 17 (Bahrain).
1440 UN Doc. CERD/C/AUS/CO/14, paras. 11 and 16 (Australia): priority concern.
1441 *Ibid.*, para. 17 (Australia): priority concern.

specific ethnic groups or people of other national origins.[1442] Legislation on mandatory sentencing, with a disparate impact on indigenous groups, is to be abrogated.[1443]

In a case of alleged discrimination in relation to housing, the CERD has held that the obligation to abstain from discrimination is not limited to the final step in the actual implementation of a particular human right, but extends to all preliminary administrative and policy-making steps which are directly connected to that implementation. A municipal council had adopted a resolution whereby it approved a plan to construct low-cost housing for the Roma inhabitants of the town. Following a petition against the resolution, the resolution was cancelled. Twenty-seven citizens of Roma ethnicity complained about the reversal of the resolution, which was in their view based on a discriminatory petition. The state argued that municipal resolutions, as purely internal organizational rules, were not binding ordinances and did not confer objective or subjective rights that could be invoked before the courts or other authorities. In its view, policy measures taken by the municipal council to secure housing for low-income citizens did not fall within the scope of ICERD, as they were part of an ongoing effort to find a conceptual solution to the problem.[1444] The Committee held however:

> that in complex contemporary societies the practical realization of, in particular, many economic, social and cultural rights, including those related to housing, will initially depend on and indeed require a series of administrative and policy-making steps by the State party's competent relevant authorities. In the present case, the council resolution clearly adopted a positive development policy for housing and tasked the mayor with pursuing subsequent measures by way of implementation.
>
> In the Committee's view, it would be inconsistent with the purpose of the Convention and elevate formalism over substance, to consider that the final step in the actual implementation of a particular human right or fundamental freedom must occur in a non-discriminatory manner, while the necessary preliminary decision-making elements directly connected to that implementation were to be severed and be free from scrutiny. As a result, the Committee considers that the council resolutions in question, taking initially an important policy and practical step towards realization of the right to housing followed by its revocation and replacement with a weaker measure, taken together, do indeed amount to the impairment of the recognition or exercise on an equal basis of the human right to housing, protected by article 5(c) of the Convention [...].[1445]

b. *The Obligation to Protect*

Protection against discrimination by non-state actors is explicitly covered by ICERD. Art. 2, para. 1 (d) ICERD obliges states parties to "prohibit and bring to an end, by

---

1442 *Ibid.*, para. 13 (Australia).
1443 *Ibid.*, para. 20 (Australia).
1444 UN Doc. CERD/C/66/D/31/2003, Communication No. 31/3003, *LR. v. Slovakia*, paras. 7.7-7.8.
1445 *Ibid.*, para. 10.

all appropriate means, including legislation as required by circumstances, race discrimination by any persons, group or organization." "To the extent that private institutions influence the exercise of rights or the availability of opportunities, the State Party must ensure that the result has neither the purpose nor the effect of creating or perpetuating racial discrimination."[1446] The CERD has emphasized the importance of adequately prohibiting and penalizing acts of racial segregation and discrimination, whether they are committed by individuals or associations:[1447] the largest possible sphere of private conduct which is discriminatory on racial or ethnic grounds is to be rendered liable to criminal sanctions.[1448] Prejudice and xenophobic stereotyping, especially in the media, are to be combated, and prejudice and discriminatory attitudes fought.[1449]

The obligation in article 2 ICERD to redress private discrimination is reinforced by a number of other provisions in the Convention, *inter alia* in the articles 4, 5 and 6 ICERD.

Article 4 ICERD features very prominently in the Committee's concluding observations. Its provisions are mandatory.[1450] Article 4 cannot be directly implemented. In order to satisfy its provisions, appropriate legislation is to be enacted that sets out sanctions to be applied to offences strictly defined under the law.[1451] This legislation is also to be effectively enforced.[1452] Article 4 ICERD requires a state party to penalize the dissemination of ideas of racial superiority, and of organized activity likely to incite persons to racial violence. In accordance with article 4 (a), the following five categories are to be penalized: (1) dissemination of ideas based on racial superiority or hatred; (2) incitement to racial hatred; (3) acts of violence against any race or group of persons of another colour or ethnic origin; (4) incitement to the latter acts; and (5) the provision of any assistance to racist activities.[1453] Failure to do so impairs implementa-

1446 UN Doc. HRI/GEN/1/Rev.7, General Recommendation XX (1996), *Non-Discriminatory Implementation of Rights and Freedoms (Art. 5)*, para. 5.

1447 UN Doc. A/56/18, para. 434 (Liberia); UN Doc. A/56/18, para. 369 (Ukraine); UN Doc. CERD/C/304/Add.85, para. 12 (Romania).

1448 UN Doc. A/56/18, para. 392 (United States).

1449 *Id.* Compare with UN Doc. CERD/C/AUS/CO/14, para. 14 (Australia).

1450 UN Doc. HRI/GEN/1/Rev.7, General Recommendation No. XV (1993), *Article 4 of the Convention*, para. 2; General Recommendation No. VII (1985), *The Implementation of Article 4 of the Convention*, para. 1. See also UN Doc. CERD/C/63/CO/11, para. 12 (United Kingdom); UN Doc. CERD/C/304/Add.102, para. 11 (United Kingdom); UN Doc. CERD/C/304/Add.19, paras. 16 and 20 (Mauritius); UN Doc. A/49/18, para. 408 (Iceland).

1451 UN Doc. CERD/C/64/CO/4, para. 9 (Libya).

1452 UN Doc. HRI/GEN/1/Rev.7, General Recommendation No. XV (1993), *Article 4 of the Convention*, para. 2. Compare with UN Doc. CERD/C/LUX/CO/13, para. 15 (Luxembourg).

1453 UN Doc. HRI/GEN/1/Rev.7, General Recommendation No. XV (1993), *Article 4 of the Convention*, paras. 3 and 5. See also UN Doc. CERD/C/63/CO/1, para. 17 (Albania); UN Doc. CERD/C/60/CO/4, para. 12 (Croatia); UN Doc. CERD/C/304/Add.62, para. 8 (Niger).

tion of article 6 ICERD on the right to effective protection and remedy.[1454] Article 4 (b) imposes the obligation on states parties to declare illegal and prohibit organizations, and also organized and all other propaganda activities, which promote and incite racial discrimination. Participation in such organizations or activities is to be recognized as an offence punishable by law.[1455] For the purposes of art. 4 (b), it is irrelevant whether or not the organization is of fascist ideology,[1456] or what its legal status is.[1457]

Time and again, the Committee has stressed that all the elements and requirements of article 4 are to be addressed, and that full effect is to be given to the provisions of article 4.[1458] Requisites of serious or flagrant circumstances or consequences,[1459] or the inclusion of a risk element,[1460] or qualification by a reference to public peace,[1461] are not in accordance with the Convention. When someone makes threats in public against the security of persons of another ethnic origin, criminal proceedings must be initiated

---

1454 UN Doc. CERD/C/304/Add.10, para. 12 (Bolivia).

1455 UN Doc. HRI/GEN/1/Rev.7, General Recommendation No. XV (1993), *Article 4 of the Convention*, para. 6. See also UN Doc. CERD/C/64/CO/9, para. 10 (Suriname); UN Doc. CERD/C/64/CO/8, para. 10 (Sweden); UN Doc. CERD/C/63/CO/8, para. 12 (Norway); UN Doc. CERD/C/63/CO/4, para. 9 (Czech Republic); UN Doc. CERD/C/62/CO/11, para. 12 (Uganda); UN Doc. CERD/C/62/CO/3, para. 22 (Fiji); UN Doc. A/56/18, para. 349 (Trinidad and Tobago); UN Doc. CERD/C/304/Add.103, para. 15 (Sweden); UN Doc. CERD/C/304/Add.93, para. 8 (Denmark); UN Doc. CERD/C/304/Add.85, para. 12 (Romania); UN Doc. CERD/C/304/Add.66, para. 13 (Finland); UN Doc. CERD/C/304/Add.64, para. 8 (Austria); UN Doc. CERD/C/304/Add.55, para. 8 (Croatia); UN Doc. CERD/C/304/Add.43, para. 16 (Russian Federation); UN Doc. CERD/C/304/Add.26, para. 18 (Belgium); UN Doc. CERD/C/304/Add.40, para. 20 (Norway); UN Doc. CERD/C/304/Add.25, para. 16 (Pakistan); UN Doc. CERD/C/304/Add.19, paras. 16 and 20 (Mauritius); UN Doc. CERD/C/304/Add.12, para. 19 (Korea); UN Doc. CERD/C/304/Add.9 (United Kingdom); UN Doc. A/50/18, para. 457 (New Zealand); UN Doc. A/49/18, para. 408 (Iceland).

1456 UN Doc. CERD/C/304/Add.67, para. 12 (Portugal).

1457 UN Doc. CERD/C/63/CO/7, para. 10 (Latvia).

1458 UN Doc. CERD/C/65/CO/3, para. 9 (Kazakhstan); UN Doc. CERD/C/64/CO/4, para. 9 (Libya); UN Doc. CERD/C/64/CO/1, para. 13 (Bahamas); UN Doc. CERD/C/63/CO/9, para. 9 (Korea); UN Doc. CERD/C/63/CO/8, para. 11 (Norway); UN Doc. CERD/C/63/CO/3, para. 12 (Cape Verde); UN Doc. CERD/C/63/CO/2, para. 12 (Bolivia); UN Doc. CERD/C/62/CO/10, para. 9 (Tunisia); UN Doc. CERD/C/62/CO/4, para. 15 (Ghana); UN Doc. CERD/C/60/CO/8, para. 18 (Lithuania); UN Doc. A/57/18, para. 461 (Yemen); UN Doc. A/57/18, para. 444 (Senegal); UN Doc. A/57/18, para. 276 (Armenia); UN Doc. A/56/18, para. 415 (Viet Nam); UN Doc. A/56/18, para. 391 (United States); UN Doc. A/56/18, para. 370 (Ukraine); UN Doc. CERD/C/304/Add.120, para. 10 (Georgia); UN Doc. CERD/C/304/Add.118, para. 8 (Bangladesh); UN Doc. CERD/C/304/Add.113, para. 12 (Algeria); UN Doc. CERD/C/304/Add.107, para. 9 (Finland); UN Doc. CERD/C/304/Add.101, para. 14 (Australia); UN Doc. CERD/C/304/Add.100, para. 8 (Bahrain); UN Doc. CERD/C/304/Add.92, para. 10 (Zimbabwe); UN Doc. CERD/C/304/Add.81, para. 15 (Chile); UN Doc. CERD/C/304/Add.80, para. 18 (Iraq); UN Doc. CERD/C/304/Add.78, para. 14 (Uruguay); UN Doc. CERD/C/304/Add.73, paras. 13 and 18 (Mongolia); UN Doc. CERD/C/304/Add.72, para. 14 (Kuwait); UN Doc. CERD/C/304/Add.55, para. 15 (Croatia); UN Doc. CERD/C/304/Add.39, para. 23 (Argentina); UN Doc. CERD/C/304/Add.33, para. 19 (Algeria).

1459 UN Doc. A/56/18, para. 242 (China).

1460 UN Doc. CERD/C/304/Add.92, para. 10 (Zimbabwe).

1461 UN Doc. CERD/C/304/Add.64, para. 8 (Austria).

with due diligence and expedition.[1462] Moreover, ethnic or racial motivation or aim for defamation, as well as acts of violence or the threat to use violence are to be made an aggravating circumstance,[1463] allowing for a more severe punishment.[1464] States parties on whose territories no organizations promoting and inciting racial discrimination hypothetically exist, are nevertheless bound by art. 4.[1465]

Art. 5 (e) (i) ICERD contains the undertaking of states to prohibit and eliminate racial discrimination in the enjoyment of the rights to work, to free choice of employment, to just and favourable conditions of work, to protection against unemployment, to equal pay for equal work, and to just and favourable remuneration. In its general recommendation on descent-based discrimination, the Committee has recommended states *inter alia* to develop or refine legislation and practice specifically prohibiting all discriminatory practices based on descent in employment and the labour market, and to take measures against private companies and other associations that investigate the ethnic background of applicants for employment.[1466] States have been encouraged to adopt or make more effective legislation prohibiting discrimination in employment and all discriminatory practices in the labour market affecting members of Roma communities, and to protect them against such practices.[1467] Full implementation of legislation prohibiting discrimination in employment and the labour market is to be ensured.[1468] Employers who recruit illegal workers are to be punished.[1469] Effective measures are to be taken to prevent and redress the problems faced by female domestic workers.[1470] Alleged discrimination is to be taken into account in the final decision on someone's dismissal.[1471]

As to article 5 (e) (iii), the Committee has held that states are to ensure that housing agencies refrain from engaging in discriminatory practices,[1472] and that they do not

---

1462 UN Doc. CERD/C/304/Add.55, para. 9 (Croatia); UN Doc. CERD/C/304/Add.45, para. 14 (Israel); UN Doc. CERD/C/42/4/1991, Communication No. 4/1991, *L.K. v. The Netherlands*, para. 6.6.

1463 UN Doc. CERD/C/65/CO/6, para. 9 (Portugal); UN Doc. CERD/C/64/CO/1, para. 13 (Bahamas); UN Doc. CERD/C/63/CO/1, para. 17 (Albania); UN Doc. A/56/18, para. 287 (Egypt).

1464 UN Doc. CERD/C/IRL/CO/2, para. 11 (Ireland); UN Doc. CERD/C/LUX/CO/13, para. 15 (Luxembourg).

1465 UN Doc. CERD/C/BHR/CO/7, para. 9 (Bahrain); UN Doc. CERD/C/304/Add.102, para. 11 (United Kingdom).

1466 UN Doc. HRI/GEN/1/Rev.7, General Recommendation XXIX (2002), *Article 1, paragraph 1, (Descent)*, paras. jj, kk and ll.

1467 UN Doc. HRI/GEN/1/Rev.7, General Recommendation No. XXVII (2000), *Discrimination against Roma*, para. 27; UN Doc. CERD/C/65/CO/2, para. 10 (Belarus).

1468 UN Doc. CERD/C/IRL/CO/2, para. 14 (Ireland).

1469 UN Doc. CERD/C/LUX/CO/13, para. 18 (Luxembourg).

1470 UN Doc. CERD/C/AZE/CO/4, para. 15 (Bahrain): priority concern.

1471 UN Doc. CERD/C/36/D/1/1984, Communication No. 1/1984, *Yilmaz-Dogan v. The Netherlands*, para. 9.3.

1472 UN Doc. CERD/C/LUX/CO/13, para. 17 (Luxembourg).

accept submissions from private landlords which would discriminate on racial grounds.[1473] For members of communities that are affected by descent-based discrimination, measures are to be taken against discriminatory practices of private owners with regard to residence and access to adequate housing.[1474]

States are also to prohibit and eliminate racial discrimination in the enjoyment of the right of access to any place or service intended for use by the general public.[1475]

The obligation to protect against racial discrimination by non-state actors has also arisen in the context of article 6 ICERD. This article requires states to ensure effective protection and remedies against racial discrimination, as well as the right to seek reparation for any damage suffered as a result of such discrimination (see further under the obligation to fulfil-facilitate).

In particular with regard to the obligation to protect, effective monitoring has been stressed of all tendencies which may give rise to racist and xenophobic behaviour,[1476] racial or ethnic segregation, and of racist incidents.[1477]

c. *The Obligation to Fulfil*

The obligation to fulfil requires states to take positive action. As explained above, the obligation to fulfil can be disaggregated into sub-obligations to facilitate, to promote and to provide.

i. To Facilitate

Most positive measures that have been recommended by CERD seem to correspond to the obligation to facilitate the enjoyment of the right to non-discrimination. Quite

1473 UN Doc. CERD/C/58/D/18/2000, Communication No. 18/2000, *F.A. v. Norway*, para. 8.

1474 UN Doc. HRI/GEN/1/Rev.7, General Recommendation XXIX (2002), *Article 1, paragraph 1, (Descent)*, para. mm; General Recommendation XXVII (2000), *Discrimination against Roma*, para. 31.

1475 UN Doc. HRI/GEN/1/Rev.7, General Recommendation XXVII (2000), *Discrimination against Roma*, para. 35; UN Doc. CERD/C/63/CO/8, para. 15 (Norway); UN Doc. CERD/C/63/CO/7, para. 17 (Latvia); UN Doc. CERD/C/63/CO/1, para. 17 (Albania).

1476 UN Doc. CERD/C/AZE/CO/4, para. 10 (Azerbaijan): priority concern; UN Doc. CERD/C/65/CO/2, para. 7 (Belarus); UN Doc. CERD/C/65/CO/1, para. 10 (Argentina); UN Doc. CERD/C/64/CO/6, para. 10 (Spain); UN Doc. CERD/C/63/CO/5, para. 13 (Finland).

1477 UN Doc. CERD/C/64/CO/2, para. 14 (Brazil); UN Doc. CERD/C/60/CO/14, para. 9 (Switzerland); UN Doc. CERD/C/60/CO/5, para. 16 (Denmark); UN Doc. CERD/C/60/CO/1, para. 13 (Austria); UN Doc. CERD/C/304/Add.117, para. 8 (Portugal); UN Doc. CERD/C/304/Add.110, para. 9 (Slovakia); UN Doc. CERD/C/304/Add.91, para. 10 (France); UN Doc. CERD/C/304/Add.88, para. 12 (Norway); UN Doc. CERD/C/304/Add.70, para. 12 (Syrian Arab Republic); UN Doc. CERD/C/304/Add.48, para. 13 (Ukraine); UN Doc. CERD/C/304/Add.44, para. 121 (Switzerland).

frequently, CERD has recommended states to adopt and implement strategies, programmes or action plans in order to address issues of racial discrimination *e.g.* in the fields of employment, education and housing,[1478] also and in particular for groups as Roma,[1479] people living in slums,[1480] or immigrant workers.[1481] Special attention has been paid to strategies and action plans to combat AIDS.[1482]

Positive measures of facilitation have been recommended in many areas. In accordance with article 5 (a) ICERD, action was recommended to mitigate difficulties with regard to interpretation services.[1483] Practical measures are to be taken to assure that ethnic minorities have equal access to state institutions,[1484] to secure due representation of minorities in the National Assembly,[1485] and to allow illiterate citizens from the most underprivileged population groups (indigenous, black or mestizo groups) to be elected to public office.[1486] Effective measures should stop racist and discriminatory speech in the media, and freedom of association is to be guaranteed without distinction as to ethnic origin.[1487] Positive measures, including strategies targeting specific groups of potential applicants, have been recommended to attract non citizens to the naturalization process.[1488]

Birth registration is to be made compulsory for all children without any discrimination.[1489]

All appropriate measures are to be taken to ensure access to work on a non-discriminatory basis.[1490] The Committee has focused in particular on employment programmes and professional training programmes for Roma,[1491] and on measures against discri-

---

1478 UN Doc. HRI/GEN/1/Rev.7, General Recommendation XXIX (2002), *Article 1, paragraph 1, (Descent)*, para. gg; General Recommendation XXVII (2000), *Discrimination against Roma*, para. 4.
1479 UN Doc. CERD/C/63/CO/11, para. 23 (United Kingdom); UN Doc. CERD/C/62/CO/9, para. 10 (Slovenia).
1480 UN Doc. CERD/C/304/Add.78, para. 15 (Uruguay); UN Doc. CERD/C/304/Add.74, para. 11 (Dominican Republic).
1481 UN Doc. CERD/C/304/Add.95, para. 7 (Spain).
1482 UN Doc. CERD/C/64/CO/9, para. 17 (Suriname); UN Doc. CERD/C/62/CO/11, para. 18 (Uganda).
1483 UN Doc. CERD/C/63/CO/8, para. 16 (Norway).
1484 UN Doc. CERD/C/65/CO/3, para. 13 (Kazakhstan).
1485 UN Doc. A/57/18,para. 278 (Armenia).
1486 UN Doc. CERD/C/64/CO/2, para. 20 (Brazil); UN Doc. CERD/C/304/Add.11, paras. 13 and 18 (Brazil).
1487 UN Doc. CERD/C/304/Add.55, para. 20 (Croatia).
1488 UN Doc. CERD/C/63/CO/7, para. 13 (Latvia).
1489 UN Doc. CERD/C/63/CO/12, para. 8 (Malawi).
1490 UN Doc. CERD/C/304/Add.40, para. 23 (Norway).
1491 UN Doc. CERD/C/63/CO/4, para. 12 (Czech Republic); UN Doc. A/57/18,para. 383 (Hungary).

mination in the labour conditions of migrant workers.[1492] Recruitment of members of minority groups, including Roma communities, into the public administration, the police and other law enforcement agencies, is to be encouraged.[1493] Special measures are equally to be taken to promote the employment of members of communities affected by descent-based discrimination in the private sectors.[1494] Special measures have been called for to promote the employment of Roma in private companies.[1495]

All appropriate measures are also to be taken to ensure access to housing on a non-discriminatory basis,[1496] in particular with regard to Roma.[1497] Measures should be devised to prevent evictions or mitigate their negative effects, in particular on the most vulnerable groups.[1498]

In the field of education, positive measures have been called for in order to integrate Roma children into the mainstream educational system,[1499] while allowing for the possibility of bilingual or mother-tongue instruction and respecting the communities' cultural identity and way of life.[1500] Recruitment of school personnel from among members of Roma communities,[1501] and sensitization of teachers and other education professionals to the social fabric and world views of Roma children and those with apparent learning difficulties may be necessary.[1502] Effective programmes are to be established to care for the educational needs of the Irish Traveller community in Great Britain and Northern Ireland.[1503]

In the context of the introduction of minority languages into the school curricula, priority in the teacher training and curriculum development programmes may be given to persons with minority languages.[1504] Measures are to be taken to ensure that

1492 UN Doc. CERD/C/60/CO/5, para. 15 (Denmark); UN Doc. CERD/C/304/Add.117, para. 10 (Portugal); UN Doc. CERD/C/304/Add.93, para. 11 (Denmark); UN Doc. CERD/C/304/Add.65, para. 16 (Republic of Korea); UN Doc. CERD/C/304/Add.49, para. 24 (Lebanon).

1493 UN Doc. HRI/GEN/1/Rev.7, General Recommendation XXVII (2000), *Discrimination against Roma*, para. 15; UN Doc. CERD/C/60/CO/1, para. 13 (Austria).

1494 UN Doc. HRI/GEN/1/Rev.7, General Recommendation XXIX (2002), *Article 1, paragraph 1, (Descent)*, paras. jj, kk and ll.

1495 UN Doc. HRI/GEN/1/Rev.7, General Recommendation XXVII (2000), *Discrimination against Roma*, para. 28.

1496 UN Doc. CERD/C/63/CO/8, para. 14 (Norway); UN Doc. CERD/C/304/Add.40, para. 23 (Norway).

1497 UN Doc. CERD/C/63/CO/4, para. 13 (Czech Republic); UN Doc. A/57/18, para. 384 (Hungary).

1498 UN Doc. CERD/C/63/CO/4, para. 13 (Czech Republic).

1499 UN Doc. CERD/C/62/CO/9, para. 11 (Slovenia); UN Doc. CERD/C/62/CO/6, para. 13 (Poland); UN Doc. A/57/18, para. 382 (Hungary).

1500 UN Doc. CERD/C/63/CO/1, para. 21 (Albania).

1501 UN Doc. CERD/C/62/CO/6, para. 13 (Poland).

1502 UN Doc. CERD/C/63/CO/4, para. 14 (Czech Republic).

1503 UN Doc. CERD/C/304/Add.9 (United Kingdom).

1504 UN Doc. CERD/C/304/Add.92, para. 11 (Zimbabwe).

minority children have access to education in their mother tongue.[1505] States are to allocate resources to facilitate publications and broadcasting in minority languages.[1506] Vulnerable groups among non-Latvian speakers, such as prisoners, sick and poor persons, should have the possibility of communicating with the relevant authorities through provision of, if necessary, translation facilities.[1507] More generally, states are to facilitate the participation of ethnic minorities in the elaboration of cultural and educational policies, and to create favourable conditions that enable persons belonging to minorities to develop their culture, language, religion, traditions and customs, and to learn or to have instruction in their mother tongue.[1508]

Measures to improve access to financial and technical support for farmers who might not otherwise qualify for land under a land reform programme have been recommended.[1509]

Appropriate measures, such as administrative measures and criminal prosecutions,[1510] are to be adopted to guarantee that access to all places and services intended for public use is not denied to anyone on the grounds of race, colour, ancestry, or national or ethnic origin.[1511] Licences to operate restaurants and discotheques should include a prohibition of racial discrimination.[1512]

Enactment of laws, making racial discrimination a criminal act, does not in itself represent full compliance with the obligations of states parties under ICERD.[1513] Guarantees of non-discrimination laid down in law, without mechanisms to monitor their application, do not on their own ensure the enjoyment of non-discrimination.[1514] Effective protection and remedies are to be offered through the competent national tribunals and other state institutions against any acts of racial discrimination, as well as the right to seek just and adequate reparation or satisfaction for any damage suffered as a result of such discrimination (art. 6 ICERD). At a minimum, this obligation requires a state's legal system to afford a remedy in cases where an act of racial discrimination has been made out, whether before the national courts or before CERD. The

---

1505 UN Doc. A/57/18, para. 280 (Armenia).
1506 UN Doc. CERD/C/63/CO/1, para. 23 (Albania); UN Doc. A/57/18, para. 281 (Armenia).
1507 UN Doc. CERD/C/63/CO/7, para. 9 (Latvia).
1508 UN Doc. CERD/C/AZE/CO/4, para. 14 (Azerbaijan).
1509 UN Doc. CERD/C/304/Add.92, para. 13 (Zimbabwe).
1510 UN Doc. CERD/C/304/Add.103, para. 17 (Sweden).
1511 UN Doc. CERD/C/63/CO/1, para. 24 (Albania); UN Doc. CERD/C/304/Add.91, para. 14 (France).
1512 UN Doc. CERD/C/304/Add.88, para. 17 (Norway).
1513 UN Doc. CERD/C/42/D/4/1991, para. 6.4, Communication No. 4/1991, *L.K. v. The Netherlands*.
1514 UN Doc. CERD/C/62/CO/8, para. 11 (Saudi Arabia); UN Doc. CERD/C/304/Add.108, para. 10 (Nepal).

failure of a state's courts to provide an effective remedy discloses "a consequential violation of article 6 of the Convention".[1515]

The Committee has warned that the absence of complaints or prosecutions for acts of racism in a country is not necessarily a positive sign, "for no State is immune to manifestations of racism."[1516] The absence of complaints and legal action by victims of racial discrimination could possibly be an indication of absence of relevant specific legislation,[1517] a lack of awareness of available legal remedies,[1518] lack of awareness of the protection against racial discrimination provided by ICERD,[1519] fear of reprisals,[1520] limited financial means, individuals' lack of confidence in the police and judicial authorities, the authorities' lack of attention or sensitivity to cases of racial discrimination,[1521] or insufficient will by the authorities to prosecute.[1522]

Time and again, CERD has stressed the need for effective remedies and for reinforcement of their effectiveness.[1523] It has urged states to ensure that appropriate provisions are available in national legislation regarding effective protection and remedies against violation of ICERD, to disseminate to the public information on the legal remedies available against those violations as widely as possible,[1524] and to strengthen training for law enforcement personnel and the legal profession in this regard.[1525] Effective remedies require strengthening the court system, the independence of the judiciary

1515 UN Doc. CERD/C/66/D/31/2003, Communication No. 31/3003, *LR. v. Slovakia*, para. 10.10.

1516 UN Doc. A/57/18, para. 402 (Mali).

1517 UN Doc. CERD/C/AZE/CO/4, para. 15 (Azerbaijan); UN Doc. CERD/C/65/CO/2, para. 12 (Belarus); UN Doc. CERD/C/64/CO/3, para. 14 (Lebanon); UN Doc. CERD/C/62/CO/5, para. 13 (Morocco); UN Doc. CERD/C/304/Add.120, para. 12 (Georgia); UN Doc. CERD/C/304/Add.96, para. 5 (Tonga).

1518 UN Doc. CERD/C/AZE/CO/4, para. 18 (Bahrain); UN Doc. A/57/18, para. 277 (Armenia); UN Doc. CERD/C/60/CO/6, para. 5 (Jamaica); UN Doc. A/56/18, para. 350 (Trinidad and Tobago).

1519 UN Doc. CERD/C/BHR/CO/7, para. 15 (Azerbaijan); UN Doc. CERD/C/304/Add.84, para. 7 (Haiti); UN Doc. CERD/C/304/Add.86, para. 13 (Guinea).

1520 UN Doc. CERD/C/64/CO/1, para. 22 (Bahamas); UN Doc. CERD/C/63/CO/7, para. 11 (Latvia).

1521 UN Doc. CERD/C/AZE/CO/4, para. 18 (Bahrain); UN Doc. CERD/C/65/CO/8, para. 20 (Tajikistan); UN Doc. CERD/C/65/CO/3, para. 19 (Kazakhstan); UN Doc. CERD/C/64/CO/5, para. 14 (Nepal); UN Doc. CERD/C/63/CO/10, para. 11 (Saint Vincent and Grenadines); UN Doc. CERD/C/63/CO/9, para. 8 (Korea); UN Doc. CERD/C/63/CO/6, para. 16 (Iran); UN Doc. CERD/C/63/CO/2, para. 17 (Bolivia); UN Doc. CERD/C/63/CO/1, para. 31 (Albania); UN Doc. CERD/C/62/CO/10, para. 10 (Tunisia).

1522 UN Doc. CERD/C/AZE/CO/4, para. 15 (Azerbaijan).

1523 UN Doc. CERD/C/304/Add.91, para. 15 (France).

1524 UN Doc. CERD/C/62/CO/10, para. 10 (Tunisia); UN Doc. CERD/C/65/CO/3, para. 19 (Kazakhstan); UN Doc. CERD/C/65/CO/2, para. 12 (Belarus); UN Doc. CERD/C/64/CO/3, para. 14 (Lebanon); UN Doc. CERD/C/62/CO/5, para. 13 (Morocco); UN Doc. CERD/C/304/Add.120, para. 12 (Georgia).

1525 UN Doc. CERD/C/65/CO/5, para. 23 (Mauritania); UN Doc. CERD/C/65/CO/4, para. 19 (Madagascar).

and the confidence of the population therein,[1526] and steps to facilitate equal access to the courts and other competent institutions for victims of racial discrimination[1527] – in particular through the effective application of a system of legal aid,[1528] exhaustive and impartial investigations into racial discrimination,[1529] measures to ensure the prosecution of persons allegedly responsible for having committed racially motivated crimes,[1530] and the implementation of consequent decisions.[1531]

In particular with regard to racially motivated acts of violence and discriminatory attitudes and practices by law enforcement officials, prompt and impartial investigations are paramount in countering them.[1532] All necessary measures to prosecute and to prevent them are to be taken.[1533] Disciplinary action only is deemed insufficient.[1534] Furthermore, the procedure relating to the investigation of complaints with respect to the work of the police is to be conducted and overseen by a body independent of the police.[1535]

Next to courts, other state institutions such as an independent national human rights institution are recommended to be established,[1536] in order to advise,[1537] to monitor and evaluate progress in the implementation of ICERD at the national and the local

---

1526 UN Doc. CERD/C/304/Add.54, paras. 14 and 20 (Cambodia); UN Doc. CERD/C/304/Add.42, para. 29 (Burundi); UN Doc. CERD/C/304/Add.34, para. 26 (Philippines); UN Doc. CERD/C/304/Add.5, para. 21 (Russian Federation).

1527 UN Doc. CERD/C/304/Add.78, para. 17 (Uruguay); UN Doc. CERD/C/304/Add.75, para. 18 (Azerbaijan); UN Doc. CERD/C/304/Add.74, para. 12 (Dominican Republic); UN Doc. CERD/C/304/Add.71, para. 19 (Costa Rica); UN Doc. CERD/C/304/Add.53, para. 21 (Cameroon).

1528 UN Doc. CERD/C/65/CO/4, para. 19 (Madagascar); UN Doc. CERD/C/63/CO/4, para. 15 (Czech Republic); UN Doc. CERD/C/304/Add.65, para. 19 (Republic of Korea); UN Doc. CERD/C/304/Add.9 (United Kingdom).

1529 UN Doc. HRI/GEN/1/Rev.7, General Recommendation XXVII (2000), *Discrimination against Roma*, para. 7; UN Doc. A/56/18, para. 336 (Sri Lanka); UN Doc. CERD/C/304/Add.54, para. 14 (Cambodia).

1530 UN Doc. CERD/C/64/CO/9, para. 20 (Suriname); UN Doc. CERD/C/304/Add.74, para. 12 (Dominican Republic); UN Doc. CERD/C/304/Add.55, para. 18 (Croatia); UN Doc. CERD/C/304/Add.54, para. 14 (Cambodia).

1531 UN Doc. CERD/C/62/CO/8, para. 11 (Saudi Arabia); UN Doc. CERD/C/304/Add.108, para. 10 (Nepal).

1532 UN Doc. CERD/C/63/CO/4, para. 11 (Czech Republic).

1533 UN Doc. CERD/C/60/CO/9, para. 17 (Moldova); UN Doc. CERD/C/60/CO/2, para. 16 (Belgium); UN Doc. A/56/18, para. 394 (United States).

1534 UN Doc. CERD/C/304/Add.94, para. 12 (Malta); UN Doc. CERD/C/304/Add.84, para. 16 (Haiti).

1535 UN Doc. CERD/C/IRL/CO/2, para. 17 (Ireland); UN Doc. CERD/C/64/CO/5, para. 15 (Nepal); UN Doc. CERD/C/63/CO/4, para. 11 (Czech Republic); UN Doc. CERD/C/60/CO/14, para. 12 (Switzerland); UN Doc. CERD/C/304/Add.107, para. 13 (Finland).

1536 UN Doc. CERD/C/BHR/CO/7, para. 12: priority concern; UN Doc. CERD/C/304/Add.84, para. 14 (Haiti); UN Doc. CERD/C/304/Add.75, para. 17 (Azerbaijan); UN Doc. CERD/C/304/Add.29, para. 13 (Bulgaria).

1537 UN Doc. A/57/18, para. 358 (Estonia).

levels,[1538] and to review complaints of human rights violations.[1539] They should be strengthened and given adequate financial support, so as to ensure their independence and effectiveness.[1540]

The CERD has further clarified the requirements of article 6 ICERD in its opinions on individual complaints. As to the investigation of complaints about racial discrimination, no discretionary power is left. In light of article 6 ICERD, accusations and complaints related to acts of racial discrimination are to be investigated properly.[1541] For example, States parties are to initiate a proper investigation into the real reasons behind a bank's loan policy vis-à-vis foreign residents, when loans are refused to non nationals, for nationality does not seem to be the most appropriate requisite for investigating a person's will or capacity to reimburse a loan. In reaction to a complaint about a bank's loan policy vis-à-vis foreign residents, whom loans were refused to because of their nationality, the Danish police and the State Prosecutor had simply accepted the explanations provided by a representative of the bank and had decided not to investigate the case further. The Committee held that the steps taken had been insufficient to determine whether or not an act of racial discrimination had taken place, and that the complainant had thus been denied an effective remedy within the meaning of article 6 ICERD in connection with article 2 (d).[1542] Similarly, when threats of racial violence are made, and especially when they are made in public and by a group, it is incumbent upon a state to investigate these with due diligence and expedition.[1543] Complaints about discrimination in the enjoyment of the right of access to public places and services are to be followed by prompt and effective police investigations.[1544] It is however sufficient that criminal complaints are lodged against those directly responsible. Criminal complaints need not to be lodged against a third party (*i.e.* a member of the political party's executive board).[1545] In conclusion, states are under a duty to initiate a proper investigation when faced with complaints of acts of racial discrimination, which should be carried out with due diligence and expeditiously and must be sufficient to determine whether or not an act of racial discrimination has occurred.

1538 UN Doc. CERD/C/65/CO/8, para. 21 (Tajikistan); UN Doc. CERD/C/65/CO/2, para. 13 (Belarus); UN Doc. CERD/C/65/CO/5, para. 24 (Mauritania); UN Doc. A/57/18, para. 358 (Estonia).

1539 UN Doc. CERD/C/63/CO/11, para. 22 (United Kingdom); UN Doc. A/57/18, para. 358 (Estonia).

1540 UN Doc. CERD/C/IRL/CO/2, para. 12; UN Doc. CERD/C/AUS/CO/14, para. 10: priority concern; UN Doc. CERD/C/64/CO/5, para. 10 (Nepal); UN Doc. CERD/C/60/CO/14, para. 13 (Switzerland).

1541 UN Doc. CERD/C/56/D/16/1999, Communication No. 16/1999, *Kashif Ahmad v. Denmark*, paras. 6.4 and 9.

1542 UN Doc. CERD/C/54/D/10/1997, Communication No. 10/1997, *Ziad Ben Ahmed Habassi v. Denmark*, paras. 9.3-9.4 and 10.

1543 UN Doc. CERDC/42/D/4/1991, Communication No. 4/1991, *L.K. v. The Netherlands*, para. 6.7.

1544 UN Doc. CERD/C/60/D/20/2000, Communication No. 20/2000, *M.B. v. Denmark*, para. 10.

1545 UN Doc. CERD/C/63/D/27/2002, Communication No. 27/2002, *Kamal Quereshi v. Denmark*, para. 7.4.

A second question the Committee had to deal with was whether there was not only an absolute obligation to *investigate*, but also to *prosecute* cases of discrimination. The Committee has submitted that the expediency principle, *i.e.* the freedom whether or not to prosecute criminal offences, is to be applied in each case of alleged racial discrimination in light of the guarantees laid down in ICERD.[1546] The expediency principle is however not called into question by article 6 ICERD. In other words, there is no absolute obligation to prosecute cases of alleged discrimination. Neither does art. 6 "impose upon States parties the duty to institute a mechanism of sequential remedies, up to and including the Supreme Court level, in cases of alleged racial discrimination."[1547]

The right to seek compensation for damage suffered as a result of racial discrimination is equally ensured by article 6 ICERD. The Committee has clarified that

> [...] the right to seek just and adequate reparation or satisfaction for any damage suffered as a result of such discrimination, which is embodied in article 6 of the Convention, is not necessarily secured solely by the punishment of the perpetrator of the discrimination; at the same time, the courts and other competent authorities should consider awarding financial compensation for damage, material or moral, suffered by a victim, whenever appropriate[1548]

The provisions of article 6 ICERD are mandatory. The right to seek just and adequate reparation for victims of racial discrimination is to be guaranteed in law and practice.[1549] States are therefore to adopt a specific statute providing for the right of individuals to seek from the courts, just and adequate reparation or satisfaction for any damage suffered as a result of acts of racial discrimination.[1550] Alternative measures to penal proceedings of obtaining reparation or satisfaction are to be offered.[1551]

In *B.J. v. Denmark*, the Committee held that being refused access to a place of service intended for the use of the general public solely on the ground of one's national or

---

1546 UN Doc. CERD/C/36/D/1/1984, Communication No. 1/1984, *Yilmaz-Dogan v. The Netherlands*, para. 9.4; UN Doc. CERD/C/42/D/4/1991, Communication No. 4/1991, *L.K. v. The Netherlands*, para. 6.5.

1547 UN Doc. CERD/C/36/D/1/1984, Communication No. 1/1984, *Yilmaz-Dogan v. The Netherlands*, para. 9.4.

1548 UN Doc. HRI/GEN/1/Rev.7, General Recommendation XXVI (2000), *Article 6 of the Convention*, para. 2.

1549 UN Doc. CERD/C/304/Add.74, para. 12 (Dominican Republic); UN Doc. CERD/C/304/Add.54, para. 20 (Cambodia); UN Doc. CERD/C/304/Add.53, para. 21 (Cameroon); UN Doc. CERD/C/304/Add.42, paras. 19 and 29 (Burundi); UN Doc. CERD/C/304/Add.34, para. 26 (Philippines); UN Doc. CERD/C/304/Add.17, para. 10 (Venezuela).

1550 UN Doc. CERD/C/304/Add.53, para. 22 (Cameroon); UN Doc. CERD/C/304/Add.13, paras. 25 and 32 (India).

1551 UN Doc. CERD/C/304/Add.107, para. 15 (Finland).

ethnic background is a humiliating experience that may merit economic compensation and cannot always be adequately repaired or satisfied by merely imposing a criminal sanction on the perpetrator:[1552]

> in accordance with article 6 of the Convention, the victim's claim for compensation has to be considered in every case, including those cases where no bodily harm has been inflicted but where the victim has suffered humiliation, defamation or other attack against his/her reputation and self esteem.[1553]

States are therefore to ensure that victims of racial discrimination seeking just and adequate reparation or satisfaction, including economic compensation, have their claims considered with due respect for situations where the discrimination has not resulted in any physical damage, but only humiliation or similar suffering.[1554]

In a case of lack of proper protection of the right to work, the use of good offices to secure alternative employment and/or other relief, were recommended by way of remedy.[1555]

ii. To Promote

The obligation to promote the right to racial equality stems from art. 2, para. 1 (e) and art. 7 ICERD. Article 7 ICERD contains the obligation to take educational and promotional measures to combat prejudices which lead to racial discrimination, and to promote understanding, tolerance and friendship among nations and racial or ethnical groups.

Public education campaigns have been recommended for a wide variety of target groups, including the general public,[1556] political leaders,[1557] agents of the state[1558] (including law enforcement officers, teachers, social workers,[1559] civil servants who

---

1552 UN Doc. CERD/C/56/D/17/1999, Communication No. 17/1999, *B.J. v. Denmark*, para. 6.3.

1553 *Ibid.*, para. 6.2.

1554 *Ibid.*, para. 7.

1555 UN Doc. CERD/C/36/D/1/1984, Communication No. 1/1984, *Yilmaz-Dogan v. The Netherlands*, para. 10.

1556 UN Doc. CERD/C/62/CO/2, para. 20 (Ecuador); UN Doc. A/56/18, para. 308 (Italy); UN Doc. A/56/18, para. 272 (Cyprus); UN Doc. CERD/C/304/Add.109, para. 15 (Czech Republic); UN Doc. CERD/C/304/Add.29, para. 19 (Bulgaria); UN Doc. CERD/C/304/Add.33, para. 24 (Algeria); UN Doc. CERD/C/304/Add.29, para. 19 (Bulgaria).

1557 UN Doc. CERD/C/62/CO/1, para. 19 (Ivory Coast).

1558 UN Doc. CERD/C/LUX/CO/13, para. 19 (Luxembourg); UN Doc. CERD/C/304/Add.53, para. 22 (Cameroon).

1559 UN Doc. CERD/C/64/CO/5, para. 20 (Nepal); UN Doc. A/57/18, para. 466 (Yemen); UN Doc. CERD/C/304/Add.29, para. 19 (Bulgaria).

deal with issues involving foreigners),[1560] and journalists and people working in the media sector.[1561] Targeted training programmes are needed for professionals, such as the legal profession[1562] and law enforcement officials[1563] (police and armed forces, as well as prison staff).[1564]

The purposes of promotional measures are multifold. On a very general level, educational campaigns want to raise awareness of human rights and of the ICERD,[1565] and in particular of issues concerning racism, xenophobia and intolerance,[1566] in order to promote understanding, tolerance and friendship[1567] and combat prejudices.[1568] More specifically, educational measures aim at increasing awareness of domestic remedies available against acts of racial discrimination, of the legal avenues for

1560 UN Doc. CERD/C/60/CO/1, para. 13 (Austria); UN Doc. CERD/C/304/Add.115, para. 11 (Germany).

1561 UN Doc. CERD/C/304/Add.107, para. 16 (Finland).

1562 UN Doc. CERD/C/65/CO/4, para. 19 (Madagascar); UN Doc. CERD/C/64/CO/2, para. 18 (Brazil); UN Doc. CERD/C/64/CO/1, para. 23 (Bahamas); UN Doc. CERD/C/63/CO/4, para. 16 (Czech Republic); UN Doc. CERD/C/62/CO/8, para. 13 (Saudi Arabia); UN Doc. CERD/C/62/CO/6, para. 10 (Poland); UN Doc. A/57/18, para. 377 (Hungary); UN Doc. CERD/C/60/CO/11, para. 19 (Qatar); UN Doc. CERD/C/60/CO/4, para. 16 (Croatia); UN Doc. CERD/C/60/CO/2, para. 19 (Belgium); UN Doc. A/56/18, para. 289 (Egypt); UN Doc. CERD/C/304/Add.109, para. 14 (Czech Republic); UN Doc. CERD/C/304/Add.47, para. 24 (Czech Republic); UN Doc. CERD/C/304/Add.43, paras. 21-22 (Russian Federation); UN Doc. CERD/C/304/Add.33, para. 23 (Algeria).

1563 UN Doc. CERD/C/AZE/CO/4, para. 17 (Azerbaijan); UN Doc. CERD/C/IRL/CO/2, para. 17 (Ireland); UN Doc. CERD/C/65/CO/6, para. 10 (Portugal); UN Doc. CERD/C/65/CO/4, para. 19 (Madagascar); UN Doc. CERD/C/65/CO/2, para. 14 (Belarus); UN Doc. CERD/C/65/CO/1, para. 9 (Argentina); UN Doc. CERD/C/63/CO/1, para. 18 (Albania); UN Doc. CERD/C/63/CO/2, para. 14 (Bolivia); UN Doc. CERD/C/63/CO/8, para. 17 (Norway); UN Doc. CERD/C/62/CO/1, para. 19 (Ivory Coast); UN Doc. CERD/C/62/CO/7, para. 13 (Russian Federation); UN Doc. A/57/18, para. 307 (Botswana); UN Doc. CERD/C/60/CO/14, para. 12 (Switzerland); UN Doc. CERD/C/60/CO/7, para. 9 (Liechtenstein); UN Doc. A/56/18, para. 336 (Sri Lanka); UN Doc. A/56/18, para. 289 (Egypt); UN Doc. CERD/C/304/Add.105, para. 10 (Slovenia); UN Doc. CERD/C/304/Add.107, para. 13 (Finland); UN Doc. CERD/C/304/Add.109, para. 14 (Czech Republic); UN Doc. CERD/C/304/Add.78, para. 18 (Uruguay); UN Doc. CERD/C/304/Add.80, para. 19 (Iraq); UN Doc. CERD/C/304/Add.84, para. 16 (Haiti); UN Doc. CERD/C/304/Add.74, para. 14 (Dominican Republic); UN Doc. CERD/C/304/Add.70, para. 15 (Syrian Arab Republic); UN Doc. CERD/C/304/Add.64, para. 17 (Austria); UN Doc. CERD/C/304/Add.43, paras. 21-22 (Russian Federation); UN Doc. CERD/C/304/Add.33, para. 23 (Algeria); UN Doc. A/56/18, para. 394 (United States).

1564 UN Doc. CERD/C/62/CO/8, para. 13 (Saudi Arabia); UN Doc. CERD/C/62/CO/2, para. 12 (Ecuador); UN Doc. CERD/C/60/CO/11, para. 19 (Qatar).

1565 UN Doc. CERD/C/64/CO/1, para. 23 (Bahamas); UN Doc. CERD/C/62/CO/1, para. 19 (Ivory Coast); UN Doc. A/56/18, para. 272 (Cyprus); UN Doc. CERD/C/304/Add.33, para. 24 (Algeria); UN Doc. CERD/C/304/Add.29, para. 19 (Bulgaria).

1566 UN Doc. CERD/C/60/CO/3, para. 19 (Costa Rica).

1567 UN Doc. CERD/C/62/CO/6, para. 14 (Poland); UN Doc. A/56/18, para. 308 (Italy); UN Doc. CERD/C/304/Add.108, para. 14 (Nepal); UN Doc. CERD/C/304/Add.29, para. 19 (Bulgaria).

1568 UN Doc. CERD/C/64/CO/6, para. 10 (Spain); UN Doc. CERD/C/63/CO/5, para. 13 (Finland); UN Doc. CERD/C/63/CO/4, para. 16 (Czech Republic); UN Doc. CERD/C/304/Add.107, para. 16 (Finland); UN Doc. CERD/C/304/Add.74, para. 13 (Dominican Republic).

obtaining compensation in cases of discrimination and of the individual complaint procedure under article 14 of the Convention,[1569] and of the importance of affirmative action programmes to address the situation of victims of descent-based discrimination.[1570] For judges and prosecutors, they are meant to sensitize them to discrimination issues,[1571] and to learn them how to address complaints of racially motivated crimes.[1572] With regard to law enforcement officials, training should improve their sensitivity to and awareness of the existence and treatment of racist crimes,[1573] train them in addressing complaints of racially-motivated crimes,[1574] ensure that in the performance of their duties they respect and protect human dignity and maintain and uphold the human rights of all persons without distinction as to race, colour, descent or national or ethnic origin,[1575] and prevent human rights violations such as arbitrary arrests, detention, and disappearances of stateless refugees and foreigners.[1576]

Inter-cultural education and instruction of international human rights standards is to be included in school curricula,[1577] and general awareness of diversity and multiculturalism is to be promoted at all levels of education.[1578] The establishment of non-denominational or multidenominational schools is to be promoted, so that no discrimination takes place with regard to the admission of pupils of all religions to schools.[1579]

With regard to Roma, tolerance is to be promoted and prejudices and negative stereotypes are to be overcome.[1580] Targeted training programmes for professionals,

1569 UN Doc. CERD/C/63/CO/4, para. 18 (Czech Republic); UN Doc. CERD/C/63/CO/5, para. 17 (Finland); UN Doc. CERD/C/63/CO/8, para. 20 (Norway); UN Doc. CERD/C/63/CO/9, para. 13 (Korea); UN Doc. CERD/C/62/CO/2, para. 18 (Ecuador); UN Doc. CERD/C/304/Add.33, para. 24 (Algeria).

1570 UN Doc. HRI/GEN/1/Rev.7, General Recommendation XXIX (2002), *Article 1, paragraph 1, (Descent)*, para. 8.

1571 UN Doc. A/57/18, para. 377 (Hungary).

1572 UN Doc. CERD/C/62/CO/6, para. 10 (Poland).

1573 UN Doc. CERD/C/64/CO/2, para. 18 (Brazil); UN Doc. CERD/C/63/CO/1, para. 18 (Albania); UN Doc. A/57/18, para. 307 (Botswana); UN Doc. CERD/C/60/CO/14, para. 12 (Switzerland); UN Doc. CERD/C/304/Add.80, para. 19 (Iraq).

1574 UN Doc. CERD/C/62/CO/6, para. 10 (Poland).

1575 UN Doc. CERD/C/AZE/CO/4, para. 17 (Azerbaijan); UN Doc. CERD/C/65/CO/6, para. 10 (Portugal); UN Doc. CERD/C/65/CO/2, para. 14 (Belarus); UN Doc. CERD/C/64/CO/6, para. 11 (Spain); UN Doc. CERD/C/62/CO/7, para. 13 (Russian Federation); UN Doc. CERD/C/60/CO/9, para. 17 (Moldova); UN Doc. CERD/C/62/CO/1, para. 19 (Ivory Coast); UN Doc. A/56/18, para. 394 (United States).

1576 UN Doc. CERD/C/304/Add.70, para. 15 (Syrian Arab Republic).

1577 UN Doc. CERD/C/64/CO/5, para. 20 (Nepal); UN Doc. CERD/C/60/CO/4, para. 16 (Croatia).

1578 UN Doc. CERD/C/63/CO/5, para. 13 (Finland).

1579 UN Doc. CERD/C/IRL/CO/2, para. 17 (Ireland).

1580 UN Doc. CERD/C/64/CO/6, para. 15 (Spain); UN Doc. CERD/C/63/CO/5, para. 16 (Finland); UN Doc. CERD/C/304/Add.91, para. 16 (France).

such as the police, judges and other public officials working with the Roma and other vulnerable groups should be organized.[1581]

iii. To Provide

The closest a state can come to actually *providing* equality might be through affirmative action. Article 1, para. 4 ICERD explicitly allows for "special measures":

> Special measures taken for the sole purpose of securing adequate advancement of certain racial or ethnic groups or individuals requiring such protection as may be necessary in order to ensure such groups or individuals equal enjoyment or exercise of human rights and fundamental freedoms shall not be deemed racial discrimination, provided, however, that such measures do not, as a consequence, lead to the maintenance of separate rights for different racial groups and that they shall not be continued after the objectives for which they were taken have been achieved.

Art. 2, para. 2 ICERD makes special measures mandatory "when circumstances so warrant"; it reads:

> States Parties shall, when the circumstances so warrant, take, in the social, economic, cultural and other fields, special and concrete measures to ensure the adequate development and protection of certain racial groups or individuals belonging to them, for the purpose of guaranteeing them the full and equal enjoyment of human rights and fundamental freedoms. These measures shall in no case entail as a consequence the maintenance of unequal or separate rights for different racial groups after the objectives for which they were taken have been achieved.

In both provisions, the temporary nature of special measures is stressed; they should not lead to the maintenance of unequal or separate rights for different racial groups and should not be continued after the objectives for which they were taken have been achieved.[1582]

Special measures are to be taken for all on a equal basis,[1583] and are to be necessary in a democratic society; they should respect the principle of fairness, and are to be grounded in a realistic appraisal of the situation of the communities concerned.[1584] They are mandatory if circumstances so warrant, such as in the case of persistent disparities,[1585] or for certain racial groups or individuals belonging to ethnic minorities

---

1581 UN Doc. CERD/C/63/CO/4, para. 16 (Czech Republic).
1582 See also UN Doc. CERD/C/62/CO/3, para. 15 (Fiji).
1583 UN Doc. CERD/C/62/CO/3, para. 16 (Fiji); UN Doc. CERD/C/62/CO/9, para. 9 (Slovenia).
1584 UN Doc. CERD/C/62/CO/3, para. 15 (Fiji).
1585 UN Doc. A/56/18, para. 399 (United States).

who are experiencing disadvantage with respect to educational achievement and other elements of their socio-economic profiles.[1586]

The goal of affirmative action is to place the beneficiaries on an equal footing with the rest of the population in the enjoyment of economic, social and cultural rights,[1587] by advancing the social, political, economic, and educational status of historically-marginalized communities.[1588]

As to the beneficiaries, the identification of an individual as belonging to a group benefiting from special measures might be based on self-identification by the individual concerned, unless justification to the contrary exists.[1589]

CERD has paid considerable attention to special measures in its concluding observations on state reports, and in some of its more recent general recommendations. The terminology varies, but by and large the notions of "special measures",[1590] "positive or affirmative action",[1591] "affirmative measures"[1592] or references to article 2, para. 2[1593] seem to have been used indiscriminately to denote the same. "Special and concrete

1586 UN Doc. CERD/C/304/Add.102, para. 20 (United Kingdom).

1587 UN Doc. CERD/C/304/Add.85, para. 15 (Romania).

1588 UN Doc. CERD/C/304/Add.76, para. 23 (Colombia).

1589 Compare with UN Doc. HRI/GEN/1/Rev.7, General Recommendation VIII (1990), *The Interpretation and Application of Article 1, paragraphs 1 and 4 of the Convention*.

1590 UN Doc. HRI/GEN/1/Rev.7, General Recommendation XXIX (2002), *Article 1, paragraph 1, (Descent)*, paras. 5, 6, 28 and 36; General Recommendation XXVII (2000), *Discrimination against Roma*, paras. 28, 29 and 41; UN Doc. CERD/C/65/CO/6, para. 13 (Portugal); UN Doc. CERD/C/65/CO/4, para. 16 (Madagascar); UN Doc. CERD/C/64/CO/5, paras. 6, 17 and 21 (Nepal); UN Doc. CERD/C/64/CO/9, para. 19 (Suriname); UN Doc. CERD/C/62/CO/3, para. 15 (Fiji); UN Doc. A/57/18, para. 303 (Botswana); UN Doc. CERD/C/60/CO/3, para. 18 (Costa Rica); UN Doc. A/56/18, para. 398 (United States); UN Doc. CERD/C/304/Add.78, para. 9 (Uruguay); UN Doc. CERD/C/304/Add.7, para. 25 (Finland).

1591 UN Doc. HRI/GEN/1/Rev.7, General Recommendation XXIX (2002), *Article 1, paragraph 1, (Descent)*, para. 8; UN Doc. CERD/C/IRL/CO/2, para. 22 (Ireland); UN Doc. CERD/C/63/CO/10, para. 10 (Saint Vincent and Grenadines); UN Doc. CERD/C/62/CO/3, paras. 16 and 18 (Fiji); UN Doc. CERD/C/62/CO/9, para. 10 (Slovenia); UN Doc. CERD/C/60/CO/3, para. 18 (Costa Rica); UN Doc. CERD/C/304/Add.110, para. 13 (Slovakia); UN Doc. CERD/C/304/Add.78, para. 9 (Uruguay); UN Doc. CERD/C/304/Add.85, para. 15 (Romania); UN Doc. CERD/C/304/Add.61, para. 14 (Nepal); UN Doc. CERD/C/304/Add.38, para. 13 (Former Yugoslav Republic of Macedonia); UN Doc. CERD/C/304/Add.29, para. 14 (Bulgaria); UN Doc. A/48/18, para. 504 (Croatia).

1592 UN Doc. CERD/C/63/CO/11, para. 24 (United Kingdom); UN Doc. CERD/C/62/CO/3, para. 15 (Fiji); UN Doc. CERD/C/304/Add.108, para. 11 (Nepal); UN Doc. CERD/C/304/Add.102, para. 20 (United Kingdom); UN Doc. CERD/C/304/Add.76, para. 23 (Colombia); UN Doc. CERD/C/304/Add.21, para. 32 (Guatemala); UN Doc. CERD/C/304/Add.16, para. 19 (Namibia); UN Doc. A/50/18, para. 394 (Mexico).

1593 UN Doc. CERD/C/304/Add.83, para. 5 (Iran); UN Doc. CERD/C/304/Add.85, para. 11 (Romania); UN Doc. CERD/C/304/Add.43, para. 20 (Russian Federation).

measures" have been referred to only once.[1594] On one occasion, affirmative action seems to have been used to indicate just one example of a broader range of special measures.[1595] A well-known affirmative action measure are quota.[1596]

Affirmative action has been called for in many fields, ranging from all rights,[1597] over representation in public services (army, police),[1598] government bodies,[1599] the legislator[1600] and the judiciary,[1601] representation in mass media,[1602] and the right to vote and to stand for elections,[1603] to economic, social and cultural rights.[1604] As "special and concrete measures" are mandatory in accordance with article 2, para. 2 ICERD in the social, economic, cultural and other fields when circumstances so warrant, the Committee has paid considerable attention to affirmative action with regard to employment,[1605] as well as education[1606] (in particular literacy[1607] and vocational[1608] training[1609]) and health.[1610]

1594 UN Doc. CERD/C/304/Add.5, para. 18 (Russian Federation).

1595 UN Doc. CERD/C/304/Add.78, para. 9 (Uruguay): "Concern is also expressed about the lack of information on special measures, such as affirmative action programmes, taken for the protection of the rights of disadvantaged ethnic groups such as Afro-Uruguayans and indigenous groups."

1596 UN Doc. CERD/C/304/Add.83, para. 5 (Iran).

1597 UN Doc. CERD/C/64/CO/5, para. 6 (Nepal); UN Doc. A/57/18, para. 303 (Botswana); UN Doc. CERD/C/304/Add.78, para. 13 (Uruguay); UN Doc. CERD/C/304/Add.29, para. 14 (Bulgaria); UN Doc. CERD/C/304/Add.7, para. 25 (Finland).

1598 UN Doc. CERD/C/62/CO/3, para. 18 (Fiji); UN Doc. CERD/C/304/Add.38, para. 13 (Former Yugoslav Republic of Macedonia).

1599 UN Doc. HRI/GEN/1/Rev.7, General Recommendation XXIX (2002), *Article 1, paragraph 1, (Descent)*, para. 28; General Recommendation XXVII (2000), *Discrimination against Roma*, para. 41; UN Doc. CERD/C/60/CO/3, para. 18 (Costa Rica).

1600 UN Doc. CERD/C/IRL/CO/2, para. 22 (Ireland); UN Doc. CERD/C/64/CO/5, para. 17 (Nepal); UN Doc. CERD/C/62/CO/9, para. 9 (Slovenia).

1601 UN Doc. CERD/C/64/CO/5, para. 17 (Nepal); UN Doc. CERD/C/60/CO/3, para. 18 (Costa Rica).

1602 UN Doc. CERD/C/64/CO/5, para. 21 (Nepal).

1603 UN Doc. HRI/GEN/1/Rev.7, General Recommendation XXIX (2002), *Article 1, paragraph 1, (Descent)*, para. 28; UN Doc. CERD/C/64/CO/5, para. 17 (Nepal).

1604 UN Doc. CERD/C/65/CO/6, para. 13 (Portugal); UN Doc. CERD/C/63/CO/11, para. 24 (United Kingdom); UN Doc. A/56/18, para. 398 (United States).

1605 UN Doc. HRI/GEN/1/Rev.7, General Recommendation XXIX (2002), *Article 1, paragraph 1, (Descent)*, para. 36; General Recommendation XXVII (2000), *Discrimination against Roma*, paras. 28-29; UN Doc. CERD/C/304/Add.110, para. 13 (Slovakia); UN Doc. CERD/C/304/Add.76, para. 23 (Colombia); UN Doc. CERD/C/304/Add.16, para. 19 (Namibia).

1606 UN Doc. CERD/C/64/CO/9, para. 19 (Suriname); UN Doc. CERD/C/304/Add.85, para. 15 (Romania); UN Doc. CERD/C/304/Add.21, para. 32 (Guatemala); UN Doc. CERD/C/304/Add.16, para. 19 (Namibia); UN Doc. A/50/18, para. 394 (Mexico).

1607 UN Doc. CERD/C/65/CO/4, para. 16 (Madagascar); UN Doc. CERD/C/304/Add.83, para. 5 (Iran).

1608 UN Doc. CERD/C/304/Add.85, para. 15 (Romania).

1609 UN Doc. CERD/C/304/Add.21, para. 32 (Guatemala); UN Doc. A/50/18, para. 394 (Mexico).

1610 UN Doc. CERD/C/65/CO/4, para. 16 (Madagascar); UN Doc. CERD/C/64/CO/9, para. 19 (Suriname); UN Doc. CERD/C/304/Add.83, para. 5 (Iran).

Target groups have included black people, including the vulnerable among them,[1611] disadvantaged or less-developed groups,[1612] vulnerable or disadvantaged ethnic and tribal groups or ethnic minorities,[1613] minority, tribal and indigenous communities,[1614] victims of descent-based[1615] or caste-based discrimination,[1616] and Roma.[1617]

d. *Conclusions*

Most recommendations of CERD in light of the obligation to respect, pertain to the revision of legislation, policies and practices. ICERD and CERD place a strong emphasis on the obligation to protect against racial discrimination by third parties. The obligation to fulfil-facilitate applies to a large number of rights and issues, and can be realized through legislation, action plans and the like. A prominent place has been given to making legal remedies and compensation available. Complaints of racial discrimination are to be investigated, but not necessarily to be prosecuted. The obligation to fulfil-provide equality is probably best reflected in affirmative action measures. These are permissible if they do not lead to the maintenance of separate rights, and are of a temporary nature. They are mandatory in the economic, social and cultural field in particular if circumstances so warrant. The CERD has recommended affirmative action in a wide variety of fields, with an emphasis on representation in political and public life, and on employment, education and health. The target groups too have been manifold, although the focus seems to have been on particularly vulnerable groups, victims of descent-based discrimination and Roma.

1611 UN Doc. CERD/C/304/Add.16, para. 19 (Namibia).

1612 UN Doc. CERD/C/64/CO/5, paras. 6, 17 and 21 (Nepal); UN Doc. CERD/C/304/Add.61, para. 14 (Nepal); UN Doc. CERD/C/304/Add.43, para. 20 (Russian Federation); UN Doc. CERD/C/304/Add.5, para. 18 (Russian Federation).

1613 UN Doc. CERD/C/304/Add.83, para. 5 (Iran); UN Doc. CERD/C/304/Add.78, para. 9 (Uruguay); UN Doc. A/48/18, para. 504 (Croatia).

1614 UN Doc. CERD/C/64/CO/9, para. 19 (Suriname); UN Doc. CERD/C/63/CO/11, para. 24 (United Kingdom); UN Doc. CERD/C/63/CO/10, para. 10 (Saint Vincent and Grenadines); UN Doc. CERD/C/62/CO/9, para. 9 (Slovenia); UN Doc. A/57/18, para. 303 (Botswana); UN Doc. CERD/C/60/CO/3, para. 18 (Costa Rica); UN Doc. CERD/C/304/Add.76, para. 23 (Colombia); UN Doc. CERD/C/304/Add.38, para. 13 (Former Yugoslav Republic of Macedonia).

1615 UN Doc. HRI/GEN/1/Rev.7, General Recommendation XXIX (2002), *Article 1, paragraph 1, (Descent)*, para. 28.

1616 UN Doc. CERD/C/304/Add.108, para. 11 (Nepal).

1617 UN Doc. HRI/GEN/1/Rev.7, General Recommendation XXVII (2000), *Discrimination against Roma*, para. 28; UN Doc. CERD/C/65/CO/6, para. 13 (Portugal); UN Doc. CERD/C/304/Add.110, para. 13 (Slovakia); UN Doc. CERD/C/304/Add.85, paras. 11 and 15(Romania); UN Doc. CERD/C/304/Add.29, para. 14 (Bulgaria); UN Doc. CERD/C/304/Add.7, para. 25 (Finland).

2. HRC

The adoption of anti-discrimination legislation has been recommended,[1618] in which discrimination is prohibited on any of the grounds enumerated in the CCPR.[1619] Like under ICERD, the insistence on the adoption of legislation under the CCPR may serve to abide by *inter alia* the obligation to respect, to protect and to fulfil-facilitate. Since the HRC has not taken the threefold typology of obligations as its framework of reference, it is hardly possible to subsume the recommendations with regard to the adoption of legislation under any of the more specific obligations, hereafter.

a. The Obligation To Respect

In its views on individual communications, the HRC has emphasized that when a state enacts legislation, that legislation and the application thereof must comply with the principle of non-discrimination, *e.g.* in the field of social security legislation,[1620] funding for private education,[1621] military pensions,[1622] marriage,[1623] or among conscientious objectors.[1624] In the two former cases, this may mean that the state is either

---

1618 UN Doc. CCPR/CO/79/PHL, para. 18 (Philippines); UN Doc. CCPR/CO/74/HUN, para. 6 (Hungary); UN Doc. CCPR/CO/73/CH, para. 10 (Switzerland); UN Doc. CCPR/CO/72/CZE, para. 10 (Czech Republic); UN Doc. CCPR/CO/71/HRV, para. 19 (Croatia); UN Doc. CCPR/CO/71/VEN, para. 23 (Venezuela); UN Doc. CCPR/C/79/Add.121, para. 13 (Guyana); UN Doc. CCPR/C/79/Add.119, para. 18 (United Kingdom – Crown Dependencies); UN Doc. CCPR/C/79/Add.62, para. 21 (Zambia); UN Doc. CCPR/C/79/Add.60, para. 23 (Mauritius); UN Doc. CCPR/C/79/Add.57, para. 23 (United Kingdom – Hong Kong).

1619 UN Doc. CCPR/CO/81/NAM, para. 22 (Namibia); UN Doc. CCPR/CO/71/HRV, para. 19 (Croatia); UN Doc. CCPR/CO/71/VEN, para. 23 (Venezuela); UN Doc. CCPR/C/79/Add.119, para. 18 (United Kingdom – Crown Dependencies).

1620 UN Doc. CCPR/C/80/D/976/2001, Communication No. 976/2001, *Derksen v. The Netherlands*, para. 9.3; UN Doc. CCPR/C/66/D/786/1997, Communication No. 786/1997, *Vos v. The Netherlands*, para. 7.4; UN Doc. CCPR/C/51/D/484/1991, Communication No. 484/1991, *Pepels v. The Netherlands*, para. 7.2; UN Doc. CCPR/C/51/D/425/1990, Communication No. 425/1990, *Doesburg Lannooij Neefs v. The Netherlands*, para. 7.2; UN Doc. CCPR/C/49/D/418/1990, Communication No. 418/1990, *Cavalcanti Araujo-Jongen v. The Netherlands*, para. 7.3; UN Doc. CCPR/C/46/D/406/1990, Communication No. 406/1990, *Oulajin and Kaiss v. The Netherlands*, para. 7.3; UN Doc. CCPR/C/44/D/395/1990, Communication No. 395/1990, *Sprenger v. The Netherlands*, para. 7.2; UN Doc. CCPR/C/44/D/415/1990, Communication No. 415/1990, *Pauger v. Austria*, para. 7.2; UN Doc. CCPR/C/35/D/218/1986, Communication No. 218/1986, *Vos v. The Netherlands*, para. 11.3; UN Doc. CCPR/C/29/D/182/1984, Communication No. 182/1984, *Zwaan-de Vries v. The Netherlands*, para. 12.4; UN Doc. CCPR/C/29/D/180/1984, Communication No. 180/1984, *Danning v. The Netherlands*, paras. 12.4-12.5; UN Doc. CCPR/C/29/D/172/1984, Communication No. 172/1984, *Broeks v. The Netherlands*, paras. 12.4-12.5.

1621 UN Doc. CCPR/C/67/D/694/1996, Communication No. 694/1996, *Waldman v. Canada*, para. 10.6.

1622 UN Doc. CCPR/C/35/D/196/1985, Communication No. 196/1985, *Gueye et al. v. France*, para. 9.5.

1623 UN Doc. CCPR/C/12/D/35/1978, Communication No. 35/1978, *Aumeeruddy-Cziffra et.al. v. Mauritius*, para. 9.2 (b): protection of the family must be equal.

1624 UN Doc. CCPR/C/48/D/402/1990, Communication No. 402/1990, *Brinkhof v. The Netherlands*, para. 9.3.

not to give any social security benefits nor any funding for private education, or to do so in a non-discriminatory way. The latter option engenders positive obligations of equal treatment on the state, in that it has to make *e.g.* sufficient funding available (see further under the obligation to fulfil).

In its concluding observations on state reports, the HRC has made clear that "gender-proofing" of all draft legislation is to be undertaken in order to ensure gender neutrality.[1625] Furthermore, discriminatory legislation is to be reviewed.[1626] Some examples are given below.

With regard to non-discrimination against women,[1627] the Committee has recommended to states to review their Family code,[1628] or Civil Code,[1629] or more specifically discriminatory legislation with regard to marriage,[1630] parental and custodial rights,[1631] ownership and inheritance,[1632] adultery,[1633] a ban on remarriage,[1634] the possibility of polygamy,[1635] and the transmission or acquisition of nationality.[1636] With regard to the Penal Code,[1637] states have been recommended to review laws on criminal offences committed against women,[1638] and the exemption for a rapist from any penalty if he subsequently marries the victim.[1639] All labour laws that discriminate against women are equally to be reviewed,[1640] and equal treatment of men and women at all levels of public service is to be ensured.[1641] Legislation that criminalizes homosexuality is to be repealed.[1642]

1625 UN Doc. A/55/40, paras. 20-21 (Ireland).
1626 UN Doc. CCPR/CO/79/LKA, para. 7 (Sri Lanka); UN Doc. CCPR/CO/75/NZL, para. 9 (New Zealand); UN Doc. CCPR/C/79/Add.28, para. 17 (Japan); UN Doc. CCPR/C/79/Add.21, para. 18 (Ireland).
1627 UN Doc. CCPR/CO/80/SUR, para. 20 (Suriname); UN Doc. CCPR/CO/79/LKA, para. 19 (Sri Lanka); UN Doc. CCPR/CO/SYR, para. 18 (Syria); UN Doc. CCPR/C/79/Add.106, para. 10 (Lesotho).
1628 UN Doc. CCPR/CO/76/TGO, para. 21 (Togo); UN Doc. CCPR/C/79/Add.33, para. 25 (Cameroon).
1629 UN Doc. CCPR/C/79/Add.72, para. 22 (Peru).
1630 UN Doc. CCPR/CO/82/MAR, para. 27 (Morocco); UN Doc. CCPR/CO/80/SUR, para. 18 (Suriname).
1631 UN Doc. CCPR/C/79/Add.43, para. 18 (Tunisia).
1632 UN Doc. CCPR/CO/81/NAM, para. 9 (Namibia); UN Doc. CCPR/CO/76/EGY, paras. 8-10 (Egypt); UN Doc. CCPR/CO/70/GAB, paras. 8-9 (Gabon).
1633 UN Doc. CCPR/CO/VEN, paras. 20-22 (Venezuela).
1634 *Idem.*
1635 UN Doc. CCPR/CO/82/MAR, para. 30 (Morocco).
1636 *Ibid.*, para. 22 (Morocco); UN Doc. CCPR/CO/75/YEM, paras. 7, 9, 11 (Yemen) (priority concern); UN Doc. CCPR/C/79/Add.43, para. 18 (Tunisia).
1637 UN Doc. CCPR/CO/76/EGY, paras. 8-10 (Egypt); UN Doc. CCPR/C/79/Add.72, para. 22 (Peru).
1638 UN Doc. CCPR/C/79/Add.48, para. 27 (Paraguay).
1639 UN Doc. CCPR/CO/72/GTM, paras. 24 (Guatemala).
1640 UN Doc. CCPR/C/79/Add.48, para. 27 (Paraguay).
1641 UN Doc. CCPR/CO/82/POL, para. 10 (Poland).
1642 UN Doc. CCPR/CO/83/KEN, para. 27 (Kenya).

As to discrimination on the basis of religion,[1643] equal participation of non-Muslims in presidential elections in predominantly Muslim countries is to be allowed,[1644] and equal status is to be given to all religious communities.[1645] Policies in the allocation of public funds to religious denominations are to be reviewed, so that all are assigned an equitable part of these funds.[1646]

Furthermore, states should allow that persons liable for military service may claim the status of conscientious objector and perform alternative service without discrimination.[1647] Alternative service should not be of a punitive character,[1648] nor be discriminatory in duration or in categories eligible for it.[1649]

Persons who only speak non-official languages used widely by the population should not be denied access to public service.[1650]

All provisions in domestic law discriminating against non citizens are systematically to be reviewed.[1651]

b. *The Obligation to Protect*

The HRC itself has referred to an obligation to protect,[1652] but that has not necessarily been in the same sense in which the obligation has been defined here, *i.e.* to protect against discrimination by third parties. On the other hand, it has referred to the obligation to protect in the latter sense, without using the notion of the obligation to protect. The HRC has requested states to inform it "about legal provisions and administrative measures directed at diminishing or eliminating discrimination in fact, which may be practised *inter alia* by private persons or bodies."[1653] Is has equally argued that "[t]he right to equality before the law and freedom from discrimination, protected by article 26, requires States to act against discrimination by public and private agencies in all fields."[1654]

1643 UN Doc. CCPR/C/79/Add.107, para. 16 (Costa Rica).
1644 UN Doc. CCPR/C/79/Add.43, para. 18 (Tunisia).
1645 UN Doc. CCPR/C/79/Add.104, para. 24 (Chile).
1646 UN Doc. CCPR/CO/81/LIE, para. 13 (Liechtenstein).
1647 UN Doc. CCPR/CO/71/DOM, para. 21 (Dominican Republic).
1648 UN Doc. CCPR/CO/82/POL, para. 15 (Poland).
1649 UN Doc. CCPR/CO/82/FIN, para. 14 (Finland).
1650 UN Doc. CCPR/CO/81/NAM, para. 21 (Namibia).
1651 UN Doc. CCPR/C/79/Add.59, para. 26 (Estonia).
1652 UN Doc. CCPR/CO/81/NAM, para. 21 (Namibia): undertake measures to protect the use of non-official languages.
1653 UN Doc. HRI/GEN/1/Rev.7, General Comment No. 18 (1989), *Non-discrimination*, para. 9.
1654 UN Doc. HRI/GEN/1/Rev.7, General Comment No. 28 (2000), *The Equality of Rights Between men and women*, para. 31.

It has been argued that article 26 CCPR involves an obligation to protect against discrimination by private persons, for it states that the law shall "guarantee to all persons equal and effective protection against discrimination on any ground."[1655] Bayefski has equally interpreted this provision as suggesting that the HRC believes states are under an obligation to protect from discrimination by private parties.[1656] Other commentators have questioned the existence of a comprehensive obligation to protect.[1657] The latter have argued that "states parties do have a duty to prevent discrimination by private persons in the public sphere where such discrimination adversely affects the rights – whether civil, political, economic, social or cultural – of the person discriminated against."[1658] In their view, "the prohibition of discrimination in the purely domestic sphere would interfere unduly with the discriminator's right to personal privacy."[1659] They therefore conclude that only discrimination by private bodies exercising public functions is probably to be protected against.[1660]

In *Nahlik v. Austria*, the HRC submitted that

> The Committee observes that under articles 2 and 26 of the Covenant the State party is under an obligation to ensure that all individuals within its territory and subject to its jurisdiction are free from discrimination, and consequently the courts of States parties are under an obligation to protect individuals against discrimination, whether this occurs within the public sphere or among private parties in the quasi-public sector of, for example, employment.[1661]

The obligation to protect against discrimination therefore clearly seems to apply at least among private parties in the *quasi-public sector*. In the afore-mentioned case, discrimination had allegedly taken place in the context of a collective agreement. This collective agreement was however regulated by law and entered only into force on confirmation by the minister. Moreover, it concerned staff of an institution of public law implementing public policy. For all these reasons, the Committee qualified the context of the alleged discrimination as the *quasi-public sector*. With reference to the drafting history of art. 26 CCPR, Nowak extends this concept of the quasi-public sector to schools, transportation, hotels, restaurants, theatres, parks, beaches etc.[1662]

The HRC initially may have hesitated to take a firm position on responsibility of states in case of failure to prevent discrimination by private actors. In *Love v. Australia*, a

---

1655 See Nowak, supra note 2, 459-460 and 475-476, and further references there.
1656 Bayefski, supra note 3, 33.
1657 Lester and Joseph, supra note 8, 566 and 582.
1658 *Ibid.*, 583.
1659 *Idem.*
1660 *Ibid.*, 594.
1661 UN Doc. CCPR/C/57/D/608/1995, Communication No. 608/95, *Nahlik v. Austria*, para. 8.2.
1662 Nowak, supra note 2, 478.

case on the compulsory age-based retirement policy of a state-owned and managed airline company, it refrained from establishing a responsibility to prevent third party discrimination by way of *obiter dictum* for example:

> In the light of the above finding that Mr Love did not suffer discrimination in violation of article 26, it is unnecessary to decide whether the dismissal was directly imputable to the State party, or whether the State party's responsibility would be engaged by a failure to prevent third party discrimination.[1663]

In its most recent general comment on the nature of the general legal obligation imposed on states parties, the HRC has unequivocally recognized the obligation to protect when certain conditions are met. The Committee has clarified that failure to protect against private actors may give rise to state responsibility, when a state has permitted or failed to take appropriate measures or to exercise due diligence to prevent, punish, investigate or redress the harm caused by such acts by private persons or entities:

> The article 2, paragraph 1, obligations are binding on States [Parties] and do not, as such, have direct horizontal effect as a matter of international law. The Covenant cannot be viewed as a substitute for domestic criminal or civil law. However the positive obligations on States Parties to ensure Covenant rights will only be fully discharged if individuals are protected by the State, not just against violations of Covenant rights by its agents, but also against acts committed by private persons or entities that would impair the enjoyment of Covenant rights in so far as they are amenable to application between private persons or entities. There may be circumstances in which a failure to ensure Covenant rights as required by article 2 would give rise to violations by States Parties of those rights, as a result of States Parties' permitting or failing to take appropriate measures or to exercise due diligence to prevent, punish, investigate or redress the harm caused by such acts by private persons or entities. States are reminded of the interrelationship between the positive obligations imposed under article 2 and the need to provide effective remedies in the event of breach under article 2, paragraph 3. The Covenant itself envisages in some articles certain areas where there are positive obligations on States Parties to address the activities of private persons or entities. [...] In fields affecting basic aspects of ordinary life such as work or housing, individuals are to be protected from discrimination within the meaning of article 26.][1664]

In the case where specialized norms have been provided for in the CCPR itself, there is no room for doubt. Article 3 for example, mandates states to end discriminatory actions in the private sector which impair the equal enjoyment of rights by men and

---

1663 UN Doc. CCPR/C/77/D/983/2001, Communication No. 983/2001, *Love v. Australia*, para. 8.4.

1664 UN Doc. HRI/GEN/1/Rev.7, General Comment No. 31 (2004), *The Nature of the General Legal Obligation Imposed on States Parties to the Covenant*, para. 8.

women.[1665] Article 20, para. 2 CCPR requires states to enact laws against hate speech, *i.e.* speech which incites discrimination on the basis of race, religion or nationality. Article 23, para. 4 CCPR imposes the obligation on states to ensure equality of rights and responsibilities of spouses to marriage, during marriage and at its dissolution. Article 24, para. 1 CCPR requires measures of protection for children.

States been recommended to curb discrimination in the private sphere, *e.g.* by introducing comprehensive anti-discrimination legislation in the private sphere,[1666] including by establishing acts of discrimination against women (such as sexual harassment in the workplace, rape) as punishable crimes,[1667] the prohibition of polygamy by law,[1668] the prohibition of female genital mutilation[1669] and the elimination of inequality of spouses with regard to marriage, divorce, devolution of property and other rights.[1670] States parties have been urged to prohibit gender discrimination by private actors in areas such as employment, education, political activities and the provision of accommodation, goods and services.[1671] Equal access to the private sector labour market and equal wages for work of equal value are to be ensured.[1672] Strong measures are to be taken to prevent trafficking and to impose sanctions on those who exploit women and children.[1673] Rehabilitation programmes are to be established for victims of trafficking.[1674] Appropriate measures are to be taken to address domestic violence cases,[1675] including the addressing of obstacles such as economic dependence on their partners that prevent women from reporting such violence,[1676] the punishment

---

1665 UN Doc. HRI/GEN/1/Rev.7, General Comment No. 28 (2000), *Article 3: The Equality of Rights Between Men and Women*, para. 4.

1666 UN Doc. CCPR/C/79/Add.104, para. 23 (Chile); UN Doc. CCPR/C/79/Add.60, para. 23 (Mauritius).

1667 UN Doc. CCPR/CO/83/ISL, para. 11 (Iceland): priority concern; UN Doc. CCPR/C/79/Add.63, para. 21 (Guatemala).

1668 UN Doc. CCPR/CO/83/KEN, para. 10 (Kenya) (priority concern); UN Doc. CCPR/CO/82/BEN, para. 10 (Benin); UN Doc. CCPR/CO/70/GAB, paras. 8-9 (Gabon); UN Doc. CCPR/CO/69/KWT, para. 8 (Kuwait).

1669 UN Doc. CCPR/CO/82/BEN, para. 11 (Benin): priority concern; UN Doc. CCPR/CO/83/KEN, para. 12 (Kenya).

1670 UN Doc. CCPR/CO/83/KEN, para. 10 (Kenya) (priority concern); UN Doc. CCPR/CO/70/GAB, paras. 8-9 (Gabon); UN Doc. CCPR/CO/69/KWT, para. 8 (Kuwait).

1671 UN Doc. HRC/GEN/1/Rev.7, General Comment No. 28 (2000), *Article 3: The Equality of Rights Between Men and Women*, para. 31.

1672 UN Doc. CCPR/CO/83/MUS, para. 8 (Mauritius); UN Doc. CCPR/CO/82/POL, para. 10 (Poland); UN Doc. CCPR/CO/82/FIN, para. 9 (Finland).

1673 UN Doc. CCPR/CO/81/SEMO, para. 16 (Serbia and Montenegro); UN Doc. CCPR/CO/74/GEO, para. 15 (Georgia).

1674 UN Doc. CCPR/CO/74/GEO, para. 14-15 (Georgia).

1675 UN Doc. CCPR/CO/83/ISL, para. 12 (Iceland).

1676 UN Doc. CCPR/CO/83/MUS, para. 10 (Mauritius).

of offenders,[1677] restraining orders,[1678] and the establishment of crisis-centre hotlines and victim support centres equipped with medical, psychological and legal facilities, including shelters for battered spouses and children.[1679]

Legislation providing for specific penalties for racial discrimination is to be adopted,[1680] and racial discrimination is to be combated in all fields of social life.[1681] Efforts to combat right-wing extremism and other expressions of xenophobia and religious intolerance are to be intensified.[1682] All persons are to be protected from discrimination on account of their religious beliefs.[1683]

In accordance with a dissenting minority of the HRC, states are under an obligation to protect against discrimination on the ground of political belief. The burden of proof in case of an allegation of discrimination in employment lies mainly with the state: the employee is to substantiate in some measure his complaint, but it is up to the state to prove positively that the different treatment was not due to discrimination (based on political opinion).[1684]

Compared to the attention CERD has paid to private discrimination in its concluding observations, the HRC seems to be much more hesitant in systematically addressing states' obligation to protect against discrimination by third parties.

c. *The Obligation to Fulfil*

The HRC has shown itself explicitly in favour of the obligation for states to take positive measures. As early as 1981, the Committee drew the attention of states to the fact

> that the obligation under the Covenant [was] not confined to the respect of human rights, but that States Parties [had] also undertaken to ensure the enjoyment of these rights to all individuals under their jurisdiction. This aspect calls for specific activities by the States parties to enable

---

1677 See most recently *e.g.* UN Doc. CCPR/CO/83/GRC, para. 7 (Greece); UN Doc. CCPR/CO/82/BEN, para. 9 (Benin); UN Doc. CCPR/CO/81/LIE, para. 8 (Liechtenstein).

1678 UN Doc. CCPR/CO/82/POL, para. 11 (Poland).

1679 UN Doc. CPR/CO/82/ALB, para. 10 (Albania); UN Doc. CCPR/CO/82/BEN, para. 9 (Benin); UN Doc. CCPR/CO/81/LIE, para. 8 (Liechtenstein); UN Doc. CCPR/CO/81/SEMO, para. 17 (Serbia and Montenegro).

1680 UN Doc. CCPR/CO/72/MCO, para. 13 (Monaco).

1681 UN Doc. CCPR/CO/81/SEMO, paras. 18 and 25 (Serbia and Montenegro).

1682 UN Doc. CCPR/CO/81/LIE, para. 9 (Liechtenstein).

1683 UN Doc. CCPR/CO/73/UK;CCPR/CO/73/UKOT, para. 14 (United Kingdom and Overseas Territories).

1684 UN Doc. CCPR/C/82/D/958/2000, Communication no. 958/2000, *Nuri Jazairi v. Canada*, para. 7 of the dissenting opinion.

> individuals to enjoy their rights. This is obvious in a number of articles (e.g. article 3 [...]), but in principle this undertaking relates to all rights set forth in the Covenant.[1685]

The obligation to fulfil, *i.e.* to take positive measures, can be disaggregated into obligations to facilitate, to promote and to provide. These sub-obligations will be dealt with in what follows.

i. To Facilitate

The obligation to facilitate equality is reflected in many recommendations to take positive measures and active steps, mainly with regard to women[1686] and minorities.[1687]

With regard to equality between women and men, administrative measures,[1688] plans and programmes of action,[1689] and targeted measures[1690] are to be taken, *inter alia* to give women access to employment and political posts.[1691] The state is to adopt positive measures in all areas "so as to achieve the effective and equal empowerment of women",[1692] *inter alia* to promote and ensure women's participation in the conduct of public affairs and in public office.[1693]

In its 1989 general comment on non-discrimination, the HRC pointed out that it is "a positive duty of States" to make certain that spouses have equal rights as required by art. 23, para. 4 CCPR.[1694] A state is therefore to take effective measures to encourage the registration of customary marriages and to grant the spouses and children of registered customary marriages the same rights as those married under civil law.[1695]

1685 UN Doc. HRI/GEN/1/Rev.7, General Comment No. 3 (1981), *Article 2: Implementation at the national level*, para. 1. This general comment was replaced in 2004.

1686 UN Doc. CCPR/CO/79/LVA, para. 14 (Latvia); UN Doc. CCPR/CO/73/UKR, para. 9 (Ukraine); UN Doc. CCPR/CO/69/KGZ, para. 13 (Kyrgyzstan); UN Doc. CCPR/C/79/Add.121, para. 13 (Guyana); UN Doc. CCPR/C/79/Add.117, para. 16 (China – Hong Kong); UN Doc. CCPR/C/79/Add.30, para. 16 (Romania); UN Doc. CCPR/C/79/Add.25, para. 21 (Iran); UN Doc. CCPR/C/79/Add.22, para. 11 (Hungary).

1687 UN Doc. CCPR/CO/74/GEO, para. 19 (Georgia); UN Doc. CCPR/CO/72/CZE, para. 9 (Czech Republic): priority concern.

1688 UN Doc. CCPR/C/79/Add.36, para. 19 (Togo).

1689 UN Doc. CCPR/C/79/Add.55, para. 26 (United Kingdom).

1690 UN Doc. CCPR/C/79/Add.93, para. 15 (Israel).

1691 UN Doc. CCPR/CO/76/TGO, para. 22 (Togo).

1692 UN Doc. HRI/GEN/1/Rev.7, General Comment No. 28 (2000), *The Equality of Rights Between Men and Women*, para. 3.

1693 *Ibid.*, para. 29. See also *e.g.* UN Doc. CCPR/CO/83/MUS, para. 8 (Mauritius); UN Doc. CCPR/CO/81/LIE, para. 7 (Liechtenstein).

1694 UN Doc. HRI/GEN/1/Rev.7, General Comment No. 18 (1989), *Non-Discrimination*, para. 5.

1695 UN Doc. CCPR/CO/81/NAM, para. 9 (Namibia): priority concern.

With regard to minorities, training in order to equip them for employment, creation of job opportunities,[1696] recruitment of their members into the police,[1697] and special training for Roma and other minority children in order to secure access to education without segregation,[1698] are just a couple of examples of how a state might facilitate equality.[1699] Positive measures, including the allocation of the requisite resources,[1700] may also be necessary to protect the identity of a minority and the rights of its members to enjoy and develop their culture and language and to practise their religion, in community with the other members of the group.[1701]

An important way in which equality can be facilitated is through remedies and recourse against violations.[1702] Remedies are to be accessible and effective,[1703] and be able to award compensation.[1704] Adequate mechanisms are to be established to receive complaints from victims and to ensure adequate investigation and prosecution of cases of racial violence and incitement to racial hatred.[1705]

The establishment of a national human rights commission might be considered,[1706] with the power to initiate legal action[1707] and to monitor the implementation of anti-discrimination legislation,[1708] in particular against women[1709] and

1696 UN Doc. CCPR/CO/78/SVK, para. 16 (Slovakia): priority concern.

1697 UN Doc. CCPR/CO/78/PRT, para. 8 (Portugal).

1698 UN Doc. CCPR/CO/78/SVK, para. 18 (Slovakia); UN Doc. CCPR/CO/72/CZE, para. 9 (Czech Republic): priority concern.

1699 Compare also with UN Doc. CCPR/CO/83/GRC, para. 18 (Greece), in which the adoption of positive measures regarding housing, employment, education and social service was recommended.

1700 UN Doc. CCPR/CO/82/FIN, para. 15 (Finland).

1701 UN Doc. HRI/GEN/1/Rev.7, General Comment No. 23 (1994), *Article 27*, para. 6.2.

1702 UN Doc. CCPR/CO/83/GRC, para. 19 (Greece); UN Doc. CCPR/CO/71/HRV, para. 19 (Croatia); UN Doc. CCPR/CO/71/VEN, para. 23 (Venezuela).

1703 UN Doc. CCPR/CO/81/SEMO, para. 18 (Serbia and Montenegro); UN Doc. CCPR/CO/78/SVK, para. 8 (Slovakia); UN Doc. CCPR/CO/70, para. 10 (Trinidad and Tobago); UN Doc. CCPR/C/79/Add.105, para. 9 (Canada); UN Doc. CCPR/C/79/Add.89, para. 15 (Zimbabwe); UN Doc. CCPR/C/79/Add.86, para. 10 (Lithuania); UN Doc. CCPR/C/79/Add.79, para. 14 (Slovakia); UN Doc. CCPR/C/79/Add.78, paras. 18-19 (Lebanon).

1704 UN Doc. CCPR/C/79/Add.80, para. 26 (France).

1705 UN Doc. CCPR/CO/82/POL, para. 17 (Poland): priority concern; UN Doc. CCPR/CO/78/SVK, para. 17 (Slovakia): priority concern.

1706 UN Doc. CCPR/CO/73/UK;CCPR/CO/73/UKOT, para. 9 (United Kingdom and Overseas Territories).

1707 UN Doc. CCPR/CO/73/CH, para. 8 (Switzerland).

1708 UN Doc. CCPR/CO/72/CZE, para. 7 (Czech Republic); UN Doc. CCPR/C/79/Add.104, para. 23 (Chile).

1709 UN Doc. CCPR/CO/78/SVK, para. 8 (Slovakia); UN Doc. CCPR/CO/73/AZE, para. 17 (Azerbaijan): priority concern; UN Doc. CCPR/CO/70/ARG, para. 15 (Argentina); UN Doc. A/55/40, paras. 20-21 (Ireland); UN Doc. CCPR/C/79/Add.105, para. 20 (Canada); UN Doc. CCPR/C/79/Add.79, para. 14 (Slovakia); UN Doc. CCPR/C/79/Add.87, para. 10 (Lithuania).

minorities.[1710] In case a non-judicial human rights body is given the power to deal with complaints of discrimination, but whereby it findings are non-binding under domestic law, there is no obligation *per se* under the CCPR to implement these non-binding findings.[1711]

ii. To Promote

The HRC has paid sustained attention to human rights education in general, but it has not put explicit emphasis on education on non-discrimination and equality. In its general comment on equality between women and men for example the Committee has indicated that education of the population and of state officials in human rights is required under the CCPR.[1712] In its concluding observations, it has stressed the need for education[1713] with regard to discrimination against women – towards the population at large (mainly with regard to customs and traditions, about women's rights and domestic violence,[1714] and female genital mutilation[1715]),[1716] and the public service (law enforcement officers, judiciary, legal profession)[1717] – with regard to sexual minorities (training to law enforcement and judicial officials),[1718] with regard to minorities and racism (through sensitization of law enforcement personnel as a matter

1710 UN Doc. CCPR/CO/80/LTU, para. 8 (Lithuania); UN Doc. CCPR/CO/78/SVK, para. 19 (Slovakia): priority concern; UN Doc. CCPR/CO/72/CZE, para. 10 (Czech Republic); UN Doc. CCPR/C/79/Add.79, para. 15 (Slovakia).

1711 UN Doc. CCPR/C/77/D/983/2001, Communication No. 983/2001, *Love v. Australia*, para. 7.5.

1712 UN Doc. HRI/GEN/1/Rev.7, General Comment No. 28 (2000), *The Equality of Rights Between Men and Women*, para. 3.

1713 UN Doc. CCPR/C/79/Add.28, para. 17 (Japan).

1714 UN Doc. CCPR/CO/83/UZB, para. 23 (Uzbekistan); UN Doc. CCPR/CO/83/GRC, para. 9 (Greece); UN Doc. CPR/CO/82/ALB, para. 10 (Albania); UN Doc. CCPR/CO/82/BEN, para. 9 (Benin); UN Doc. CCPR/CO/81/SEMO, para. 17 (Serbia and Montenegro).

1715 UN Doc. CCPR/CO/83/KEN, para. 12 (Kenya).

1716 UN Doc. CCPR/CO/76/TGO, para. 22 (Togo); UN Doc. CCPR/CO/74/GEO, para. 13 (Georgia); UN Doc. CCPR/CO/73/AZE, paras. 17 (priority concern) and 18 (Azerbaijan); UN Doc. CCPR/CO/71/UZB, paras. 19-20 (Uzbekistan); UN Doc. CCPR/CO/70/ARG, para. 15 (Argentina); UN Doc. CCPR/CO/69/KGZ, para. 13 (Kyrgyzstan); UN Doc. CCPR/CO/KWT, paras. 7-8 (Kuwait); UN Doc. CCPR/CO/73/UKR, para. 9 (Ukraine); UN Doc. CCPR/C/79/Add.116, paras. 9-11 (Cameroon); UN Doc. CCPR/C/79/Add.107, para. 20 (Costa Rica); UN Doc. CCPR/C/79/Add.70, para. 23 (Switzerland); UN Doc. CCPR/C/79/Add.59, para. 29 (Estonia); UN Doc. CCPR/C/79/Add.53, para. 21 (Latvia); UN Doc. CCPR/C/79/Add.42, para. 8 (Nepal); UN Doc. CCPR/C/79/Add.36, para. 19 (Togo); UN Doc. CCPR/C/79/Add.35, para. 15 (Jordan); UN Doc. CCPR/C/79/Add.33, para. 25 (Cameroon).

1717 UN Doc. CCPR/CO/79/PHL, para. 13 (Philippines); UN Doc. CCPR/C/79/Add.55, para. 26 (United Kingdom).

1718 UN Doc. CCPR/CO/82/POL, para. 18 (Poland).

of priority,[1719] media campaigns[1720] and primary and secondary education[1721]),[1722] with regard to religions (through awareness campaigns for the public at large)[1723], and with regard to caste-based discrimination.[1724] Women themselves are to be sensitized about the prohibition of polygamy.[1725]

iii. To Provide

The CESCR Committee has made clear that in case of the right to education, the obligation to provide prevails over the other obligations.[1726] Fully in line with this, the HRC has emphasized the need to provide education to girls and women in order to eliminate gender discrimination.[1727]

The question has arisen whether a state is to provide the same level of funding in light of the principle of equality. In *Blom v. Sweden*, the HRC decided that a state is not to provide the same level of funding to private education as it does to public education, when private education is not subject to state supervision.[1728] In *Waldman v. Canada*, the Committee held that funding religious schools of one minority but not of other minorities in a comparable situation, constituted discrimination.[1729] In our view, the latter case means that the principles of non-discrimination and equality on themselves do not oblige a state to fund religious education of minorities. However, if a state decides to fund one type of religious education of minorities, it is to refrain from discrimination and to so for all minorities in a comparable situation.[1730] A difficult

---

1719 UN Doc. CCPR/CO/83/GRC, para. (Greece): priority concern; UN Doc. CCPR/CO/74/HUN, para. 7 (Hungary): priority concern; UN Doc. CCPR/CO/78/PRT, para. 8 (Portugal): priority concern.

1720 UN Doc. CCPR/CO/80/DEU, para. 20 (Germany); UN Doc. CCPR/C/79/Add.58, para. 23 (Sweden); UN Doc. CCPR/C/79/Add.30, para. 14 (Romania).

1721 UN Doc. CCPR/CO/74/SWE, para. 13 (Sweden); UN Doc. CCPR/C/79/Add.58, para. 23 (Sweden); UN Doc. CCPR/C/79/Add.37, para. 18 (Italy); UN Doc. CCPR/CO/74/HUN, para. 7 (Hungary): priority concern; UN Doc. A/55/40, paras. 27-28 (Ireland).

1722 UN Doc. CCPR/CO/83/GRC, para. 19 (Greece).

1723 UN Doc. CCPR/CO/74/HUN, para. 14 (Hungary); UN Doc. CCPR/CO/74/GEO, para. 17 (Georgia).

1724 UN Doc. CCPR/C/79/Add.42, para. 8 (Nepal).

1725 UN Doc. CCPR/CO/82/BEN, para. 10 (Benin).

1726 UN Doc. HRI/GEN/1/Rev.7, General Comment No. 13 (1999), *The Right to Education (Art. 13)*, para. 48: states have the principal responsibility for the direct provision of education in most circumstances; they have an enhanced obligation to fulfil-provide regarding the right to education.

1727 UN Doc. CCPR/CO/76/TGO, para. 22 (Togo); UN Doc. CCPR/CO/76/EGY, para. 7 (Egypt); UN Doc. CCPR/CO/69/KGZ, para. 13 (Kyrgyzstan).

1728 UN Doc. CCPR/C/32/D/191/1985, Communication No. 191/1985, *Blom v. Sweden*, para. 10.3. See also supra.

1729 UN Doc. CCPR/C/67/D/694/1996, Communication No. 694/96, *Waldman v. Canada*, paras. 10.5-10.6.

1730 A similar argument has been made with regard to positive measures in favour of minorities: equality is to be observed as regards the treatment between different minorities (UN Doc. HRI/GEN/1/Rev.7, General Comment No. 23 (1994), *Article 27*, para. 6.2).

issue is whether equal treatment in this situation might be restored by "equalizing down", *i.e.* by lowering the rights of those better treated to the level of the victim of discrimination (in the *Waldman* case, this would have meant ending funding for Roman Catholic religious education).[1731] As pointed out by Scheinin in its individual opinion in *Waldman v. Canada*, a state may well have an obligation to fund religious education of minorities under another substantive right (*i.e.* article 27).[1732] In line with this conclusion, the HRC has recommended in its concluding observations on the allocation of public funds to religious denominations that they all were to be assigned an equitable part of the funds,[1733] and that all recognized religions were to enjoy the same advantages.[1734]

As to affirmative action in order to provide equality, the HRC's general comment on non-discrimination suggest that affirmative action may be mandatory:

> The Committee also wishes to point out that the principle of equality sometimes requires States parties to take affirmative action in order to diminish or eliminate conditions which cause or help to perpetuate discrimination prohibited by the Covenant. For example, in a State where the general conditions of a certain part of the population prevent or impair their enjoyment of human rights, the State should take specific action to correct those conditions.[1735]

Affirmative action seems to be required to correct *de facto* discrimination. It is of a temporary nature, but may last as long as it is needed to correct the *de facto* discrimination:

> Such action may involve granting for a time to the part of the population concerned certain preferential treatment in specific matters as compared with the rest of the population. However, as long as such action is needed to correct discrimination in fact, it is a case of legitimate differentiation under the Covenant.[1736]

In *Stalla Costa v. Uruguay*, the HRC had to decide whether preferential access to public service for persons who had been dismissed from public service for political reasons by the previous government, amounted to discrimination. It held that the measure was to be considered as a measure of redress and therefore not discriminatory.[1737] In

---

1731 An element in support of this might be found with Lemmens, supra note 142, 90: if positive action is required, and several policy options lay open for the legislator, a judge is not in a position to force the legislator to take a particular option.

1732 UN Doc. CCPR/C/67/D/694/1996, Communication No. 694/96, *Waldman v. Canada*, concurring opinion of Scheinin, para. 5.

1733 UN Doc. CCPR/CO/81/LIE, para. 13 (Liechtenstein).

1734 UN Doc. CCPR/CO/81/BEL, para. 26 (Belgium).

1735 UN Doc. HRI/GEN/1/Rev.7, General Comment No. 18 (1989), *Non-Discrimination*, para. 10.

1736 *Idem.*

1737 UN Doc. CCPR/C/30/D/198/1985, Communication No. 198/1985, *Stalla Costa v. Uruguay*, para. 10.

Jacobs v. Belgium, the question arose whether gender quota for appointment of non-justices to the High Council of Justice (at least 4 out of 11 had to be of a different sex) were permissible. The Committee concluded that the requirement was objective and reasonably justifiable, and that it did not amount to a disproportionate restriction of candidates' right of access, on general terms of equality, to public office. It thereby stressed the fact that only just over one third of the candidates was submitted to the gender clause. One may wonder whether the conclusions of the Committee would have been different had the gender clause been stricter, requiring for example 50% of the candidates to be of each sex. This case makes clear what the criteria are to gauge the permissibility of affirmative action; the measure is to be objective and reasonably justifiable, and to be proportional with the aim pursued.[1738] A law banning advertising in another language than French in Quebec was found not to be in violation of article 26 CCPR; the affirmative action argument was however rejected as a justification for limiting freedom of expression.[1739]

The HRC has been much more restrictive than CERD in recommending affirmative action measures. It has limited itself to suggesting affirmative action with regard to women, in order to ensure their participation in the conduct of public affairs and in public office,[1740] as well as in social and economic life,[1741] and exceptionally also with regard to minorities (mainly Roma).[1742]

d. *Conclusions*

Anti-discrimination legislation has been considered a *conditio sine qua non* for the fulfilment of obligations under the principles of equality and non-discrimination. The obligation to respect has received ample attention of the HRC; a variety of discriminatory laws have been recommended to be reviewed. The obligation to protect against discrimination by third parties has been unequivocally recognised in a 2004 general comment; state responsibility for private discrimination may arise when a state has permitted or failed to take appropriate measures or to exercise due diligence to

---

1738 UN Doc. CCPR/C/81/D/943/2000, Communication No. 943/2000, *Jacobs v. Belgium*, para. 9.5.

1739 UN Doc. CCPR/C/47/D/359/1989, Communication No. 359/89 and 385/1989, *Ballantyne, Davidson & Mcintyre v. Canada*, para. 11.4.

1740 UN Doc. HRI/GEN/1/Rev.7, General Comment No. 28 (2000), *Article 3: The Equality of Rights Between Men and Women*, para. 29.

1741 UN Doc. CPR/CO/82/ALB, para. 11 (Albania): priority concern; UN Doc. CCPR/CO/72/GTM, para. 25 (Guatemala); UN Doc. CCPR/C/79/Add.52, para. 22 (Ukraine); UN Doc. CCPR/C/79/Add.50, paras. 30 and 38 (United States of America); UN Doc. CCPR/C/79/Add.40, para. 16 (Slovenia); UN Doc. CCPR/C/79/Add.39, para. 20 (Cyprus).

1742 UN Doc. CCPR/CO/80/DEU, para. 21 (Germany) and UN Doc. CCPR/CO/78/PRT, para. 20 (Portugal): in favour of Roma with regard to housing, employment, education and social services; UN Doc. CCPR/C/79/Add.50, paras. 30 and 38 (United States of America).

prevent, punish, investigate or redress the harm caused by such acts by private persons or entities. Under the obligation to fulfil-facilitate, the availability of remedies has been an important concern. Like CERD, the HRC has paid attention to the establishment of a national human rights commission in this regard. The HRC has been very selective and restrictive in recommending affirmative action under the obligation to fulfil-provide: it has done so only with regard to women and minorities, in fairly general terms, and only to a handful of states.

The HRC seems to focus on two groups in particular when spelling out obligations under the principles of equality and non-discrimination, *i.e.* women and minorities (Roma).

3. CESCR COMMITTEE

As the Committee made clear early in its history, it may be difficult to respect, protect and fulfil the right to non-discrimination and equality effectively in the absence of a sound legislative foundation.[1743] Specific anti-discrimination framework legislation is to be adopted if absent,[1744] and provisions in the domestic legal order with respect to the prohibition of discrimination in accordance with article 2, para. 2 CESCR are to be strengthened.[1745] As to racial discrimination, *criminal* legislation is required.[1746]

With regard to gender equality,[1747] a constitutional prohibition of discrimination on grounds of sex is to be included,[1748] and comprehensive anti-discrimination legislation in accordance with article 2, paras. 2 and 3 CESCR is to be adopted.[1749] Specific legislative measures are required to prohibit all forms of gender-based discrimination[1750] in all fields of civil, political, economic, social and cultural life.[1751]

1743 UN Doc. HRI/GEN/1/Rev.7, General Comment No. 3 (1990), *The Nature of States Parties' Obligations*, para. 3.

1744 UN Doc. E/C.12/1/Add.108, para. 39 (Serbia and Montenegro).

1745 UN Doc. E/C.12/1/Add.77, para. 27 (Ireland); UN Doc. E/C.12/1/Add.65, para. 22 (Ukraine); UN Doc. E/C.12/1/Add.46, para. 29 (Jordan).

1746 UN Doc. E/C.12/1/Add.16, para. 31 (Dominican Republic).

1747 UN Doc. E/C.12/1/Add.92, para. 28 (Yemen).

1748 UN Doc. E/C.12/1/Add.86, para. 29 (Luxemburg); UN Doc. E/C.12/1/Add.75, para. 20 (Jamaica).

1749 UN Doc. E/C.12/1/Add.108, para. 43 (Serbia and Montenegro); UN Doc. E/C.12/1/Add.81, para. 22 (Slovakia); UN Doc. E/C.12/1/Add.80, para. 37 (Trinidad and Tobago); UN Doc. E/C.12/1994/19, para. 35 (UK: Hong Kong); UN Doc. E/C.12/1/Add.79, para. 31 (United Kingdom).

1750 UN Doc. E/C.12/1995/15, para. 25 (Ukraine).

1751 UN Doc. E/C.12/1/Add.65, para. 23 (Ukraine); UN Doc. E/C.12/1/Add.46, para. 30 (Jordan).

a. *The Obligation to Respect*

The obligation to respect imposes a duty on the state to abstain from discrimination. It has been stressed in particular with regard to sex/gender discrimination. Amendment and abolition of gender discriminatory laws and practices has been recommended in general wordings,[1752] and more specifically with regard to discriminatory provisions in criminal law,[1753] family law,[1754] commercial law[1755] and labour laws.[1756] In many cases, suggestions with a considerable degree of detail have been made, for example with regard to the more severe punishment of women for adultery and "honour crimes",[1757] indecent dress and being on the street after dusk,[1758] the low legal age of marriage for girls, and the unequal treatment of women insofar as personal, property, succession and social security laws are concerned,[1759] taxation, allocation of seeds and family allowances,[1760] the "cohabitation rule" in the unemployment insurance regime,[1761] divorce law,[1762] inheritance,[1763] citizenship law not granting women the same right as men to transmit citizenship to their foreign-born spouses,[1764] laws permitting men to marry without the acknowledgement or consent of the partner,[1765] and discrimination in the acquisition and transmission of nationality.[1766] States have equally been encouraged to respect equality by providing for the same age of retirement for women

---

1752 UN Doc. E/C.12/2005/3, General Comment No. 16 (2005), *Article 3: The Equal Right of Men and Women to the Enjoyment of All Economic, Social and Cultural Rights*, para. 5; UN Doc. E/C.12/1/Add.98, para. 33 (Kuwait); UN Doc. E/C.12/1/Add.95, para. 33 (Democratic People's Republic of Korea); UN Doc. E/C.12/1/Add.75, para. 20 (Jamaica); UN Doc. E/C.12/1/Add.25, para. 40 (Netherlands); UN Doc. E/C.12/1/Add.23, para. 39 (Nigeria); UN Doc. E/C.12/1/Add.17, para. 30 (Iraq); UN Doc. E/C.12/1/Add.16, para. 32 (Dominican Republic); UN Doc. E/C.12/1/Add.4, para. 29 (El Salvador); UN Doc. E/C.12/1995/14, para. 15 (Mauritius); UN Doc. E/C.12/1995/7, para. 29 (Philippines); UN Doc. E/C.12/1994/5, para. 18 (Morocco).

1753 UN Doc. E/C.12/1/Add.87, para. 52 (Brazil).

1754 UN Doc. E/C.12/1/Add.106, paras. 37-38 (Zambia); UN Doc. E/C.12/1/Add.71, para. 29 (Algeria); UN Doc. E/C.12/1/Add.55, para. 16 (Morocco); UN Doc. E/C.12/1/Add.40, para. 32 (Cameroon); UN Doc. E/C.12/1/Add.3, para. 28 (Guatemala).

1755 UN Doc. E/C.12/1/Add.105, para. 46 (Chile); UN Doc. E/C.12/1/Add.40, para. 32 (Cameroon).

1756 UN Doc. E/C.12/1/Add.1, para. 22 (Paraguay).

1757 UN Doc. E/C.12/1/Add.63, para. 31 (Syrian Arab Republic).

1758 UN Doc. E/C.12/1/Add.48, para. 34 (Sudan).

1759 UN Doc. E/C.12/1/Add.63, para. 31 (Syrian Arab Republic); UN Doc. E/C.12/1/Add.28, para. 19 (Cyprus). Compare with UN Doc. E/C.12/2005/3, General Comment No. 16 (2005), *Article 3: The Equal Right of Men and Women to the Enjoyment of All Economic, Social and Cultural Rights*, paras. 27 and 28.

1760 UN Doc. E/C.12/1/Add.62, para. 38 (Senegal).

1761 UN Doc. E/C.12/1/Add.54, para. 22 (Belgium).

1762 UN Doc. E/C.12/1/Add.44, para. 33 (Egypt).

1763 UN Doc. E/C.12/1/Add.36, para. 22 (Tunisia).

1764 UN Doc. E/C.12/1995/17, para. 22 (Algeria).

1765 UN Doc. E/C.12/1995/6, para. 16 (Suriname).

1766 UN Doc. E/C.12/1/Add.28, para. 19 (Cyprus).

and men,[1767] and by revising pension plans and social security benefits to ensure gender equality.[1768] Persistent *de facto* gender inequality in the pension system is to be remedied to the maximum possible extent.[1769] Equal remuneration and equal opportunity for promotion in employment should be subject to no considerations other than those of seniority and competence.[1770]

Discriminatory legislation on grounds of nationality too has been required to be revised,[1771] *i.e.* to allow foreign workers to enrol in the vocational guidance and training courses to which national workers were entitled,[1772] or to avoid discrimination against children born to women married to non nationals.[1773] Israel has been asked to review its re-entry policies for Palestinians who wished to re-establish their domicile in their homeland, "with a view to bringing such policies level with the Law of Return as applied to Jews."[1774] Objective criteria are to be established for the granting of citizenship,[1775] and measures to reduce unemployment and to promote entrepreneurship are to be undertaken in a non-discriminatory manner.[1776] Financial obstacles to post-secondary education for low-income students are to be addressed without any discrimination on the basis of citizenship status.[1777] Educational material that is discriminatory is to be removed.[1778] A state is to abstain from discriminatory treatment within the housing sector towards persons belonging to ethnic minorities, refugees and asylum seekers.[1779]

Discriminatory practices on the basis of origin against internal migrants is to be ceased.[1780]

1767 UN Doc. E/C.12/2005/3, General Comment No. 16 (2005), *Article 3: The Equal Right of Men and Women to the Enjoyment of All Economic, Social and Cultural Rights*, para. 26; UN Doc. E/C.12/1/Add.82, para. 41 (Poland).

1768 UN Doc. E/C.12/1/Add.29, para. 30 (Germany).

1769 UN Doc. E/C.12/1/Add.67, para. 51 (Japan).

1770 UN Doc. E/C.12/1/Add.82, para. 39 (Poland).

1771 UN Doc. E/C.12/1/Add.107, para. 95 (China); UN Doc. E/C.12/1/Add.97, para. 33 (Greece); UN Doc. E/C.12/1/Add.90, para. 34 (Israel); UN Doc. E/C.12/1/Add.34, para. 24 (Denmark).

1772 UN Doc. E/C.12/1/Add.53, para. 19 (Portugal).

1773 UN Doc. E/C.12/1/Add.44, para. 33 (Egypt).

1774 UN Doc. E/C.12/1/Add.27, para. 36 (Israel).

1775 UN Doc. E/C.12/1/Add.74, para. 22 (Croatia).

1776 *Ibid.*, para. 23 (Croatia).

1777 UN Doc. E/C.12/1/Add.31, para. 49 (Canada).

1778 UN Doc. E/C.12/1/Add.74, para. 37 (Croatia).

1779 UN Doc. E/C.12/1994/7, para. 14 (Belgium).

1780 UN Doc. E/C.12/1/Add.107, para. 91 (China).

The CESCR Committee has also taken a firm position on discriminatory legislation against children born out of wedlock,[1781] which is to be repealed. Discriminatory provisions in statutes relating to persons with disabilities are equally to be abolished.[1782]

As to the fields in which equality is to be respected, the Committee has emphasized in its general comments the need to refrain from discrimination with regard to education, health and water. A state is to respect the right to non-discrimination by ensuring the right of access to public educational institutions and programmes on a non-discriminatory basis as a core obligation under the right to education.[1783] It is to make primary and basic education free and compulsory for all without discrimination on the grounds of gender, ethnicity, religion or social status.[1784] With regard to public funding to private educational institutions, a state must take care that such funding is without discrimination on any of the prohibited grounds.[1785] Furthermore, discrimination against Roma children is to be eliminated by removing them from "special schools" and integrating them into the mainstream of the educational system.[1786]

With regard to the right to health:

> In particular, States are under the obligation to *respect* the right to health by, *inter alia*, refraining from denying or limiting equal access for all persons, including prisoners or detainees, minorities, asylum seekers and illegal immigrants, to preventive, curative and palliative health services; abstaining from enforcing discriminatory practices as a State policy; and abstaining from imposing discriminatory practices relating to women's health status and needs.[1787]

A subsidized health-care system is thus to be extended to asylum-seekers without discrimination.[1788] A national health strategy is to incorporate the principles of non-discrimination and equal access to health facilities and services.[1789] A state is to ensure that a system of subsidies in the health sector does not discriminate against the most disadvantaged and marginalized groups.[1790] Furthermore, laws, policies and practices

---

1781 UN Doc. E/C.12/1/Add.101, para. 38 (Malta); UN Doc. E/C.12/1/Add.24, para. 24 (Sri Lanka); UN Doc. E/C.12/1/Add.22, para. 21 (Luxemburg); UN Doc. E/C.12/1/Add.18, para. 19 (Uruguay).

1782 UN Doc. E/C.12/1/Add.67, para. 52 (Japan).

1783 UN Doc. HRI/GEN/1/Rev.7, General Comment No. 13 (1999), *The Right to Education (Art. 13)*, para. 57.

1784 UN Doc. E/C.12/1/Add.66, para. 57 (Nepal).

1785 UN Doc. HRI/GEN/1/Rev.7, General Comment No. 13 (1999), *The Right to Education (Art. 13)*, para. 54; UN Doc. E/C.12/1/Add.43, para. 35 (Italy).

1786 UN Doc. E/C.12/1/Add.76, para. 44 (Czech Republic).

1787 UN Doc. HRI/GEN/1/Rev.7, General Comment No. 14 (2000), *The Right to the Highest Attainable Standard of Health (Art. 12)*, para. 34.

1788 UN Doc. E/C.12/1/Add.43, para. 32 (Italy).

1789 UN Doc. E/C.12/1/Add.77, para. 35 (Ireland).

1790 UN Doc. E/C.12/1/Add.75, para. 47 (Colombia).

in relation to HIV/AIDS are to be non-discriminatory,[1791] and legislation and all necessary measures are to be adopted to prevent and abstain from discrimination against persons who are HIV-positive.[1792]

Also, a state is to refrain from engaging in any practice or activity that denies or limits equal access to adequate water.[1793]

b. The Obligation to Protect

The CESCR itself does not explicitly mention the obligation for states to protect against discrimination, but the CESCR Committee has referred to this obligation,[1794] particularly in relation to gender (with regard to employment),[1795] race,[1796] disability,[1797] age (with regard to employment and occupation),[1798] and political opinion.[1799] Legislative measures are to be taken (*i.e.* for the protection against discrimination of Roma[1800] and children born out of wedlock[1801]), also to penalize some forms of conduct – in particular with regard to racial discrimination[1802] – and educational campaigns and programmes are to be carried out.[1803]

In its recent general comment on gender discrimination, the Committee has elucidated the scope of the obligation to protect in light of article 3 CESCR:

> The obligation to protect requires States parties to take steps aimed directly towards the elimination of prejudices, customary and all other practices that perpetuate the notion of inferiority or superiority of either of the sexes, and stereotyped roles for men and women. States parties' obligation to protect under Article 3 of the ICESCR includes *inter alia*, the respect and adoption

1791 UN Doc. E/C.12/1/Add.44, para. 38 (Egypt).

1792 UN Doc. E/C.12/1/Add.29, para. 35 (Germany); UN Doc. E/C.12/1/Add.13, para. 40 (Russian Federation).

1793 UN Doc. HRI/GEN/1/Rev.7, General Comment No. 15 (2002), *The Right to Water (Arts. 11 and 12 of the International Covenant on Economic, Social and Cultural Rights)*, paras. 12 (c) (iii) and 21.

1794 Sepúlveda, supra note 108, 390. See *e.g.* UN Doc. E/C.12/1/Add.57, para. 33 (Honduras).

1795 UN Doc. E/C.12/1/Add.22, para. 18 (Luxemburg); UN Doc. E/C.12/1/Add.13, para. 31 (Russian Federation).

1796 UN Doc. E/C.12/1/Add.73, para. 9 (Croatia); UN Doc. E/C.12/1/Add. 58, para. para. 30 (China: Hong Kong).

1797 UN Doc. HRI/GEN/1/Rev.7, General Comment No. 5 (1994), *Persons with Disabilities*, para. 11.

1798 UN Doc. HRI/GEN/1/Rev.7, General Comment No. 6 (1995), *The Economic, Social and Cultural Rights of Older People*, para. 22.

1799 UN Doc. E/C.12/1993/17, para. 8 (Germany).

1800 UN Doc. E/C.12/1/Add.43, para. 23 (Italy); UN Doc. E/C.12/1/Add.35, para. 27 (Ireland).

1801 UN Doc. E/C.12/1/Add.67, para. 41 (Japan); UN Doc. E/C.12/1/Add.55, para. 47 (Morocco); UN Doc. E/C.12/1994/5, para. 23 (Morocco).

1802 UN Doc. E/C.12/1/Add.82, para. 35 (Poland); UN Doc. E/C.12/1/Add.54, para. 21 (Belgium); UN Doc. E/C.12/1/Add.16, para. 31 (Dominican Republic).

1803 Sepúlveda, supra note 108, 391; see *e.g.* UN Doc. E/C.12/1/Add.53, para. 18 (Portugal).

> of constitutional and legislative provisions on the equal right of men and women to enjoy all human rights and the prohibition of discrimination of any kind; the adoption of legislation to eliminate discrimination and to prevent third parties from interfering directly or indirectly with the enjoyment of this right; the adoption of administrative measures and programmes, as well as the establishment of public institutions, agencies and programmes to protect women against discrimination.[1804]

As the Committee has stressed in its concluding observations, harmful traditional practices for women and girls are to be eliminated.[1805] Domestic violence is to be criminalized.[1806] Boys and girls are to be protected from practices that promote child marriage, marriage by proxy, or coercion.[1807] Female genital mutilation is to be prohibited.[1808] Legislation is to be promulgated for the standardization of minimum wages.[1809] Also, discrimination against immigrants and refugees, especially in the workplace, is to be prevented.[1810] Measures are to be taken to prevent sexual harassment in the workplace.[1811]

Anti-discrimination legislation is to be effectively monitored:[1812] states are to monitor compliance by the private sector with national legislation on working conditions through an effectively functioning labour inspectorate.[1813]

The Committee has emphasized the obligation to protect in particular with regard to health, education and water. In its general comment on persons with disabilities, it held:

> In a context in which arrangements for the provision of public services are increasingly being privatized and in which the free market is being relied on to an ever greater extent, it is essential that private employers, private suppliers of goods and services, and other non-public entities be subject to both non-discrimination and equality norms in relation to persons with disabilities. [...]This is not to imply that legislative measures will always be the most effective means of seeking to eliminate discrimination within the private sphere. Thus, for example, the Standard

1804 UN Doc. E/C.12/2005/3, General Comment No. 16 (2005), *Article 3: The Equal Right of Men and Women to the Enjoyment of All Economic, Social and Cultural Rights*, para. 19.

1805 UN Doc. E/C.12/1/Add.106, para. 45 (Zambia).

1806 UN Doc. E/C.12/1/Add.102, para. 30 (Denmark).

1807 UN Doc. E/C.12/2005/3, General Comment No. 16 (2005), *Article 3: The Equal Right of Men and Women to the Enjoyment of All Economic, Social and Cultural Rights*, para. 27.

1808 *Ibid.*, para. 29.

1809 UN Doc. E/C.12/1/Add.25, para. 58 (Netherlands).

1810 UN Doc. E/C.12/1/Add.70, para. 29 (Sweden).

1811 UN Doc. E/C.12/1/Add.107, para. 17 (China).

1812 UN Doc. E/C.12/1/Add.109, para. 27 (Norway).

1813 UN Doc. E/C.12/2005/3, General Comment No. 16 (2005), *Article 3: The Equal Right of Men and Women to the Enjoyment of All Economic, Social and Cultural Rights*, para. 24.

> Rules place particular emphasis on the need for States to "take action to raise awareness in society about persons with disabilities, their rights, their needs, their potential and their contribution.[1814]

It repeated this concern, *i.e.* the obligation to ensure that not only the public health sector but also private providers of health services and facilities comply with the principle of non-discrimination in relation to persons with disabilities, in its general comment on the right to health.[1815] In the same general comment, it clarified that states have a special obligation to prevent any discrimination on internationally prohibited grounds in the provision of health care and health services, especially with respect to the core obligations of the right to health.[1816] Obligations to *protect* include, *inter alia*, the duty of states to adopt legislation or to take other measures ensuring equal access to health care and health-related services provided by third parties.[1817] A state is to ensure that women in the reproductive age are not discriminated against in the private health-care system.[1818]

A similar obligation to protect has been identified with regard to the right to education (in light of the freedom of individuals to establish schools)[1819] and water. With regard to the latter, states have a special obligation to prevent any discrimination on internationally prohibited grounds in the provision of water and water services.[1820] They are to adopt the necessary and effective legislation and other measures to restrain, for example, third parties from denying equal access to adequate water.[1821]

c. *The Obligation to Fulfil*

The obligation to fulfil can be understood in terms of sub-obligations to facilitate, to promote and to provide.[1822]

1814 UN Doc. HRI/GEN/1/Rev.7, General Comment No. 5 (1994), *Persons with Disabilities*, para. 11.

1815 UN Doc. HRI/GEN/1/Rev.7, General Comment No. 14 (2000), *The Right to the Highest Attainable Standard of Health (Art. 12)*, para. 26.

1816 *Ibid.*, para. 19.

1817 *Ibid.*, para. 35.

1818 UN Doc. E/C.12/1/Add.105, para. 57 (Chile).

1819 UN Doc. HRI/GEN/1/Rev.7, General Comment No. 13 (1999), *The Right to Education (Art. 13)*, para. 30.

1820 UN Doc. HRI/GEN/1/Rev.7, General Comment No. 15 (2002), *The Right to Water (Arts. 11 and 12 of the International Covenant on Economic, Social and Cultural Rights)*, para. 15.

1821 *Ibid.*, para. 23.

1822 See also UN Doc. E/C.12/2005/3, General Comment No. 16 (2005), *Article 3: The Equal Right of Men and Women to the Enjoyment of All Economic, Social and Cultural Rights*, para. 17.

i. To Facilitate

The obligation to facilitate requires the state to take positive measures to assist individuals to enjoy the right to non-discrimination and equality. States are encouraged to take all effective measures, both legislative and practical, to prohibit discrimination in all fields of economic, social and cultural life.[1823] All appropriate preventive and penal measures are to be taken to combat effectively all forms of racial discrimination.[1824] Similarly, all effective measures are to be taken to ensure equality between men and women in all fields of life.[1825]

Protective measures, which are of unlimited duration, may be considered to be taken in fulfilment of this obligation. The Committee has recommended protective measures in favour of pregnant women,[1826] persons with disabilities[1827] and older persons.[1828]

The right to equality may also be facilitated through the provision of judicial or other effective remedies:[1829]

> [...] some obligations, such as (but by no means limited to) those concerning non-discrimination, in relation to which the provision of some form of judicial remedy would seem indispensable in order to satisfy the requirements of the Covenant.[1830]

Specific remedies are to be made available to women victims of sexual discrimination.[1831] Institutions are to be established to provide protection and assistance to

---

1823 UN Doc. E/C.12/1/Add.104, para. 41 (Azerbaijan); UN Doc. E/C.12/1/Add.87, para. 44 (Brazil); UN Doc. E/C.12/1/Add.84, para. 18 (Solomon Islands); UN Doc. E/C.12/1/Add.62, para. 35 (Senegal); UN Doc. E/C.12/1/Add.45, para. 25 (Republic of Congo); UN Doc. E/C.12/1/Add.17, para. 29 (Iraq); UN Doc. E/C.12/1993/7, para. 8 (Iran).

1824 UN Doc. E/C.12/1/Add.2, para. 17 (Spain).

1825 UN Doc. E/C.12/1/Add.106, para. 39 (Zambia); UN Doc. E/C.12/1/Add.104, para. 42 (Azerbaijan).

1826 UN Doc. E/C.12/1/Add.30, para. 31 (Switzerland); UN Doc. E/C.12/1/Add.37, para. 30 (Bulgaria); UN Doc. E/C.12/1/Add.28, para. 19 (Cyprus).

1827 UN Doc. E/C.12/1/Add.42, paras. 12 and 25 (Georgia); UN Doc. E/C.12/1/Add.9, para. 12 (Portugal: Macau); UN E/C.12/1/Add.35, para. 27 (Ireland).

1828 UN Doc. HRI/GEN/1/Rev.7, General Comment No. 6 (1995), *The Economic, Social and Cultural Rights of Older People*, para. 10; UN Doc. E/C.12/1/Add.37, para. 26 (Bulgaria).

1829 UN Doc. E/C.12/2005/3, General Comment No. 16 (2005), *Article 3: The Equal Right of Men and Women to the Enjoyment of All Economic, Social and Cultural Rights*, para. 21; General Comment No. 5 (1994), *Persons with Disabilities*, para. 16; General Comment No. 3 (1990), *The Nature of States Parties' Obligations*, para. 5.

1830 UN Doc. HRI/GEN/1/Rev.7, General Comment No. 9 (1998), *The Domestic Application of the Covenant*, para. 9.

1831 UN Doc. E/C.12/1/Add.17, para. 30 (Iraq); UN Doc. E/C.12/1/Add.16, para. 32 (Dominican Republic).

victims of discrimination,[1832] who should receive compensation from employers who act illegally.[1833]

A state institution responsible for the promotion and protection of gender equality is to be established.[1834]

The implementation of legislation and policies is an important instrument,[1835] also in achieving gender equality.[1836] Implementation of legislation and policies has been emphasized in particular in the field of employment, including representation of women at various levels of the government, political representative bodies and public administration,[1837] labour conditions and wages,[1838] prohibition of the dismissal of pregnant women and the criminalisation of sexual harassment.[1839] Enforcement of legislation has also been stressed with regard to the minimum legal age for marriage of 18 years, inheritance laws affecting women,[1840] and access to education.[1841]

The effective enforcement of legislation and programmes to put an end to discrimination has occasionally also been recommended with regard to racism,[1842] for minority groups and low-caste people,[1843] and for people with disabilities.[1844]

Thematically, gender discrimination has received most attention from the Committee. States are to pursue policies designed to achieve full equality between men and women in all areas of economic, social and cultural life.[1845] They are to include a gender

---

1832 UN Doc. E/C.12/1995/15, para. 25 (Ukraine).

1833 UN Doc. E/C.12/1/Add.13, para. 31 (Russian Federation).

1834 UN Doc. E/C.12/1/Add.107, para. 118 (China).

1835 UN Doc. E/C.12/1/Add.99, para. 28 (Spain); UN Doc. E/C.12/1/Add.31, para. 46 (Canada).

1836 UN Doc. E/C.12/1/Add.92, para. 28 (Yemen); UN Doc. E/C.12/1995/6, para. 16 (Suriname).

1837 *Idem*; UN Doc. E/C.12/1/Add.81, para. 23 (Slovakia).

1838 UN Doc. E/C.12/1/Add.103, para. 38 (Italy); UN Doc. E/C.12/1/Add.67, paras. 42 and 44 (Japan); UN Doc. E/C.12/1/Add.66, para. 42 (Nepal); UN Doc. E/C.12/1/Add.57, para. 32 (Honduras); UN Doc. E/C.12/1/Add.53, para. 20 (Portugal); UN Doc. E/C.12/1/Add.8, para. 19 (Finland); UN Doc. E/C.12/1/Add.5, para. 14 (Guinea); UN Doc. E/C.12/1/Add.4, para. 31 (El Salvador); UN Doc. E/C.12/1/Add.2, para. 13 (Spain); UN Doc. E/C.12/1/Add.1, para. 24 (Paraguay).

1839 UN Doc. E/C.12/1/Add.47, para. 23 (Mongolia).

1840 UN Doc. E/C.12/1/Add.24, para. 24 (Sri Lanka).

1841 UN Doc. E/C.12/1/Add.2, para. 13 (Spain).

1842 UN Doc. E/C.12/1/Add.103, para. 35 (Italy).

1843 UN Doc. E/C.12/1/Add.66, para. 46 (Nepal); UN Doc. E/C.12/1/Add.24, para. 25 (Sri Lanka).

1844 UN Doc. E/C.12/1/Add.107, para. 47 (China); UN Doc. E/C.12/1/Add.27, para. 38 (Israel).

1845 UN Doc. E/C.12/1/Add.105, para. 36 (Chile); UN Doc. E/C.12/1/Add.80, para. 45 (Trinidad and Tobago); UN Doc. E/C.12/1/Add.78, para. 30 (Benin); UN Doc. E/C.12/1/Add.74, paras. 24 and 26 (Croatia); UN Doc. E/C.12/1/Add.62, para. 38 (Senegal); UN Doc. E/C.12/1/Add.60, para. 31 (Bolivia); UN Doc. E/C.12/1/Add.40, para. 32 (Cameroon); UN Doc. E/C.12/1/Add.38, para. 32 (Argentina); UN Doc. E/C.12/1/Add.19, para. 24 (United Kingdom); UN Doc. E/C.12/1/Add.18,

equality perspective in legislation, especially in relation to the right to work, family related rights and the right to education.[1846] Appropriate legislative and administrative measures are to be adopted,[1847] non-discrimination policies are to be developed and effective steps are to be taken to enforce such measures and policies.[1848] Gender mainstreaming is to be introduced into all legislation in accordance with the provisions of CESCR.[1849] Effective measures, including programmes which explicitly target parents and measures to address the economic, social and cultural factors that are the root causes of the problem,[1850] have been recommended to eliminate gender disparity in enrolment rates both at primary and secondary education levels.[1851] The necessary resources are to be allocated to enable administrative bodies which have been created to foster gender equality, to function effectively and to apply a gender perspective in legislation and in society.[1852]

Employment and labour conditions enjoy a particular attention,[1853] with recommendations to take effective measures to facilitate equality of labour conditions, representation in higher positions in political representative bodies, public services and administration,[1854] wages (equal pay for work of equal value),[1855] and the level of participation

---

para. 23 (Uruguay); UN Doc. E/C.12/1/Add.17, para. 30 (Iraq); UN Doc. E/C.12/1/Add.16, para. 32 (Dominican Republic); UN Doc. E/C.12/1/Add.12, para. 17 (Zimbabwe); UN Doc. E/C.12/1/Add.4, para. 29 (El Salvador); UN Doc. E/C.12/1/Add.1, para. 22 (Paraguay); UN Doc. E/C.12/1994/16, para. 16 (Austria).

1846 UN Doc. E/C.12/1/Add.93, para. 30 (Guatemala); UN Doc. E/C.12/1/Add.78, para. 44 (Benin); UN Doc. E/C.12/1/Add.66, para. 42 (Nepal); UN Doc. E/C.12/1/Add.57, para. 32 (Honduras); UN Doc. E/C.12/1993/7, para. 8 (Iran).

1847 UN Doc. E/C.12/1/Add.45, para. 26 (Republic of Congo).

1848 UN Doc. E/C.12/1/Add.61, para. 20 (Togo).

1849 UN Doc. E/C.12/1/Add.71, para. 29 (Algeria).

1850 UN Doc. E/C.12/1/Add.44, para. 40 (Egypt).

1851 UN Doc. E/C.12/1/Add.84, para. 29 (Solomon Islands).

1852 UN Doc. E/C.12/1/Add.101, para. 29 (Malta); UN Doc. E/C.12/1/Add.59, para. 37 (Republic of Korea).

1853 UN Doc. E/C.12/1/Add.91, para. 37 (Moldova); UN Doc. E/C.12/1/Add.62, para. 40 (Senegal); UN Doc. E/C.12/1/Add.39, para. 19 (Armenia); UN Doc. E/C.12/1/Add.7/Rev.1, para. 23 (Belarus); UN Doc. E/C.12/1995/13, para. 24 (Norway).

1854 UN Doc. E/C.12/1/Add.97, para. 34 (Greece); UN Doc. E/C.12/1/Add.67, para. 42 (Japan).

1855 UN Doc. E/C.12/1/Add.109, para. 30 (Norway); UN Doc. E/C.12/1/Add.107, para. 48 (China); UN Doc. E/C.12/1/Add.105, para. 37 (Chile); UN Doc. E/C.12/1/Add.102, para. 25 (Denmark); UN Doc. E/C.12/1/Add.101, para. 32 (Malta); UN Doc. E/C.12/1/Add.100, para. 38 (Ecuador); UN Doc. E/C.12/1/Add.93, para. 30 (Guatemala); UN Doc. E/C.12/1/Add.92, para. 31 (Yemen); UN Doc. E/C.12/1/Add.91, para. 37 (Moldova); UN Doc. E/C.12/1/Add.89, para. 21 (Iceland); UN Doc. E/C.12/1/Add.88, para. 27 (New Zealand); UN Doc. E/C.12/1/Add.87, para. 45 (Brazil); UN Doc. E/C.12/1/Add.86, para. 34 (Luxemburg); UN Doc. E/C.12/1/Add.81, para. 26 (Slovakia); UN Doc. E/C.12/1/Add.80, para. 40 (Trinidad and Tobago); UN Doc. E/C.12/1/Add.75, para. 37 (Colombia); UN Doc. E/C.12/1/Add.58, para. 35 (China: Hong Kong); UN Doc. E/C.12/1/Add.54, para. 23 (Belgium); UN Doc. E/C.12/1/Add.34, para. 25 (Denmark); UN Doc. E/C.12/1/Add.31, para. 53 (Canada); UN Doc. E/C.12/1/Add.28, para. 19 (Cyprus); UN Doc. E/C.12/1/Add.24, para. 25 (Sri Lanka); UN Doc. E/C.12/1995/4, para. 12 (Portugal).

in the labour market[1856] and in decision-making.[1857] Women are to be encouraged to choose occupations and professions which are traditionally held by men and are better remunerated.[1858] Article 3 read together with article 7 CESCR (the right to enjoy just and favourable conditions of work) requires states to take adequate policies for childcare and care of dependent family members.[1859] Article 3 in combination with article 9 CESCR requires guaranteeing adequate maternity leave for women, paternity leave for men, and parental leave for both men and women.[1860]

With regard to discrimination based on nationality too, effective measures are to be taken, *e.g.* with regard to inequality between Jewish and non-Jewish sectors,[1861] non national workers[1862] and persons with immigrant background.[1863] Effective measures are equally to be taken to ensure equal opportunities to indigenous peoples,[1864] (ethnic)[1865] minorities,[1866] including Roma,[1867] in many fields, especially with regard to employment, housing, health and education. More effective steps are recommended to combat *de facto* discrimination based on religion.[1868]

1856 UN Doc. E/C.12/1/Add.109, para. 30 (Norway); UN Doc. E/C.12/1/Add.101, para. 32 (Malta); UN Doc. E/C.12/1/Add.86, para. 34 (Luxemburg); UN Doc. E/C.12/1/Add.76, para. 35 (Czech Republic); UN Doc. E/C.12/1/Add.70, para. 30 (Sweden); UN Doc. E/C.12/1/Add.68, para. 37 (Germany); UN Doc. E/C.12/1/Add.30, para. 32 (Switzerland); UN Doc. E/C.12/1/Add.25, paras. 22, 39 and 56 (Netherlands).

1857 UN Doc. E/C.12/1/Add.102, para. 25 (Denmark).

1858 UN Doc. E/C.12/1/Add.109, para. 30 (Norway).

1859 UN Doc. E/C.12/2005/3, General Comment No. 16 (2005), *Article 3: The Equal Right of Men and Women to the Enjoyment of All Economic, Social and Cultural Rights*, para. 24. Compare with *e.g.* UN Doc. E/C.12/1/Add.109, para. 33 (Norway); UN Doc. E/C.12/1/Add.103, para. 44 (Italy); UN Doc. E/C.12/1/Add.101, para. 33 (Malta).

1860 UN Doc. E/C.12/2005/3, General Comment No. 16 (2005), *Article 3: The Equal Right of Men and Women to the Enjoyment of All Economic, Social and Cultural Rights*, para. 26.

1861 UN Doc. E/C.12/1/Add.90, para. 37 (Israel); UN Doc. E/C.12/1/Add.27, para. 34 (Israel).

1862 UN Doc. E/C.12/1/Add.16, para. 34 (Dominican Republic); UN Doc. E/C.12/1995/3, para. 19 (Republic of Korea).

1863 UN Doc. E/C.12/1/Add.109, para. 27 (Norway).

1864 UN Doc. E/C.12/1/Add.100, para. 34 (Ecuador); UN Doc. E/C.12/1/Add.93, para. 29 (Guatemala); UN Doc. E/C.12/1/Add.60, para. 30 (Bolivia); UN Doc. E/C.12/1/Add.14, para. 30 (Peru); UN Doc. E/C.12/1/Add.1, para. 21 (Paraguay).

1865 UN Doc. E/C.12/1/Add.100, para. 36 (Ecuador); UN Doc. E/C.12/1/Add.87, para. 44 (Brazil); UN Doc. E/C.12/1/Add.74, paras. 21 and 36 (Croatia); UN Doc. E/C.12/1/Add.30, para. 33 (Switzerland); UN Doc. E/C.12/1/Add.25, para. 22 (Netherlands); UN Doc. E/C.12/1/Add.19, para. 24 (United Kingdom).

1866 UN Doc. E/C.12/1/Add.79, para. 31 (United Kingdom); UN Doc. E/C.12/1/Add.74, para. 20 (Croatia); UN Doc. E/C.12/1/Add.67, para. 40 (Japan); UN Doc. E/C.12/1/Add.63, para. 30 (Syrian Arab Republic).

1867 UN Doc. E/C.12/1/Add.103, para. 46 (Italy); UN Doc. E/C.12/1/Add.82, para. 36 (Poland); UN Doc. E/C.12/1/Add.81, para. 22 (Slovakia); UN Doc. E/C.12/1994/4, para. 15 (Romania).

1868 UN Doc. E/C.12/1/Add.19, para. 24 (United Kingdom).

Plans are to be established, including a study of specific actions to be taken, to ensure equal access to education by all sectors of society.[1869]

Particular situations in which positive, facilitating measures are required include the occurrence of evictions[1870] and the imposition of economic sanctions.[1871] Equal access for all to the underlying determinants of health, such as nutritiously safe food and potable drinking water, basic sanitation and adequate housing and living conditions is to be ensured.[1872] Similarly, a national strategy should give particular attention to the need to prevent discrimination in access to food or resources for food. According to the Committee, this would include:

> guarantees of full and equal access to economic resources, particularly for women, including the right to inheritance and the ownership of land and other property, credit, natural resources and appropriate technology; measures to respect and protect self-employment and work which provides a remuneration ensuring a decent living for wage earners and their families (as stipulated in article 7 (a) (ii) of the Covenant); maintaining registries on rights in land (including forests).[1873]

Equal access to international food aid is to be ensured for more vulnerable groups. They should also enjoy priority in food programmes.[1874]

ii. To Promote

The obligation to promote concerns education and awareness-raising. Awareness about international anti-discrimination standards is to be increased among judges and other members of the legal profession.[1875] The creation of a culture of tolerance has been recommended with regard to women, ethnic groups, asylum seekers and immigrants.[1876]

1869 UN Doc. E/C.12/1/Add.59, para. 42 (Republic of Korea).

1870 UN Doc. HRI/GEN/1/Rev.7, General Comment No. 7 (1997), *The Right to Adequate Housing (Art. 11(1) of the Covenant: Forced Evictions*, para. 10.

1871 UN Doc. HRI/GEN/1/Rev.7, General Comment No. 8 (1997), *The Relationship between Economic Sanctions and Respect for Economic, Social and Cultural Rights*, para. 10.

1872 UN Doc. HRI/GEN/1/Rev.7, General Comment No. 14 (2000), *The Right to the Highest Attainable Standard of Health (Art. 12)*, para. 36.

1873 UN Doc. HRI/GEN/1/Rev.7, General Comment No. 12 (1999), *The Right to Adequate Food (Art. 11)*, para. 26.

1874 *Ibid.*, para. 38.

1875 UN Doc. E/C.12/1/Add.108, para. 39 (Serbia and Montenegro).

1876 UN Doc. E/C.12/1/Add.53, para. 18 (Portugal).

In order to attain gender equality,[1877] including equal remuneration for work of equal value,[1878] states have been recommended to carry out large-scale public campaigns to promote understanding among the general public about human rights of women,[1879] to develop awareness of the problem of discrimination[1880] and about gender equality,[1881] to prevent and combat discriminatory treatment and negative societal attitudes, particularly within the family,[1882] and to eliminate gender-based prejudices and traditional practices that are harmful to women and girls.[1883] Resources are to be allocated to carry out a range of activities in the fields, *inter alia*, of juvenile and adult education.[1884]

Inter-ethnic dialogue and tolerance among different ethnic groups,[1885] and information and education campaigns are to be organized,[1886] in order to raise awareness of the dimensions of discrimination,[1887] to promote intercultural understanding and tolerance,[1888] and to eliminate discrimination against Roma.[1889] Awareness-raising campaigns and educational programmes have also been recommended, to prevent and combat discrimination with regard to marginalized and vulnerable groups in society,[1890] HIV-positive people[1891] and persons with a mental illness.[1892]

1877 UN Doc. E/C.12/1/Add.94, para. 42 (Russian Federation); UN Doc. E/C.12/1/Add.91, para. 35 (Moldova); UN Doc. E/C.12/1/Add.71, para. 29 (Algeria); UN Doc. E/C.12/1/Add.17, para. 30 (Iraq); UN Doc. E/C.12/1/Add.16, para. 32 (Dominican Republic).

1878 UN Doc. E/C.12/1/Add.85, para. 37 (Estonia).

1879 UN Doc. E/C.12/1/Add.59, para. 43 (Republic of Korea); UN Doc. E/C.12/1995/15, para. 25 (Ukraine).

1880 UN Doc. E/C.12/1/Add.30, para. 31 (Switzerland); UN Doc. E/C.12/1995/6, para. 16 (Suriname).

1881 UN Doc. E/C.12/1/Add.107, para. 118 (China); UN Doc. E/C.12/1/Add.101, para. 29 (Malta).

1882 UN Doc. E/C.12/1/Add.46, para. 30 (Jordan); UN Doc. E/C.12/1/Add.28, para. 19 (Cyprus); UN Doc. E/C.12/1994/5, para. 18 (Morocco).

1883 UN Doc. E/C.12/1/Add.107, para. 45 (China).

1884 UN Doc. E/C.12/1995/3, para. 18 (Republic of Korea).

1885 UN Doc. E/C.12/1/Add.91, para. 34 (Moldova).

1886 UN Doc. E/C.12/1/Add.16, para. 31 (Dominican Republic).

1887 UN Doc. E/C.12/1/Add.97, para. 32 (Greece).

1888 UN Doc. E/C.12/1/Add.108, para. 64 (Serbia and Montenegro); UN Doc. E/C.12/1/Add.102, para. 24 (Denmark).

1889 UN Doc. E/C.12/1/Add.76, para. 29 (Czech Republic).

1890 UN Doc. E/C.12/1/Add.92, para. 27 (Yemen).

1891 UN Doc. E/C.12/1/Add.94, para. 62 (Russian Federation).

1892 UN Doc. E/C.12/1/Add.58, para. 45 (China: Hong Kong).

Fields in which the obligation to promote assumes particular importance concern *inter alia* equal access to social benefits and social services,[1893] and equal opportunity for all in education, including in vocational education.[1894]

iii. To Provide

The obligation to provide has been said to be applicable "when individuals or groups are unable, for reasons beyond their control, to realize the right themselves by the means at their disposal" (see above).

In this book, affirmative action is considered to be a measure that corresponds to this obligation to fulfil-provide. No definition for affirmative action is given under the CESCR or by the CESCR Committee,[1895] though it has been argued that affirmative action is implicitly referred to in the CESCR.[1896] The Committee has asserted the need for affirmative action on a few occasions, most recently in its 2005 general comment on gender equality. In its view:

> [t]emporary special measures may sometimes be needed in order to bring disadvantaged or marginalized persons or groups of persons to the same substantive level as others. [...] [T]he application of the principle of equality will sometimes require that States parties take measures in favour of women in order to attenuate or suppress conditions that perpetuate discrimination.[1897]

Affirmative action does not contravene the principle of equality if used only to the extent necessary to achieve the objective of equality by redressing *de facto* discrimination:

> The obligation in the case of such a vulnerable and disadvantaged group is to take positive action to reduce structural disadvantages and to give appropriate preferential treatment to people with disabilities in order to achieve the objectives of full participation and equality within society for all persons with disabilities.[1898]
>
> Because appropriate measures need to be taken to undo existing discrimination and to establish equitable opportunities for persons with disabilities, such actions should not be considered

[1893] UN Doc. E/C.12/1/Add.96, para. 40 (Lithuania).
[1894] UN Doc. E/C.12/2005/3, General Comment No. 16 (2005), *Article 3: The Equal Right of Men and Women to the Enjoyment of All Economic, Social and Cultural Rights*, para. 30; UN Doc. E/C.12/1/Add.64, para. 40 (Panama).
[1895] Sepúlveda, supra note 108, 386.
[1896] Craven, supra note 1019, 186; Bayefski, supra note 3, 29.
[1897] UN Doc. E/C.12/2005/3, General Comment No. 16 (2005), *Article 3: The Equal Right of Men and Women to the Enjoyment of All Economic, Social and Cultural Rights*, paras. 15 and 35.
[1898] UN Doc. HRI/GEN/1/Rev.7, General Comment No. 5 (1994), *Persons with Disabilities*, para. 9.

> discriminatory in the sense of article 2 (2) of the International Covenant on Economic, Social and Cultural Rights as long as they are based on the principle of equality and are employed only to the extent necessary to achieve that objective.[1899]

> As long as these measures are necessary to redress *de facto* discrimination [...], such differentiation is legitimate.[1900]

Furthermore, and fully in line with the case-law of other Committees, the CESCR Committee has held that affirmative action should not lead to the maintenance of unequal or separate standards for different groups, and should not be continued after the objectives for which they were taken, have been achieved:

> The adoption of temporary special measures intended to bring about de facto equality for men and women and for disadvantaged groups is not a violation of the right to non-discrimination with regard to education, so long as such measures do not lead to the maintenance of unequal or separate standards for different groups, and provided they are not continued after the objectives for which they were taken have been achieved.[1901]

> As long as these measures [...] are terminated when *de facto* equality is achieved, such differentiation is legitimate.[1902]

In its general comment on gender equality, the Committee acknowledges one exception to the principle that temporary special measures in favour of women are legitimate, in light of the principle of proportionality, *i.e.* when reasons specific to an individual male candidate tilt the balance in his favour. Whether that is the case is to be assessed objectively, "taking into account all criteria to the individual candidates."[1903]

Reference has been made to special programmes[1904] and a fellowship system for individuals belonging to disadvantaged groups.[1905]

1899 *Ibid.*, para. 18.

1900 UN Doc. E/C.12/2005/3, General Comment No. 16 (2005), *Article 3: The Equal Right of Men and Women to the Enjoyment of All Economic, Social and Cultural Rights*, para. 15.

1901 UN Doc. HRI/GEN/1/Rev.7, General Comment No. 13 (1999), *The Right to Education (Art. 13)*, para. 32.

1902 UN Doc. E/C.12/2005/3, General Comment No. 16 (2005), *Article 3: The Equal Right of Men and Women to the Enjoyment of All Economic, Social and Cultural Rights*, para. 15.

1903 *Ibid.*, para. 15, footnote 9.

1904 UN Doc. HRI/GEN/1/Rev.7, General Comment No. 13 (1999), *The Right to Education (Art. 13)*, para. 16, (e); General Comment No. 12 (1999), *The Right to Adequate Food (Art. 11)*, para. 13.

1905 UN Doc. HRI/GEN/1/Rev.7, General Comment No. 13 (1999), *The Right to Education (Art. 13)*, para. 26.

Sepúlveda noticed in 2003 that the Committee did not make any distinction between protective action, which is of unlimited duration, and affirmative action, which is supposed to be temporary in character. It has done so however in its 2005 general comment on gender equality, in which it submitted that "[t]emporary special measures should be distinguished from permanent policies and strategies undertaken towards equality of men and women."[1906] Nor has the Committee been precise on the type of affirmative action required, *i.e.* specific benefits, a quota system or other measures.[1907] It can therefore be concluded that the kind of measures is left to the discretion of the state.[1908] This was confirmed by the Committee itself, which accepted that the nature, duration and application of affirmative action measures is to be designed with reference to the specific issue and context, and to be adjusted as circumstances require.[1909]

Affirmative action has been favoured with regard to persons with disabilities,[1910] women,[1911] indigenous people,[1912] (ethnic) minorities[1913] and disadvantaged groups.[1914] With regard to women, affirmative action was recommended to improve working conditions for women and to ensure equal pay for work of equal value,[1915] to ensure the participation of women in decision-making,[1916] and to guarantee ideological pluralism in education and equality of opportunities of men and women in that field.[1917] Affirmative action should also be of help to reverse the devastating effects of discrimination against the indigenous populations.[1918]

1906 UN Doc. E/C.12/2005/3, General Comment No. 16 (2005), *Article 3: The Equal Right of Men and Women to the Enjoyment of All Economic, Social and Cultural Rights*, para. 35.

1907 Sepúlveda, supra note 108, 387-388. Quota were favoured *e.g.* in UN Doc. E/C.12/1/Add.27, para. 15 (Israel).

1908 *Ibid.*, 404.

1909 UN Doc. E/C.12/2005/3, General Comment No. 16 (2005), *Article 3: The Equal Right of Men and Women to the Enjoyment of All Economic, Social and Cultural Rights*, para. 36.

1910 UN Doc. HRI/GEN/1/Rev.7, General Comment No. 5 (1994), *Persons with Disabilities*, paras. 9 and 18; UN Doc. E/C.12/1/Add.107, para. 121 (China); UN Doc. E/C.12/1/Add.27, para. 15 (Israel).

1911 UN Doc. E/C.12/2005/3, General Comment No. 16 (2005), *Article 3: The Equal Right of Men and Women to the Enjoyment of All Economic, Social and Cultural Rights*, para. 15; General Comment No. 13 (1999), *The Right to Education (Art. 13)*, para. 32; UN Doc. E/C.12/1/Add.107, para. 17 (China); UN Doc. E/C.12/1/Add.94, para. 48 (Russian Federation); UN Doc. E/C.12/1993/17, para. 10 (Germany); UN Doc. E/C.12/1/Add.1, para. 24 (Paraguay).

1912 UN Doc. E/C.12/1/Add.3, para. 27 (Guatemala).

1913 UN Doc. E/C.12/1/Add.9, para. 19 (Portugal: Macau).

1914 UN Doc. HRI/GEN/1/Rev.7, General Comment No. 13 (1999), *The Right to Education (Art. 13)*, para. 32.

1915 UN Doc. E/C.12/1/Add.102, para. 25 (Denmark); UN Doc. E/C.12/1/Add.94, para. 48 (Russian Federation); UN Doc. E/C.12/1/Add.1, para. 24 (Paraguay).

1916 UN Doc. E/C.12/1/Add.102, para. 25 (Denmark).

1917 UN Doc. E/C.12/1993/17, para. 10 (Germany).

1918 UN Doc. E/C.12/1/Add.3, para. 27 (Guatemala).

All in all, the Committee does not seem to have developed as yet, a clear policy under which circumstances and in favour of which groups it recommends affirmative action.

The obligation to provide has been emphasized sometimes outside the context of affirmative action. With respect to equality of access to health care and health services, states have been said to have a special obligation to provide those who do not have sufficient means with the necessary health insurance and health-care facilities.[1919] With regard to domestic violence against women, which is considered to be a form of gender-based discrimination, states are under the obligation to provide victims with access to safe housing, remedies and redress of physical, mental and emotional damage (see also under the obligation to protect).[1920]

d. Conclusions

The CESCR Committee, like other Committees, deems anti-discrimination legislation indispensable for the fulfilment of all types of obligations. It has emphasized most the obligation to respect equality with regard to women, non nationals and children born out of wedlock. The obligation to protect against private discrimination has been elaborated most explicitly in the fields of education, health and water. The main instruments may be legislation and monitoring thereof. In order to fulfil-facilitate equality, implementation of legislation is very important. Affirmative action has acquired growing attention, but the Committee does not seem to have developed as yet a clear policy when and in favour of whom to recommend it.

4. CEDAW COMMITTEE

As was pointed out before, the incorporation of the principle of equality (here of women and men) in domestic legislation may serve to fulfil several obligations. As no specification has usually been made by the CEDAW Committee itself, this recommendation is treated here by way of introduction.

1919 UN Doc. HRI/GEN/1/Rev.7, General Comment No. 14 (2000), *The Right to the Highest Attainable Standard of Health (Art. 12)*, para. 19.

1920 UN Doc. E/C.12/2005/3, General Comment No. 16 (2005), *Article 3: The Equal Right of Men and Women to the Enjoyment of All Economic, Social and Cultural Rights*, para. 27. Compare with *e.g.* UN Doc. E/C.12/1/Add.109, para. 34 (Norway); UN Doc. E/C.12/1/Add.108, para. 50 (Serbia and Montenegro); UN Doc. E/C.12/1/Add.107, para. 57 and 122 (China); UN Doc. E/C.12/1/Add.104, para. 49 (Azerbaijan); UN Doc. E/C.12/1/Add.102, para. 31 (Denmark).

The principle of equality of women and men is to be incorporated in the constitution and legislation,[1921] in order to progress towards *de jure* equality, as an essential prerequisite for achieving *de facto* equality of women.[1922] CEDAW is to be fully integrated into domestic law,[1923] and to be enforceable in courts.[1924] The definition of discrimination contained in article 1 of the Convention, *i.e.* discrimination that has the effect or purpose of adversely affecting women's human rights[1925] ("direct and indirect discrimination"),[1926] is to be fully reflected in national legislation.[1927] States are also to ensure that CEDAW is directly applicable within the national legal order.[1928]

1921 UN Doc. CEDAW/C/GAB/CC/2-5, para. 19 (Gabon); UN Doc. CEDAW/C/DZA/CC/2, para. 22 (Algeria); UN Doc. A/58/38 (part II), para. 99 (Brazil); UN Doc. A/58/38 (part I), para. 303 (Luxembourg); UN Doc. A/58/38 (part I), para. 109 (Switzerland); UN Doc. A/57/38 (part III), para. 314 (Hungary); UN Doc. A/57/38 (part III), para. 226 (Barbados); UN Doc. A/57/38 (part II), para. 146 (Belgium); UN Doc. A/57/38 (part I), paras. 374 and 376 (Russian Federation); UN Doc. A/56/38 (part I), para. 133 (Maldives); UN Doc. A/55/38 (part II), para. 92 (Moldova); UN Doc. A/55/38 (part I), para. 169 (Jordan); UN Doc. A/54/38/Rev.1 (part II), para. 95 (Georgia); UN Doc. A/54/38/Rev.1 (part I), para. 284 (China); UN Doc. A/54/38/Rev.1 (part I), para. 232 (Thailand); UN Doc. A/54/38/Rev.1 (part I), para. 114 (Kyrgyzstan); UN Doc. A/52/38/Rev.1 (part II), para. 214 (Luxembourg); UN Doc. A/52/38/Rev.1, para. 69 (Morocco).

1922 UN Doc. A/58/38 (part I), para. 250 (El Salvador).

1923 UN Doc. A/58/38 (part II), para. 406 (New Zealand); UN Doc. A/58/38 (part II), para. 161 (Morocco); UN Doc. A/58/38 (part I), para. 206 (Kenya); UN Doc. A/57/38 (part II), para. 320 (Denmark); UN Doc. A/57/38 (part II), para. 231 (Zambia); UN Doc. A/57/38 (part II), para. 40 (Suriname); UN Doc. A/55/38 (part II), para. 94 (Moldova); UN Doc. A/54/38/Rev.1 (part II), paras. 301 (United Kingdom and Northern Ireland); UN Doc. A/53/38/Rev.1 (part I), para. 69 (Azerbaijan); UN Doc. A/52/38/Rev.1, para. 69 (Morocco).

1924 UN Doc. CEDAW/C/PAR/CC/3-5, para. 21 (Paraguay); UN Doc. CEDAW/C/WSM/CC/1-3, para. 21 (Samoa); UN Doc. CEDAW/C/LAO/CC/1-5, para. 18 (Laos); UN Doc. A/51/38, para. 88 (Iceland).

1925 UN Doc. UN Doc. A/58/38 (part I), para. 159 (Congo); UN Doc. A/58/38 (part I), para. 109 (Switzerland); UN Doc. A/57/38 (part III), para. 385 (Yemen); UN Doc. A/57/38 (part III), para. 314 (Hungary); UN Doc. A/57/38 (part III), para. 226 (Barbados); UN Doc. A/57/38 (part II), para. 193 (Tunisia); A/55/38 (part II), paras. 182-183 (Iraq).

1926 UN Doc. A/58/38 (part II), para. 358 (Japan); UN Doc. A/56/38 (part II), para. 163 (Guyana); UN Doc. A/54/38/Rev.1 (part I), para. 316 (China-Hong Kong); UN Doc. A/54/38/Rev.1 (part I), para. 284 (China); UN Doc. A/52/38/Rev.1 (part II), para. 172 (Israel).

1927 UN Doc. CEDAW/C/TUR/CC/4-5, para. 21 (Turkey); UN Doc. CEDAW/C/PAR/CC/3-5, para. 21 (Paraguay); UN Doc. CEDAW/C/ITA/CC/4-5, para. 20 (Italy); UN Doc. CEDAW/C/GAB/CC/2-5, para. 19 (Gabon); UN Doc. CEDAW/C/DZA/CC/2, para. 22 (Algeria); UN Doc. CEDAW/C/WSM/CC/1-3, para. 21 (Samoa); UN Doc. CEDAW/C/LAO/CC/1-5, para. 18 (Laos); UN Doc. A/58/38 (part II), para. 161 (Morocco); UN Doc. A/57/38 (part I), paras. 374 and 376 (Russian Federation); UN Doc. A/57/38 (part I), para. 236 (Iceland); UN Doc. A/57/38 (part I), para. 187 (Uruguay); UN Doc. A/57/38 (part I), para. 140 (Trinidad and Tobago); UN Doc. A/57/38 (part I), para. 88 (Estonia); UN Doc. A/57/38 (part I), para. 47 (Fiji); UN Doc. A/56/38 (part II), para. 119 (Guinea); UN Doc. A/56/38 (part I), para. 254 (Mongolia); UN Doc. A/56/38 (part I), para. 167 (Uzbekistan); UN Doc. A/56/38 (part I), para. 88 (Kazakhstan); UN Doc. A/55/38 (part II), para. 92 (Moldova); UN Doc. A/55/38 (part I), para. 360 (Belarus); UN Doc. A/55/38 (part I), para. 169 (Jordan); UN Doc. A/54/38/Rev.1 (part II), para. 139 (Nepal); UN Doc. A/54/38/Rev.1 (part II), para. 51 (Belize); UN Doc. A/53/38/Rev.1 (part II), para. 227 (Tanzania); UN Doc. A/53/38/Rev.1 (part II), para. 116 (South Africa); UN Doc. A/53/38/Rev.1 (part I), para. 250 (Bulgaria); UN Doc. A/53/38/Rev.1 (part I), para. 199 (Czech Republic); UN Doc. A/53/38/Rev.1 (part I), para. 69 (Azerbaijan).

1928 UN Doc. A/58/38 (part I), para. 410 (Norway); UN Doc. A/58/38 (part I), para. 59 (Albania).

a. *The Obligation to Respect*

The obligation to respect is reflected in a number of provisions of CEDAW. In accordance with article 2 (d), states are to refrain from engaging in any act or practice of discrimination against women and to ensure that public authorities and institutions shall act in conformity with this obligation. They also commit themselves to modifying or abolishing existing laws and regulations, and to repeal penal provisions, which constitute discrimination against women (art. 2 (f) and (g) CEDAW).

In order to respect the principle of non-discrimination, states are to refrain from discriminatory law and practices. Their constitutions and legislation should comply with the principles of CEDAW.[1929] States are to review all existing laws and amend discriminatory provisions in consultation with women's groups,[1930] so that they are compatible with CEDAW.[1931] States have been urged to establish a concrete programme and timetable for a legal reform process and to activate fully the body established for the purpose of reviewing the discriminatory aspects of the various codes.[1932] Amendments may be necessary for example, in the Civil Code,[1933]

1929 UN Doc. HRI/GEN/1/Rev.7, General Recommendation No. 23 (1997), *Political and Public Life*, paras. 41 and 47 (a).

1930 UN Doc. A/57/38 (part II), para. 191 (Tunisia).

1931 UN Doc. CEDAW/C/TUR/CC/4-5, para. 26 (Turkey); UN Doc. A/58/38 (part II), para. 302 (Ecuador); UN Doc. A/58/38 (part I), para. 161 (Congo); UN Doc. A/58/38 (part I), para. 61 (Albania); UN Doc. A/57/38 (part III), para. 130 (Uganda); UN Doc. A/57/38 (part II), paras. 231, 235 and 251 (Zambia); UN Doc. A/57/38 (part II), para. 42 (Suriname); UN Doc. A/57/38 (part I), para. 275 (Sri Lanka); UN Doc. A/57/38 (part I), para. 142 (Trinidad and Tobago); UN Doc. A/56/38 (part I), para. 256 (Mongolia); UN Doc. A/56/38 (part I), para. 212 (Jamaica); UN Doc. A/55/38 (part II), para. 181 (Iraq); UN Doc. A/55/38 (part II), para. 46 (Cameroon); UN Doc. A/55/38 (part I), para. 401 (Luxembourg); UN Doc. A/55/38 (part I), para. 167 and 171 (Jordan); UN Doc. A/54/38/Rev.1 (part I), para. 333 (China-Hong Kong); UN Doc. A/54/38/Rev.1 (part I), para. 74 (Algeria); UN Doc. A/53/38/Rev.1 (part II), para. 193 (Panama); UN Doc. A/53/38/Rev.1 (part II), para. 118 (South Africa); UN Doc. A/53/38/Rev.1 (part I), para. 200 (Czech Republic); UN Doc. A/52/38/Rev.1, para. 142 (Saint Vincent and the Grenadines); UN Doc. A/52/38/Rev.1 (part II), para. 357 (Italy); UN Doc. A/52/38/Rev.1 (part I), para. 71 (Morocco); UN Doc. A/50/38, para. 104 (Bolivia); UN Doc. A/49/38, para. 541 (Ecuador); UN Doc. A/49/38, para. 184 (Guyana).

1932 UN Doc. CEDAW/C/GAB/CC/2-5, para. 23 (Gabon); UN Doc. CEDAW/C/WSM/CC/1-3, para. 23 (Samoa).

1933 UN Doc. CEDAW/C/GAB/CC/2-5, para. 23 (Gabon); UN Doc. CEDAW/C/DZA/CC/2, paras. 24 and 26 (Algeria); N Doc. A/56/38 (part II), para. 74 (Singapore); UN Doc. A/56/38 (part II), para. 119 (Guinea); UN Doc. A/53/38/Rev.1 (part I), para. 352 (Dominican Republic); UN Doc. A/49/38, para. 79 (Guatemala); UN Doc. A/52/38/Rev.1, para. 191 (Turkey); UN Doc. A/52/38/Rev.1, para. 174 (Turkey).

Criminal Code,[1934] nationality law,[1935] labour law,[1936] property law[1937] and immigration law.[1938]

Many discriminatory provisions in civil law pertain to marriage[1939] and family law:[1940] on polygamy,[1941] on the choice of surnames for married couples,[1942] on domicile rights of spouses,[1943] on legal guardianship and the age for guardianship,[1944] on property rights during marriage and equal rights to property on divorce,[1945] on adultery,[1946] divorce,[1947] remarriage after divorce[1948] and *de facto* relationships.[1949] Special attention has been paid to an equal minimum age for marriage.[1950] Discrimination in law against women with regard to inheritance and succession is to be abstained from.[1951] Laws which prevent women from concluding contracts in their own names, from travelling alone

1934 UN Doc. CEDAW/C/GAB/CC/2-5, para. 23 (Gabon); UN Doc. A/49/38, para. 79 (Guatemala); UN Doc. A/52/38/Rev.1, para. 174 (Turkey).

1935 UN Doc. CEDAW/C/DZA/CC/2, para. 26 (Algeria); UN Doc. A/53/38/Rev.1 (part I), para. 352 (Dominican Republic); UN Doc. A/52/38/Rev.1, para. 174 (Turkey).

1936 UN Doc. A/53/38/Rev.1 (part I), para. 352 (Dominican Republic).

1937 UN Doc. A/58/38 (part I), para. 179 (Congo); UN Doc. A/53/38/Rev.1 (part II), para. 236 (Tanzania); UN Doc. A/52/38/Rev.1 (part II), para. 405 (Australia); UN Doc. A/52/38/Rev.1 (part II), para. 123 (Namibia).

1938 UN Doc. A/57/38 (part II), paras. 342 and 346 (Denmark).

1939 UN Doc. CEDAW/C/WSM/CC/1-3, para. 35 (Samoa); UN Doc. A/57/38 (part II), para. 68 (Suriname); UN Doc. A/54/38/Rev.1 (part II), para. 139 (Nepal).

1940 UN Doc. A/58/38 (part I), para. 183 (Congo); UN Doc. A/57/38 (part III), para. 393 (Yemen); UN Doc. A/57/38 (part I), para. 205 (Uruguay); UN Doc. A/57/38 (part I), para. 67 (Fiji); UN Doc. A/56/38 (part II), para. 313 (Nicaragua); UN Doc. A/54/38/Rev.1 (part I), para. 92 (Algeria); UN Doc. A/50/38, para. 154-155 (Chile).

1941 UN Doc. A/55/38 (part I), para. 175 (Jordan).

1942 UN Doc. A/58/38 (part II), paras. 371-372 (Japan).

1943 UN Doc. A/58/38 (part I), para. 137 (Switzerland).

1944 UN Doc. A/58/38 (part II), para. 163 (Morocco).

1945 UN Doc. A/54/38/Rev.1 (part II), para. 222 (Chile).

1946 UN Doc. A/49/38, para. 240 (Madagascar).

1947 UN Doc. A/58/38 (part II), para. 163 (Morocco); UN Doc. A/56/38 (part I), para. 329 (Egypt); UN Doc. A/50/38, para. 154-155 (Chile).

1948 UN Doc. A/58/38 (part II), paras. 371-372 (Japan); UN Doc. A/58/38 (part I), para. 319 (Luxembourg); UN Doc. A/56/38 (part II), para. 47 (Andorra); UN Doc. A/54/38/Rev.1 (part II), para. 222 (Chile).

1949 UN Doc. A/53/38/Rev.1 (part II), para. 278 (New Zealand).

1950 UN Doc. A/58/38 (part II), paras. 371-372 (Japan); UN Doc. A/58/38 (part I), para. 61 (Albania); UN Doc. A/57/38 (part III), para. 450 (Mexico); UN Doc. A/57/38 (part III), para. 197 (Guatemala); UN Doc. A/57/38 (part III), para. 334 (Hungary); UN Doc. A/57/38 (part III), para. 395 (Yemen); UN Doc. A/57/38 (part III), para. 489 (Peru); UN Doc. A/58/38 (part II), para. 268 (France); UN Doc. A/57/38 (part I), para. 205 (Uruguay); UN Doc. A/57/38 (part I), para. 158 (Trinidad and Tobago); UN Doc. A/56/38 (part I), para. 56 (Burundi); Doc. A/55/38 (part II), para. 114 (Moldova); UN Doc. A/55/38 (part II), para. 319 (Romania).

1951 UN Doc. A/55/38 (part I), para. 83 (India); UN Doc. A/53/38/Rev.1 (part II), para. 236 (Tanzania); UN Doc. A/50/38, para. 341 (Uganda); UN Doc. A/49/38, para. 240 (Madagascar).

and from choosing their place of residence should be revoked.[1952] Legislation on names is to be reviewed.[1953] Laws restricting family planning activities, thereby limiting women's access to family planning,[1954] are to be repealed.[1955]

Discriminatory laws on nationality are to be amended,[1956] so that mothers can transmit their nationality to their children in the same way that fathers can,[1957] and female and male spouses who marry foreigners be treated equally.[1958]

Women are to be ensured the full protection of penal law on equal terms with men.[1959] Discriminatory provisions with regard to adultery,[1960] provisions excusing a man or other male relative who kills or injures his wife or his female kin caught in the act of adultery,[1961] provisions penalizing prostitutes[1962] and imposing forced medical control of prostitutes,[1963] and provisions on marital immunity relating to rape[1964] and the mitigation of the sentence in case the rapist marries the victim,[1965] are to be repealed. The practice of virginity examinations in cases of alleged rape is equally to be reviewed.[1966] The law on abortion is to be reappraised with a view to its liberalization and decriminalisation,[1967] at least for physical or mental health reasons of woman and

1952 UN Doc. A/55/38 (part I), paras. 172-173 (Jordan).

1953 UN Doc. A/57/38 (part II), para. 166 (Belgium); UN Doc. A/56/38 (part II), para. 224 (The Netherlands).

1954 UN Doc. A/58/38 (part I), para. 175 (Congo).

1955 UN Doc. A/58/38 (part I), para. 175 (Congo); UN Doc. A/57/38 (part II), para. 64 (Suriname); UN Doc. A/55/38 (part I), para. 228 (Congo).

1956 UN Doc. A/58/38 (part I), para. 218 (Kenya); UN Doc. A/57/38 (part II), para. 255 (Zambia); UN Doc. A/56/38 (part II), para. 75 (Singapore); UN Doc. A/54/38/Rev.1 (part II), para. 139 (Nepal); UN Doc. A/54/38/Rev.1 (part I), para. 248 (Thailand); UN Doc. A/52/38/Rev.1, para. 241 (Venezuela); UN Doc. A/52/38/Rev.1, para. 200 (Turkey).

1957 UN Doc. A/54/38/Rev.1 (part I), paras. 83-84 (Algeria).

1958 UN Doc. A/58/38 (part II), para. 163 (Morocco); UN Doc. A/56/38 (part II), para. 125 (Guinea); UN Doc. A/56/38 (part I), para. 331 (Egypt); UN Doc. A/55/38 (part I), paras. 172-173 (Jordan).

1959 UN Doc. A/52/38/Rev.1 (part II), para. 306 (Argentina); UN Doc. A/52/38/Rev.1 (part I), para. 192 (Turkey); UN Doc. A/51/38, para. 127 (Paraguay).

1960 UN Doc. A/56/38 (part I), para. 347 (Egypt); UN Doc. A/56/38 (part I), para. 56 (Burundi).

1961 UN Doc. A/57/38 (part III), para. 391 (Yemen); UN Doc. A/55/38 (part I), paras. 178-179 (Jordan).

1962 UN Doc. A/56/38 (part II), para. 181(Guyana); UN Doc. A/56/38 (part I), para. 347 (Egypt); UN Doc. A/54/38/Rev.1 (part I), para. 289 (China); UN Doc. A/54/38/Rev.1 (part I), para. 168 (Liechtenstein); UN Doc. A/53/38/Rev.1 (part I), para. 414 (Mexico).

1963 UN Doc. A/53/38/Rev.1 (part I), para. 74 (Azerbaijan).

1964 UN Doc. A/54/38/Rev.1 (part II), para. 62 (Belize); UN Doc. A/54/38/Rev.1 (part I), para. 192 (Greece).

1965 UN Doc. A/57/38 (part I), para. 197 (Uruguay).

1966 UN Doc. A/52/38/Rev.1, para. 195 (Turkey).

1967 UN Doc. HRI/GEN/1/Rev.7, General Recommendation No. 24 (1999), *Article 12 of the Convention on the Elimination of All Forms of Discrimination against Women – Women and Health*, para. 31 (c); UN Doc. A/56/38 (part II), para. 48 (Andorra); UN Doc. A/55/38 (part II), para. 60 (Cameroon); UN Doc. A/54/38/Rev.1 (part II), para. 139 (Nepal); UN Doc. A/54/38/Rev.1 (part II), para. 57 (Belize); UN Doc. A/53/38/Rev.1 (part I), para. 408 (Mexico); UN Doc. A/53/38/Rev.1 (part II), para.

child.[1968] The requirement of spousal consent for abortion,[1969] and that health officials report women who undergo abortions to law enforcement agencies[1970] are to repealed. Mitigation of the sentence in case of induced abortion, in order to protect the honour of the perpetrator, the spouse and a close relative, is to be reconsidered as well.[1971]

Outdated and discriminatory labour laws and policies are to reviewed,[1972] in an effort to allow for women's participation in the labour market on a footing of genuine equality with men.[1973] Existing occupational health and safety legislation and standards are to be amended and all such standards that directly or indirectly discriminate against women are to be repealed.[1974] Existing restrictions on women's access to employment, particularly those based on stereotypical assumptions concerning women's work, are to be reviewed.[1975] The legal requirement of the husband's authorization of a wife's paid employment is to be revoked.[1976] Legal provisions regarding the retirement age of women and men[1977] and women's employment in police and the fire brigade should be reviewed in order to eliminate discrimination against women.[1978]

Discrimination with regard to full social security coverage between married and unmarried women or any disparities among women as regards the eligibility to benefits[1979] are to be abolished,[1980] and discriminatory laws to be amended, such as those providing for the reduction of pay during maternity leave.[1981]

340 (Peru); UN Doc. A/53/38/Rev.1 (part I), para. 426 (Mexico); UN Doc. A/53/38/Rev.1 (part I), para. 349 (Dominican Republic); UN Doc. A/53/38/Rev.1 (part I), para. 159 (Zimbabwe); UN Doc. A/52/38/Rev.1 (part II), para. 319 (Argentina); UN Doc. A/52/38/Rev.1 (part II), para. 127 (Namibia); UN Doc. A/52/38/Rev.1 (Part I), para. 148 (Saint Vincent and the Grenadines); UN Doc. A/51/38, para. 131 (Paraguay); UN Doc. A/50/38, para. 446 (Peru); UN Doc. A/50/38, para. 158 (Chile).

1968 UN Doc. A/57/38 (part I), para. 283 (Sri Lanka); UN Doc. A/55/38 (part I), para. 181 (Jordan); UN Doc. A/54/38/Rev.1 (part II), para. 229 (Chile); UN Doc. A/52/38/Rev.1 (Part I), para. 148 (Saint Vincent and the Grenadines); UN Doc. A/50/38, para. 446 (Peru).

1969 UN Doc. A/52/38/Rev.1 (Part I), para. 196 (Turkey).

1970 UN Doc. A/54/38/Rev.1 (part II), para. 229 (Chile).

1971 UN Doc. A/57/38 (part I), para. 197 (Uruguay).

1972 UN Doc. CEDAW/C/WSM/CC/1-3, para. 29 (Samoa); UN Doc. A/57/38 (part III), para. 144 (Uganda); UN Doc. A/57/38 (part II), para. 249 (Zambia); UN Doc. A/57/38 (part II), para. 60 (Suriname); UN Doc. A/57/38 (part I), para. 57 (Fiji); UN Doc. A/55/38 (part I), para. 185 (Jordan).

1973 UN Doc. A/57/38 (part III), para. 442 (Mexico).

1974 UN Doc. A/56/38 (part I), para. 102 (Kazakhstan); UN Doc. A/55/38 (part II), para. 108 (Moldova); UN Doc. A/55/38 (part I), para. 374 (Belarus); UN Doc. A/54/38/Rev.1 (part II), para. 110 (Georgia).

1975 UN Doc. A/52/38/Rev.1, para. 79 (Morocco).

1976 UN Doc. A/55/38 (part I), para. 226 (Congo).

1977 UN Doc. A/56/38 (part II), para. 271 (Viet Nam).

1978 UN Doc. A/57/38 (part III), para. 282 (Greece).

1979 UN Doc. A/56/38 (part I), para. 216 (Jamaica).

1980 UN Doc. A/51/38, para. 65 (Cyprus).

1981 UN Doc. A/55/38 (part I), para. 226 (Congo).

Legislation limiting women's political participation in public life is to be repealed.[1982]

All victims of trafficking are to benefit from stay permits on grounds of social protection,[1983] and gender-related forms of persecution are to be recognized in the determination of refugee status.[1984]

States should also refrain from discrimination against children born out of wedlock.[1985]

b. *The Obligation to Protect*

The obligation to protect against discrimination by non-state actors is very prominent under CEDAW. Art. 2, para. 1 (e) CEDAW obliges states parties to take all appropriate measures to eliminate discrimination against women by any person, organization or enterprise. Art. 2 thus imposes accountability on the state party for action by the private sector, private organizations or political parties. This obligation to redress private discrimination is reinforced by many other provisions.

States have been encouraged by the CEDAW Committee to adopt legislation in order to make the standards of the Convention applicable to *non-state* action and inaction.[1986] States are encouraged to take more active and proactive measures to bring about changes in the traditional patriarchal attitudes on gender-role stereotyping[1987] and to modify or eliminate customs and cultural and traditional practices that discriminate against women, so as to promote women's full enjoyment of their human rights.[1988]

With regard to the family, states have been encouraged to secularize and codify law on family relations and marriage,[1989] thereby incorporating only those customary and religious laws and practices that promote gender equality and the empowerment of women.[1990] In case customary marriage is preserved, rights of wife and children are to be safeguarded by law.[1991] Legislation is to be enacted in order to prohibit traditional customs and practices which are in violation of women's fundamental rights, such

---

1982 UN Doc. A/56/38 (part II), para. 220 (Netherlands); UN Doc. A/56/38 (part I), para. 131 (Maldives).
1983 UN Doc. CEDAW/C/ITA/CC/4-5, para. 32 (Italy).
1984 *Ibid.*, para. 36 (Italy).
1985 UN Doc. A/58/38 (part II), paras. 371-372 (Japan); UN Doc. A/52/38/Rev.1 (part II), para. 223 (Luxembourg).
1986 UN Doc. A/57/38 (part I), para. 47 (Fiji); UN Doc. A/55/38 (part I), para. 67 (India).
1987 UN Doc. CEDAW/C/LAO/CC/1-5, para. 38 (Laos).
1988 UN Doc. CEDAW/C/GAB/CC/2-5, para. 31 (Gabon).
1989 UN Doc. A/53/38/Rev.1 (part II), para. 230 (Tanzania); UN Doc. A/52/38/Rev.1 (part II), para. 173 (Israel); UN Doc. A/51/38, para. 154 (Ethiopia).
1990 UN Doc. A/53/38/Rev.1 (part I), para. 157 (Zimbabwe).
1991 UN Doc. A/49/38, paras. 364-3655 (Zambia); UN Doc. A/49/38, para. 241 (Madagascar).

as dowry, the levirate, polygamy, inheritance, early and forced marriage and female genital mutilation.[1992] Consent of the woman is to be made a prerequisite for genital examinations under all circumstances; any crime committed in the name of custom or honour is to be classified as aggravated homicide and severest penalties are to be provided for by law.[1993] Measures are to be taken to prevent and prohibit early marriage,[1994] including by the introduction of a minimum age of marriage.[1995] The minimum age for marriage for women is to be raised to 18 years,[1996] "in line with article 1 of the Convention on the Rights of the Child, which defines a child as being below the age of 18, and the provision on child marriage in article 16, paragraph 2, of CEDAW."[1997]

States have also the obligation to protect women against gender-based violence:

> Under general international law and specific human rights covenants, States may also be responsible for private acts if they fail to act with due diligence to prevent violations of rights or to investigate and punish acts of violence, and for providing compensation.[1998]

This was repeated in *A.T. v. Hungary*, in which the Committee concluded that

> the obligations of the State party that are set out in article 2(a), (b) and (e) of the Convention extend to the prevention of, and protection from violence against women and, in the instant case, remain unfulfilled and constitute a violation of the author's human rights and fundamental freedoms, particularly here right to security of person.[1999]

Adequate legislative and structural measures are to be taken to protect women who are victims of domestic and sexual violence.[2000] States are to ensure that violence against

---

1992 UN Doc. A/58/38 (part II), para. 105 (Brazil); UN Doc. A/58/38 (part I), para. 208 (Kenya); UN Doc. A/57/38 (part II), para. 338 (Denmark); UN Doc. A/55/38 (part II), para. 54 (Cameroon); UN Doc. A/55/38 (part I), para. 215 (Congo); UN Doc. A/55/38 (part I), para. 167 (Jordan); UN Doc. A/53/38/Rev.1 (part II), para. 118 (South Africa); UN Doc. A/50/38, para. 341 (Uganda).

1993 UN Doc. CEDAW/C/TUR/CC/4-5, para. 26 (Turkey).

1994 UN Doc. CEDAW/C/LAO/CC/1-5, para. 40 (Laos); UN Doc. A/58/38 (part I), para. 183 (Congo); UN Doc. A/57/38 (part I), para. 100 (Estonia).

1995 UN Doc. A/56/38 (part I), para. 353 (Egypt); UN Doc. A/56/38 (part I), para. 136 (Maldives).

1996 UN Doc. A/57/38 (part III), para. 65 (Armenia).

1997 UN Doc. A/58/38 (part II), para. 163 (Morocco); UN Doc. A/57/38 (part III), para. 450 (Mexico); UN Doc. A/57/38 (part III), para. 197 (Guatemala); UN Doc. A/57/38 (part III), para. 334 (Hungary); UN Doc. A/57/38 (part III), para. 395 (Yemen); UN Doc. A/57/38 (part III), para. 489 (Peru); UN Doc. A/58/38 (part II), para. 268 (France). Compare with UN Doc. CEDAW/C/PAR/CC/3-5, para. 27 (Paraguay).

1998 UN Doc. HRI/GEN/1/Rev.7, General Recommendation No. 19 (1992), *Violence Against Women*, para. 9.

1999 Communication No. 2/2003, *A.T. v. Hungary*, para. 9.3.

2000 UN Doc. A/56/38 (part I), para. 96 (Kazakhstan); UN Doc. A/55/38 (part I), para. 2708 (Burkina Faso).

women constitutes a crime punishable under criminal law,[2001] that all allegations of domestic violence are investigated "promptly, thoroughly, impartially and seriously",[2002] that perpetrators are prosecuted and punished with the required severity and speed, and that women victims of violence have immediate means of redress and protection.[2003] The latter includes safe and prompt access to justice, including free legal aid where necessary, and available, effective and sufficient remedies and rehabilitation.[2004] Offenders are to be provided with rehabilitation programmes and programmes on non-violent resolution methods.[2005] Severe penalties for sexual violence and abuse of women and girls are to be considered,[2006] in particular within the family.[2007] Provision should be made for the prosecution of offenders even in the absence of a complaint by the victim.[2008] In particular with regard to domestic violence, exclusion orders are to be provided for.[2009] Penal law on rape is to be amended[2010] so as to

2001 UN Doc. HRI/GEN/1/Rev.7, General Recommendation No. 12 (1989), *Violence Against Women*, para. 3.

2002 Communication No. 2/2003, *A.T. v. Hungary*, para. 9.6 II (vi).

2003 UN Doc. CEDAW/C/PAR/CC/3-5, para. 25 (Paraguay); UN Doc. CEDAW/C/GAB/CC/2-5, para. 27 (Gabon); UN Doc. CEDAW/C/CRO/CC/2-3, para. 32 (Croatia); UN Doc. CEDAW/C/WSM/CC/1-3, para. 25 (Samoa); UN Doc. CEDAW/C/TUR/CC/4-5, para. 28 (Turkey); UN Doc. CEDAW/C/ITA/CC/4-5, para. 32 (Italy); UN Doc. CEDAW/C/LAO/CC/1-5, para. 38 (Laos); UN Doc. A/58/38 (part II), para. 362 (Japan); UN Doc. A/58/38 (part II), para. 207 (Slovenia); UN Doc. A/58/38 (part II), para. 169 (Morocco); UN Doc. A/58/38 (part II), para. 113 (Brazil); UN Doc. A/58/38 (part II), para. 55 (Costa Rica); UN Doc. A/58/38 (part I), para. 731 (Albania); UN Doc. A/58/38 (part I), para. 212 (Kenya); UN Doc. A/58/38 (part I), para. 167 (Congo); UN Doc. A/57/38 (part III), para. 276 (Greece); UN Doc. A/57/38 (part III), para. 136 (Uganda); UN Doc. A/57/38 (part II), para. 239 (Zambia); UN Doc. A/57/38 (part II), para. 239 (Zambia); UN Doc. A/57/38 (part II), para. 195 (Tunisia); UN Doc. A/57/38 (part I), para. 195 (Uruguay); UN Doc. A/57/38 (part I), para. 59 (Fiji); UN Doc. A/56/38 (part II), para. 259 (Viet Nam); UN Doc. A/56/38 (part II), para. 135 (Guinea); UN Doc. A/56/38 (part I), para. 138 (Maldives); UN Doc. A/56/38 (part I), para. 96 (Kazakhstan); UN Doc. A/55/38 (part II), para. 307 (Romania); UN Doc. A/55/38 (part I), para. 411 (Luxembourg); UN Doc. A/54/38/Rev.1 (part II), para. 102 (Georgia); UN Doc. A/54/38/Rev.1 (part I), para. 376 (Colombia); UN Doc. A/54/38/Rev.1 (part I), para. 286 (China); UN Doc. A/54/38/Rev.1 (part I), para. 243 (Thailand); UN Doc. A/54/38/Rev.1 (part I), para. 190 (Greece); UN Doc. A/53/38/Rev.1 (part II), para. 234 (Tanzania); UN Doc. A/53/38/Rev.1 (part I), para. 411 (Mexico); UN Doc. A/53/38/Rev.1 (part I), para. 202 (Czech Republic); UN Doc. A/52/38/Rev.1, para. 300 (Philippines); UN Doc. A/52/38/Rev.1, para. 241 (Venezuela); UN Doc. A/52/38/Rev.1 (part II), para. 64 (Armenia); UN Doc. A/51/38, para. 58 (Cyprus); UN Doc. A/50/38, para. 99 (Bolivia).

2004 Communication No. 2/2003, *A.T. v. Hungary*, para. 9.6 II (vii). In this case, the Committee ordered the state to give a safe home, appropriate child support and legal assistance, and reparation proportionate to the physical and mental harm undergone and to the gravity of the violations of her rights.

2005 Communication No. 2/2003, *A.T. v. Hungary*, para. 9.6 II (viii).

2006 UN Doc. A/57/38 (part I), para. 246 (Iceland).

2007 UN Doc. A/52/38/Rev.1 (part II), para. 220 (Luxembourg).

2008 UN Doc. A/53/38/Rev.1 (part I), para. 255 (Bulgaria).

2009 UN Doc. A/57/38 (part I), para. 98 (Estonia); UN Doc. A/55/38 (part II), para. 151 (Lithuania); UN Doc. A/57/38 (part III), para. 322 (Hungary). See also Communication No. 2/2003, *A.T. v. Hungary*, para. 9.6 II (v).

2010 UN Doc. A/57/38 (part I), para. 100 (Estonia).

explicitly define rape as sexual intercourse without consent,[2011] to criminalize marital rape[2012] and to increase the penalty for rape.[2013]

Incest is to be included as a specific crime in penal legislation.[2014] Trafficking, exploitation of prostitution, pornography and sexual exploitation of children and adolescents should be strictly penalized,[2015] and law enforcement is to be strengthened.[2016]

Women and girls are to be protected from discrimination in education because of pregnancy, through both legislative provisions and adequate policy measures.[2017]

Labour law protection is to be extended to domestic employees[2018] and workers in the free-trade zone areas.[2019] The prohibition of direct and indirect discrimination with regard to access and opportunities is to be fully integrated into labour legislation,[2020] covering *inter alia* discrimination in hiring, promotion, employment conditions and dismissal.[2021] Protection against wage discrimination is equally to be offered.[2022] Parties to collective agreements should be encouraged to apply the principle of equal

---

2011 UN Doc. A/57/38 (part III), para. 334 (Hungary); UN Doc. A/57/38 (part III), para. 96 (Czech Republic); UN Doc. A/57/38 (part I), para. 98 (Estonia); UN Doc. A/55/38 (part II), para. 151 (Lithuania).

2012 UN Doc. A/57/38 (part III), para. 96 (Czech Republic); UN Doc. A/57/38 (part II), para. 54 (Suriname); UN Doc. A/57/38 (part I), para. 285 (Sri Lanka); UN Doc. A/56/38 (part II), para. 259 (Viet Nam); UN Doc. A/54/38/Rev.1 (part I), para. 324 (China-Hong Kong); UN Doc. A/52/38/Rev.1 (part II), para. 120 (Namibia).

2013 UN Doc. A/58/38 (part II), para. 362 (Japan); UN Doc. A/57/38 (part III), para. 96 (Czech Republic); UN Doc. A/53/38/Rev.1 (part I), para. 415 (Mexico).

2014 UN Doc. A/58/38 (part II), para. 362 (Japan); UN Doc. A/57/38 (part III), para. 477 (Peru); UN Doc. A/57/38 (part I), para. 334 (Portugal).

2015 UN Doc. A/58/38 (part II), paras. 312 and 314 (Ecuador); UN Doc. A/58/38 (part I), para. 71 (Albania); UN Doc. A/57/38 (part III), para. 185 (Guatemala); UN Doc. A/57/38 (part III), para. 146 (Uganda); UN Doc. A/57/38 (part III), para. 51 (Armenia); UN Doc. A/57/38 (part I), para. 65 (Fiji); UN Doc. A/55/38 (part I), para. 220 (Congo); UN Doc. A/51/38, para. 299 (Ukraine).

2016 UN Doc. CEDAW/C/GAB/CC/2-5, para. 29 (Gabon); UN Doc. A/55/38 (part I), para. 77 (India).

2017 UN Doc. A/57/38 (part II), para. 58 (Suriname); UN Doc. A/54/38/Rev.1 (part II), para. 227 (Chile); UN Doc. A/54/38/Rev.1 (part II), para. 53 (Belize).

2018 UN Doc. CEDAW/C/PAR/CC/3-5, para. 31 (Paraguay); UN Doc. A/56/38 (part II), para. 78 (Singapore); UN Doc. A/52/38/Rev.1 (part II), para. 313 (Argentina).

2019 UN Doc. A/56/38 (part I), para. 230 (Jamaica).

2020 UN Doc. A/57/38 (part III), para. 244 (Barbados); UN Doc. A/57/38 (part III), para. 57 (Armenia); UN Doc. A/57/38 (part II), para. 201 (Tunisia); UN Doc. A/56/38 (part II), para. 46 (Andorra); UN Doc. A/55/38 (part II), para. 108 (Moldova); UN Doc. A/55/38 (part I), para. 366 (Belarus); UN Doc. A/55/38 (part I), para. 312 (Germany).

2021 UN Doc. A/57/38 (part I), para. 384 (Russian Federation).

2022 UN Doc. A/57/38 (part II), para. 100 (Saint Kitts and Nevis); UN Doc. A/54/38/Rev.1 (part II), para. 156 (Nepal); UN Doc. A/54/38/Rev.1 (part I), para. 332 (China-Hong Kong).

remuneration for work of equal value.[2023] Action is to be taken against employers who discriminate against women on grounds of pregnancy.[2024]

Sexual harassment occurring in the workplace in the private sector should be legally addressed and penalized,[2025] and women should be empowered to take action with regard to sexual harassment.[2026]

Protection is also to be offered against discrimination in political and public life:

> State parties are under an obligation to take all appropriate measures, including the enactment of appropriate legislation that complies with their Constitution, to ensure that organizations such as political parties and trade unions, which may not be subject directly to obligations under the Convention, do not discriminate against women and respect the principles contained in articles 7 and 8.[2027]

c. *The Obligation to Fulfil*

Throughout the text, CEDAW indicates that legislation is not sufficient to realize equality for women, and that a variety of positive measures is required. Many articles indicate clear positive measures to be taken in order to (mainly) facilitate gender equality.

i. To Facilitate

A variety of measures have been suggested to facilitate equality. On a general level, a gender perspective is to be mainstreamed within all ministries, and procedures are to be established for assessing the impact of such mainstreaming.[2028] A comprehensive

---

2023 UN Doc. HRI/GEN/1/Rev.7, General Recommendation No. 13 (1989), *Equal Remuneration for Work of Equal Value*, para. 3.

2024 UN Doc. A/53/38/Rev.1 (part I), para. 416 (Mexico).

2025 UN Doc. A/58/38 (part II), para. 65 (Costa Rica); UN Doc. A/57/38 (part III), para. 477 (Peru); UN Doc. A/57/38 (part III), para. 322 (Hungary); UN Doc. A/57/38 (part III), para. 144 (Uganda); UN Doc. A/57/38 (part I), para. 57 (Fiji); UN Doc. A/52/38/Rev.1 (part II), para. 314 (Argentina); UN Doc. A/51/38, para. 63 (Cyprus).

2026 UN Doc. A/57/38 (part III), para. 278 (Greece); UN Doc. A/57/38 (part I), para. 152 (Trinidad and Tobago).

2027 UN Doc. HRI/GEN/1/Rev.7, General Recommendation No. 23 (1997), *Political and Public Life*, para. 42. In this general recommendation, the CEDAW Committee went even further by also identifying direct obligations for trade unions and political parties, *i.e.* "to demonstrate their commitment to the principle of gender equality in their constitutions, in the application of those rules and in the composition of their memberships with gender-balanced representation on their executive boards [...]. (para. 34).

2028 UN Doc. CEDAW/C/GAB/CC/2-5, para. 19 (Gabon); UN Doc. A/57/38 (part I), para. 144 (Trinidad and Tobago); UN Doc. A/57/38 (part I), para. 211 (Uruguay).

national strategy and plan of action for the full implementation of all the provisions of the Convention is to be elaborated and implemented.[2029] Laws, policies and programmes with regard to the family should affirm and incorporate the principle of equality and partnership between women and men and the full realization of women's human rights.[2030] Legislation and policies should cover the more subtle utilization of and support for traditional sex role stereotypes in the family, in employment, in politics and in society.[2031]

States are "to encourage the provision of the necessary supporting social services to enable parents to combine family obligations with work responsibilities and participation in public life, in particular through promoting the establishment and development of a network of child-care facilities." (article 11, para. 2 (c) CEDAW). In order to facilitate equality in household tasks and child care between men and women, other means than revising the law on maternity leave are to be developed to increase men's participation in household tasks and child care.[2032] Measures allowing for the reconciliation between family and professional responsibilities are to be strengthened and promoted, including awareness-raising for equal sharing of domestic and family tasks between women and men.[2033] The availability of sufficient childcare places and an uninterrupted long school day are to be ensured.[2034]

A comprehensive strategy should be adopted to combat trafficking of women,[2035] including increased international, regional and bilateral cooperation, the introduction of measures aimed at improving the economic situation of women so as to reduce their vulnerability to traffickers; rehabilitation and reintegration measures for women and girls who have been victims of trafficking,[2036] protection and support to enable women and girls to provide testimony against their traffickers;[2037] and training of border police and law enforcement officers in order to provide them with the requisite skills to

---

2029 UN Doc. CEDAW/C/GAB/CC/2-5, para. 19 (Gabon).
2030 UN Doc. A/57/38 (part III), para. 393 (Yemen).
2031 UN Doc. A/57/38 (part I), para. 96 (Estonia).
2032 UN Doc. A/51/38, para. 94 (Iceland).
2033 UN Doc. CEDAW/C/ITA/CC/4-5, para. 30 (Italy); UN Doc. CEDAW/C/CRO/CC/2-3, para. 28 (Croatia).
2034 UN Doc. CEDAW/C/TUR/CC/4-5, para. 36 (Turkey); UN Doc. A/56/38 (part II), para. 204 (The Netherlands).
2035 UN Doc. A/58/38 (part II), para. 209 (Slovenia).
2036 UN Doc. CEDAW/C/CRO/CC/2-3, para. 38 (Croatia); UN Doc. CEDAW/C/PAR/CC/3-5, para. 29 (Paraguay); UN Doc. A/56/38 (part I), para. 98 (Kazakhstan).
2037 UN Doc. A/58/38 (part I), para. 71 (Albania); UN Doc. A/57/38 (part II), para. 50 (Suriname); UN Doc. A/57/38 (part I), para. 396 (Russian Federation).

recognize and provide support for victims of trafficking.[2038] The demand for prostitution should be discouraged.[2039]

Measures are to be taken to increase the representation of women in elected and appointed bodies in all areas of political and public life at all levels.[2040]

Priority is to be accorded to the education of girls and women.[2041] Specific programmes should be established to reduce female illiteracy, promote the access of girls to all levels of education[2042] and to prevent their dropping out of school.[2043] Measures may include incentives for parents to send girls to school and the recruitment of women teachers.[2044] The mainstreaming of gender perspectives in curricula and textbooks is to be strengthened, the training of teaching staff in regard to gender equality issues to be enhanced, and diversification of the educational choices of men and women,[2045] and a public dialogue on the educational choices girls and women make and their subsequent opportunities and chances in the labour market to be encouraged.[2046]

De facto equal opportunities for women and men in the labour market is to be ensured through, *inter alia*, effective implementation of labour legislation.[2047] Efforts to address the impediments women face in entering the labour force and to implement measures to promote the reconciliation of family and work responsibilities between women and men are to be stepped up.[2048] A forward-looking equal employment opportunities law is to be adopted, with effective enforcement procedures, sanctions for non-compliance and remedies.[2049] Formal and informal mechanisms for the resolution of labour disputes through appropriate representation of women are to be strengthened.[2050]

2038 UN Doc. A/58/38 (part I), para. 71 (Albania).

2039 UN Doc. CEDAW/C/CRO/CC/2-3, para. 38 (Croatia); UN Doc. CEDAW/C/LAO/CC/1-5, para. 32 (Laos).

2040 UN Doc. CEDAW/C/TUR/CC/4-5, para. 32 (Turkey); UN Doc. CEDAW/C/ITA/CC/4-5, para. 28 (Italy); UN Doc. CEDAW/C/CRO/CC/2-3, para. 36 (Croatia); UN Doc. CEDAW/C/WSM/CC/1-3, para. 27 (Samoa); UN Doc. CEDAW/C/LAO/CC/1-5, para. 34 (Laos). See also article 7 CEDAW.

2041 UN Doc. CEDAW/C/TUR/CC/4-5, para. 34 (Turkey); UN Doc. A/55/38 (part I), para. 268 (Burkina Faso). See also article 10 CEDAW.

2042 UN Doc. CEDAW/C/TUR/CC/4-5, para. 34 (Turkey); UN Doc. CEDAW/C/PAR/CC/3-5, para. 37 (Paraguay); UN Doc. A/55/38 (part I), para. 224 (Congo).

2043 UN Doc. A/57/38 (part III), para. 387 (Yemen); UN Doc. A/56/38 (part I), para. 58 (Burundi).

2044 UN Doc. A/56/38 (part II), para. 127 (Guinea); UN Doc. A/57/38 (part II), para. 247 (Zambia).

2045 UN Doc. CEDAW/C/TUR/CC/4-5, para. 34 (Turkey).

2046 UN Doc. CEDAW/C/CRO/CC/2-3, para. 34 (Croatia).

2047 *Ibid.*, para. 28 (Croatia). See also article 11 CEDAW.

2048 UN Doc. CEDAW/C/DZA/CC/2, para. 40 (Algeria); UN Doc. CEDAW/C/WSM/CC/1-3, para. 29 (Samoa).

2049 UN Doc. A/57/38 (part I), para. 384 (Russian Federation); UN Doc. A/55/38 (part II), para. 313 (Romania); UN Doc. A/52/38/Rev.1 (Part I), para. 115 (Slovenia).

2050 UN Doc. CEDAW/C/LAO/CC/1-5, para. 36 (Laos).

Occupational segregation is to be corrected through concrete measures,[2051] *i.e.* through education, training and retraining measures, and better use of enforcement mechanisms.[2052] Discrimination against part-time workers in relation to overtime is to be eliminated,[2053] and full social security benefits should be extended to part-time workers, the majority of which are women.[2054] Policies and active measures are to be taken to accelerate the eradication of pay discrimination against women,[2055] including job evaluations, collection of data, further study of the underlying causes for the wage gap and provision of increased assistance to social partners in collective wage bargaining, in particular in determining wage structures in sectors dominated by women.[2056] Proactive measures are also to be taken to encourage more women to apply for high-ranking posts,[2057] including in decision-making in politics, the economy and academia.[2058] Measures are recommended to encourage women to become entrepreneurs, facilitate access to credits and loans, and technology for women.[2059] Remedial measures regarding any disadvantageous impact on women of economic reforms, including on women in the civil service, may have to be taken.[2060]

Maternity leave with pay is to be made mandatory,[2061] whereas parental leave for fathers should be made possible and encouraged.[2062]

Access to health-care facilities and medical assistance by trained personnel, particularly in rural areas and particularly for post-natal care, may have to be increased.[2063] Health services are to be improved and expanded,[2064] *inter alia* through the introduction of a holistic view of women's health[2065] and the implementation of a life-cycle approach to women's health.[2066] Programmes to combat traditional practices which affect

---

2051 UN Doc. A/52/38/Rev.1, para. 202 (Turkey).
2052 UN Doc. CEDAW/C/CRO/CC/2-3, para. 28 (Croatia).
2053 UN Doc. A/56/38 (part II), para. 214 (The Netherlands).
2054 UN Doc. CEDAW/C/ITA/CC/4-5, para. 30 (Italy).
2055 *Id.*
2056 UN Doc. A/56/38 (part II), para. 341 (Sweden); UN Doc. A/52/38/Rev.1, para. 246 (Venezuela).
2057 UN Doc. A/58/38 (part II), para. 260 (France).
2058 UN Doc. A/56/38 (part II), para. 218 (The Netherlands).
2059 UN Doc. CEDAW/C/LAO/CC/1-5, para. 36 (Laos); UN Doc. A/53/38/Rev.1 (part I), para. 259 (Bulgaria).
2060 UN Doc. CEDAW/C/LAO/CC/1-5, para. 36 (Laos).
2061 UN Doc. A/58/38 (part I), para. 133 (Switzerland); UN Doc. A/57/38 (part I), para. 57 (Fiji); UN Doc. A/56/38 (part II), para. 169 (Guyana). Compare with article 11, para. 2 (b) CEDAW. See also further under the heading of the obligation to fulfil-provide.
2062 UN Doc. A/58/38 (part II), para. 412 (New Zealand); UN Doc. A/57/38 (part III), para. 244 (Barbados).
2063 UN Doc. CEDAW/C/TUR/CC/4-5, para. 38 (Turkey).
2064 UN Doc. CEDAW/C/LAO/CC/1-5, para. 26 (Laos); UN Doc. A/49/38, para. 242 (Madagascar).
2065 UN Doc. A/55/38 (part II), para. 204 (Iraq).
2066 UN Doc. A/55/38 (part II), para. 159 (Lithuania).

women's health should be expanded.[2067] Family planning and reproductive health policy and programmes, including the availability and accessibility of affordable modern contraceptive means to both women and men need to be improved.[2068]

Appropriate measures and special programmes are to be implemented to address poverty amongst women, particularly the most vulnerable women, including elderly women, women with children, women with disabilities, Roma and migrant women, and rural women,[2069] and to support the full integration of rural women in national development.[2070] The promotion of gender equality is to be made an explicit component of a national development plan and policies, in particular those aimed at sustainable development.[2071] The needs and concerns of rural women are to be fully integrated in the formulation and implementation of sectoral policies and programmes.[2072]

An important way of facilitating the realization of equality is through complaints and monitoring mechanisms. Effective, adequate, accessible and affordable enforcement and complaints procedures should be provided for,[2073] through judicial[2074] (including constitutional)[2075] and quasi-judicial mechanisms[2076] (such as an ombudsman).[2077] Legal

2067 UN Doc. A/49/38, para. 725 (Senegal).

2068 UN Doc. CEDAW/C/PAR/CC/3-5, para. 33 (Paraguay); UN Doc. CEDAW/C/WSM/CC/1-3, para. 31 (Samoa); UN Doc. CEDAW/C/LAO/CC/1-5, para. 26 (Laos); UN Doc. A/56/38 (part II), para. 303 (Nicaragua). See also article 12 CEDAW.

2069 UN Doc. CEDAW/C/ITA/CC/4-5, para. 35 (Italy); UN Doc. CEDAW/C/GAB/CC/2-5, para. 39 (Gabon); UN Doc. A/57/38 (part I), para. 388 (Russian Federation); UN Doc. A/53/38/Rev.1 (part II), para. 385 (Korea); UN Doc. A/53/38/Rev.1 (part II), para. 136 (South Africa); UN Doc. A/53/38/Rev.1 (part I), para. 403 (Mexico); UN Doc. A/53/38/Rev.1 (part I), para. 257 (Bulgaria).

2070 UN Doc. CEDAW/C/PAR/CC/3-5, para. 35 (Paraguay); UN Doc. A/55/38 (part I), para. 189 (Jordan).

2071 UN Doc. CEDAW/C/WSM/CC/1-3, para. 35 (Samoa).

2072 UN Doc. CEDAW/C/DZA/CC/2, para. 42 (Algeria). See also article 14 CEDAW.

2073 UN Doc. CEDAW/C/DZA/CC/2, para. 28 (Algeria); UN Doc. CEDAW/C/GAB/CC/2-5, para. 21 (Gabon); UN Doc. A/58/38 (part I), para. 63 (Albania); UN Doc. A/57/38 (part III), para. 314 (Hungary); UN Doc. A/57/38 (part III), para. 132 (Uganda); UN Doc. A/57/38 (part III), para. 88 (Czech Republic); UN Doc. A/57/38 (part II), para. 282 (Ukraine); UN Doc. A/57/38 (part II), para. 193 (Tunisia); UN Doc. A/57/38 (part I), paras. 374 and 376 (Russian Federation); UN Doc. A/57/38 (part II), para. 237 (Zambia); UN Doc. A/57/38 (part I), para. 344 (Portugal); UN Doc. A/57/38 (part I), para. 238 (Iceland); UN Doc. A/57/38 (part I), para. 47 (Fiji); UN Doc. A/56/38 (part II), para. 119 (Guinea); UN Doc. A/56/38 (part II), para. 89 (Singapore); UN Doc. A/55/38 (part I), para. 360 (Belarus); UN Doc. A/55/38 (part I), para. 310 (Germany); UN Doc. A/55/38 (part I), para. 212 (Congo); UN Doc. A/53/38/Rev.1 (part II), para. 373 (Korea).

2074 UN Doc. A/56/38 (part II), para. 163 (Guyana); UN Doc. A/55/38 (part II), para. 46 (Cameroon); UN Doc. A/55/38 (part I), para. 401 (Luxembourg); UN Doc. A/54/38/Rev.1 (part I), para. 284 (China); UN Doc. A/54/38/Rev.1 (part I), para. 114 (Kyrgyzstan).

2075 UN Doc. A/56/38 (part I), para. 2126 (Jamaica).

2076 UN Doc. A/57/38 (part III), para. 88 (Czech Republic).

2077 UN Doc. A/56/38 (part I), para. 94 (Kazakhstan); Doc. A/55/38 (part II), para. 108 (Moldova); UN Doc. A/52/38/Rev.1, para. 110 (Slovenia).

aid to women is to be offered,[2078] and funds should be made available for equality test cases under all jurisdictions.[2079] Effective remedies are also to be ensured against indirect discrimination[2080] and discrimination by non-state actors in the private sphere and the private sector.[2081]

Space is to be created for autonomous women's and human rights organizations.[2082]

The effective application and implementation of the laws on gender equality is to be monitored,[2083] and the effectiveness and impact of legislation and policies to be regularly assessed,[2084] with a view to taking corrective action when and if necessary.[2085] All programmes are to include mechanisms for the assessment of outcomes of their implementation and the evaluation of their effectiveness and the extent of their outreach as well.[2086]

A particular obligation with regard to CEDAW is that national machinery is required to ensure effective gender mainstreaming in all sectors of government,[2087] to coordinate

2078 UN Doc. CEDAW/C/CRO/CC/2-3, para. 32 (Croatia); UN Doc. A/58/38 (part I), para. 356 (Canada); UN Doc. A/57/38 (part I), para. 344 (Portugal); UN Doc. A/55/38 (part I), para. 360 (Belarus); UN Doc. A/54/38/Rev.1 (part I), para. 284 (China).

2079 UN Doc. A/58/38 (part I), para. 356 (Canada).

2080 UN Doc. A/55/38 (part I), para. 360 (Belarus); UN Doc. A/54/38/Rev.1 (part II), para. 51 (Belize).

2081 UN Doc. A/54/38/Rev.1 (part II), para. 51 (Belize); UN Doc. A/53/38/Rev.1 (part I), para. 156 (Zimbabwe).

2082 UN Doc. CEDAW/C/LAO/CC/1-5, para. 40 (Laos).

2083 UN Doc. CEDAW/C/PAR/CC/3-5, para. 31 (Paraguay); UN Doc. A/58/38 (part II), para. 99 (Brazil); UN Doc. A/56/38 (part II), para. 121 (Guinea); UN Doc. A/54/38/Rev.1 (part I), para. 284 (China); UN Doc. A/49/38, para. 726 (Senegal).

2084 UN Doc. CEDAW/C/CRO/CC/2-3, para. 24 (Croatia); UN Doc. A/57/38 (part III), para. 428 (Mexico); UN Doc. A/55/38 (part II), para. 185 (Iraq); UN Doc. A/54/38/Rev.1 (part I), para. 362 (Colombia).

2085 UN Doc. CEDAW/C/PAR/CC/3-5, para. 38 (Paraguay); UN Doc. A/54/38/Rev.1 (part II), para. 191 (Ireland). See UN Doc. A/58/38 (part II), para. 254 (France); UN Doc. A/57/38 (part III), para. 232 (Barbados); UN Doc. A/56/38 (part II), para. 295 (Nicaragua); UN Doc. A/55/38 (part II), para. 262 (Cuba); UN Doc. A/55/38 (part I), para. 306 (Germany); UN Doc. A/56/38 (part II), para. 50 (Andorra); UN Doc. A/54/38/Rev.1 (part II), para. 264 (Spain); UN Doc. A/53/38/Rev.1 (part II), para. 272 (New Zealand); UN Doc. A/52/38/Rev.1 (part II), paras. 398-399 (Australia); UN Doc. A/52/38/Rev.1, para. 304 (Philippines).

2086 UN Doc. A/54/38/Rev.1 (part I), para. 117 (Kyrgyzstan).

2087 UN Doc. CEDAW/C/ITA/CC/4-5, para. 22 (Italy); UN Doc. CEDAW/C/LAO/CC/1-5, para. 20 (Laos); UN Doc. A/56/38 (part I), para. 175 (Uzbekistan).

the overall policy level for women,[2088] to promote gender equality[2089] and to lead the Government's efforts to implement the Convention[2090].[2091] National machinery should exist at all levels,[2092] be autonomous, and with the requisite powers, visibility and resources.[2093] The mandates and the responsibilities of the different mechanisms related to gender and the interaction among them should be clearly defined.[2094] Special attention is to be paid as to where this machinery is placed within the government structure to make it as effective as possible.[2095] It should be high-level,[2096] have the necessary authority,[2097] and be sufficiently integrated into the political system.[2098]

2088 UN Doc. CEDAW/C/ITA/CC/4-5, para. 24 (Italy); UN Doc. A/58/38 (part II), para. 304 (Ecuador); UN Doc. A/56/38 (part I), para. 94 (Kazakhstan); UN Doc. A/52/38/Rev.1, para. 72 (Morocco); UN Doc. A/51/38, para. 257 (Hungary); UN Doc. A/50/38, para. 450 (Peru); UN Doc. A/49/38, para. 542 (Ecuador).

2089 UN Doc. A/54/38/Rev.1 (part I), para. 318 (China-Hong Kong); UN Doc. A/53/38/Rev.1 (part II), para. 120 (South Africa); UN Doc. A/53/38/Rev.1 (part I), para. 339 (Dominican Republic); UN Doc. A/53/38/Rev.1 (part I), para. 152 (Zimbabwe); UN Doc. A/52/38/Rev.1 (part II), para. 61 (Armenia); UN Doc. A/51/38, para. 56 (Cyprus).

2090 UN Doc. A/55/38 (part II), para. 1002 (Moldova); UN Doc. A/53/38/Rev.1 (part I), para. 200 (Czech Republic).

2091 UN Doc. A/58/38 (part I), para. 254 (El Salvador); UN Doc. A/58/38 (part I), para. 113 (Switzerland); UN Doc. A/57/38 (part III), para. 471 (Peru); UN Doc. A/57/38 (part III), para. 316 (Hungary); UN Doc. A/57/38 (part II), para. 284 (Ukraine); UN Doc. A/57/38 (part I), para. 191 (Uruguay); UN Doc. A/57/38 (part I), para. 144 (Trinidad and Tobago); UN Doc. A/56/38 (part II), para. 165 (Guyana); UN Doc. A/53/38/Rev.1 (part I), paras. 152 and 164 (Zimbabwe).

2092 UN Doc. A/50/38, para. 550 (Russian Federation); UN Doc. A/50/38, para. 214 (Mauritius).

2093 For recent recommendations on this, see UN Doc. CEDAW/C/CRO/CC/2-3, para. 27 (Croatia); UN Doc. A/58/38 (part II), para. 205 (Slovenia); UN Doc. A/58/38 (part II), para. 179 (Morocco); UN Doc. A/58/38 (part I), para. 226 (Kenya); UN Doc. A/58/38 (part I), para. 113 (Switzerland); UN Doc. A/58/38 (part I), para. 67 (Albania); UN Doc. A/57/38 (part III), para. 316 (Hungary); UN Doc. A/57/38 (part III), para. 230 (Barbados); UN Doc. A/57/38 (part III), para. 179 (Guatemala); UN Doc. A/57/38 (part III), para. 90 (Czech Republic); UN Doc. A/57/38 (part II), para. 284 (Ukraine); UN Doc. A/57/38 (part II), paras. 44 and 46 (Suriname);UN Doc. A/57/38 (part I), para. 378 (Russian Federation); UN Doc. A/57/38 (part I), para. 277 (Sri Lanka); UN Doc. A/57/38 (part I), para. 191 (Uruguay); UN Doc. A/57/38 (part I), para. 144 (Trinidad and Tobago); UN Doc. A/57/38 (part I), para. 92 (Estonia); UN Doc. A/56/38 (part II), para. 311 (Nicaragua); UN Doc. A/56/38 (part II), para. 255 (Viet Nam); UN Doc. A/56/38 (part I), para. 175 (Uzbekistan); UN Doc. A/56/38 (part II), para. 165 (Guyana); UN Doc. A/56/38 (part I), para. 94 (Kazakhstan).

2094 UN Doc. A/58/38 (part I), para. 226 (Kenya); UN Doc. A/57/38 (part II), paras. 44 and 46 (Suriname); UN Doc. A/57/38 (part I), para. 378 (Russian Federation); UN Doc. A/54/38/Rev.1 (part I), para. 116 (Kyrgyzstan).

2095 UN Doc. A/53/38/Rev.1 (part I), para. 251 (Bulgaria).

2096 UN Doc. A/54/38/Rev.1 (part I), para. 318 (China-Hong Kong); UN Doc. A/53/38/Rev.1 (part II), para. 285 (New Zealand); UN Doc. A/52/38/Rev.1, para. 72 (Morocco); UN Doc. A/51/38, para. 257 (Hungary); UN Doc. A/49/38, para. 542 (Ecuador).

2097 UN Doc. A/55/38 (part I), para. 1875 (Jordan); UN Doc. A/53/38/Rev.1 (part I), para. 339 (Dominican Republic); UN Doc. A/53/38/Rev.1 (part I), para. 152 (Zimbabwe).

2098 UN Doc. A/56/38 (part II), para. 311 (Nicaragua); UN Doc. A/55/38 (part II), para. 1002 (Moldova); UN Doc. A/52/38/Rev.1, para. 244 (Venezuela); UN Doc. A/51/38, para. 128 (Paraguay); UN Doc. A/50/38, para. 450 (Peru); UN Doc. A/49/38, para. 542 (Ecuador).

ii. To Promote

As early as 1987, the CEDAW Committee insisted on education and public information programmes to help eliminate prejudices which hinder women's equality.[2099]

Information and education campaigns may be targeted at different groups. A first target group is women themselves, or particular groups of women (such as migrant women or indigenous women).[2100] They should be educated about the content of CEDAW[2101] and about legal remedies.[2102] In order to promote women to positions of power, special training programmes for women, including leadership training, are to be organized.[2103] Mentoring, networking and support systems may facilitate women's entry into public life.[2104]

Secondly, there are some professional target groups which comprehensive, gender-sensitive awareness-raising and education should be offered to, such as law enforcement agencies (judges, lawyers and police),[2105] military personnel,[2106] teachers, social

2099 UN Doc. HRI/GEN/1/Rev.7, General Recommendation No. 3 (1987), *Education and Public Information Campaigns.* Repeated in General Recommendation No. 19 (1992), *Violence Against Women*, para. 24 (f). Compare with UN Doc. CEDAW/C/TUR/CC/4-5, para. 30 (Turkey); UN Doc. CEDAW/C/ITA/CC/4-5, para. 26 (Italy); UN Doc. CEDAW/C/GAB/CC/2-5, para. 31 (Gabon); UN Doc. CEDAW/C/DZA/CC/2, para. 36 (Algeria); UN Doc. CEDAW/C/WSM/CC/1-3, para. 35 (Samoa); UN Doc. CEDAW/C/LAO/CC/1-5, para. 28 (Laos).

2100 UN Doc. CEDAW/C/PAR/CC/3-5, para. 37 (Paraguay); UN Doc. A/51/38, para. 100 (Iceland).

2101 UN Doc. CEDAW/C/PAR/CC/3-5, para. 37 (Paraguay); UN Doc. A/53/38/Rev.1 (part I), para. 423 (Mexico).

2102 UN Doc. CEDAW/C/CRO/CC/2-3, para. 22 (Croatia); UN Doc. CEDAW/C/PAR/CC/3-5, para. 21 (Paraguay); UN Doc. A/57/38 (part I), para. 90 (Estonia); UN Doc. A/54/38/Rev.1 (part I), para. 196 (Greece).

2103 UN Doc. CEDAW/C/DZA/CC/2, para. 38 (Algeria); UN Doc. A/57/38 (part II), para. 286 (Ukraine); UN Doc. A/57/38 (part II), para. 56 (Suriname); UN Doc. A/57/38 (part I), para. 150 (Trinidad and Tobago); UN Doc. A/57/38 (part I), para. 104 (Estonia); UN Doc. A/56/38 (part II), para. 253 (Viet Nam); UN Doc. A/56/38 (part II), para. 133 (Guinea); UN Doc. A/56/38 (part I), para. 90 (Kazakhstan).

2104 UN Doc. A/54/38/Rev.1 (part II), para. 190 (Ireland).

2105 UN Doc. CEDAW/C/ITA/CC/4-5, para. 20 (Italy); UN Doc. A/58/38 (part II), para. 530 (Costa Rica); UN Doc. A/58/38 (part II), para. 107 (Brazil); UN Doc. A/57/38 (part II), para. 193 (Tunisia); UN Doc. A/57/38 (part I), para. 90 (Estonia); UN Doc. A/56/38 (part II), para. 257 (Viet Nam); UN Doc. A/54/38/Rev.1 (part II), para. 199 (Ireland); UN Doc. A/53/38/Rev.1 (part II), para. 230 (Tanzania); UN Doc. A/53/38/Rev.1 (part I), para. 422 (Mexico); UN Doc. A/52/38/Rev.1 (part II), para. 357 (Italy); UN Doc. A/52/38/Rev.1 (part I), para. 194 (Turkey); UN Doc. A/52/38/Rev.1 (part I), para. 108 (Slovenia); UN Doc. A/51/38, para. 296 (Ukraine); UN Doc. A/51/38, paras. 90 and 97 (Iceland); UN Doc. A/51/38, para. 66 (Cyprus).

2106 UN Doc. A/55/38 (part I), para. 118 (Myanmar).

workers and health personnel,[2107] journalists and the mass media,[2108] policy-makers, administrators[2109] and parliamentarians.[2110] Education in women's rights is to be provided in all schools and university systems.[2111] Finally, the general public is to be targeted through educational programmes, the revision of curricula and textbooks, the formulation of positive symbolic messages and mass media campaigns, to overcome traditional stereotypes regarding the role of women and men in the society[2112] and to change the attitudes of men and women in order to achieve *de facto* equality in all spheres of life.[2113]

The CEDAW Committee has called for education and information in particular fields such as health, child rearing, violence against women, employment etc. Sex education and family planning education is to be organized, in which the shared responsibility of men and women is stressed.[2114] Age-appropriate sex education is to be introduced

2107 UN Doc. A/55/38 (part I), para. 73 (India); UN Doc. A/53/38/Rev.1 (part I), paras. 152-153 (Zimbabwe); UN Doc. A/53/38/Rev.1 (part I), paras. 77-78 (Azerbaijan); UN Doc. A/52/38/Rev.1 (part II), para. 225 (Luxembourg).

2108 UN Doc. A/53/38/Rev.1 (part II), para. 318 (Peru); UN Doc. A/53/38/Rev.1 (part II), para. 195 (Panama).

2109 UN Doc. A/54/38/Rev.1 (part II), para. 144 (Nepal); UN Doc. A/54/38/Rev.1 (part I), paras. 360 and 364 (Colombia); UN Doc. A/54/38/Rev.1 (part I), para. 233 (Thailand).

2110 UN Doc. A/58/38 (part I), para. 410 (Norway); UN Doc. A/57/38 (part III), para. 314 (Hungary).

2111 UN Doc. A/53/38/Rev.1 (part I), paras. 77-78 (Azerbaijan); UN Doc. A/52/38/Rev.1, para. 270 (Denmark); UN Doc. A/52/38/Rev.1, para. 73 (Morocco).

2112 UN Doc. A/58/38 (part I), para. 412 (Norway); UN Doc. A/57/38 (part III), para. 234 (Barbados); UN Doc. A/57/38 (part I), para. 330 (Portugal); UN Doc. A/56/38 (part II), para. 295 (Nicaragua); UN Doc. A/56/38 (part II), para. 251 (Viet Nam); UN Doc. A/56/38 (part I), para. 218 (Jamaica); UN Doc. A/56/38 (part I), para. 135 (Maldives); UN Doc. A/55/38 (part II), para. 192 (Iraq); UN Doc. A/55/38 (part I), para. 404 (Luxembourg); UN Doc. A/54/38/Rev.1 (part II), para. 154 (Nepal); UN Doc. A/54/38/Rev.1 (part II), para. 100 (Georgia); UN Doc. A/54/38/Rev.1 (part I), paras. 360 and 364 (Colombia); UN Doc. A/54/38/Rev.1 (part I), para. 121 (Kyrgyzstan); UN Doc. A/53/38/Rev.1 (part II), para. 230 (Tanzania); UN Doc. A/53/38/Rev.1 (part I), paras. 152-153 (Zimbabwe); UN Doc. A/52/38/Rev.1 (part II), para. 455 (Bangladesh); UN Doc. A/52/38/Rev.1 (part II), para. 65 (Armenia); UN Doc. A/52/38/Rev.1 (part I), para. 245 (Venezuela); UN Doc. A/52/38/Rev.1 part I), para. 193 (Turkey); UN Doc. A/52/38/Rev.1, para. 113 (Slovenia); UN Doc. A/51/38, para. 95 (Iceland); UN Doc. A/50/38, para. 341 (Uganda).

2113 UN Doc. A/58/38 (part II), para. 530 (Costa Rica); UN Doc. A/49/38, para. 725 (Senegal); UN Doc. A/49/38, para. 543 (Ecuador); UN Doc. A/49/38, para. 367 (Zambia).

2114 UN Doc. A/57/38 (part II), para. 58 (Suriname); UN Doc. A/57/38 (part I), paras. 158 and 160 (Trinidad and Tobago); UN Doc. A/54/38/Rev.1 (part II), para. 57 (Belize); UN Doc. A/54/38/Rev.1 (part I), para. 208 (Greece); UN Doc. A/54/38/Rev.1 (part I), para. 137 (Kyrgyzstan); UN Doc. A/53/38/Rev.1 (part II), para. 342 (Peru); UN Doc. A/53/38/Rev.1 (part II), para. 92 (Slovakia); UN Doc. A/53/38/Rev.1 (part I), para. 349 (Dominican Republic); UN Doc. A/53/38/Rev.1 (part I), para. 205 (Czech Republic); UN Doc. A/53/38/Rev.1 (part I), para. 161 (Zimbabwe); UN Doc. A/52/38/Rev.1 (part II), para. 267 (Antigua and Barbados); UN Doc. A/52/38/Rev.1 (part I), para. 147 (Saint Vincent and the Grenadines); UN Doc. A/52/38/Rev.1 (part I), para. 119 (Slovenia).

as part of the school curriculum,[2115] with a particular focus on teenage conception and pregnancy,[2116] and abortions among adolescents.[2117] Special information programmes relating to sexually transmitted diseases, especially HIV/AIDS, need to be set up.[2118] Specific training programmes are needed to educate health professionals[2119] on gender sensitivity[2120] and the right of women, freely and without coercion, to choose means of contraception.[2121]

With regard to family work and rearing of children, women and men are to be educated towards a culture of shared obligations and responsibilities of family work and the rearing of children.[2122] The role of men in caring and their responsibility for parenting should be highlighted.[2123]

Public sensitization campaigns should be organized to deal with stereotypical attitudes that are amongst the root causes of violence against women,[2124] and to create zero tolerance in society with regard to violence against women.[2125] Public awareness is to be raised on the issue of domestic violence against women,[2126] through utilization of the media, popular music, theatre and so on, with the cooperation of civil society.[2127] Training should be offered to professional groups whose work is relevant in the context of violence against women,[2128] such as the judiciary, law enforcement officers, lawyers,

---

2115 UN Doc. A/57/38 (part II), para. 58 (Suriname); UN Doc. A/55/38 (part II), para. 315 (Romania); UN Doc. A/55/38 (part II), para. 159 (Lithuania); UN Doc. A/55/38 (part II), para. 110 (Moldova); UN Doc. A/54/38/Rev.1 (part II), para. 57 (Belize); UN Doc. A/54/38/Rev.1 (part I), para. 208 (Greece).

2116 UN Doc. A/54/38/Rev.1 (part II), para. 310 (United Kingdom and Northern Ireland).

2117 UN Doc. A/54/38/Rev.1 (part II), para. 266 (Spain).

2118 UN Doc. CEDAW/C/WSM/CC/1-3, para. 31 (Samoa); UN Doc. CEDAW/C/LAO/CC/1-5, para. 30 (Laos); UN Doc. A/54/38/Rev.1 (part II), para. 59 (Belize); UN Doc. A/51/38, para. 224 (Cuba).

2119 UN Doc. A/53/38/Rev.1 (part I), para. 205 (Czech Republic).

2120 UN Doc. A/54/38/Rev.1 (part I), para. 300 (China).

2121 UN Doc. A/53/38/Rev.1 (part I), para. 410 (Mexico).

2122 UN Doc. A/54/38/Rev.1 (part II), para. 184 (Ireland); UN Doc. A/53/38/Rev.1 (part I), para. 112 (Croatia); UN Doc. A/52/38/Rev.1 (part II), para. 356 (Italy); UN Doc. A/52/38/Rev.1 (part I), para. 193 (Turkey). Compare with article 5 (b) CEDAW: "ensure that family education includes a proper understanding of maternity as a social function and the recognition of the common responsibility of men and women in the upbringing and development of their children [...].".

2123 UN Doc. CEDAW/C/LAO/CC/1-5, para. 22 (Laos); UN Doc. A/52/38/Rev.1 (part II), para. 269 (Antigua and Barbados); UN Doc. A/52/38/Rev.1 (part II), para. 65 (Armenia).

2124 UN Doc. A/53/38/Rev.1 (part II), para. 165 (Nigeria); UN Doc. A/53/38/Rev.1 (part II), para. 122 (South Africa).

2125 UN Doc. A/55/38 (part II), para. 264 (Cuba); UN Doc. A/55/38 (part I), para. 370 (Belarus); UN Doc. A/52/38/Rev.1, para. 120 (Slovenia).

2126 UN Doc. CEDAW/C/TUR/CC/4-5, para. 28 (Turkey); UN Doc. CEDAW/C/LAO/CC/1-5, para. 38 (Laos); UN Doc. A/53/38/Rev.1 (part II), para. 80 (Slovakia); UN Doc. A/52/38/Rev.1 (part II), para. 359 (Italy).

2127 UN Doc. A/53/38/Rev.1 (part I), para. 255 (Bulgaria).

2128 UN Doc. A/53/38/Rev.1 (part I), para. 202 (Czech Republic).

health professionals and the media.[2129] They should be fully sensitized to all forms of violence against women and be adequately trained to respond to them.[2130] A legal education campaign directed at women is desirable, so that they are better aware of their rights.[2131]

In the field of employment, campaigns need to be initiated to guarantee equality of treatment in the workplace,[2132] including equal pay for work of equal or comparable worth,[2133] to encourage the reporting and elimination of sexual harassment in the workplace[2134] and to alert particularly vulnerable groups of women to potential dangers when seeking work overseas.[2135] Awareness-raising campaigns on the importance of women's participation in political and public life and decision-making positions, are to be carried out.[2136]

Aggressive educational campaigns and massive social awareness campaigns are to be organized to encourage women's education.[2137]

iii. To Provide

Rather exceptionally, the Committee has recommended to directly "provide" equality, for example by providing for coverage of abortion by social security,[2138] by insisting

---

2129 UN Doc. A/57/38 (part II), para. 195 (Tunisia); UN Doc. A/57/38 (part I), para. 195 (Uruguay); UN Doc. A/56/38 (part II), para. 259 (Viet Nam); UN Doc. A/56/38 (part II), para. 135 (Guinea); UN Doc. A/56/38 (part I), para. 96 (Kazakhstan); UN Doc. A/55/38 (part II), para. 264 (Cuba); UN Doc. A/55/38 (part I), para. 370 (Belarus); UN Doc. A/55/38 (part I), para. 320 (Germany); UN Doc. A/55/38 (part I), para. 271 (Burkina Faso); UN Doc. A/54/38/Rev.1 (part II), para. 313 (United Kingdom and Northern Ireland); UN Doc. A/54/38/Rev.1 (part II), para. 264 (Spain); UN Doc. A/54/38/Rev.1 (part I), para. 286 (China); UN Doc. A/54/38/Rev.1 (part I), para. 190 (Greece); UN Doc. A/54/38/Rev.1 (part I), para. 123 (Kyrgyzstan); UN Doc. A/54/38/Rev.1 (part I), para. 80 (Algeria); UN Doc. A/53/38/Rev.1 (part II), para. 375 (Korea); UN Doc. A/53/38/Rev.1 (part II), para. 328 (Peru); UN Doc. A/53/38/Rev.1 (part I), para. 303 (Indonesia); UN Doc. A/52/38/Rev.1 (part II), para. 454 (Bangladesh); UN Doc. A/52/38/Rev.1 (part II), para. 121 (Namibia); UN Doc. A/52/38/Rev.1 (part I), para. 120 (Slovenia); UN Doc. A/52/38/Rev.1 (part II), para. 64 (Armenia). See also Communication No. 2/2003, *A.T. v. Hungary*, para. 9.6 II (iv).

2130 UN Doc. CEDAW/C/CRO/CC/2-3, paras. 22 and 32 (Croatia); UN Doc. CEDAW/C/PAR/CC/3-5, para. 25 (Paraguay); UN Doc. CEDAW/C/ITA/CC/4-5, para. 32 (Italy); UN Doc. CEDAW/C/GAB/CC/2-5, para. 27 (Gabon); UN Doc. CEDAW/C/TUR/CC/4-5, para. 28 (Turkey); UN Doc. CEDAW/C/WSM/CC/1-3, para. 25 (Samoa).

2131 UN Doc. A/55/38 (part I), para. 271 (Burkina Faso).

2132 UN Doc. A/53/38/Rev.1 (part II), para. 198 (Panama).

2133 UN Doc. A/51/38, para. 62 (Cyprus).

2134 UN Doc. A/53/38/Rev.1 (part II), para. 379(f) (Korea).

2135 UN Doc. A/53/38/Rev.1 (part I), para. 346 (Dominican Republic).

2136 UN Doc. CEDAW/C/TUR/CC/4-5, para. 32 (Turkey); UN Doc. CEDAW/C/ITA/CC/4-5, para. 28 (Italy); UN Doc. CEDAW/C/GAB/CC/2-5, para. 35 (Gabon); UN Doc. CEDAW/C/WSM/CC/1-3, para. 27 (Samoa).

2137 UN Doc. A/54/38/Rev.1 (part II), para. 142 (Nepal); UN Doc. A/53/38/Rev.1 (part II), para. 200 (Panama).

2138 UN Doc. A/55/38 (part I), para. 276 (Burkina Faso).

on the allocation of adequate resources to improve the status of women's health, in particular with regard to maternal and infant mortality,[2139] by offering legal aid,[2140] medical assistance and rehabilitation and counselling services,[2141] and shelters[2142] to victims of domestic violence, or by requiring the father under parental leave legislation to take part of the leave.[2143]

Unlike most other core human rights treaties, CEDAW provides for protective measures ("special measures") in art. 4, para. 2, *i.e.* measures aimed at protecting maternity. In line with this, states are obliged[2144] to ensure to women, appropriate services in connection with pregnancy, confinement and the post-natal period (art. 12, para. 2 CEDAW). The rationale behind this non-identical treatment for women and men are biological differences between women and men.[2145] As a consequence, protective measures are of a permanent nature, in contrast to temporary special measures (see below).[2146] Maternity leave can therefore not be considered as a measure of affirmative action.[2147]

In its concluding comments, the CEDAW Committee has only occasionally referred to special measures, such as protection for maternity without discrimination under article 4, paragraph 2 of the Convention,[2148] or special measures to reduce maternal mortality rates and protect women's right to life.[2149] The Committee seems to be very reluctant to urge for special measures. It has rather tended to express concern about over-protective measures for pregnancy and motherhood,[2150] and "paternalistic restrictions imposed by the labour laws, which were aimed at protecting maternity and resulted in the legal limitation of women's employment opportunities and choices".[2151]

2139 UN Doc. CEDAW/C/TUR/CC/4-5, para. 38 (Turkey).

2140 UN Doc. A/57/38 (part III), para. 322 (Hungary); UN Doc. A/57/38 (part I), para. 98 (Estonia); UN Doc. A/55/38 (part II), para. 151 (Lithuania).

2141 UN Doc. CEDAW/C/TUR/CC/4-5, para. 28 (Turkey); UN Doc. CEDAW/C/GAB/CC/2-5, para. 27 (Gabon); UN Doc. CEDAW/C/DZA/CC/2, para. 32 (Algeria); UN Doc. CEDAW/C/WSM/CC/1-3, para. 25 (Samoa).

2142 UN Doc. CEDAW/C/TUR/CC/4-5, para. 28 (Turkey); UN Doc. CEDAW/C/PAR/CC/3-5, para. 25 (Paraguay); UN Doc. CEDAW/C/ITA/CC/4-5, para. 32 (Italy); UN Doc. CEDAW/C/CRO/CC/2-3, para. 32 (Croatia); UN Doc. CEDAW/C/WSM/CC/1-3, para. 25 (Samoa); UN Doc. A/55/38 (part II), para. 151 (Lithuania); UN Doc. A/54/38/Rev.1 (part I), para. 80 (Algeria).

2143 UN Doc. A/52/38/Rev.1, para. 115 (Slovenia).

2144 On the mandatory character of this provision, see Joseph, Schultz and Castan, supra note 53, 729.

2145 UN Doc. HRI/GEN/1/Rev.7, General Recommendation No. 25 (2004), *On Article 4, paragraph 1, of the Convention on the Elimination of All Forms of Discrimination against Women – Temporary Special Measures*, para. 16.

2146 *Id.*

2147 UN Doc. A/52/38/Rev.1 (part II), para. 103 (Namibia).

2148 UN Doc. A/57/38 (part II), para. 60 (Suriname); UN Doc. A/53/38/Rev.1 (part II), para. 198 (Panama); Doc. A/53/38/Rev.1 (part I), para. 185 (Czech Republic).

2149 UN Doc. A/52/38/Rev.1, para. 78 (Morocco).

2150 UN Doc. A/53/38/Rev.1 (part I), para. 196 (Czech Republic).

2151 UN Doc. A/52/38/Rev.1 (part II), para. 58 (Armenia).

The CEDAW Committee has paid considerable attention to affirmative action, "temporary special measures" as it is called in art. 4, para. 1 CEDAW.[2152] The terminology has varied. Very exceptionally, references have been made to article 4 of the Convention,[2153] temporary measures,[2154] special temporary measures of affirmative action,[2155] or positive action.[2156] Much more common in use are references to article 4.1,[2157] to temporary special measures,[2158] to affirmative action,[2159] or to temporary special

2152 UN Doc. E/CN.4/2004/40, *Analytical study of the High Commissioner for Human Rights on the fundamental principle of non-discrimination in the context of globalization*, para. 15.

2153 UN Doc. A/52/38/Rev.1 (part II), para. 265 (Antigua and Barbados); UN Doc. A/49/38, para. 446 (Barbados).

2154 UN Doc. A/52/38/Rev.1, para. 112 (Slovenia).

2155 UN Doc. A/53/38/Rev.1 (part I), para. 155 (Zimbabwe).

2156 UN Doc. A/55/38 (part I), para. 81 (India); UN Doc. A/54/38/Rev.1 (part II), para. 306 (United Kingdom and Northern Ireland).

2157 UN Doc. A/58/38 (part II), para. 165 (Morocco); UN Doc. A/57/38 (part III), para. 1430 (Uganda); UN Doc. A/57/38 (part III), para. 290 (Greece); UN Doc. A/57/38 (part III), para. 191 (Guatemala); UN Doc. A/57/38 (part II), para. 98 (Saint Kitts and Nevis); UN Doc. A/56/38 (part I), para. 51 (Burundi); UN Doc. A/55/38 (part II), para. 196 (Iraq); UN Doc. A/55/38 (part II), para. 98 (Moldova).UN Doc. A/54/38/Rev.1 (part II), paras. 301 (United Kingdom and Northern Ireland); UN Doc. A/54/38/Rev.1 (part II), para. 104 (Georgia).UN Doc. A/54/38/Rev.1 (part I), para. 88 (Algeria).

2158 UN Doc. CEDAW/C/WSM/CC/1-3, para. 27 (Samoa); UN Doc. A/58/38 (part I), para. 372 (Canada); UN Doc. A/57/38 (part III), para. 387 (Yemen); UN Doc. A/57/38 (part III), para. 288 (Greece); UN Doc. A/57/38 (part I), para. 279 (Sri Lanka); UN Doc. A/57/38 (part I), para. 106 (Estonia); UN Doc. A/57/38 (part I), para. 94 (Estonia); UN Doc. A/56/38 (part I), para. 300 (Finland); UN Doc. A/56/38 (part I), para. 260 (Mongolia); UN Doc. A/56/38 (part I), para. 220 (Jamaica); UN Doc. A/56/38 (part II), para. 133 (Guinea); UN Doc. A/56/38 (part I), para. 90 (Kazakhstan); UN Doc. A/56/38 (part II), para. 253 (Viet Nam).UN Doc. A/56/38 (part I), para. 135 (Maldives); UN Doc. A/55/38 (part II), para. 270 (Cuba); UN Doc. A/55/38 (part II), para. 181 (Iraq); UN Doc. A/54/38/Rev.1 (part II), para. 190 (Ireland); UN Doc. A/54/38/Rev.1 (part II), para. 98 (Georgia); UN Doc. A/54/38/Rev.1 (part I), para. 234 (Thailand); UN Doc. A/53/38/Rev.1 (part II), para. 270 (New Zealand); UN Doc. A/54/38/Rev.1 (part I), para. 119 (Kyrgyzstan); UN Doc. A/53/38/Rev.1 (part II), para. 231 (Tanzania); UN Doc. A/53/38/Rev.1 (part I), para. 254 (Bulgaria); UN Doc. A/53/38/Rev.1 (part I), para. 201 (Czech Republic); UN Doc. A/53/38/Rev.1 (part II), para. 163 (Nigeria); UN Doc. A/53/38/Rev.1 (part II), paras. 128 and 130 (South Africa); UN Doc. A/53/38/Rev.1 (part II), paras. 76 and 88 (Slovakia); UN Doc. A/53/38/Rev.1 (part I), para. 254 (Bulgaria); UN Doc. A/52/38/Rev.1 (part II), para. 266 (Antigua and Barbados); UN Doc. A/52/38/Rev.1 (part II), para. 215 (Luxembourg); UN Doc. A/52/38/Rev.1 (part II), paras. 62 and 63 (Armenia); UN Doc. A/52/38/Rev.1, para. 1136 (Slovenia); UN Doc. A/52/38/Rev.1, para. 302 (Philippines); UN Doc. A/52/38/Rev.1, para. 267 (Denmark); UN Doc. A/53/38/Rev.1 (part II), para. 231 (Tanzania); UN Doc. A/52/38/Rev.1, para. 199 (Turkey); UN Doc. A/52/38/Rev.1, para. 115 (Slovenia); UN Doc. A/50/38, para. 551 (Russian Federation).

2159 UN Doc. A/56/38 (part II), para. 46 (Andorra); UN Doc. A/55/38 (part II), para. 232 (Austria); UN Doc. A/55/38 (part I), para. 65 (India).UN Doc. A/54/38/Rev.1 (part I), para. 322 (China-Hong Kong); UN Doc. A/54/38/Rev.1 (part I), para. 234 (Thailand); UN Doc. A/53/38/Rev.1 (part I), para. 110 (Croatia); UN Doc. A/53/38/Rev.1 (part I), para. 72 (Azerbaijan); UN Doc. A/52/38/Rev.1 (part II), para. 463 (Bangladesh); UN Doc. A/52/38/Rev.1 (part II), para. 355 (Italy); UN Doc. A/52/38/Rev.1 (part II), para. 122 (Namibia); UN Doc. A/51/38, para. 92 (Iceland); UN Doc. A/49/38, para. 661 (New Zealand); UN Doc. A/49/38, para. 317 (The Netherlands).

measures in accordance with article 4, paragraph 1, of the Convention.[2160] References to the latter in combination with general recommendation 25 have become predominant since the adoption of the general recommendation on temporary special measures in 2004.[2161] The equivalence of temporary special measures and affirmative action has been confirmed.[2162]

The Committee has mainly clarified its viewpoints on temporary special measures in its 2004 general recommendation on the topic.[2163] Earlier, it had defined temporary special measures as the establishment of programmes that advantage women more than men, which require undermining formal equality for a certain period of time in

---

2160 UN Doc. CEDAW/C/CRO/CC/2-3, para. 34 (Croatia); UN Doc. A/58/38 (part II), para. 408 (New Zealand); UN Doc. A/58/38 (part II), para. 368 (Japan); UN Doc. A/58/38 (part II), para. 328 (Ecuador); UN Doc. A/58/38 (part II), para. 260 (France); UN Doc. A/58/38 (part II), paras. 211 and 213 (Slovenia); UN Doc. A/58/38 (part II), para. 121 (Brazil); UN Doc. A/58/38 (part II), para. 59 (Costa Rica).UN Doc. A/58/38 (part I), para. 311 (Luxembourg); UN Doc. A/58/38 (part I), para. 169 (Congo); UN Doc. A/58/38 (part I), para. 131 (Switzerland); UN Doc. A/58/38 (part I), paras. 75 and 79 (Albania); UN Doc. A/57/38 (part III), paras. 475 and 481 (Peru); UN Doc. A/57/38 (part III), para. 403 (Yemen); UN Doc. A/57/38 (part III), para. 328 (Hungary); UN Doc. A/57/38 (part III), para. 326 (Hungary); UN Doc. A/57/38 (part III), para. 288 (Greece); UN Doc. A/57/38 (part III), para. 144 (Uganda); UN Doc. A/57/38 (part III), paras. 92 and 100 (Czech Republic); UN Doc. A/57/38 (part II), para. 294 (Ukraine); UN Doc. A/57/38 (part III), para. 242 (Barbados); UN Doc. A/57/38 (part III), para. 138 (Uganda); UN Doc. A/57/38 (part III), para. 43 (Armenia); UN Doc. A/57/38 (part II), paras. 328 and 330 (Denmark); UN Doc. A/57/38 (part II), para. 286 (Ukraine); UN Doc. A/57/38 (part II), para. 249 (Zambia); UN Doc. A/57/38 (part II), para. 199 (Tunisia); UN Doc. A/57/38 (part II), para. 96 (Saint Kitts and Nevis); UN Doc. A/57/38 (part II), para. 56 (Suriname); UN Doc. A/57/38 (part I), paras. 384 and 382 (Russian Federation); UN Doc. A/57/38 (part I), para. 338 (Portugal); UN Doc. A/57/38 (part I), para. 244 (Iceland); UN Doc. A/57/38 (part I), para. 201 (Uruguay); UN Doc. A/57/38 (part I), para. 104 (Estonia); UN Doc. A/57/38 (part I), para. 51 (Fiji); UN Doc. A/56/38 (part II), para. 345 (Sweden); UN Doc. A/56/38 (part II), para. 218 (The Netherlands); UN Doc. A/56/38 (part I), para. 341 (Egypt); UN Doc. A/56/38 (part I), paras. 171 and 183 (Uzbekistan); UN Doc. A/57/38 (part I), para. 150 (Trinidad and Tobago); UN Doc. A/55/38 (part II), para. 1062 (Moldova); U Doc. A/55/38 (part II), para. 302 (Romania); UN Doc. A/55/38 (part II), para. 238 (Austria); UN Doc. A/55/38 (part I), para. 273 (Burkina Faso); UN Doc. A/55/38 (part I), para. 222 (Congo); UN Doc. A/55/38 (part I), para. 183 (Jordan); UN Doc. A/54/38/Rev.1 (part II), para. 190 (Ireland); UN Doc. A/54/38/Rev.1 (part II), para. 152 (Nepal); UN Doc. A/54/38/Rev.1 (part I), para. 370 (Colombia); UN Doc. A/54/38/Rev.1 (part I), paras. 322 and 330 (China – Hong Kong); UN Doc. A/54/38/Rev.1 (part I), para. 293 (China); UN Doc. A/54/38/Rev.1 (part I), para. 165 (Liechtenstein); UN Doc. A/54/38/Rev.1 (part I), para. 119 (Kyrgyzstan).

2161 UN Doc. CEDAW/C/TUR/CC/4-5, paras. 32 and 34 (Turkey); UN Doc. CEDAW/C/ITA/CC/4-5, paras. 28, 30 and 35 (Italy); UN Doc. CEDAW/C/CRO/CC/2-3, paras. 28 and 36 (Croatia); UN Doc. CEDAW/C/PAR/CC/3-5, paras. 19, 31 and 37 (Paraguay); UN Doc. CEDAW/C/GAB/CC/2-5, paras. 19, 33 and 35 (Gabon); UN Doc. CEDAW/C/DZA/CC/2, paras. 34, 38, 40 and 42 (Algeria); UN Doc. CEDAW/C/WSM/CC/1-3, paras. 27 and 29 (Samoa); UN Doc. CEDAW/C/LAO/CC/1-5, paras. 24 and 34 (Laos).

2162 UN Doc. A/53/38/Rev.1 (part I), para. 234 (Bulgaria).

2163 For background reading, see Ineke Boerefijn, Fons Coomans, Jenny Goldschmidt, Rikki Holtmaat and Ria Wolleswinkel (eds.), *Temporary Special Measures. Accelerating de facto Equality of Women under Article 4(1) UN Convention on the Elimination of All Forms of Discrimination Against Women*, Antwerp, Intersentia, 2003.

order to achieve *de facto* equality in the long term.[2164] The application of temporary special measures is therefore closely related to the realization of *de facto* or substantive equality.[2165] It is considered as one of the means to realize *de facto* or substantive equality for women, rather than an exception to norms of non-discrimination and equality,[2166] and as part of a necessary strategy directed towards the achievement of *de facto* or substantive equality, irrespective of any proof of past discrimination.[2167] Special temporary measures are said to be *mandatory*, if they can be shown to be necessary and appropriate in order to accelerate the achievement of the overall, or a specific goal of, women's *de facto* or substantive equality.[2168]

The function of special temporary measures is to *accelerate de facto* equality, *e.g.* to accelerate the modification and elimination of cultural practices and stereotypical attitudes and behaviour,[2169] or access to equal participation or redistribution of power and resources.[2170]

Both elements, *i.e.* (*de facto*)[2171] equality[2172] and acceleration,[2173] had been highlighted before in numerous concluding comments. Affirmative action has been requested "where women's de facto equality had not been improving at the desired pace."[2174] Reasons for this lack of progress in realizing *de facto* equality have been sought in structural and indirect discrimination against women.[2175]

2164 *Idem.*

2165 Compare with the text of article 4, para. 1 CEDAW: "aimed at accelerating de facto equality between men and women".

2166 UN Doc. HRI/GEN/1/Rev.7, General Recommendation No. 25 (2004), *On Article 4, paragraph 1, of the Convention on the Elimination of All Forms of Discrimination against Women – Temporary Special Measures*, para. 14.

2167 *Ibid.*, para. 18.

2168 *Ibid.*, para. 24.

2169 *Ibid.*, para. 38.

2170 *Ibid.*, paras. 18 and 39.

2171 UN Doc. CEDAW/C/DZA/CC/2, paras. 34 and 42 (Algeria); UN Doc. A/58/38 (part II), para. 412 (New Zealand); UN Doc. A/58/38 (part I), para. 311 (Luxembourg); UN Doc. A/54/38/Rev.1 (part I), para. 330 (China-Hong Kong); UN Doc. A/53/38/Rev.1 (part II), para. 270 (New Zealand); UN Doc. A/53/38/Rev.1 (part II), para. 75 (Slovakia); UN Doc. A/53/38/Rev.1 (part I), para. 254 (Bulgaria); UN Doc. A/52/38/Rev.1 (part II), para. 265 (Antigua and Barbados); UN Doc. A/52/38/Rev.1 (part I), para. 145 (Saint Vincent and the Grenadines).

2172 UN Doc. A/58/38 (part II), paras. 121 and 131 (Brazil); UN Doc. A/55/38 (part II), para. 181 (Iraq); UN Doc. A/53/38/Rev.1 (part I), para. 155 (Zimbabwe); UN Doc. A/52/38/Rev.1, para. 108 (Slovenia).

2173 UN Doc. A/57/38 (part I), para. 106 (Estonia); UN Doc. A/54/38/Rev.1 (part I), para. 165 (Liechtenstein); UN Doc. A/49/38, para. 239 (Madagascar).

2174 UN Doc. A/53/38/Rev.1 (part I), para. 110 (Croatia); UN Doc. A/52/38/Rev.1 (part II), para. 355 (Italy).

2175 UN Doc. A/54/38/Rev.1 (part II), para. 190 (Ireland); UN Doc. A/53/38/Rev.1 (part II), para. 75 (Slovakia).

Special temporary measures are qualified "special" as they are meant to accelerate the achievement of a *concrete* goal for women of *de facto* or substantive equality. Being designed to serve a specific goal,[2176] they fundamentally differ from general social policies to improve the situation of women.[2177] Therefore, a clear distinction is to be made between measures aimed at eliminating discrimination, and temporary special measures aimed at accelerating equality.[2178]

Some limitations to the use of special temporary measures apply. First and foremost, "states parties have an obligation to ensure that temporary special measures are clearly designed to support the principle of equality and therefore comply with constitutional principles which guarantee equality to all citizens."[2179] Secondly, affirmative action should not be implemented at random, but only "if necessary and most appropriate under the circumstances",[2180] and to the extent that there is an objective and reasonable justification.[2181] Thirdly, affirmative action measures are by definition of a temporary nature. This is made very clear in art. 4, para. 1 CEDAW itself, which stipulates that they should "in no way entail as a consequence the maintenance of unequal or separate standards; these measures shall be discontinued when the objectives of equality of opportunity and treatment have been achieved." The CEDAW Committee has clarified in its general recommendation that the duration is to be determined by its functional result: temporary special measures are justified until the desired results have been achieved and sustained for some period of time.[2182] The impact of temporary special measures is therefore regularly to be evaluated, so as to ensure that they lead to the desired goals.[2183] In relation to health in particular, states should carefully distinguish between measures of an ongoing and permanent nature and those of a temporary

2176 UN Doc. HRI/GEN/1/Rev.7, General Recommendation No. 25 (2004), *On Article 4, paragraph 1, of the Convention on the Elimination of All Forms of Discrimination against Women – Temporary Special Measures*, para. 21.

2177 *Ibid.*, paras. 19 and 26.

2178 UN Doc. A/58/38 (part II), para. 131 (Brazil).

2179 UN Doc. HRI/GEN/1/Rev.7, General Recommendation No. 23 (1997), *Political and Public Life*, para. 15.

2180 UN Doc. HRI/GEN/1/Rev.7, General Recommendation No. 25 (2004), *On Article 4, paragraph 1, of the Convention on the Elimination of All Forms of Discrimination against Women – Temporary Special Measures*, para. 39; UN Doc. A/58/38 (part II), para. 260 (France); UN Doc. A/58/38 (part II), para. 121 (Brazil); UN Doc. A/57/38 (part III), para. 288 (Greece); UN Doc. A/56/38 (part II), para. 218 (Netherlands); UN Doc. A/56/38 (part I), para. 300 (Finland).

2181 UN Doc. A/53/38/Rev.1 (part II), para. 320 (Peru).

2182 UN Doc. HRI/GEN/1/Rev.7, General Recommendation No. 25 (2004), *On Article 4, paragraph 1, of the Convention on the Elimination of All Forms of Discrimination against Women – Temporary Special Measures*, para. 20.

2183 UN Doc. CEDAW/C/WSM/CC/1-3, para. 27 (Samoa).

nature.[2184] The temporary nature of affirmative action distinguishes temporary special measures from protective measures: whereas the former are per definition temporary, the latter are per definition of a permanent character.[2185] An earlier retirement age for women than for men *e.g.* cannot be regarded as a measure of affirmative action.[2186]

Temporary special measures may come under very different forms and through a wide variety of legislative,[2187] executive, administrative and other regulatory instruments, policies and practices, such as outreach or support programmes; allocation and/or reallocation of resources;[2188] preferential treatment (*e.g.* scholarships to girl students)[2189]; targeted recruitment, hiring and promotion; numerical goals connected with time frames;[2190] and quota systems.[2191] The choice depends on the context and the specific goal the measures aim to achieve. Quotas have been expressly advocated for in order to achieve gender balance in public and political bodies,[2192] and access to

2184 UN Doc. HRI/GEN/1/Rev.7, General Recommendation No. 25 (2004), *On Article 4, paragraph 1, of the Convention on the Elimination of All Forms of Discrimination against Women – Temporary Special Measures*, para. 37.

2185 Compare with UN Doc. A/53/38/Rev.1 (part II), para. 321 (Peru); UN Doc. A/53/38/Rev.1 (part II), para. 75 (Slovakia).

2186 UN Doc. A/53/38/Rev.1 (part I), para. 234 (Bulgaria).

2187 UN Doc. A/54/38/Rev.1 (part II), paras. 301 (United Kingdom and Northern Ireland).

2188 UN Doc. A/52/38/Rev.1, para. 267 (Denmark).

2189 UN Doc. CEDAW/C/GAB/CC/2-5, para. 33 (Gabon).

2190 UN Doc. A/58/38 (part I), para. 372 (Canada); UN Doc. A/57/38 (part III), para. 288 (Greece); UN Doc. A/57/38 (part I), para. 384 (Russian Federation); UN Doc. A/57/38 (part I), para. 94 (Estonia); UN Doc. A/55/38 (part II), para. 238 (Austria); UN Doc. A/55/38 (part II), para. 141 (Lithuania); UN Doc. A/55/38 (part II), para. 98 (Moldova); UN Doc. A/54/38/Rev.1 (part I), para. 234 (Thailand); UN Doc. A/54/38/Rev.1 (part I), para. 88 (Algeria); UN Doc. A/53/38/Rev.1 (part I), para. 110 (Croatia); UN Doc. A/53/38/Rev.1 (part II), para. 76 (Slovakia); UN Doc. A/53/38/Rev.1 (part I), para. 201 (Czech Republic); UN Doc. A/52/38/Rev.1 (part II), para. 355 (Italy); UN Doc. A/52/38/Rev.1 (part I), para. 267 (Denmark); UN Doc. A/52/38/Rev.1 (part I), para. 116 (Slovenia); UN Doc. A/52/38/Rev.1 (part I), para. 199 (Turkey); UN Doc. A/52/38/Rev.1 (part I), para. 115 (Slovenia).

2191 UN Doc. HRI/GEN/1/Rev.7, General Recommendation No. 25 (2004), *On Article 4, paragraph 1, of the Convention on the Elimination of All Forms of Discrimination against Women – Temporary Special Measures*, para. 22. Compare with General Recommendation No. 5 (1988), *Temporary Special Measures*.

2192 UN Doc. HRI/GEN/1/Rev.7, General Recommendation No. 23 (1997), *Political and Public Life*, para. 29; UN Doc. A/57/38 (part III), para. 403 (Yemen); UN Doc. A/57/38 (part III), para. 288 (Greece); UN Doc. A/57/38 (part III), para. 191 (Guatemala); UN Doc. A/57/38 (part III), para. 43 (Armenia); UN Doc. A/57/38 (part I), para. 94 (Estonia); UN Doc. A/56/38 (part II), para. 88 (Singapore); UN Doc. A/56/38 (part I), para. 341 (Egypt); UN Doc. A/56/38 (part I), para. 300 (Finland); UN Doc. A/55/38 (part II), para. 238 (Austria); UN Doc. A/55/38 (part I), para. 273 (Burkina Faso); UN Doc. A/55/38 (part I), para. 183 (Jordan); UN Doc. A/54/38/Rev.1 (part II), para. 106 (Georgia); UN Doc. A/54/38/Rev.1 (part I), para. 119 (Kyrgyzstan); UN Doc. A/53/38/Rev.1 (part II), para. 377 (Korea); UN Doc. A/53/38/Rev.1 (part II), para. 132 (South Africa); UN Doc. A/53/38/Rev.1 (part II), para. 75 (Slovakia); UN Doc. A/52/38/Rev.1 (part II), para. 463 (Bangladesh); UN Doc. A/53/38/Rev.1 (part II), para. 128 (South Africa); UN Doc. A/52/38/Rev.1, para. 116 (Slovenia); UN Doc. A/51/38, para. 129 (Paraguay); UN Doc. A/50/38, para. 100 (Bolivia).

education.[2193] Supportive mechanisms, in particular educational and training programmes, can accompany and sustain affirmative action programmes.[2194]

Although the Committee recognizes that the establishment of quotas and other temporary special measures to promote women are often controversial,[2195] states have been called upon to include in their domestic legislation provisions that allow for the adoption of temporary special measures,[2196] to proactively[2197] introduce[2198] them in a short-term and long-term framework,[2199]and to strengthen existing affirmative action programmes,[2200] to review their negative attitude towards such concepts and provisions as temporary special measures,[2201] and to ensure the effective monitoring of the implementation of all affirmative action policies and programmes.[2202]

The CEDAW Committee has recommended temporary special measures rather frequently in general ("in all spheres of society";[2203] "the political, economic and social life of the country";[2204] "in all necessary areas"),[2205] or in more specific domains such as education, the economy,[2206] politics, employment,[2207] and health.[2208]

2193 UN Doc. A/57/38 (part III), para. 403 (Yemen); UN Doc. A/57/38 (part III), para. 288 (Greece); UN Doc. A/57/38 (part III), para. 191 (Guatemala); UN Doc. A/57/38 (part III), para. 43 (Armenia); UN Doc. A/57/38 (part I), para. 94 (Estonia); UN Doc. A/56/38 (part I), para. 300 (Finland); UN Doc. A/55/38 (part I), para. 273 (Burkina Faso); UN Doc. A/55/38 (part I), para. 183 (Jordan); UN Doc. A/54/38/Rev.1 (part II), para. 106 (Georgia); UN Doc. A/54/38/Rev.1 (part I), para. 119 (Kyrgyzstan); UN Doc. A/53/38/Rev.1 (part II), para. 377 (Korea); UN Doc. A/53/38/Rev.1 (part II), para. 132 (South Africa); UN Doc. A/53/38/Rev.1 (part II), para. 75 (Slovakia); UN Doc. A/52/38/Rev.1 (part II), para. 463 (Bangladesh); UN Doc. A/53/38/Rev.1 (part II), para. 128 (South Africa); UN Doc. A/52/38/Rev.1, para. 116 (Slovenia); UN Doc. A/50/38, para. 100 (Bolivia).

2194 UN Doc. A/58/38 (part I), para. 169 (Congo); UN Doc. A/53/38/Rev.1 (part II), para. 128 (South Africa); UN Doc. A/52/38/Rev.1 (part II), para. 463 (Bangladesh); UN Doc. A/52/38/Rev.1 (part II), para. 114 (Namibia).

2195 UN Doc. A/53/38/Rev.1 (part II), para. 75 (Slovakia).

2196 *Ibid.*, para. 31; UN Doc. A/57/38 (part II), para. 282 (Ukraine); UN Doc. A/57/38 (part I), para. 88 (Estonia); UN Doc. A/56/38 (part I), para. 167 (Uzbekistan).

2197 UN Doc. A/53/38/Rev.1 (part II), para. 270 (New Zealand).

2198 UN Doc. A/57/38 (part I), para. 382 (Russian Federation); UN Doc. A/56/38 (part I), para. 220 (Jamaica); UN Doc. A/55/38 (part I), para. 75 (India).

2199 UN Doc. A/56/38 (part I), para. 135 (Maldives).

2200 UN Doc. A/57/38 (part III), para. 191 (Guatemala).

2201 UN Doc. A/54/38/Rev.1 (part II), para. 98 (Georgia).

2202 UN Doc. A/52/38/Rev.1 (part II), para. 119 (Namibia).

2203 UN Doc. CEDAW/C/GAB/CC/2-5, para. 19 (Gabon); UN Doc. CEDAW/C/DZA/CC/2, para. 34 (Algeria); UN Doc. A/53/38/Rev.1 (part I), para. 155 (Zimbabwe).

2204 UN Doc. A/52/38/Rev.1 (part II), para. 215 (Luxembourg).

2205 UN Doc. A/53/38/Rev.1 (part I), para. 254 (Bulgaria).

2206 UN Doc. A/57/38 (part I), para. 106 (Estonia); UN Doc. A/56/38 (part II), para. 218 (Netherlands); UN Doc. A/52/38/Rev.1, para. 108 (Slovenia).

2207 UN Doc. HRI/GEN/1/Rev.7, General Recommendation No. 25 (2004), *On Article 4, paragraph 1, of the Convention on the Elimination of All Forms of Discrimination against Women – Temporary Special Measures*, para. 37; General Recommendation No. 5 (1988), *Temporary Special Measures.*

2208 UN Doc. A/55/38 (part I), para. 75 (India).

Specific temporary special measures may be needed to eliminate multiple discrimination.[2209]

In the field of employment,[2210] both in the public and private sectors,[2211] temporary special measures should be used to create employment opportunities for women,[2212] including special credit and loan programmes for women entrepreneurs,[2213] in order to accelerate the achievement of *de facto*[2214] equal opportunities for women and men in the labour market.[2215] Affirmative action has equally been called for to help integrate women in full-time employment and to avoid limiting their participation in the workforce to part-time, insecure or lower paid jobs;[2216] to increase the number of women in the formal workforce;[2217] to improve the representation of women in non-traditional fields of employment[2218] and to overcome sex segregation of the labour market;[2219] to reduce unemployment among women[2220] (mainly through the use of quotas in job creation schemes to a degree proportional to the unemployment rate for women);[2221] to ensure that women and men receive equal pay for work of equal value;[2222] and to ensure that women are present at all levels of employment, including

2209 UN Doc. HRI/GEN/1/Rev.7, General Recommendation No. 25 (2004), *On Article 4, paragraph 1, of the Convention on the Elimination of All Forms of Discrimination against Women – Temporary Special Measures*, para. 12.

2210 UN Doc. CEDAW/C/CRO/CC/2-3, para. 28 (Croatia); UN Doc. CEDAW/C/DZA/CC/2, para. 40 (Algeria); UN Doc. CEDAW/C/WSM/CC/1-3, para. 29 (Samoa); UN Doc. A/57/38 (part I), para. 94 (Estonia); UN Doc. A/56/38 (part II), para. 345 (Sweden); UN Doc. A/56/38 (part II), para. 46 (Andorra); UN Doc. A/55/38 (part I), para. 75 (India); UN Doc. A/54/38/Rev.1 (part II), para. 98 (Georgia); UN Doc. A/53/38/Rev.1 (part I), para. 254 (Bulgaria); UN Doc. A/52/38/Rev.1, para. 145 (Saint Vincent and the Grenadines); UN Doc. A/52/38/Rev.1, para. 108 (Slovenia); UN Doc. A/49/38, para. 317 (The Netherlands).

2211 UN Doc. A/56/38 (part II), para. 345 (Sweden); UN Doc. A/54/38/Rev.1 (part I), para. 88 (Algeria); UN Doc. A/53/38/Rev.1 (part II), para. 270 (New Zealand).

2212 UN Doc. A/57/38 (part III), para. 144 (Uganda); UN Doc. A/53/38/Rev.1 (part II), para. 377 (Korea); UN Doc. A/57/38 (part II), para. 249 (Zambia).

2213 UN Doc. A/52/38/Rev.1 (part II), para. 62 (Armenia).

2214 UN Doc. A/57/38 (part III), para. 100 (Czech Republic); UN Doc. A/58/38 (part I), para. 131 (Switzerland).

2215 UN Doc. CEDAW/C/ITA/CC/4-5, para. 30 (Italy); UN Doc. A/58/38 (part II), para. 412 (New Zealand); UN Doc. A/58/38 (part II), para. 370 (Japan); UN Doc. A/58/38 (part II), para. 213 (Slovenia); UN Doc. A/58/38 (part I), para. 75 (Albania); UN Doc. A/57/38 (part III), para. 328 (Hungary); UN Doc. A/57/38 (part II), para. 294 (Ukraine); UN Doc. A/56/38 (part I), para. 183 (Uzbekistan).

2216 UN Doc. A/53/38/Rev.1 (part II), para. 231 (Tanzania); UN Doc. A/49/38, para. 661 (New Zealand).

2217 UN Doc. CEDAW/C/PAR/CC/3-5, para. 31 (Paraguay).

2218 UN Doc. A/57/38 (part II), para. 328 (Denmark); UN Doc. A/54/38/Rev.1 (part I), para. 119 (Kyrgyzstan).

2219 UN Doc. A/55/38 (part II), para. 270 (Cuba); UN Doc. A/53/38/Rev.1 (part II), para. 88 (Slovakia); UN Doc. A/52/38/Rev.1, para. 115 (Slovenia).

2220 UN Doc. A/55/38 (part II), para. 270 (Cuba); UN Doc. A/52/38/Rev.1, para. 267 (Denmark).

2221 UN Doc. A/54/38/Rev.1 (part II), para. 106 (Georgia); UN Doc. A/54/38/Rev.1 (part I), para. 88 (Algeria); UN Doc. A/53/38/Rev.1 (part II), para. 132 (South Africa); UN Doc. A/52/38/Rev.1, para. 116 (Slovenia).

2222 UN Doc. A/52/38/Rev.1, para. 267 (Denmark).

decision-making positions and leadership roles in the public and private sectors in all fields of employment,[2223] including high-ranking posts in academia.[2224]

The use of temporary special measures has been encouraged also in political and public life,[2225] in order to ensure political representation of women in elected and appointed bodies,[2226] and in decision-making positions at all levels.[2227] Affirmative action has been

2223 UN Doc. A/58/38 (part II), para. 408 (New Zealand); UN Doc. A/58/38 (part II), para. 328 (Ecuador); UN Doc. A/58/38 (part II), para. 260 (France); UN Doc. A/58/38 (part I), para. 311 (Luxembourg); UN Doc. A/57/38 (part III), para. 481 (Peru); UN Doc. A/57/38 (part III), para. 138 (Uganda); UN Doc. A/57/38 (part I), para. 384 (Russian Federation); UN Doc. A/57/38 (part I), para. 244 (Iceland); UN Doc. A/56/38 (part II), para. 253 (Viet Nam); UN Doc. A/56/38 (part II), para. 133 (Guinea); UN Doc. A/56/38 (part I), para. 341 (Egypt); UN Doc. A/56/38 (part I), para. 220 (Jamaica); UN Doc. A/56/38 (part I), para. 90 (Kazakhstan); UN Doc. A/54/38/Rev.1 (part I), para. 119 (Kyrgyzstan); UN Doc. A/53/38/Rev.1 (part II), para. 76 (Slovakia); UN Doc. A/53/38/Rev.1 (part I), para. 201 (Czech Republic); UN Doc. A/52/38/Rev.1, para. 267 (Denmark); UN Doc. A/51/38, para. 92 (Iceland); UN Doc. A/49/38, para. 446 (Barbados).

2224 UN Doc. A/57/38 (part III), para. 288 (Greece); UN Doc. A/56/38 (part II), para. 218 (Netherlands); UN Doc. A/55/38 (part II), para. 232 (Austria); UN Doc. A/54/38/Rev.1 (part I), para. 330 (China-Hong Kong); UN Doc. A/52/38/Rev.1, para. 267 (Denmark).

2225 UN Doc. HRI/GEN/1/Rev.7, General Recommendation No. 25 (2004), *On Article 4, paragraph 1, of the Convention on the Elimination of All Forms of Discrimination against Women – Temporary Special Measures*, para. 37; UN Doc. HRI/GEN/1/Rev.7, General Recommendation No. 23 (1997), *Political and Public Life*, para. 15. With regard to representation at the international level and participation in the work of international organizations, see UN Doc. HRI/GEN/1/Rev.7, General Recommendation No. 8 (1988), *Implementation of Article 8 of the Convention*. See concluding comments in UN Doc. CEDAW/C/ITA/CC/4-5, para. 28 (Italy); UN Doc. CEDAW/C/PAR/CC/3-5, para. 19 (Paraguay); UN Doc. A/57/38 (part III), para. 191 (Guatemala); UN Doc. A/57/38 (part III), para. 92 (Czech Republic); UN Doc. A/57/38 (part I), para. 382 (Russian Federation); UN Doc. A/57/38 (part I), para. 338 (Portugal); UN Doc. A/57/38 (part I), para. 201 (Uruguay); UN Doc. A/57/38 (part I), para. 94 (Estonia); UN Doc. A/56/38 (part II), para. 88 (Singapore); UN Doc. A/55/38 (part II), para. 238 (Austria); UN Doc. A/55/38 (part II), para. 196 (Iraq); UN Doc. A/55/38 (part II), para. 98 (Moldova); UN Doc. A/55/38 (part I), para. 273 (Burkina Faso); UN Doc. A/55/38 (part I), para. 183 (Jordan); UN Doc. A/54/38/Rev.1 (part II), para. 225 (Chile); UN Doc. A/54/38/Rev.1 (part II), para. 190 (Ireland); UN Doc. A/54/38/Rev.1 (part II), para. 152 (Nepal); UN Doc. A/54/38/Rev.1 (part II), paras. 104 and 98 (Georgia); UN Doc. A/54/38/Rev.1 (part I), para. 370 (Colombia); UN Doc. A/54/38/Rev.1 (part I), para. 322 (China-Hong Kong); UN Doc. A/54/38/Rev.1 (part I), para. 119 (Kyrgyzstan); UN Doc. A/53/38/Rev.1 (part II), para. 231 (Tanzania); UN Doc. A/53/38/Rev.1 (part I), para. 254 (Bulgaria); UN Doc. A/53/38/Rev.1 (part I), para. 110 (Croatia); UN Doc. A/53/38/Rev.1 (part I), para. 72 (Azerbaijan); UN Doc. A/52/38/Rev.1 (part II), para. 355 (Italy); UN Doc. A/52/38/Rev.1 (part II), para. 266 (Antigua and Barbados); UN Doc. A/52/38/Rev.1 (part II), para. 63 (Armenia); UN Doc. A/52/38/Rev.1 (part I), para. 199 (Turkey); UN Doc. A/52/38/Rev.1 (part I), para. 145 (Saint Vincent and the Grenadines); UN Doc. A/51/38, para. 60 (Cyprus); UN Doc. A/49/38, para. 446 (Barbados).

2226 UN Doc. CEDAW/C/TUR/CC/4-5, para. 32 (Turkey); UN Doc. CEDAW/C/CRO/CC/2-3, para. 36 (Croatia); UN Doc. CEDAW/C/DZA/CC/2, para. 38 (Algeria); UN Doc. CEDAW/C/WSM/CC/1-3, para. 27 (Samoa); UN Doc. A/58/38 (part I), para. 127 (Switzerland); UN Doc. A/57/38 (part III), para. 242 (Barbados); UN Doc. A/55/38 (part I), para. 273 (Burkina Faso); UN Doc. A/52/38/Rev.1 (part II), para. 463 (Bangladesh).

2227 UN Doc. CEDAW/C/GAB/CC/2-5, para. 35 (Gabon); UN Doc. CEDAW/C/LAO/CC/1-5, para. 34 (Laos); UN Doc. A/58/38 (part II), para. 408 (New Zealand); UN Doc. A/58/38 (part II), para. 368 (Japan); UN Doc. A/58/38 (part II), para. 211 (Slovenia); UN Doc. A/58/38 (part II), para. 165

recommended with regard to the public administration,[2228] in particular its senior management,[2229] other governmental or government-appointed bodies, such as those dealing with business and economic matters,[2230] state-owned enterprises,[2231] the diplomatic service[2232] and in particular high ranks of the diplomatic service,[2233] and the judiciary.[2234] A wide range of measures is mentioned in general recommendation No. 23, including recruiting, financially assisting and training women candidates, amending electoral procedures, developing campaigns directed at equal participation, setting numerical goals and quotas and targeting women for appointment to public positions such as the judiciary or other professional groups that play an essential part in the everyday life of all societies. Furthermore, states should ensure that temporary special measures adopted by some political parties, including setting aside for women a certain minimum number or percentage of positions on their executive bodies – ensuring that there is a balance between the number of male and female candidates nominated for election, and ensuring that women are not consistently assigned to less favourable constituencies or to the least advantageous positions on a party list – are specifically permitted under anti-discrimination legislation or other constitutional guarantees of equality.[2235]

(Morocco); UN Doc. A/58/38 (part II), para. 59 (Costa Rica); UN Doc. A/58/38 (part I), para. 372 (Canada); UN Doc. A/58/38 (part I), para. 274 (El Salvador); UN Doc. A/58/38 (part I), para. 169 (Congo); UN Doc. A/58/38 (part I), para. 79 (Albania); UN Doc. A/57/38 (part III), para. 444 (Mexico); UN Doc. A/57/38 (part III), para. 403 (Yemen); UN Doc. A/57/38 (part III), para. 326 (Hungary); UN Doc. A/57/38 (part III), para. 288 (Greece); UN Doc. A/57/38 (part III), para. 92 (Czech Republic); UN Doc. A/57/38 (part II), para. 286 (Ukraine); UN Doc. A/57/38 (part II), para. 199 (Tunisia); UN Doc. A/57/38 (part II), para. 96 (Saint Kitts and Nevis); UN Doc. A/57/38 (part II), para. 56 (Suriname); UN Doc. A/57/38 (part I), para. 338 (Portugal); UN Doc. A/57/38 (part I), para. 150 (Trinidad and Tobago).UN Doc. A/57/38 (part I), para. 51 (Fiji); UN Doc. A/56/38 (part II), para. 218 (Netherlands); UN Doc. A/56/38 (part I), para. 171 (Uzbekistan); UN Doc. A/56/38 (part I), para. 51 (Burundi); UN Doc. A/55/38 (part II), para. 302 (Romania); UN Doc. A/54/38/Rev.1 (part I), para. 322 (China-Hong Kong); UN Doc. A/54/38/Rev.1 (part I), para. 293 (China); UN Doc. A/53/38/Rev.1 (part I), para. 201 (Czech Republic); UN Doc. A/52/38/Rev.1 (part II), para. 63 (Armenia); UN Doc. A/52/38/Rev.1, para. 302 (Philippines); UN Doc. A/52/38/Rev.1 (part I), para. 112 (Slovenia); UN Doc. A/50/38, para. 551 (Russian Federation).

2228 UN Doc. A/55/38 (part II), para. 141 (Lithuania); UN Doc. A/52/38/Rev.1 (part II), para. 463 (Bangladesh).

2229 UN Doc. A/51/38, para. 60 (Cyprus); UN Doc. A/50/38, para. 100 (Bolivia).

2230 UN Doc. A/53/38/Rev.1 (part II), para. 128 (South Africa).

2231 UN Doc. A/57/38 (part I), para. 104 (Estonia).

2232 UN Doc. A/57/38 (part III), para. 1430 (Uganda); UN Doc. A/57/38 (part III), para. 290 (Greece); UN Doc. A/57/38 (part II), para. 98 (Saint Kitts and Nevis); UN Doc. A/49/38, para. 446 (Barbados).

2233 UN Doc. A/57/38 (part III), para. 290 (Greece); UN Doc. A/57/38 (part II), para. 330 (Denmark); UN Doc. A/51/38, para. 60 (Cyprus).

2234 UN Doc. A/55/38 (part I), para. 81 (India); UN Doc. A/53/38/Rev.1 (part II), para. 163 (Nigeria); UN Doc. A/53/38/Rev.1 (part II), para. 130 (South Africa);UN Doc. A/52/38/Rev.1 (part II), para. 122 (Namibia).

2235 UN Doc. HRI/GEN/1/Rev.7, General Recommendation No. 23 (1997), *Political and Public Life*, para. 33. Compare with UN Doc. A/53/38/Rev.1 (part II), para. 377 (Korea) (minimum quota of 30 per cent representation of women in political parties) and UN Doc. A/53/38/Rev.1 (part II), para. 76 (Slovakia).

Temporary special measures in the field of education[2236] have been recommended in particular to increase enrolment of girls at all levels,[2237] and to give them equal access to education,[2238] including high quality education and training; to overcome the clustering of female students in certain disciplines at schools and universities and to diversify their educational choices;[2239] to address higher drop-out rates;[2240] and to accelerate women's representation in educational decision-making.[2241]

Temporary special measures have been mentioned rather exceptionally in the area of encouraging men to devote more time to child care and housework,[2242] the eradication of poverty among women, especially rural women,[2243] and the elimination of discrimination against certain groups of women, such as ethnic minority women,[2244] indigenous women,[2245] Dalit women and girls,[2246] and more generally vulnerable groups of women, including Roma and migrant women.[2247]

d. *Conclusions*

Strong emphasis is put on the elimination of discriminatory legislation in the CEDAW Committee's concluding comments. As *de jure* equality is considered a necessary prerequisite for achieving *de facto* equality of women, detailed recommendations have been given to review discriminatory legislation in all fields of life. Commensurate with the detailed provisions in CEDAW itself, positive measures (to fulfil-facilitate) have been stressed in the Committee's concluding comments. The CEDAW Committee has been remarkably restrictive in recommending protective measures. This might be explained by the Committee's concern that a "policy of gender equality in compliance with the Convention will require the recognition that women can have various roles in society, not only the important role of mother and wife, exclusively responsible for children and the family, but also as an individual person and actor in her

---

2236 UN Doc. CEDAW/C/TUR/CC/4-5, para. 34 (Turkey); UN Doc. CEDAW/C/LAO/CC/1-5, para. 24 (Laos); UN Doc. A/57/38 (part I), paras. 94 and 106 (Estonia); UN Doc. A/55/38 (part I), para. 75 (India); UN Doc. A/52/38/Rev.1, para. 108 (Slovenia).

2237 UN Doc. CEDAW/C/GAB/CC/2-5, para. 33 (Gabon); UN Doc. A/58/38 (part I), para. 171 (Congo).

2238 UN Doc. A/57/38 (part III), para. 387 (Yemen); UN Doc. A/55/38 (part I), para. 65 (India).

2239 UN Doc. CEDAW/C/CRO/CC/2-3, para. 34 (Croatia); UN Doc. A/55/38 (part II), para. 141 (Lithuania); UN Doc. A/54/38/Rev.1 (part I), para. 330 (China-Hong Kong); UN Doc. A/52/38/Rev.1, para. 1136 (Slovenia).

2240 UN Doc. A/57/38 (part III), para. 387 (Yemen); UN Doc. A/52/38/Rev.1 (part II), para. 176 (Israel).

2241 Doc. A/55/38 (part II), para. 1062 (Moldova).

2242 UN Doc. A/52/38/Rev.1, para. 267 (Denmark).

2243 UN Doc. A/57/38 (part III), para. 475 (Peru).

2244 UN Doc. A/54/38/Rev.1 (part II), para. 306 (United Kingdom and Northern Ireland).

2245 UN Doc. CEDAW/C/PAR/CC/3-5, para. 37 (Paraguay).

2246 UN Doc. A/55/38 (part I), para. 75 (India).

2247 UN Doc. CEDAW/C/ITA/CC/4-5, para. 35 (Italy); UN Doc. CEDAW/C/CRO/CC/2-3, para. 30 (Croatia).

community and in the society in general."[2248] Persistence of the emphasis on women's role as mothers, together with an extensive protection provided to women as mothers, may tend to perpetuate sex role stereotypes and reduce the father's role and responsibility in the upbringing of children.[2249] The obligation to fulfil-promote has been developed rather strongly as well, and the Committee has paid sustained attention to it. It has focused on awareness of women, training and sensitization of professional groups, and awareness of the general public. Affirmative action ("temporary special measures") is prominently present in the CEDAW Committee's work. Is has been well-developed conceptually, and been recommended in a wide range of fields in which gender-based discrimination occurs.

5. CRC COMMITTEE

States are to prevent, prohibit and eliminate all forms of discrimination against children and to ensure equal opportunities for their full participation in all spheres of life.[2250] The specific obligations that ensue from this general obligation will be analysed in terms of obligations to respect, to protect and to fulfil.

The amendment and adoption of legislation may take place in response to the obligations to respect, to protect or to fulfil-facilitate. Some attention is therefore paid to legislative measures by way of introduction, without subsuming them to one of the more specific obligations.

As a general principle, a state is to "[a]mend the existing legislation and [to] adopt new laws to ensure that all children within its territory enjoy all rights set out in the Convention without discrimination, in accordance with article 2."[2251] Full compatibility

2248 UN Doc. A/57/38 (part II), para. 48 (Suriname); UN Doc. A/57/38 (part III), para. 234 (Barbados). Compare with UN Doc. A/56/38 (part I), para. 169 (Uzbekistan); UN Doc. A/57/38 (part I), para. 148 (Trinidad and Tobago); UN Doc. A/53/38/Rev.1 (part I), paras. 184-185 (Czech Republic).

2249 UN Doc. A/53/38/Rev.1 (part I), para. 233 (Bulgaria); compare with UN Doc. A/55/38 (part I), para. 405 (Luxembourg); UN Doc. A/54/38/Rev.1 (part II), para. 179 (Ireland); UN Doc. A/54/38/Rev.1 (part I), para. 280 (China); UN Doc. A/53/38/Rev.1 (part II), para. 74 (Slovakia).

2250 UN Doc. CRC/C/15/Add.263, para. 42 (Mongolia); UN Doc. CRC/C/15/Add.262, para. 19 (Norway).

2251 UN Doc. CRC/C/15/Add.260, para. 37 (Nepal); UN Doc. CRC/C/15/Add.257, para. 30 (Nigeria); UN Doc. CRC/C/15/Add.253, para. 29 (The Bahamas); UN Doc. CRC/C/15/Add.249, para. 24 (Albania); UN Doc. CRC/C/15/Add.242, para. 28 (Botswana); UN Doc. CRC/C/15/Add.240, para. 19 (France); UN Doc. CRC/C/15/Add. 235, para. 22 (Sao Tome and Principe); UN Doc. CRC/C/15/Add.223, paras. 28-29 and 31 (Indonesia); UN Doc. CRC/C/15/Add.222, para. 20 (Georgia); UN Doc. CRC/C/15/Add.213, paras. 25-26 (Kazakhstan); UN Doc. CRC/C/15/Add.207, para. 26 (Sri Lanka); UN Doc. CRC/C/15/Add.205, para. 28 (Cyprus); UN Doc. CRC/C/15/Add.200, para. 23 (Viet Nam); UN Doc. CRC/C/15/Add.184, para. 20 (St. Vincent and the Grenadines); UN Doc. CRC/C/15/Add.165, para. 26 (Gambia).

and conformity of national legislation and practices with the CRC is to be ensured.[2252] In case the principle of non-discrimination is not yet incorporated in domestic law, steps are to be taken to that effect.[2253] It should be possible to invoke the principle of equality before the courts.[2254]

Furthermore, it is important that all prohibited grounds of discrimination under the CRC (*i.e.* race, colour, language, political or other opinion, national or ethnic origin, disability, birth or other status) are explicitly included in domestic legislation.[2255] Particular attention has been paid to the ground of disability.[2256]

a. *The Obligation to Respect*

States are to respect the rights in the CRC for each child within their jurisdiction without discrimination of any kind.[2257] They are recommended to revise or rescind legislation where necessary, to prevent and eliminate discrimination.[2258] They have been

---

2252 UN Doc. CRC/C/15/Add.240, para. 19 (France); UN Doc. CRC/C/15/Add.222, para. 22 (Georgia); UN Doc. CRC/C/15/Add.219, paras. 24-25 (Brunei Darussalam); UN Doc. CRC/C/15/Add.209, paras. 7-8 (Syrian Arabic Jamahiriya); UN Doc. CRC/C/15/Add.177, para. 22 (Guinea-Bissau); UN Doc. CRC/C/15/Add.172, para. 26 (Mozambique); UN Doc. CRC/C/15/Add.81, para. 30 (Czech Republic); UN Doc. CRC/C/15/Add.76, para. 33 (Algeria); UN Doc. CRC/C/15/Add.70, para. 24 (Syrian Arab Republic); UN Doc. CRC/C/15/Add.62, para. 17 (Uruguay); UN Doc. CRC/C/15/Add.47, para. 14 (Yemen); UN Doc. CRC/C/15/Add.54, para. 28 (Lebanon); UN Doc. CRC/C/15/Add.43, para. 28 (Germany); UN Doc. CRC/C/15/Add.42, para. 17 (Ukraine); UN Doc. CRC/C/15/Add.41, para. 16 (Italy); UN Doc. CRC/C/15/Add.16, para. 14 (Romania).

2253 UN Doc. CRC/C/15/Add.112, para. 17 (Mexico); UN Doc. CRC/C/15/Add.85, para. 25 (Ireland).

2254 UN Doc. CRC/C/15/Add.40, para. 25 (Sri Lanka); UN Doc. CRC/C/15/Add.25, para. 18 (Indonesia); UN Doc. CRC/C/15/Add.13, para. 15 (Mexico).

2255 UN Doc. CRC/C/15/Add.197, paras. 31-32 (Korea); UN Doc. CRC/C/15/Add.210, paras. 23-24 (Jamaica); UN Doc. CRC/C/15/Add.186, paras. 25-26 (Netherlands Antilles); UN Doc. CRC/C/15/Add.179, para. 28 (Niger); UN Doc. CRC/C/15/Add.175, para. 25 (Bahrain); UN Doc. CRC/C/15/Add.148, paras. 9-10 (Saudi Arabia); UN Doc. CRC/C/15/Add.128, para. 32 (Cambodia); UN Doc. CRC/C/15/Add.126, para. 21 (Norway); UN Doc. CRC/C/15/Add.125, para. 30 (Jordan); UN Doc. CRC/C/15/Add.116, paras. 30-31 (Sierra Leone); UN Doc. CRC/C/15/Add.96, para. 17 (Kuwait); UN Doc. CRC/C/15/Add.94, para. 17 (Iraq); UN Doc. CRC/C/15/Add.92, paras. 9 and 27 (Luxembourg); UN Doc. CRC/C/15/Add.90, para. 14 (Japan); UN Doc. CRC/C/15/Add.85, paras. 11 and 18 (Libya); UN Doc. CRC/C/15/Add.69, paras. 8 and 28 (Myanmar); UN Doc. CRC/C/15/Add.2, para. 7 (Sweden).

2256 UN Doc. CRC/C/15/Add.246, para. 22 (Angola); UN Doc. CRC/C/15/Add.227, para. 31 (Netherlands and Aruba); UN Doc. CRC/C/15/Add.222, para. 21 (Georgia); UN Doc. CRC/C/15/Add.184, para. 20 (St. Vincent and the Grenadines); UN Doc. CRC/C/15/Add.153, para. 23 (DRC). This does not come as a surprise, for the CRC Committee has devoted particular attention to disability-based discrimination more generally (see higher, chapter III).

2257 UN Doc. HRI/GEN/1/Rev.7, General Comment No. 5 (2003), *General Measures of Implementation of the Convention on the Rights of the Child (Arts. 4, 42 and 44, para. 6)*, para. 12.

2258 UN Doc. CRC/C/15/Add.249, para. 24 (Albania); UN Doc. CRC/C/15/Add.212, para. 26 (Syrian Arab Republic); UN Doc. CRC/C/15/Add.211, para. 26 (Morocco); UN Doc. CRC/C/15/Add.209, paras. 23-24 (Syrian Arabic Jamahiriya); UN Doc. CRC/C/15/Add.196, para. 24 (Estonia); UN Doc.

asked to end or eliminate discrimination,[2259] *inter alia* against vulnerable groups of children,[2260] such as children living/working on the streets and children belonging to minority groups,[2261] non-autochthonous Roma,[2262] children without residence permits,[2263] girls,[2264] and children born out of wedlock.[2265] Particular attention is to be paid to discrimination based on religious beliefs.[2266] Amendment of citizenship laws have been recommended,[2267] in order to allow transmission of nationality through fathers and mothers,[2268] and through unmarried as well as married fathers.[2269] With regard to gender-based discrimination, particular attention has been paid to access to education,[2270] inheritance and property rights,[2271] and the minimum age for marriage. With a reference to general comment No. 21 of the CEDAW Committee, the latter has been recommended to be increased with and without parental consent to 18 years, for both girls and boys.[2272] Concerning children born out of wedlock, the focus has been on inheritance and citizenship rights and birth registration, as well as discriminatory terminology.[2273]

CRC/C/15/Add.195, para. 27 (Israel); UN Doc. CRC/C/15/Add.183, para. 22 (United Arab Emirates); UN Doc. CRC/C/15/Add.175, para. 27 (Bahrain); UN Doc. CRC/C/15/Add.163, para. 30 (Qatar); UN Doc. CRC/C/15/Add.161, para. 25 (Oman); UN Doc. CRC/C/15/Add.157, para. 31 (Bhutan); UN Doc. CRC/C/15/Add.148, paras. 10, 24 and 32 (Saudi Arabia); UN Doc. CRC/C/15/Add.147, para. 26 (Lesotho); UN Doc. CRC/C/15/Add.145, para. 30 (Egypt); UN Doc. CRC/C/15/Add.125, para. 30 (Jordan); UN Doc. CRC/C/15/Add.123, paras. 22 and 36 (Iran); Doc. CRC/C/15/Add.57, paras. 10 and 25 (Nepal); UN Doc. CRC/C/15/Add.55, paras. 12 and 22 (Zimbabwe).

2259 UN Doc. CRC/C/15/Add.166, para. 28 (Paraguay); UN Doc. CRC/C/15/Add.133, para. 27 (Burundi).

2260 UN Doc. CRC/C/15/Add.100, para. 17 (Guinea); UN Doc. CRC/C/15/Add.89, para. 34 (Fiji); UN Doc. CRC/C/15/Add.78, para. 40 (Laos); UN Doc. CRC/C/15/Add.29, para. 23 (Philippines).

2261 UN Doc. CRC/C/15/Add.128, para. 28 (Cambodia).

2262 UN Doc. CRC/C/15/Add.230, para. 23 (Slovenia).

2263 UN Doc. CRC/C/15/Add.110, para. 51 (Russian Federation).

2264 UN Doc. CRC/C/15/Add.148, para. 9 (Saudi Arabia); UN Doc. CRC/C/15/Add.107, para. 17 (Chad).

2265 UN Doc. CRC/C/15/Add.258, para. 20 (Philippines); UN Doc. CRC/C/15/Add.250, para. 23 (Luxembourg); UN Doc. CRC/C/15/Add.51, para. 22 (Korea); UN Doc. CRC/C/15/Add.40, para. 28 (Sri Lanka).

2266 UN Doc. CRC/C/15/Add.190, para. 27 (Sudan); UN Doc. CRC/C/15/Add.148, para. 9 (Saudi Arabia).

2267 UN Doc. CRC/C/15/Add.255, para. 27 (Togo); UN Doc. CRC/C/15/Add.236, para. 33 (Liberia); UN Doc. CRC/C/15/Add.220, para. 31 (Singapore).

2268 UN Doc. CRC/C/15/Add.221, para. 40 (Bangladesh).

2269 UN Doc. CRC/C/15/Add. 188, para. 23 (United Kingdom).

2270 UN Doc. CRC/C/15/Add.128, para. 28 (Cambodia).

2271 UN Doc. HRI/GEN/1/Rev.7, General Comment No. 3 (2003), *HIV/AIDS and the Rights of the Child*, para. 30. See also UN Doc. CRC/C/15/Add.141, para. 24 (Comoros).

2272 UN Doc. HRI/GEN/1/Rev.7, General Comment No. 4 (2003), *Adolescent Health and Development in the Context of the Convention on the Rights of the Child*, para. 16.

2273 UN Doc. CRC/C/15/Add.231, para. 25 (Japan); UN Doc. CRC/C/15/Add.129, para. 24 (Malta).

b. The Obligation to Protect

The obligation to protect against violations of the principle of non-discrimination by third parties may very often be covered by recommendations to amend or adopt legislation. The CRC Committee has for example, recommended to ensure through legislation that all children within a state's jurisdiction enjoy all the rights set out in the CRC without discrimination.[2274] It has insisted on the criminalization and punishment of racially motivated acts.[2275] Protective measures have been recommended with regard to *inter alia* children of migrant families in irregular situations,[2276] indigenous children,[2277] children with disabilities[2278] and children infected with and affected by HIV/AIDS.[2279] This obligation seems however to have been developed much less by the CRC Committee than by the other Committees.

c. The Obligation to Fulfil

A state is to ensure the rights in the CRC to each child within its jurisdiction without discrimination of any kind.[2280] This obligation to fulfil can be disaggregated into obligations to facilitate, to promote and to provide.

i. To Facilitate

Facilitation of the right to non-discrimination can occur for instance, through the adoption of appropriate legislation, the implementation of existing legislation, and the application of the principle of non-discrimination in policies and programmes.

The CRC Committee has recommended the adoption of appropriate legislation that explicitly prohibits all forms of discrimination, and in greater detail.[2281] Similarly, it has insisted on full and effective implementation of existing laws and policies guaranteeing the principle of non-discrimination,[2282] in particular also to prevent and combat

---

2274 UN Doc. CRC/C/15/Add.202, para. 26 (Haiti).

2275 UN Doc. CRC/C/15/Add.214, para. 13 (San Marino); UN Doc. CRC/C/15/Add.198, para. 21 (Italy); UN Doc. CRC/C/15/Add.196, para. 24 (Estonia).

2276 UN Doc. CRC/C/15/Add.265, para. 19 (Costa Rica).

2277 UN Doc. CRC/C/15/Add.261, para. 74 (Ecuador).

2278 UN Doc. CRC/C/15/Add.258, para. 56 (Philippines).

2279 *Ibid.*, para. 65 (Philippines).

2280 UN Doc. HRI/GEN/1/Rev.7, General Comment No. 5 (2003), *General Measures of Implementation of the Convention on the Rights of the Child (Arts. 4, 42 and 44, para. 6)*, para. 12.

2281 UN Doc. CRC/C/15/Add.247, paras. 26-27 (Antigua and Barbuda); UN Doc. CRC/C/15/Add.224, para. 22 (Guyana).

2282 UN Doc. CRC/C/15/Add.264, para. 28 (Nicaragua); UN Doc. CRC/C/15/Add.263, para. 23 (Mongolia); UN Doc. CRC/C/15/Add.261, para. 29 (Ecuador); UN Doc. CRC/C/15/Add.260, para. 37 (Nepal); UN Doc. CRC/C/15/Add.258, paras. 20, 56 and 65 (Philippines); UN Doc.

persistence in practice of discrimination.[2283] Effective law enforcement is to be ensured.[2284]

The CRC has also paid consistent attention to the application of the principle of non-discrimination in all political, judicial and administrative decisions and in projects, programmes, services and reconstruction activities that have an impact on all children, in particular vulnerable groups of children.[2285] In other words, the principle of non-discrimination is to be applied in planning and policy making at every level, as well as in actions taken by social and health welfare and educational institutions, courts of law and administrative authorities.[2286]

CRC/C/15/Add.257, para. 30 (Nigeria); UN Doc. CRC/C/15/Add.251, para. 21 (Austria); UN Doc. CRC/C/15/Add.250, para. 20 (Luxembourg); UN Doc. CRC/C/15/Add.247, para. 26 (Antigua and Barbuda); UN Doc. CRC/C/15/Add.245, para. 24 (Equatorial Guinea); UN Doc. CRC/C/15/Add.244, para. 27 (Kyrgyzstan); UN Doc. CRC/C/15/Add.241, para. 30 (Brazil); UN Doc. CRC/C/15/Add.239, para. 28 (People's Republic of Korea); UN Doc. CRC/C/15/Add.238, para. 22 (Dominica); UN Doc. CRC/C/15/Add. 236, para. 24 (Liberia); UN Doc. CRC/C/15/Add.228, paras. 28 and 34 (India); UN Doc. CRC/C/15/Add.227, para. 31 (Netherlands and Aruba); UN Doc. CRC/C/15/Add.224, para. 22 (Guyana); UN Doc. CRC/C/15/Add.222, para. 22 (Georgia); UN Doc. CRC/C/15/Add. 216, para. 23 (New Zealand); UN Doc. CRC/C/15/Add.207, para. 26 (Sri Lanka); UN Doc. CRC/C/15/Add.204, para. 21 (Eritrea); UN Doc. CRC/C/15/Add.199, para. 26 (Romania); UN Doc. CRC/C/15/Add.194, para. 28 (Poland); UN Doc. CRC/C/15/Add.174, para. 23 (Malawi); UN Doc. CRC/C/15/Add.149, para. 33 (Palau); UN Doc. CRC/C/15/Add.141, para. 24 (Comoros); UN Doc. CRC/C/15/Add.138, para. 29 (Central African Republic); UN Doc. CRC/C/15/Add.133, para. 27 (Burundi); UN Doc. CRC/C/15/Add.131, para. 28 (Djibouti); UN Doc. CRC/C/15/Add.130, para. 25 (Suriname); UN Doc. CRC/C/15/Add.124, para.25 (Georgia); UN Doc. CRC/C/15/Add.115, para. 31 (India); UN Doc. CRC/C/15/Add.99, para. 16 (Belize); UN Doc. CRC/C/15/Add.97, para. 18 (Thailand).

2283 UN Doc. CRC/C/15/Add.240, para. 19 (France); UN Doc. CRC/C/15/Add.116, para. 31 (Sierra Leone).

2284 UN Doc. CRC/C/15/Add.228, para. 30 (India); UN Doc. CRC/C/15/Add.218, para. 26 (Madagascar); UN Doc. CRC/C/15/Add.202, para. 26 (Haiti); UN Doc. CRC/C/15/Add.193, para. 24 (Burkina Faso); UN Doc. CRC/C/15/Add.181, para. 23 (Tunisia); UN Doc. CRC/C/15/Add.169, para. 24 (Lebanon); UN Doc. CRC/C/15/Add.159, para. 26 (Mauritania); UN Doc. CRC/C/15/Add.155, para. 23 (Ivory Coast); UN Doc. CRC/C/15/Add.115, para. 33 (India).

2285 UN Doc. CRC/C/15/Add.215, para. 22 (Canada); UN Doc. CRC/C/15/Add.207, para. 24 (Sri Lanka); UN Doc. CRC/C/15/Add.201, para. 29 (Czech Republic); UN Doc. CRC/C/15/Add.135, para. 24 (United Kingdom – Overseas Territories); UN Doc. CRC/C/15/Add.134, para. 21 (United Kingdom – Isle of Man); UN Doc. CRC/C/15/Add.128, para. 26 (Cambodia); UN Doc. CRC/C/15/Add.113, para. 16 (Mali); UN Doc. CRC/C/15/Add.111, para. 14 (Vanuatu); UN Doc. CRC/C/15/Add.106, para. 14 (Benin); UN Doc. CRC/C/15/Add.104, para. 17 (St. Kitts and Nevis); UN Doc. CRC/C/15/Add.102, para. 17 (Yemen); UN Doc. CRC/C/15/Add.100, para. 16 (Guinea); UN Doc. CRC/C/15/Add.99, para. 15 (Belize); UN Doc. CRC/C/15/Add.97, para. 17 (Thailand); UN Doc. CRC/C/15/Add.96, para. 16 (Kuwait); UN Doc. CRC/C/15/Add.94, para. 16 (Iraq); UN Doc. CRC/C/15/Add.92, para. 28 (Luxembourg); UN Doc. CRC/C/15/Add.90, para. 35 (Japan); UN Doc. CRC/C/15/Add.89, para. 33 (Fiji); UN Doc. CRC/C/15/Add.86, para. 32 (Micronesia); UN Doc. CRC/C/15/Add.75, para. 34 (Paraguay).

2286 UN Doc. CRC/C/15/Add.205, para. 26 (Cyprus); UN Doc. CRC/C/15/Add.202, para. 24 (Haiti); UN Doc. CRC/C/15/Add.199, para. 24 (Romania); UN Doc. CRC/C/15/Add.197, para. 29 (Korea); UN Doc. CRC/C/15/Add.196, para. 22 (Estonia); UN Doc. CRC/C/15/Add. 192, para. 25 (Moldova); UN Doc. CRC/C/15/Add. 191, para. 28 (Ukraine); UN Doc. CRC/C/15/Add. 189, para. 24

The right to equality can also be facilitated through the establishment of complaints and monitoring mechanisms.[2287] Accessible, prompt and effective mechanisms to monitor, receive and address complaints of discrimination are therefore to be established.[2288] Children and their parents who have been victims of discrimination should be able to seek recourse through the judicial system,[2289] and persons who violate non-discrimination provisions of the law should be prosecuted.[2290]

Overall coordination of the implementation of the CRC within a state party is required, with a view to decreasing and eliminating any possibility of disparity or discrimination in the implementation of the CRC and to ensuring that the CRC is fully respected in all parts of the territory of a state.[2291]

States are encouraged to take all necessary measures[2292] or to make greater efforts[2293] to ensure that all children within their jurisdiction enjoy all the rights set out in the CRC without discrimination.[2294] Measures to reduce economic, social and regional

---

(Seychelles); UN Doc. CRC/C/15/Add. 187, para. 28 (Argentina); UN Doc. CRC/C/15/Add. 185, para. 26 (Spain); UN Doc. CRC/C/15/Add. 180, para. 26 (Belarus); UN Doc. CRC/C/15/Add. 179, para. 26 (Niger); UN Doc. CRC/C/15/Add. 176, para. 26 (Andorra); UN Doc. CRC/C/15/Add. 175, para. 23 (Bahrain); UN Doc. CRC/C/15/Add. 174, para. 21 (Malawi); UN Doc. CRC/C/15/Add. 173, para. 25 (Chile); UN Doc. CRC/C/15/Add.171, para. 23 (Gabon); UN Doc. CRC/C/15/Add.170, para. 32 (Greece); UN Doc. CRC/C/15/Add.168, para. 27 (Cape Verde); UN Doc. CRC/C/15/Add.166, para. 26 (Paraguay); UN Doc. CRC/C/15/Add.159, para. 24 (Mauritania); UN Doc. CRC/C/15/Add.154, para. 25 (Guatemala); UN Doc. CRC/C/15/Add.152, para. 28 (Turkey); UN Doc. CRC/C/15/Add.146, para. 19 (Lithuania); UN Doc. CRC/C/15/Add.142, para. 21 (Latvia).

2287 UN Doc. CRC/C/15/Add.259, para. 26 (Bosnia and Herzegovina); UN Doc. CRC/C/15/Add.226, para. 24 (Germany); UN Doc. CRC/C/15/Add.148, para. 17 (Saudi Arabia).

2288 UN Doc. CRC/C/15/Add.157, para. 31 (Bhutan).

2289 UN Doc. CRC/C/15/Add.170, para. 34 (Greece).

2290 UN Doc. CRC/C/15/Add.133, para. 27 (Burundi).

2291 UN Doc. CRC/C/15/Add.240, para. 9 (France); UN Doc. CRC/C/15/Add.182, para. 10 (Switzerland); UN Doc. CRC/C/15/Add.101, para. 7 (Sweden); UN Doc. CRC/C/15/Add.98, para. 8 (Austria); UN Doc. CRC/C/15/Add.50, para. 22 (Iceland); UN Doc. CRC/C/15/Add.37, para. 20 (Canada).

2292 UN Doc. CRC/C/15/Add.219, para. 27 (Brunei Darussalam); UN Doc. CRC/C/15/Add.178, para. 19 (Belgium); UN Doc. CRC/C/15/Add.161, para. 27 (Oman); UN Doc. CRC/C/15/Add.145, para. 32 (Egypt); UN Doc. CRC/C/15/Add.140, para. 20 (Slovakia); UN Doc. CRC/C/15/Add.136, para. 21 (Tajikistan).

2293 UN Doc. CRC/C/15/Add.218, para. 26 (Madagascar); UN Doc. CRC/C/15/Add.217, para. 30 (Pakistan); UN Doc. CRC/C/15/Add.214, para. 13 (San Marino); UN Doc. CRC/C/15/Add.206, para. 22 (Zambia); UN Doc. CRC/C/15/Add.193, para. 24 (Burkina Faso); UN Doc. CRC/C/15/Add.171, para. 25 (Gabon); UN Doc. CRC/C/15/Add.164, para. 26 (Cameroon); UN Doc. CRC/C/15/Add.157, para. 29 (Bhutan).

2294 UN Doc. CRC/C/15/Add.217, para. 30 (Pakistan); UN Doc. CRC/C/15/Add.203, para. 23 (Iceland); UN Doc. CRC/C/15/Add.179, para. 28 (Niger); UN Doc. CRC/C/15/Add.175, para. 29 (Bahrain); UN Doc. CRC/C/15/Add.167, para. 27 (Uzbekistan); UN Doc. CRC/C/15/Add.163, para. 33 (Qatar); UN Doc. CRC/C/15/Add.92, para. 27 (Luxembourg).

disparities should be increased or intensified.[2295] A proactive and comprehensive strategy has been recommended more generally in recent times.[2296] All necessary proactive measures are to be undertaken to combat societal discrimination.[2297] Social services are to be prioritized and targeted to children belonging to (the marginalized and) most vulnerable groups, through a proactive and comprehensive strategy.[2298] To that effect, existing disparities in the enjoyment by children of their rights are to be evaluated carefully and regularly, and on the basis of that evaluation the necessary steps are to be undertaken to prevent and combat discriminatory disparities through proactive measures.[2299] Monitoring of the situation of particular groups of children is to be taken place in order to be able to develop, on the basis of the results of this monitoring, comprehensive proactive strategies containing specific and well-targeted actions aimed at preventing and eliminating all forms of discrimination.[2300] Gender impact

---

2295 UN Doc. CRC/C/15/Add.137, para. 33 (Colombia); UN Doc. CRC/C/15/Add.110, para. 25 (Russian Federation); UN Doc. CRC/C/15/Add.93, para. 18 (Ecuador).

2296 UN Doc. CRC/C/15/Add.264, para. 28 (Nicaragua); UN Doc. CRC/C/15/Add.263, para. 23 (Mongolia); UN Doc. CRC/C/15/Add.261, para. 29 (Ecuador); UN Doc. CRC/C/15/Add.260, para. 37 (Nepal); UN Doc. CRC/C/15/Add.258, paras. 20, 56 and 65 (Philippines); UN Doc. CRC/C/15/Add.257, para. 30 (Nigeria); UN Doc. CRC/C/15/Add.252, para. 26 (Belize); UN Doc. CRC/C/15/Add.251, para. 21 (Austria); UN Doc. CRC/C/15/Add.250, para. 20 (Luxembourg); UN Doc. CRC/C/15/Add.245, paras. 23-24 (Equatorial Guinea); UN Doc. CRC/C/15/Add.244, para. 27 (Kyrgyzstan); UN Doc. CRC/C/15/Add. 241, para. 30 (Brazil); UN Doc. CRC/C/15/Add.239, para. 28 (People's Republic of Korea); UN Doc. CRC/C/15/Add.238, para. 221 (Dominica); UN Doc. CRC/C/15/Add.236, para. 24 (Liberia); UN Doc. CRC/C/15/Add. 235, para. 22 (Sao Tome and Principe); UN Doc. CRC/C/15/Add.227, para. 31 (Netherlands and Aruba); UN Doc. CRC/C/15/Add.224, para. 22 (Guyana); UN Doc. CRC/C/15/Add.223, para. 31 (Indonesia); UN Doc. CRC/C/15/Add.221, para. 29 (Bangladesh); UN Doc. CRC/C/15/Add. 216, para. 23 (New Zealand); UN Doc. CRC/C/15/Add.207, para. 25 (Sri Lanka); UN Doc. CRC/C/15/Add.204, para. 21 (Eritrea); UN Doc. CRC/C/15/Add.194, para. 28 (Poland).

2297 UN Doc. CRC/C/15/Add.220, para. 24 (Singapore); UN Doc. CRC/C/15/Add.197, para. 32 (Korea).

2298 UN Doc. CRC/C/15/Add.266, para. 33 (Yemen); UN Doc. CRC/C/15/Add.263, para. 23 (Mongolia); UN Doc. CRC/C/15/Add.260, para. 37 (Nepal); UN Doc. CRC/C/15/Add.218, para. 26 (Madagascar); UN Doc. CRC/C/15/Add.217, para. 30 (Pakistan); UN Doc. CRC/C/15/Add.206, para. 21 (Zambia); UN Doc. CRC/C/15/Add.202, para. 26 (Haiti); UN Doc. CRC/C/15/Add.198, para. 21 (Italy); UN Doc. CRC/C/15/Add. 193, para. 24 (Burkina Faso); UN Doc. CRC/C/15/Add.179, para. 27 (Niger); UN Doc. CRC/C/15/Add.178, para. 19 (Belgium); UN Doc. CRC/C/15/Add.175, para. 29 (Bahrain); UN Doc. CRC/C/15/Add.171, para. 24 (Gabon); UN Doc. CRC/C/15/Add.167, para. 27 (Uzbekistan); UN Doc. CRC/C/15/Add.164, para. 26 (Cameroon); UN Doc. CRC/C/15/Add.163, para. 33 (Qatar); UN Doc. CRC/C/15/Add.161, para. 27 (Oman); UN Doc. CRC/C/15/Add.157, para. 28 (Bhutan); UN Doc. CRC/C/15/Add.145, para. 32 (Egypt); UN Doc. CRC/C/15/Add.136, para. 21 (Tajikistan).

2299 UN Doc. CRC/C/15/Add.259, para. 26 (Bosnia and Herzegovina); UN Doc. CRC/C/15/Add.243, para. 23 (Croatia); UN Doc. CRC/C/15/Add. 226, para. 24 (Germany); UN Doc. CRC/C/15/Add.198, para. 21 (Italy); UN Doc. CRC/C/15/Add.182, para. 22 (Switzerland).

2300 UN Doc. CRC/C/15/Add.251, para. 24 (Austria); UN Doc. CRC/C/15/Add.213, para. 28 (Kazakhstan); UN Doc. CRC/C/15/Add.208, para. 22 (Solomon Islands); UN Doc. CRC/C/15/Add.192, para. 27 (Moldova); UN Doc. CRC/C/15/Add.191, para. 30 (Ukraine); UN Doc. CRC/C/15/Add.188, para. 23 (United Kingdom); UN Doc. CRC/C/15/Add.187, para. 30 (Argentina); UN Doc. CRC/C/15/Add.185, para. 28 (Spain); UN Doc. CRC/C/15/Add.180, para. 29 (Belarus); UN Doc. CRC/C/15/Add.173, para. 27 (Chile); UN Doc. CRC/C/15/Add.166, para. 28 (Paraguay); UN Doc. CRC/C/15/Add.154, para. 27 (Guatemala); UN Doc. CRC/C/15/Add.152, para. 30 (Turkey).

studies or other studies have been suggested in order to identify the causes of discrimination,[2301] and to prepare policies.[2302] Concerted efforts at all levels may have to be taken to address social inequalities by reviewing and reorienting policies, including increasing budgetary allocations for programmes targeting the most vulnerable groups.[2303] In consultation with the media, a code of conduct may be developed with a view to eliminating stereotyping and stigmatization of minority and/or ethnic groups in the media.[2304]

States have explicitly been asked to implement the recommendations of other UN Committees,[2305] and to seek assistance from the UN and the international community.[2306]

Muslim countries have been requested to undertake all possible measures to reconcile the interpretation of Islamic texts with fundamental human rights,[2307] including by considering the practice of other states that had been successful in reconciling fundamental rights with Islamic texts.[2308]

The CRC Committee has mainly insisted on effective and proactive measures with regard to equal access to basic services, such as education and health, as well as welfare and other social services.[2309]

With regard to health, adequate access to health-care services for all children without discrimination has been a central concern.[2310] Health facilities, goods and services

2301 UN Doc. CRC/C/15/Add.153, para. 23 (Democratic Republic of Congo); UN Doc. CRC/C/15/Add.133, para. 27 (Burundi).

2302 UN Doc. CRC/C/15/Add.228, para. 34 (India); UN Doc. CRC/C/15/Add.200, para. 23 (Viet Nam); UN Doc. CRC/C/15/Add.203, para. 23 (Iceland).

2303 UN Doc. CRC/C/15/Add.228, para. 26 (India); UN Doc. CRC/C/15/Add.181, para. 23 (Tunisia); UN Doc. CRC/C/15/Add.169, para. 24 (Lebanon); UN Doc. CRC/C/15/Add.159, para. 26 (Mauritania); UN Doc. CRC/C/15/Add.155, para. 23 (Ivory Coast); UN Doc. CRC/C/15/Add.119, para. 24 (Armenia); UN Doc. CRC/C/15/Add.115, para. 29 (India).

2304 UN Doc. CRC/C/15/Add.259, para. 26 (Bosnia and Herzegovina).

2305 UN Doc. CRC/C/15/Add.178, para. 19 (Belgium); UN Doc. CRC/C/15/Add.153, para. 23 (Democratic Republic of Congo).

2306 UN Doc. CRC/C/15/Add.153, para. 23 (Democratic Republic of Congo); UN Doc. CRC/C/15/Add.125, para. 32 (Jordan).

2307 UN Doc. CRC/C/15/Add.183, para. 22 (United Arab Emirates); UN Doc. CRC/C/15/Add.163, para. 31 (Qatar); UN Doc. CRC/C/15/Add.161, para. 25 (Oman).

2308 UN Doc. CRC/C/15/Add.148, para. 24 (Saudi Arabia); UN Doc. CRC/C/15/Add.145, para. 30 (Egypt).

2309 UN Doc. CRC/C/15/Add.243, paras. 61-62 (Croatia); UN Doc. CRC/C/15/Add.227, para. 31 (Netherlands and Aruba); UN Doc. CRC/C/15/Add.186, para. 26 (Netherlands Antilles); UN Doc. CRC/C/15/Add.170, para. 34 (Greece); UN Doc. CRC/C/15/Add.96, para. 17 (Kuwait); UN Doc. CRC/C/15/Add.80, para. 30 (Uganda); UN Doc. CRC/C/15/Add.73, para. 32 (Ghana).

2310 UN Doc. CRC/C/15/Add.140, para. 36 (Slovakia).

should be known and easily accessible (economically, physically and socially) to all adolescents, without discrimination.[2311] States parties must ensure that [health] services are provided to the maximum extent possible to all children living within their borders, without discrimination, and that they sufficiently take into account differences in gender, age, and the social, economic, cultural and political context in which children live.[2312] Appropriate resources are to be allocated and comprehensive policies and programmes to be developed to improve the health situation of all children without discrimination, in particular by focusing more on health promotion and prevention,[2313] and on primary health care and decentralizing the health-care system.[2314] Laws, policies, strategies and practices are to address all forms of discrimination that contribute to increasing the impact of the epidemics.[2315]

As to education, recommendations have focused in particular on indigenous, Roma and migrant children, and on children with disabilities. For indigenous children, efforts are to be geared towards providing for compulsory and free primary education, eradicating illiteracy and ensuring the availability of bilingual education. Moreover, greater efforts are to be made in training qualified teachers.[2316] Roma children are to be integrated into mainstream education, so that special assistance and support for Roma children can be provided at regular classes.[2317] The right of migrant children to have access to scholarships and to take part in students councils is to be ensured.[2318] Public education policy and school curricula are to reflect in all their aspects the principle of full participation and equality, and children with disabilities are to be included in the mainstream school system to the extent possible.[2319]

More generally speaking, stronger emphasis is to be placed on public education.[2320] The curriculum is to ensure that the child's freedom of religion can be fully realised in the educational system without any discrimination.[2321] With a view to create an

---

2311 UN Doc. HRI/GEN/1/Rev.7, General Comment No. 4 (2003), *Adolescent Health and Development in the Context of the Convention on the Rights of the Child*, para. 37.

2312 UN Doc. HRI/GEN/1/Rev.7, General Comment No. 3 (2003), *HIV/AIDS and the Rights of the Child*, para 18.

2313 UN Doc. CRC/C/15/Add.187, para. 47 (Argentina); UN Doc. CRC/C/15/Add.142, para. 36 (Latvia).

2314 UN Doc. CRC/C/15/Add.173, para. 40 (Chile); UN Doc. CRC/C/15/Add.166, para. 38 (Paraguay); UN Doc. CRC/C/15/Add.159, para. 38 (Mauritania); UN Doc. CRC/C/15/Add.154, para. 41 (Guatemala); UN Doc. CRC/C/15/Add.152, para. 52 (Turkey).

2315 UN Doc. HRI/GEN/1/Rev.7, General Comment No. 3 (2003), *HIV/AIDS and the Rights of the Child*, para. 7.

2316 UN Doc. CRC/C/15/Add.265, para. 19 (Costa Rica); UN Doc. CRC/C/15/Add.58, para. 37 (Guatemala).

2317 UN Doc. CRC/C/15/Add.230, para. 23 (Slovenia).

2318 UN Doc. CRC/C/15/Add.265, para. 19 (Costa Rica).

2319 UN Doc. CRC/C/15/Add.258, para. 56 (Philippines).

2320 UN Doc. CRC/C/15/Add.169, para. 49 (Lebanon).

2321 UN Doc. CRC/C/15/Add.265, para. 26 (Costa Rica).

environment of tolerance, peace and understanding of cultural diversity shared by all children, so as to prevent intolerance, bullying and discrimination in schools and society at large, Bosnia-Herzegovina was recommended to harmonize its educational system throughout the country, and to eliminate the system of "schools-under-one-roof".[2322]

A special focus has been on the most disadvantaged or vulnerable groups of children.[2323]

ii. To Promote

The CRC Committee's recommendations in observance of the obligation to promote relate to general promotional measures, and to training of specific professional groups.

The Committee's view on information campaigns for the general public was well summarized in its concluding observations to Uruguay:

> Information campaigns on children's rights will contribute to ensuring visibility to children within Uruguayan society and to changing negative attitudes towards children. Such campaigns should aim at eradicating discriminatory attitudes towards children, especially those belonging to vulnerable and marginalized groups, and enhancing respect for their fundamental rights. In this regard, the Committee underlines the importance of the general principles of the Convention, namely the best interests of the child, the child's participation and respect of his or her views, respect of the principle of non-discrimination and the right to life, survival and development to the maximum extent, which should guide and inspire all training and information programmes in this area.[2324]

Comprehensive public education campaigns[2325] (involving religious leaders)[2326] have been recommended time and again to prevent and combat all forms of discrimi-

2322 UN Doc. CRC/C/15/Add.259, para. 59 (Bosnia and Herzegovina).

2323 UN Doc. CRC/C/15/Add.249, para. 35 (Albania); UN Doc. CRC/C/15/Add.150, para. 23 (Dominican Republic); UN Doc. CRC/C/15/Add.127, para. 22 (Kyrgyzstan); UN Doc. CRC/C/15/Add.125, para. 32 (Jordan); UN Doc. CRC/C/15/Add.123, para. 24 (Iran); UN Doc. CRC/C/15/Add.122, para. 18 (South Africa); UN Doc. CRC/C/15/Add.120, para. 16 (Peru); UN Doc. CRC/C/15/Add.117, para. 15 (Costa Rica); UN Doc. CRC/C/15/Add.112, para. 18 (Mexico); UN Doc. CRC/C/15/Add.109, para. 18 (Venezuela); UN Doc. CRC/C/15/Add.108, para. 24 (Nicaragua); UN Doc. CRC/C/15/Add.106, para. 15 (Benin); UN Doc. CRC/C/15/Add.105, para. 19 (Honduras); UN Doc. CRC/C/15/Add.102, para. 18 (Yemen); UN Doc. CRC/C/15/Add.95, para. 17 (Bolivia); UN Doc. CRC/C/15/Add.93, para. 18 (Ecuador); UN Doc. CRC/C/15/Add.85, para. 34 (Ireland); UN Doc. CRC/C/15/Add.81, para. 32 (Czech Republic); UN Doc. CRC/C/15/Add.45, para. 21 (Portugal); UN Doc. CRC/C/15/Add.33, para. 25 (Denmark); UN Doc. CRC/C/15/Add.31, para. 27 (Poland); UN Doc. CRC/C/15/Add.25, para. 22 (Indonesia); UN Doc. CRC/C/15/Add.13, para. 18 (Mexico).

2324 UN Doc. CRC/C/15/Add.62, para. 17 (Uruguay).

2325 UN Doc. CRC/C/15/Add.260, para. 37 (Nepal); UN Doc. CRC/C/15/Add.215, para. 22 (Canada).

2326 UN Doc. CRC/C/15/Add.218, para. 26 (Madagascar).

nation,[2327] or negative societal attitudes and practices,[2328] to sensitize society to the situation and needs of children within the society and particularly within the family,[2329] and to develop a culture of tolerance.[2330] In light of article 29 CRC on the aims of education, states are to establish adequate programmes and activities with a view to create an environment of tolerance, peace and understanding on cultural diversity, to prevent intolerance, bullying and discrimination in schools and society at large.[2331]

Specifically-targeted educational and training activities have been recommended with regard to discrimination based on HIV/AIDS,[2332] ethnic origin[2333] (indigenous children,[2334] Roma children,[2335] minorities[2336]), national origin[2337] (children of migrant workers and refugee and asylum-seeking children,[2338] non-residents[2339]), social origin,[2340] religion or other belief,[2341] caste,[2342] gender,[2343]

2327 *Id.*; UN Doc. CRC/C/15/Add.202, para. 26 (Haiti); UN Doc. CRC/C/15/Add.181, para. 23 (Tunisia); UN Doc. CRC/C/15/Add.172, para. 26 (Mozambique); UN Doc. CRC/C/15/Add.169, para. 24 (Lebanon); UN Doc. CRC/C/15/Add.159, para. 26 (Mauritania); UN Doc. CRC/C/15/Add.155, para. 23 (Ivory Coast); UN Doc. CRC/C/15/Add.138, para. 29 (Central African Republic); UN Doc. CRC/C/15/Add.133, para. 27 (Burundi).

2328 UN Doc. CRC/C/15/Add.215, para. 22 (Canada); UN Doc. CRC/C/15/Add.196, para. 24 (Estonia); UN Doc. CRC/C/15/Add.195, para. 27 (Israel); UN Doc. CRC/C/15/Add.193, para. 24 (Burkina Faso); UN Doc. CRC/C/15/Add.178, para. 19 (Belgium).

2329 UN Doc. CRC/C/15/Add.119, para. 24 (Armenia).

2330 UN Doc. CRC/C/15/Add.243, para. 22 (Croatia); UN Doc. CRC/C/15/Add.170, para. 34 (Greece).

2331 UN Doc. CRC/C/15/Add.243, para. 58 (Croatia).

2332 UN Doc. HRI/GEN/1/Rev.7, General Comment No. 3 (2003), *HIV/AIDS and the Rights of the Child*, para. 7. See also UN Doc. CRC/C/15/Add.264, para. 51 (Nicaragua); UN Doc. CRC/C/15/Add.255, para. 53 (c) (Togo); UN Doc. CRC/C/15/Add.245, para. 51 (Equatorial Guinea); UN Doc. CRC/C/15/Add.115, para. 51 (India); UN Doc. CRC/C/15/Add.23, para. 20 (Norway).

2333 UN Doc. CRC/C/15/Add.157, para. 31 (Bhutan); UN Doc. CRC/C/15/Add.117, para. 15 (Costa Rica); UN Doc. CRC/C/15/Add.108, para. 24 (Nicaragua); UN Doc. CRC/C/15/Add.105, para. 19 (Honduras).

2334 UN Doc. CRC/C/15/Add.233, para. 64 (Panama).

2335 UN Doc. CRC/C/15/Add.249, para. 24 (Albania); UN Doc. CRC/C/15/Add.198, para. 53 (Italy); UN Doc. CRC/C/15/Add.81, para. 32 (Czech Republic).

2336 UN Doc. CRC/C/15/Add.233, para. 25 (Panama); UN Doc. CRC/C/15/Add.231, para. 25 (Japan).

2337 UN Doc. CRC/C/15/Add.198, para. 53 (Italy); UN Doc. CRC/C/15/Add.143, para. 21 (Liechtenstein); UN Doc. CRC/C/15/Add.117, para. 15 (Costa Rica).

2338 UN Doc. CRC/C/15/Add.233, para. 25 (Panama); UN Doc. CRC/C/15/Add.231, para. 25 (Japan); UN Doc. CRC/C/15/Add.209, paras. 25-26 (Libyan Arabic Jamahiriya).

2339 UN Doc. CRC/C/15/Add.220, para. 24 (Singapore).

2340 UN Doc. CRC/C/15/Add.233, para. 25 (Panama).

2341 UN Doc. CRC/C/15/Add.148, para. 32 (Saudi Arabia); UN Doc. CRC/C/15/Add.123, para. 36 (Iran).

2342 UN Doc. CRC/C/15/Add.228, para. 28 (India); UN Doc. CRC/C/15/Add.115, para. 31 (India).

2343 UN Doc. CRC/C/15/Add.246, para. 22 (Angola); UN Doc. CRC/C/15/Add.233, para. 25 (Panama); UN Doc. CRC/C/15/Add.231, para. 25 (Japan); UN Doc. CRC/C/15/Add.220, para. 24 (Singapore); UN Doc. CRC/C/15/Add.228, para. 34 (India); UN Doc. CRC/C/15/Add.117, para. 15 (Costa Rica); UN Doc. CRC/C/15/Add.115, para. 33 (India); UN Doc. CRC/C/15/Add.108, para. 24 (Nicaragua); UN Doc. CRC/C/15/Add.105, para. 19 (Honduras); UN Doc. CRC/C/15/Add.70, para. 25 (Syrian Arab Republic).

disability,[2344] and birth (out of wedlock)[2345]. As to gender discrimination, public education campaigns should also pay attention to discrimination within the family,[2346] and eliminate stereotyping in terms of traditional roles of men and women in society.[2347] They should be also targeted towards boys and men.[2348] Educational programmes that support and promote the idea of joint parental responsibility should be set up.[2349]

A particular characteristic of the CRC seems to be its emphasis on the involvement of political, religious and community leaders,[2350] specifically with regard to discrimination based on caste,[2351] gender[2352] and birth.[2353]

2344 UN Doc. CRC/C/15/Add.261, para. 50 (Ecuador); UN Doc. CRC/C/15/Add.258, para. 56 (Philippines); UN Doc. CRC/C/15/Add.233, para. 25 (Panama); UN Doc. CRC/C/15/Add.231, para. 25 (Japan); UN Doc. CRC/C/15/Add.220, para. 24 (Singapore); UN Doc. CRC/C/15/Add.129, para. 38 (Malta); UN Doc. CRC/C/15/Add.128, para. 49 (Cambodia); UN Doc. CRC/C/15/Add.120, para. 16 (Peru); UN Doc. CRC/C/15/Add.117, para. 23 (Costa Rica); UN Doc. CRC/C/15/Add.108, para. 24 (Nicaragua); UN Doc. CRC/C/15/Add.105, para. 28 (Honduras); UN Doc. CRC/C/15/Add.102, para. 18 (Yemen); UN Doc. CRC/C/15/Add.100, para. 28 (Guinea); UN Doc. CRC/C/15/Add.94, para. 24 (Iraq); UN Doc. CRC/C/15/Add.91, para. 40 (Maldives); UN Doc. CRC/C/15/Add.90, para. 41 (Japan); UN Doc. CRC/C/15/Add.89, para. 40 (Fiji); UN Doc. CRC/C/15/Add.88, para. 33 (DPR Korea); UN Doc. CRC/C/15/Add.81, para. 30 (Czech Republic).

2345 UN Doc. CRC/C/15/Add.212, para. 26 (Syrian Arab Republic); UN Doc. CRC/C/15/Add.209, paras. 23-24 (Libyan Arabic Jamahiriya).

2346 UN Doc. CRC/C/15/Add.266, para. 33 (Yemen); UN Doc. CRC/C/15/Add.228, para. 30 (India); UN Doc. CRC/C/15/Add.219, para. 25 (Brunei Darussalam); UN Doc. CRC/C/15/Add.211, para. 26 (Morocco); UN Doc. CRC/C/15/Add.183, para. 22 (United Arab Emirates); UN Doc. CRC/C/15/Add.175, para. 27 (Bahrain); UN Doc. CRC/C/15/Add.167, para. 31 (Uzbekistan); UN Doc. CRC/C/15/Add.163, para. 31 (Qatar); UN Doc. CRC/C/15/Add.161, para. 25 (Oman); UN Doc. CRC/C/15/Add.148, para. 24 (Saudi Arabia); UN Doc. CRC/C/15/Add.145, para. 30 (Egypt); UN Doc. CRC/C/15/Add.136, para. 23 (Tajikistan); UN Doc. CRC/C/15/Add.127, para. 26 (Kyrgyzstan); UN Doc. CRC/C/15/Add.115, para. 33 (India); UN Doc. CRC/C/15/Add.11, para. 16 (Costa Rica).

2347 UN Doc. CRC/C/15/Add.205, para. 28 (Cyprus).

2348 UN Doc. CRC/C/15/Add.221, para. 29 (Bangladesh).

2349 UN Doc. CRC/C/15/Add.263, para. 32 (Mongolia).

2350 UN Doc. CRC/C/15/Add.212, paras. 26 and 47 (Syrian Arab Republic); UN Doc. CRC/C/15/Add.209, paras. 23-24, 40 (Libyan Arabic Jamahiriya); UN Doc. CRC/C/15/Add.195, para. 27 (Israel).

2351 UN Doc. CRC/C/15/Add.228, para. 28 (India).

2352 UN Doc. CRC/C/15/Add.266, para. 33 (Yemen); UN Doc. CRC/C/15/Add.228, para. 30 (India); UN Doc. CRC/C/15/Add.211, para. 26 (Morocco); UN Doc. CRC/C/15/Add.183, para. 22 (United Arab Emirates); UN Doc. CRC/C/15/Add.175, para. 27 (Bahrain); UN Doc. CRC/C/15/Add.163, para. 31 (Qatar); UN Doc. CRC/C/15/Add.161, para. 25 (Oman); UN Doc. CRC/C/15/Add.148, para. 24 (Saudi Arabia); UN Doc. CRC/C/15/Add.145, para. 30 (Egypt); UN Doc. CRC/C/15/Add.125, para. 30 (Jordan); UN Doc. CRC/C/15/Add.124, para. 22 (Iran); UN Doc. CRC/C/15/Add.115, para. 33 (India).

2353 UN Doc. CRC/C/15/Add.212, para. 26 (Syrian Arab Republic); UN Doc. CRC/C/15/Add.209, paras. 23-24 (Libyan Arabic Jamahiriya).

The effectiveness of measures to raise awareness for the prevention and combating of discrimination and promoting tolerance is to be evaluated.[2354]

Training has been recommended in particular towards the legal profession, and more especially the judiciary, with regard to gender-sensitivity.[2355]

iii. To Provide

Affirmative action – special measures as they are called under the CRC – has been considered permissible and necessary under certain circumstances. It is recalled that one of the general principles of the CRC is the non-discrimination obligation. In the view of the Committee

> This non-discrimination obligation requires States actively to identify children and groups of children the recognition and realisation of whose rights may demand special measures. [...] It should be emphasized that the application of the non-discrimination principle of equal access to rights does not mean identical treatment. A general comment by the Human Rights Committee has underlined the importance of taking special measures in order to diminish or eliminate conditions that cause discrimination.[2356]

The CRC Committee does not seem to use uniform language: it has referred to affirmative action,[2357] affirmative measures,[2358] special temporary programmes,[2359] preferential treatment,[2360] and more recently to special measures.[2361]

2354 UN Doc. CRC/C/15/Add.63, para. 24 (United Kingdom – Hong Kong).

2355 UN Doc. CRC/C/15/Add.266, para. 33 (Yemen); UN Doc. CRC/C/15/Add.219, para. 25 (Brunei Darussalam); UN Doc. CRC/C/15/Add.211, para. 26 (Morocco); UN Doc. CRC/C/15/Add.183, para. 22 (United Arab Emirates); UN Doc. CRC/C/15/Add.175, para. 27 (Bahrain); UN Doc. CRC/C/15/Add.163, para. 31 (Qatar); UN Doc. CRC/C/15/Add.161, para. 25 (Oman); UN Doc. CRC/C/15/Add.148, para. 24 (Saudi Arabia); UN Doc. CRC/C/15/Add.145, para. 30 (Egypt).

2356 UN Doc. HRI/GEN/1/Rev.7, General Comment No. 5 (2003), *General Measures of Implementation of the Convention on the Rights of the Child (Arts. 4, 42 and 44, para. 6)*, para. 12. This was confirmed in para. 30: "As noted above (para. 12), the non-discrimination principle does not prevent the taking of special measures to diminish discrimination."

2357 UN Doc. CRC/C/15/Add.195, para. 27 (Israel); UN Doc. CRC/C/15/Add.140, paras. 21 and 24 (Slovakia).

2358 UN Doc. CRC/C/15/Add.115, para. 31 (India).

2359 UN Doc. CRC/C/15/Add.228, paras. 31-32 (India).

2360 UN Doc. CRC/C/15/Add.199, para. 55 (Romania).

2361 UN Doc. CRC/C/15/Add.243, para. 71 (Croatia); UN Doc. CRC/C/15/Add.241, para. 30 (Brazil); UN Doc. CRC/C/15/Add.230, para. 49 (Slovenia); UN Doc. CRC/C/15/Add.228, para. 28 (India). This is also the terminology used in general comment No. 5, see above.

Affirmative action has been recommended with regard to ethnic groups,[2362] minorities,[2363] Roma,[2364] untouchables[2365] and refugees.[2366]

The Committee does not seem to want affirmative action to be based on specific grounds of discrimination, but rather on needs and rights:

> While welcoming the special temporary programmes and other activities to improve the enjoyment of rights by girls and vulnerable groups such as children belonging to Scheduled Castes and Tribes, the Committee expresses its concern at the possibility that other children in situations similar to that of those groups are not receiving the same benefits.[2367]

> The Committee further recommends that the State party start to develop special programmes for the allocation of educational and other benefits that are based on child's needs and rights rather than on the basis of sex, caste or tribe, or any other characteristic that may result in unjustifiable discrimination.[2368]

The inclusion of specified goals and timetables has been recommended, "in order to evaluate their success and justify their continuation, expansion and dissemination."[2369]

d. *Conclusions*

The CRC Committee has – generally speaking – refrained from very detailed recommendations on specific obligations. It has paid considerable attention to the obligation of states to refrain from discrimination, and to the obligation to fulfil-promote. Obligations to protect, to fulfil-facilitate and fulfil-provide have remained relatively underdeveloped. The Committee has not put strong emphasis on affirmative action. Affirmative action has been recommended with regard to certain groups such as ethnic groups, minorities, Roma, untouchables and refugees, but quite remarkably not with regard to girls.

[2362] UN Doc. CRC/C/15/Add.241, para. 30 (Brazil).
[2363] UN Doc. CRC/C/15/Add.243, para. 71 (Croatia).
[2364] UN Doc. CRC/C/15/Add.230, para. 49 (Slovenia); UN Doc. CRC/C/15/Add.140, paras. 21 and 24 (Slovakia).
[2365] UN Doc. CRC/C/15/Add.228, para. 28 (India); UN Doc. CRC/C/15/Add.115, para. 31 (India).
[2366] UN Doc. CRC/C/15/Add.199, para. 55 (Romania).
[2367] UN Doc. CRC/C/15/Add.228, para. 31 (India).
[2368] *Ibid.*, para. 32 (India).
[2369] *Id.*

C. CONCLUSIONS

The obligations arising from the principles of non-discrimination and equality have been analysed from the perspective of the threefold typology of state obligations now commonly applied to economic, social and cultural rights. States are thus to respect, to protect and to fulfil (facilitate, promote, provide) equality.

Not all Committees have emphasized the same obligations to the same extent. All seem however, to recognize the importance of comprehensive anti-discrimination legislation.

The obligation to respect most often leads to recommendations to review and/or repeal discriminatory legislation or practices. All Committees have stressed this obligation, albeit in varying degrees of detail, and with respect to a wide and diverse range of issues. The CRC Committee may have issued the least focused and specific recommendations in this regard.

The obligation to protect against discrimination by third parties has equally been acknowledged by all Committees, albeit to a strongly different degree. The two Committees supervising a specific non-discrimination treaty (*i.e.* the CERD and the CEDAW Committee) have been very explicit on the obligation to protect. This is hardly surprising, as both ICERD and CEDAW contain explicit provisions on the prevention of and protection against private discrimination. The HRC too has explicitly confirmed the obligation of states to protect against private discrimination. Failure to protect against private actors may give rise to state responsibility, when a state has permitted or failed to take appropriate measures or to exercise due diligence to prevent, punish, investigate or redress the harm caused by such acts by private persons or entities.

The obligation to fulfil-facilitate, which most references to positive measures probably correspond to, has equally been elaborated upon most by the CERD and CEDAW Committee. The latter has been restrictive in recommending protective measures of motherhood though. The CEDAW Committee's approach of considering women as full-fledged actors, who do not need too much protection distinguishes it from other Committees, who may tend to consider women more as a vulnerable group in need of special protection. All Committees have emphasized the need for complaints and monitoring mechanisms.

All Committees have drawn attention to the obligation to fulfil-promote. Most often, both awareness-raising among the general public, and training of specific target groups have been recommended *e.g.* the legal profession. The CRC Committee quite uniquely has suggested to involve community leaders in awareness-raising activities.

The obligation to fulfil-provide may be best reflected in affirmative action measures. The HRC, the CESCR Committee and the CRC Committee have been either restrictive, or at least unsystematic in recommending affirmative action. The CEDAW Committee on the other hand has been most specific, both conceptually and practically. Quite remarkably, the CRC Committee does not seem to encourage affirmative action for girls.

The most prominent theme in common to the Committees (albeit to a considerably lower degree to CERD) is gender-based discrimination. Although some obligations may be recurrent under all treaties, divergent opinions exist on what the principles of non-discrimination and equality on the basis of sex/gender mean in practice. This conclusion may be even more true for other grounds of discrimination. Therefore, the provisional conclusion drawn at the end of chapter III on the prohibited grounds of discrimination, seems to have been confirmed in this chapter.

While there are unmistakably common elements in the way the Committees understand the obligations ensuing from the principles of non-discrimination and equality, there is less spontaneous harmonization and convergence than expected, and each Committee tends to take its own approach. This may have become most evident with regard to affirmative action. While the CEDAW Committee frequently recommends affirmative action measures to accelerate *de facto* equality for women in all fields of life, other Committees have been much more restrictive, or do not have as yet developed any policy. The CRC Committee seems to have been most reluctant in recommending affirmative action measures.

CHAPTER V. GENERAL CONCLUSIONS

A. NON-DISCRIMINATION AND EQUALITY: A MIXED PICTURE

Detailed conclusions have been drawn at the end of each chapter. These conclusions will not be repeated in full detail. Suffice it to recall the major insights here.

Our initial research hypothesis was that the principles of non-discrimination and equality, which feature prominently in most of the UN core human rights treaties, might have been interpreted and applied quite similarly by most of the UN treaty bodies. This hypothesis has not been confirmed unequivocally by the research undertaken in this book. The degree of convergence seems lower than might have been expected in the case of so-called congruent provisions, *i.e.* provisions most UN core human rights treaties have in common.[2370]

After all, the lack of a strongly harmonized approach towards non-discrimination and equality may be less surprising than it looks at first sight, for the treaty provisions themselves do not necessarily enshrine strong incentives for a convergent approach. Notwithstanding some clear communalities, they also differ quite strongly on a number of other points (see chapter I).

Similarly, while all Committees have by now started to refer to the pragmatic definition of discrimination in terms of unequal treatment of similar cases without a reasonable and objective justification (*i.e.* without a legitimate aim, and/or without proportionality between the unequal treatment and the aim), their understanding of discrimination and equality still strongly differs. In fact, only the HRC has had the opportunity to really use this definition repeatedly in the handling of individual complaints, and to build up a more or less consistent body of case-law. Differences among the Committees become even more apparent in the way they use or do not use qualifiers like intentional, indirect or structural discrimination (see chapter II).

2370 We may therefore not be able to fully subscribe to Joseph's, Schultz's and Castan's expectation "that the HRC is heavily influenced by ICERD and CEDAW precedents in its interpretation of the relevant ICCPR guarantees [...]" (see Joseph, Schultz and Castan, supra note 53, 680).

The same conclusion – that no unequivocal confirmation of convergence and harmonisation can be found, but rather that some elements point to convergence and similarity, while others point to divergence and difference – was confirmed at the end of the third chapter, in which the prohibited grounds of discrimination were examined. Though the Committees share a fair number of grounds, different grounds have received different emphasis and attention from different Committees, so that no general conclusions on convergence can be drawn. An exception to this general conclusion may have to be made with regard to gender discrimination, which at least three Committees have developed a largely similar approach to.

As to the obligations that ensue from the principles of non-discrimination and equality, an attempt has been made in the fourth chapter to structure the obligations along a threefold typology, *i.e.* obligations to respect, protect and fulfil. The latter disaggregates into sub-obligations to facilitate, promote and provide. While the identification of obligations is very often case and country-specific, this typology of obligations has nevertheless allowed to draw comparisons between the Committees' approaches. The conclusion at the end of this chapter was once more ambiguous. On the one hand, some obvious commonalities appeared: all Committees insist on comprehensive anti-discrimination legislation and the primary duty of states to abstain from discrimination. All Committees have also recognized that legislation and abstention from discrimination is not sufficient, and that positive measures may be required to realize *de facto* equality. Therefore, they have stressed the need for promotional measures, and for a wide range of measures that facilitate equality, ranging from the implementation of legislation and the availability of remedies to action plans, the allocation of resources and targeted policies. On the other hand, only some of the Committees have attributed detailed attention to the obligation to protect against private discrimination. Divergence among the Committees may be well illustrated most clearly by their approach to affirmative action. While gender discrimination has in many ways been most representative for harmonisation and convergence, recommendations on affirmative action measures in order to redress gender inequality have revealed an interpretational gap between the CEDAW Committee on the one hand, and the HRC and CESCR Committee on the other hand.

How do these conclusions affect current reform proposals to include the provisions on non-discrimination and equality as so-called congruent provisions in a common core document, in the context of the reporting procedure?

B. UN REFORM AND THE COMMON CORE DOCUMENT

The idea behind the common core document is to alleviate to some extent the burden of reporting for states that are a party to many if not all core UN human rights treaties, by allowing them to report on a number of issues in a single document for use by all Committees, the so-called common core document.[2371] The provisions on non-discrimination and equality were identified in 2004 as congruent provisions amenable for inclusion in the common core document.[2372] In our book on the Committees' procedures,[2373] the lead argument was that streamlining of procedures was most likely to be successful if it could build upon spontaneous harmonisation that had already taken place. The conclusion there was that this spontaneous harmonisation and convergence had indeed taken place, and that attempts to streamline procedures were therefore likely to succeed. With regard to non-discrimination and equality, our conclusions do not point as strongly to spontaneous harmonisation that is already happening. How might this impact on the current reform proposals?

First of all, it may render it more difficult to strike a consensus as to which information on non-discrimination and equality be included in the common core document. Committees may feel that their particular perspective and concerns are not given enough attention. The "possible weakening of specificities and particularities"[2374] seems to be a common concern regarding the proposed inclusion of congruent provisions in the common core document of all Committees. The HRC and CEDAW Committee have further explicitly voiced this concern specifically with regard to non-discrimination and equality.[2375]

Secondly, if reporting on the so-called congruent provisions of non-discrimination and equality in a common core document materializes, it would be extremely important to avoid the risk of equalizing down, *i.e.* of degenerating the rich interpretation and standards of the different Committees to the smallest common denominator.[2376]

2371 For more information on the common core document, see higher in the introduction.

2372 This was reconfirmed in UN Doc. HRI/MC/2005/3, *Harmonized Guidelines on Reporting under the International Human Rights Treaties, Including Guidelines on a Common Core Document and Treaty-Specific Targeted Documents. Report of the Secretariat*, paras. 70-72.

2373 Supra, note 1.

2374 *Report by Mr Filali, Rapporteur of the Third Inter-Committee Meeting on Discussions in the Treaty Bodies Concerning the Draft Harmonized Reporting Guidelines.*

2375 *Idem* for the HRC; for the CEDAW Committee, see UN Doc. HRI/MC/2005/6/Add.1, *Comments and Suggestions Concerning the Draft Harmonized Guidelines on Reporting under the International Human Rights Treaties. Addendum*, paras. 26-33.

2376 Compare with UN Doc. HRI/MC/2005/6/Add.1, *Comments and Suggestions Concerning the Draft Harmonized Guidelines on Reporting under the International Human Rights Treaties. Addendum*, para. 26.

Our conclusions on the only partial harmonisation of non-discrimination and equality standards that has so far taken place, should not be interpreted necessarily though as firm objections against inclusion in the common core document.[2377] To the contrary, if the two above-mentioned concerns (respect for particularities and no equalizing down) are properly taken into account,[2378] inclusion of the non-discrimination and equality provisions in the common core document may be a major incentive for the Committees to critically reflect on their current practices. Inclusion in the common core document may invite further harmonisation as well as a more explicit division of labour among the UN treaty bodies.

First of all, inclusion may and will invite further harmonisation of the interpretation of the principles of non-discrimination and equality, for all Committees will receive basically the same information (with the exception of information that is specific to one single treaty).[2379] They will inevitably be challenged to check which observations and suggestions other Committees have given to the state concerned in reaction to that information. It is to be expected (or at least to be hoped) that this will enhance the Committee's knowledge of each other's comments and recommendations, and consequently also the harmonisation of their interpretation and practices with regard to non-discrimination and equality.

Secondly, inclusion of the principles of non-discrimination and equality in the common core document might encourage the Committees to explicitly establish a clearer division of tasks. At present, there is a considerable degree of overlap. The HRC for instance, also deals explicitly and in great detail with issues of racial discrimination and gender-based discrimination, while the former is within the core mandate of CERD, and the latter of the CEDAW Committee.[2380] The HRC, CESCR Committee, CEDAW Committee and CRC Committee alike have expressed concern about gender

---

2377 The inclusion of any congruent substantive provisions in the common core document still seems to be a major contentious issue, as the fourth Inter-Committee Meeting agreed on the need to submit this question to a technical working group to be established, see *Decisions and Recommendations of the fourth Inter-Committee Meeting*, III.

2378 This seems already to be the case in the 2005 revised version of the draft harmonized guidelines, as prepared by the Secretariat. They explicitly provide that not all information on non-discrimination and equality is to be included in the common core document. States can reserve information for treaty-specific documents, with this limitation that the treaty-specific document for one treaty should not contain information which is also to be included in another treaty-specific document. Secondly, where the specific standards differ, states are to address the issue in the common core document according to the most progressive or protective standard (see UN Doc. HRI/MC/2005/3, *Harmonized Guidelines on Reporting under the International Human Rights Treaties, Including Guidelines on a Common Core Document and Treaty-Specific Targeted Documents. Report of the Secretariat*, paras. 57 and 58).

2379 See supra note 2379.

2380 Compare with: "[...] it is arguable that the ICCPR obligations essentially subsume those of ICERD and CEDAW [...].," see Joseph, Schultz and Castan, supra note 53, 680.

discriminatory minimum ages for marriage, and about discrimination against children born out of wedlock. Inclusion of the principles of non-discrimination and equality in the common core document holds potential for complementarity and rationalisation of the Committees' work. Issues of racial discrimination might therefore be reserved to the CERD, and those of gender discrimination to the CEDAW Committee. Both Committees have already done most of the standard-setting in the past on these issues, and it is to be expected that specific issues of racial or gender discrimination will be included by states in the treaty-specific documents for respectively CERD and the CEDAW Committee.

As to the other grounds of discrimination, the HRC might focus on discrimination based on political or other opinion (the issue of discrimination against conscientious objectors can be mentioned here) and on religion. The CESCR Committee might prioritize discrimination based on social status. Discrimination against children born out of wedlock and discrimination on the ground of disability, could be the exclusive realm of the CRC Committee. The CMW Committee might take up issues of discrimination based on migrant, asylum seeking or refugee status.

Furthermore, the HRC might (continue to) focus on discrimination in relation to civil and political rights, the CESCR Committee on discrimination in the field of economic, social and cultural rights, the CRC Committee on discrimination against children and the CMW Committee on discrimination against migrants and members of their families.[2381] In sum, inclusion in the common core document may help the Committees to delineate their respective mandates, and to focus on their core mandate (as defined in fact by the treaty the implementation of which they supervise).

If more treaty bodies can receive individual complaints in the near future, a similar division of tasks might materialize in dealing with complaints about violations of the principles of non-discrimination and equality.[2382]

2381 This would be fully in line with the accessory nature of the non-discrimination and equality provisions in most core UN human rights treaties.

2382 Currently, of the Committees discussed, only the CERD, the HRC and the CEDAW Committee can receive individual complaints. An Optional Protocol providing for a complaints procedure for violations of economic, social and cultural rights is under consideration with the Commission on Human Rights. The CMW contains provisions on an individual complaints procedure, but states need to opt in explicitly for these provisions to be applicable. No plans for the establishment of an individual complaints procedure under the CRC exist.

www.ingramcontent.com/pod-product-compliance
Ingram Content Group UK Ltd.
Pitfield, Milton Keynes, MK11 3LW, UK
UKHW051926100926
8556IPUK00022B/1396

9 789050 95500